A History of the Manx Church

(1698—1911)

by

Canon J D Gelling

The Manx Heritage Foundation

To the Memory of
Archdeacon Kewley
A great Archdeacon and a great Manxman

Published by the Manx Heritage Foundation,
P.O. Box 1986, Douglas, Isle of Man.

First published 1998

ISBN No 0 952 4019 4 0

Layout and typesetting by The Manx Heritage Foundation
Cover design by Ruth Sutherland
Photographs courtesy of Manx National Heritage
Eight Views of Manx Churches courtesy of the estate of
Miss F M C Kermode

Cover and plates printed by Mannin Media
Copied and bound by The Copy Shop

Foreword

The Reverend Canon John Gelling has been both a servant and a student of the Church in Man during his professional life.

This book is the result of lengthy research and careful reading, and will add greatly to the history of the Island's parishes and the policies of its senior churchmen. It contains a wealth of information from the days of that doyen of Bishops, Thomas Wilson, and gives an insight into the development of the Church and the Island.

It has been my privilege to serve the diocese of Sodor and Man as Bishop since before Canon Gelling retired from active parochial ministry, and I have thus been able to benefit from his wisdom, academic expertise and courtesy. It affords me much pleasure to commend this book for serious consideration as an important contribution to the fascinating Story of Man and the impact of religion upon it.

I would also like to place on record the debt of gratitude which the Isle of Man owes to Canon Gelling for his zealous and unstinting work in handing to us the fruits of his labour.

+ ——Noel Sodor and Man.

+Noel Sodor and Man.
BISHOP

PREFACE

This History was not originally written for publication - if it had been I would have approached the subject in a rather different way. Over the years I had collected a considerable amount of material concerning the Manx Church and the late Bishop Attwell pressed me very much to put this into narrative form and deposit it in the Diocesan office, simply to preserve the information. This accounts for its being rather strictly factual and for the absence of references.

Eventually a number of friends (especially Mr John Crellin, CP), suggested that it should be made available to the Manx people and not just gather dust on an office shelf and this view was supported by the Manx Heritage Foundation and the Centre for Manx Studies.

Primary sources are Parish Registers, Diocesan Records, the Atholl Papers (for Bishops Richmond, Mason, Crigan and Murray) and, for most of the nineteenth century, contemporary newspapers. Some information was also obtained verbally from individuals who remembered the closing years of the last century, notably the late Archdeacon Kewley, the late Canon Quine and the late Mr Harold Hughes-Games, son of Archdeacon Hughes-Games.

Secondary sources are:-
Life of Bishop Wilson by Cruttwell (1781);
Life of Bishop Wilson by Stowell (1819);
Life of Bishop Wilson by Keble (1863) - by far the fullest and best;
Memoirs of Bishop Hildesley by Weeden Butler (1799);
Life & Memoirs of W. A. Shirley by T. Hill;
Account of the Diocese of Sodor & Man (Harrison);
Histories of the Isle of Man by Train and A. W. Moore.

I wish to thank the Manx Heritage Foundation for undertaking and supervising the publication of this work, the Centre for Manx Studies (especially Dr Fenella Bazin), and the staff of the Manx Museum Library for much help; and also two individuals, Miss M. Moore, who gave me invaluable help in the early stages by sorting out and filing the material and Mrs Ann Kelly who, when I had temporary eye trouble, made a fair copy of the whole manuscript. I must also thank Mrs Muriel McVaney who put the whole manuscript onto disc and did some editing, work for which I am most grateful; Mrs Celia Salisbury Jones who proof read the final manuscript and marked up the names and subjects for the index; and finally to Mr Bill Snelling and Mrs Pat Burgess for constructing the index on computer.

I am also most grateful to parishes who lent me photographs of former vicars, to the Manx National Heritage Library for lending a number of photographs and pictures and to various individuals, especially the late Miss Margaret Kermode, who lent a large number of photographs &c., belonging to her late father, Canon Kermode.

J D Gelling
Crosby, 1998.

Contents

Foreward v
Preface vi
Illustrations viii

Bishop Wilson 1
    The Parishes under Wilson 16

Bishop Hildesley 29
    The Parishes under Hildesley 36

Bishops Richmond and Mason 41
    The Parishes under Richmond and Mason 42

Bishop Crigan 46
    The Parishes under Crigan 47

Bishop Murray 52
    The Parishes under Murray 58

Bishop Ward 63
    The Parishes under Ward 66

Bishops Bowstead, Pepys and Short 78
    The Parishes under Bowstead, Pepys and Short 82

Bishops Shirley and Auckland 90
    The Parishes under Shirley and Auckland 94

Bishop Powys 104
    The Parishes under Powys 130

Bishop Hill 156
    The Parishes under Hill 165

Bishop Bardsley 180
    The Parishes under Bardsley 183

Bishop Straton 194
    The Parishes under Straton 199

Bishop Drury 214
    The Parishes under Drury 215

Appendix I (Biographical details of the Clergy) 221

Appendix II (Parish Clergy) 243

Index 255

The Illustrations

between pages 146—147

Plate 1

Bishop Wilson 1698—1755

Bishop Wilson's birthplace at Burton near Neston, Cheshire

A drawing of Bishopscourt by Daniel King in 1651

Plate 2

Bishop Hildesley 1755—1772

The Revd James Wilks (1719—1777), Rector of Ballaugh and Vicar General

The Revd Philip Moore (1705—1783), editor of the Manx Bible

The Revd Evan Christian (1744—1811), Vicar of Patrick and Vicar General

Plate 3

Bishop Crigan 1784—1813

Bishopscourt after Bishop Crigan's alterations (1784—1788)

Bishop Murray 1814—1827

Bishopscourt after Bishop Murray's alterations of 1814

Plate 4

Bishop Ward 1828—1838

Revd J T Clarke, 1799—1888, Vicar of St Mark's

Revd William Drury, 1808—1887, Vicar of Braddan

Plate 5

The state of the Manx Church when Bishop Ward arrived in 1828

Plate 6

A series of views of Manx churches built during the episcopacy of Bishop Ward

Kirk Lonan Church, with the Tomb of the Revd. Hugh Stowell

Baldwin Chapel, which, during the Week, serves, by means of screens, as separate School Houses

Plate 7

Dawby Chapel, also used as a School House

Kirk Onchan Church

Plate 8
Ballaugh Church
Sulby Chapel, also used as a School House

Plate 9
Lezayre Church
Kirk Michael Church, with the Tomb of the celebrated Bishop Wilson

Plate 10
Bishop Short 1841—1846
Bishop Shirley 1847
Bishop Auckland 1847—1854
Revd John Alcock, Chaplain of St Barnabas', 1848—1852
Richard Jebb, 1808—1884, Vicar General

Plate 11
Bishop Powys 1854—1877
Bishop Hill 1877—1887
Revd William Gill, 1797—1871, Vicar of Malew
Archdeacon Gill, 1830—1912, Son of Revd William Gill
Revd Thomas Gill, 1836—1894, Chaplain of St Mark's and of Malew. Son of Revd William Gill
Revd J Hughes-Games, Archdeacon 1886—1895

Plate 12
Bishop Bardsley 1887—1892
Bishop Straton 1892—1907
Bishop Drury 1907—1911
Revd John Howard 1817—1892, Vicar of Onchan
Archdeacon Kewley 1860—1941
Canon Quine, 1856—1940, Vicar of Lonan, and Mrs Quine

Chapter 1

BISHOP WILSON 1698-1755

On the 6th April 1698 a small group of Clergy and prominent laymen gathered at Derbyhaven (then a thriving port) to welcome their new Bishop, Thomas Wilson, who had left England on the 2nd April. They accompanied him to the capital, Castletown, where he paid his respects to the Governor, Colonel Nicholas Stanley, and preached his first sermon in his new diocese, on the 'barren fig tree'. Four days later he set off on horseback (there were no carriages on the Island in those days), with the Governor and other high officials, and made his way on rough tracks over the mountains to Peel, the Cathedral City. There he was, on the 11th April, installed as Bishop by Samuel Wattleworth, Vicar of German and Vicar General (1694-1703), and later Archdeacon who, being a Manx speaker, and knowing only a little English, conducted the service in Latin. It was a momentous day in the history of this diocese.

In 1697 the Lord of Mann, William Stanley, 9th Earl of Derby failed to persuade Wilson, then his domestic Chaplain at his English seat at Knowlsey in Lancashire, to accept nomination as Bishop as Wilson felt himself unworthy, but soon after this Archbishop Sharp of York protested to William III about the long vacancy, and the King peremptorily ordered Derby to make a nomination or he would choose a Bishop himself. Derby again offered it to Wilson, with greater insistence and this time he was successful (27th November 1697).

Derby presented Wilson to William III, who sent the Archbishop of York an order under the Great Seal to consecrate him. Wilson was consecrated by Sharp and the Bishops of Chester and Norwich in the Savoy Chapel on the 16th January 1698 (Epiphany II). On that day Wilson wrote in his diary the text "Son of Man I have made thee a watchman to the house of Israel" (Ezekiel 3.¹⁷). In the same month the Archbishop of Canterbury made him DCL, Oxford University made him DD and Cambridge made him DD in 1707. Derby had offered him the Parish of Badlesworth, Yorkshire to hold in plurality with Sodor and Man to help him financially, but Wilson

refused as a matter of principle as it would involve non residence and plurality. The income of the see was only £300 per annum, so that nearly all previous Bishops, and some later ones had kept whatever preferments they had held in England.

Thomas Wilson was born on Sunday, 20th December 1663 (Advent 4) at Burton near Neston, Cheshire. He was the sixth of the seven children (five boys and two girls) of Nathaniel Wilson, a farmer, and his wife Alice, whom he later described as "honest parents, fearing God". In 1681 he entered Trinity College, Dublin, and for a while studied medicine. He graduated B A in 1686 and was persuaded by the Reverend Michael Hewetson (later Archdeacon of Armagh) to enter the ministry, and on the 29th June 1686 he was made deacon by Bishop Moreton of Kildare, although at 22 he was under the canonical age and he had no title. He was ordained alone, there being no other candidate. It must have been a long service because first of all Kildare Cathedral was consecrated, then came a confirmation, and then the ordination. From Hewetson he received advice which he remembered all his life and gave to the Manx Clergy - to read over the ordination service, and the 39 articles once a year; to observe the laws of the Church and her festivals and fasts as far as possible; to say Mattins and Evensong either publicly or privately each day; and always to behave reverently in Church, not to turn his back to the altar in service time, to bow at the Name of Jesus whenever it is mentioned, to turn east in the Gloria and Creeds and to make obeisance going into or out of the Church or on approaching or leaving the Altar.

On the 10th February 1688 Wilson became curate to his maternal uncle, Dr Sherlock the Rector of Winwick, and was given responsibility for Newchurch, a chaplaincy within the parish. He found the church deserted and the fabric very neglected. He had free board with the Rector and a stipend of £30 per annum of which he gave a tenth to charity, later increased to one fifth. On Sherlock's death on the 20th June 1689 Wilson remained Curate for three more years under the Reverend Thomas Bennet, then Fellow, later Master, of University College, Oxford. Bennet was often non-resident and died in May 1692. On 20th October 1689 Wilson received priest's orders from Bishop Stratford of Chester and in 1692 he became domestic chaplain to the 9th Earl of Derby, and tutor to his only son, still at the same stipend, although he was also made Master of Lathom Alms House at a salary of £20 per annum. Derby formed a high opinion of his chaplain, and it was due to him, as we have seen, that Wilson was nominated as Bishop of Sodor and Man, having never had a parish of his own, and with his experience limited to a curacy and a chaplaincy.

The long vacancy in the see made Wilson's inheritance difficult. He found Bishopscourt and St German's Cathedral in ruins, many Churches and vicarages in a bad state of repair, the clergy slack and often ignorant and the people poor and uneducated, speaking a language which he did not understand, and finding their chief occupation in smuggling. He began with Bishopscourt. On Bishop Parr's death in 1643 it had become the Earl of Derby's summer seat, and it was at this time, in the troubled days of the Civil War, that he had built a large rectangular rampart and ditch around the house, with a gateway in the west, and bastions at the four corners. In 1651 there was a rebellion against the Countess of Derby, during which the house was captured, and from then until the Restoration in 1660 it was the headquarters of the Commissioners sent by Cromwell to govern the Island. Bishop Levinz had called the house his Patmos, and refused to live there so that only the tower and chapel were intact, but Wilson turned it into a fine residence with gardens, fruit trees and about 1,000 trees at a cost of £1,400, of which Wilson paid £1,200 and the Earl of Derby the rest. Its original name was Balicury, later Ballachurry, and it was the residence of Bishop Simon as early as 1230. The 13th century Orry's Tower has walls 10 feet thick in places and was once surrounded by a ditch, probably for the defence of the road running north. The marshy nature of the surrounding land would also strengthen it as a defensive post. The exact date when Bishopscourt became the episcopal residence, and why this particular site was chosen, is uncertain. There are remains of a Bishop's residence adjoining St German's Cathedral, and it is possible that the Church

was unable to retain this. The central hall was the outstanding feature of Wilson's work. He began by raising the roof, built a new doorway into it, and removed the external staircase. A new block was built onto the west end, a farm was laid out and the barns, stables, outhouses and cottages were either built or repaired.

Above all Wilson rebuilt Bishopscourt chapel, under which once flowed the stream (now diverted), dividing the parishes of Kirk Michael and Ballaugh. Frequent disputes arose as to which of the parishes the Bishop and his household belonged, but in 1678 Bishop Bridgman laid down, presumably on good grounds, that the chancel was in Ballaugh and the rest in Michael. Wilson also made Bishopscourt a kind of theological seminary for ordinands.

With St German's Cathedral he was less successful. He had found the chancel in good repair, and the nave had recently been reroofed, but the transepts and tower were roofless. By 1710 the roof of the nave had again fallen in, and in 1728, when Wilson wanted to mend the roof Governor Horton forbade him to do the work. Soon after Wilson's death even the chancel was ruinous.

The Manx Church had not recovered from the Commonwealth period. The system of land tenure, which made the Manx people tenants at will of the Lord of Man, led to disorder and sedition arising from smuggling. It also checked spiritual development, despite the somewhat lukewarm efforts of the clergy.

His long episcopate saw a great improvement in the spiritual and academic standard of the clergy, and some of the men he appointed turned out to be among the greatest figures in the Manx Church. His choice of vicars was always limited by the need to have Manx speakers, and another obstacle was that most parishes were in the gift of the Lord of Man, and the Earls of Derby often chose men unsympathetic to Wilson's point of view. He expected a very high standard of character and conduct from the clergy as essential to the credibility of their preaching, but his own example made such precept unnecessary. He never tired of urging them to visit the people and instruct the children. On occasion, however, he could act decisively with the clergy, one of whom he suspended for immoral behaviour and another of whom he removed from his orders for a similar offence. One of the causes of the poor standard of clergy he inherited was the fact that their stipends were miserably poor but Wilson did his best to remedy this from his own resources. By the neglect of former incumbents, tithe had been allowed to lapse and a practice had crept in of excluding the estates of the chief civil officers from tithe and this was soon claimed by them as a right. Clergy and Church wardens would be taken to task vigorously if the Chancel, Font or Communion linen did not meet with his approval.

He insisted on proper parish registers being kept. To raise the educational standard of the clergy he established parochial libraries in 1699, with the help of a friend, Dr Thomas Bray. For these he bought books each time he visited England, but after 1740 there were few additions. These libraries have now disappeared, although in 1731 Convocation made each Vicar responsible for that of his own parish and in 1734 Tynwald made this legal.

An Act of 1696 compelled the clergy to live in their parish, but several parishes had no vicarage, while others were in ruins. An Act of 1734 set up a fund to pay a man on leaving a parish two thirds of what he had paid in building improvements and repairs and he was to receive the remaining third from his successor. Dilapidations were to be assessed by four sworn men appointed by the Bishop or the Archdeacon.

Wilson rebuilt and restored nearly all the Churches and built two new ones, St Matthew's and Castletown. New vicarages were built and older ones repaired. To all this work he contributed liberally from his stipend of £300 per annum, and he raised much money in England. In the case of three parishes, Braddan, German and Patrick, he bought a glebe for the vicar. Up to his 80th year he was a familiar figure riding about the diocese, and all his life he took at least one service each Sunday except when he was ill. Often he would join a congregation unannounced. When he was 91 he asked to be excused from Tynwald on account of his age. At the end of one long list of donations he quoted Nehemiah 5¹⁹ (Remember unto me, O my God, for good, all that I have done for this people).

It was one of the duties of Churchwardens, dating from the earliest times, to present in the Vicar General's Court those who had transgressed the laws and customs of the church, though this was interpreted very widely to include unbecoming behaviour in church, and almost anything of which the Churchwardens disapproved. Sentences of the court varied considerably, from imprisonment in the crypt of St German's Cathedral (for serious offences) to a caution in minor cases, but the most usual penalty was to perform a penance, usually in church, wearing a white robe. The clergy themselves were not exempt from the power of the Churchwardens to present, and a number of cases recorded. Presentments were very common before and during Bishop Wilson's episcopate, but with the partial breakdown of ecclesiastical disipline under Bishop Hildesley and his successors they became gradually less common, except during Bishop Murray's time, and nowadays they have ceased altogether. On the 6th September 1700 Wilson laid down the duties of Churchwardens as follows:

(1) To present the Minister or Parish Clerk "if they neglected their duty or if the Minister frequented Ale houses 'more than for his honest necessity'".

The Clerk's duty was to ring the bell, to raise the psalms (either in person or by deputy) and to attend the minister when visiting the sick, and at baptisms, weddings and funerals.

(2) To present parishioners who profaned the Sabbath by drinking, gambling, sporting or doing unnecessary work and those absent from Church.

(3) To present parents and masters who failed to send their children and servants to be catechised.

(4) To present those guilty of sorcery, charms, fornication, adultery, incest and swearing.

(5) To present those who do not apply legacies to the Church for the purpose intended.

(6) To keep the Church chancel and Churchyard in good repair, to provide service books, a chalice and bread and wine and to ensure that marriages, baptisms and burials are registered.

(7) To present anyone encroaching on the glebe or churchyard.

(8) To present those of 16 or over who do not take Holy Communion.

(9) To present couples not married who live together.

(10) To present those not paying their Church dues.

(11) To present the Sumner if he does not keep dogs out of Church.

(12) To present anyone carrying tales from house to house and sowing discord.

(13) To ensure that the schools are diligently kept, and prayers read on Wednesdays and Fridays.

The Churchwardens were asked "Does the Minister lead a disorderly or irregular life, giving an evil example by frequenting places where strong liquor is sold or such loose company?" [sic].

In the field of education Wilson was a pioneer. In 1672 the Earl of Derby had made the clergy responsible for educating the children in their parishes, the Church being used as a school and ordered all his tenants to send their children to school. Wilson, however, realised that this was a great burden on the clergy, so he allowed them to appoint a lay person as schoolmaster or schoolmistress provided such person was licensed by him as suitable. He disapproved of the Church being used for classes, so he made the Churchwardens of each parish responsible for providing a school. He took his full share in providing the money for this and was greatly helped by his friend, Lady Elizabeth Hastings, until her death in 1739. By 1755 there were Church schools all over the diocese, and parents who did not send their children to school were fined in the Church courts. He was a prime mover in the first Education Act (1703) which set up schools in each parish which the clergy had to visit every quarter. His episcopate produced no Sunday Schools, however.

Wilson was the son of a farmer, and his knowledge of farming came as a revelation to the Manx countryfolk who had made little progress in this direction for centuries. Many came to Bishopscourt to learn modern farming methods such as crop rotation, and Bishopscourt farm became a model for the Island. Breeds of farm animals were improved and a mill was established at Bishopscourt.

1739-41 were years of famine, but Wilson was able to feed the poor with the produce of his own land. Throughout his life he was a friend to the poor, and as he kept open house they crowded to him. To avoid scroungers he made those seeking relief bring a note of recommendation from their vicar. His table was covered with the produce of his own farm and garden and there was no extravagance. He kept a "poor drawer" in his desk, a "poor chest" in his granary and a "poor wardrobe" in his house, so that whether they needed money, food or clothes he could help. He also kept a collection of spectacles for the poor. Much of his charity to the poor was given in kind, and tailors and shoemakers were kept busy at Bishopscourt. The story is told that, to avoid anything like luxury, he only wanted one button and loop on his cloak, until the tailor said that if everyone did the same the button maker would starve, whereupon the Bishop at once changed his mind. "He kept beggars from everyone's door but his own". The doors of Bishopscourt were never locked, simply left on the latch. His domain must have been one of industry, goodness and simplicity. He used his stipend with such care and skill that he was able to help the poor and distressed throughout the Island. He used to send agents to every fair to buy flannels and linen for the poor.

His early study of medicine was put to good use and he kept a store which he distributed free to the poor, with advice. In his early years here he was the only doctor on the Island. In urging sanitary reform, the lack of which was the origin of so much disease, he was far ahead of his time.

The winter of 1739-40 was very cold, with 10 weeks of frost, and due to a drought in 1739 corn was so scarce that the British Government forbade the export of grain. The Island at this time depended on England for grain, as so many farmers were engaged in smuggling that the land was not properly cultivated. To alleviate the distress the Bishop's son, Dr Thomas Wilson, managed to buy from Holland two shiploads of grain, and this, together with the produce of Bishopscourt farm, Wilson distributed to the poor in limited quantities at half price or free. Dr Wilson then petitioned the King and obtained the lifting of the embargo to a certain extent and for a few months. In 1741 Wilson gave away over 500 bushels of barley, and bought whatever corn he could and sold it cheaply. The same thing happened in 1744 when the harvest was bad, imported corn very dear, and many sheep and cattle died in the wet and cold. To make matters worse, in 1741 pestilence followed the famine in the form of a violent diarrhoea which Wilson treated with laudamum. He was worn out with visiting and tending the sick who flocked to Bishopscourt from all quarters for healing, but by these measures he must have saved hundreds from dying of starvation or disease.

All his life Wilson fearlessly denounced smuggling, the cause of much crime, and thereby drew upon himself abuse from its many and powerful supporters.

From an early date in his episcopate Wilson realised that most of the people spoke Manx, and were unable to follow a service in English. Some of the clergy were bilingual, and could translate into Manx as they read the Service, but he was aware that this was barely satisfactory, and that the only real solution was to have the Bible and the Prayer Book translated into Manx. This project was only partly realised when Wilson died, and it was left to his successor, Hildesley, to bring it to a conclusion, but a start was made. Wilson clearly found Manx difficult, though he took pains to learn it, but he learned enough for baptism, confirmation and the blessing, and could greet the people in Manx. He could speak it fairly well latterly, but never preached in Manx. During his imprisonment in Castle Rushen in 1722 he gave much thought to this matter and planned to have at least the four Gospels and Acts translated into Manx. This was done by the Revd William Walker, but only 53 copies of St Matthew were printed, at Wilson's own expense, for the use of the Clergy. In 1707 he printed a catechism in Manx (probably also done by Walker) and English, which differed from the prayer book catechism in that it consisted of questions by the candidate and answers from the instructor. In 1714 he also issued his Form of Prayer for the Herring Fishery in Manx.

Perhaps Wilson's greatest contribution to the welfare of the Island was the Act of Settlement of 1703 (called the Manx Magna Carta) approved by Convocation on the 3rd February and by Tynwald on the 4th February 1704 with the support of the Earl of Derby. From the start of his episcopate he realised that the feudal tenures aimed at by Derby, which gave no compensation for improvements, and which robbed the farmers of any security, were disastrous for the Island. An Act of Tynwald in 1645 had accepted an offer from Derby of a 21 years tenancy for all tenants, but as they were uncertain of the tenancy after 21 years, no improvements were made and the soil became exhausted. By this Act, which restored to the Manx their ancient tenure, the tenant became owner of his land which he could in future sell or pass on to his children, on payment of the Lord's rent which could not be raised. The wisdom of this was seen in a marked growth of prosperity among farmers which benefited the whole community.

Second only in importance to this came the Ecclesiastical Constitutions which were accepted by Convocation on 3rd February 1703 and, after being passed by Tynwald in 1704 became Statute Law. They were designed for the better government and discipline of the Manx Church and were a summary and simplification of existing canon law and the traditional rules for the Manx church as drawn up at Synods in 1239, 1291 and 1350. These canons were enforced by various penances, by fines or by imprisonment. It was at this Convocation that it was enacted that Convocation should meet at Bishopscourt on the Thursday in Whit week, or, if the Bishop was away, as soon as possible after his return.

The First Canon dealt with proper preparation for confirmation. The Second laid down that only those who had been confirmed could take Holy Communion, though in the event of the Bishop's absence or illness a person could receive the sacrament on producing a certificate from the Archdeacon, or one of the Vicars General, that he was fully prepared for confirmation. The Third made confirmation essential for marriage or being a godparent; any clergyman taking a marriage had to require a certificate of confirmation from either of the two who came from another parish. Canon Four said that churchwardens had to keep a record of all unconfirmed children and servants, who had to come to Evensong for at least half an hour, to be instructed in the catechism by the vicar. Those who did not come were fined, parents being answerable in this respect for their children and employers for their servants.

Canon Five laid down that anyone who incurred the censures of the Church and, having done penance, repeated the offence, should not be allowed simply to do penance again (the custom hitherto) until he had given proof of his genuine repentance. During this time he was not allowed to enter the Church, but had to stand at the Church door on Sundays and Holy Days during Mattins and Evensong until the vicar was sufficiently convinced of his penitence and amendment to give him a certificate, (signed also by the churchwardens and the senior members of the congregation) which was to go to the Bishop. If he failed to obtain such certificate within three months he was to be excommunicated, and no one was to speak to him. During this three months he was forbidden to leave the Island. Heavy penalties were laid down for any minister or churchwardens who failed in this respect.

Canon Six concerned admission to Holy Communion, and here Wilson took his stand on the rubric preceding the service in the Prayer Book. The full force of ecclesiastical censure was directed on any clergyman who admitted a person of bad character to the sacrament contrary to the rubric. Canon Seven ordered Churchwardens to present anyone who received or paid rent on a Sunday and Canon Eight ended the practice of commuting penances for a money payment.

Canon Nine reflected Wilson's lifelong passion for education. All children, when old enough had to be sent to school, and parents neglecting to do so had to pay to the schoolmaster a fine of one shilling a quarter. A lesser fine was imposed where children attended irregularly. Wilson realised that there were times in the year, like harvest, when poor parents had to keep their children at home to help in the fields, but these children had to attend the parish church an hour before Evensong on the third Sunday of the month to be taught by the schoolmaster. The schoolmasters received a salary plus sixpence a quarter from the parents of every child whom they taught to read English, and nine pence per quarter for each child taught to write. No payment, however, was expected from parents who were genuinely unable to pay. Each vicar had to visit the school once a quarter and report on the progress of each child. In all this Wilson was nearly two centuries ahead of his time. Finally Canon Ten laid down that after Evensong on the last Sunday of each month the vicar and wardens had to enter the names of all who had failed to attend church without a proper reason, of all parents and employers who failed to send their children and servants to be catechised, and of parents who did not send their children to school. The right of making canons, which Convocation had exercised since 1229, was expressly recognised.

In these constitutions Wilson clearly tried to return to the primitive discipline of the Church. They made ecclesiastical offences an offence against the state, and he had no hesitation in enforcing them even against the highest in the land. Until Governor Horne came in 1715 temporal and spiritual authorities worked together, and convictions in the Church

Court were enforced by the civil power. The Clerk of the Rolls was imprisoned for refusing to pay tithe, and Archdeacon Wattleworth was suspended both as Archdeacon and as Rector of Andreas, for refusing to carry out the Bishop's sentence on one of his parishioners. Laymen and women who offended against Church Law had to do penance either at the parish Church or in the marketplace or to submit to such penalties as the bridle. More serious cases were punished by imprisonment in the crypt under St German's Cathedral and, though more rarely, by excommunication. Women suspected of immorality had to swear themselves innocent at the altar (though this must often have led to perjury) and occasionally, as in the famous case of Catherine Kinrade, were dragged through the water by a man in a boat pulling them by the hair. Sometimes Wilson would be unexpectedly generous as when he gave permission to Christopher Hampton of Braddan to marry again, as his wife had been sentenced to 7 years in prison for lamb stealing, and his children were motherless.

Despite all these efforts for the spiritual and moral welfare of his people, Wilson realised at the end of his life that he had failed. Even his own servants were in some cases offenders, and the many people who, year by year, performed penance, were proof that the system had not worked. Like Cromwell and the Puritans, Wilson learned that it was impossible to improve and elevate human nature by laws and penalties, and that moral teaching without the great evangelical truths, though enforced either by penances or Canon Law, could not bring about moral improvement. Ecclesiastical discipline in England had been virtually ended by the 1689 Toleration Act and Wilson, coming after it, was swimming against the tide. His episcopate was a rearguard action, gallant but unavailing, and by 1755 his disciplinary system had more or less collapsed through the opposition of successive Governors.

Wilson's strongly held views on the authority and independence of the Church were bound to bring him into conflict with the State. Governor Alexander Horne did all possible to impede ecclesiastical discipline. He was not a bad man, but was coarse, of limited intelligence and ability, and was jealous of his own rights. He was at first on good terms with Wilson, and often spent several weeks at Bishopscourt. In 1716 Mary Henricks, wife of an innkeeper in Douglas, was convicted of adultery in the Church Courts, and was ordered to do penance, but when she refused she was excommunicated (22nd October 1716) and ordered to be arrested by the civil authority and sent to St German's prison. Horne made no attempt to arrest her after she had appealed to him but consulted Derby, thus raising the point of whether by law the Earl was supreme in purely spiritual cases. Derby decided that Mrs Henricks and the Bishop should both appear before him in London on the 23rd December 1716. This Wilson refused to do, or even to be represented, saying that there was no appeal in a case like this so the case dropped and early in 1717 Derby ordered that the lady should be exempt from ecclesiastical penalties, and that this order be published in Braddan Church (her parish Church) and in Douglas Market. Wilson's point was that appeals from the Church Courts should go to the Archbishop of York, not to the Lord of the Isle. In the reign of James I an Act of Parliament had given the Island to the Earl of Derby, but it contained a Clause saving to the Archbishop of York and his successors "All metropolitical jurisdiction, in all points, and to all purposes and effects" over Sodor and Man. On this clause Wilson based his contention that appeals from the Church Courts should go to the Archbishop of York, and also on the terms of an Act of 1542 which had put Sodor and Man under the jurisdiction of York. The Governor, however, construed his refusal to appear before Derby as contempt of court, and on the 19th February 1718, in conjunction with Deemsters Mylrea and Moore and two other officials (John Rowe the Comptroller and William Sedden the Water Bailiff) fined the Bishop £10. Wilson reacted by asking that the Deemsters and the House of Keys, together with him and the two Vicars General should decide the question of who should hear such appeals. Horne refused, saying that Derby alone as "Metropolitan and Chief of the Holy Church of this Isle" could and should decide the point. After an abortive interview with the Governor on the 3rd March, Wilson appealed to Derby against the fine. In August 1719 Derby remitted the fine on the basis of the 1542 Act, but did not censure the Governor, who maintained his point that Derby was Head of the Manx Church as well as Lord of the Isle.

Mary Henricks, from whom the whole dispute arose, remained excommunicate, with all that it involved, until March 1723 when she asked to be received back into the Church. Wilson agreed, subject to her doing penance in six parish churches. There is no doubt that those who were opposed to Church discipline used her as a tool.

In 1722 rumours, evidently with some foundation, circulated regarding the treatment of prisoners in Castle Rushen. Wilson obtained the backing of the Keys in protesting to the Governor, but the Bishop had chosen his ground badly, as Horne at once retaliated with a criticism of the conditions under which ecclesiastical prisoners were kept in the crypt of St German's Cathedral. This famous prison was doubtless roughly contemporary with the building of the chancel by Bishop Simon in 1229, and is 34 feet by 18 feet, vaulted, barrel shaped with 13 ribs. It is reached by a narrow staircase of 18 steps built into the south wall of the chancel, and as it was open to the north wind in the barred opening overlooking the harbour the prisoners must have suffered terribly from damp and cold. Wilson was also allowed to use other rooms in Peel Castle for prisoners. In law only the Bishop could commit people to this prison, but in fact he delegated this right to his Vicars General, who were the judges in the Church Courts. In the 18th century these courts had the right to try cases which, if still an offence, are now heard in the civil courts - sorcery, absence from Church or school, sleeping in church, desecrating Sundays and Holy Days, slander, bad language, drunkenness, matrimonial cases and immorality. It was the claims of these courts which led to the most serious clash between Wilson and the civil power.

In 1719 Mrs Jane Horne, wife of the Governor, accused Mrs Rebecca Puller, whom she disliked, of improper intimacy with Sir James Poole, a Liverpool Alderman living in Castletown. The chaplain at Castletown from 1719-25 was Robert Horrobin, formerly curate of Warrington, who had been appointed Rector of Andreas and Archdeacon by Derby in 1719, but as Chaplain to the Governor he lived in Castletown. Late in 1720, in a sermon preached at Castletown on St Matthew, 16[27] he said:

(1) That the clergy had assumed for themselves the power to forgive sins.
(2) That priestly absolution is virtually useless.
(3) That the words 'whosoever sins ye remit' applied only to the apostles.

7

(4) That the clergy only had authority to declare the terms on which God will forgive sins.

(5) That salvation was for all, irrespective of belief in Christ and that a man could be saved by good deeds.

(6) That the divinity of Christ was doubtful.

Early in 1721 a certain Thomas Harley complained to Wilson that Horrobin was preaching heresy. Horrobin, encouraged by John Rowe, denounced Harley as an injurious man and a calumniator, and refused Wilson's request for a copy of the sermon in question. Wilson therefore summoned Harley and Horrobin to appear before him and his Vicars General (Walker and Curghey) and Registrar Woods in St John's Chapel on 21st March 1721. The hearing was continued at Santan on 27th April, but no decision was reached. Horrobin refused to hand over the sermon, but Harley had told Wilson the main points.

On 31st October 1721 Horrobin barred Mrs Puller from Holy Communion partly because of Mrs Horne's accusation, and partly because she openly critised his sermons. She appealed to Wilson, but conciliation failed, so Wilson called a special Convocation on the 29th November at which he asked the views of the clergy on Horrobin's sermon, urging them to speak freely. Here Horrobin repeated Mrs Horne's accusation against Mrs Puller. At a Consistory Court held at Kirk Michael on the 5th December Mrs Puller and Sir James Poole appeared before Wilson with friends who were prepared to swear to their innocence and they themselves took a solemn oath that they were innocent. No evidence of their guilt was produced, so Wilson cleared both of them of the charge. He and the Vicars General charged Mrs Horne with slander and ordered her to acknowledge her offence in St Mary's, Castletown, or be imprisoned in St German's crypt until she gave bonds to perform public penance. Wilson and his advisors were wrong in condemning Mrs Horne without a hearing, but she treated the court order with complete contempt so Wilson banned her from Holy Communion. Ignoring this, she attended a service early in 1722 when Horrobin, in defiance of the Bishop's ban administered the sacrament to her. Horrobin had refused Wilson's order to apologise to Mrs Puller after she was found innocent, maintaining that every parish priest had the right to refuse Holy Communion to a person of bad character.

Convocation that year fell on the 11th May and Wilson suspended Horrobin both as Archdeacon and as Rector of Andreas until he had given satisfaction to the Church as regards preaching heresy, and admitting Mrs Horne to Holy Communion while under censure. All the clergy except Vicar Bridson of Marown supported the suspension. Horrobin's sermon showed that he was ignorant of theology, but he was described by those who knew him as well meaning and even kindly.

Horrobin had the right of appeal against this to the Archbishop of York, but, perhaps feeling that the Archbishop would support the Bishop, he appealed instead to the Governor, claiming that the households of the Lord and the Governor were exempt from ecclesiastical discipline. On the 20th June 1722 Horne ordered Wilson to withdraw his suspension of Horrobin, but Wilson ignored this, so Horne closed Castletown Chapel for several months. Horne, seeing his chance of striking a blow at Wilson and the whole system of spiritual Courts, waited at the end of a Tynwald Court in Castle Rushen on 25th June 1722 until most of the members had gone home, then brought forward Horrobin's appeal and, declaring the suspension illegal, proceeded in the name of the whole Tynwald Court, to impose a fine of £50 on the Bishop and £20 on each of his two Vicars General for contempt of Court. They refused to pay as a matter of principle, so on 29th June all three were committed to Castle Rushen on the grounds that they were unwilling to conform to the laws of the Island. In prison Wilson obtained a statement from the Keys that they were not party to the fine, and did not consider the Church Courts tyrannical. By Horne's orders the Bishop's imprisonment was made as rigorous as possible, and he was denied the services of his housekeeper, Mrs Heywood, or of any of his servants. He and the Vicars General were treated as those guilty of high treason with only jailers in attendance. Wilson was imprisoned by himself in the guardhouse to the left of the entrance to the keep and the Vicars General in one to the right of it. They were allowed no visitors or letters. Wilson's cell was dark and damp and it caused chronic rheumatism in his right hand which made writing difficult for the rest of his life, as he had to grip the pen in his hand instead of his fingers. Several hundred people assembled daily under his barred window to hear him preach.

This high handed action of the Governor, defeated its own end by arousing the fury of the people, who considered Wilson to be the defender of the Island's liberties. They surrounded the Castle and threatened to pull down the Governor's house and were only dissuaded from this by Wilson himself. Meanwhile Wilson, on the advice of Archbishop Dawes of York, sent a petition to the King in Council asking for release and for the actions of the Governor to be declared null and void. He offered to give security for the payment of the fines if they proved to be legal. The appeal was laid before the Privy Council on the 19th July and on the 22nd July they sent the Bishop's petition to Horne, ordering him to answer Wilson's complaint and to allow him and his Vicars General free access to any documents they desired. The English Attorney General was told to ask Derby if the prisoners could be released on giving security for the payment of the fines. Derby's reply (29th July) was virtually a disclaimer of any knowledge of Horne's doings (though he tried to defend them) and he followed this up (31st July) with an abusive letter to Wilson, and sent a copy to Horne with instructions to proclaim it throughout the Island. On the 2nd August the legal advisers to the Privy Council advised the release of the three men on payment of the fine, and the Privy Council agreed to this on the 7th August. These instructions did not reach Horne till the 29th August, and on the 31st, when the fines were paid, he released them with a very bad grace. This was greeted with general rejoicing. People lined the route from Castle Rushen to Bishopscourt, strewing flowers (Wilson refused to let them strew garments) and seeking his blessing. The procession was three miles long and included four hundred leading Manx people on horseback. Bonfires on many of the hills proclaimed that the Bishop was once more free to live and work among his people. The Kirk Michael people prepared a bonfire of their own to greet him.

After Wilson's release the Governor continued to intercept his and the Vicars General's letters to England, and the promise to allow them free access to documents (with a view to an appeal) was largely evaded. He also continued his policy of pinpricks - for example on three occasions Captain Mercer, Constable of Peel Castle, refused to allow a burial in the Cathedral, which had been authorised by the Bishop,

on the grounds that the people concerned had no licence from the Governor.

It was the 4th July 1724, however, before the whole issue was finally settled by the Privy Council. At first it was suggested that in order to obtain their release the three men should pay their fines, but in the end Horne's proceedings were declared illegal, the fines were cancelled and Wilson removed Horrobin's suspension. No order, unfortunately, was made as to the costs of about £1,600 which proved a severe strain on Wilson's resources and left him permanently impoverished, despite a fund which raised £264 which was set up to help him. George I offered to translate him to the richer see of Exeter but Wilson declined. When Wilson declined this offer the King promised to defray his expenses out of the privy purse, but he died before he could do so.

Horrobin petitioned the Bishop against his suspension on 20th December 1722, but it was not until 6th November 1723 that Wilson accepted his unreserved submission, which was read by Vicar General Curghey to the southern clergy at Malew on 25th November. In February 1726 Horrobin obtained leave to visit England on urgent business, and on 25th May 1727 he resigned. His resignation removed a thorn in Wilson's flesh.

The net result of the whole episode was the beginning of Wilson's immense popularity, and the permanence of the Church Courts during his lifetime, though the fight against the claims of the Church Courts went on. His imprisonment certainly increased his influence over the clergy.

Horne was undoubtedly guilty of highhanded conduct, and the Keys were firmly on Wilson's side, but he could honestly claim to have acted with the consent of the Council and of the legal officers. In setting aside the decision of a Church Court he had exceeded his powers, as the Privy Council pointed out in their judgement and they also observed that the Tynwald Court which had sentenced the Bishop and his Vicars General was not properly constituted. On this latter point they were probably wrong, and their judgement omitted any reference to the two main points raised by the case, namely, whether this appeal from the Church Court was to the Archbishop of York or to the Earl of Derby, and whether the Governor was right in claiming that his officials and household were exempt from the jurisdiction of the

Church Courts.

From April 1723 to October 1724 Wilson and Walker had been in England for his appeal to the Privy Council and on the 18th July 1723 the parties were heard by Counsel. On the 17th December 1723 the Privy Council had referred the whole matter to the Attorney General and the Solicitor General, on whose advice their judgement was based.

Two more disputes between Horne and Wilson arose when the Governor in 1720 broke with long custom by refusing to supply a soldier to conduct those sentenced in the Church Courts to St German's prison.

Horne was succeeded as Governor on 3rd October 1723, by John Lloyd, a low type of man and a drunkard. From the start he opposed Wilson, and within a month he refused the services of a soldier to commit to prison a man named Wainwright, under censure for adultery, on the plea that he was a soldier in the Governor's service. He gave similar orders to the Captain of the Garrison at Peel Castle. He insisted on the immunity of state officials from the jurisdiction of the Church Courts, and even appointed known bad characters to these offices so that they would enjoy the immunity. He showed his petty mindedness by banning all rejoicing and celebrations when Wilson returned from his successful appeal to the Privy Council.

The last straw came on the 12th March 1725, when, despite it being a Sunday, he not only spent the morning hunting, but rode through several parishes, and even through Douglas, with his retinue during the time of morning service. This affront to ordinary decency so aroused public opinion that Derby at once dismissed him. Before this, two men of bad character, Wattleworth (grandson of Archdeacon Samuel Wattleworth) and Looney 'married' a widower to his niece, (with whom he was living), in a public house. The woman died soon afterwards and the widower and both men were excommunicated. After the Court hearing Vicar General Curghey was rescued by the mob from Wattleworth's vengeance, but Lloyd took no action. Freedom from church censures were claimed by the soldiers and retainers of the Lord, and Lloyd would write to Wilson excusing them from censure. In 1724 Thomas Heywood was excommunicated for fathering an illegitimate child, and he planned to shoot Wilson and his Vicar

General, knowing that the Governor would shield him from the consequences, and this belief led to several threats against Wilson's life. Lloyd's reaction was to appoint Heywood Captain of the Douglas fort, to protect him from Church censure. In the same year a man who had publicly cursed the Bishop was given a post in Peel Castle garrison. Francis Davenport, who was imprisoned in Castle Rushen for drinking the devil's health, was allowed to escape.

Before the next Governor arrived Wilson, on the 24th June 1725, asked the Deemsters and the Keys to give a ruling on whether Horne and Lloyd had the power to refuse the use of soldiers to enforce the sentences of the Church Courts. They decided that they had not this power, but when Governor Thomas Horton, a country squire and a magistrate from Chadderton, arrived in October 1725 he declined to be bound by this, and on several occasions refused a soldier for this purpose. Though an abler man than Horne and Lloyd he was of bad character, and did everything he could to break down the system of Church discipline, with considerable success. He used his influence with Derby to have clergymen who were opposed to Wilson appointed to Crown livings.

The Bishop's chief executive officer in the 18th century was the Sumner General. He was mainly responsible for presentments, and sometimes he was also parish clerk or schoolmaster. He dealt with the estates of deceased persons and collected fines imposed by the Church Courts and tithe arrears. He had to keep dogs out of Church during service, and in 1735 the Curate of Arbory asked if the Sumner1 was not obliged to attend funerals, as the barking of dogs drowned the service. He did well out of the office, for when gathering the wool tax with horse and sack he received a lamb and a fleece from the tithe. For escorting an offender to gaol he received four pence and often hired out the penitent's white sheet at four pence a time. He had to arrange for the swearing in of Church wardens and to empanel the Chapter Quest - 4 'honest and sufficient' men, who met every three or four weeks with the Vicar as chairman and were bound by oath to report and present anyone alleged to have broken canon law. He dealt with matrimonial problems, but the power of divorce was only rarely used by the Church.

In 1712 Wilson appointed as Sumner General Thomas Corlett of Ballaugh. In April 1727 the Chancery Court, instigated by Horton, inhibited him from acting and appointed in his place William Christian of Jurby, who was to hold office for 21 years, but Wilson refused to admit him. The Bishop appealed unsuccessfully to the Deemsters, the Keys and the King in Council, and it is from this time that a decline in the powers and functions of the Church Courts can be dated, so that at Wilson's death, and certainly by the end of the century, their jurisdiction was limited to matrimonial and testamentary matters, and this remained the case until 1884, when these functions were transferred to the High Court. Henceforth the Sumner General was appointed by the Governor on behalf of the Lord.

Other cases of dispute with successive Governors lay in their policy of ordering notices to be read in Churches without the Bishop's authority, and in Wilson's policy of reducing or remitting fines imposed by the Civil Courts on appeal to the Church Courts. As such fines went to the Lord of the Isle, this policy was bound to bring him into collision with Derby. The Governors made purely spiritual offences recognisable in the Civil Courts and ecclesiastical censures were often evaded by appeals to the Civil Courts.

In 1721 a book called 'The Independent Whig' was brought into the Island on behalf of Derby and began circulating. It was a collection of essays by Thomas Gordon, a freethinker, which violently attacked religion, morality and Church authority, cast doubt on the teaching of the gospels and abused the clergy. John Stevenson, M.H.K., of Balladoole, a friend of Wilson, sent a copy to the Bishop. For this he was imprisoned in Castle Rushen by Governor Horne, who must have known about its circulation. He was only released when Wilson returned it to the Governor, with a protest against Stevenson's imprisonment, and against the Governor for harbouring so 'damnable' a book. The Revd William Ross, schoolmaster at Castletown, was imprisoned for three days for refusing to put the book in Castletown library. In June 1721 the Governor ordered an appeal for charity on behalf of William Watterson (whose family were starving) to be read in the southern churches. Governor Mawdsley, early in Wilson's episcopate, had agreed that no briefs should be read in churches without the Bishop's prior consent. Vicar Woods of Malew was handed this brief by Sedden (the Water Bailiff) at 9 a.m. on Sunday, 18th June, but as he

refused to read it without first consulting the Bishop, and translating it into Manx he was, next morning, fined £3-6-8d and imprisoned for a week by the Governor and Deemster Moore. He was not allowed to make a defence, or given a public hearing, but he was released the following Saturday evening. Wilson complained about the Governor's action in Tynwald, but to no avail, and when Woods did not pay the fine he was imprisoned again and, in his own words, "exposed to the rigour, vermin and stench of a cold damp and loathsome room without bed or fire". After he had been there a short time Wilson paid the fine. At Convocation (17th May 1722) Wilson asked the clergy if it had not been the custom for the Governor to send any notices for reading in church to the Bishop and via him to the clergy and they agreed that this was so. After this time the Governor's claim to issue notices not approved by Wilson to be read in church was dropped, and in 1725 Woods' fine was repaid.

In 1722 Henry Halsall of Castletown admitted to adultery with Jane Macnameer, the Governor's Housekeeper, and was sentenced to seven days in St German's prison and ordered to do penance on three Sundays. He was eventually restored to the Church on doing one Sunday's penance at Malew, and the lady fled to England. The Governor brought Halsall to trial by Court Martial because he, as a soldier, had submitted to Church censure without his permission and for disregarding the immunity of soldiers of the garrison from Church censure, and was sentenced to be discharged with ignominy. Wilson protested, and asked for the Keys to be summoned so that he could show that Halsall had broken no law in submitting to Church censure. He also said that in Manx law no one was immune from Church censure. The Governor told all the soldiers of the garrisons at Peel, Douglas, and Castletown that they would be severely punished if they submitted to Church censure. He also helped people under Church censure to leave the Island.

While all this was happening Wilson was greatly inconvenienced by the personal hostility of one of his clergy, the Revd William Bridson. In May 1721 he sent a message to Vicar William Gell of Onchan that he could prove Gell and the Bishop to be liars. He also gave Holy Communion to Henry Balfour, who was under Church censure, declaring the censure to be illegal. For this he was suspended at a

Consistory Court (consisting of the Bishop, the two Vicars General and six other clergy) held at Kirk Michael on the 27th June 1721, but two months later he apologised, and the suspension was lifted on the 29th August. He continued to trouble Wilson, however, by supporting the Governor against him, and by supporting Derby in his disputes with the Bishop. For this he was rewarded by Derby, who appointed him to the Crown livings of Lezayre (1727) Bride (May 1729) and Ballaugh (July 1729).

Wilson met Governor Horton soon after his arrival in 1725 and found him very prejudiced against the Church and its laws and discipline and against Churchmen. He at once refused the use of soldiers to help with Church discipline, and thwarted Church discipline in every way. For a while Wilson's relations with Horton were quite good, but he showed much rudeness to the Bishop and heavily fined Wilson's supporters for trivial offences. On one occasion Wilson was summoned to meet Horton at Castletown but after the long journey found that he had gone out hunting. His anti-Church policy encouraged immorality, and the worst criminals were protected. He once arrived drunk to see the Bishop. The Churches were treated with contempt, and when in May 1728 Wilson ordered the Sumner General to employ a slater to repair the Cathedral roof Horton stopped it. In 1730 he removed the roof timbers from the Cathedral to build new stables for his horses at Castletown, and they were shipped from Peel. "I know not what will come of this" wrote Wilson in his journal, but later he added "I now know what happened. The ship which carried the timber was lost on her next voyage, and the Governor's son lost his sight in the smallpox".

There was a sequel to the case of Thomas Heywood. In March 1726 he was presented for giving a party marked by cursing, drunkenness and blasphemy. Horton at once declared the presentment null and void and showed his favour to Heywood by hunting with him and publicly dining with him. In April 1730 Derby, who claimed that the Lord's retainers were exempt from Church discipline, pardoned Heywood, remitted all disabilities imposed by the Church Courts, and restored all his rights and liberties. Heywood showed this to the Governor (May 1730) who, on the advice of his senior officials and the Deemsters, ordered the Vicar of Braddan (the

Revd John Curghey) to read it in Church in Manx and English, and ordered the Chaplain of Castletown (the Revd William Ross) to read it in Church in English, and they did so. Wilson then told Curghey that he had to read out, in Manx and English, that Heywood was still excommunicate, and that everyone must avoid his company under threat of excommunication. Heywood now began interrupting Church services with his soldiers, and to show that he thought himself no longer excommunicate began attending Church services beginning with Bishopscourt Chapel, but Wilson told him that the service could not go on, as he was excommunicate. On the morning of the 21st June 1730 he came to Braddan Church whereupon the Vicar stopped the service, so Heywood returned in the afternoon with soldiers, and seems to have been admitted. On the 24th June he attended St John's Church with the Governor for the customary service before the proclamation of the laws from Tynwald Hill. Wilson said that there could be no service while Heywood was there, and although Horton threatened that if the Bishop refused to read prayers he would do so at his peril, there was no service.

In 1726 Anthony Halsall, the Chaplain of St Matthew's, criticised Deemster Moore who, on the instructions of Governor Horton, had refused a jury of enquiry to find out who had broken the windows of the Church. For this he was tried by Horton and his officials and put in the pillory and fined £10 but on appeal to Derby the sentence was quashed on a legal technicality. In November 1727 the Sumner of Braddan was imprisoned for presenting a certain William Christian for adultery. In 1728 Ross, Chaplain of Castletown, was ordered by the Governor not to catechise children, and on Easter Monday 1729 Vicar Woods of Malew was not allowed to read prayers in St Mary's in the absence of a chaplain. On the 6th December 1731 Horton sequestered the tithes of Santan and ordered the parishioners, not to pay anything to the Curate, the Revd John Cosnahan, who had been turned out of his office to make way for the Revd Paul Crebbin, a nominee of Horton.

Horton left in 1736, and in his last years he was rather more co-operative, though he still refused to help Wilson to enforce ecclesiastical discipline. But the continued opposition which he and Derby offered to the Church Courts had its effect, and in Wilson's last twenty years they gradually fell into disuse, and the discipline became largely voluntary. This is shown by the fact that from 1720-1736 1,450 people were dealt with in the Chapter and Consistory Courts, but only 68 from 1736-1755. The discipline had worked well until 1714 when the Governors had supported it.

In 1734 Tynwald abolished corbs, that is certain customary payments due from a retiring incumbent (or from the executors of an incumbent who had died in office) to his successor, in addition to the payment of dilapidations.

Wilson's relations with Derby's Governors were bad, apart from the first three Nicholas Stanley, James Cranston (1701-3) and Robert Mawdsley (1703-14) who helped him to pass the Act of Settlement. This ended when the 10th Earl died on the 1st February 1736. The Island then passed to James Murray, 2nd Duke of Atholl (1690-1764), great-grandson of James Stanley, Earl of Derby, and with this transfer to Atholl all Church and State disputes ended. He appointed as Governor Captain James Murray, who remained until 1744, then came Patrick Lindsey (1744-51) and Basil Cochrane (1751-61) and the Bishop's relations were good with all three.

In 1666 Derby sold the Impropriate Tithes (the tithes of Rushen Abbey) to Bishop Barrow and Archdeacon Fletcher in trust, to augment stipends and maintain schoolmasters. They were bought with money raised by Barrow in England for the benefit of the Manx Clergy, and of education in the Island. They were subject to the charge of maintaining and repairing the chancels of the churches of the parishes whence such tithes were derived. There were some doubts as to Derby's right to sell them, so to secure the title the grant was made by Derby to the Bishop and the Archdeacon of certain lands in Lancashire as collateral security. When Derby's Isle of Man property came to Atholl in 1736 the lands in Lancashire and other property went to Edward, Earl of Derby. Atholl seized the Impropriate Tithes and evicted the Bishop and Archdeacon and the other trustees. Suits were at once instituted in the English Court of Chancery, in which it was decided that Atholl was entitled to the Impropriate Tithes and that the trustees should be indemnified from the collateral security which yielded £219 per annum. In 1809 Derby was threatened with a Court action to pay an increased annual

sum in proportion to the increased value of the Impropriate Tithes. He offered a lump sum of £16,000 to be quit of future annual payments, and this was agreed. This was invested in land, so in future the Impropriate Fund consisted of the annual rents and profits of this land. Bishop Barrow had been determined to recover for the Manx Church some part of the tithes of which she had been robbed at the Reformation. The Earl, as Impropriator, agreed to surrender the tithe of the ten parishes belonging to him. He and the Archdeacon and their assigns were given a lease for 10,000 years with a payment of £130 each thirty years. This became due in 1698, and Wilson paid it to prevent the lease from being forfeited.

Wilson attached great importance to the proper preparation of ordinands and took them to live with him at Bishopscourt for a year prior to ordination. He devoted much time to teaching them the Greek New Testament. For most of his episcopate he ordained men in some Church before a congregation, but in his old age he held the ordinations in Bishopscourt Chapel.

He worked ceaselessly in the interests of the clergy both as regards material and spiritual matters. He found in 1698 that the average stipend was £17 per annum, and by 1730 it had only risen to £25 per annum. He added to their glebes and contributed to repairs and improvements to the vicarages. He kept in regular touch with them, and many of them were invited to Bishopscourt for days and even weeks. He stressed to them the importance of house to house visiting, which he considered their most important pastoral task. His ascendancy over them was due, less to his being the Bishop, than from his personal holiness. He advised them to encourage their people to have family prayers, even if only to say the Lord's Prayer. He insisted that Holy Communion be administered regularly, not just three times a year. While physically able to do so he made a general visitation of the diocese four times a year. He recommended them to read the service for ordaining priests each Ember week, and tried hard to raise the rather lax standards of the clergy. On the 10th June 1699 the Kirk Michael Churchwardens presented their vicar, Henry Norris, for immorality, and he was suspended from his office until he had cleared himself and shown proper repentance. This he seems to have done, because on the 12th October 1699 Wilson convened the clergy to German Church and there restored Norris. When he died in 1717 Wilson took his funeral, so his conduct afterwards must have been satisfactory.

At the end of his life he succeeded in obtaining for the clergy the renewal of the Royal Bounty, which had been suspended for several years. In 1730 he set up a fund to provide for clergy, widows and children in the diocese, and started it off with £100.

He required of the clergy the highest standards of character and conduct, without which their teaching would be ineffective.

Wilson firmly opposed non-residence, but in November 1724 he allowed Vicar John Christian of Jurby to live in his own house adjoining the Church instead of in the vicarage because of his large family and many servants. He started the fisherman's service at the start of the herring season. When the boats were ready to set out on their first night's fishing, Wilson would come from Bishopscourt on his little shaggy Manx pony. Then, while the boats would be lying in the harbour with sails set, waiting for the tide, the men would gather on the shore. Surrounded by their wives and children they would kneel on the sand while the Bishop read the service and gave the blessing standing in an old boat.

On the 18th June 1705, with the Governor's approval, he ordered that in public services of the Church this petition be included in the Litany and always used in the Church "That it may please thee to give and preserve to our use the kindly fruits of the earth, and to restore and continue to us the blessings of the seas, so as in due time we may enjoy them". It was still used in most Manx Churches as late as 1900.

On 24th April 1741 Wilson ordered the clergy to revive beating of the parish boundaries in Rogation week, saying prayers for the crops at various places. The Collects to be used were those for Quinquagesima, Lent III and Septuagesima, and the Prayers for Rain (if needed), in time of Dearth and Famine, and In Time of War, and the last two petitions of the Litany. Psalm 103 was to be said by the Minister alone. The custom had evidently lapsed but although Wilson's instructions were obeyed for a time, beating of the bounds later took place only at long and irregular intervals.

In Wilson's later years the conduct of some of the clergy was a great worry to him. Between 1736 and 1755 six were suspended, either for drinking, neglecting Sunday services, embezzling money or for immorality. In 1735 he had to complain to the clergy about irregular marriages, hasty reading of the prayers and neglect of the parish libraries and Communion vessels.

Some of the clergy were unaware of anything happening in the wider world. In the reign of George I Wilson once travelled over the mountains to Lonan. He arrived late, and heard the Vicar reading prayers for William and Mary. This was probably John Taubman, Vicar of Lonan 1686-1720.

Wilson's Manx Catechism (full title The Principles and Duties of Christianity) was published on 30th May 1707. It is an instruction, not a translation, of the Prayer Book Catechism. Wilson and Hildesley could both say the Commandments and the Blessing in Manx.

In 1742 Wilson made 15 the minimum age for confirmation, perhaps to prevent boys and girls being rushed into marriage against their will, though earlier he confirmed his own son at Ballaugh when he was 13.

Wilson laid great stress on Christian morals and the need to obey the teaching of the Church. To the question "What must I do to be saved?" he would have replied "Repentance, amendment of life and conformity to the teaching of the Church" but it is remarkable that nowhere does he mention the need for conversion or Christ's atoning sacrifice as a means of salvation. His writings show that he attached great importance to the efficacy of the sacrament administered by episcopally ordained priests; to apostolical succession; and to absolution by a priest. Denial of this last point was one of the charges against Horrobin. He believed strongly that only work undertaken with a conscious reliance on the power of God had any real effect or value - "Without God's special blessing your best purposes and all your endeavours will come to nothing. 'We have toiled all the night and 'taken nothing' will be found true by everyone who tries to manage without the aid of God's Holy Spirit. Beg of God a blessing on yourself and your work every day of your life." He was a lifelong reader of the Bible, and he advised those reading it to implore the help of the Holy Spirit for true understanding of it, and to take all Scripture as spoken to yourself. His devotional book on the Lord's Supper was published in 1734. He remained evangelical and Low Church despite his belief in priestly absolution, and longed for the first Prayer Book of Edward VI to be brought back into use.

Wilson took an active part on Sundays in the parishes until he was about 80, and even at this age he preached on Palm Sunday, administered Holy Communion on Easter Eve and again at Peel on Easter Sunday (when there were 300 communicants), on the following Sunday at Kirk Michael and on the next Sunday he took the whole service at Jurby. In 1729 he gave Holy Communion on Easter Sunday, singlehanded, to about 250 at Kirk Michael. Until about 1745 he would often ride to distant parts of the diocese. Horseback was virtually the only means of transport in Wilson's time, though he is said to have imported the first carriage into the Island. Douglas and Castletown could only be reached from Bishopscourt by bridle path over the mountains. In 1739 he rode to Peel on a stormy day to preach, and rode on horseback until he was 80, but after 1749 he used a carriage and took drives around Orrisdale. After 1743 he confined himself to his immediate duties, but continued confirming until 1753, though always at Kirk Michael, Ballaugh or Bishopscourt, to which the candidates had to come.

Family Prayers in Bishopscourt Chapel were held at 6 a.m. in the summer and 7 a.m. in the winter, and always in the evening. He usually took them himself, and neither guests nor work could interrupt them. He used to spend three hours of each day in prayer, in the morning, at noon and in the evening.

Out of a stipend of £300 Wilson gave generously to churches, vicarages and parishes. He gave £40 to begin the building of St John's Chapel in 1699, and in 1719 he and Rector William Walker shared the cost of the steeple on Ballaugh Church. He gave £10 towards St Matthew's Church (1708) and in 1712 he built a new vicarage at Arbory by making a contribution and by taking the services himself without a fee during the year's interregnum after Vicar Robinson. The parish also made a contribution. He used to leave his horse, during the service, in a field just above Parville.

In 1744 he endowed Jurby with a meadow. In 1743 a new vicarage was built at Kirk Michael and

Wilson bought 18 acres of glebe for the parish. In 1704 he gave a new east window to Braddan Church and in 1705 provided the parish with a new vicarage. In 1706 he gave £5 towards the rebuilding of Ballure Chapel and £5 towards the building and enlargement of Lezayre Church. In 1715 he gave a new vicarage to Rushen and subscribed generously towards the building of Patrick Church. In 1722 he gave £5 towards a new vicarage at Santan and paid for the steeple for the Church. These are only examples, as such gifts were made almost annually, so that in his last years he was giving away 60% of his income.

To help his older clergy, Wilson several times dispensed with the strict observance of Canon Law. Thus in December 1740 he agreed to a request from Vicar William Gell of Onchan for his son to assist him (virtually as a lay reader) because of his impaired health and eyesight, and in October 1749 he licensed William Kewin, schoolmaster and parish clerk of Bride, to help Rector Matthias Curghey, who could not get a Curate, and whose age and failing sight made it impossible for him to read the whole service. In January 1750 he allowed John Christian, an ordinand, to help his father, Vicar Thomas Christian of Marown, whose health had prevented him from doing his parish duties for nearly a year. In 1751 Wilson pointed out to the Archbishop of York that there were no ordinands of canonical age and received permission to ordain men provided they were 21.

Wilson was tolerant of other faiths and his services were often attended by Catholics and Methodists. He allowed the Quakers freedom of worship, but most of them emigrated.

During Wilson's episcopate the Archdeacon was appointed by Derby, and the Archdeacon appointed his own Official (always a clergyman). The two Vicars General were nominated by the Bishop, each having authority throughout the Island, though in practice the northern half was allotted to one, and the southern half to the other.

Wilson found the practice of burials in Church and in the Chancel and under the family pew widespread, but whenever he consecrated a church he made an order banning such burials.

In 1698 Wilson went to England, and on the 27th October was married by licence to Mary Patten in Winwick Church by Vicar Henry Finch. Wilson had met her while Curate of Newchurch. She was born on 16th July 1674. They returned to the Island the following April, this long absence being probably due to Bishopscourt not yet being habitable, but their married life was short. Mrs Wilson's health seems not to have been good and she died at Warrington on the 7th March 1705 and was buried there. Wilson had taken her to Cheshire in the hope that her native air would do her good. She left a son, Thomas, but three other children, a boy and two girls, had died in infancy. The Bishop never remarried. He lost his father on the 29th May 1702 and his mother died, aged 84, on 16th August 1708, but Mrs Heywood acted as his housekeeper from 1717 until her death in November 1752.

Wilson was a man of Christian humility, sincerity and zeal. He had great tact, commonsense, and a deep faith, combined with great aptitude for business. He was a great believer in family prayers. He was firm but gentle, and soon won his people's love, respect and confidence. He was indifferent to material things and used to say "Nature wants little and grace wants less". His deep seriousness was united with habitual cheerfulness, but he never forgot the sanctity of his office, nor could others forget it. He observed his birthday and New Year's Day with great solemnity, but especially the anniversary of his ordination, when he always read along with other things 1 Timothy $3^{8,9,10}$, 4^{12-16}, and 6^{20-21}. He would never sit in the House of Lords, saying that the church should have nothing to do with the state, but his predecessor, Levinz, used to sit there in his episcopal robes. Cardinal Fleury, the chief minister in the French Government, lived, like Wilson, to a great age, and much wanted to see him, so he wrote a letter. Wilson's reply gave Fleury such a high opinion of him that, in the war with France (1740-48), he gave orders that no French warship was to attack the Isle of Man.

In his later years, especially after 1750, Wilson suffered from attacks of gout and after 1743 his eyes gave trouble, though they yielded to treatment to some extent. As late as 1754 he held an ordination and consecrated a church. From 1753 his mind began to fail, and in January 1755, the Governor wrote to Atholl saying that the Bishop's memory and judgement had gone. It was either this, or spiritual exaltation which underlay the incident when he said to Henry Corlett, who was reading the Greek New Testament to him, that he could see angels in the trees outside the study window at Bishopscourt.

The immediate cause of his death was a chill caught while walking in the avenue of elms north of the chapel (which he had planted) on a cold damp day after evening prayers and he died about 4 a.m. on Friday, the 7th March 1755 (the anniversary of his wife's death), aged 91. His last illness was peaceful and he died, as he had lived, praising God in Psalms and verses from the Te Deum. Shortly before his death he said, "whatever sins I have committed that are not yet forgiven, Lord, pardon me for Jesus Christ's sake". His coffin was made some years before from an elm he had planted soon after his arrival, and he asked in his Will to be buried opposite the east window of Kirk Michael Church, hoping that his example would deter others from 'the indecent custom of burying the bodies of their friends in the House of God'. He asked that his grave should be nine feet deep and walled around with bricks. He left a legacy to the poor of each parish and £5 to each of his Vicars General (Radcliffe and Moore). His funeral, on the 11th March was attended by people from every town, village and parish, and it was a day of mourning throughout the Island. His coffin was carried from Bishopscourt to Kirk Michael in relays. The service was taken by the Vicar, the Revd James Wilks, and the sermon was preached by the friend and companion of his later years, the Revd Philip Moore, the text being "the righteous shall be had in everlasting remembrance". (Psalm 112^6).

Spencer Walpole wrote "As a Bishop, Wilson lived some centuries too late; as a statesman he was a century before his time". His episcopate remains the outstanding one in the history of our diocese, and his name is still a household word.

The Parishes under Wilson

ANDREAS is the only one of the ancient parishes named after an apostle, but it was probably originally dedicated to a Celtic saint, and the change to Andreas may have been made under Scottish influence. It is a Crown living. The Church is unique among the ancient ones in that it is in the centre of the parish. The Rectory was rebuilt in 1666 and although added to and altered it remains basically the same building. Andreas is one of the three rectories in the Island and until 1978 (except for 1938-64) the Rector was Archdeacon of Man. The Archdeacon and Rector on Wilson's arrival was Archippus Kippax. He was succeeded on 10th June 1700 by Christopher Marsden, but his tenure of the office was short. The new Rector and Archdeacon was Samuel Wattleworth.

His successor was Robert Horrobin. It was an unhappy time for the parish, as Horrobin quarrelled with Wattleworth, the Curate, who did not even live in the parish. There was no service in Manx, there had been no regular school for 12 years. The children were not catechised and Baptisms were in English. The last Archdeacon and Rector under Wilson was John Kippax.

Once at a confirmation at Andreas, Wilson made a public complaint to the churchwardens about the state of the altar cloth. There was no flagon or alms dish. Two months later he ordered the churchwardens to supply an altar cloth by next Candlemas Day, on penalty of a fine of half a crown each.

ARBORY the name is a corruption of St Cairbre, a disciple of St Patrick, to whom the original church was dedicated when built in 1358. Cairbre gave his name to the parish, but the present church is dedicated to St Columba. The old church stood to the south of, and parallel with the present one. The record of vicars goes back to 1291, further than any other parish in the Island. The original churchyard had no access from the main road, but was entered by the gate opposite Parville. In 1712 Bishop Wilson, helped by the parish, raised money for a new vicarage, which stood until demolished in 1862. It stood just inside the gate of the churchyard, near the Cunningham grave, and some of its stones were used for the 1862 house. The removal of the old vicarage provided extra space (consecrated in 1863) in the burial ground. Until the early years of this century water for baptisms came from the well at Ballacross. Arbory is a Crown living.

The Vicar, on Wilson's arrival, was Samuel Robinson, appointed in 1680. In April 1713 was succeeded by Robert Parr. He and William Bridson were the only two clergy on Derby's side in his dis-

pute with Wilson and in March 1723 he was rewarded by being appointed Rector of Bride, then one of the best livings in the diocese. In June 1714 one of the churchwardens was severely censured by the Bishop for refusing to buy enough Communion wine for the previous Whit Sunday, resulting in sixteen people being unable to communicate. Derby seems now to have left Arbory vacant for three years, as it was not until June 1726 that Charles Wattleworth, Curate of Andreas, was appointed.

He was succeeded by John Quayle, who was Vicar from July 1728 until 1748. He seems to have neglected the Church, as a visitation in 1743 reported that the pulpit, reading desk and several seats were broken, the west door needed repair, the floor was uneven and full of holes, the chest needed a lock, and the church fence was partly broken down.

The last Vicar of Arbory in Wilson's time was John Moore. The great event of his incumbency was the building of the present parish church, but that was under Bishop Hildesley.

BALLAUGH is one of the three rectories on the Island, and is a Crown Living. The church is first mentioned in a Papal Bull of 1231. The Burial register begins in 1598 (the oldest in the diocese), the Baptismal register in 1607 and the Marriage register in 1695. These registers became very dilapidated over the years and their preservation is due to the Revd Thomas Howard (Rector from 1836-76) who copied them into a bound book. In 1717 the church was enlarged at the instigation of Bishop Wilson, an extra 21' being added to the east end, the cost being met by the Bishop, except for £12 paid by the parish. The foundation of this extension was laid on 19th June 1717 by Wilson. In addition the gable was added, adorned by two pilasters springing from the porch, and surmounted by a bell tower. The Bishop and Rector Walker paid for the tower and Wilson also gave at this time the two Jacobean chairs in the sanctuary. The church walls contain material from earlier churches. The present north side windows are not older than the 18th century, and replace two small openings. The Manx people firmly believed in Jeremiah's prophecy that evil came from the north, so there were few or no windows in the north wall of the old Manx churches. The leaning pillars are not earlier than the 18th century, the weather cock is 19th century and the sundial is 1813. The font is built into a window ledge, and is made out of a block of sandstone. It cannot be dated, but it is clearly very old. A cross cut in relief is the only decoration, and the Manx inscription is "Ta un chiarn, un Credjue, un Vashtey, un Jee as Ayr jeh ooilley" (There is one Lord, one Faith, one Baptism, one God and Father of all).

The Rector in 1698 was Henry Lowcay. In the Burial register for 1700 we read "The reverend, pious and eminently learned Henry Lowcay MA who led his life so that he might be justly termed and esteemed a true pattern of primitive piety"

His successor, William Walker was one of the outstanding men of the Manx Church. He was born in Ballaugh on the 18th February 1679, the son of Thomas Walker of Lezayre, who died soon after his birth, leaving the family in straitened circumstances. At the age of 13 we find him a manservant at Balladoole, Arbory, and one day, when driving a horse pulling an empty sledge to the cornfield, he became so absorbed in a book that the horse ran furiously across the lawn opposite Balladoole house. His employer, Mr John Stevenson, MHK, (later Speaker), saw the incident, stopped the horse, and was so impressed with the boy's desire to learn that he sent him at his own expense to Castletown Grammar School, and for this Walker remained grateful for the rest of his life.

He also, in some way, attracted the notice of Bishop Wilson, who made him deacon on the 11th March 1700 when he was only 21. The 1522 Ordinal made 21 the minimum age for a deacon and 25 for a priest, but Canon 34 of 1604 laid down 23 for a deacon and 24 for a priest, while recognising the Archbishop of Canterbury's right to issue a faculty for a deacon (not a priest) to be ordained under age. This evidently happened in Walker's case, and he was ordained priest on 31st May 1702. On Lowcay's death, Wilson appointed him Rector of Ballaugh, but as he was still only a deacon the living was kept vacant until the 10th June 1703, during which time Matthias Curghey acted as Curate from 1698-1703. Ballaugh, being a rectory, was one of the best livings in the diocese, but Wilson doubtless appointed him to have him near Bishopscourt to help in administering the diocese, having evidently noticed the young man's qualities. In 1712, on the death of Robert Parr of

Lezayre, Wilson appointed him Vicar General and from then on they worked closely together. He entered fully into the Bishop's plans for building and restoring churches and made generous contributions to this work from his own pocket. After 1722 he made several journeys to London in connection with Wilson's law suit, and in recognition of the ability he showed in this matter, Archbishop Wake of Canterbury conferred the Lambeth LLD on him in July 1728. Wilson possibly asked for this with a view to Walker succeeding him as Bishop. On his return home after receiving this degree, seeing his mother in the crowd by the Rectory door, he at once dismounted and knelt before her for a blessing, an action characteristic of his simplicity and humility.

Walker's mother married again, but her second husband was a drunkard. They lived with Walker, who found his stepfather a severe trial, but for his mother's sake he put up with it.

Walker was a man of great wisdom and courage, with a judicial mind, and a temper which nothing could ruffle. His noble character was long remembered, as was his wonderful knack of being able to extend the right kind of sympathy to all he met. He was one of the most learned and respected men on the Island. He undertook a major restoration of the rectory and the outbuildings at great personal cost, having found them virtually ruinous. The rectory probably stands on or near the site where a clerical dwelling has stood for 700 years. He left money in his will to build a new parochial school (the children having hitherto been taught in the Church) and in 1721 he gave four acres for use of the parish schoolmaster in perpetuity and to build a house for him.

In 1714 there were complaints that the seating in the church was not properly regulated, and two of the wardens had nowhere to sit. Walker therefore asked Deemster Mylrea, Thomas Curlot, (Sumner General), William Curlot (Parish Clerk) and the other two wardens to make a full investigation and report to him. This was done and the matter was apparently settled.

Walker made the following note in the Baptismal register on the 15th March 1709. "This day Dr Thomas Wilson, Lord Bishop of this Isle, issued a decree enforcing a former decree of the Lord Bishop Bridgman obliging all the tenants of the Bishop's Domain who are inhabitants within the precincts of

Ballaugh, to come to the said church as to their proper parochial church, and to perform all parochial duties as other parishioners do. Note: This is the final result of long and tedious controversies between the Vicar of Kirk Michael (Norris) and myself. The papers relating to this debate are in the church chest, and the originals of the two decrees are in the Lord Bishop's Registry. March 24th-16 families (being all that lived within the parish) have conformed to the above decree".

Walker died on the 18th June 1729, aged 50, and was buried in the chancel on the 20th under a stone with a Latin epitaph composed by the Bishop, who preached at the funeral on Philippians 1[21] (For me to live is Christ, and to die is gain). The site of the grave was opposite the altar gate, outside the rail, but in the 19th century restoration of the church the stone disappeared.

The Revd William Bridson, who succeeded him as rector, was an entirely different kind of man. We have already met him as a favourite of Derby (to whom he owed his move to one of the best livings in the diocese) because of his opposition to, and dislike of, Wilson. He was regarded with neither love nor respect by his parishioners. He neglected the rectory buildings, which he left in a bad state of repair.

In his place in 1751 came the Revd Philip Moore.

He became Curate of Bride on a stipend of £26 per annum. As a young man he was high spirited and while curate of Marown he masqueraded as a ghost in St Trinian's one night to frighten the people and show them how foolish they were to believe in the buggane. The parishioners later found out that it was Moore. While Curate of Marown he was reproved by Wilson for frivolous conduct of a kind not expected in a clergyman. Apart from the St Trinian's incident, he was accused of writing a sarcastic letter ridiculing the other clergy. Wilson accepted his apology in both cases.

At his own request he was not ordained priest until 23rd September 1739 because he disagreed with the statement in the 39 Articles that salvation was impossible for the heathen. This ordination took place in St Matthew's, of which he had been appointed chaplain in 1736, and where he remained until 1765, combining this with the Mastership of the Grammar School which he retained until his death. He was an open pluralist and combined this post with being

Rector of Ballaugh (1751-1760) and Rector of Bride (1760-1783). This did not please his parishioners and both at Ballaugh and Bride complaints were made that the services were not being provided, even though the people paid tithe. From time to time he provided a Curate, and once the Ballaugh churchwardens presented him in the Vicar General's Court for neglect of duty. Only the influence of Bishop Hildesley saved him from censure.

BALLURE CHURCH is on the site of an old treen chapel and burial ground which was for centuries a place for worship. It is first mentioned in 1637 and a burial in 1611 is recorded, but the Church in its present form dates from the 1706 restoration undertaken by Bishop Wilson. It had previously been rebuilt by Bishop Parr in 1639-1640. A further restoration and enlargement took place in 1743, and was so thorough that a consecration deed was prepared, and it was reconsecrated on the 9th June 1745. It was originally a chapel of ease to Maughold, and was built at the request of Ramsey residents (where there was no church until 1822), who, in order to reach their parish church of Maughold, had a long and difficult journey which involved crossing the Ballure river, often a raging torrent. It is variously called St Mary's and St Catherine's. The Chaplains were appointed by the Vicar of Maughold.

In Wilson's time the church was used as a school, and in 1712 James Knipe, the schoolmaster, was licensed to conduct the services. He remained until 1747 when the first ordained Chaplain was appointed in the person of the Revd Thomas W. J. Woods.

BRADDAN is one of the seventeen ancient parishes, the Bishop being patron, and the name is a corruption of Brenainn, one of the old Irish Saints. The churchyard is much older than the church, which in its present form is 1773, though the site is a Keeil dating back to the 5th or 6th century. The present church incorporates parts of older buildings, but the date of the pre-1773 church is unknown. A gallery was erected in 1737, and it was decided that the cost of this and future work would be paid for in proportion two thirds by the parish and one third by Douglas. The gallery was "for the good of the inhabitants and the cottage holders of Douglas" because the pews were all appropriated to the various farms and estates in the parish, and there were no free seats for the poor or for people living in detached houses. In 1704 Bishop Wilson put in a new east window, and the floor was flagged; then in 1735 he gave £6 towards a new vicarage, and on the 20th March 1739 he gave £20 for buying a glebe. Like all the old Manx churches there is no division between chancel and nave. The site of this new vicarage, which adjoined the church, proved unhealthy however, so in 1742 Tynwald, in response to a petition from the Vicar and Wardens, passed an Act enabling the glebe lands and vicarage to be moved to a more wholesome site three quarters of a mile from the church. To this new vicarage Wilson gave £15 in 1741.

The white marble sundial is a replacement (1860). The church has two bells, a treble and a tenor, the latter dated 1780. The present altar is not the original one. The large monument on the north wall (1843) necessitated breaking up the window opposite the door. The gallery was extended in 1861. The font, in the north west corner, is one of the few wall fonts left on the Island. Originally there was a stove in the chancel, and one near the west door, both set up in 1852. The first organ was installed in 1837 and a later organ was transferred to the new church in 1876, then to St Luke's, Baldwin in 1894, where it remained until 1916. There is now no organ in the church. The old churchyard was closed for burials in 1921.

The Vicar, when Wilson came, was the Revd Robert Fletcher, who had been appointed on the 14th November 1696, but he was a man of bad character, who was accused by his wife (and widely suspected) of unchastity. He also perjured himself, for on 5th June 1698 he appeared with compurgators and swore his innocence. In March 1702 he was again charged and could not deny his guilt, so the Bishop called on him to resign and stand trial, but he confessed and asked for another chance. This was granted, but he continued to offend, so at a Court held in Douglas in April 1704 he was stripped of his deacon's and priest's orders and dismissed from the ministry.

He was succeeded by John Curghey, a man of very different stamp. On one occasion, however, he incurred the Bishop's displeasure when in 1716 a penitent came without the necessary white sheet, and was allowed by the Vicar to wrap himself in the altar cloth. Wilson ordered that this cloth was never again to be used on the altar, and that Curghey was to replace it at his own expense.

On the 30th October 1733 John Cosnahan was appointed Vicar and remained until his death in June 1750. In 1731 Wilson wished to appoint him to Santan, but Derby, the Patron, declined, so the Bishop, who had great faith and trust in Cosnahan, made him Vicar General, though still a Curate, and later Vicar of Braddan. Derby and Governor Horton acquiesced in this, and thereby tacitly restored to Wilson the right to appoint his own Vicar General. Like some of his contemporaries he tended to neglect church property, and at a visitation in 1738 the Archdeacon found the Prayer Book "old and not legible in many places".

Joseph was Vicar from the 4th October 1750 until his death in September 1768, aged 43. On the 17th May 1756 he wrote in his diary "The sum of 2 shillings per week, being as near the tenth of my whole income from the church as I can well conjecture, I am resolved, by the grace of God, from this time henceforth to lay by every Lord's Day for the use of the poor, namely for those whom my Lord God shall judge most worthy of it. I thank God for this good thought and resolution - and the Lord reward me and mine". Then comes an entry for the 14th August, 1758 "I have since altered this method, and, according to my old custom, pay the tenth of my weekly receipts, let it be more or less".

BRIDE is a Crown Living, and the name comes from St Bridget, to whom the old church was dedicated. It was a 12th century building which stood in the old part of the churchyard about thirty yards east of the present church, its site being marked by a weeping elm tree. It was typical of old Manx churches in having no windows on the north side, and in being approximately three times as long as it was broad (54' x 16'). It had a single bell turret at the west end, and the gallery (erected by Bishop Hildesley in 1772) was reached by an external staircase at the west end. There was a door in the south wall, and another (reserved for the Rector) in the chancel. It had a three decker pulpit and sat 150 people. Apart from the altar candles there was no lighting, as Evensong was in the afternoon. The registers start in 1693. The old church was demolished in 1870 when the present one was built. Baptismal water for the old church came from

Chibbyr Vreeshey, due north of the building.

On Wilson's arrival in 1698 the living was vacant, the Revd John Christian (Rector since 1687) having recently become Vicar of Jurby. The vacancy lasted until 1700 when the Revd John Parr was appointed (25th October). He was ill for most of the winter of 1722-23, and most of the Sunday duty was done by Wilson in person. He was succeeded by Robert Parr (29th March 1723) who died in 1729. Derby then appointed the Bishop's persistent opponent, the Revd William Bridson as Rector (15th May 1729) but on the 17th October he was appointed Rector of Ballaugh. Bride and Ballaugh were then two of the best livings in the Island, this being clearly Derby's reward to Bridson for opposing Wilson. During his short incumbency at Bride he had rooms and stables at Ballakilley. There was no rectory at this time, a fact which probably accounts for the frequent complaint of the parishioners that the rectors were non-resident.

His successor was Matthias Curghey. The last rector under Wilson was William Mylrea (24th July 1754).

CASTLETOWN The old Grammar School was founded as a chapel about 1250 and became the Grammar School in 1698 when, on the 16th July, Wilson laid the foundations of a new chapel almost on the site of what was, until recently, St Mary's Parish Church. It was paid for, with Derby's agreement, out of the revenues which had accumulated during the vacancy in the see prior to Wilson's coming, and was consecrated on Friday, 11th April 1701 in Derby's presence. On this occasion Vicar Woods of Malew (in whose parish the chapel was built) read the service and Archdeacon Marsden preached. The money for building was administered by four commissioners appointed by Derby - the Bishop, Samuel Wattleworth, Richard Stevenson and Thomas Huddleston. This 1698 church had no tower or belfry, though a little steeple was added in 1800, and the bell of the old chapel in Castle Rushen was hung in it. It was served by a chaplain and an assistant chaplain and although they acknowledged a certain dependence on Malew, there were many disputes between the Malew and Castletown clergy regarding fees, and the legality of baptisms in Castletown Chapel.

The first chaplain was James Makon, who remained until 1719. He preached things unpalatable to the Governor, who asked Wilson to dismiss him, and in his place came Robert Horrobin. During Horrobin's suspension, Wilson authorised the Revd William Ross, the schoolmaster, to officiate, but the Governor thereupon locked the chapel, and refused to give Ross the keys, despite the Bishop's protest. It remained locked for three and a half years until July 1725. The chaplaincy of John Kippax lasted only a month (August to September 1727 when he went to Andreas), then Ross became chaplain in his own right and remained until his death on the 4th October 1754, aged 86. In 1718 he and Makon were accused of papist teaching and appeared before the Bishop and some senior clergy in St German's Cathedral on the 15th October, but after explaining their views they were acquitted. Castletown being a royal chaplaincy, Atholl appointed the chaplain, but after the death of Ross he kept it vacant until 1758. The population of Castletown was 785 at this time.

GERMAN St German's Cathedral was begun in the 12th century, and was the Cathedral church of the Norse diocese of Man and the Isles. In addition to this it was also the parish church until 1799, and a burial ground for German. There was a burial there as late as 1869. It is less than half the length of Hereford (which is the smallest English cathedral) and is Gothic in style. Between 1692 and 1697 the Cathedral (except the tower) was reroofed with slate and generally repaired at great expense, to meet which Derby kept the see vacant between Bishop Levinz's death on the 31st January and the appointment of Wilson. The crypt was used as a prison for offenders against church discipline until 1780. During the 18th century Peel people claimed and received the right of burial in the Cathedral, and the last recorded marriage there was that of Edward Trevor and Mary Savage on the 27th September 1753. In 1791 Vicar Corlett of German said that in 1765 all the Cathedral, except the Choir was dilapidated and unfit for Divine Service, but the chancel was roofed, the windows and seats were in good condition and the stone altar in good repair and railed in, but since then the chancel had gone completely to ruin, and was almost roofless.

St Peter's, the old parish church in the market

place, was built about 1550, on the site of a still older church, as a chapel of ease to the Cathedral. It is said to have been built after a boat carrying a coffin for burial in the Cathedral overturned in the harbour on a windy day, and was carried out to sea. The parishioners of German and Patrick formerly worshipped in Peel Castle, those from German in the Cathedral and those from Patrick in the more ancient St Patrick's Church. Until 1729 St Peter's Church was the parish church of both German and Patrick, sharing one Vicar. The south aisle was reserved for Patrick people. The earliest dated headstone in the churchyard was 1595, and the registers start in 1667. In 1714 Feltham said that the church was 81' x 59', with side galleries (the west gallery built in 1764, and the south gallery in 1778) and could seat 600. The patron of German is the Bishop. The Vicar on Wilson's arrival was Samuel Wattleworth (see under Andreas) and he was succeeded by Matthias Curghey. He seems to have been German's first resident Vicar. John Woods (son of Vicar Woods of Malew) was inducted on the 20th September 1730. He had been ordained by Wilson in 1717 as Curate of Kirk Michael, where there was no Vicar from the death of Henry Norris in 1717 until 1735, as Derby declined to appoint, so Woods had a heavy responsibility for a newly ordained Curate. On the 30th October 1729 he succeeded Robert Parr as Vicar General, but Governor Horton refused to swear him in, saying that he had Derby's positive orders not to do so, hence Wilson had him sworn in by the then Vicar General, John Curghey (13th February 1730). On the 4th April Horton warned him not to act as Vicar General at his peril, but he remained in office. As a result Derby said that he would never appoint Woods to any parish of which he was patron. Wilson described Woods as "a man of singular sobriety, integrity, veracity, probity and piety". He is said to have been fond of acting as Godfather to children whom he baptised.

The incumbency of John Craine was very short (from 28th July 1741 until his death on the 4th April 1742), aged 26, less than three months after his marriage to Margaret Woods who also died young in 1747. On Easter Sunday 1742 Wilson ordained in German Church as Deacon and Curate, the Revd James Wilks, born on 26th July 1719 in Santan, his parents being John Wilks, blacksmith at Ballasalla, and Margaret Moore. He was to become one of the outstanding clergy of the century. One of his achievements as Vicar was to obtain a piece of land at St John's, (then in the Parish of German) to build there the first school in the neighbourhood. In 1745 he was sent by the Bishop to Dublin to obtain arrears of interest on some money left to the Academic Fund by Bishop Barrow which had been invested in property in Dublin. Wilks was successful in this mission.

The last Vicar under Wilson was Robert Christian, who was appointed on the 4th November 1752 and died on the 26th December 1754 aged 27. He was ordained in 1750 as Curate of Ballaugh and, though only a Deacon, had been Curate in charge between Rectors Bridson and Moore. German then remained vacant for four years.

JURBY is a parish in the gift of the Bishop, as the eastern third of the parish was formerly the Bishop's barony. A church stood near the site of the present one (built in 1813) in the middle of the churchyard, in the 13th century. The Burial register dates from 1606 and the Baptismal register from 1613. Most of Wilson's episcopate was covered by the long incumbency (1698 until his death early in 1747) of the Revd John Christian who had been Rector of Bride. He was succeeded by Samuel Gell, but in March 1748 he became Vicar of Lonan. There then seems to have been an interregnum of three years before William Crebbin was appointed Vicar on the 9th August 1751.

In 1744 there was trouble when the wardens put up nails in the church for hats without the permission of the Vestry.

LEZAYRE is a Crown Living, and the largest in area of the seventeen ancient parishes. Wilson found the church ruinous, and rebuilt a church on the same site in 1704, though the chancel was not completed until 1723. He gave £5 towards the cost. This church stood in the eastern part of the churchyard, on a level site now covered with graves, about two thirds of the way up from the road, and its east end came to within about five feet of the eastern boundary of the churchyard. It was evidently larger than other churches of the time as it was 84' long (including a chancel 22.5 feet long) and 20.5 feet broad. There was a gallery with four pews on each side at the west end and one central aisle. There were four windows on the south

22

side and one, very high up, on the north side. There was a door at the west end, another on the north side near the chancel and a three decker pulpit. On the north side of the chancel was the vicarage pew, and on the south side the Ballakillingan pew. It seated 250. The main entrance to the churchyard was the gate in the lane running up to the cottage on the east side. Lezayre Cross stood right opposite this entrance and all funerals passed around it on the east and north side before entering the churchyard. An old plan marking this route calls it the 'Ancient Funeral Way'. From 1704-8 there were no seats in the church, but in February 1708, at a meeting attended by the Bishop and the Archdeacon, the seats were apportioned to the quarterlands of the parish, and inhabitants of the quarterlands were ordered to make their seats by the following Easter, failing which the churchwardens would make them and send the owners the bill, those who would not pay being threatened with St German's prison. One result of this was that the seats were of all shapes and sizes. Over the front door was a stone inscribed "To the honour of the Sacred Trinity this church was rebuilt AD 1704. The Right Revd Dr Ts Wilson, the Bishop; Mr Robert Parr, Vicar General, Minister; James Christian, John Curghey, Edmund Curlett and Robert Curghey, Churchwardens". The registers begin in 1736.

On Wilson's arrival the Vicar was Robert Parr, who was buried at Lezayre on 3rd December 1712. After a year's interregnum Henry Allen became Vicar on the 13th April 1714, and remained until he moved to Maughold in October 1726. His stipend in 1725 was £25 per annum without a house. After him came William Bridson, January 1727-May 1729 when he went to Bride. His successor was Matthias Curghey. He built a vicarage in 1735 at a cost of £68-6s-5d, plus £3-12s-7d for a cow house, but he does not seem to have kept the church in very good order. A visitation and report by the Vicar General on the 8th July 1743 said that the laths on the chancel roof were rotten, the altar was loose and needed to be made firm, the chancel window needed mending, several seats in the chancel and nave were broken and the Altar Prayer Book and the lectern Bible were "much decayed". There was no hearse cloth for burials, there were several holes in the roof and the churchyard fence needed repairing. On the 26th July 1750 another visitation reported loose boards, broken seats stored

in the church and several large stones lying loose in the chancel. These latter were probably memorial stones for the Curgheys of Ballakillingan, who for generations had a pew in the chancel and were buried there. The floor under the altar was described as rugged and uneven, the altar rails loose, and the chancel steps in very bad order. On the other hand he was an able parish priest. His stipend in 1761 was £27 plus the glebe, £2 more than in 1729.

In 1756 the Sumner, Thomas Killip, was presented in the Vicar General's Court for failing to keep dogs out of the church.

LONAN is a Crown Living. The church near Groudle is very old, especially the west end, which is about 12th century but about 4' below its foundations were found the foundations of a much older building, probably of the 7th or 8th century. The north door, now blocked up, may have been the entrance then when the inside floor was evidently on a lower level. The east and west ends show no bond between their walls until about 4' below ground level. The former window on the south side was blocked up. On the south side of the west end, near the dividing wall with the present church is a leper slant. In accordance with the idea that evil came from the north, (Jeremiah 1[14]) there is only one small window on the north side. As was the custom at the time the length was three times the breadth (54' x 18') but originally it was much shorter, and the extension eastward, when it became a parish church in the 12th century, was probably made by the monks of Rushen Abbey, who were the patrons of the living. The east gable was taken down and the church extended 29' eastward. Some time after this the south door in the new part was blocked up, and two doors put in the older west end.

In 1733 the parishioners petitioned the Bishop to have a new parish church, vicarage and outbuildings built in a more convenient part of the parish and Tynwald, in response, passed an Act for this purpose on the 25th June 1733. A larger church was also needed as the population of Lonan in 1726 was 547. The new church was consecrated on the 25th March 1735 by Bishop Wilson, who preached on II Chronicles 6[40], 7[15], and at the same service he ordained Thomas Christian and Nathaniel Curghey Deacon. The consecration deed forbade the use of the Church as a school, and forbade burials in the church or within one yard of the outside wall. The church was built in about 17 months, as the ground had been marked out on the 24th October 1733. It was 63.5' x 19.5', and was set due east and west. Unfortunately the former church at Groudle was allowed to become ruinous. By this time Governor Horton had become more co-operative and encouraged the building of the new church and the raising of the necessary funds.

The Vicar on Wilson's arrival was John Taubman. After the sort of interregnum which was common in Crown livings at the time, Robert Radcliffe was appointed Vicar in 1725 and remained until 1735. In November 1732 Radcliffe presented his whole parish (except those families living near the church) in the Vicar General's Court for not attending on the festivals of the church. They were ordered to be admonished from the pulpit. Edward Moore (see under Kirk Michael) was Vicar for a few months, then from 1735-1753 the parish was left in charge of the Curate, Nathaniel Curghey.

MALEW is a Crown living, and the church dates from the early 14th century. The north transept, (to accommodate the Castle Rushen garrison) and the chancel were added in 1781. The nave is therefore the oldest part. The old bell was presented by William Earl of Derby in 1677, so the church has two bells, the second being the passing bell used only at funerals. As with most old Manx churches there were originally no windows on the north side. The registers start in 1649. The parish contained Castle Rushen, Rushen Abbey and Castletown, then the capital, hence it was the most important in the diocese.

There were only two vicars during Wilson's episcopate. The first was John Woods. We have already noted his imprisonment in 1721, but in August 1719 he had also been imprisoned in Castle Rushen for refusing to give up a document to the Governor until he had the Bishop's authority to do so. John Quayle was appointed on the 17th March 1739 and died in June 1758 aged 72.

MAROWN is a Crown Living, and the only one of the seventeen ancient parishes which does not at some point touch the sea. Within the parish is the ancient church of St Trinian's, now a ruin. The original site goes back perhaps as far as the 5th century, and in its walls are many fragments of Irish-Norman work which evidently belonged to a still older church on the site. The present building (which is a chantry, not a parish church) is 13th century. It is dedicated to the Holy Trinity, and is said to have been built by a Scotsman who escaped a storm at sea and vowed to build a church in whichever country he landed safely. About 1750 it was decided to re-roof the church, slates were brought from Barrule quarry, and a ship was chartered to bring wood from England, but the ship sank off the Island and the plan was dropped. When old Marown church was extended westwards some of the moulded archstones of St Trinian's were taken and used for this work.

The oldest part of Marown old church, dedicated to St Runius, is 12th century, when it would almost certainly be built as the parish church. The oldest part is the north wall (in which there is no window), the east end being much more recent. The entrance was through a door in the south wall, near the south west corner. The site of this door was opened up in 1906. Although blocked on the inner face the opening can be seen in the outside wall, with the beam holes for the oak bars which secured the door. When the present entrance was built during the westward extension about 1754 this south west doorway was made into a window. Another doorway in the south wall led into the chancel, but it was demolished with the chancel in 1850 because the east end had become unsafe. Traces of the old chancel can still be seen. The old entrance to the churchyard and stile were in the south wall, opposite the old door. During the 1754 extension a gallery was built for those who provided the music, with an outside staircase which still remains, though the gallery was removed in 1850 and the door into it was bricked up. The lines of some of the alterations can be seen in the stone work. This westward extension made the church 15' longer, and is marked by thinner walling. The original church was 45' x 18'. The moulded jamb stones of the west doorway are obviously much earlier, and probably came from St Trinian's, and so too may the massive masonry which flanks the top of the stairs to the gallery, and the carved and moulded stones in the walls. The steeple was probably built in the 1754 extension. The two windows in the south wall are a later addition. In 1850 the north west window was removed and the east gable (after the demolition of the chancel) was closed by a light stone wall with a central opening through which coffins at funerals could be carried out more easily than through the west door, but in 1906 this opening was built up, as funerals were no longer held at the old church.

The original font was in the north west corner and about 1822, to make room for the vicarage pew, it was removed to a position outside the north west corner and a window was made in the north wall. The gap left by the font was made into a window, which was sealed in 1850. Baptisms were then performed in a much smaller font. In 1906 the font was restored to its original position, and a smaller font, dating from the 12th or 13th century, and found buried in the churchyard near the old sundial, was placed with it.

After the building of the present parish church in 1853 the old church was only used for funerals, the continued right of burial there having been secured by Act of Tynwald on the 16th March 1846. Until 1862 it was lit only by candles. By 1889 it was badly dilapidated as the windows were broken, the floor had fallen in and rabbits had scattered the bones of those buried under the church; but in this year it was extensively repaired and was restored to use in 1959.

In 1698 the Vicar was Robert Fletcher; his successor was Evan Gill. Then came Wilson's inveterate foe, William Bridson. Matthias Curghey was appointed on the 18th September 1728, but his incumbency was very short, as he too moved to Lezayre in the following February. At a confirmation on the 28th July 1728 Wilson reproved the churchwardens publicly for having "so scurvy a Communion tablecloth and the floor within the Communion rail so scandalously out of order". There now seems to have been a vacancy of five years during which the Bishop took most of the duty himself, putting aside the stipend as a fund for rebuilding the church. On the 4th March 1734 Thomas Christian became Vicar. He had been ordained in 1733 as Curate of German, and was priested at the consecration of Lonan Church (25th March 1735) so he must have been Vicar of Marown while still a Deacon. He was an able man with scholarly interests and strong political views. During the rebellion led by the Young Pretender in 1745-46 he expressed Jacobitical views, and in May

1746 he was suspended, but was restored in the following month after apologising and affirming his loyalty to the Crown. Like many of Wilson's clergy, he seems to have allowed the Church and its furniture to deteriorate, as the Vicars General (John Cosnahan and Edward Moore), in a visitation report in 1743, said that there was no case for books or linen, a carpet was needed for the sanctuary, there was nothing to cover the elements, the lectern Bible was tattered, the Prayer Book on the reading desk needed to be rebound, there was no font cover, no hearse cloth for burials, the stile needed repairing and the church needed whitewashing. He was also told to repair the vicarage which then stood on the Vicar's glebe on the high land west of the church.

He was succeeded by his son, John Christian, who inherited his ability and scholarly interests, but his incumbency was mainly under Wilson's successors.

ST MATTHEW'S The original Church was built in 1641, but it was demolished early in Wilson's episcopate and a new one built, to the cost of which the Bishop gave £10. He consecrated it on Tuesday, 21st September, 1708, using for the first time his own "Office for the Dedication of Churches" and preaching on Exodus 20²⁴. From this date the Chaplain and the Master of the Grammar School were always the same person because of endowments given for the Chaplain and Schoolmaster. By the Deed of Consecration Wilson reserved to himself and his successors, as patrons of Braddan (the mother Church) the right of appointing the Chaplain - though his predecessors had always done so. The Deed of Consecration appointed as trustees the Vicar of Braddan and the Chaplain. Until the building of St George's it was the only church in Douglas, and as such it served a great purpose, in view of the distance to the parish church (Braddan). No district or cure of souls was assigned to it. The Church faced the end of what is now James Street. At the west end was a gallery, supported by pillars, in which the choir sat, and in the church was a very grand square pew, covered with a canopy and surrounded by curtains, which was occupied by the Duke of Atholl. There were about 50 pews, and the church held about 350. There was a three-decker pulpit, and on the south side was an old pulpit only used by the Bishop. When this church was demolished in 1897 it was found to be without foundations.

The first Chaplain of the new church was Samuel Robinson, who remained until 1714, when he was succeeded by Peter Lancaster. He left in 1716, then came Anthony Halsall.

After the short Chaplaincy of Thomas Birkett (1732-36), Philip Moore was appointed and began his long and distinguished career of 47 years as Chaplain and Schoolmaster. By 1783 he had educated all the Manx clergy except four, and all respected and loved him. He was a very good classical scholar, and one of the men to whom we owe most in the work of translating the Manx Bible. His wife died in 1768, and he died at Douglas after only a few hours illness, on the 22nd January 1783, aged 77, his health undermined since 1773 by his work on the Manx Bible.

MAUGHOLD is a Crown Living, formerly in the patronage of Furness Abbey, and the church is probably more in its original form than any of the ancient parish churches. It is a type of early English church, of simple oblong construction, with a small, very ancient, chancel, and a belfry at the west end. No part is earlier than the 11ᵗʰ century, but it is unlikely to be the first church on the site. It seems to have been rebuilt about 1275. The original church was shorter than the present one, and ended where traces of the old north door can be seen near the outside steps to the gallery. There was also a south door. The church was extended eastwards on two separate occasions, the first before 1500 and the second before 1650. The western half of the church is thus the oldest. The Irish Romanesque arch with nail head moulding over the west door is probably 11ᵗʰ or 12ᵗʰ century. The west door was opened in 1708, replacing the north and south doors, and at the same time the font was moved into the north wall. Its size suggests that it was intended for total immersion of babies, and it is probably early Norman, though the fact that there is no ornamentation prevents exact dating. In the south wall are two sandstone windows (11ᵗʰ or 12ᵗʰ century) which were uncovered during major repair work in 1860, and were restored to their present condition in 1901. A former east window, dismantled in 1900 and now built into the gable behind the Altar, is of St Bee's sandstone, the same as the two ancient windows in the south wall. The modern east window is a replica of the former one.

The two side windows at the east end are contemporary with the old east window. Before 1900 they had been partly filled in, but were in that year restored to their original shape. The Registers go back to 1647.

In 1698 the Vicar was Thomas Allen. He was the third of five generations of the Allen family (who came from Norwich) who were Vicars successively from 1625 to 1754. In his diary Wilson described him as "a diligent pastor, of a serious, grave, sober behaviour, kind to his neighbours and to the poor, and very hospitable to all others ......, always resident upon his cure, and always contented with his condition", and in his funeral sermon he described him as "laborious and exemplary". After his death Wilson licensed the son of William Ross, (Chaplain of Castletown), as Curate, but he died on the 10th November 1726, and on the 24th January 1727, Derby appointed Henry Allen (nephew of Thomas) as Vicar. In 1732 Wilson wrote to him saying that he wished it to be stated in future whether marriages were performed by licence (and whose licence) or by banns. In 1744 he was presented by his churchwardens for making a gap in the churchyard wall to drive his cattle from the churchyard, where he grazed them, to the glebe. He was succeeded by his son Thomas.

KIRK MICHAEL is a Crown Living, and the Registers start in 1611-the older ones being copied out in 1712 by Vicar Norris, as they had been mutilated during the Commonwealth period. In 1299 we find a reference to Skeeylley Mayl, that is the parish church for Michael, which very probably stood on the site of the most notable of the nine of ten treen churches which are known to have stood in the parish. The large number of stone graves near the old church show that burials took place here well before 1100.

The original, 12ᵗʰ century, church was in the centre of the ancient burial ground, which was surrounded on three sides by the Vicar's ancient glebe and the clerk's glebe. The church seated about 300 people and was plain and rectangular, with a small tower at the west end and a gallery, admission to which was from the tower. For lighting each person carried his own candle. Dr Thomas Wilson, son of the Bishop, rebuilt the chancel in 1776, and part of it still stands. Near it are the graves of Bishops Wilson,

Hildesley, Crigan and Thornton-Duesbery. Wilson used to attend Kirk Michael Church and the congregation used to wait kneeling outside the church for his blessing.

The Vicar on Wilson's arrival was Henry Norris. The stipend in his time was £24 per year. He died on 23rd January 1717.

There followed an interregnum of 18 years, the longest of the many such resulting from Derby's slackness in nominating to Crown livings, unless it be that he and the Bishop, who were never on good terms, were unable to agree on a new incumbent. During this period the parish was served by a Curate, John Woods, whom we have met as Vicar of German (1730-40) and who seems to have continued to look after Michael after going to German. On the 21st May 1735 John Allen, the Curate of Lonan, was appointed Vicar, but soon afterward he became ill and died on the 10th July. In his place came Edward Moore. He was held in high esteem by Wilson. While Vicar of Michael he lived at the White House as there was no Vicarage, but in 1743 the Glebe Farm was bought and presented to the parish by Dr Thomas Wilson, on condition that the parishioners afterwards built on the land a vicarage equal in size to that at Braddan. In May 1741 he was taking a service of Holy Communion in Kirk German Church, and refused the Sacrament to Major General John Christian, Constable of Peel Castle, on the grounds that he was the father of an illegitimate child. Christian complained to the Bishop, who endorsed Moore's action and the incident shows that the claim that the Lord's dependents were exempt from ecclesiastical discipline had been dropped.

ONCHAN is a Crown Living, and the name is, correctly Conchan, that is the Irish Saint Conchenn, though the church is now dedicated to St Peter. The Baptismal register starts in 1627, the Burial register in 1647 and the Marriage register in 1698. The original church (12th or 13th century) stood under the tree at the bottom of the present churchyard. The pre-1833 church stood within 50 yards north of the west door of the present one, and the marks of the gateway (later blocked up) to what was then the churchyard can still be seen where the wall bends just below the vicarage gate. There had originally been a stile at this point, but in 1756 the parishioners complained of having had to pay for replacing it with a gate, as it was in such a bad state of repair that pigs and other animals stepped over it at will; while the Vicar, who wished to let his horse graze in the churchyard, had blocked the stile to prevent the horse straying.

The Vicar in 1698 was Evan Gill, who had been appointed on the 20th June 1686, and moved to Marown in September 1701. In 1698 the Sumner was presented in the Vicar General's Court "for not keeping out dogs, or hanging the dogs which frequent the church on Sundays". He was followed by William Gell, and he was succeeded by his son Samuel, who had been his curate, and who was Vicar until his removal to Lonan in 1759.

PATRICK is in the patronage of the Bishop. The original church was on St Patrick's Isle, there having been no church in Patrick since the Reformation, but by 1710 it was ruinous, and the Patrick people had to attend German Church, so in that year Wilson called a meeting to discuss building a new church, and offered considerable financial help. On October 20th 1710 Tynwald passed the necessary Act, and at the same time relieved the people of Patrick of their share in maintaining German Church which they had paid while using it. This Act virtually authorised the Bishop to use lead from St German's Cathedral for roofing the new church and some of the lead was sold to help with the cost. The building was completed by 1714 and was consecrated on the 29th June 1714 with a dedication to the Holy Trinity. It was 75' x 19', and had a wing with a pewed gallery. By the Deed of Consecration burials in the church were forbidden, as was also its use as a school. Part of the foundations can still be seen in the old churchyard. Wilson gave £50 to endow the living, and personally paid for the pulpit, reading desk, Clerk's seat, vicarage pew, altar, carpet, rails and the registers, which begin in 1714. The school was built in 1716. On one of the corner pillars of the churchyard, overlooking the Peel to Glen Maye road, is a sundial dated 1740, inscribed with Job 3[19] in English and Manx.

In 1714 the Vicar was Matthias Curghey, who was also Vicar of German. He continued to hold both parishes but when he went to Bride in 1729 Patrick was given its own Vicar in the person of Robert Radcliffe. In 1743 he was suspended for two months for performing a secret marriage. He owned

Knockaloe and was buried at Patrick.

RUSHEN is a Crown Living. The Baptismal and Burial registers begin in 1713, the Marriage register in 1757 and the Confirmation register in 1821. There has been a church on the site since at least the 13th century. The original school at the church gate, of which the Parish Clerk was the Master, was built with Wilson's help in 1734 to end the practice of school being held in the Church, and it remained in use until 1861, when it was demolished to make room for graves, the parish school having been built in 1860. By 1715 the Vicarage was in ruins so Wilson collected, and gave personally, enough to build a new one.

The Vicar in 1698 was John Parr, who had been appointed on the 25th June 1691. He became Rector of Bride in 1700 and, after an interval of three years, was succeeded on the 24th June 1703 by Matthias Curghey. For most of Curghey's incumbency the Curate in charge was Thomas Christian, who had been Curate of Ballaugh. He was a man of unsatisfactory character, and in June 1699 he had been suspended for a short time after being found guilty of an offence in the civil court. In 1702 he was fined £5 (later reduced to 50 shillings) for stealing goods from the 'Lucy' which had been wrecked in Castletown Bay and for buying goods knowing them to have been stolen from this ship. In September 1711 he was ordered to appear at a Consistory Court at Kirk Michael to answer a charge of adultery with Dorothy Cornish of Arbory. Most of the clergy were present to hear the evidence. He admitted the charge, and as it was the last of a number of charges of adultery he was deprived of his Orders. In March 1728, as part of his dispute with Wilson, Governor Horton encouraged Christian's son to put pressure on the Bishop to restore his father to the ministry, but without success.

The next Vicar was named Thomas Christian, and he held the Living from 1713 until 1727. He was succeeded by John Quayle 1729-39. Then in 1734 came the long curacy and incumbency of Nicholas Christian (1748-82). In May 1746 he had been suspended for a month for marrying a girl of 13 and a boy of 12 behind locked doors in Arbory Church. The girl, Isobel Lowey, was the heiress of Lingague, Rushen. He was again suspended in 1756 for performing a clandestine marriage. The stipend in his time was £30 per annum, but by 1788 it had risen to £45-10s-7d.

SANTAN, a Crown Living, is the smallest of the 17 ancient parishes, and its dedication is to St Sanctan, an early Irish Bishop - not, as was once thought, to St Anne, the Mother of the Virgin Mary. The church stands on the site of an ancient Keeil. The north side was rebuilt in 1703, the south side in 1715 and the gable and steeple in 1725, when the church was enlarged, the steeple being paid for by Wilson. This latter work was finished on the 29th July 1725, after which the seats were allocated by the churchwardens with the help of four sworn men. The steps around the font were allocated to the poor. A new bell was set up on the 9th April 1720. A new vicarage, towards which Wilson gave £5, was built in 1722.

The Vicar in 1698 was John Cosnahan. After his death, Derby then kept the parish vacant for seven years, until Paul Crebbin was appointed on the 2nd July 1731, to begin an incumbency of 33 years.

A Visitation by the Vicars General took place on the 5th July 1743 and revealed some slackness on the part of the Vicar and his churchwardens. The report laid down that the font should be repaired and a cover made, and that in future household vessels should not be used for baptisms, but that the water should be poured into the font as laid down by the rubric. The wardens were ordered to provide a new surplice, a white linen altar cloth, proper Communion linen and a hearse cloth for funerals.

Chapter 2

BISHOP HILDESLEY 1755-1772

Wilson's successor, Mark Hildesley, was one of the 16 children of the Revd Mark Hildesley, who, at the time of his son's birth, was Vicar of Sittingbourne, Kent and who died in 1726 as Rector of Houghton, Hampshire. The future Bishop was born at Marston, near Sittingbourne, on the 9th December 1698, and was baptised two days later. His mother lived until the 25th November 1745, when she died aged 70. He went to Charterhouse School, London, in 1710, and in 1717 entered Trinity College, Cambridge, of which he became a Fellow in 1723. He graduated in 1720, and was made Deacon in 1722 and Priest in 1723. In 1723 he became domestic chaplain to Lord Cobham, and from 1725 to 1730 he was Curate of Yelling, Hampshire. In February 1730 he became Rector of Hitchin (of which the patrons were the Master and Fellows of Trinity College) where he remained until his consecration. From January 1733 he acted as private chaplain to Viscount Bolingbroke, who appointed him, in November 1735 Rector of Holwell, about 3 miles from Hitchin. He held Holwell in commendam until September 1767, when he gave it up, and became Master of Sherburn Almshouse, near Durham. To this he was presented by the Bishop of Durham and he retained the post until his death. His salary as Master was £450 per annum, and besides relieving him from all money worries, it enabled him to give more in charity, especially to clergy widows and orphans, for whom he felt a special responsibility. In his first year at Hitchin, he had 158 funerals due to an outbreak of the plague. He could not afford a Curate until 1735, and he worked so hard that he injured his health. Holwell had been much neglected by the previous Rector, but Hildesley pulled it together by faithful visiting and by his personal character. He preached alternately with his Curate in the two parishes, and at this time he preached from memory or from short notes. He attached great importance to work with young people. On arrival at Hitchin he had to spend a good deal on the Rectory, and as the living was poor he had to take boarding pupils, varying in number from four to six. In October 1731 he married at Hitchin, Elizabeth Stoker, and had a son and a daughter who both died in infancy.

The appointment of the Bishop of Sodor and Man rested with the Duke of Atholl, who then owned the Island. He consulted Archbishop Secker of Canterbury and Bishop Trevor of Durham, who both recommended Hildesley because of his pastoral qualities. On the 1st April 1755 Cambridge University created him DD and he was consecrated in Whitehall Chapel on the 27th April 1755 by Archbishop Hutton of York, assisted by the Bishops of Durham, Carlisle and Chester. On his journey from Hitchin to London for his consecration he was robbed by a highwayman of the money he was carrying (£4-14s-6d) and a watch worth 9 guineas. Hildesley could not face a farewell gathering of parishioners but when he left Hitchin for the Isle of Man the streets were crowded with people who wished to show their respect. He embarked at Whitehaven, but the ship was driven by winds towards the Welsh coast and had to shelter for five days at Beaumaris, so the whole journey took ten days. The last cargo of his belongings did not reach him until mid-September. He landed at Ramsey, where he was met by a firing of cannon, and by people wading up to their knees in the sea to greet him. On the 8th August he was enthroned in St German's Cathedral, the roof having been repaired for the occasion.

Hildesley was a man of modest means, and he was shocked by the number and amount of payments he had to make in connection with his election and consecration. These came to £304, and his removal costs were £123. Goods and furnishings for Bishopscourt came to £255, and he bought from Wilson's estate the stock and grain in the farms for £245 - a total of over £900, double his £450 stipend as Bishop.

He had been reluctant to leave Hitchin, and the Bishop of Lincoln, in whose diocese Hitchin then was, was sorry to lose him, considering him to be his ablest incumbent. Hildesley realised, however, that the

29

invitation to the Isle of Man had come at the right time, as his heavy work with parish and pupils was beginning to tell on him. His responsibility as a Bishop was greater, but the work was less, and his duties at Durham could be done by a deputy.

On arrival at Bishopscourt he soon realised that he would need to be a farmer, as he had inherited about ten horses and as many cows, some heifers, a small flock of sheep, many acres of farmland and three large stacks of good hay. About 1770 he imported a fine Holderness bull and heifer and presented them to the Clerk of the Rolls, Thomas Quayle, with the request that they be used to improve the breed of cattle in the Island. Beer and cider were brewed at Bishopscourt, and bacon and herrings were cured. The Bishop's Demesne made him self-supporting in food. By long tradition the Bishop's tenants had to pay to the new Bishop one ox, or a payment for each quarterland. Hildesley chose the ox.

The new Bishop was described as rather above medium height, with small, regular features. His voice was clear but not sonorous. He was elegant in his person and dress, and cheerful, but polite, in manner. His tastes were simple, he was unassuming and was a tireless worker, his whole day being run to a rigid timetable. He was hospitable but was abstemious in eating and temperate as regards wine. He was particularly happy in the presence of naval and military men. He was invariably careful to avoid giving offence, or causing anyone embarrassment, by his conversation, and deplored the current habit of swearing. If he had a fault, it was that he was generous and unsuspecting, and unscrupulous people could impose on him. He was sociable and loved company, so it is not surprising that he felt lonely in the Island, especially after the death, on the 27th February 1763, of his wife, who had been in failing health for two months. On the day of her funeral at Kirk Michael Hildesley gave £5 to the Vicar to distribute to the poor, thus breaking with the bad custom of giving out free drink on these occasions. On the day of his own funeral he had ordered that £5 worth of barley be given to the local poor. After his wife's death his sister Hester came to keep house for him. It is perhaps true to say that he never really reconciled himself to life on the Island, or found it easy, and he wearied of the isolation and monotony.

Hildesley made it his great aim to tread in Bishop Wilson's footsteps, and he showed his clergy, by his own example, a pattern of the most diligent discharge of duty. He kept no chaplain, so he took the services and preached every Sunday in Bishopscourt Chapel. He set the clergy a high standard of manners and conduct and he did all possible to raise their stipends.

His loneliness was much relieved by Philip Moore, who, like the Bishop, was a good classical scholar, and to whom he wrote weekly. There was in those days no postal service in the Island, and letters were taken by travellers. Mrs Moore did his shopping for him. Hildesley also missed the newspapers and those he received were always old. His isolation at Bishopscourt was physical as well as mental and spiritual, as the roads were only bridle paths. He could get to Ramsey and the south in his carriage, but the only road to Douglas, (except via Ramsey or Peel) was over the mountains, as the road to Ballacraine did not exist. So difficult was it to obtain a barber from Douglas that Hildesley had his valet instructed in barbering. He does not seem to have ridden around the diocese, as did Wilson, but on medical advice he rode for two hours every day before dinner. Judging by his letters, it is probably true to say that he was homesick for the whole of his episcopate, yet he refused several offers of an English diocese, so great was his love for the Manx people. He was a man of great spirituality as witness the morning prayer he composed for his household.

The following incident may conclude the subject of his character. Once while on holiday in Scarborough he found in his room a sheet of paper on which the following words were written, probably by a former parishioner:

If to paint folly till her friends despise,
Or virtue till her foes would fain be wise.
If angel sweetness, if a Christlike mind,
That melts with Jesus over all mankind,
If this can make a Bishop - and it can -
Though lawn were wanting, Hildesley's the man.

The Bishop kept this, and it was found among his papers, but on it he had written "From vainglory in the applause of men, Deus me liberat et conservat".

Hildesley found a diocese of 19,136 people. Under Wilson, a long tradition of reverence for the Bishop had continued, and he was always approached on bended knee, but Hildesley abolished this custom.

He found the churches so small and crowded that worshippers regularly fainted, so he made it his policy to enlarge them where possible. He also found the clergy poorly paid, the average stipend being £30-£40 per annum, and to help them he appointed them as proctors for collecting the tithe, whereby they got a percentage. By the end of his episcopate the stipends had risen to £60 per annum. He also did all possible for clergy widows and orphans. He was impressed from the start by the strict observance of the rubrics in church services, everyone kneeling and rising at the customary points. On the 16th September 1765 he wrote that all the clergy save one had visited him, and he thought them decent, sensible, and well-behaved men. Six hundred Easter communicants was common in a parish, showing that communicant life was strong. He took a great interest in Kirk Michael, as the parish in which he lived, and besides being generous to the poor, he added two side galleries to the parish church and built the court house. He aimed at continuing the spirit of Wilson's episcopate, and he gave the clergy an example of strict attention to duty. He formed for Bishopscourt Chapel a choir of twenty poor children, ten boys and ten girls, whom he fed and clothed at his own expense.

From the start Hildesley did his best to maintain Wilson's system of church discipline. It was not easy, as it had been little regarded in Wilson's later years, and the penalties had become much milder, most cases being dismissed, or ending with a warning to the offender. In 1758 he ordered that no one under church censure, and who had not received Holy Communion could be married without his permission, and the clergy were instructed to issue certificates for those to be married in another parish, this certificate being based on personal knowledge, or on the certain knowledge of two responsible people. This was really Canon 3 of the Ecclesiastical Constitutions of 1703 in different words.

There were many presentments under Hildesley for non-observance of Sundays and Saints' Days and he particularly tried to prevent secular work on Ash Wednesday and Good Friday, personally reproving some men he once found ploughing on Ash Wednesday during service time, but they answered that it was the general practice in the Island. On asking the two Vicars General if this was so, they replied that it was, and that even the late Vicar General Walker had

done so. They added, however, that prayers were read in Church at 8 a.m. on these two days to enable people to attend before going to work. In the light of this Hildesley was surprised to find that all work stopped on the 2nd February (Purification) and the 25th March (Annunciation).

After Hildesley's death church discipline rapidly declined, and presentments were mainly for moral offences. Attempts to enforce attendance at church virtually ceased.

In 1796 Bishop Crigan asked the opinion of the clergy as to whether it might be better for Tynwald to empower the Church courts to impose fines rather than censures, and they agreed, some saying that censures had done little to check immorality. But Crigan, in his dilatory manner, made no such request to Tynwald, and at his death in 1813 the whole system of church discipline had collapsed. A few penances were imposed under Bishop Murray, and as late as 1825 he excommunicated a man for a moral offence.

On the 16th May 1761 Hildesley issued an important directive to churchwardens and the Chapter Quest:

(1) To present the minister and the parish clerk if they neglected their duty. Each incumbent had to preach one sermon each Sunday; to catechise the young people in the parish each Sunday afternoon, and only to admit to Holy Communion those who had been confirmed or who were ready to be confirmed; to visit the sick; and to live soberly as to be a pattern of religion and virtue to his whole parish. He was to be presented if he frequented ale houses more than for his honest necessity.

The clerk's duty was to ring the bell; to attend the Vicar on sick visits, baptisms and burials; and to raise the Psalm or get someone else to do it.

(2) They were to present anyone who profaned Sunday by absence from Church, irreverent behaviour in Church, going to the alehouse, gambling, playing games, and doing any work not wholly necessary.

(3) Parents, guardians and masters who did not send their children to be catechised were to be presented.

(4) They were to present those guilty of immorality, swearing, and taking God's name in vain.

(5) They were to present the parents of children un-

der 14 who profaned Sunday by playing games, and anyone who provided music for dancing on Saturday nights, which went on into the early hours of Sunday.

(6) To see that legacies to the church were properly used, to provide good service books for the congregation, to ensure that there were decent Communion vessels and a supply of bread and wine, and to keep a proper record of weddings and baptisms.

(7) To present the former churchwardens and Quest men if they had been negligent.

(8) To present all persons of 16 and over who did not take Holy Communion.

(9) To present the Sumner if he did not keep dogs out of the church.

(10) To present all drunkards, and those who carry tales from house to house.

These were to be read in every church on the 1st January, 1st April, 1st July and the 1st October.

Hildesley also wrote a small tract called 'Plain Instructions for young persons in the principles of the Christian Religion, a Method of Confirmation Preparation'.

He took great trouble with his ordinands, whom he gathered at Bishopscourt once a month. He was very particular about their dress, he expected them, and the clergy, to wear wigs, and stressed that the clergy were to maintain a proper standard of manners, speech and dress.

Hildesley allowed Methodists to attend Holy Communion, but would not allow local preachers to preach in the churches. He thought highly of John Wesley personally, and was once heard to express a wish that the Manx clergy had some of his zeal.

The bad relationship between Church and State which had marked so much of Wilson's episcopate ceased under Hildesley mainly because of the different characters of the two men, but also because the system of church discipline, which had been the underlying cause of Wilson's disputes with the Governors, was tacitly being allowed to drop. Basil Cochrane was Governor from 1751-61, and John Wood from 1761-65, in which year, on the 7th March, the Duke of Atholl sold the Island to the British Crown for £70,000 and an annuity of £2,000. He retained, however, the right to appoint the Bishop and the Archdeacon. This step was taken by the Brit-ish Government to stamp out smuggling, which was rife in the Island. John Hope became Governor in 1765 and remained until 1776.

In 1757 an Act of Tynwald confirmed and continued to the Bishop and his successors the ancient right of granting special licences to marry at any time and place (a power possessed in England only by the Archbishop of Canterbury) and which still exists. This Act was mainly concerned with applying to the Island the provisions of Lord Hardwicke's Marriage Act of 1753. Before 1757 Manx people of any age could marry at will without banns or licence.

In 1757 a visitation of the diocese was made on Hildesley's instructions by the two Vicars General and the Episcopal Registrar, two or three churches being visited each day. They came with twelve questions, of which the first three - concerning the fabric and contents of the church, the churchyard and the vicarage - were answered by the officials themselves, while numbers four to twelve, which concerned glebe, libraries, benefactions, baptisms, Holy Communion, preaching, schools and perambulation of the parish, were answered by the incumbent. The fact that most of the churches took two years (three years in the case of Rushen) to carry out the work ordered shows that the visitation was very necessary. The floor of German church was in a bad state, with dead bones, skulls and pieces of coffin visible. The roof of Lonan church was only kept on by sods and ropes, while the roof of Maughold church was virtually non-existent. The walls of Onchan church which were supposed to be white, were described as 'green and squalid'. Maughold had no Bible, and in many parishes, especially German, the registers were in bad condition. The surplice at Santan was said to be 'foul and dirty' and orders were given that it be washed once a quarter. At Bride there was no rectory and the Rector lived at Ballakilley. The Vicar of Rushen was also Schoolmaster, and at Braddan the school was held in the church. The Vicar of Michael preached in Manx generally, the Vicar of Jurby nearly always, and the Rector of Bride four Sundays in five, but there were no Manx sermons in Douglas or Ramsey. Holy Communion was usually celebrated four times a year. Perambulation of the parish took place every Ascension Day in Arbory, but elsewhere once every five years or more.

There were two Church courts in the 18th century. The Circuit or Chapter Court was presided over by one of the Vicars General, and was usually held in the parish church, going from parish to parish. The Consistory Court, presided over by the Bishop, usually met in Kirk Michael and dealt with more serious cases. In fairness to these Courts they were less concerned with punishing offenders than with helping them to amend their lives, and they were quite impartial in dealing with high and low, rich and poor. First offenders were often acquitted. The sentence of excommunication, which could only be imposed by the Bishop, was much feared, as an excommunicate person was boycotted by the whole community and often became destitute. Between 1709 and 1819 it was imposed twentyfour times, but seems usually to have been lifted after a few years. The Chapter Quest consisted of four parishioners elected to help the churchwardens to trace offenders, and to deal with matters which required a knowledge of the parish. They and the churchwardens met on the last Sunday of each month to give the charges to the Vicar. A common offence was illegally ringing the church bell. An assessment was made on all pew holders for repairs to the church, and the collection of this cess was a fruitful source of trouble. The Quest died out with the decay of church discipline.

In Wilson's time the fish tithe was regularly paid, with much grumbling, but in 1767 some fishermen at Kirk Michael and Peel refused to pay. The Manx Courts decided against them, (3rd July 1767) so they appealed to the Privy Council, at which hearing the Revd James Wilks represented the Bishop (14th April 1769). This appeal failed, and the heavy costs ruined the fishermen, but they continued to refuse to pay, and after 1770 no further attempt was made to collect the tithe.

But the greatest achievement of Hildesley's episcopate was the translation of the Bible and Prayer Book into Manx. Before and during Wilson's time the services were read from the English Prayer Book, or translated (with varying degrees of accuracy) by the clergy. At his first Convocation in 1755 Hildesley said that he would like the Catechism printed in Manx and urged the clergy to learn the language properly. Copies of the Psalms in Manx were sent to the clergy to make copies for their parishioners. At the 1758 Convocation he laid down that not more than one Psalm, or part of a Psalm, should be sung in English

on a Sunday or Holy Day 'which I think full sufficient for ye ease and comfort of ye minority who are supposed to understand it' and that the sermon should be in Manx, especially in the country churches, though he allowed the Vicar to use his discretion as regards the language of the rest of the service. In 1761 he asked the clergy to preach in English or Manx in proportions suitable to their congregation. The practice under Wilson seems to have been for the sermons generally to have been in Manx, and the rest of the service partly in Manx and partly in English. Hildesley was surprised that there was no Manx literature or grammar apart from St Matthew's Gospel and Catechism. He strongly condemned those who thought that to know Manx was hardly respectable. He insisted on children and confirmation candidates learning the Catechism in Manx, and he himself was soon able to read part of the service, to take confirmations, to celebrate Holy Communion, and to give the blessing in Manx, but he always spoke it with an English accent.

He was very fond of the language and Dr John Kelly's Manx Dictionary and Manx Grammar were compiled primarily at the Bishop's request for his own use, but he never mastered Manx to the extent that Wilson had done.

Wilson and his Vicars General had, as we have seen, planned a Manx Translation of the Bible during their imprisonment in Castle Rushen, and possibly St Matthew's Gospel was translated, but it was not printed until 1748, and the edition was limited to 50 copies for the clergy, paid for by Wilson personally. The other three Gospels and Acts had been translated by 1755, but not published. The Revd William Crebbin of Jurby, who lived with Wilson for 12 months after his ordination in 1743, told the Revd Thomas Cubbon of Maughold that during this period the Gospels, Acts and part of the Prayer Book, had been translated. Cubbon, in a letter to Weeden Butler (Hildesley's biographer) dated 17th March 1798 said that he was unable to find out, even from the papers of the Revd James Wilks, his father-in-law) who originally translated the Gospels, but he then added the above information from Crebbin, who felt sure that all were in the handwriting of William Walker. Whoever translated them, they were found among Wilson's papers in manuscript, but prepared for the press, and Hildesley, after they had been revised by

Matthias Curghey and Wilks, had them printed in 1763, but only for the clergy.

In July 1762 the Society for the Propagation of Christian Knowledge gave Hildesley £100 towards the printing of the Manx Bible, and various friends in England made contributions. In August Archbishop Drummond of York urged Hildesley to have a translation made of the Liturgy, saying that he did not favour the custom of translating the Bible and Prayer Book into Manx on the spur of the moment. In 1763 Wilson's Form of Prayer for the Herring Fishery appeared and in 1765 came the four Gospels and Acts for general use. The Prayer Book, in a limited edition for the clergy, appeared in 1765, and an edition for the public in 1768. Meanwhile, the rest of the New Testament had been printed in 1767. It is remarkable that in translating the Prayer Book no use seems to have been made of Bishop Phillip's translation of 1610, even though its language was now largely obsolete and it had never been printed.

The Manx New Testament and Prayer Book were well received and widely read, and the feelings of ordinary people were perhaps summed up by a poor woman in Kirk Michael, who, listening to her son read the Manx Bible said, "we have sat in darkness until now". Hildesley was so pleased with this reception that in 1765 he determined to proceed with the Old Testament. To save time he divided it up between the clergy. Genesis-Deuteronomy was printed in April 1770, Joshua-Job inclusive came in March 1771 and the rest of the Old Testament, with the Wisdom of Solomon and Ecclesiasticus were delivered to Hildesley in November 1772.

A revised edition of the New Testament appeared in 1775, in one volume with the Old Testament, but only 40 copies were printed as it was intended only for the clergy. The rest of the Apocrypha, (Tobit, Judith, Baruch, Susann, Bel and the Dragon) were discovered in the Manx Museum in 1978, and have been published. The Bible was printed in Whitehaven, and while bringing Volume 2 of the Old Testament for printing, Dr Kelly was shipwrecked on the 19th March 1771 in a storm off the Cumberland coast on which the ship had been driven, but managed to hold it above the water for 5 hours before being rescued. The New Testament, virtually the same as in 1775, was reprinted in 1810, 1815 and 1825; and in 1819 the whole Bible (without the Apocrypha) was pub-lished in one volume by the British and Foreign Bible Society. This 1819 edition did not correct even obvious errors which had crept into the text of the 3-Volume SPCK Bible of which it is a copy.

The tradition that the Prayer Book was translated by William Walker (at least in part) is incorrect, as the Minutes of the 1761 Convocation show clearly that it had just been translated by Robert Radcliffe, Matthias Curghey, Paul Crebbin, James Wilks, John Christian, William Mylrea, Philip Moore, Nicholas Christian and William Crebbin.

We owe the inception of the Manx Bible to Hildesley, but most of the editorial work was done by Philip Moore, helped by Dr Kelly. Moore was rather reluctant to undertake the work, but he said later that it had been one of the happiest periods of his life. They, with Curghey, revised and corrected the Old Testament, Wilks and Curghey revised the Gospels and Acts, Curghey revised the Epistles and Revelation and Wilks the Liturgy. Kelly corrected the Bible for the press. The Prayer Book was revised by Curghey, Moore and Wilks and was corrected for the press by Thomas Corlett.

The Manx Bible claims on the title page to have been made from the original Hebrew and Greek, but it is very doubtful whether the Manx Clergy who translated it were familiar with these languages. Probably however Philip Moore, who was a classical scholar, had mastered them both, so the claim may be justified. Archibald Cregeen, the Manx scholar, estimated that the Manx Bible and Prayer Book had preserved only about two thirds of the language, but they fixed the orthography of Manx in a way which would never have been possible otherwise. This had been very unsystematic, as is clear from the 1748 edition of St Matthew, the 1707 Catechism, and Bishop Phillip's Prayer Book. Moore's revision aimed at strengthening and purifying the Manx.

It is a great tribute to the Manx Clergy who undertook this laborious work of translation that, poverty-stricken though many of them were, they refused any payment, even when the Society for the Propagation of Christian Knowledge asked the Bishop to try and induce them to accept something. Thomas Corlett, who travelled to London to correct the printed copy was offered 30 guineas to cover his expenses, but would only accept 20.

One important fact about the Manx translation

is that (mainly, perhaps, through Philip Moore), it embodied the progress of Biblical studies up to about 1765, which gave it an advantage in this respect over the Authorised Version of 1611. The Manx Bible and Prayer Book gave new life to the Manx Church, and this was especially important in view of the Methodist revival which was soon to reach the Island, and which might have proved disastrous to the church had not the Manx translations been made. English people in the Island, and a few sophisticated persons were indifferent or hostile to the Manx Bible, but it and the Prayer Book soon became treasured by the Manx People.

However by the middle of the 19th century Manx services were only held every other Sunday instead of three Sundays a month, and were dropped altogether before 1900. The last person to hold Manx services regularly was the Revd John Qualtrough, Vicar of Arbory from 1859-75, and Rector of Bride from 1875 until his death in 1879.

The translators of the Manx Bible, as far as they are known, were as follows:

BOOKS	TRANSLATED BY

GENESIS
Archdeacon William Mylrea (jointly) and Robert Radcliffe   Vicar: Patrick.
EXODUS
Henry Corlett   Vicar: German
LEVITICUS
Nicholas Christian   Vicar: Rushen
NUMBERS
William Crebbin   Vicar: Jurby
DEUTERONOMY
John Moore   Vicar: Arbory
JOSHUA
James Wilks   Vicar: Kirk Michael
JUDGES & RUTH
Robert Quayle   Curate: Braddan
I SAMUEL
Samuel Gell   Vicar: Lonan
II SAMUEL
Joseph Cosnahan   Vicar: Braddan
I KINGS
Thomas Quayle   Vicar: Onchan
II KINGS
John Christian Vicar: Marown

I CHRONICLES
Daniel Gelling   Vicar: Malew
II CHRONICLES
John Gill   Vicar: Lezayre
EZRA & NEHEMIAH
Thomas Cubbon   Vicar: Santan
ESTHER
John Crellin   Chaplain: Ballure
JOB
Thomas Corlett   Curate: Bride
PSALMS
John Gill and Philip Moore, perhaps with some help from Matthias Curghey & Robert Radcliffe
PROVERBS
Thomas Woods   Vicar: Maughold
ECCLESIASTES
Charles Crebbin   Curate: St Matthew's
SONG OF SOLOMON
William Clucas   Curate: Marown
EZEKIAL
Nicholas Christian   Vicar: Rushen
DANIEL
Philip Moore   Rector: Bride
THE MINOR PROPHETS
William Fitzsimmons, Minister of Episcopal Chapel in Edinburgh
I CORINTHIANS
William Mylrea   Rector: Andreas
II CORINTHIANS
Nicholas Christian   Vicar: Rushen
I & II THESSALONIANS
Daniel Gelling Vicar: Malew
TITUS & PHILEMON
Samuel Gell   Vicar: Lonan
I & II PETER
Joseph Cosnahan   Vicar: Braddan
I,II & III JOHN
Thomas Quayle   Vicar: Onchan
REVELATION
John Crellin & Henry Corlett (Jointly).

It is not known who translated Isaiah, Jeremiah and Lamentations, but it was probably Philip Moore. The rest of the New Testament Epistles were probably translated by James Wilks.

Another achievement of Hildesley's was the Manx Fund, which he raised to provide Bibles and Prayer Books for the Churches.

On the 20th February 1760, when the Seven Years War between England and France was raging, a naval engagement took place between ships commanded respectively by Elliot and Thurot off Ramsey. Hildesley is said to have watched the fight from a hillock near the entrance to Bishopscourt Glen. After his victory Elliot put into Ramsey Bay, and invited the Governor, the Bishop and other notabilities on to his ship.

For some years before his death Hildesley had been aware that his health was failing. In October 1771 he was taken seriously ill, and though he recovered, a general weakness returned in March 1772. In June it was noticed that his old liveliness had gone, and that he was obviously finding business difficult. On Saturday, 28th November 1772 he received the last part of the Manx Bible, and sang the Nunc Dimittis with his family.

On the following evening he preached in Bishopscourt Chapel on the uncertainty of human life, referring to people who had died suddenly, and urging his hearers to be ready to meet God. Next Day, after dining at 4 p.m. in his normal good spirits with his family and the Revd Henry Corlett he suddenly had a stroke on the left side, and became unconscious. He lingered in this state for a week and died about 1 a.m. on Monday, 7th December. He was buried with his wife at Kirk Michael on the 10th December. In his will he asked that his funeral service and the sermon should be in Manx (this was done by Philip Moore) and that he should be buried as near as possible to Bishop Wilson. With \characteristic consideration for his clergy he said that he only expected those living nearby to attend the funeral, and even then only if it was convenient, if they were in good health, and if it was a fine day. He asked that the funeral be at 10 a.m. on the fourth day after his death, and that the burial should take place before the service in church which, he said, "was the place designed for the living and not for the dead". He expressed the wish that all the tenants of the Bishop's demesne should attend, and that each should be given a crown. He forbade any entertainment after the funeral, but instructed his executors (his sister Hester and James Wilks) to provide a plain meal for his tenants and for the parish clerk. Only the names and dates of death of him and his wife were to be engraved on the tombstone. He left a small legacy to each parish, and provided for his servants, saying that they were to receive one guinea for every year they had spent in his service.

Archdeacon Moore considered Hildesley a good and useful Bishop, but felt that he owed much to the achievements and work of his predecessor. To follow a man of Wilson's personality, spirituality and calibre, and one whose episcopate was so long, could not have been easy, and the fact that Hildesley was such a successful Bishop in his own right, shows the man he was. He brought much needed peace to the diocese, and ended once and for all the disputes between church and state which, although forced on Wilson, had been bad for the church and for the spiritual life of the diocese. The passage of time has enabled us to see his qualities, which were admittedly less striking than those of Wilson, but the fact that they are so often grouped together as two of the outstanding Bishops of Sodor and Man, speaks for itself.

The Parishes under Hildesley

ANDREAS John Kippax was Rector and Archdeacon on Hildesley's arrival, and he was succeeded on his death in 1760 by William Mylrea, who was appointed on the 18th July. In 1769 he was presented for not reading the Oeil Voirrey service on Christmas Eve 1768. As it was not observed in all the parishes, Mylrea asked Bishop Hildesley either to order its general use or to suppress it. In the end the Vicar General's Court decided that the incumbent was not bound to attend the Oeil Voirrey.

ARBORY The incumbency of John Moore (1748-91) covered the whole of Hildesley's episcopate. By his time the old church, built in 1328, which stood in the churchyard south of the present church, was very dilapidated, and on the 20th October 1757 Tynwald passed an Act to build a new church. The Duke of Atholl gave his assent to this on the 24th February 1758. During the building baptisms took place in Rushen or Malew. The work was temporarily held up when the ship bringing slates for the roof was wrecked off the Calf of Man. When the church was completed there was a dispute between the church-wardens and Governor Cochrane (representing the Duke of Atholl) as to who should pay for it. In the end the Duke agreed to pay for the chancel, but stipulated that it was to be no bigger than the chancel of the old church, while the churchwardens raised the remaining money by cess. The altar steps and the pinnacle stones were from Pooilvaish. The 1759 roof remained good until 1924.

The consecration was fixed for the 1st November 1759, and the clergy were invited by means of a messenger on horseback, who managed to visit all the vicarages in two days. The Bishop's text was Leviticus 26² and he ended with the words "this is none other than the House of God". The consecration deed forbade burials in the church.

Vicar Moore seems to have had the sad lack of respect for what is seemly in church which characterised some of the 18th century Manx clergy, and in 1766 Hildesley reproved him for the bad state of the churchyard and of the offertory basins.

BALLAUGH Philip Moore moved to Bride in November 1760, and was succeeded by Matthias Curghey who was inducted on 24th February 1761. He was Vicar General in his later years. His last illness seems to have been short as he married a couple on the 8th December 1770, and died at 5 a.m. on Saturday 19th January 1771. He left £12 as capital of which the interest was to be paid to the parish schoolmaster, but the churchwardens lent it on insufficient security, and £4 was lost.

It was probably in his time that, at the request of the parishioners, a rear gallery and two side galleries were added to the church, the former reached by outside steps on either side of the porch. At this time Holy Communion was only celebrated four times a year, and it is recorded that in 1757 there were 494 Easter Communicants, over a third of the population of the parish. Most services were in Manx. The various festivals of the church meant little to Manx people at this time, and in 1769 the churchwardens presented the whole parish for not being in church on Holy Days.

BALLURE The chaplain in 1755 was Thomas Woods (1747-54). His successor was Daniel Gelling,

who was appointed on the 27th October 1756 and remained until 1761. On the morning of the 2nd March 1760 Hildesley held in Ballure church a service of thanksgiving for Elliott's defeat of the French naval force under Thurot, but Elliott and his men were unable to attend as they had to guard their many prisoners. For this service Hildesley wrote a Prayer of Thanksgiving. On Gelling's appointment to Malew in July 1761 John Crellin was appointed Chaplain and remained until he became Vicar of Kirk Michael in 1771.

BRADDAN On the death of Joseph Cosnahan, Thomas Woods became Vicar on the 23rd December 1768. In 1769 the churchwardens were presented for not providing enough wine the previous Christmas Day. There was only half a bottle in the vestry. A full bottle had been left as a reserve at Pat Cubbon's alehouse near the church, but when sent for it was half empty. Warden Thomas Quine explained that he had given part of it to a woman who was taken ill in the alehouse.

BRIDE The Rector on Hildesley's arrival was William Mylrea, who moved to Andreas in 1760. His place was taken (14th November 1760) by Philip Moore, who remained until his death on the 22nd January 1783. He rarely resided either at Ballaugh or Bride, and this was particularly resented in Bride where his curates were often themselves non-resident and neglected the services.

The Parish Clerk was the only effective representative of the church in Moore's time. Moore was very Low Church, ignored Ash Wednesday, Lent and Saints' Days, and did not always have a service on Maundy Thursday or Good Friday. He was rather sarcastic in manner, but this was to some extent a screen for a sensitive and emotional temperament. His introspection was morbid, he continually blamed himself for real or imaginary faults, and was always afraid of incurring criticism or anger.

CASTLETOWN There was an interregnum of nearly four years after the death of William Ross before Thomas Castley was appointed as Chaplain and Master of the Grammar School on the 31st January 1758. He remained until his death in 1807.

GERMAN After the death of Robert Christian in 1754 there was no Vicar until Robert Brew was appointed on the 15th April 1758. He had been the Curate of Andreas, but his incumbency was too short for him to make his mark on the parish as he died in 1760. His successor, Henry Corlett was Vicar until his death on the 15th November 1801. He came to live with Wilson in Bishopscourt as an ordinand in August 1753, and was the companion of Wilson in his last illness - the Bishop died in his arms. He was one of the outstanding churchmen of the century. The fear of losing the Impropriate Tithe made it difficult to obtain clergy, and in August 1754 Wilson gave Corlett (who was then 18) a licence "to read the prayers and services of the church as by law established, and also to read a homily or some other practice or instructive book as you shall be directed by the Vicars General of the Isle for the time being, in such churches or chapels as you shall be desired by the said Vicars General to whom we require you to give all obedience". This was virtually a lay reader. On these terms he went in 1755 as Curate at Ballaugh, and was presumably made Deacon by Hildesley when he had attained the canonical age. As the Rector, Philip Moore, was non-resident, Corlett lived in the rectory. At Peel he lived in a house in Crown Street which he once lent to Bishop Richmond during some repairs at Bishopscourt.

JURBY William Crebbin's long incumbency (1751-1803) covered the whole of Hildesley's episcopate. It was an uneventful period in the parish. The gateway to the churchyard, replacing a stile, was made in 1751. In the same year Hildesley paid for the re-slating of the chancel, but the population of Jurby was increasing, and it was becoming clear that the church was not big enough.

LEZAYRE Matthias Curghey went to Ballaugh in 1761, and his place was taken by John Gill. Hildesley had found the church and furniture in a frightful condition. The chancel roof was in ruins and dangerous. The floor of the sanctuary was uneven, the rails loose and tottering, and the chancel steps in bad order. There was no offertory basin. In 1762 Hildesley officiated in the church, but as the Bible and Prayer Book were so badly worn, he was unable to proceed with the service. In 1758 Hildesley instructed the Vicar and Wardens to do the repairs. In 1760 the north wall and the roof were restored and rebuilt, and by 1766 the church was in good repair. In 1761 the Parish Clerk, Thomas Corlett, was presented for not raising and singing the Psalms, and Vicar Gill was presented for forbidding Corlett to do so.

LONAN On the death of Nathaniel Curghey in 1759 Samuel Gell was appointed Vicar. After the building of the new parish church in 1733-35 the old church at Groudle was completely neglected and became ruinous.

MALEW On the death of John Quayle in June 1758 John Gill was appointed Vicar (19th April 1759) but in 1761 he moved to Lezayre and was succeeded by Daniel Gelling. In 1761 he was presented for not living in the Vicarage. This was in ruins and he told the Vicar General that he was quite willing to live in the Vicarage when one was provided.

ST MARK'S Hildesley's episcopate was not a great period of church building as was Bishop Wilson's, or later, Bishop Ward's, but it saw the building of the new church at Arbory, and the church at St Mark's, in the parish of Malew, which was consecrated on the 23rd June 1772, six months before Hildesley's death, and was doubtless named after him. The sermon was preached by Philip Moore on St Luke 7⁵. The Baptismal register begins in July 1772. Before 1772 the 400 or so people in the area were far from the parish church or from any school, and the roads were poor, so it was decided to build a church and school and to raise money to endow a chaplain and schoolmaster. They were encouraged by Hildesley, who, with his sister, gave about £500, £284 of which was spent on buying a glebe. The people successfully petitioned Governor John Wood for permission to invite subscriptions. The church was built on a site called Dreem-freaie, near to where the parish of Malew touches the boundaries of Marown and Santan. The piece of land was bought from Nicholas Taggart for £3-3s-0d on the 7th October 1771, and the yearly rent to the Lord (the Duke of Atholl) was fixed at 1 farthing. The Vicar of Malew, Daniel Gelling, agreed to the building of St Mark's Church on condition that the chaplain did not interfere with the rights and privileges of the parish church. The final bill for building and furnishing the church was £280-7s-1d. Hugh Cosnahan, MHK of Ballakew and Thomas Faragher of Shenvalley were appointed as trustees, and the first two churchwardens were William Taggart of Cordeman and Christopher Bridson of Ballavervane. The Deed of Consecration vested the appointment of the chaplain in the Bishop, although no Deed was executed by the Vicar of Malew giving the Bishop this right. It also forbade burials in the church or within a yard of the church walls. Seats in the church were sold for £10 each.

On completion of the church the trustees set about building a house for the chaplain (costing £151-15s-6½d) and buying some glebe. Wages paid for work on the church and the chaplain's house were - carpenters and masons one shilling a day, labourers 7 pence a day and cartage 2 shillings and 4 pence a day.

The stipend in 1772 was set at £21-7s-6d per annum and it was decided that as soon as a school could be built the chaplain would be appointed schoolmaster, and would be able to augment his stipend by fees from the school. A kind of parochial district was assigned to St Mark's which included parts of Patrick, Santan, Marown and Malew, though when Foxdale Church was built these areas of Patrick were transferred to Foxdale.

The first chaplain was David Harrison.

MAROWN John Christian became Vicar on the 27th February 1753. On his tomb is the rhyme
In wit facetious, humorous to his end,
    A good companion and a steady friend.
He was a scholarly man. Like many of the 18th century clergy he allowed the church and its furnishings to fall into bad order, perhaps due to poverty as much as to negligence. A visitation in 1758 said that the pulpit was very indifferent; the floor of the reading desk was in bad order; there was no font cover; no proper place for communicants to kneel at the altar; the register was "all loose and in leaves"; the surplice was "shamefully old and tattered"; there was no hearse cloth or offertory basin; and the space within the altar rails needed flagging and boarding - this latter work Vicar Christian did at his own expense. The Vicar was ordered to transcribe into a new book so much of the old registers as was legible, and the wardens were ordered to buy a new surplice.

It was stated that the south stile of the churchyard was so high as to be dangerous for elderly people, so an order was made for its closure, and for a gateway to be made at the west corner. These instructions were never fully carried out, as the stile was not built up and is still there.

In 1765 the population of the parish was 658, but by 1776 it had risen to about 700, and there were 120 houses in the parish. Good Friday communicants were 182 in 1765, 194 in 1766 and 237 in 1771. In 1757 the average collection at Holy Communion was 14 shillings, and in this year there were about 350 Easter Communicants, about 200 at Whitsun and about 200 at Christmas. Vicar Christian preached in Manx twice a month and beat the bounds of the parish every five years.

ST MATTHEW'S In 1765 Philip Moore, who was schoolmaster and Chaplain and Rector of Bride gave up the chaplaincy and was succeeded by Charles Crebbin. He was succeeded in 1770 by Robert Quayle, who remained until 1791.

MAUGHOLD On Hildesley's arrival the Vicar was Thomas W. J. Woods. Between 1757 and 1761 he rebuilt, and much improved, the vicarage. In the burial register for 1756 is an entry for a certain Daniel Kerruish who was killed by falling down the cliff while going to the beach to gather edible seaweed on Sunday morning, 16th October. Vicar Woods wrote in the margin "From a profanation of the Sabbath, and from sudden unprepared and eternal death, good Lord deliver us. Amen". He was succeeded on the 7th March 1769 by Thomas Cubbon who remained as Vicar until 1814, this 45 years incumbency being typical of the faithfulness of the Manx Clergy in the 17th and 18th centuries.

KIRK MICHAEL James Wilks, who was Vicar when Hildesley became Bishop, remained until September 1771 when he became Rector of Ballaugh. In 1759 he was presented by Kirk Michael Chapter Quest for letting his cattle graze in the churchyard.

ONCHAN Samuel Gell was succeeded by Thomas Quayle, who was appointed on 19th April 1759 and remained Vicar until his death on 9th March 1798. On 11th November 1761 he was married by

Hildesley in Bishopscourt Chapel to Grissel, daughter of the Revd William Ross, chaplain of Castletown, but on the 28th July 1768 she was killed in her bed, at the age of 57, by a thunderbolt which came in at the window. A major restoration of the church at the request of the parishioners took place in 1757 to 1760 by which time the walls of the chancel had become so ruinous as to be a danger to the congregation. The church was enlarged and a gallery added, but being only 56' x 15' it was still too small.

PATRICK On the death of Robert Radcliffe, Evan Christian was appointed Vicar (9th October 1769) and remained until 1808.

RUSHEN The long incumbency of Nicholas Christian (1748-82) covered the whole of Hildesley's episcopate.

SANTAN Vicar Crebbin died on 26th August 1764 and was succeeded on 7th February 1765 by Thomas Cubbon, who in 1769 was succeeded by Charles Crebbin. A visitation on 20th July 1758 by Vicars General Cosnahan and E. Moore mentioned that several seats were out of order and that others were "rugged and uneven", that the door lock needed repairing, that the altar rail and the back of the pulpit were loose, that the roof needed repair, that there was no hearse cloth, that a new bier was needed and also a new Prayer Book for the reading desk and a new collection plate. The chancel was ordered to be whitewashed, and the surplice was described as "foul and dirty" and orders were given that it be washed once a quarter.

The 1722 vicarage was unsuitable and inconvenient and had been little used by Vicars, so it was rebuilt in 1769.

Chapter 3

BISHOPS RICHMOND 1773-1780 and MASON 1780-1783

The new Bishop was Richard Richmond LLD, Vicar of Walton on the Hill, Lancashire and chaplain to the Duke of Atholl. The Duchess nominated him on the 23rd January 1773. He was consecrated on Sunday, 14th February 1773 in the Chapel Royal, Whitehall, by Archbishop Drummond of York, assisted by the Bishops of Durham, Ely and Chester. Richmond was the last Bishop to be enthroned in St German's Cathedral. His health was not good, and this caused him to be absent from the diocese for long periods while he was taking the waters at Bath and Buxton, and he was away when Atholl visited the Island in 1779. He was considered to be an eloquent preacher, but he was perhaps our most secular-minded Bishop and was said to have been remarkable only for his unbending haughtiness.

The first five years of his episcopate were occupied by a dispute with his tenants at Bishopscourt. By long tradition they had to pay a new Bishop one ox or a money payment for each quarterland and Richmond demanded the money. The tenants maiantained that the choice was theirs, and in October 1778 the Manx Chancery Court decided the point in their favour. Richmond decided not to appeal to the Privy Council, as he felt that, even if his appeal were allowed, he would have to pay his own costs, reckoned at £100.

Until 1773 the tithes were let to the clergy, who acted as their own proctors for collecting them in their parishes. Richmond, however, put the tithes up to public auction and let them to the highest bidder, who in turn re-let them, often at inflated prices. The clergy were irritated and dissatisfied by this arrangement and preferred the previous system which had been started by Hildesley. As they ceased to act as proctors they lost their fees.

On the 16th July 1776, before John Wesley came to the Island in 1777, Richmond sent a pastoral letter to the clergy regarding the Methodist preachers, whom he described as "unordained, unauthorised and unqualified persons from other countries". He asked the clergy to do all possible to dissuade their people from going to Methodist services, but if they still continued to do so the clergy were to find out their names, and if they were Schoolmasters, Parish Clerks or anyone else holding a licence from the Bishop, they were to give their names to the Bishop and the Vicars General within a month. If any Methodist preachers came to Communion they were to be repelled and the Bishop notified within fourteen days. He also forbade John Wesley to preach from Manx pulpits. It had little effect, as in 1778 there were about 600 Methodists on the Island and by 1781 this had risen to 1,597.

Under Richmond ecclesiastical discipline rapidly declined, the few cases brought before the Church Courts being cases of immorality and all attempts to enforce attendance at Church almost ceased. Richmond died in London on 4th February 1780.

His successor was George Mason, nominated by the Dowager Duchess of Atholl, and enthroned at Castletown. He found Bishopscourt almost ruinous and unfit for habitation, due doubtless to Richmond's long absences. The hall needed urgent attention to roof, floor and joists. Mason liked the house and was determined to repair it, but he seems to have done little, and after his death the south wall of the tower was so ruinous that it needed taking down to the foundations. Mason's personal character made him unfitted for his office. He appointed as his Vicars General Charles Crebbin (St George's) and William Clucas (Malew). He continued Richmond's opposition to the Methodists, and, on one occasion, after he had attacked them in a sermon at St George's, John Cowell, the Parish Clerk (who was a Methodist Local Preacher) gave out as the hymn

> In vain, O man of lawless might,
> Thou boast'st thyself in ill.
> Since God, the God in whom I trust
> Vouchsafes His favour still.
> The wicked tongue doth slanderous tales
> Maliciously devise;
> And sharper than a razor whet
> It wounds with treacherous lies.

Next day Mason took revenge by rebuking Cowell for preaching when he did not understand Greek or Hebrew, but Cowell answered that he knew English and Manx well enough to make men understand that he was calling them to repentance.

Mason was criticised for using his spiritual position against his political opponents. Early in 1783 he planned to enlarge several churches but in April he became ill with what seemed to be cancer, and died at 2 a.m. on the 8th December.

He was buried in Kirk Michael Churchyard.

The Parishes under Richmond and Mason

ANDREAS William Mylrea remained Rector and Archdeacon under Richmond and Mason.

ARBORY John Moore remained Vicar under Richmond and Mason.

BALLAUGH Matthias Curghey was succeeded as Rector by James Wilks.

The galleries which were formerly in Ballaugh Old Church were added in 1776 for the school children of the parish, thanks to a bequest from Hildesley's sister, Hester. The pulpit and reading desk were erected in 1772.

Wilks had been very intimate with Bishop Wilson, who depended on him very much in his later years. He was one of Wilson's Executors, and was also Executor for Hildesley, with the Bishop's sister. Wilks is described as straightforward, but cautious. In 1769 he was appointed one of the two Vicars General.

The fish tithe had ceased to be collected about 1750, but some of the clergy tried to revive it, and about 1756 disputes arose.

The Vicars General were asked to ascertain the legal position, and they obtained from the Manx courts a declaration in favour of the clergy in 1769. The fishermen thought that the Revestment Act of 1765 had ended the old statute law on which the fish tithe was based. The dispute caused much ill-feeling in Ballaugh and Michael, and in 1771 a crowd of about 60, led by Thomas Cowley, forced their way into Ballaugh Rectory and jostled Wilks daughter, Elizabeth. In asking the Governor for protection, Wilks said that he dared not leave the house. Cowley was imprisoned in Castle Rushen, and bound over to keep the peace. As we have seen the opposition to the fish tithe was so strong that it was soon allowed to lapse. An interesting point is that the Rector of Ballaugh had in the past received the fish tithe on condition that he conducted a short service on Ballaugh shore before the boats put to sea.

Wilks was succeeded as Rector by Daniel Gelling who was appointed by Atholl despite Richmond's opposition. In 1781 he entertained John Wesley to breakfast at the Rectory, and he and Vicar Corlett of German seem to have been the only two clergy who defied Mason's ban on any dealings with Wesley and his movement. On June 4th Wesley preached in the open air to a huge congregation which included the Rector and his wife, sister and daughter. Gelling experimented with growing turnips on the glebe and his new methods were soon adopted all over the Island.

Gelling's son, John Caesar Gelling, became High Bailiff of Ramsey, and his daughter married her father's Curate, Thomas Stephen, (later Vicar of Marown and then of Patrick) and was the mother of J. C. (later Deemster) Stephen.

BALLURE John Bridson became Chaplain in 1771 and remained until 1783.

BRADDAN T. W. J. Woods was Vicar from December 1768 until February 1786. In May 1773 he and the Wardens told the Ecclesiastical Court that the roof and part of the gable seemed to be ruinous and dangerous. The Court ordered it to be viewed by a jury of experienced workmen, but their decision is not preserved. They seem to have decided that it would be better to build a new and larger church, but a major restoration took place, and the date on the tower is 1774.

BRIDE Philip Moore was Rector (mostly non-resident) from 1760 to 1783. The gallery was given by Bishop Hildesley in 1772.

CASTLETOWN Thomas Castley continued his long incumbency under Richmond and Mason.

GERMAN Henry Corlett was Vicar throughout these two episcopates. He was one of the few Island clergy who was friendly to the Methodists, and in 1777 he told John Wesley that he would gladly have asked him to preach if the Bishop had not forbidden it. In 1781 one of the churchwardens was presented for lending the Communion vessels to Wesley for use at one of his meetings, but the charge was dismissed, as the plaintiff failed to appear. At this time in German Holy Communion was only celebrated five times a year, on Good Friday, Easter Eve, Easter Sunday, Whit Sunday and Christmas Day, but in 1782 Trinity Sunday was added to this list. Corlett said that he could always fill his church by preaching one of Bishop Wilson's sermons in Manx.

ST GEORGE'S The building of this church was the most important event of these two episcopates. Bishop Hildesley had early recognised the need for another church in Douglas, and following a sermon which he preached at a meeting which he held in Douglas on the 26th October 1761, it was decided to build a new church. The Bishop appointed trustees to collect money and proceed with the building. Very soon enough money came in (or was promised) to justify making a start, but the Revestment Act dealt a serious blow at smuggling, hence at the prosperity of the Douglas merchants and by 1765 £700 had been spent and there was no more to pay the workmen, so, with the roof partly on, work stopped. By 1775 however, the need for a new church in Douglas became more pressing as St Matthew's was not adequate, so in 1775 Bishop Richmond launched appeals in London, Liverpool and Bath which raised £418. On the 20th February 1776 he appointed new trustees to get on with the building and another £800 was raised. Unfortunately, when Richmond died he was insolvent and £160 of donations which had been paid into his personal account was lost. In 1776 therefore work was resumed, and the church was finished on the 24th November 1780 and consecrated on Saturday, 29th September 1781, on which day the first baptism was held.

The Douglas merchants gave the organ, which came from Dublin. The dedication to St George was probably a compliment to Bishop Mason. By the Deed of Consecration the Bishop reserved to himself and his successors the right to appoint the chaplain, though no Deed was executed by the Vicar of Braddan (in whose parish St George's then was) giving the Bishop this right. It was challenged by the Vicar, the Revd T. W. J. Woods, who appointed Julius Cosnahan as Chaplain. The matter came before the Metropolitan Court at York, but the death of both Vicar and Bishop caused the suit to lapse. The Bishop has always been the Patron.

The original building was very different from the St George's we know today. The early part (pre 1776) was simple and primitive, with only a single roof, but the parts built after 1776 show a knowledge of design and skilled workmanship. There is a tradition that the silver Communion service, dated 1777, was given by the fourth Duke of Atholl. The Church was probably modelled on old St Matthew's. There were no galleries, and an apse instead of a chancel. The first Chaplain was Charles Crebbin, who was also Vicar of Santan. His annual stipend was £100, that of the organist £15, the Clerk £10 and the Sexton £5.

It is the only Douglas church with a graveyard, which was bought in 1811 from John Moore in return for two pews (rented at £9-3s-0d per annum) and a plot in the churchyard. The wall encircling it was built the same year.

In 1788 a debt of £297-7s-5d remained, and the various creditors received 5% on their claims until 1818, but friction arose from paying interest out of church revenues, and by an Act of Visitation dated 3rd October 1818, Bishop Murray appointed five new trustees and directed the appropriation of the funds, without reserving anything to pay the interest on the debt.

JURBY William Crebbin's long incumbency continued under Richmond and Mason.

LEZAYRE John Gill was succeeded by Thomas Corlett. At Bride he did not even reside in the parish, and had to be ordered by Hildesley to visit the parish three times a week, including Sundays and Holy Days. He was considered to have the best knowledge of Manx of anyone in the Island and in 1765 he was sent to London as corrector of the press which was printing the Manx Bible.

In 1780 he was excommunicated and suspended by Bishop Mason for an offence with another man's wife. In 1781 he petitioned the Bishop for restoration to the peace of the church and to his office. This was granted at a hearing in Kirk Michael before the Bishop and the other clergy who had been summoned to attend.

LONAN Samuel Gell remained Vicar under Richmond and Mason.

MALEW Daniel Gelling was succeeded by William Clucas, who was inducted on 31st March, 1778.

ST MARK'S When David Harrison was appointed Vicar of Malew in 1783 he was succeeded by John Moore.

MAROWN John Christian was succeeded by his son Thomas, the third Vicar from the same family. He was inducted on 24th November 1780, the interregnum of 14 months being clearly due to Bishop Richmond's absence and death. He was a very athletic man and was considered to be the best long jumper in the district. In 1796 he published a translation into Manx of Milton's Paradise Lost. The population of the parish in his time was about 700.

ST MATTHEW'S Robert Quayle's Chaplaincy continued under Richmond and Mason.

MAUGHOLD The long incumbency of Thomas Cubbon (1769-1814) covered the Richmond-Mason period.

KIRK MICHAEL John Crellin became Vicar on 4th November 1771 and remained until his removal to Bride in 1798.

In 1774 John Shimmin, schoolmaster at Kirk Michael, fell foul of Bishop Richmond, to whom he had presented a petition which the Bishop thought "extremely improper and disrespectful". Richmond licensed John Clague, the Curate, as schoolmaster in his place.

ONCHAN Thomas Quayle remained Vicar under these two Bishops. On the 4th February 1781

he performed the marriage of Captain Bligh (of the Bounty) to Elizabeth Betham, daughter of the English Collector of Customs at Douglas, who lived in a house at the foot of Summerhill.

PATRICK The incumbency of Evan Christian (1769-1808) covered these two episcopates.

RUSHEN In 1773 the church was described as tottering and ruinous. Hildesley, shortly before his death had drawn attention to the deterioration of the fabric, and soon afterwards a jury of builders and joiners inspected the church and advised re-building, not only because of its dilapidated state, but also because it was too small. Following on this Bishop Richmond consented to the proposed work on 8th December 1774. A vestry meeting held in May 1775 decided that the church should be extended so as to measure 64 feet x 22 feet; that the west gable should be removed, and about 20 feet, including two new windows, should be added to the length of the church prior to the re-building of the west gable and the bell tower. Before this the door had been on the north side, but a door and porch were to be built at the west end, though the old north door was not walled up. Further work in 1775 was the removal of the old roof, and before the new roof was put on the walls were raised in height. A gallery was built, reached by an outside staircase and a door high in the north wall. Dormer windows were built level with the eaves in the north and south walls to give light in the gallery. Between 1775 and 1790 the church was further lengthened at the east end by 18 feet and in this extension windows with round heads, of the same shape and size as those in the side walls, were put in at the junction of the old and new walls, but these were soon replaced by doorways, the one in the north wall leading to the vicarage pew, and that in the south wall leading to the Gawne pew. This meant that the chancel was darkened, so in 1839 the vestry decided to insert new windows on the east side of the former positions. They also decided to brick up the door in the north wall.

Nicholas Christian was succeeded by John Clague. His appointment to Rushen was due to the influence of Peter Heywood of the Nunnery, steward to the Duke of Atholl. Clague asked Heywood to put his name forward. Clague fought hard to get better stipends for the Manx Clergy, and to preserve Manx Gaelic, which even then was decaying. Clague was a rigorous enforcer of church discipline, and insisted on Sabbath breakers and immoral women standing sheeted in church while he denounced their sins from the pulpit. He had no patience with belief in fairies and other superstitions. He had a weakness for lawsuits. He took boarding pupils at £12 per annum and his wife took two girls, daughters of merchants in the West Indies, as boarding pupils to eke out his stipend of £42 per annum. Often he would gather the fishermen of Port Erin and Port St Mary on the shore, and read Bishop Wilson's Prayer for the Herring Fishery, and he regularly prayed earnestly for the blessings of the sea. When the Duke of Atholl asked the Manx Clergy to advise the fishermen to fish on Saturday night Clague refused, as it would lead to desecration of Sunday by drying fish and repairing nets, thus keeping them from church. He loved to preach on the repentance and return of the Prodigal Son. His neighbour at Ballakilley, Robert Callow, who poisoned his pigeons, and annoyed and insulted him in every way, suffered a stroke which made him drag his leg permanently and this was considered to be retribution. Clague made a versified translation of many of the Psalms into Manx and was very interested in astronomy. He wore a wig, and both he and his wife, who was a great help to him, were very much of the old school. On her death he fell into the hands of mercenary relatives, who showed little regard for his comfort.

SANTAN Charles Crebbin was Vicar throughout the Richmond-Mason period. He rebuilt the Vicarage in 1769, and largely rebuilt the church in 1774. The Vicarage Well, about 16 feet deep, was sunk in the very dry summer of 1775.

Chapter 4

BISHOP CRIGAN 1784-1813

Bishop Mason was succeeded by Claudius Crigan, who was born in 1743, the son of a tailor in Omagh, Co. Tyrone. He became Chaplain to an infantry regiment which spent some time in the West Indies, and while there he married a widow, Mary Harmon, the daughter of a rich planter, who brought him a fair dowry. Her family owned slaves and to the end of his life Crigan favoured slavery as a system. As a result of the dowry he felt able to leave the army and was appointed Rector of St Anne's, Liverpool.

When the Duke of Atholl sold the Isle of Man to the British Government in 1765 the Duchess had reserved the right to appoint the Bishop of Sodor and Man. She had appointed Richmond and Mason, and, in 1784 she wrote to the Home Secretary claiming this right. Crigan had been brought to her notice by one of his parishioners, Mrs Calcraft, who had once been employed by the Duchess. She wanted money for making the nomination, and Mrs Calcraft asked Crigan if he would be 'grateful' for being appointed. He appeared to agree, and duly became Bishop, but when, later on, the Duchess asked for the money through Mrs Calcraft, Crigan told her that simony was forbidden by Canon Law and threatened to lay before the Privy Council some passages from letters to Mrs Calcraft from the Duchess which he possessed. The circumstances of his appointment became known, and for a long time he was subjected to much criticism and abuse. It appeared that some years before the Duchess had ceded her right of patronage to the Duke, and this caused further doubt on the legality of the appointment.

The Duchess had appointed Crigan as a stop gap until her son, Lord George Murray (later Bishop of St David's), should be old enough to be consecrated, and that would not be until 1791. The Duchess believed that Crigan was in delicate health, but in fact he outlived Lord George, who died in 1803, aged 42.

Crigan was a good theologian, with a great knowledge of the classics, acquired at Trinity College, Dublin, which he entered in 1759. He was honest, and

his life and polished manners gained him the respect of the diocese. He was a good preacher, benevolent, affable to all, and devoted to his family. He had serenity, cool wisdom and steady piety, while his fixed principles sustained him in his last illness. He had, as the Duchess thought, had a period of bad health, but the air of the Isle of Man, and his freedom from money worries, did him much good. His stipend never exceeded £1,000 per annum, but he was satisfied with it. It must be said, however, that he lacked all energy of mind, and was too easy going, so the diocese made no progress in his episcopate of 29 years.

He was consecrated Bishop on 24th February 1784, and was enthroned at Castletown on 16th May. Thereafter he dressed in a suit of black velvet, and wore a powdered wig. He found Bishopscourt very dilapidated and took up the matter with Mason's executors, a course of which the Duchess of Atholl disapproved. The matter went to Chancery Court, and a jury was asked to inspect it, with the result that in 1787 the tower was re-roofed and partly rebuilt. Over the years he did much to make Bishopscourt more comfortable, and more like a family home. While this work was going on (1784-88) he lived in a small house in Peel. Crigan rebuilt and repaired the ruinous parts of the house and the outbuildings. His improvements were concentrated on the tower - the crenellations were removed or hidden, and the defective south east wall was rebuilt, enabling six new sash windows to be provided on the three main floors. The interior was divided by lath and plaster partitions into smaller rooms with fireplaces served by a central brick flue. The roof was replaced on a new line. The tower thus lost its stark appearance on the south side. Originally the staircase to the upper tower was built inside the massive double walls. Although a more modern staircase now leads to the hall gallery and the first and second floor rooms, the entrance to the old staircase remains, converted to a large cupboard. The tower once contained a secret room, reached from the old staircase. Crigan said that the work was "a very severe expense" but he added "it will not only be a convenient, but a comfortable place".

On 5th May 1790 Crigan, bearing in mind that perambulating parish boundaries had begun to fall into disuse, wrote to all the clergy telling them that on the following Sunday (9th May Rogation Sunday) they were to give notice that on Ascension Day they would walk the parish bounds (or part of them in large parishes) and desiring the people to come as well. Crigan gave as his reasons:

(1) To secure the parish boundaries.
(2) To give public acknowledgement to God for all His blessings by sea and land and especially for the fruits of the earth which by then were beginning to appear.
(3) To pray for seasonable weather.
(4) To pray to God to preserve them from all infections diseases and unusual mortality among men and beasts, and from the rage of enemies.

Crigan also suggested that the minister should read Psalm 103 from time to time, and in other places to pronounce openly the curse in Deuteronomy 27[17.]

In 1797 Crigan and Archdeacon Murray protested against the confiscation of St German's Cathedral by the Duke of Atholl and the British Crown. Crigan wished to make St George's the Cathedral. Confirmations under Crigan must have been very rare, as we read that about 700 candidates were confirmed at St John's on 22nd November 1802.

Crigan died at Bishopscourt at 10 a.m. on 5th April 1813 aged 70, and on 8th April was buried in Kirk Michael churchyard with his wife, who had died on 26th February 1812 aged 68. On their tomb are the words "the righteous shall be had in everlasting remembrance". Atholl allowed his family to live in Bishopscourt until a house could be got ready for them.

The Parishes under Crigan

ANDREAS William Mylrea died 14th September 1787 aged 64, and was succeeded by Lord George Murray.

By 1798 the parish church was ruinous though still in use. A special vestry meeting was held on 19th February 1800 attended by the Duke of Atholl, representing the Archdeacon. It was decided that in view of the state of the church, and that it was so small (only 55 x 18'), application be made to Tynwald for an Act to permit a new one to be built, and this was passed on 6th March 1800. It said that no burial was to take place in the church or within 12 feet of the walls. The new church was to be built in or near the south side of the churchyard, and the nave was to be big enough for two aisles and three rows of pews, each seating eight people. Materials from the old church were to be used, and the cost was to be met by cess and donations, but the Rector was to pay for the chancel. It was some years before the new church was built. The site of the old church is unknown.

Archdeacon Murray was succeeded on 18th July 1803 by Lord Charles Aynsley. He was succeeded by his nephew, George Murray, on the 29th September 1808, but he too seems to have been non-resident

until he succeeded Bishop Crigan in 1813.

ARBORY Vicar Moore was succeeded by John Christian but nothing of note happened during his incumbency.

BALLAUGH Rector Gelling was succeeded by Daniel Mylrea, son of William Mylrea, on 17th February 1802. He was Curate of Andreas (1785-99). As the Rector, Archdeacon Murray was non-resident. Mylrea lived in the rectory and paid Murray £5-16s-0d per annum as rent which included the outhouses and glebe. He was generous and hospitable, and lived as a father to his parishioners, charitable to the poor and a friend of the friendless. In 1814 he became Rector of Andreas.

BALLURE The Chaplains of Ballure changed rapidly, and there were eight during Crigan's episcopate. John Bridson was succeeded by Daniel Mylrea (1783-85), then John Bridson served again from 1785-89. It was during Bridson's chaplaincy that a large barrel organ was installed in 1787-the first instrument of its kind to be used in a Manx Church. He was succeeded by Nicholas Christian (1789-90) later Vicar

47

of Kirk Michael and then of Patrick. Then came Henry Maddrell (1790-1803), later Vicar of Lezayre. He was followed by William Sturt (1803-4) who seems to have left the Island, as apparently did Robert Craine (1804-7). Thomas Howard held the chaplaincy from 1807-09 and was succeeded by Alexander Gelling (1809-16) who outlived Crigan.

BRADDAN Vicar Woods died in February 1786, and was succeeded on the 21st March by his nephew, Julius Cosnahan. After him came John Moore. Robert Quayle was appointed to succeed him on 19th January 1792. His successor was Thomas Howard. He was an officer in the Manx Fencibles which he entered in 1804 and left in 1806 after serving with them in Ireland. He was much loved by his men. At St George's he started a service at 6 a.m. for men going to work. He was diligent and tireless in his parish work, and was described as being cheerful, gentle, firm, gentlemanly and affectionate, tall, with a fine presence and lovable face. He was a decided evangelical, and was one of the best and holiest of men, with great wisdom and simple faith. His kindly benevolence made him loved in the parish.

BRIDE Philip Moore was succeeded on 31st May 1783 by William Clucas. His successor was John Crellin. At Bride he was the first man in the parish to grow turnips. As there was then no rectory he lived at, and farmed, Ballakesh, until he built Thurot Cottage for himself. The next Rector was John Bridson. His incumbency at Bride was uneventful.

CASTLETOWN Thomas Castley died in 1807 after being Chaplain for 49 years, and was succeeded as Vicar and Schoolmaster by Joseph Brown. In 1811 an organ was installed. The first organist was Philip Caley (now only remembered by a beautiful psalm chant) who was appointed in 1815 and remained in the post until 1863.

GERMAN In 1761 a Royal Commission of Enquiry was set up at the request of the Duke of Atholl to consider the state of St German's Cathedral, and the Commissioners came to the Island to take evidence. On 21st October 1791 Crigan and Vicar General Christian issued a Memorial saying that in 1772 Bishop Richmond had asked Governor Wood to or-der a jury to examine the Cathedral and estimate the cost of repairs. This Wood did, but afterwards he refused the Bishop and the jury access to the Cathedral. Since then the Bishop had been refused access, so Crigan and Christian asked that as the Cathedral was so dilapidated as to be useless, it should be repaired and ownership given back to the Bishop.

Vicar Corlett told the Commissioners appointed in 1791 that all the Cathedral except the Choir was very dilapidated and had been unfit for worship since 1765, when the chancel had been roofed. At that time the windows and seats were in good order and the stone altar had been railed in. Richmond's enthronement in 1773 was the last in the Cathedral where all previous Bishops had been enthroned. Until 1772 Corlett had taken funerals in the Cathedral, but since then the chancel had gone completely to ruin, it was mostly unroofed, and the doors and windows, and everything inside, had been taken away.

In 1775 Corlett assured John Cook, one of the earliest Methodist preachers here, that he would welcome him, and let him use his house, but in 1798 he quarrelled with Cook, and in his last years was unfriendly to the Methodists.

In 1798 the morning service was said in Manx and English on Alternate Sundays. Corlett died on 15th November 1801, aged 65, and was succeeded by James Gelling, who was appointed on 23rd November.

On 19th February 1813 the Vicar and many parishioners sent a petition to the Archbishop of York asking to be allowed to build a new church, as the present one was ruinous - and hoping that a permanent minister could be appointed to St John's.

ST GEORGE'S Charles Crebbin remained Chaplain throughout Crigan's episcopate. On 15th November 1778 an organ was bought for £100, the first in any church in the Island. In 1781 a scheme was started to clear some of the debt on the building. The seats were classified, and every subscriber of 25 guineas was entitled to a first class seat and 15 guineas for a second class seat, etc. The scheme paid for the organ and continued to raise money until 1808, when Crigan abolished it.

In September 1808 it was announced that the pews in St George's would be let by public auction for a term of seven years.

JURBY William Crebbin died on 19th November 1803 aged 86 after being Vicar for 52 years, and was succeeded by John Nelson. His daughter, Esther, published in 1839 a volume of poems called 'Island Minstrelsy', all marked by nobility, but also by deep melancholy, due probably to her poor health. She died on 21st March 1843, aged 32.

T. E. Brown thought highly of her poems and wrote "Often I think of her and her early death; and Bride seems to me a shrine of splendid promise and aspirations, unfulfilled save in God. My father thought her poems worthy of Milton. And all that was breathed in and bred from the Bride hills and the long stretches of the Ayre".

The main event of Nelson's incumbency was the building of the new parish church. As far back as 1756 the roof was reported to be in very bad condition and in 1806 the whole church was beyond repair, so it was decided to build a new one. The old church, 60' by 14', stood in the middle of the churchyard and was like the vicarage, of the utmost simplicity. In 1757 Hildesley had reslated the chancel and improved the poor lighting at the west end, the rest of the church being repaired by the parishioners.

In 1806 Nelson read a notice in church, in Manx and English, calling a parish meeting to consider building a new church, and to apply for an Act of Tynwald to authorise it. The old church was to be demolished, and the new church to be built on the south side of the churchyard. Tynwald passed the Act on 20th February 1813, and the church was completed by the end of the year, but was not consecrated until 8th December 1829. Bishop Murray gave £150, but most of the money came from an assessment on the parish. Material from the old church was incorporated in the new one. Outside the churchyard was an area of unconsecrated ground for the burial of suicides.

LEZAYRE Thomas Corlett was not wholly satisfactory as Vicar. At the end of 1789 he ceased filling in Baptism and Burial registers, but continued to enter marriages. In 1803 the parents of these children asked Vicar Maddrell and the churchwardens to call a meeting of parishioners to receive the name of each child baptised between 1789 and 1803. This meeting was held in the church in October 1803 and the names given were, after careful enquiry, entered in the register. In 1789 Corlett admitted that he had upset the congregation by reading the whole service in English, but said that it was done on Bishop Crigan's orders.

In 1789 Crigan ordered another chalice to be provided, the church to be whitewashed, the seats in the chancel to be made uniform, some necessary flagstones to be put in the aisle, and the surplice to have a new neck. Vicar Corlett said that they could not afford another chalice, having just bought a new bell, but by 1793 two chalices had been bought.

The new Vicar was Henry Maddrell. He lived alone with an old housekeeper. He kept cattle and sheep on the Glebe, and looked after them himself. He was a byword for his miserly, parsimonious character, and in many respects set a bad example to his people - for instance he thought nothing of putting in his hay or corn on a Sunday. In June 1811 he was appointed Archdeacon's Official on the resignation of John Nelson. During his incumbency the church became ruinous, the school was roofless, and his successor had to rebuild the vicarage, even though Maddrell claimed to have rebuilt it and the outhouses at a cost of nearly £300. In 1831 the population of Lezayre was 1,976 and the stipend was £90.

LONAN Samuel Gell died in January 1802 after being Vicar for forty-three years, and was buried at Lonan. In 1797 he had been presented by the churchwardens for not entering burials and baptisms in the register. His successor was Hugh Stowell. In 1808 he established the first Sunday School in the Island. Stowell was a man of deep personal piety, respected and loved by all, and he was later a great help to Bishop Ward in raising money for church building by a tour through England in 1829.

He was early intended for the church and owed much to the religious influence of his mother, formerly Ann Brown, aunt of the Revd Robert Brown, and great aunt of T. E. Brown. On 23rd April 1793 he was ordained Priest at Bishopscourt and wrote in his diary "This was an awful day to me; never shall I forget the strong emotions which I felt on the occasion, and I pray God to imprint on my heart and memory the solemn vows which I then took". In summer he rose at 5 a.m. and spent half an hour in deep and solemn devotion.

He increased the number of pupils in the Douglas Grammar School, and increased the congregation of St Matthews by having a Manx service and sermon each Sunday. His health was never very good, however, and his request in 1802 for a move to a country parish led to his going to Lonan. He corrected the 1810 edition of the Manx New Testament. The other clergy looked on him as a model of faithfulness as a minister, and all respected his deep seriousness and sincerity. He was a strong evangelical, and was a forceful and eloquent preacher.

MALEW David Harrison was appointed on 25th June 1783, and remained until he went to Lonan in 1817. As there was no vicarage in Malew he lived at Big Tree House in Castletown, the site of the former Malew Street Chapel, where his son, Bowyer Harrison (later Vicar of Maughold), was born.

ST MARK'S David Harrison was succeeded by John Moore (1783-86) who was appointed Vicar of Braddan in 1786. He was succeeded by John Gell who was appointed as Lay Reader at St Mark's in late 1783 by Governor Dawson and Archdeacon Mylrea, Bishop Mason having just died. Previous to this he had spent some years at sea. In 1784 he became the first man to be ordained by Bishop Crigan. He remained Chaplain until 1809 with one short break in 1796-7, then left to serve a curacy in Liverpool. He was described as kind hearted and benevolent. By 1784 the stipend had been raised to £30 per annum, and it remained so until 1827, but nothing was done to the fabric of the church.

MAROWN In 1790 Vicar Christian was suspended by Bishop Crigan for drunkenness, frequenting public houses and keeping bad company. An Ecclesiastical Court document stating that Mr Christian "having quitted the retirement enjoined upon him by His Lordship, and returned to the scene of his unfortunate connections, has promised to repair to Kirk Bride and submit himself to the guidance of his brother-in-law, the Revd William Clucas, during the period of his probation". Another document of 1796 says that he was "degraded by being dismissed from the church" and a Curate, John Bridson, was put in his place, but he remained Vicar until he was finally unfrocked on 31st January 1799.

Bridson replaced him, being appointed on the 3rd

September. Christian seems to have lived at Ballakilley and Feltham describes a Vicarage near the church as being in ruins in 1797. During his last illness Christian misread a doctor's prescription and took a fatal overdose of the medicine.

Vicar Bridson's father, William, had been Vicar of Marown from 1713-27. John Bridson became Rector of Bride in 1808 and was succeeded by Thomas Stephen, appointed on 27th March, who remained Vicar until he went to Patrick in 1827. Stephen was a good classical scholar, and wrote much poetry, one poem, 'Cre ta gloyr' being considered one of the best Manx poems.

ST MATTHEW'S Robert Quayle became Vicar of Braddan in 1791 and was succeeded by the Chaplain of Ballure, Nicholas Christian, who stayed until 1797. The next Chaplain was Hugh Stowell, who became Vicar of Lonan in 1802. He began holding a Manx service each Sunday for the poor of Douglas, which always filled the church.

After him came John Kewley, who died on 3rd November 1810, aged 38. The last chaplain under Crigan was Joseph Qualtrough.

MAUGHOLD Thomas Cubbon's incumbency just outlasted Crigan's episcopate as he was appointed Vicar of Lonan on 3rd May 1814. He had been blind since 1825, but despite this he performed his duties most conscientiously. About 1774 the gallery was erected, but in 1780 the church was described as being so ruinous as to endanger the health of worshippers. Cubbon was respected throughout the Island as a clergyman and as Vicar General for his uprightness and integrity.

KIRK MICHAEL John Crellin was succeeded by Daniel Mylrea in 1799, but early in 1802 he moved to Ballaugh and Nicholas Christian took his place on 15th March 1802. He was made one of the Vicars General in 1808, and early in 1809 he moved to Patrick. In 1806 he had been presented by the Churchwardens for not reading prayers in the church on every Holy Day. His successor, Thomas Harrison, was appointed on 25th November 1808 and died on 2nd February 1818.

ONCHAN Thomas Quayle was succeeded on

27th April 1798 by John Cannell. He was a fluent Manx speaker. In 1803 he was presented by the churchwardens for calling a troublesome parishioner a mule. In his time Holy Communion was only celebrated five times a year - on Good Friday, Easter Sunday, Whit Sunday, Christmas Eve and Christmas Day.

Edward Craine was appointed on 29th March 1810 and began an incumbency of 37 years which was to see the building of the new parish church.

PATRICK Evan Christian died on 14th June 1808, aged 62 after being Vicar for 39 years, and was buried at Patrick. His successor was Nicholas Christian who was appointed on 8th November 1808, but died on 29th December 1811 aged 45. He was succeeded by John Cottier, who was appointed on 3rd January 1812.

RUSHEN John Clague's 34 years as Vicar co-incided almost exactly with Crigan's episcopate.

SANTAN Charles Crebbin's long incumbency outlasted Crigan's episcopate. It saw the rebuilding of the church and chancel in 1774, but in 1812 the church was reported to be in bad condition and the chancel ruinous. Crebbin's incumbency saw the burial of Daniel Teare, an Andreas man, and a vagrant all his life, who died on 9th December 1787, aged 110.

The parish clerk in Manx churches had to read the psalms for the day, line by line, in Manx, the people then singing the line with him, but in 1798 one of the Santan churchwardens complained that the clerk, John Crebbin, read out the first two lines only of the psalm (or that part of the psalm which was to be sung) and often sang two, three or four verses, which was useless to the congregation. When he refused the churchwarden's request to follow the usual practice, he was ordered by the Vicar General's Court to do so.

Chapter 5

BISHOP MURRAY 1814-1827

The appointment of Crigan's successor lay with the fourth Duke of Atholl (1755 - 1830). The patronage of the Bishopric was originally in the Stanley family, then passed to the Duke of Atholl. In 1825 the British Government bought the patronage of the Bishopric and of 14 parishes from Atholl for £100,000. He had shown unblushing nepotism in his church appointments in the Isle of Man, notably that of his brother as Rector of Andreas and Archdeacon in 1787 and of another brother, Lord Charles Aynsley, to the same positions in 1803. On 29th September 1808 he appointed as Aynsley's successor, his nephew, George Murray, who was barely of age to receive priest's orders (24). But the limit was reached when, on Crigan's death, he kept the see vacant for a year so that he could appoint his nephew as Bishop, though it was with the consent of the two Archbishops. When Atholl offered the see to Murray he said that the character and dignity of the office had been "so unfortunately lowered" by Mason and Crigan.

Born on the 12th January 1784, Murray was only 29 when Crigan died and the minimum canonical age for a Bishop is 30. He was consecrated on 6th March 1814 by Archbishop Vernon Harcourt of York in Whitehall Chapel, the sermon being on Ephesians 2⁹. Murray was the eldest of the seven children of Lord George Murray, Bishop of St David's, and his wife, Anne Charlotte Grant, and was born at Farnham in Surrey. He was ordained in 1807 as Curate of Burnham, which he held in plurality with his office of Rector of Andreas. He was nominated Bishop by Atholl on 16th April 1813, only 11 days after Crigan's death, and accepted the post on 5th May. He was educated at Christchurch, Oxford, and graduated in 1806. After his consecration the degree of DD was conferred on him (April 1814) by Oxford University.

Murray was described as noble looking, of engaging manners, and of benevolent disposition, dignified and gentlemanly in his bearing. He admired the scenery of the Isle of Man, especially Sulby Glen. He gave much charity unostentatiously, and after leaving the Island he continued to send money to several poor people living near Bishopscourt. He was an eloquent preacher. He disliked the intoning of prayers, the Psalms, the creed and especially the Litany, saying that it prevented people from understanding the words properly. He was never popular with the Manx people or with many of the clergy, due probably to a certain haughtiness of manner which suggested that he looked down on them socially. His relationship to the Duke of Atholl led him to interfere in the politics of the Island and in patronage. Some of his more unfortunate actions, notably his attempt to extend the tithe, were sometimes attributed to his strong-willed and often domineering wife, Lady Sarah Hay-Drummond, daughter of the 10th Earl of Kinnoull, whom he married on 9th May 1811, and who outlived the Bishop, dying in July 1874 after a short illness, aged 86. They had five sons and nine daughters.

Murray found Bishopscourt, which had been unoccupied for a year, especially the outbuildings, in rather a bad state, and reckoned that he would need to spend a thousand pounds on it, though he described the interior as comfortable and convenient. The Duke of Atholl lent him some of this. In a letter to Atholl he said that the house was "uninhabitable" and at first he considered removing the site, but he could not raise the money and Tynwald would not let him sell part of the tithes. Crigan had tried to make the house more like a country gentleman's residence by removing or concealing the battlements, but Murray, helped by the architect, Thomas Brine, tried to restore the house in the gothic style which was then fashionable. He replaced the battlements, tudorised the windows, and demolished the medieval chapel, replacing it by one in the Georgian gothic style on the north side of the tower. He added a new drawing room and upper room, and removed the main entrance to the west side of the hall.

In the garden the Civil War fortifications were partly landscaped, though about half of them were destroyed, and many trees and shrubs were planted, mainly under the direction of Lady Sarah Murray, to whom the gardens owed much. This restoration lasted from 1814-18. The terrible stench which greeted him on arrival at Bishopscourt was reduced when 47 dead rats, some decomposed, were removed from various corners. Archdeacon Mylrea said that he had never seen such a rat-infested place.

Two barrow-loads of crows' nests were taken from the chimney in the entrance hall, where no fire had been lit for many years because it smoked. While all this work was being done Murray tried to rent Fort Anne, but without success, and eventually he and his family became the Duke's guests at Castle Mona. When Atholl appointed Murray as Bishop, he made him promise to reside continuously for the first two years and after that for at least nine months each year. He did not, in fact, leave the Island until April 1818 when he took a three months holiday, returning in July after a passage of 24 hours from Holyhead, to be welcomed by the ringing of the bells of St George's and St Matthew's.

In December 1814 Murray wrote to Atholl that the clergy were on the whole active and zealous, though one or two were hopeless drunkards.

Among the works undertaken by Murray in his early years here was the making of a lime kiln on the shore adjoining Bishopscourt, and a small jetty at the mouth of the glen where ships could moor with cargoes of lime from the south of the Island. He also made the more northerly road from Orrisdale to the main road, known as the Deemster's road, because Deemster Crellin lived there then.

Soon after Murray's arrival Bishop Crigan's family claimed £500 for improvements at Bishopscourt, on the basis of the findings of a jury appointed to consider the dilapidations. They reckoned that these would cost £170, and estimated Crigan's improvements at £513, leaving Murray £343 to pay Crigan's executors. He refused to pay, on the grounds that Hildesley had not been asked to pay the £1,400 which Wilson had spent on the house. A Council, consisting of the Governor, the Clerk of the Rolls and the two Deemsters upheld the Crigan family's claim. Murray said that he would appeal, so the Council sought advice from England but in the end Crigan's executors said that they would be satisfied with £170, which Murray paid.

Bishop Murray and his wife gave much to charity, and he distributed in the Island not only his sti-pend but his personal resources, to such an extent that, though he was modest in his personal tastes, it was said that he had to borrow £1,000 from the bank when he left in 1827. No-one ever accused him of personal greed in the tithe dispute, and the memory of his charities lived long in Kirk Michael and around Bishopscourt. Another example of his interest in the welfare of the people came in 1823, when he became President of an organisation in Douglas to arrange work for the poor who were willing to work, but could find no employent. It was very successful. He also tried to improve education on the Island.

Murray and his family arrived on the Island after a pleasant 20 hours crossing from Liverpool to Douglas on the 'William Leece', which he had hired, on the 4th April 1814, and was greeted by the ringing of church bells. He had asked the Archdeacon to enthrone him in time to enable him to take part in the Easter Services and it was his wish to be enthroned in St George's. This took place on the 7th April and afterwards he entertained the clergy to dinner at Castle Mona where he was staying. On 15th June he held his first confirmation in St George's when there were 350 candidates. He normally held an all-Island confirmation in St George's every three years. His first Convocation was in St George's on the 2nd June, when the sermon was preached by Vicar John Nelson of Jurby. Afterwards the clergy were invited to a meal at Castle Mona.

In June 1817 there was a severe smallpox epidemic on the Island and Murray was obliged to obtain the backing of the Government in enforcing a ban on bringing the bodies, often in an advanced state of putrefaction, into church. People had even brought them in during services.

In July 1825 Murray wrote to SPCK saying that the Manx Bible and Prayer Book were no longer needed, but that there was a demand for the Bible and Prayer Book in English. Murray opposed the introduction of the Corn Laws into the Island, as they raised the price of flour and led to riots in Douglas and Peel in October 1821.

But the most fateful event of Murray's episcopate was the great dispute over the tithes, which alienated whole sections of the people from the church, and led them to join the Methodists and which virtually made it essential for Murray to be translated to another diocese.

Tithe on cereal crops had never been popular but the fact that the clergy, who were mostly liked by their people, collected their own tithe had induced the farmers to pay. The clergy never collected the potato tithe as it was the poor man's main food. Much of the trouble was due to the tactless and unscrupulous agents employed by Atholl and Murray to collect the tithes. Chief of these was James McCrone (1767-1840) who had been in business in Glasgow for about 25 years, and had for most of that time acted as Collector of Government Taxes for Glasgow, Lanarkshire and Renfrewshire. He came to the Island in 1818 as Murray's tithe agent and in 1820 he became Atholl's tithe agent. He was a devoted Presbyterian and started a Presbyterian church in Fort Street (known as McCrone's Gospel Shop) which was the origin of St Andrew's in Finch Road. On Sunday 17th May 1840 he was returning home from church in a trap drawn by a half-broken horse which ran away, and at the corner of Marina Terrace the trap was upset and McCrone and his daughter were thrown out. The girl was badly injured and McCrone died of his injuries a week later. He is buried at Onchan. Mrs McCrone, who distrusted the horse, had refused to get into the trap. He was not of good character, having been at one time charged with perjury re the tithes on Castleward, though he had been found not guilty. He was undoubtedly Murray's evil genius throughout the dispute.

His other advisor was William Roper, whom he had made a Vicar General in 1824, despite a long tradition in the diocese that this office was held by a clergyman who was scholarly and of good character. Roper had started life as a lawyer in Ireland, but after being made bankrupt twice he came to the Island to avoid being thrown into a debtors' prison. In 1822 he was admitted by Atholl to the Manx Bar, a move which was bitterly opposed by the whole legal profession. In 1825 Deemster Christian petitioned Governor Smelt (who was no friend of Atholl or Murray) to have him removed from the Manx Bar because of his wholly unprofessional behaviour. Smelt did as the Deemster asked, but in 1826 Atholl and Murray successfully put pressure on the British Government to have him reinstated.

It is fair to say that Murray's raising of the tithes was at least in part due to a desire to improve the stipends of the clergy which were very low. As ex-

amples, he raised the tithes of Braddan from £220-£390, of Patrick from £160-£250, and of Onchan from £35-£60. He hoped to raise the tithes of the Bishopric to £3,000. Bishop Crigan had never received more than £1,000 of tithe, and this was the Bishop's income in 1813, but since about 1790 the tithe demand had increased tenfold and this had, of course, held back the development of Manx agriculture. In 1815 the tithes were worth £3,000, but Murray wished to commute them for £6,000, which was far in excess of their real value, and when the opposition of the Manx farmers and of Tynwald made this impossible, he revived a claim (dormant since Bishop Wilson's time) to a tithe on all green crops, potatoes, turnips, etc. Had the tithes been commuted for £6,000 it could have been of advantage to both the Church and the Manx people, but Tynwald rejected it, probably because they thought the amount excessive. When the tithes were eventually commuted in 1839 it was for £5,000.

Murray could not have chosen a worse time. 1816 was a very wet year, with few dry days between March and November. Harvesting could not begin until late September and some of the corn crop was not cut until late October, a month of snow and frost. November and December were marked by gales and very heavy rain, which damaged the crops, and made the wheat unsuitable for bread, so there was great distress throughout the Island.

In 1712 Bishop Wilson had introduced a potato tithe. Before then it seems that tithe had been paid on green crops and cereal crops but since then no attempt had been made to collect the tithe on green crops or potatoes. The clergy had, however, suffered loss of income by the fact that during the 18th century farmers were increasingly turning from growing cereals to growing potatoes and turnips. Wilson's potato tithe lapsed after his death, and another financial blow to the clergy was the fact that for many years it had been impossible to collect the fish tithe owing to the opposition of the fishermen, even though an Order in Council in 1769 had stated that it was legal.

In 1817 Murray decided to clear up the whole matter once and for all, and in May he filed a test case in the Manx Court of Exchequer claiming potato and turnip tithe from Robert Farrant of Ballamoar, Jurby, and in 1819 the Court decided in the Bishop's favour. In 1821 he won another test case against Caesar Tobin of Ballameanagh. In 1818 he had applied without success to the Home Secretary in Lord Liverpool's government (Lord Sidmouth) for troops from England to enforce the fish tithe which he planned to revive.

Robert Farrant had meanwhile died, but his son, William, and Tobin, decided to appeal to the Privy Council on the ground that potatoes, turnips and root crops had never been subject to tithe. Judgement was not given until 24th June 1825 when the Privy Council confirmed the decision of the Manx Court of Exchequer.

On 28th April 1823 Atholl offered in Tynwald, on behalf of Murray and the Clergy, to commute the tithes of the whole Island for £6,000, leaving the actual levying and payment of the tithes to be worked out by Tynwald, and on the 14th May 1823 Tynwald appointed a committee for this purpose. They began by asking the Captains of the Parishes for a valuation of the crops in their parishes based on an average of 1820, 1821 and 1822. It had been noticed that green crops had been included in the £6,000 offered by the Duke as a basis for commutation, and in view of this, and a judgement from Deemster Cosnahan that potatoes and turnips were not titheable, the committee asked for, and obtained, a reduction to £5,000 (October 1823). The committee had asked the clergy for details of their tithe, but the vicars of eight parishes (Maughold, Lonan, Patrick, German, Marown, Michael, Malew and Arbory) declined to answer. The Captains of the Parishes were next asked to call meetings of farmers to discuss the proposed commutation, and most were in favour, probably because of a widespread belief, which proved correct, that the question of the tithe on green crops would be decided in favour of the Bishop and clergy.

A clause in the reduction of the tithes from £6,000 to £5,000 had given landowners and farmers the right to redeem their tithes at 25 years purchase. But early in 1824 Murray suddenly said that he would not agree to this redemption clause, so the landowners and farmers withdrew their agreement to the whole plan and Tynwald decided not to proceed (February 1824). The figure of £6,000 or even £5,000 was certainly excessive. The Committee of Tynwald had assessed the tithes at £4,000 a year, reduced to £3,550, allowing for the cost of collection.

The decision of the Privy Council left Murray free to proceed with the tithe on green crops, and McCrone was eager to implement it. But it was a time of great hardship on the Island. The 1825 herring fishing had been a failure, and this made the poor people even more dependent than usual on potatoes. The green crop and potato crop were very poor in both 1825 and 1826. In July 1825 the Bishop ordered a notice to be read in all churches that in November he would draw a potato tithe of 12 shillings an acre. This compared with 3 shillings an acre in England and 2/6 an acre in Ireland. Governor Smelt believed that the farmers would willingly have paid 3 shillings an acre, even though potatoes (and herrings) were the main food of the poor. The Island, like Britain, was suffering from the after-effects of the long Napoleonic Wars, the Corn Laws kept up the price of grain, and hence of bread, and in addition Atholl and Murray had been increasing rents. The Bishop's announcement united all sections of the community against him. John Nelson, Vicar of Santan, supported Murray over the potato tithe, and had been one of the first of the clergy to demand it, but this caused such anger in the parish that he had to take refuge in Douglas.

McCrone and his assistants seemed to have lost all sense of proportion following the decision of the Privy Council. In 1826, for example, they demanded a tithe of geese, and in December 1825, a tithe of calves. There was, it is true, an ancient Act which imposed a tithe on lambs, calves and colts, but it was not payable if the owner had less than five of the animal concerned. Murray intended that the green crop tithe should only be paid by those who cultivated one or more acres of the crop, but McCrone levied it even on widows and other poor people who had as little as a quarter of an acre. Even tithes of cocks and hens were being demanded by McCrone and his agents, though all this was probably without Murray's knowledge. One question was whether the tithe should be levied on calves which had been **bought** as well as on those which had been **reared** but McCrone claimed both. Vicar General Cubbon, though nearly ninety, said that he could never remember a tithe on calves. When cases came before him Cubbon refused to impose costs on the poor farmers, so Murray asked the other Vicar General, Roper, to impose them. McCrone and his agents brought people to court for the most petty reasons, doubtless knowing the inconvenience this would cause, and many felt that his motive was to induce the farmers to pay the tithe in money.

Although Murray was legally, and by ancient statute, entitled to the tithe on green crops, it was folly to revive something which had lapsed for nearly a century, and it destroyed his popularity in the diocese. An instance of this occurred one Sunday in October 1825 when Murray had arranged to officiate at a service of Holy Communion in Kirk Michael church. It was then the custom for the parishioners to stand in two lines leading to the church to receive the Vicar. Murray was received in complete silence and without any marks of respect, but Vicar Brown, who followed him, was well received. Several people seeing that the Bishop was to take the service, left the church. Relations between Bishop and Vicar were already strained because of Brown's refusal to collect the tithe on green crops due to him. Murray, angry at the Vicar's attitude, said that he would demand a potato tithe from the glebe. Brown told the tithe agent to be present while he dug his potatoes, but the agent refused, so the Bishop's tithe was left on the ground, where they eventually rotted. The Bishop then took Brown to court, but lost his case. Many other clergy also refused to levy the green crop tithe.

Another cause of complaint was that the tithe agents usually failed to attend on the days when the farmers notified them (as required by law) that they were cutting their corn or digging their potatoes. This meant that corn and potatoes had to be left on the field until the agents came, and the corn was often spoiled.

In October 1825 collection of the green crop tithe began. The mood of the farmers should have been clear to Murray and McCrone, because wherever they went there were poles by the road decorated with potatoes and turnips. The 1825 potato crop was one of the worst in living memory.

Trouble began in two separate areas, the south and the west. At first it seemed in the south that McCrone and his agents would be allowed to collect the tithe, but their high-handed manner led to a fight with some farm servants on Kentraugh, the spark that lit the fuse being a stone thrown by one of the agents at a woman in the crowd which had collected. The agents were hopelessly outnumbered and were badly beaten by the infuriated labourers, the carts which

they had brought for carrying away the tithe were smashed and the horses let loose. The agents appealed for protection to Mr Edward Gawne, JP, who owned Kentraugh, but he had little sympathy with the Bishop's policy, and would only promise to reprimand his men next morning. The agents, now in fear for their lives, fled to Port St Mary, where they passed an anxious night with angry men surrounding the house.

An attempt was now made to restore order by High Bailiff Kelly, of Castletown, who went to Port St Mary next day with three policemen, and managed to arrest three of the men's leaders, whom they brought back and imprisoned in Castle Rushen. Mr Gawne and the High Bailiff now thought that they would be able to make further arrests, believing that resistance had been broken, but when an attempt was made next day the police and High Bailiff were strongly opposed and forced to retire, after one man who had been arrested was freed by the crowd (Monday October 31st). The police tried again next day, and this time McCrone sent with them Murray's gardener, Cobb, who was carrying a pistol, but he was intercepted near Ballagawne gardens and badly beaten. Stones were thrown at the police, who once again had to retreat. The High Bailiff now considered the situation to be so serious that he asked the Governor for soldiers, and a party was sent under Captain Bissett with orders to look for the ringleaders. This they did for that day and the next, but without result. On Thursday a rumour spread that the mill at the Smelt was being used to store tithe potatoes and a large and hostile crowd assembled and began moving towards Castletown (then the capital) where the Governor and Council (including the Bishop) were in session. The meeting was suddenly interrupted by High Bailiff Kelly, who rushed in and said that the mob was approaching Castletown. A decision had to be made quickly, and it was decided to send the Coroner of Rushen (Archibald Cregeen, author of the Manx Dictionary) to meet them. Their demands were much more reasonable than might have been expected, as they told Cregeen that it was quite wrong for the Bishop to draw tithe when the potato crop had failed, but they offered to pay all other tithes or a money equivalent. They asked for the release of those imprisoned in Castle Rushen earlier in the week, for the potato tithe to be dropped, and for a general pardon.

They offered to pay for all damage done.

After the Council broke up, Murray had remained behind with Deemster Christian, as he had been told that the leaders wished to present a petition to him. He waited until 6 p.m. but as this information proved to be incorrect he set off for Douglas. Before leaving, Deemster Christian advised him to drop the potato tithe because the poor crop was causing great distress among a people largely dependent on potatoes for food. That night in Douglas the Bishop's wife and her mother urged him to accept the Deemster's advice. Murray seems to have been unaware of the distress caused by the failure of the potato crop until the Deemster told him, and this doubtless influenced his decision. Next morning, Friday, 4th November, the Bishop returned to Castletown, where the situation was tense, as a big crowd waited outside the Castle to hear his next move, many armed with pitchforks and other weapons. As a precaution the gates of the Castle were closed on the Governor's orders, and soldiers could be seen on the walls. Murray seems to have hoped for a declaration of Martial Law, but this would have been impossible with the few troops on the Island. Eventually the Bishop announced that he would not claim the potato tithe that year, though whether this was due to fears for his life or regard for the poor remains unknown. This defused the situation and the Governor, who was personally popular, induced the crowd to go home. The southern parishes later kept their promise to pay for damage done in the past week.

In the west of the Island the protests occurred mainly in the parish of Patrick, where several hundred men banded together. A rumour spread that tithed potatoes were stored in a shed at the vicarage, so the crowd burned the shed, together with two carts used for collecting the tithe which belonged to the Bishop. Their next target was Knockaloe, farmed by a Mr Kennedy and his son. Their object was to avenge themselves on the son, who had helped McCrone's agents to collect the tithe. They attacked the house and badly damaged it, then set fire to the stacks in the yard. When daylight dawned Mr & Mrs Kennedy and their son were forced to accompany the crowd to Peel, but on the way they met the High Bailiff of Peel, who took a conciliatory line, and promised to persuade the Bishop to remit the potato tithe, at least for that year. With this assurance the men

went home. About three weeks later those who had led the trouble in Patrick were arrested, and two of them, John Kermode and William Hudgeon, were tried and convicted for arson at the Kennedy's farm and transported to Botany Bay for life.

Meanwhile a crowd of men, estimated at 5,000 from the north of the Island, marched to Bishopscourt on Monday 7th November. They were armed, and the situation seemed dangerous, as threats against the Bishop were increasing daily. He had returned to Bishopscourt from Castletown on Friday, 4th November, having asked the Governor for military protection. This was granted and a small guard arrived on Saturday evening, November 5th, but it was quite clear that they would be helpless against the mob. It is noteworthy that in this crisis Murray's tenants did what they could to help, even though it meant leaving their families unprotected. Stones were carried up to the roof, anything that could be used as a weapon was brought into the house and barricades were erected at all the doors and windows. The great fear, of course, was that an attempt would be made to set the house on fire. On 9th November, however, the Bishop and his family managed to slip out and made their way over the mountains to Douglas, the ladies in carriages, with the Bishop, two friends, and 23 soldiers, all armed, going ahead on horseback. After an anxious journey they reached Castle Mona safely. The High Bailiff of Peel told Murray that he had now no option but to give up the potato and green crop tithe permanently and this he did, though with a bad grace, realising that he had under-estimated the strength of feeling against these tithes among the Manx people. On 3rd October 1826 the Bishop announced that because a drought had caused a failure of the crops he would not demand the potato and turnip tithes that year, and in fact they were never again levied.

Murray had left the Island in June 1826 and did not return until March 1827, one of the results of this being that those who were employed by him were out of work. Some of the clergy wrote asking him to return, but he refused, on the ground that the riots had endangered his life. He left the Island for the last time on 16th August 1827. It was clear that he could not continue as Bishop here, and on 4th October it was announced in the local press that he had been translated to Rochester. He held this see until his death, after a long illness, at his London home on 16th February 1860. He was the last Bishop to wear the episcopal wig. In 1847 he was one of twelve bishops who protested to the Prime Minister, Lord John Russell, about the appointment of Dr Hampden to be Bishop of Hereford, his theological views being suspect - without any real reason.

On arriving in Rochester Murray found that his predecessors had left the episcopal revenues in such a bad state that he would lose nearly £5,000 per annum for the first two or three years. Probably to compensate him for this he was appointed Dean of Worcester in March 1828. On the whole he was popular in Rochester.

In May 1827 the Duke of Atholl sent an agent, William Pettman, to see whether agreement could be reached on commuting the tithes, but the obvious question of whether this would include, by implication, potatoes and green crops, was left unanswered. Although the highest value of the tithes in any one year had been £4,200, Pettman valued them at £11,000, calculated not on what the land actually produced, but on what it **could** produce. The parishes were not told the sum they would be asked to pay in lieu of tithes, so most rejected the idea of commutation.

In August 1827 Atholl's share of the tithe was transferred to the Crown and the British Government sent an agent, William Courtney, to assess the situation. Despite the decision of the Privy Council that the tithe owner had the right to a tithe on green crops, he realised that the farmers would never pay it. He asked the Government for further instructions, but meanwhile he told McCrone that no tithe was to be imposed on green crops grown in gardens or on any land less than an acre in extent, and that instead of calculating the actual value of the tithe on green crops, he was to accept a commutation of 1/- per acre. Murray had asked for 12/- per acre.

There can be no doubt that there was little support or sympathy for Murray from the governing classes of the Island. Governor Smelt was never on good terms with the Duke of Atholl and only supported the Bishop as far as his duty required. There

seems to have been no communication between them during the crisis. In 1825 the Captains of the Parishes had held meetings, with the agreement of the magistrates, in which men signed a bond not to take or pay any kind of tithe for two years. Murray tried to prosecute three of the Captains, two of whom where Members of the House of Keys, but all Smelt did was to express disapproval of their action in private. The Bishop's wife openly complained that those in authority, like magistrates, or Members of the House of Keys, had done nothing to end the disorder.

Murray's episcopate saw a decline in church discipline, mainly due to Roper who was Vicar General from 1824-28. For example he refused to take action against those who desecrated Sunday, and on one occasion he rejected as "frivolous" a presentment for cursing and swearing, but penances imposed by the Church Courts continued until 1825. Murray was the last Bishop to excommunicate anyone, the victim being John Noe of Lezayre, who had committed a moral offence, and who died the same year. Tradition in the parish said that the Vicar suspended the service at the graveside until permission to proceed had been obtained by a messenger sent to Bishopscourt. Sentences of excommunication had been imposed in the past, and were greatly feared, as the sentence was taken literally, and the victims were often reduced to destitution.

In 1818 Lord Sidmouth, the Home Secretary, doubted the propriety of Atholl, who was non-resident, appointing clergy to Crown livings in the Island, even with the Bishop's advice. The Atholl Papers show, however, that in nearly every case he adopted the Bishop's recommendation.

Murray's relations with the Methodists were bad, and on one occasion he made an unsuccessful attempt to prevent those not licensed by him from teaching. His later career showed that he was an able man, and his troubles in the Island arose from the fact that he was too young and inexperienced when appointed. He meant well, but was undoubtedly autocratic.

The Parishes under Murray

ANDREAS When Rector George Murray was appointed Bishop in 1814 he was succeeded as Rector

and Archdeacon by Daniel Mylrea, Rector of Ballaugh. The main event of his incumbency was the building of a new church, as the old one was ruinous and too small. A special vestry meeting was held on 19th February 1800 which was attended by the patron, the Duke of Atholl, at which it was decided to apply to Tynwald for the necessary Act for a new church. This was passed on 6th March but building did not start for some years, probably due to lack of funds. The Act of Tynwald laid down that material from the old church was to be used for building, that the cost was to be met by cess and donations, that the Rector was to pay for the chancel, and that no burial was to take place in the church or within 12 feet of its walls. It was to be built in or near the south side of the churchyard and the nave was to be big enough for two aisles and three rows of pews, each pew seating eight people. The site of the former church has disappeared. The new church was consecrated by Bishop Murray in November 1821. Mylrea was still Rector when Murray was translated to Rochester.

ARBORY John Christian, described by Murray as being one of the best of the clergy, was succeeded on 4th March 1816 by Alexander Gelling, whose long incumbency lasted until his death in 1859.

BALLAUGH Hugh Stowell, Vicar of Lonan, was appointed to Ballaugh on 20th April, 1814, and remained there until his death in 1835. He was one of the earliest advocates of temperance (not total abstinence) in the Island. His Life of Bishop Wilson was written at Ballaugh in 1819.

BALLURE In 1822 St Paul's was consecrated as a daughter church of Maughold, and in future Ballure was simply a Chapel of Ease in the parish. Its last three Chaplains were Bowyer Harrison (1816-18), John Kaye (1818 until his death on 17th March 1819), and Philip Corlett (1819 until his death on 1st October 1825 aged 30) who became in 1822 the first Chaplain of St Paul's.

After the building of St Paul's, Ballure quickly became dilapidated, but it was extensively restored by William Kermode (Chaplain of St Paul's 1843-1871) in 1851 at a cost of £323. The dedication was changed from St Mary to St Catherine. The font was installed in 1867 and the altar rails and font cover came from St Paul's. The east window was given in memory of George Paton, the beloved Vicar of St

Paul's from 1871-1900, and the small circular windows at the west end are a memorial to his daughter Jessie. In the latter part of the century the only service was Evensong at 3 p.m. on Sundays during the summer.

BRADDAN Thomas Howard remained Vicar throughout Murray's episcopate, In 1816 the churchyard on the road to the Strang was bought.

BRIDE Thomas Cubbon was appointed Rector on 18th April 1817, and remained until his death on 19th January 1828, aged 89. His health had failed, however, and he engaged a retired priest, John Gell, to run the parish. Gell occupied the rectory as Cubbon was non-resident. In May 1825 the 'Manx Patriot' accused him of immorality and drunkenness but the Bishop brought an action for libel on Gell's behalf which was successful, the editor John Sumner being fined £5 and imprisoned in Castle Rushen for 3 months. Gell was in fact, well liked in Bride.

At the 1824 Vestry meeting, one of the four wardens elected, a Mr Scott, was not a member of the Church of England. This was quite legal, but the other wardens refused to act with him so the Vicar General ordered the old wardens to remain in office for another year.

CASTLETOWN Joseph Brown was appointed Vicar of Kirk Michael in 1818, and was succeeded by Thomas Thimbleby. The great event of his chaplaincy was the building of St Mary's Church. On 10th June 1817 Murray wrote to Atholl saying that Castletown Chapel was quite inadequate for the growing population and suggesting that an extra aisle be built on the town side. He said that many people who could not find a seat in the church were going to the Methodists. Thimbleby lived just long enough to see it consecrated by Bishop Murray on Easter Sunday 1826. Murray preached on Psalm 95[6]. The Castletown people were very annoyed that the consecration had taken place without any vestry meeting being called. On June 22, 1822 a Vestry meeting had decided that the 1698 chapel should be demolished (which was done in 1824) and rebuilt. A report ordered by the Vestry on 4th June said that the roof and walls were ruinous and dangerous. In order to obtain a bigger site some adjoining plots of land were bought. On 19th April 1824 (Easter Monday) the foundation of the new church was laid by Governor Smelt, who was eventually buried beneath the altar. The cost of the new St Mary's was £1,675-6s-8 ½d, of which one third was paid by the Government and the rest was raised by the sale of pews. The lesson at the laying of the foundation stone was Ezra 3$^{6-12}$, read by the Revd G. Parsons, who succeeded Thimbleby as Chaplain in 1827, while the prayers were taken by the Revd A. Holmes, who used a prayer written by Bishop Wilson for such occasions. The architect was Thomas Brine of Castletown. The square pews were formerly occupied by officers of the garrison and their families, and the narrow pews outside the Communion rail were for the Bishop and the Duke of Atholl. The Governor's pew was in the gallery, which was normally occupied by the garrison. 334 people could be seated on the ground floor.

One Sunday in 1826 the Manx Arms was put up in front of the organ gallery, but was taken down by the Parish Clerk. A Vestry meeting was held the following Wednesday and was told that the Bishop had ordered the Arms to be removed when he consecrated the church. It was finally resolved that the Arms (after having certain laurel leaves, which had been painted around them, removed) should be put up again. Thimbleby only agreed to sign the resolution if he was allowed to add that he disagreed with it. Parsons, then Thimbleby's Curate, agreed to sign it.

GERMAN James Gelling was Vicar from 1801-8th July 1838 when he died suddenly aged 66. About 1811 he became Master of Peel Grammar School, which had been established about 1774, but after running it efficiently for some years he neglected it, and most of the pupils left. The people of Peel petitioned the House of Keys to have him removed and a better successor appointed, but in response to this Bishop Murray set up a Court of Enquiry. This met on 26th November 1824, under Vicar General Roper, in St John's Chapel, and its terms of reference were wide viz: to investigage Gelling's conduct and character as Master of the school. Joseph Brown, Vicar of Kirk Michael, acted as secretary. The Court recommended that he should continue as Master, a decision which was very unpopular in Peel.

Although Peel people claimed the right of inter-

ment in the Cathedral, by 1828 the burial ground there was used only for sailors found drowned. The Cathedral was damaged in 1815 when some of its stonework was used to build a two gun battery in the Castle. The last oak timbers of the roof were blown down in a great gale on 10th October 1824. Bishop Crigan owned some remains of the Cathedral stained glass.

The population of the parish in 1831 was 1,791, and the stipend £90 per annum.

ST GEORGE'S Charles Crebbin died on 4th December 1817, and a week later it was announced that John Christian, who had been Curate since 1811, was to succeed him.

JURBY John Nelson left in 1818 to become Vicar of Santan, and was succeeded by John Harrison. He was an excellent Manx scholar, especially on Manx folklore, but also of the language which he largely learned from his parishioners. He was able to give much information to Archibald Cregeen, author of the Manx Dictionary, who lodged with him for three months. In 1831 the population of Jurby was 1,097 and the stipend £90 per annum.

A great character in Jurby while Harrison was Vicar was the Sumner, Juan Lewin, who was born in Lonan, but came to Jurby about 1800 and died there in 1857, aged 89. He was a tailor by trade, a Methodist Local Preacher and a bachelor and lived alone in a small cottage on the Summerhill Road. He was tall, with craggy rugged features and long flowing hair. He believed that the sin of man was bringing the world to destruction, and his message was one of warning and dire prediction. He believed that God spoke to man in wind and tempest and on stormy days and nights he would walk about the parish with his Sumner's staff, knocking on cottage doors, and urging the inmates to repent.

LEZAYRE Henry Maddrell's long incumbency outlasted Murray's episcopate.

LONAN Vicar Stowell moved to Ballaugh in April 1814, and was succeeded on 3rd May by Thomas Cubbon who moved to Bride in 1817. On 18th April 1817 David Harrison succeeded him but his incumbency was short as he died suddenly on 27th February 1824 aged 77. On the 1st April Joseph Qualtrough became the new Vicar.

MALEW William Christian was appointed on 18th April 1817 to succeed David Harrison. He remained nominally Vicar until his death on 22nd March 1830 aged 59, but his personal character and neglect of duty led to many complaints from the churchwardens to the Bishop and on 11th July 1827 Murray called together an Ecclesiastical Court consisting of himself, William Roper and John Nelson (the two Vicars General) and Thomas Howard to meet in Douglas. The Court, after a hearing lasting an hour, suspended Christian for three years, and banned him from officiating after that time unless he obtained certificates from five beneficed clergymen as to his good reputation and qualifications to resume duty. He obtained these certificates, but the churchwardens said that his conduct had been such as to preclude him from again holding a cure of souls, and in the end he was deprived of his orders. At the next Easter Vestry the churchwardens proposed that the legal costs of £40-11s-11d should be a charge on the parish, but this was rejected by a large majority. The matter went to Court, which decided that the charge was not the responsibility of the parish, and should not be levied by assessment.

ST MARK'S John Gell was succeeded by two chaplains in quick succession, Patrick Kneale and John Cottier, whose dates are uncertain. Edward Craine was Chaplain from 1814-20 when he was succeeded by William Duggan. He was the only son of a fairly wealthy widowed mother, but he found the greatest difficulty in bringing up a family of six sons and two daughters on the tiny stipend at St Mark's. His mother kept them from starvation, but her means did not reach to enabling him to farm the glebe.

MAROWN Thomas Stephen remained Vicar until 1827 when he moved to Patrick. In 1812 he succeeded Nicholas Christian as one of the Vicars General but he resigned in 1824. Due to standing surety for a relative he became financially embarrassed, and feeling that this was improper for a Vicar General he resigned. He suffered a personal tragedy on New Year's Eve 1821 when his three year old daughter was burned to death after her clothes caught light from the fire.

ST MATTHEW'S Robert Brown, father of T. E. Brown, the poet, was appointed Chaplain and Master of the Grammar School in 1817, and remained until May 1832. He was a scholar, and a faithful and conscientious parish priest. His favourite subject was Church history. He was very evangelical, always in earnest and preached a simple Gospel. According to his son he was characterised by deep melancholy. Though a great reader, he would not allow a novel in the house, but after about 1834 he was partially blind owing to cataracts. He was a heavy pipe smoker and kept very late hours, often until 3 a.m. He is described as a man of courtly manners. His stipend was £52-9s-2d plus £60 as Master of the school, but on this he kept his mother, his wife, five children and two servants. He wrote two hymn tunes, called Braddan and Hatford, and in 1826 published a volume of poems. In 1822 a correspondent in the Manx Sun complained that the morning service was very late in starting, and that sometimes the bell was not rung until 11.20 or even 11.30.

MAUGHOLD On 20th April 1814 John Edward Harrison was appointed to succeed Thomas Cubbon, but his incumbency was short as he went to Jurby in 1818. He was followed by Bowyer Harrison, who was appointed on 4th April 1818, and began what was to be the longest incumbency of the 19th century in the Manx church, lasting 53 years until his death in 1871. From the start he gained the love and respect of his parishioners and retained it until the end. The stipend in 1821 was £108-9s-5 3/4d, and the population of the parish in 1831 was 1,341.

KIRK MICHAEL On the death of Thomas Harrison, David Brown was appointed Vicar, and began an incumbency of 42 years during which the Church School (1839) the Vicarage (1846) the buildings on the Glebe Farm and the Court House (1835) were built. The stipend in 1829 was £100 per annum. In 1826 it was decided at a Vestry meeting that as the steeple was decayed and dilapidated it should be partly taken down and an inspection made of the remainder to see if it should all come down.

ONCHAN The main event of Edward

Craine's long incumbency was the building of the new church, but this took place under Bishop Ward.

PATRICK John Cottier's incumbency was an unhappy period in the history of the parish, as he was unfrocked for drunkenness in June 1827.

ST PAUL'S This and Andreas were the only two churches built in the episcopate of Bishop Murray. The original Trust Deed is dated 20th October 1820, but plans to build a church had begun in 1819, and since 1814 people had been raising money. Murray gave £100. This Deed appointed as trustees the Northern Deemster, the Archdeacon and the High Bailiff of Ramsey and their successors. The cost of the building was met by subscriptions and a grant of £300 from the Incorporated Society for the Enlargement of Churches on condition that 100 free seats were provided for the poor. A pew was allotted to the Duke of Atholl, and another to the Bishop. There was no glebe or endowment and the chaplain's income came solely from pew rents. There were 68 rented pews in 1822 at £1-4s-0d per annum each. Murray, who had obtained the land from Atholl, consecrated the church on Sunday 18th August 1822 preaching on Psalm 95⁶ on which occasion the collection was £18. The patronage was rested in the Bishop.

Philip Corlett died in 1825 and was succeeded by Archibald Holmes. Holmes' stipend was £50 plus pew rents.

RUSHEN Joseph Qualtrough was appointed to succeed John Clague on 13th April 1816 and remained vicar until 1824 when he went to Lonan. His stipend was £91-0s-7d. In May 1824 he was sued by Richard Sansbury of Port St Mary for 13 shillings for ½ ton of coal, but in Court he successfully pleaded the Statute of Limitation. His successor, William Corrin, was appointed on 1st April 1824. He is believed to have been the original of Parson Gale in T. E. Brown's poem.

Until 1850 he had no curate, but no duty was neglected. In the 1832 cholera epidemic he spent his time with the sick and dying and eventually contracted it himself. He was a total abstainer, and was one of the founders of the temperance movement on the Island. He was an able man, cheerful, charitable to the poor and hospitable, while his preaching was described as earnest and evangelical. He saw the death of his wife and of several children, but met these losses with a serene and unshakeable faith. His wise and commonsense advice was sought by many, and he had a wonderful gift of sympathy which enabled him to enter into the amusements of young people and the problems of those who were older. He entered in to the work of both the farmers and the fishermen. In 1847 he was offered the Rectory of Bride (a better living) but refused, saying that he was too fond of his parishioners to leave them. He wanted Oliver Goldsmith's words "He never left, nor wished to leave, the place" inscribed on his tombstone. The memorial to him in the parish church was put up in 1860.

SANTAN On the death of Charles Crebbin, John Nelson was appointed to succeed him on 4th April 1818. His support for Bishop Murray in the tithe dispute obliged him to leave the parish and live in Douglas, where he stayed for 3 years until his appointment as Rector of Bride in 1830. In December 1827 he was appointed one of the Vicars General. He seems to have resigned as Vicar of Santan, because on 12th April 1827 Thomas Kewley was appointed to succeed him.

Chapter 6

BISHOP WARD 1828-1838

Soon after Murray's departure, Sodor and Man was offered to Bishop John Sumner of Chester, but he refused, so it was then offered to William Ward by Lord Goderich, the Prime Minister, to whom Ward had once been private tutor. Ward also was at first inclined to refuse, but he accepted in January 1828. He was allowed to retain both his livings in England and his Canonry of Wilford *in commendam* because of the poverty of the see of Sodor and Man, and his removal expenses, and for work on Bishopscourt.

Ward was born on 29th September 1762 at Saintfield, near Belfast, and was educated at Ballynahinch School. In 1782 he went to London to teach in a private school. On 17th February 1788 he was made Deacon in Duke Street Chapel, Westminster, by Bishop Halifax of Gloucester and later received Priest's orders from Bishop Porteus of London. It was Bishop Porteus who early recognised Ward's integrity and ability and who obtained for him the post of tutor to the sons of the widowed Duchess of Grantham, the younger of whom was Prime Minister as Lord Goderich from August 1827 until January 1828. He must have received Priest's orders early in 1789, as in that year Porteus appointed him to Mayfair Chapel. In 1798 he became Vicar of Myland on the outskirts of Colchester, a parish where few previous vicars had resided and where he built a parish school and a House of Industry. In October 1805 he married Miss Anne Hammersley, and had two sons and five daughters, but of these the elder son, Thomas, died in 1829, as a student at Cambridge, the eldest daughter, Charlotte, died in 1828, and a younger daughter, Annabel, died as an infant in 1817. The marriage was conducted by Bishop Fisher of Exeter, later Bishop of Salisbury. In 1812 Ward became Vicar of the small parish of Alphanstone, Essex. He remained at Myland until 1818 when he became Rector of Great Horkesley, Essex, where he remained until his appointment to Sodor and Man. In 1827 Goderich advised the King to exercise the right (acquired from the Duke of Atholl) to appoint

the Bishop of Sodor and Man. The Crown had purchased from Atholl all his rights as Lord of the Island, including all those connected with the Church. In commending Ward to the King, Goderich wrote "I know his zeal, his devotion to his sacred profession, his upright and pious mind and I was confident that he would undertake the duties of the see with an unalterable determination to perform them".

Ward was consecrated on 9th March 1828 by Archbishop Vernon Harcourt of York, Bishop Howley of London and by Bishop George Murray, now of Rochester. His arrival in the Isle of Man was delayed by the death of his daughter, Charlotte, but he landed at Douglas on Saturday, 20th September 1828, after a passage in the 'Majestic' and was cordially received by the many people who had assembled on the pier, including Deemster Christian, High Bailiff Quirk and several of the clergy. Bells rang, cannon were fired and bonfires were lit on the Quay. He went to the British Hotel, (kept by Mrs Dixon) in the market place where rooms had been reserved for him. Next day he attended St George's in the morning and St Matthew's in the evening. When he left for Bishopscourt next morning the people drew his carriage to Peel Road and when they left he addressed them from the carriage and was given three hearty cheers. At St John's he was met by the Governor and then drove to Bishopscourt. He visited Castletown on 24th October. The whole town was up early and in a bustle. The members of the Castletown Artificers Friendly and Philanthropic Societies marched for nearly a mile along the Malew road to meet him with banners flying and bands playing. When about 1.30 p.m. the Bishop's carriage and four came into sight the horses were taken out of the shafts and the coach drawn into the town amid great cheering. Ward repeatedly raised his hat and waved to the people. He called on Governor Smelt, then was sworn in as a member of the Council by the Clerk of the Rolls, John MacHutchin, and a loyal address was presented by the Castletown people. He was enthroned in St Mary's, Castletown by Archdeacon

Mylrea on 27th October. It was to have been at 11 a.m.; but due to some misunderstanding it was 12.30 before the Bishop came across from Castle Rushen. All the clergy attended and the Revd G. Parsons, Chaplain of Castletown, read Mattins. On 18th November he paid his first to Peel and the crowd which turned out to greet him took the horses out of the carriage and drew it into the town. On 30th November he held his first ordination in St George's.

Ward soon realised that accommodation in the existing churches was inadequate. The population was about 50,000 but the churches could only seat 9,000. Douglas had 7,000 people but the churches there could only seat 1,300. Many churches were very dilapidated but Ward found that he could get no help in church building from the Church Commissioners, the Church Building Society or the Church Enlarging Society. He therefore in 1829 appointed Rector Stowell of Ballaugh as Missionary to England with the task of raising money for Ward's Fund (for building and enlarging churches). To this fund Ward gave £100, and gave ten pounds to every church built, repaired or enlarged, but no subscription came from the Duke of Atholl. There was an especial need for a church in Douglas for the poor, who were almost entirely excluded because no seating was asigned to them, most of the pews being rented, and therefore private property. It was said that individuals in St Matthew's rented up to twelve pews, which were kept locked. Ward's Fund had been partly intended to provide free seats for the poor in churches, but to some extent failed to achieve this.

Ward's episcopate saw more church building than any other save Bishop Wilson's, as the parish churches of Kirk Michael, Ballaugh, Lezayre, Lonan, Onchan and St Barnabas' date from this period, besides St Stephen's, Sulby, St Luke's, Baldwin and St James', Dalby. Altogether Ward raised nearly £9,000 in England and £4,000 on the Island, for church building, besides spending his own money for the purpose, so that he died poorer than when he came.

Stipends in 1830 were nearly £100 per annum. The see, including the land, was valued at £3,500. In 1830 Ward proposed to Tynwald to commute the tithes due to himself and the clergy for £6,000 per annum, but Tynwald would only agree to £5,000. In 1820, 1821 and 1822 the average value of the tithe for Bishop and clergy was £3,164, after deducting collect-

ing expenses, but, in order to help the clergy Ward rejected the £5,000 offer and stuck to £6,000 (April 1830). The Tithe Commutation Act did not come until after Ward's death.

An epidemic of cholera started in December 1831, and reached its height in September 1832, causing many deaths, but by the end of the year it was confined to the south of the Island. Ward appointed January 1st 1833 as a Day of Thanksgiving for the end of the cholera, but attendance in the churches was less than expected. Archdeacon Philpot then appointed 30th October 1833 as a second Day of Thanksgiving and this time it was taken much more seriously, business of any kind being suspended and the churches well attended.

The later years of Ward's episcopacy were darkened by the threat of the diocese being merged with Carlisle. In 1835 a Committee was appointed by the English Government "to revise the boundaries of the various dioceses in England and the amounts of the revenues". As a result of its recommendations Parliament passed the Established Church Act in 1836 which said, among other things, that at the next vacancy Sodor and Man should be joined to Carlisle as it had too few parishes to justify a Bishop. The Bill passed the House of Lords on 1st August 1836. On 15th March 1836 a meeting of the clergy had been held at Kirk Michael to discuss the proposed merger. The intention was to petition Tynwald not to deprive the Island of a Bishop, but to increase clergy stipends. Failing that, it was suggested that the revenues of the Bishopric, if suppressed, should be used for education and clergy stipends, and not go off the Island. Finally it was agreed to take no action until the intentions of the British Government were known. Ward drew up a masterly memorial against it, another was sent by Archdeacon Philpot and most of the clergy (December 1837). Another came from the Manx Bar and a fourth was based on petitions which had been sent to every town and village in the Island in May 1836, which were signed by 1600 people. The clergy said in their petition "As to enriching the parochial clergy by the spoils of their Bishop, your petitioners dislike the principle and dread the example". The object of the proposed merger was probably to benefit the Manx Clergy. 14 of the 17 parishes were Crown Livings and in these the Crown was the lay impropriator of the great tithes, the vicars of these parishes deriving their stipends from the small tithes, and a fund created long ago by Bishop Barrow. It was calculated that if the Government gave up £518 per annum out of the £800 per annum which the great tithes yielded, stipends could be raised to £150. The Bishop received the great tithes in the other four livings, and Ward said that if Sodor and Man was preserved as a separate diocese he would contribute enough of the great tithes to raise the stipend of these four parishes to £150 per annum.

The reasons Ward gave in his memorial for retaining the independence of the see were:
(1) The antiquity of the see.
(2) Its geographical position.
(3) The Manx were a distinct people with their own laws and legislature.
(4) The Bishop was needed in Tynwald and there were certain duties which the Archdeacon could not do.
(5) The Bishop was in a position to give poor relief.
(6) The Bishop was needed for moral and spiritual reasons.

He concluded "But it shall never be said that the last of this long line of Bishops stood by with folded arms, without an effort, in the name of God, to arrest the stroke before it fell".

To reverse an Act of Parliament must have seemed an almost impossible task, especially as it had been supported by prominent figures like Archbishop Howley of Canterbury, though Bishop Murray had strongly opposed it in the House of Lords. Another powerful ally was the Earl of Ripon, formerly Lord Goderich, Ward's former pupil, who, on 14th December 1837, presented the memorials and petitions in the Lords, and he gained the support of the Prime Minister, Lord Melbourne. Among the petitions which Ripon presented were some from the clergy of Chester, Bath and Wells, Winchester, Ripon, Norwich and from the Masters and graduates of several Oxford and Cambridge Colleges. In January 1838 Ripon introduced a Bill in the House of Lords excluding Sodor and Man from the Established Church Act. On 9th February Archbishop Howley asked Ripon to defer this Bill, as Tynwald had told him of their desire to retain a Bishop in view of their regard for Ward. On 22nd February Ripon announced that the Ecclesiastical Commissioners had decided to recommend the continuance of Sodor and Man as a separate diocese. This good news came too late for Ward, however, as he died at Great Horkesley Rectory on Friday, 26th January 1838. His eysight had become so bad that in July 1836 he left the Island never to return, to undergo an operation for cataract by Mr Alexander, the leading eye surgeon of his day, but, though the operation on 14th June 1837 was successful, his health gradually deteriorated until his death.

In 1834 Ward established a floating chapel for seamen in Douglas harbour. It was a frigate which was a present from the Admiralty following a request from Ward to his friend Earl de Grey, who was First Lord of the Admiralty in Sir Robert Peel's first ministry. He bought an old chapel in Ramsey, and intended to open it as a second church, to be called St Peter's, to meet the needs of Ramsey. He appointed Samuel Page, who was shortly to be ordained, as the first Chaplain, but the Chaplain of St Paul's, Archibald Holmes, protested so strongly that the plan was dropped. Other plans which came to nothing were to establish a Clergy Training College, to restore St German's Cathedral or build a new one, and to restore Rushen Abbey.

Ward took a leading part in establishing King William's College. He contributed £100 to the building and paid for the chapel, which was opened for public worship on Sunday 6th September 1835 when sermons were preached by the Principal, the Revd E. Wilson and the Vice-Principal, the Revd R. Dixon.

Ward was anxious to raise the low stipends of the clergy, and used the episcopal tithes to raise the value of the four livings in his gift to £150 per annum, hoping that the Government would do the same for the Crown Livings out of the Impropriate Tithes which had been taken from the clergy and vested in the Crown. Ward did all possible to persuade the British Government to release them to augment clergy stipends. These Impropriate Tithes were originally in the hands of Lord Derby, but had been taken by the first Duke of Atholl when the Island came under his rule. Ward considered that Atholl had robbed the Manx Church, and that the attempt of the 5th Duke to deprive the Church of Bishop Barrow's estate was the cause of the poverty of the Manx clergy.

When Archdeacon Mylrea died in 1832 Governor Smelt wanted to replace him by Hugh Stowell, Rector of Ballaugh, and sent his name to the Home Secretary, Lord Melbourne, but Ward said that he wanted "A man of business" and succeeded in having Benjamin Philpot, Chaplain of St George's, appointed.

As a man, Ward was kindly and liberal, with great zeal and energy. He continued to wear the episcopal wig when other bishops were abandoning theirs, due to the unpopularity they had gained by their opposition to the Reform Bill of 1832. At Great Horkesley he only celebrated Holy Communion at Christmas, Easter, Whitsun and on the Sunday nearest to his birthday, September 29th. He did not have his children confirmed until they were at least 16. He was a great supporter of the British and Foreign Bible Society, which had been founded in 1804. He believed that cheap liquor was the curse of the Island.

In 1834 Ward wrote, "We only want to believe in God the Father Almighty, and in Jesus Christ His only Son and all the other articles of our belief, and we shall be no more afraid of the madness of the people or other waves of this troublesome world, than we are of the raging of the sea when we stand on Orrisdale cliffs, the summit of Snaefell or the top of South Barrule".

Mrs Ward worked hard to help the poor of the district, and the door of Bishopscourt was open to rich and poor. She died on 1st April 1841 in Dorset and was buried with her husband at Great Horkesley. In June 1838 there had been a sale at Bishopscourt of most of the furniture, horses, carriages, harness, colts, brood mares, ponies, many cattle, a pair of ploughing oxen, sixty to seventy pigs, 300-400 sheep and many farm implements.

In October 1833 Archdeacon Philpot made a visitation as follows:

Monday, 21st October
    Lezayre: 11 a.m.; St Paul's: 1 p.m.; Maughold: 3 p.m.

Tuesday, 22nd October
    Lonan: 10 a.m.; Onchan: 12.30 p.m.; Braddan: 2 p.m.; Marown: 4 p.m.

Wednesday, 23rd October
    St George's: 8 a.m.; St Matthew's: 8.30 a.m.; St Barnabas': 9 a.m.; Santan: 12 noon; Castletown: 2 p.m.; Malew: 4 p.m.

Thursday, 24th October
    St Mark's: 9 a.m.; Arbory: 11 a.m.; Rushen: 2 p.m.

Friday, 25th October
    Patrick: 10 a.m.; German: 11.30 a.m.; Michael: 3 p.m.; Ballaugh: 4 p.m.

Monday, 28th October
    Jurby: 11 a.m.; Bride: 2 p.m.; Andreas: 3.30 p.m.

The clergy were sent a detailed questionnaire covering the fabric, furniture, books, vestments, vessels, the churchyard (e.g.: are bodies ever buried nearer to the surface than 4 feet?), the parsonage, the glebe lands, the parochial library, benefactions, fees of the Minister, Parish Clerk and Sexton, baptism, the sacrament of Holy Communion (e.g.: do you exclude wrongdoers?), the services (e.g.: how often are Manx services held?), Parish schools, walking the bounds and registers. A terrier and inventory had to be drawn up. Churchwardens were required to attend, and to state if there was any complaint against the Vicar, did he reside in the parish, were they careful in making presentments, did they prevent brawling and indecent conduct in the church and churchyard and did they take action against people loitering about the churchyard during services?

On 27th August 1830 Ward held a confirmation at Andreas and at the end of the sermon he told the children to go straight home, and not to resort to a public house, as had been the custom.

The Parishes under Ward

ANDREAS The Rector on Ward's arrival was Daniel Mylrea who died on 29th March 1832 after being long confined to the house and latterly to bed. He lived at Braust, and spent his last years in private. A hugh crowd from all over the Island attended his funeral at Andreas on 2nd April. He had a kind and gentle character, and had never raised the tithe. The sale of Mylrea's furniture and stock included 10 feather beds, an Ayrshire bull, 9 milking cows, 12 bullocks and calves, 4 working horses, 2 colts, a foal, 11 sheep, 3 lambs, 1 tup, 5 pigs, many geese, 3 ploughs, 3 harrows, 4 carts, plough harness, cart harness and a carriage and harness.

He was succeeded as Rector and Archdeacon by Benjamin Philpot who was inducted on 22nd May 1832 and resigned in August 1839 because of his wife's ill health. As Archdeacon he took open air services in many parts of the Island, riding miles on his horse,

Captain, and when he held these services at Andreas he had to fill the passages in the Rectory to put up those who came from far to hear him. Bishop Ward disapproved of these open air services, but allowed them. During Ward's absences in England to raise money for church building, and during his last 2 years of ill health, Philpot was in charge of the diocese. Andreas Rectory was too small for his family and servants, so he rented Braust. He became very popular in Andreas, and his congregation, small at first, grew, thanks to the return of many Methodists to the church. He found 33 public houses in Andreas but he managed to close down 31 of them, with the support of Mr Kneale, the Captain of the Parish, who refused to renew their licences. This gained Philpot many enemies, and he received threatening letters, but he ignored them and rode alone to evening meetings, and often to Douglas and other parts of the Island. He did much sea fishing, and practised herbal medicine for the benefit of his parishioners. He began monthly meetings of the clergy at Braust, feeding them and putting them up for the night, but support for these soon evaporated. He provided a room, a bed and washing facilities for homeless wanderers. Andreas Rectory was occupied by divinity students, and was called the Minor Prophet's House. Philpot farmed the glebe and had a flock of sheep, several cows and horses, and a large stock of pigs and poultry. His household used two sheep a week, the wool being made into blankets and the fat into candles. He and his neighbours killed a bullock in turn and shared the meat. There was some wrecking by lighting fires on the shore, and Philpot would often ride to the shore on a stormy night to put them out. Philpot learned enough Manx to read the service but not enough to preach.

In 1836 Mrs Philpot finally left the Island for health reasons. On Ward's death many hoped that Philpot would succeed him as Bishop, but he told Archbishop Howley, who sounded him out, that he would not accept the position even if offered. In 1838 he decided to resign, partly to rejoin his wife and partly for the sake of his children's education, but he agreed to stay another year at Bishop Bowstead's request. He preached his last sermon at Andreas on Sunday, 4th August 1839 on the text "I have a message from God for thee" (Judges 3²⁰) to a congregation of about 1,000.

His departure was deeply regretted and in 1840 his parishioners sent him a copy of Matthew Henry's Commentary on the Bible. The clergy to a man signed an address in which they spoke of his faithful and efficient discharge of his duties, his efforts to help everything tending to advance the material and spiritual welfare of the Manx people and the kindness with which he treated the clergy individually. He exchanged livings with the Revd J. C. Hall and became Rector of Cressingham, Norfolk. Shortly before he left, Philpot gave a party in the grounds of Peel Castle for 500 children from Peel, Patrick and St John's. It was a fine day and Vicar Carpenter of St Barnabas' preached to them on the feeding of the Five Thousand. He retired in 1874 to Putney and in 1878 moved to Surbiton, Surrey where he died on 28th May 1889 aged 98. His health failed in the last 6 months, but the beautiful old-world courtesy of his manners, and his faculties, remained until the end. In August 1879, when 89, he visited Douglas and preached in St George's on Sunday, 17th August. He returned in July 1881 and visited Archdeacon Moore. At 97 he baptised a grandson and in his nineties he often took services and occasionally preached. His end was hastened by the death of his eldest son.

Philpot had no taste or aptitude for music. All his life he opposed card playing. He greatly fancied himself as a preacher, usually basing his sermons on the Old Testament especially the prophets. He always had good relations with the Methodists. He was interested in Manx ways and customs, and recorded some of them. One of the clergy told him that he never allowed a candle in the house between Lady Day and Michaelmas as "we would be sitting up too late if we had lights". Philpot once found a household in bed asleep at 7 p.m. No-one would cross a bridge at 9 p.m. as it was believed that witches occupied bridges briefly at that hour. House fires were everywhere put out on 30th April and fresh ones laid on the 1st May when they were lit by rubbing two sticks together. Philpot did many works of charity of which only the recipient knew at the time. He combined industry, piety and the graces of social life. During the severe gale of 19th October 1838 he had an accident near Kirk Michael, when the horse he was driving upset the trap into a ditch, but neither he nor the horse was injured, and the trap was undamaged.

ARBORY Alexander Gelling's long incumbency covered the whole of Ward's episcopate.

BALLAUGH Hugh Stowell was Rector until his death on 14th October 1835. The most important event of his incumbency was the building of the new parish church. On 24th April 1830 the Bishop presided at a vestry meeting at which it was decided to build a new and larger church, but the proposal was only carried by 110 votes to 84, the Bishop and Rector voting for, but two of the four churchwardens (Thomas Cowley and Stephen Kneale) voting against. The reason for building a new church was that the old church was ruinous, that it was too small and that it was too far from the village. The necessary Act of Tynwald was passed on 20th September 1830, and on Monday, 10th May 1831 at 12 noon, the Bishop laid the foundation stone on a site of his own choice - a field known as Magher y Raad Vooar (field of the high road) which had been given free by Thomas Corlett of Ballaterson. A large crowd asssembled for the ceremony, and on seeing Ward's coach draw near to the bridge, the villagers took out the horses and pulled the coach themselves. The same thing happened when he left. The architect was John Welsh of Douglas, and Stowell rather sourly described it as "The best of his bad designs". It cost £1,714-6s-7d of which Ward's Fund contributed £1,134-6s-7d and £580 was paid by assessment on the parish. It was consecrated by Ward on Thursday 27th September 1832, and on that day Stowell noted in the register that the church had been consecrated "after much delay and many obstacles". It seats 700. The stipend at this time was £200.

Stowell's death, aged 67, was a great loss to the Manx Church and, indeed, to the Island as a whole. He combined great ability, untiring industry, and great humility, teaching his people by example as well as by preaching. He was a gentleman, a scholar and a Christian. In 1828 Ward wrote of him "Mr Stowell is truly a man of God, one of the few which remain of the genuine Wilson School. He will come up to the highest idea you have formed of the simplicity, gentleness, humility, meekness and sincerity of primitive Christians, possessing not much knowledge of this world, but rich in the knowledge and temper of the blessed world to come, an orthodox sound churchman of the old school. May God bless and reward

all those who will take him by the hand and forward pious objects. God *will* bless and reward them, the mouth of Christ has spoken it. He that receiveth a prophet in the name of a prophet shall receive a prophet's reward".

Stowell was succeeded in May 1836 by Thomas Howard who began an incumbency of 40 years. He and Stowell had been great friends, and on his deathbed Stowell asked Howard, if at all possible, to succeed him as Rector. Howard's early months were marred by the death of his wife on 24th July 1836, aged 42. In the Burial Register he wrote of her "She was a humble and devoted follower of our Lord and Saviour Jesus Christ. In life and in death Christ was her all in all. May I die the death of the righteous, and may my last end be like hers".

ST BARNABAS' In 1829 a group of Douglas people petitioned the Bishop for a new church and Ward obtained from the Crown some land for its site and a chaplain's house. This was to be held in trust perpetually by the Bishop on behalf of the parishioners of Braddan. The patronage was vested in the trustees (who had the right to appoint one of the two churchwardens, the other one being appointed by the Chaplain), by the Deed of Consecration dated 12th December 1832. The Trust Deed, dated 3rd April 1832, was prepared by Dr Stephen Lushington, one of the leading ecclesiastical lawyers in the kingdom. Ward attached great importance to the building of St Barnabas', as the population of Douglas was growing, and he contributed £216-13s-0d for it out of a grant of many thousand pounds given to him by a Mr Gordon of London, who became one of the three Trustees. The architect was John Welsh, and it was built in the Early English style with two tiers of galleries. It was expressly for the poor of Douglas, and all seats under the galleries were free. It held 1500 people, and the dedication to St Barnabas was Ward's wish.

The foundation stone was laid by Ward at 12 noon on 11th June 1832 (St Barnabas's Day) and he consecrated the church at noon on Wednesday, 12th December 1832, the sermon being preached by Archdeacon Philpot on Exodus 3[2,3], and the service being read by William Carpenter, the first Chaplain. The weather was not good, so fewer people came than was expected. After the congregation had left the

Bishop celebrated Holy Communion for the clergy.

William Carpenter was appointed by the trustees at a stipend of £200, and he soon filled the church. 500 seats were crowded with the poor of Douglas, but all classes, from the highest in the Island to the poorest fisherman, came in multitudes to hear him because, although a scholar, his sermons were so plain that all could understand them. They were irresistible in their appeal to heart and mind, so that his parishioners idolised him, and hung on every word. His preaching was described as homely, yet vigorous, with plenty of illustration. Once when money was needed for work on the church, he said one Sunday evening from the pulpit "I want £150, and I will be in the vestry tomorrow and expect you will bring it to me". He got it all.

Dr Carpenter's deeply spiritual nature, and his wholesome influence, were felt all over Douglas, especially in the churches, yet he never lost his somewhat diffident simplicity and unfailing kindness. His tireless energy remained to the end, and, always in earnest, he set a wonderful example as a man of God. He was a supporter (and often the originator) of every good work in and around Douglas. For example, the establishment of the House of Industry (now the Ellan Vannin Home), was largely due to him and he founded, and worked hard to raise the money for the Hospital Dispensary in Fort Street for the sick and poor and the Sailors' Home and St Barnabas' Schools. His people, high and low, looked on him as a true Father in God whose advice they regularly sought and always followed. He was a welcome visitor in their homes at any hour and whatever they were doing, and he visited Methodists as well as his own people. On 11th September 1833 the parish presented him with a gold watch inscribed "A small tribute of respect and esteem from a few of the congregation of St Barnabas' chapel to their truly beloved Pastor, Rev. Wm. Carpenter". He used to have a service on New Year's Day, and in the evening a meeting was held for prayer in the school room attended by anything up to 600 people some of whom had walked 5 miles or more. A Douglas resident spoke of him as "the man whose name will never be forgotten by any who knew him in this Island". He was always ready to help the poor with money, and used to say "All that a man has in the world is what he gives away". The ship which Ward bought as a floating chapel in Doug-

las harbour was in Carpenter's charge, and for many years it was well attended, but eventually had to be broken up.

BRADDAN In April 1836 Howard was succeeded as Vicar by Robert Brown. From 1832-36 he seems to have acted a priest in charge of Braddan for his great friend, Howard. He had hoped to be appointed Chaplain of St Barnabas' in 1832. Brown found that the services at Braddan were at 10.30 a.m. and 3 p.m. and by immemorial custom there was a Manx service every other Sunday, but by 1846 these had dwindled to one a month. He had to learn his Manx sermons by heart, and to avoid mistakes he preached them on Saturday evening to John Creer, the schoolmaster. He knew no Manx on his appointment, but learned it. After the failure of his eyesight he also had to memorise his English sermons. They are said to have been beautiful in their diction and expression, yet with a real warmth. He ignored Ash Wednesday and Lent, never observed Saints Days and never read the Athanasian Creed. In 1836 some parishioners gave him a cow for Christmas in return for his refusal to make a charge for opening graves. In his day the Vicarage was a simple Manx cottage, with the parlour on the left of the front door and the kitchen on the right. It stood to the west of the vicarage built by Vicar Drury. The stipend in Brown's time was £90 per annum, derived mainly from tithe, which was often paid in kind.

In August 1837 Mr Dale of Leece Lodge loaned an organ to the church, and on 28th August 1839, two sermons were preached to raise enough money to buy it. Twenty pounds 4 shillings was given.

On October 22nd 1833 Archdeacon Philpot made a visitation and told the churchwardens to extend the churchyard, but they did not do so. In January 1834 he wrote to them reminding them that it was their duty to provide a decent burial place for all who die in the parish, but nothing was done in Brown's time.

BRIDE Rector Cubbon was succeeded on 19th May 1830 by John Nelson. By 1837 he appears to have got into debt, and Bishop Ward ordered that the tithes due to him be put into the hands of trustees who were told to use them to pay Nelson's debts. His incumbency outlasted Ward's episcopate.

CASTLETOWN George Stickler Parsons succeeded Thimbleby in November 1827, and began an incumbency of 28 years. Parsons was a lovable man, and, like his wife, very good to the poor, to the extent that he used to scatter stones over his glebe field so that he could pay poor people to pick them off. He did not hesitate to reprove anyone who was behaving badly in church. In his will he remembered the aged and sick of Castletown, and also left money for widows of Manx clergy. On 11th January 1845 the Manx Sun reported that Parsons, with his usual liberality, gave a large quantity of beef, mutton, potatoes and coal to the poor of Castletown.

Parsons claimed that St Mary's was a Royal or Free Chapel, and therefore exempt from the Archdeacon's visitations. The various Bishops agreed that it was a Royal Chapel, but denied that it was exempt from visitations. But in 1860, after Parson's death the Court of Exchequer decided that the Chapel was the property of the Queen and therefore exempt from visitations by the Bishop or the Archdeacon.

Parsons made systematic pastoral visits all over the town, and ministered regularly to the prisoners in Castle Rushen, then used as a prison. He said in 1851 that the average morning congregation was 350, and 380 in the evening out of a population of 2,531. The chapel could seat 920 but only 600 in comfort.

On 28th November 1832 Governor Smelt, who had held the office since 1805, died, and was buried under the altar. He was a regular worshipper at St Mary's.

From August to October 1832 90 people died of cholera in Castletown, the last to die being Dr Richard Jones on 15th October. He had faithfully attended most of the cases, and his death was considered a great loss to the community. On 6th June 1833 Ward confirmed 537 people at Castletown, many, no doubt, coming from the other southern parishes.

ST GEORGE'S Within a month of John Christian's death Benjamin Philpot was nominated to succeed him (10th August 1827). He has been introduced already under Andreas. Bishop Murray offered him St George's, saying that the Manx clergy as a body lacked social and educational qualifications, and he wanted a gentleman and a scholar. Philpot came to the Island with 5 children and nurses and servants, and on arrival they were met in the open sea in Douglas bay by boats on a pouring wet night, and landed on the quay to find what quarters they could. He spent some days with the Murrays at Castle Mona but as St George's had no vicarage he had to find his own house. For eighteen months he lived in Douglas, but in the summer of 1829 he moved to a house at Oakhill.

As a nominee of the Bishop, and a stranger to the diocese, Philpot was at first unpopular. The parish was in chaos as Christian had neglected it, and had spent his last months in Ballasalla, but Philpot at once set out to work to revive it. He started Sunday Schools and lectures to young men, and gave open air sermons in outlying places which drew increasing numbers, and made him unpopular with the clergy. He regularly visited the poorest parts of the parish and knew no moral or physical fear. He appealed to people by his quiet, courteous manner, and his freedom from vanity or ambition for promotion, but he was not afraid to speak his mind. He opened a soup kitchen and worked hard to relieve destitution. Drink, which was duty free, was the curse of the whole town, and he, with Vicar Howard of Braddan, was among the earliest temperance workers in the Island though few of the clergy supported them. Philpot was not a total abstainer but he only drank moderately. He was a small eater and needed only 5 hours sleep. He greatly increased the congregations at St George's and as early as March 1828 a lady wrote to the Manx Sun saying what benefit had come to St George's through his ministry. In 1834 the congregation presented him with a silver salver in recognition of all he had done for the parish.

In December 1828 Ward decided that he could no longer keep the disreputable Roper as one of the Vicars General, because he was Irish and a layman (though a barrister) and replaced him by Philpot. In July 1825 Roper had been dismissed from the Manx Bar by the Governor, whom he had criticised in the press. Until Murray's time the office had for centuries been held by a Manx clergyman and the fact that Philpot was not Manx involved him in a storm of abuse and unpopularity. One of his first acts as Vicar General was to abolish the practice of doing penance in a white sheet in the chancel. In 1829 Philpot, with Clerk of the Rolls McCutchin, met to choose the site of King William's College. On 23rd April

1832 he said the prayers at the laying of the foundation stone of the Tower of Refuge by Sir William Hillary. Many were on the rock and many others, bare-headed, were in boats around. On 27th May 1832 he preached his last sermon in St George's, before going to Andreas, on Acts 20[32]. Murray had invited Philpot to accompany him to Rochester on his translation in 1828, so highly did he think of him.

GERMAN James Gelling remained Vicar throughout Ward's episcopate.

JURBY John Harrison remained Vicar throughout Ward's episcopate.

LEZAYRE Vicar Maddrell neglected the church building, and on 30th December 1829 a meeting of the chief landowners in the parish was held in church to consider building a new one. They decided to ask the Bishop to appoint a jury to inspect and report on the present church. Ward appointed two masons and two carpenters, who reported on 5th January 1830 that part of the south wall projected about 2½ inches into the church and that the north wall projected out by 2½ inches. As regards the roof, the beams in the wall were rotten and the rafters, laths and slates were decayed. The floor and some of the pews were in need of repair. Other reports on the church said that the wind blew through the chinks, the seats were worm-eaten and the roof and steeple were ready to fall in. The Archdeacon, after a visitation on 21st October 1833, reported that the roof, the walls and the altar were ruinous and the pulpit and reading desk were in bad order. The Manx Prayer Book was torn and in leaves.

A Vestry meeting on 26th March 1830 decided to build a new church and to levy a cess of £10 per quarterland. Another meeting on 6th December 1830, decided that the new church should be big enough to seat 724 people and should be high enough to contain galleries if they were needed in future. Soon after 1835 a gallery was needed, as there was not space for 75 quarterland pews and a few free ones, but no money was available so parts of the chancel were sold in which buyers could make private pews. These were removed early in the present century. The pews were not allotted until 1838.

The church cost £680, and the architect was John Welsh. Ward made a contribution from his Fund, and the Manx Government paid for the chancel. The new church was built against the wishes of many parishioners, who thought that the old church was large enough. It was alleged that only new arrivals in the parish favoured a new church. Those who opposed it may have been right, as the population of the rural parts of the Island was falling, and the building of St Stephen's, Sulby in 1839 and of St Olave's, Ramsey in 1862 took many people from the parish church.

The church was consecrated on 14th July 1835 by Bishop Ward, and the old church was demolished the same year. The site of the old church formed part of the churchyard.

LONAN The main event of Joseph Qualtrough's long incumbency was the building of the new parish church on the site of the church built in 1733 to replace the old church at Groudle. At a Vestry meeting held in church on 21st October 1829 it was stated that the church was too small, and ruinous beyond repair. Ward had offered £100 from his Fund, it was anticipated that the Crown would pay for the chancel and it was hoped to raise some money by the sale of materials from the present church. It was decided to ask Tynwald to impose cess on the quarterlands, intacks, mills, etc.

The size of the church was due to the fact that for each quarterland there had to be a six seater pew, in addition to pews for the intacks and for the poor, and in the end the church seated about 500 people. There was no gallery, but a small choir gallery was built in 1862. In April 1830 Tynwald passed the Act authorising the building of the new church. The Architect was John Taggart of Douglas, and the contract for building it, at a cost of £640 was given to James Moore who was a churchwarden.

Bishop Ward laid the foundation stone on Thursday 20th May 1830 at 2 p.m. He arrived an hour earlier so as to allow time for a service which was conducted by the Vicar. A large gathering of parishioners witnessed the ceremony and their reception of the Bishop showed how popular he was. Despite disputes with the builder, which at one time brought work to a halt, the Church was consecrated by Ward on 14th May 1835.

The Act of Tynwald authorising the building of the present church said that the old church at Groudle had to be demolished but this remained a dead letter, due, no doubt, to its being so remote and to the Manx people of the time being reluctant to commit what they would consider to be a sacrilege. After 1733, however, the old church was neglected, and was not restored until 1895.

In 1831 the population of Lonan was 1,823 and the stipend was £134-5s-0d.

ST LUKE'S Bishop Ward was deeply perturbed that there was no Anglican place of worship in the Baldwin valleys, then part of the parish of Braddan. He had obtained nearly £1,000 from the Government for building schoolrooms and it was his own idea to annex a chapel with sliding doors. On 17th November 1834 he visited Baldwin with his son and daughter to choose a site, and, with the help of the local people, the building was completed in less than 18 months. On Wednesday, 14th May 1836, the day of the consecration of the east end (the schoolroom part was not consecrated), Ward set off from Castle Mona, where he had stayed overnight, and at the foot of the hill he mounted a black pony, the people preceding and following him with flags and banners. He robed in Mr Frere's house then walked to the site in a blustering wind. The school part was used until the Education Act of 1870, the Chaplain superintending the teaching. It stands on the site of an ancient Keeil dedicated to St Abban which has long since disappeared. The cross on the west end was put there in 1896 and replaced a chimney. Philip Caine, known as Phillie the Desert, and mentioned in the song 'The Manx Wedding' is buried in the churchyard. He died in a house now under Baldwin reservoir, having spent his life in Baldwin where he was born.

For the first few years St Luke's seems to have been looked after by the Vicar or Curate of Braddan, but on 13th November 1840 Thomas Caine was appointed the first Chaplain. Caine was a faithful pastor who was beloved by all for his quaint and hearty, yet kindly, manner, and for his sympathy with the farmers. He founded the Manx teetotal movement and travelled all over the Island preaching total abstinence. He was a great house to house visitor, and was always to be found where there was illness or trouble. Every alternate Sunday he preached and conducted the service in Manx.

MALEW Following the unfrocking of William Christian, William Gill was appointed Vicar on 7th September 1830 and began a memorable ministry lasting until his death in 1871. On any count he was one of the outstanding Manx clergymen of the century. On 7th November 1820 he married, in Ballaugh Old Church, Anne, the eldest daughter of Rector Stowell. On the wedding morning the special licence had not yet arrived, so Gill rode from Ballaugh to Douglas to get it, only to find that the Vicar General had gone to Castletown. There he found him, got the licence, and set off back to Ballaugh, but darkness soon came on and heavy snow began to fall. In those days there were no lamps in the church as Evensong was in the afternoon, so the marriage had to be conducted by the light of torches, and the couple had to spend the night at the rectory. Anne Stowell's mother had died when she was 16, so she kept house for her father and brought up the younger children.

Gill found the glebe a bog, which he drained, and as there was no vicarage he raised £500 to build one (the largest subscription was £2) and also rebuilt the parish schoolhouse.

Gill was tall with a strong frame, and abundant white hair, and was reserved and quiet, but with a sense of humour. His judgement and fairness were recognised by all, and, unlike the other Manx clergy, he was a High Churchman. He was an ideal parish priest, as he had love for all, and was devoted to the welfare of his people. He was a great visitor, always on foot, especially to the poor. He could rarely be persuaded to preach in another parish, and so great was his attachment to his home and to the Island that he only left them when official duties called him away - e.g. his work over many years as Diocesan Inspector of Schools and his being on two occasions elected as Proctor for the clergy in York Convocation. He was also secretary of the Diocesan Association, founded by Bishop Bowstead.

Gill was an accomplished Manx Scholar. He edited the Manx-English part of Kelly's Manx Dictionary, helped the Revd J. T. Clarke to compile the English-Manx part, and revised the entire work for publication in 1866. In 1859 he edited Kelly's Manx Grammar which had been finished in 1804. He was the official translator into Manx of the laws proclaimed on 5th July from Tynwald Hill, a very laborious task because until 1865 these were read in full, not in the present summary form.

Gill was a man of iron self discipline, who avoided luxury or self indulgence in any form. He rose early, ate the simplest food, was a non-smoker and total abstainer and even as an old man he would only sit on a hard chair. He was hardly ever ill. After lunch on Saturdays he retired to his study where he remained in prayer and meditation until the first Sunday service. On a stipend of less than £200 he managed to give to the poor (for whom he kept almost open house), to enable his four sons to attend university, a fifth to qualify for the Bar and to educate his four daughters. The self denial which this involved must have been intense.

His hard work in the parish won universal respect. He was a great believer in education and gave particular attention to his day and Sunday Schools, besides doing much for education generally in the Island. This interest in education may have arisen from his lifelong love of children. He was a friend of John Keble, who stayed at Malew Vicarage several times. One of Gill's dreams (never realised) was to have one hymn book for the whole diocese.

He put a stained glass east window in Malew Church, and several people ceased to attend, considering this a step towards Rome.

On the Sunday after its installation a lady said to Gill, "I saw the devil behind you in the pulpit this morning". "Indeed, madam" he replied quietly and courteously "you must be better acquainted with him than I am, for I would not know him if I saw him".

Gill was unhappy about King William's College Chapel being built in his parish, and went so far as to ask Lord John Russell, then a member of the British Government, not to sanction it.

Almost as well known in the parish as the Vicar himself was John Clague, who was his manservant for 50 years, and who lived in a small cottage in one of the glebe fields near the Cross Four Ways.

Mrs Anne Gill was a woman of great strength of character, who was loved by everyone in the parish. She was hospitable and generous, yet managed her large family with equanimity. After her husband's death she went to live at Sandymount, Castletown, which had been built by an aunt of Gill and given to him. There she died, aged 89, on 11th July 1886, cared for by her two servants, Janet and Jane, who had been with her for 35 years. She was buried at Malew, the service being attended by the Bishop, the Archdeacon and most of the clergy.

ST MARK'S A new era for St Mark's opened with the appointment as Chaplain on 29th July 1827 of John Thomas Clarke, who remained there until 1864 and gave the chaplaincy the continuity which it had hitherto lacked. His was one of Murray's last appointments.

As a young man he set up two schools for adults in which he personally taught 150 pupils, but these ended when he moved to Castletown to study for Holy Orders.

The situation which he found at St Mark's was as discouraging as it could well be. The village was almost unapproachable (especially in winter) for want of good roads. A little money had been left in the Trust Fund, after building the chapel, and the trustees had tried to repair the roads but for many years little had been done to the fabric of the church or the parsonage, due to the rapid succession of young chaplains whose main aim was to get a parish of their own. The stipend was £30 per annum, partly from pew rents, and had remained unchanged since 1784. But Clarke was a man of strong will, who faced with undaunted perseverance the almost hopeless prospect, and worked tirelessly. At times, however he must have been depressed, for he wrote "never was a clergyman of the Church of England appointed to a more deplorably wretched situation in the church than that at St Mark's". Though opened for worship in 1772 the church was in some respects unfinished, and was uncomfortable for the congregation. The floor was clay instead of wood, and dust fell through the floorboards of the gallery onto those below. The inside remained undecorated, and most of the pews lacked doors and kneeling boards.

The parsonage had been built on the ruins of a cottage and on a very damp and unhealthy part of the glebe. It comprised three rooms on the ground floor, with a loft running the length of the house. The bare roof could be seen in the bedrooms, and about one third of the whole building was occupied by a cowhouse, above which was a hay loft, and the cowhouse smells penetrated to the living rooms. The walls were full of rat holes and from one of these in the foundation of the west gable water from a spring always flowed, while another spring from the ashpit ran past the kitchen fireplace. Both the gables bulged. It is small wonder that few of the previous chaplains had lived in the house, and had lodged where they could. The glebe was mountainous, covered with gorse and rocks, and had never been cultivated.

Clarke said that his first reaction was to resign his Orders and take a secular job to enable him to support his family, "But God ordained it otherwise and overruled the temptation to the benefit of St Mark's and I hope to the glory of His own great Name. In the midst of melancholy reflection, but under the influence of a prayerful frame of mind for wisdom to direct me, I became solemnly impressed with the conviction that deserting the Church of God would be a dereliction of duty which would haunt my mind with awful forbodings of futurity and plant my dying pillow with excruciating anguish. I started from my reveries and determined in the name of God to attempt the augmentation of my living, by soliciting subscriptions from a Christian public to erect a new parsonage and to cultivate my glebe lands. From the text 'Behold, how great a matter a little fire kindleth' I believed that great results frequently arose out of small beginnings. I reflected, situated as I was, even if I did fail in such a laudable design, that the world at large would sympathise with me. At all events, I believed that God, in the hollow of whose omnipotent hand man, and the purposes of man, are safely lodged, would go before me and make the crooked places straight, would break in pieces the gates of brass and cut in sunder the bars of iron. That He would say to St Mark's, as He did to the city of Judah 'Thou shalt be built and I will raise the decayed places thereof'. Under this impression I communicated my thoughts to my much lamented friend, Bishop Ward, and by his encouragement and under his auspices, I commenced. The sequel of this history of St Mark's constrains me to acknowledge the goodness and power of God, and to declare my firm belief that my success has been from the Lord that maketh all things".

Clarke held his first Vestry meeting on 7th April 1828 and persuaded those present to buy a new Manx Bible and a new Register, into which he copied all the baptisms and funerals contained in a little register which was tattered beyond repair. Other books in the church could be rebound.

Towards the end of 1828 Clarke obtained permission from Ward to demolish the old parsonage, barn and cowhouse and build a new one in a more suitable place: as much material from the old buildings as possible was to be used. The money came from subscriptions, including £20 from Ward, £2 from the Governor and £23-8s-6d from the clergy. On 18th December 1828 the two Vicars General, Nelson and Philpot, held a Consistory Court at Kirk Michael which ordered the Sumner of Malew to form a jury of two carpenters and two stonemasons to report on the old parsonage. They advised that it be demolished, as it was beyond repair and in every way unsuitable. Work began at once and was helped by the sympathy felt for Clarke and his family by the people of St Mark's. This found practical expression in the form of help with the work and the loan of horses. By mid-1830 there was a new parsonage and new outbuildings (stable, cowhouse, potato house and granary) and to supply water a well was sunk 39 feet deep. On 19th August Bishop Ward came to see the new buildings, and considered that the new parsonage compared favourably with any other in the diocese. In 1835 Clarke added a new kitchen and back kitchen with a view to starting a small boarding school. He also built a cottage on the glebe for a workman who would, he hoped, help him with farming the glebe. In 1831 Clarke made the first of several visits to England to raise the necessary funds for his work of re-building and raised £400.

In April 1830 Clarke made several exchanges of pews with a view to keeping all seven free seats together at the west end. Ward bought these for £100 and directed that it be invested to augment the Chaplain's stipend. He also gave £30 for the repair and maintenance of the church.

MAROWN Thomas Stephen's successor was William Duggan. He seems to have only been Curate in charge until 1840 and Stephen, who had become Vicar of Patrick, may have held both parishes until 1840. In the registers of Marown Duggan described himself as Curate (October 1827-June 1828) then as officiating Minister (June-December 1828) then as Minister of Marown (January 1829-February 1840) and thereafter as Vicar.

ST MATTHEW'S Robert Brown was succeeded on 14th June 1832 by John La Mothe Stowell. He was left fatherless when young, and was brought up by his relative, Rector Stowell of Ballaugh. As a youth he could recite the Sermon on the Mount in Greek, and wished to be ordained, but as there seemed to be no chance of this he studied for the Manx Bar with his uncle Thomas Stowell, Clerk of the Rolls. But he soon won an exhibition to Queen's College, Oxford, where he graduated in 1825. In the same year he was made Deacon by Bishop Legge of Oxford, and was later ordained priest by Bishop Barrington of Durham. After a Curacy at Egglingham in Northumberland, and a period as Chaplain in the household of Mr George Raikes, he came to St Matthew's, and soon afterwards began part time teaching at the newly founded King William's College. He was a good man, kind and genial. His first wife, Eliza, died on 11th May 1839, and on the 8th November 1842 he married at Gosport Miss Mary Pattison, who died on 13th April 1855. On 16th January 1854 a meeting was held to discuss the possible demolition of the church to enlarge the market place but it was agreed that if it was demolished another church should be built. In October 1835 Bishop Ward agreed to its removal provided the pew owners would give up their claim, and £500 be raised for building a new church.

MAUGHOLD Bowyer Harrison's long incumbency covered Ward's whole episcopate.

KIRK MICHAEL The old parish church was in bad repair and a Vestry meeting was held on 28th May 1833 at which Archdeacon Philpot presided as the Bishop was ill. The intack owners wished to be put on the same footing as those in other parishes as regards seatings and cess and they agreed to having a new church if this was granted. But there was some objection from the quarterland owners, and this led to the meeting being adjourned until a committee (which was then appointed) could report. This meeting was held on 19th July 1833 at which Bishop Ward presided. It was decided to build a new church on the Vicar's ancient glebe, and some land, called Corneil ny Killagh was bought for the Vicar to replace his glebe. Ward contributed half the cost from his Building Fund, and the other half was raised by assessments on the quarterlands. Tynwald agreed to the new church being built in the Michael Church Act of 5th April 1834.

The architect was Mr John Welsh of Birmingham. The church holds 650 people. Provision was made for a gallery if needed in future. The Bishop's pew, and the vicarage pew, each numbered 1 adjoin the chancel. The church was big enough to provide a pew for each quarterland, and a pew or pews, in the usual proportion, for the intack mills and cottages in the parish. Each pew was to be at least 8 feet long. There was a three decker pulpit which stood where the present lectern and pulpit are now. The wall around the churchyard was partly built with material from the old church. Originally there were 114 pews, 57 in the north transept and north aisle and 57 in the south transept and south aisle. Seats 2, 3, 4 and 5 on each side were for widows and orphans, but these were removed in 1853 to make room for the pulpit, reading desk, and clerk's desk when the position of the three decker pulpit was altered and other seats substituted. The church was consecrated on Thursday 11th June 1833, which happened to be the Thursday in Whit week, when the annual Convocation of the clergy is held, and after lunch at Bishopscourt, Ward and the clergy walked to Kirk Michael for the consecration.

ONCHAN The old church, even though it had a gallery, was too small, and as early as 1760 the walls and roof were considered likely to collapse, to the danger of the congregation. On 22nd December 1829 a meeting was held in church at which it was decided that, in view of the condition of the church, a new and bigger one should be built, capable of seating 500 people and high enough for side galleries to be erected if they should ever be needed in future. Mr John Banks of Ballanahow, the Captain of the Parish, agreed to give a piece of his land of the same size as the part of the Vicar's glebe field on which the new church was to be built. This was to compensate the vicar for the loss of part of his glebe.

The church cost £819-13s-6d. £156-2s-6d came in the form of donations, including £150 from Ward's Fund for building churches. Ward, the Vicar and Deemster Heywood each gave £10. Tynwald gave £250 and £240 came from an assessment laid on the parish at the rate of £5 per quarterland. Mills, cottages and intacks were assessed in proportion. Parishioners who subscribed were given pews, depending on how much they subscribed. Three pews were allotted to the poor in the west end gallery, and three others were set aside in the nave for visitors. Any surplus pews were to be rented and the money was to go to the parish Sunday School for the benefit of the children. Tynwald approved the building of a new church, dedicated to St Peter, on the 5th May 1830. and on the 8th July 1830, at 12 noon, Bishop Ward laid the foundation stone and gave £1 to treat the Sunday School children. This site was not unanimously accepted, however, and finally it was decided to build on the present site, so the Bishop had to return on 30th August and lay the foundation stone again. The church was completed in about 3 years, the architect being Mr John Welsh, and was dedicated on 4th September 1833 in a service lasting 3 hours. The sermon was given by Vicar Craine, and afterwards Mr Banks provided a cold meal for the Bishop and clergy. On 21st March 1839 Tynwald passed an Act for building a new vicarage on the Vicar's glebe. This was built in 1842 and cost £546-18s-9d of which £482-6s-6d was subscribed, mostly at £1 per person. Nearly all the clergy subscribed. The former vicarage was sold for £100 but even so there was a deficit even though Ward gave £10 and Bishop Short later gave £10.

PATRICK After the unfrocking of Vicar Cottier, Thomas Stephen, Vicar of Marown, was appointed Vicar on 9th July 1827, one of Bishop Murray's last appointments. It seems to have been a period of decline in Patrick, which then included Foxdale as well as Dalby. Out of 2,000 in the parish there were 700 communicants in 1825 but by 1833 this had fallen to 200. In 1833 Stephen lamented that the children were rarely taken to church "their parents having no care about them or authority over them". This was in reply to Archdeacon Philpot, who made a visitation in October 1833.

Further points from Stephen's reply were that the wardens seldom attended church, nor did the Sumner - "He may as well belong to a Turkish Mosque for any attention he pays to the church". Asked by the Archdeacon whether he had made any improvements in the glebe he said, "Yes, for which I expect neither reward nor thanks". In reply to a question as to whether he excluded from Holy Communion all drunkards, swearers, Sabbath-breakers and immoral

people, he said that there was no need to do so, as they seldom or never came to church unless to a burial or, occasionally, as a godparent. The services were at 8 a.m., 10 a.m., and 2 p.m. on Sundays when they were in Manx, and at 9 a.m., 11 a.m. and 3 p.m. when they were in English, but Stephen only preached once a Sunday "for want of a congregation". He told Philpot that he had at first given two sermons a Sunday and a weeknight lecture, but both were deserted due to the popularity of the Methodists and that chapels of ease were needed at Foxdale and Dalby. We further learn from this visitation that the baptism fee was 6d, marriage 2/6, burial 1/-. The stipend was £143-8s-7d. This rather sad picture shows how the tithe troubles in Bishop Murray's time had reduced support for the church.

Stephen was a classical scholar and a poet, and in 1842 wrote one of the earliest guides to the Isle of Man. He is described as being very caustic.

ST PAUL'S The ministry of Archibald Holmes covered the whole of Ward's episcopate. Holmes was both loved and respected in Ramsey. The west gallery, mainly for the musicians, was built in 1830. In the Irish famine of 1830-31 Holmes and the Methodist Minister made a house to house collection which raised £13.

RUSHEN William Corrin was Vicar during Ward's years. In August 1829 Ward visited Kentraugh, home of the Gawne family, and on the Sunday preached in the parish church to a large congregation. The population of Rushen in 1831 was 2,732 and by 1841 it had risen to 3,044. The stipend in 1831 was £91-0s-7d.

On the 3rd January 1828 Thomas Kinnish aged 58, married Margaret Gale, aged 21. The procession to and from the church was followed by a forsaken sweetheart of the bride, gaily decorated with green laurels, causing great amusement to the large crowd of spectators.

Up to and including Corrin's incumbency a large three decker pulpit stood halfway down the south side of the church facing the Gawne family pew on the north side. The congregation sat in high-backed box pews. This arrangement lasted until the re-ordering of the church in 1868-9. In Corrin's time the church was unheated even in winter, though rushes were strewed on the roughly flagged floor to prevent worshippers having to stand on the cold flagstones.

A Vestry meeting on the 26th October 1831 decided to extend the churchyard by buying part of Balnahowe meadow on the north side. This extension was consecrated by Ward on 7th June 1833. The 1832 Vestry meeting decided that the expenses incurred by the cholera epidemic should be assessed on the parish.

The 1715 vicarage, built with money raised by Bishop Wilson was replaced in 1839. The foundation stone was laid on 18th March, and it was completed later in the year.

SANTAN Thomas Kewley, Curate of Patrick, was appointed Vicar on 12th April 1827. Kewley is described as being mercenary, and interested in his fees, but he won the esteem and affection of his parishioners, who showed it by erecting his tombstone in the churchyard when he died on 12th April 1835, aged 39. On it is inscribed "Remember them that have the rule over you". (Hebrews 13[7]).

The population of Santan in 1831 was 798, and the stipend was £90 per annum.

Kewley was succeeded by Samuel Gelling, who was appointed on 24th June 1835, and was Vicar until his death on 4th November 1865, aged 66. He was described as hospitable, simple and kindly and was a competent Hebrew scholar. In August 1841 he became involved in a dispute with the churchwardens who kept the Communion wine locked up. The matter was settled when new wardens were elected, but there seems to have been temporary bad feeling as Archdeacon Hall, on his 1841 visitation, regretted that the churchwardens did not attend. In 1842 it was proposed at the vestry meeting that in future there should be two services in English for every one in Manx, but it was decided to keep to having alternative services as hitherto.

Chapter 7

BISHOPS BOWSTEAD 1838-40   PEPYS 1840-41
and SHORT 1841-46

Ward was succeeded as Bishop by James Bowstead. He was born in Cumberland on 1st May 1801 and graduated from Corpus Christi College, Cambridge, in 1824. He became BD in 1834 and DD on becoming Bishop. He was made deacon in 1826 by Bishop Sparke of Ely and in 1827 received priest's orders from Bishop Percy of Carlisle. From 1824-38 he was a Fellow of his college, and a tutor from 1832-38. He also held several appointments in the Church - Curate of Grantchester in 1829, Examining Chaplain to Bishop Allen of Bristol in 1834, and Rector of Rettendon, Essex in 1837. He was strongly Liberal in politics, and in 1834 he signed a petition for the abolition of religious tests for admission to the University. He was very protestant, and anti-tractarian. He was a bachelor, due to a disappointment early in life. While on a reading holiday in Scotland he fell in love with the daughter of a minister, but decided not to propose until he should come back in the next year, but when he returned he found that she had just married. He was a man of extensive learning, of deep humility and honesty of purpose.

In 1838 the clergy petitioned Tynwald to be excused from collecting their tithe, as it caused friction with their parishioners. Finally they were allowed £50 each for collecting it. The British Government put off the appointment of a new Bishop until the tithes were commuted, so Tynwald passed a Bill in 1839 commuting the tithes of the Island for £5,050. This Tithe Commutation Act took effect at Easter 1841, and was based on the amount of tithe payable by the landowner in the previous seven years, and on the average price of cereals sold to the miller. This had the support of the clergy, who had met at St John's on the 29th March 1837 and had agreed unanimously to commute the tithe on the basis of the average of the last seven years, to vary according to the price of corn. In 1838 the Archdeacon and some of the clergy said that it was Bishop Ward's intention to augment some of the poorer livings from the Bishop's tithe, and they obtained the approval of the Archbishop of York (as guardian of the spiritualities of the see dur-

ing the vacancy) and of Tynwald. Bowstead on his arrival at once agreed to give up part of his tithe for this purpose. This enabled clergy stipends to be raised from £90 to £141 per annum. The Bishop's stipend was now £1,515, the Rectors of Ballaugh and Bride £303 each, the Rector of Andreas £707, and the Chaplain of St Jude's, when built, £101. Tynwald was clearly more or less obliged to pass the Tithe Commutation Act in order to obtain a Bishop and to ensure that the diocese remained independent.

Bowstead was consecrated at Lambeth Palace on 23rd July 1838 by Archbishop Howley of Canterbury, assisted by the Bishops of Ely, Hereford and Lincoln, and on 6th August he paid homage to the Queen. On 22nd August he crossed to the Isle of Man on the 'Queen of the Isle' and was received with hearty cheers on landing. On the following Sunday morning he preached at St George's on behalf of the day and Sunday Schools on Proverbs 22[6]. He stayed for a few days at Castle Mona, then set off for Bishopscourt on the 27th. At Ballacraine he was met by a group of gentlemen on horseback, who escorted him to Kirk Michael, where, at the Courthouse, a large crowd had assembled, headed by Vicar Brown and Vicar Harrison of Jurby. The Bishop was so pleased with his reception that he asked Mr Gee, of the Mitre Hotel, to give the parishioners 2 barrels of his best ale, from which many toasts were drunk. Had it not been Ballaugh Fair Day many more people would have been at Michael. As the Bishop was about to leave, the people unharnessed the horses and drew the carriage to Bishopscourt. On 5th September he was enthroned in St Mary's, Castletown, by Archdeacon Philpot and the Revd G. Parsons, the Chaplain. The clergy and other officials having assembled at the Court House, walked in procession to St Mary's and at the door the mandate was read by the Revd J. Brown (Episcopal Registrar) after which the Bishop was conducted into the Chapel by Brown and the Archdeacon's Official, (Rector Nelson of Bride) and led to his throne. Parsons then read Mattins, after which Bowstead celebrated Holy

Communion. The procession then returned to the courthouse, where the oaths were administered by the Clerk of the Rolls, and addresses of welcome were read by the High Bailiff of Castletown, on behalf of the townspeople, and by Rector Howard of Ballaugh on behalf of the clergy, to both of which Bowstead replied. He then invited 20 prominent people to dine with him and made a very good impression by his kind and genial manner and by his conversation. Next day a deputation from King William's College consisting of the Principal, (the Revd A. Philips), the Vice-Principal (the Revd R. Dixon) and the third master (the Revd J. E. Stowell) went to Bishopscourt to present a congratulatory address, and were invited to dinner. On 9th September he preached in St Paul's, Ramsey on Ecclesiastes 11[6]. On 24th September 200 sheep belonging to him were landed at Douglas, and from 25th September until 20th October he was in England. His return late on Saturday 20th October was adventurous as the weather was so bad that the ship could only land him and his two servants on the beach at Bride. Not knowing the road, they made their way along the beach in the direction of Ramsey on a dark and stormy night, but they were none the worse for it.

Bowstead's first ordination was on 24th March 1839 in Bishopscourt Chapel, when, among others, William Kermode was made Deacon and John Qualtrough was ordained Priest. The candidates had been examined on the two previous days. The Archdeacon preached and the sermon was so good that the Bishop had it printed.

Bowstead worked hard to raise the standard of education in the parish schools, but his greatest achievement was the formation of the Diocesan Association, said to have been suggested to him by Deemster Christian, or, in another version, by William Carpenter. It was established at a public meeting in Castletown on 16th July 1839 and the first two secretaries were Rector Howard of Ballaugh and Vicar Carpenter of St Barnabas'. Its object was to provide chapels of ease, chaplains and chaplains' houses in outlying districts with the necessary endowments, and to further it Bowstead held meetings in the chief towns. It led in the first few years to the building of chapels at Dalby, Cronk y Voddy, Port St Mary, Sulby, and the Dhoon and of parsonages at Dalby, St John's, St Jude's and Cronk y Voddy. For example,

grants made in 1852 were Sulby £60, Foxdale £60, Baldwin £30, Port St Mary £30, Cronk y Voddy £20 and Laxey £15. In 1853 when subscriptions were tending to fall off, the grants were Sulby £60, Foxdale School house (where services were held for the miners) £60, Baldwin £30, Cronk y Voddy £25, Laxey £15 and the Dhoon £30.

Archdeacon Philpot described Bowstead as "a very suitable man, truly an enlightened Christian, of a clear perception and vigorous mind". They worked very well together and found each other congenial company. Once, while riding together near the Point of Ayre, Bowstead was thrown from his horse and fell heavily, sustaining slight concussion. Philpot attributed the Bishop's early death to this accident. When Bowstead left, Philpot bought all his carriages and horses and the contents of his wine cellar.

The only place of worship to be consecrated by Bowstead was the chapel at Dalby, dedicated to St James. Work on it had begun under Bishop Ward, and it was consecrated on 7th April 1839, the Bishop preaching on Psalm 118[24]. In September 1840 after he had left the Island Bowstead presented the chapel with a set of Communion Vessels.

On 5th November 1839 Bowstead gave a treat to the workmen on Bishopscourt farms and estate, when about 40 men and their families had a meal of roast beef and plum pudding with plenty of ale.

In late December 1839 it became known that Bowstead had been translated to Lichfield. On 2nd January 1840 a deputation of three Methodist Ministers and three Circuit Stewards presented him with an Address expressing their regret that he was leaving, especially in view of all that he had done to encourage education and to further morality and religion among the Manx people and thanking him for his kindly attitude to the Methodists. The Anglican clergy also gave him an Address, expressing appreciation of his pleasant manner, firm character, zeal, discretion and Christian love and tolerance. In reply Bowstead spoke of the tranquility, happiness and freedom from party strife in the diocese.

He left the Island on 7th January 1840 on the 'Queen of the Isle', and was seen on board by all the clergy and many leading lay people. In his short episcopate he had endeared himself to all by his humility, mildness, consistent character, hospitality, pleasant manner, intellectual ability, strong principles, honesty of purpose and sincere piety, and his departure was regretted by everyone.

Bowstead was an enthusiastic horseman, and intended to ride from Liverpool to Lichfield, but his horse was suffering from the effects of the sea voyage, and soon after setting off he fell and rolled onto his rider who had been thrown to the ground. There was no apparent bad effect and his first few months at Lichfield were full of activity, but by April it was clear that his spine had been injured, and a long and painful illness ensued, culminating in his death at Clifton, near Bristol, on 11th October, 1843. He is buried at Eccleshall. For three years he had been unable to carry out his duties.

Bowstead's successor was Henry Pepys, brother of the Earl of Cottenham, who, in 1841, was Lord Chancellor in Lord Melbourne's government. Born in 1783, he entered Trinity College, Cambridge and after graduating he became a Fellow of St John's. From 1818-27 he was Rector of Aspeden, Hertfordshire, holding this in plurality with Moreton, Essex, from 1822-40. In 1827 he became Rector of Westmill, Hertfordshire and was also Prebendary of Wells. He was appointed to Sodor and Man in January 1840, and was consecrated in Whitehall Chapel by Archbishop Vernon Harcourt of York on 1st March, In 1824 he married Miss Maria Sullivan, who lived until 1885, and by whom he had two sons and two daughters. He did not arrive in the Island until April, but in February he sent £550 to help the stipends of the Manx clergy and wrote to Archdeacon Hall to say that any tithe he received above £1,500 would go to the clergy. He added that he might not be able to maintain the same hospitality or to give as much to charity, as his predecessors.

He arrived at Douglas on the 'Mona's Isle' on Monday, 27th April. The High Bailiff unfurled his flag on Harold Tower, as did Sir William Hillary on Fort Anne. He was greeted on board by the Archdeacon, some of the clergy and Mr George Dumbell, the banker, who took him in his carriage to Castle Mona. Two days later he and his family set out for Bishopscourt, and at Kirk Michael he was welcomed by the Northern Deemster, the Vicars of Kirk Michael and Jurby, the Rector of Ballaugh and some other notables. Also there were the Headmaster of the school and his pupils and the Sunday School children with their teachers, headed by the band of the Friendly

Society. Almost the whole village turned out and they drew the Bishop's carriage to Bishopscourt, after taking out the horses, to enthusiastic cheering from those lining the road. The cordiality with which Pepys acknowledged this was widely noticed, and on reaching Bishopscourt he spoke courteously to those who had followed him. He was enthroned at Castletown on Friday 1st May at 12 noon and a departure from tradition was that the mandate of consecration, and the induction into the temporalities was read and carried out outside the door of the church. Inside, the Archdeacon read the Litany and led the Bishop to his throne, where he said "By virtue of this mandate I install thee on the throne or customary seat assigned to the Bishop of Sodor and Man, in the name of the Father, the Son and the Holy Ghost. The Lord preserve thee in thy going out and coming in, now and always; mayest thou advance in truth and holiness and use the office now delegated to thee by God for the glory of His name, the salvation of souls and the honour and advantage of the Church and when at length thy functions shall cease, may God of His infinite mercy give thee the life and crown eternal, through Jesus Christ our Lord". At the end of the service the Bishop gave his blessing, then went to the Courthouse for the taking of the oaths. An address was presented by the people of Castletown, to which Pepys gave a short reply and he then entertained the clergy to lunch. Archdeacon Hall made a speech of welcome, to which the Bishop replied, saying that he hoped that they would consider him as a brother rather than a father, and that they would not hesitate to seek his advice when needed. He added that it would not be easy to follow Bowstead, who had been so loved and respected.

Pepys aimed at preaching in one of the parish churches each Sunday, but his time here was too short for him to make any real impression on the diocese, as he was translated to Worcester and left the Island on 4th May 1841. He had, however revived S.P.C.K. in the diocese, and had given much in charity to the poor, the clergy, the schools and the church. Before leaving he received an Address from the clergy in which they referred to him as "not being a lord over God's heritage but an example to his flock". "While firmly holding your own opinions you have set us the example of neither acting unkindly towards those who differ from us, nor opposing their opinions with violence of language or bitterness of feeling. You have taught us to be pitiful, courteous, tenderhearted and compassionate".

Pepys was a man of polished manners in whom the bishop and the gentleman were beautifully blended. He was never known to commit a mean or harsh action, and his cheerful benevolence at once put people at ease and gained their confidence. He won the affection of his people and the esteem of all the clergy by his kindness and his invariable Christian courtesy. He remained Bishop of Worcester until his death on 13th November 1860.

He was succeeded by Thomas Vowler Short, son of Archdeacon Short of Cornwall, and was born in Dawlish, Devon, on 16th September 1790. After education at Westminster School he entered Christ Church Oxford in 1809, where he took a first class degree in Classics and Mathematics. He was ordained in 1813 by Bishop Jackson of Oxford and was a tutor of his college. He became Vicar of Cowley (1816-23), Vicar of Stockleigh Pomeroy, Devon (1823-26) and Vicar of Kingsworthy, Hampshire (1826-34). All this time he remained tutor of Christ Church and did his best to improve the system of examinations in the university which, before the University Comission of 1852, left much to be desired, and was in some respects farcical. In 1829 he left the college and went to live in his parish of Kingsworthy. In 1834 he became Rector of St George's Bloomsbury, where he showed himself to be a conscientious parish priest. In 1837 he was made deputy Clerk of the Closet to Queen Victoria.

In May 1841 Short visited the Island and made a good impression by his learning and courtesy. The 'Manx Sun' commented (bearing in mind the short episcopates of Bowstead and Pepys) "We only hope he will not vanish before we have time to become acquainted with him". He was consecrated by Archbishop Vernon Harcourt of York, assisted by the Bishops of London and Ripon, on Sunday, 6th June in the Chapel Royal, Whitehall. The Prime Minister, Sir Robert Peel, attended, and the sermon was preached by Short's brother. He arrived in the Island on 15th July on the 'Mona's Isle' commanded by Captain Quayle, and was received by several clergy and notables, then went straight to Bishopscourt. On 10th July he had been presented by his parishioners with a piece of plate, valued at 200 guineas, and with

an inscription ending "From his parishioners, grateful for his ministrations among them, and regretting his departure, but rejoicing in his advancement, and sincerely respecting the zeal and tenderness, the single-heartedness and charity of his character".

He was enthroned in St Mary's, Castletown on Monday, 26th July and in his sermon he asked clergy and laity to help him restore the diocese to that state of wholesome ecclesiastical discipline in which Bishop Wilson had left it. At 3 p.m. he entertained the clergy to lunch in the George Hotel and the 'Manx Sun' commented on his benevolence and the unflinching attachment he declared to the Church of England, and said that it all promised well.

Short's interest in education soon became apparent. In September 1841 he gave 45 volumes to King William's College library, and on 22nd September he held a meeting at Bishopscourt of parochial and other schoolmasters, the object being to ascertain the various methods of teaching, especially in the parochial schools and to afford an opportunity of suggesting to the teachers several plans, which, Short thought, would improve education. He advised them to form, without delay, a scholastic society for mutual instruction and information and steps were taken to set up a schoolmasters' library (which Short also suggested) by setting up a committee and starting a subscription list. Short promised to look into the claims of the parish schoolmasters to part of Bishop Barrow's Fund. This first meeting was attended by about 70 teachers, who were received with the Bishop's usual courtesy and hospitality, as he invited them to lunch and the whole thing was voted so successful that the meeting at Bishopscourt became an annual event.

In March 1842 Short sent a circular letter to the clergy urging proper preparation for confirmation. In reporting this, the 'Manx Sun' regretted the fact that the old system of catechising children in church had almost died out though Archdeacon Hall was trying to revive it in Andreas. Short offered to confirm at more frequent intervals rather than have children not properly prepared.

In September 1842 a memorial was sent to the Governor (Colonel John Ready) and the Bishop asking that men appointed to Crown livings should be able to conduct services and preach in Manx, as many people in the diocese did not understand English. It was signed by Thomas Howard (Ballaugh), John Nelson (Bride), Joseph Qualtrough (Lonan), William Duggan (Marown), John Cannell (St Matthew's), Edward Craine (Onchan), Bowyer Harrison (Maughold) and John Stowell (German).

In 1846 Short commented "that the churchwardens, generally speaking, do not keep their accounts very regularly" and on 17th October 1846 the 'Manx Sun' reported that Short had been translated to St Asaph and that same evening he crossed to the mainland. His final departure was on 12th December, when he received an Address from the Archdeacon and clergy expressing their regret at losing him and their affectionate personal respect for him. It referred to his untiring zeal, patient industry, generous liberality and faithful integrity. It spoke of his work for King William's College after the fire of 1844, and the improved schools and parsonages and chaplains' houses which had been built in his time, enabling the vicar to live among his people. Short, who had considerable private means, undoubtedly contributed to these achievements without seeking publicity. He also received an Address from the people of Peel.

Short was very active and conscientious in carrying out his duties, and throughout his episcopate he set himself to further the spiritual welfare of his diocese and to improve the parochial schools. For this latter purpose he aimed at engaging qualified teachers. He was honest and kindly, but impetuous and sometimes indiscreet in speech. An example of this was on one occasion at Convocation he described the Methodists as those who "lead the people from their parish churches". He disliked the Methodists and this ended the good relations which had been created by Bowstead and Pepys, and to some extent by Ward.

He liked the Manx people and observed that there was no better material than Manxmen, and that with a hundred Manxmen he would not be afraid to go to the end of the world.

He enforced Church discipline as far as possible, but he failed to revive presentments by churchwardens, as public opinion, supported by the local press, was against it. He approved of the Diocesan Association, and gave it generous financial support.

For some years prior to 1846 Short had administered the diocese of St Asaph, as the Bishop, William Carey, was in feeble health and unable to perform his duties so it was no surprise when, on Carey's death in 1846, Short was chosen to succeed him. He remained at St Asaph until 1870 where he was loved and respected, even by the Methodists, and where he regularly spent half his stipend on the needs of the diocese. But his health was poor from about 1866, so he resigned and went to live with his brother-in-law, Archdeacon Wickham, Vicar of Gresford. He died on 13th April 1872, aged 81. In 1833 he married the widow of the Revd J. C. Conybeare, but she died at the Palace at St Asaph, aged 57, on 16th August, 1848. During his years at St Asaph he regularly put flowers on her grave.

The Parishes under Bowstead, Pepys and Short

ANDREAS Philpot was succeeded as Rector and Archdeacon by John Cecil Hall. He was a man of the highest character, who was a great help to the younger clergy both in the wise advice he gave them and in his readiness to support them in times of difficulty or distress. In March 1840 Rector Howard of Ballaugh and Vicar Harrison of Jurby expressed to him the warm appreciation and thanks of the clergy for all that he was doing for them.

Archdeacon Hall died on 8th February 1844, aged 40, as a result of typhus fever, contracted while visiting a sick parishioner.

He was respected and loved by everyone. He was buried at Andreas, and his wife was later buried with him. "In thy presence is fulness of joy" is inscribed on the headstone.

He was succeeded in April by Joseph Christian Moore, who was Rector and Archdeacon for 42 years, and to whom the Manx Church probably owes more than to any other individual. Moore felt deeply the responsibility of taking a parish with so little experience. His enthusiasm and hard work in founding schools, and restoring his church made him widely known and he was soon appointed Rural Dean of South Derbyshire. Queen Adelaide, widow of William IV, often came to stay with Lord Howe, at Gopsal, near Measham, and she was so impressed by his management of his schools that she, with the support of Queen Victoria, asked the Home Secretary, Sir George Grey, to appoint him Archdeacon (a Crown appointment in Sodor and Man). Moore only accepted after anxious consideration, as his severance from Measham was a great grief to him. On leaving the parish the people gave him a silver salver and a silver breakfast service. He set off for the Isle of Man on Easter Monday 1844, having adopted the text "My presence shall go with thee and I will give thee rest". On his arrival Bishop Short said "Well you have come. You are not at all the man I wanted but we must make the best of it". They soon learned to value and esteem each other and became firm friends.

All his life Moore had a deep reverence for Bishop Wilson. As a parish priest he was very much of the old school, and was rather quaint in his ways and manner, one example of this being his habit, both in church and at family prayers. of making comments on the lessons, often very pointed, while reading them. He never married. He was very opposed to the eastward position at Holy Communion, as his views were very evangelical. He used to say "Defend the outworks of the citadel of faith".

Moore was a true gentleman, hence attractive and popular with all classes. He made Andreas Rectory famous for its quiet and enjoyable hospitality. He had a quaintness of speech which many found very appealing. His sound commonsense and wisdom came out in the pulpit, on the platform, in private talk, and in the Legislative Council. All recognised his deep personal piety and severe self-discipline. He was a firm believer in the destiny of the church, a strong upholder of the ordained ministry and a lover of the prayer book.

Archdeacon Moore had substantial private means, and spent much of it on the church and the rectory. He found the rectory rather dilapidated on his arrival, but he repaired it at his own cost, and made the 30 acres of glebe pay, even though he employed four men at it, in addition to three women in the house. He had the church painted and re-roofed. He had a great aptitude for business, and both as Rector and Archdeacon, he proved to be a good administrator. He was a good chairman, and usually came off best at Vestry meetings, which were sometimes difficult, then in the evening he always invited the old and new churchwardens to dinner at the rectory. In a quiet way he gave financial help to young Manxmen who

were training for the ministry. He set about repairing relations between Anglicans and Methodists which had suffered under Bishop Short. His voice in church was clear and although he was not particularly eloquent as a preacher, he had firm moral principles, feared no-one and had no hesitation in rebuking from the pulpit those involved in any trouble in the parish during the week. He was a non-smoker, and although not teetotal, he was alive to the misery caused by drunkenness, and would reprove in no uncertain terms anyone who got drunk. On Andreas Fair Day (December 11th) he used to give 10 shillings to the local publican to close his doors at 4 p.m. He was a diligent visitor, especially to those who were ill or in trouble, and throughout his life he helped the poor. He always gave more than his stipend in charity. He chose a grave plot for himself near the church door and in later life often stood there in deep thought.

His sermons were thoughtful and original, without ornament and with racy Manx humour, but wise and forceful. He would go over and over again the same words if he felt them to be interesting and applicable to his hearers. He often quoted passages from the old English divines, whom he greatly admired. His slow sing-song voice was well known. He was very frank in his views about things "new and therefore not true" and he was wholly uninfluenced by the Tractarian Movement. His churchmanship was middle of the road, but he was strict on points which he considered important and which he invariably observed, e.g. his strict observance of Sunday. He was above party and always maintained good relations with the Methodists, but he could be unsparing when talking about faithless churchmen. To him the Establishment of the Church was vitally important, and he used to say that he could imagine no other state of affairs for the church. He was a devoted parish priest, and his kind, simple, genial character quickly won the affection and respect of his parishioners, with whom he remained popular all his life. His sound commonsense and wise judgement were widely recognised by the clergy, by Tynwald, (of which the Archdeacon was then a member) and by the trustees of King William's College and gave him great influence throughout the Island. He was a thorough Manxman and it was his joy to serve the Island in both church and state, but he was shrewd and his years in England had enabled him to know the world. He had a great love of order and had a strong faith in prayer. His views were liberal and he lost no opportunity of improving the material and moral condition of the people, his main interests being to develop farming, trade and education. In his early and middle years he would ride about the diocese, paying surprise visits to the schools, examining the children and making suggestions as to how the teaching could be improved. By these means he made his presence felt all over the Island. Apart from his restoration of Andreas church he took an active part in church building and the churches of St John's, Cronk y Voddy, St Thomas' and Laxey owed much to his hard work.

In his home life Moore preserved the old ways. Visitors to the Rectory were impressed by its order and simplicity and his decent regard for the past. Between him and his household there was goodwill and affectionate devotion and an atmosphere of peace. He said family prayers with them morning and evening.

Moore considered that his two years of service under Bishop Short was one of the most valuable experiences of his life.

He was the trusted adviser of Bishops Eden and Hill, and to some extent of Bishop Powys, and his goodness and integrity made him the sheet anchor of the diocese during the troubles of Powys' episcopate and in the last few years of Powys' life when he was ill and mostly non-resident. In 1880 there were signs that Moore's health was failing and between then and his death in 1886 he had to resign one duty after the other.

On the 23rd April 1845 Archdeacon Moore was presented to the Queen at a levée by the Home Secretary, Sir James Graham. On the evening of 25th June 1845 he entertained the choir and several parishioners to tea on the rectory lawn, and after the meal the choir performed various pieces of music. Every summer he treated the choir to a day out. The Chapel of King William's College was re-opened after the fire on 29th May 1845, on which occasion Archdeacon Moore preached and then gave the prizes.

ARBORY The long incumbency of Alexander Gelling covered these three episcopates.

BALLAUGH Thomas Howard remained Rec-

tor under Bowstead, Pepys and Short.

ST BARNABAS' In May 1842 the ladies of the church presented Carpenter with a tea service worth 60 guineas. A new organ was bought in 1842. In 1844 several leading people wanted Carpenter to succeed Hall as Archdeacon.

BRADDAN Archdeacon Hall, in a visitation in September 1841, stressed the necessity of having a cemetery near Douglas, as the existing churchyard was quite inadequate. The churchyard around the old church, which is much older than the church, was the only burial place for the whole of Douglas, apart from St George's. Hall also forbade the Sumner from calling Coroners' sales, etc. in the churchyard on Sunday mornings.

In July 1840 Vicar Brown called a Vestry meeting to consider a letter from the Governor saying that two lunatics (natives of Braddan) were confined in Castle Rushen and had no means of support. He understood that all parishes were compelled by law to support their own poor, and hoped that the Vestry would consider the matter. The meeting decided that all the poor of the parish were entitled to a share of the poor's money, but they were not aware of any law compelling the parish to maintain its poor. A reply was sent to the Governor that they would try to have the two people concerned removed to England.

In December 1841 Brown was presented with a clerical gown and a silver watch by some parishioners and in May 1842 he was given a parlour suite.

In September 1842 a meeting of parishioners decided to discontinue the practice of bringing the dead into church on Sundays before the afternoon service. On 20th April 1846 a Vestry meeting was held to discuss the best means of extending the burial ground, which was full. Sir George Drinkwater of Kirby refused to sell any land adjoining the existing churchyard as he did not want it to come nearer his home. Sir John Buchan, however, was willing to sell any of his land north west of the main road, so the Vestry agreed to buy 1½ acres from him, and a committee was appointed for the purpose. Douglas paid two thirds of the cost of the new burial ground and the parish one third. One third of the ground was allowed to be sold, from the proceeds of which town and parish were to be recompensed in proportion to their contribution.

At a Vicar General's Court on 27th May 1846 one of the Churchwardens told the Bishop (who was present) that many people claiming seats in the chancel were in the habit of locking their doors, so that, when they did not attend, the seats had to remain vacant. They were much needed, especially in summer, so Bishop Short was asked if he would authorise them to remain unlocked. The Bishop agreed that it was a great inconvenience, but that although he would not go into the case while sitting in Court, he said he would enquire into it if the Vestry would draw up a statement of the case.

The nearness of the church to Douglas inevitably led to vandalism. In October 1845 an unsuccessful attempt was made to rob the safe, in 1846 window panes were broken and in March 1849 vandals forced the door off its hinges, ransacked the church, damaged the organ and the clock and stole the Vicar's surplice, the collecting boxes and the weights of the clock (one of which was later found).

Vicar Brown's end was tragic, although for some years he had been nervous and inclined to epilepsy. Saturday 28th November 1846 was a dark and cold day, with light falls of snow driven by a strong wind. Brown's son, Hugh, (who had greatly distressed his father by becoming a Methodist, and at present had charge of a chapel in Myrtle Street, Liverpool), had been visiting his parents. As night fell the wind rose to a gale and a blizzard began, but Hugh, who intended to return to Liverpool that night, set off at 6 p.m. to walk to Douglas. The Vicar, although not well, was so worried that after a while he set out to try to overtake his son and persuade him not to travel that night, but 150 yards from the vicarage he collapsed in the snow. His Scottish manservant, who was devoted to him, was returning from Douglas in a trap and when the pony suddenly stopped and refused to budge, he got out and found the Vicar lying in the road. He was alive, but died before he could be moved. He was 54. A contributory cause was, no doubt, the severe shock of losing one son on 7th October 1846 and another on 11th November, but he had recovered so much as to have prepared his sermons for the following Sunday, though for the two preceeding Sundays he had handed over the services to his Curate. He is buried in the southwest corner of the churchyard, and the funeral sermon was preached by Thomas Howard.

Brown was kind, genial and just, and a most conscientious parish priest. The friend of all, he was beloved and admired by all. His death left the family in very straitened circumstances, as there was only £109 in the bank. However, Colonel Goldie Taubman started a fund for them to which the Governor gave £5, Bishop Short £20, the Archdeacon £20 and many of the clergy lesser amounts. The parish raised £350 and this, with certain church charities, eventually gave Mrs Brown an annual income of £128. She and her youngest children moved to Castletown to live with her sister.

BRIDE John Nelson's incumbency covered these three episcopates.

CASTLETOWN The disastrous fire at King William's College occurred on Sunday morning, 14th January 1844. The Chapel (then in the main building), the Tower, the Library and the Principal's house and furniture were all destroyed. The fact that there was no fire engine nearer than Douglas meant a delay of several hours, and despite all the efforts of local people the building was nearly gutted, only the walls remaining standing. During the rebuilding, the pupils and Masters attended the services at Castletown church, and on the Sunday after the fire the service was one of thanksgiving that no-one had lost their life. Bishop Short preached in the morning and the Revd G. Parsons, the chaplain, in the evening.

ST JAMES' This church, a daughter church of Patrick, was planned and begun under Bishop Ward, but was consecrated by Bishop Bowstead - that is the part to be used as a church was consecrated but not the part to be used as a school, as in St Luke's, Baldwin. The first Chaplain was William Kermode, who became one of the outstanding Manx clergymen of the century. At Dalby he had a Sunday congregation of anything up to 300, but he was unable at first to find suitable lodgings and seems to have lived at Patrick Vicarage with Vicar Stephen. They used to help each other to souse their head under the pump, one working the handle. Before leaving he put in hand the building of a chaplain's house. He lamented his habit of lying in bed in the morning and of attending parties and playing cards. He wrote in his diary "I am set here as an example, and shall I descend from the height I ought to occupy to mingle with the gay and idle frivolities of the world?"

He was succeeded as Chaplain by George Caesar Stephen, son of Vicar Thomas Stephen, who remained until 1858.

ST GEORGE'S Philpot was succeeded by Thomas Howard in May 1832, and until 1836, when he became Rector of Ballaugh, he combined the Chaplaincy with being Vicar of Braddan. He was succeeded at St George's by Francis Hartwell. He lived in Finch Road during his chaplaincy. He suffered from ill health and his Curate, William McGill, did most of the work of the parish.

On 5th June 1839 Bishop Bowstead held a confirmation in St George's for the town of Douglas and confirmed 380 candidates

In October 1845 vandals broke into the church and did considerable damage and in 1846 window panes were broken.

On the tombstone of Hartwell and his wife are the words "They were lovely and pleasant in their lives, and in their death they were not divided. May their children be followers of their faith and may their last end be like theirs".

GERMAN James Gelling's successor was John La Mothe Stowell, who was appointed on 28th March 1839 and remained Vicar until June 1880. He built a Vicarage, assisted financially by Bishop Short and Archdeacon Moore, the foundation being laid on 13th February 1846 on a site presented by the Bishop. The schools in Peel owed much to his unflagging interest. Bishop Short considered German Parish Church too small. Extensive repairs had been undertaken in 1820, but in 1844, when the church had to be re-roofed and restored, the Bishop offered £300 out of his own pocket towards a new church, besides paying for the chancel, but the parishioners refused.

ST JUDE'S was built as a daughter church of Andreas. The Act of Tynwald authorising the building was dated 21st March 1839 and the patronage was vested in the Rector of Andreas. It seats 250. The land was given by William Christian of Ballachurry, and two pews were assigned to him and his heirs.

Subscribers of £10 who were resident in the parish and non-resident subscribers of £15 were given one pew for themselves and their heirs. One third of the seats were reserved for the poor, and one third of the pews not disposed of were to be let, and the income applied to keeping the church in repair. It was consecrated by Bishop Short on 25th November 1841, he being the preacher in the morning and Dr Carpenter of St Barnabas' in the evening. One eighth of the Andreas tithes (£101) was assigned to St Jude's as stipend for the Chaplain. In 1844 the parsonage was begun with funds provided by the Diocesan Association.

The first Chaplain was William Drury, who remained until he became Vicar of Braddan in 1847. He was deeply respected at St Jude's and became one of the best known and best loved of the Manx clergy. St Jude's Church, parsonage and school were built mainly through his efforts. Bishop Pepys, before he left, gave St Jude's a valuable Communion set in addition to two previous large donations.

JURBY Vicar Harrison continued through these three episcopates.

LEZAYRE When Vicar Maddrell died on 23rd July 1842 a parishioner wrote to the 'Manx Sun' hoping that the new Vicar would be a Manx speaker. "The comfort, the consolation which the old Manx parishioners receive from having the rites of the church administered to them on their deathbeds, in their native language, is far beyond what I have power to describe".

The new Vicar was John Henry La Mothe (5 December 1842). On becoming Vicar he found the house and outhouses so ruinous that he obtained permission to demolish them, and to use the sum awarded for dilapidations as part payment for the building of a new vicarage which cost £471.

In July 1845 he was succeeded by William Bell Christian. Christian was a man of distinguished appearance, of polished and courtly manners, a thorough gentleman, of sterling character, kind to all, and universally respected. He suffered the death of his first three wives, so was married four times. He had a large family, and although he added a room to the vicarage he was still unable to accommodate them comfortably, so in 1853 he was allowed to live at

Milntown to which he had succeeded in 1852. He was the last of the family to occupy it.

LONAN   Joseph Qualtrough's long incumbency covered these three episcopates.

ST LUKE'S   Thomas Caine remained the chaplain under these three Bishops.

MALEW   From 1840-54 the Revd Gilmour Harvey, a master at King William's College, acted as unpaid Curate for William Gill, preaching and visiting the sick and poor. In return for this he was presented on 7th November 1854, with a purse containing 100 sovereigns, and Scott's six volume Commentary on the Bible.

The deputation which presented it consisted of the Revd R. Dixon (Principal of King William's College), Vicar Gill, the Clerk of the Rolls, and the High Bailiff of Castletown. In February 1842 Gill was presented by his parishioners with a new set of clerical robes.

Evensong at Malew at this time was in the afternoon, and in the evening the Vicar and his family sang hymns.

ST MARK'S   J. T. Clarke continued his herculean labours for his people and to make the chaplaincy more attractive in future. In November 1828, to improve the convenience of the glebe, he made an exchange of road with the adjoining proprietors, John Callister of Shenvalley and Esther Callister of Cleigh Rouyr. In 1841 he bought a new glebe of 21 acres for £308 and made new roads on the glebe for £33. 8 miles of draining cost £188 while 5,000 yards of fencing, blasting rocks and general outlay on the glebe came to £391. A new wash house in the Chaplain's house and a pigsty and henhouse cost £15, while excavating a well cost £23. In 1845-6, helped by Bishop Short, a new schoolhouse and schoolmaster's house were built, together with two cottages whose rent would form a repair fund for the school. These all cost £403.

The new glebe of 21 acres, part of Cleigh Rouyr was bought at a public auction in order to secure a legacy of £100 from the estate of Bishop Ward which was conditional on the land being bought for a new glebe. This brought the glebe up to 60 acres, divided into 15 fenced fields. Bishop Pepys lent £50 to help pay for the new glebe.

Ward's legacy and Pepys' loan liquidated the debt on the glebe. In February 1841 Clarke went to London where, under the auspices of Bishops Bowstead and Pepys, who were then in the capital, he was able to collect enough money to repay Pepys' loan and to assist in putting the new glebe into cultivation. Archbishop Howley of Canterbury gave him £20. Bishop Short said that Clarke had achieved in one short trip to London what all his influence could not accomplish. The purchase of the new glebe enabled Clarke to make better use of the exchange of road with the Callisters in 1828, and also enabled him to exchange 12½ acres of the new glebe for 12½ acres belonging to Thomas Moore of Cleigh Rouyr, in order to make each property more convenient by having the Cleigh Rouyr main high road as the boundary, and to have the old road into the glebe meadow levelled.

In building the new schoolhouse and masters' house, Clarke persuaded the National Society for Education in London to extend their work to the Isle of Man by altering their Charter which had confined their work to England and Wales. They gave £70 and Clarke also obtained £30 from the British Government. The school had 100 day pupils, who all attended Sunday School.

In 1843 Clarke successfully fought a legal battle to recover part of the fairground for the church. The wall around the churchyard, thus extended, was built in 1863. Clarke's efforts secured a Post Office for St Mark's, and many miles of drainage in the district were on his initiative. Another achievement was to start a country Library, which in 1846 was the largest on the Island. The new chaplain's house cost £184-9s -10¹/4d and the outbuildings, consisting of a stable for 3 horses, a cow house for 8 cows with a hayloft, a cart shed and a potato house with a loft for a granary cost £111-17s-0d.

In February 1835 Clarke advertised in the 'Manx Sun' that he had furnished his newly built glebe house to accommodate a limited number of boarding pupils at £16 per annum, and also offered to board three or four pupils of King William's College and transport them there and back for £18 per annum.

By establishing a capital of £3,000 Clarke was able to increase the endowment of the chaplaincy from £40 in 1840 to £68 in 1851, to £87 in 1861 and to £90 in 1864.

MAROWN At a meeting in September 1841 it was decided to build a new church, but no site was fixed. The report of a jury dated 29th February 1844 said that the old church was beyond repair. Further Vestry meetings were held on 13th March and 9th April 1844, but the final decision to build was not taken until a Vestry meeting on 27th December 1844. Philip Killey, a brewer in Douglas, gave land on the estate of Ballawilleykilley for the building of a church, the conveyance being dated 4th May 1844.

On 16th March 1846 Mr Jeffcot, on behalf of Vicar Duggan and the wardens, presented a petition in Tynwald to build a new church in Marown, and said that notices had been sent to Messrs. Alex. Spittall and William Kelly, as the lay impropriators, to pay for the building of the chancel in the new Church. Mr Bluett (for Spittall and Kelly) said that he would not oppose the notices, but that there were other lay impropriators in the parish who should also have been made parties and he insinuated that the present church was not the real parish church of Marown, at which a Member of the House of Keys observed that if there was not a parish church in Marown it was high time that there was one. The Bill to build a new church laid down that there were to be about 400 seats, with eight pews reserved for the poor, and that there were to be no burials in the church or within 12 feet of the walls. The Bill was passed by Tynwald on 3rd November 1846 and the Act is dated 26th February 1847.

ST MATTHEW'S Brown was succeeded as Chaplain and Headmaster of the Grammar School by John La Mothe Stowell. He was succeeded by Samuel Gelling and he by John Cannell, who began a faithful chaplaincy of 38 years.

MAUGHOLD Bowyer Harrison remained Vicar under these three Bishops.

KIRK MICHAEL In 1840 Bishop Pepys granted a petition from the parishioners that the services should be said in Manx twice a month.

The old Vicarage had been built on land bought by Bishop Wilson, but by 1844 it was beyond repair, and was condemned as such by a jury of carpenters and masons. It was therefore decided to build a new one, and Vicar Brown began collecting subscriptions.

In 1843 Bishop Short presented a Bible and Prayer Book to the church.

ONCHAN Edward Craine's long incumbency ended on 26th April 1847 when he died after being ill for six months, and was buried at Onchan on 1st May. He had actually resigned on 7th February. There were hopes that John Cannell, Chaplain of St Matthew's, would succeed him, but as there was a vacancy in the see following the death of Bishop Shirley, Archdeacon Moore appointed John Baylis, Vicar of Bloxwich, Staffs, to take charge of Onchan for seven weeks.

PATRICK Thomas Stephen died at the vicarage on Friday, 30th April 1842 after a very short illness, as he had preached and taken the usual services the previous Sunday.

He was succeeded as Vicar by Archibald Holmes (5th October 1842), the Chaplain of St Paul's, Ramsey. He was a good, kindhearted man who faithfully discharged his duties.

ST PAUL'S After Holmes' appointment to Patrick, William Kermode succeeded him (12th October 1843) and began a chaplaincy of 28 years which was a "golden age" for St Paul's. As there was no vicarage he lived at No. 73 Parliament Street (Holmes had lived in Waterloo Road). Early and late he attended to the church, the poor, and the sick. In 1840, when Curate of Lezayre in charge of north Ramsey, he was the main mover in forming Ramsey Health Association to preserve public health. He was described as one of the men with whom it was always safe to consult in times of anxiety and perplexity. A Vestry meeting on 18th March 1844 decided to build the north and south transepts, over which were erected the present galleries. Kermode had urged this as soon as he became chaplain and, with characteristic energy he had begun raising money. The north transept was ready by 28th July and the south transept by the 1st September, the total cost being £435. The west end gallery had been built in 1830 for the school children, helped by a grant from Ward's Fund.

Kermode found that there was no vicarage, glebe or endowment and the only income was about £65 per annum from pew rents. He built the parsonage, paying one third of the cost himself, and giving the site, part of his Claghbane estate which he had inherited.

RUSHEN In 1839 a new vicarage was built at a cost of £450. The top floor was not added until 1881.

SANTAN Samuel Gelling's long incumbency covered these three episcopates.

ST STEPHEN'S owed its inception to Bishop Ward, but he died before the foundation stone was laid on 4th June 1838 by his son, the Revd W. P. Ward. St Stephen's was opened on 24th November 1839 and the collection (£6) went towards buying a Communion Set and other necessaries. Archdeacon Hall celebrated Holy Communion and Bishop Bowstead preached on I Chronicles 29 ⁹. The day was wet and windy, so the congregation was comparatively small. The first Chaplain was the Curate of Lezayre, John Qualtrough, who was appointed on 15th November 1839 and he proved to be energetic and capable. In November 1840 William Kermode gave £3 from his limited stipend towards what was needed for a choir at St Stephen's.

Chapter 8

BISHOPS SHIRLEY 1847 and AUCKLAND 1847-54

The see was first offered to Dr John Graham, Master of Christ's College, Cambridge, and from 1849-65 Bishop of Chester, but he declined so Bishop Short was succeeded by Walter Augustus Shirley. He was born at Wexford, Co. Mayo, on 30th May 1797, the son of a clergyman, and in later life he wrote "If I have been in any measure preserved from the evils which surrounded me, it has been owing the prayers and the constant, affectionate and judicious advice of my beloved parents". In 1798 the family moved to England and young Shirley entered Winchester College in 1809. The second master was Dr Williams (later Warden of New College, Oxford) to whom Shirley was always grateful for his kindness and encouragement. Williams was just, impartial and kind, without ceasing to inspire respect. In 1815 Shirley entered New College and on graduating in 1819 he was elected a Fellow. In 1820 he was ordained to his Fellowship and received Priest's orders in 1821. Meanwhile his father had become Rector of Woodford, Northants, and Shirley became his Curate. There followed two more curacies, and in 1828 he succeeded his father as Vicar of the family living of Shirley, where he lived until 1847, except for 1838-9 when he held the rectory of Whiston, near Rotherham, on the presentation of the Earl of Effingham, to whom also he became chaplain. In 1839 he presented himself to the other family living, Brailsford, which adjoined Shirley. As Rector he celebrated Holy Communion once a quarter. On 4th September 1827 he married Miss Maria Waddington, the wedding being in the British Embassy Chapel in Paris, where most of the bride's family lived. They had a son and a daughter. Mrs Shirley died on 10th January 1854.

At Whiston he found a congregation of 40 in a church which seated 800, but he soon filled it. On his return to Shirley and Brailsford he took charge of the adjoining parishes of Yeaveley and Osmaston and employed three curates. In December 1840 he was appointed Archdeacon of Derby by Bishop Bowstead of Lichfield, which then included Derbyshire. In

November 1846 he was offered the see of Sodor and Man and at once visited the Island with Bishop Short. They had a rough passage on 27th November, lasting from 9.30 a.m. until 6 p.m. and were met on the pier by Archdeacon Moore and Dr Carpenter of St Barnabas'. They stayed at Derby Castle. Short was a good sailor but neither he nor Shirley could face a meal at sea. They left on 12th December. Shirley was consecrated in Whitehall Chapel on 10th January 1847, but as Archbishop Vernon Harcourt of York was 89 and infirm (he died later in the year) the Crown issued a Commission to the Bishops of Carlisle (Percy), Lichfield (Lonsdale) and St Asaph (Short) to consecrate him. The sermon was preached on Revelations 2 [1-3] by an old friend, the Revd Thomas Hill, who succeeded Shirley as Archdeacon of Derby, and became his biographer. Shirley had preached his farewell sermon to his parishioners on 3rd January on Hebrews 7 [1-2].

He arrived in Douglas on the 'King Orry' on Tuesday evening, 26th January and was enthroned in St Mary's, Castletown on 1st February. He was amused by the fact that part of the oath he had to take was to abjure the Pretender. His reply to an address from the people of Castletown, which included a tribute to Bishop Short, was described by the 'Manx Sun' as "manly, unaffected and sincere". Afterwards Governor Hope hospitably entertained him and the clergy to lunch at Government House, then in Castletown.

In one of his early letters Shirley wrote "The Bishop's duties here are much more varied than in England and though on a small scale, require much wisdom and thoughtful discretion". On 31st January he preached at St George's in the morning and at Braddan in the afternoon and on 2nd February took his seat in Tynwald.

His early impressions of his diocese were not wholly favourable. The low stipends of the clergy, and the need for them to be able to speak Manx, made new appointments difficult. He found the churches, including Bishopscourt Chapel "cold and empty" and realised that Methodism was much stronger than in England. He summed it up in the words "The church is at a very low ebb". He did, however, admire the scenery, especially the sands on Orrisdale shore. In a letter to his parents on 8th February he described the Manx language as "An unmitigated portion of the curse of Babel".

The most pressing question facing him was the fact that the growing town of Douglas was only part of the parish of Braddan and there was a growing feeling that it should be made a separate parish or parishes. The death of Vicar Brown in November 1846 seemed to afford an opportunity to resolve the problem, and in February 1847 Shirley moved in Tynwald that a committee of the Legislature be appointed to draw up the boundary of a proposed parish of Douglas to make all civil and ecclesiastical arrangements and report back to Tynwald. The Committee he proposed was Attorney General Ogden and Archdeacon Moore from the Legislative Council and the Speaker and a member with local knowledge from the Keys. This was carried, but owing to the ensuing death of the Bishop nothing happened. Later in the month Shirley took his only confirmation, at St Paul's, Ramsey, when there were 29 candidates.

Oxford University had nominated Shirley as Bampton Lecturer for 1847 and on 3rd March he left the Island to deliver the first two on 14th and 21st. On the 26th he and Mrs Shirley went to stay with a friend at Naseby, Northants. and he spoke at a meeting for the Pastoral Aid Society. Either at this meeting or on the journey from Oxford, he caught a chill and next morning he felt **unwell** and had a heavy cold, but he preached that day on II Corinthians 6[1] - his last sermon. On returning he complained of pain in his limbs, but next day he and his wife set off for the Isle of Man. Things were not helped by an hour's wait on a railway platform in a piercing wind which thoroughly chilled him, but they had a good crossing to Douglas, which the Bishop spent in conversing with passengers and playing with some children. Every effort was made by the staff at Bishopscourt to warm the house, but it still felt cold when the travellers arrived on the evening of 1st April and he still felt unwell. Mrs Shirley knew no doctors on the Island, but next day she found a chemist who, after examining the Bishop, said there was no cause for alarm. His condition deteriorated, however, and on 9th April

Dr Young was summoned from Peel. He at once diagnosed advanced pneumonia and said that the Bampton lectures must be given up, so a medical certificate was sent to the Vice-Chancellor of Oxford. On 13th April Dr Kemp was called in to give a second opinion and he confirmed Dr Young's diagnosis. From then on Dr Young stayed at Bishopscourt and did all possible for his patient. On the evening of the 14th Vicar Brown of Kirk Michael administered Holy Communion to the Bishop, his wife and son, Dr Young and the household. Shirley's daughter was desperately trying to get a passage to the Island, as she was in England. She eventually arrived on 16th, accompanied by the Bishop's aged parents. On the 15th and 16th he felt much better and Dr Kemp held out some hope. On Sunday morning, April 18th, he read the Litany with Dr Young, but early on Monday morning new and alarming symptoms appeared, and he died at 8 a.m. on Wednesday, 21st April, aged 49. His body was taken to England on the 'Ben my Chree' and buried in a vault in Shirley Church, the Bishop of Lichfield taking the committal (April 29th). Archdeacon Moore represented the Manx clergy. Mrs Shirley and her family left the Island early in June. Shirley's parents were left destitute, as he was their only child (a sister had died young) and they were dependent on him. However, the Government heard of their plight and the father was appointed Vicar of Brailsford. Bishop Shirley's episcopate lasted two months and nineteen days, the shortest in the history of the diocese.

Shirley was learned, zealous, with a deep love for, and reliance on, God, though in many ways he was self-reliant, despite his humility. All his life he set a high value on Sunday as a time of rest and spiritual refreshment and would mildly check worldly conversation in his own family. He once wrote, "we must expect that many will reject and oppose our messsage, because the truth is unwelcome to them. Indeed it would be a mark of evil upon us were it otherwise, for it is only of the false prophets that all men have spoken well". He had an ardent desire to be useful to his flock, and was much loved by those in the Island who knew him. St Paul's, Derby, was built by public subscription, as a memorial to him.

Shirley was replaced by the Hon. Robert John Eden, the youngest son of William, first Lord Auckland and his wife Eleanor Elliott. He was born on

10th July 1799, educated at Eton and Magdalene College, Cambridge and made Deacon in 1823 and ordained Priest in 1824. He was Curate of Eyam, Derbyshire (1823-25), Rector of Hertingfordbury, Herts (1825-35), and Vicar of Battersea (1835-47). He was Chaplain to King William IV (1831-37) and to Queen Victoria from 1837-47. On 15th September 1825 he married Miss Mary Hunt, who was greatly loved by the Manx people while Eden was Bishop. They had a son and four daughters.

As early as 1st May 1847 the 'Manx Sun' announced his appointment. He spent a few days on the Island before his consecration at Whitehall Chapel on 25th May by the aged Archbishop of York, assisted by Bishops Sumner of Chester, Wilberforce of Oxford and Percy of Carlisle. He arrived on the Fleetwood steamer on 22nd June, and was described as tall and good looking. He went straight to Bishopscourt, his wife and family following on 29th June. They were met by the Bishop and travelled in his carriage to Bishopscourt. The same day he had been enthroned in St Mary's, Castletown by the Archdeacon, who preached on St John 20[21,] after which Governor Hope entertained him and the clergy to lunch. He took his seat in Tynwald on 8th July.

On 20th September 1847 the Royal yacht, with Queen Victoria and the Prince Consort on board, anchored in Ramsey Bay. The Archdeacon and High Bailiff Tellett of Ramsey went aboard, and when they learned that the yacht would stay for some hours, they returned to shore and sent word to the Governor and the Bishop. The latter arrived in less than an hour, and went aboard with Deemster and Miss Christian, the Archdeacon and the Chaplain of St Paul's, William Kermode, and his wife. It was on this occasion that the Prince Consort landed, and walked to the top of the hill on which the Albert Tower (named after him), now stands. The foundation stone of the Tower was laid on Easter Monday, 24th April 1848 by Mrs Eden.

On 28th September 1847 Eden held his first confirmation, at Lonan, when 70 were confirmed. On 13th December Kirk Michael Church Choir was invited to Bishopscourt, where they sang some anthems and hymns, had a meal, and passed a happy evening.

On 2nd November 1848 Eden sent the following letter to the clergy.

Reverend and Dear Sir,

It having pleased the Almighty during the past year to bless the inhabitants of this Island with a most abundant supply of fish, and graciously permitted us to gather in the fruits of a good harvest, I am desirous that you should observe Sunday 19th November as a Day of Thanksgiving for these mercies. I would suggest that you should exhort your brethren to partake on that day of the Holy Sacrament; to remember the poor at the offertory and to unite in thanksgiving to Him who has "restored and continued to us the blessings of the sea", granting to us a sufficient supply of the fruits of the ground and has, up to this time, warded off from our Island "the pestilence that walketh in darkness and the sickness that destroyeth at noonday" and should impress upon them that "blessed are the people who have the Lord for their God"

I remain,
Reverend Dear Sir,
Yours very faithfully,
R. J. Sodor and Man.

On 1st January 1849 Eden's older brother, George, died suddenly and as he was unmarried the Bishop succeeded him as third Lord Auckland. Henceforth he signed himself "Auckland, Sodor and Man". This is the only case of a peer of the realm being Bishop of Sodor and Man, and of someone being a member of Tynwald and of the House of Lords. He sat as a peer in the House of Lords, but wore no episcopal robes until he became Bishop of Bath and Wells.

In October 1849 it was rumoured that Auckland was to be translated to the vacant see of Llandaff. Manx people complained that it was a disrespect to their church to appoint Bishops, only to move them to something better at the first chance. They were looked on as birds of passage, and there is no doubt that the rapid changes of the last decade had adversely affected the office of Bishop in the public mind. By 1849 Auckland's uprightness, faithfulness and Christian benevolence had gained him the good opinion of all.

Thursday 15th November 1849 was appointed by the Governor (at the request of the Bishop) as a day of Public Thanksgiving for the fact that the cholera in England had only visited part of the Island for a short time. The Bishop asked that at least part of the collections should go to the dependants of the cholera victims.

In January 1850 Auckland went to England for a short holiday, as he had not been well, but returned in February much improved. He was very interested in education and in March 1850 he appointed Diocesan Inspectors to visit the parish schools, and visited them himself from time to time. He also preached regularly in the churches.

On 14th November 1850 the clergy met in Douglas on the summons of the Archdeacon and addressed petitions to the Crown and to the Bishop against the recent action of Pope Pius IX in dividing England into dioceses, each with its Bishop. Auckland replied that he was not really worried, and that the best answer to this was to ensure that people, and especially children, were well grounded in the faith. He believed that the clergy would achieve more by quiet attentions to duty than by preaching against the Pope. Nevertheless meetings against the "Papal agression" were held in various places.

On 17th January 1851 the Bishop gave an excellent supper to Kirk Michael choir at Bishopscourt. The rest of the evening was spent in various amusements, interspersed with the singing of anthems and sacred music. The 'Manx Sun' reported that the party broke up at a "seasonable hour"

Auckland asked that Sunday 3rd October 1852 should be observed as a Day of Thanksgiving for the abundant harvest and good harvest weather. From March until June 1852 he had been on holiday in England. On 28th December 1852, as he was returning from Ramsey, the Bishop stopped to speak to a farmer, whose horse kicked out viciously and gave him a compound fracture of the leg. It did not heal as well as expected, so on 25th April 1853 he went to London to obtain expert attention. On 1st May prayers were offered for him in the churches. The treatment to induce the fractured bone to unite proved to be severe and by mid-June he still could not walk, but he returned on 30th August much improved, and in early September held the annual Convocation at Bishopscourt, transferred from Whit week.

The wreck of the 'Lily' on Kitterland occurred during a gale on 28th December 1852, and in the subsequent explosion 29 lives were lost and 24 children lost their father. The Bishop gave £20 to the Disaster Fund, Lady Auckland £5, Vicar Corrin of Rushen £3, the Archdeacon £10 and Bishop Short £10.

In July 1853 a Scripture Readers' Association was formed for Douglas with the Bishop as Patron and the Archdeacon as Vice-Patron.

On 2nd November 1853, as was customary at the end of the harvest, the Bishop entertained the tenants and labourers on his domain to a harvest supper. He presided over a meal of roast beef, plum pudding and ale with his usual geniality and courtesy, and in the evening there was a dance which his daughters attended for a short time.

In August 1853 Auckland gave £25 for a proposed chapel at Foxdale and £20 each to provide parsonages for St George's and St Barnabas'. On 3rd January 1854 he gave a lecture on 'Health and Longevity' at Ramsey Courthouse in aid of Ramsey Literary Institution and Reading Room. He showed a considerable knowledge of physiology and anatomy, and urged sanitary reforms in the town. Considering the bad weather there was a good audience, which included the Archdeacon and Vicar General Corlett.

Wednesday 26th April 1854 was kept as a day of national humiliation and fast because of the Crimean War. Ordinary occupations were suspended and services held in all churches and chapels, the collections being mostly for soldiers' wives and children. Vicar Hawley of St George's preached on Ezekiel 21 [8,9,10] in the morning and in the evening on II Chronicles 20[3]; Vicar Gray of St Barnabas' preached on Daniel 9[19] and Vicar Drury of Braddan preached on Jerememiah 13[15-17].

On 24th February 1854 the Bishop and his family went to London, and in late May it was announced that he had been translated to Bath and Wells. A Memorial to the Queen was at once drawn up on the Island and widely signed, asking that Dr William Carpenter (Vicar of St Barnabas 1832-48) be appointed the new Bishop. Auckland returned to the Island on 9th June, and was met at Ramsey by the Archdeacon and some clergy. Much good feeling was shown by the Ramsey people and cannon were fired as a mark of respect. On 12th June he attended his last prizegiving at King William's College and on 14th June Convocation was held at which, after a sermon by the Archdeacon, the Bishop gave an affectionate and impressive farewell charge. The clergy then presented an Address, as did the people of Douglas later, speaking of his simple dignity, his unwearied exertions and of all that was due to his example and precepts. The people of Foxdale sent him an appreciative Address, and he also received one from the teachers in the Island - something quite unprecedented - which spoke of his inestimable services to education, e.g. in appointing diocesan inspectors of religious education in schools. The teachers recalled that one of his first acts had been to ask the Council for Education in London to send an inspector to report on the schools. Canon Mosely had come and had reported that 26 had no maps or blackboards, simply books, benches and desks. Auckland also received from friends and the schools a service of plate worth £150. A condition had been attached to the subscription list limiting the amount which could be given. After the Bishop's reply to this last presentation the people were too affected to applaud.

The people of Ramsey and district took the opportunity of his final departure from Ramsey on 20th June to present him with an Address read by Deemster Drinkwater, to which the Bishop replied. This Address spoke of the dignified way in which he had discharged his duties; of his courtesy and kindness and of his zeal for education and for the general advancement of the community. A large party accompanied him to the pier, and he embarked on the 'Manx Fairy' at 8.30 a.m. He was enthroned at Bath and Wells on 21st July, where he remained until his resignation on 6th September 1869. He died on April 25th 1870 and Lady Auckland on 25th November

1872. He suffered much from gout in his last years and never really recovered from an ankle injury sustained in a fall from his horse just before leaving the Island.

Auckland won the esteem of all classes and denominations by his unaffected piety, kindness, and genial courteous manners. He showed much wisdom and commonsense in his rule of the Church, and, though strict and conscientious, he was a liberal churchman, and never showed any hostility to Methodists or Roman Catholics, who all loved him. He had no pomposity, but could be gracefully firm and dignified when called on to exercise his authority. Typical of him was the way in which, almost every day, he brought in person a can of soup and other good things to a sick old man, a Roman Catholic, in Kirk Michael. He attended scrupulously to his duties in church and state. He exercised an unostentatious benevolence and did his best to provide clergy and churches in parts of the Island where spiritual ministrations were lacking. He was said to have been loved, for what he was personally, by every man, woman and child in the diocese, and there was widespread regret when he left. Auckland's policy was to let the diocese run itself without interference from him (provided things were going properly). In these 30 years (1847-77) which included the troubled episcopate of Bishop Powys, the sheet anchor and ruling spirit of the diocese was Archdeacon Moore, to whom the Manx Church owes an unpayable debt.

The Parishes under Shirley and Auckland

ANDREAS In January 1847 Archdeacon Moore called a meeting to raise funds for the poor of the parish, and promised to contribute £50 if the parishioners could raise £100 or more. £150 was quickly raised. On 26th February 1847 Tynwald passed an Act authorising the enlargement of the churchyard from glebe land.

ARBORY Alexander Gelling's long incumbency continued under Auckland.

BALLAUGH In 1849 the old church was re-roofed, and the porch and the bell tower were re-

stored at a cost of £125. James Cregeen, Parish Clerk and Schoolmaster for 28 years, died in March 1849 aged 48. In 1850 the font and the pulpit in the parish church were removed from the chancel.

ST BARNABAS' William Carpenter left on 19th March 1848 to become Vicar of St Jude's, Liverpool, but he returned to preach his last sermon on Sunday evening, 23rd April, to an immense congregation. The text of this, and of his first sermon in 1832, was Acts 20[28]. His departure from St Barnabas' was widely and deeply regretted, by the clergy as well as by the laity. He received a cheque for £400, subscribed by people from all over the Island. At the presentation Attorney General Ogden said "You had better make that cheque payable only in Liverpool for if Dr Carpenter can cash it here, he will give away half of it before he leaves". The Archdeacon and clergy presented him with an Address and the Steam Packet gave him free passages on their ships in the hope that it might induce him to visit the Island more often. The day he left the pier was thronged with people, and he walked four times up and down shaking hands.

In October 1866 a memorial to him was erected on the north side of the chancel in St Barnabas' which said "To the memory of the Rev. W. Carpenter DD, first incumbent of this parish, and for fifteen years the devoted and laborious pastor of the flock. Publicly and from house to house, he ceased not to teach and to preach Christ crucified. In his large-hearted benevolence he founded the House of Industry, St Barnabas' schools, St Thomas' Church and Christ Church Maughold, and originated schemes of spiritual good. Through eighteen years of absence he was remembered as the spiritual father of many and the friend of all, and is loved, honoured and lamented. He entered into rest on Christmas Eve, 1865, at St Paul's Vicarage, Penzance in his sixtieth year. Revelations 14^{15}".

Carpenter was succeeded by John Alcock who was appointed on 27th July 1848. He had been recommended to the trustees of St Barnabas' by Dr Carpenter. He always used the collect for Advent III before the sermon. Before giving the text he would look around the congregation and then, putting a small Bible in the palm of his left hand, he would cover it with his right hand saying "The word of God as you will find it written in" whatever the text was. He was loved by the people and although St Barnabas' sat 1200 people it was usually full in his time.

On 24th June 1849 Dr Carpenter paid a visit and preached for an hour on Romans 1^{11}. In the summer of 1849 the Church was painted and cleaned, the services being held in the Wellington Hall. Alcock preached his last sermon on 30th May 1852, and asked that the large sum raised as a present for him should go to pay a debt for work on the church and that the surplus should go to the schools. He left on 3rd June, but returned to preach at the anniversary on 9th July 1854.

Alcock was succeeded by Joseph Henry Gray, who was appointed on 24th June 1852. He often held services for the young, and was a man of great ability, but he was not a peacemaker.

In October 1853 a piece of land was bought near Mona Terrace, Finch Road, for a vicarage, which had hitherto been the Hermitage on Peel Road. The Church was closed for several weeks in the autumn of 1853 for repairs and decoration, and was re-opened on 20th November, the Archdeacon preaching in the morning and the Vicar in the evening.

BRADDAN   Vicar Brown's death raised an important issue. Braddan was the mother church of Douglas, which was still part of the parish and had three churches, St Matthew's, St George's and St Barnabas', increased to four when St Thomas' was built in 1849. Bishop Short had long felt that Douglas should be separated from Braddan and made into at least one separate parish, so one of his last acts, in consultation with Archdeacon Moore, was to draw up "A Bill to provide for the appointment of an Incumbent to the Vicarage of Braddan" and the Speaker introduced it into Tynwald on 15th December 1846. The Bill recognised the need to separate Douglas from Braddan, but accepted the fact that Braddan could not be kept vacant until this was done, so its main clause read "that any further appointment to the office of Vicar of the Parish of Braddan shall be made subject to such measures and regulations as may hereafter be enacted by Act of Tynwald, with respect to the said Parish, and with a view to divide the said Parish and to create the town of Douglas, and any portion of the adjoining country, into a separate and independent Parish and to provide for the patronage of the Parish so to be erected". This Act, with the support of Bishop Shirley, was passed on 26th February 1847, and next day William Drury, Chaplain of St Jude's, was appointed Vicar, and was inducted on 1st April. He accepted the parish under the terms of this Bill. William Drury (or Parson Drury, as he was affectionately known all over the Island), thus began a ministry at Braddan which lasted 40 years and made him one of the best known and best loved clergymen in the Island. For many years he worked his large parish without a curate, and knew everyone in it. A big man, he had immense physical powers and wonderful endurance, and when there was no chaplain at

St Luke's, Baldwin, he thought nothing of walking the 12 miles there and back to take the 8 a.m. service, before taking the morning and afternoon services at Braddan, preaching on Douglas Quay at 5 p.m. and finishing with a schoolroom service at Cronkbourne, besides baptisms, and often a wedding or funeral, then common on a Sunday.

His sermons on the quay attracted large numbers, many of them non-churchgoers. Later he had a horse, Dumple, which was almost as well known in the parish as the Vicar. He worked hard in Douglas and would gladly walk there to visit a sick person after a full day. He often walked 20 miles a day visiting. His striking personality and deep earnestness attracted many visitors who would otherwise have heard no spiritual message. His preaching was based on his firm faith in the Bible as the Word of God, and he once said that if the Bible had stated that Jonah swallowed the whale he would believe it. He was the last Vicar of Bradddan to speak Manx, and his Manx sermons drew crowds of people. But his great influence sprang less from his untiring work than from his sympathy and generosity (every beggar found him an easy victim), and his willingness and desire to pray with all and sundry anywhere and at any time. He loved the Island and the Manx people, and delighted in talking broad Manx. Long before his death he had become an institution. A. W. Moore, the Manx historian, who knew Drury well, wrote of him "The memory of this excellent man will remain in the hearts of his countrymen without assistance from any pen".

On 1st August 1849 St Thomas' Church was opened and licensed for worship but was not consecrated. Bishop Auckland appointed as the first Chaplain, W. D. Carter, who left in 1851 and was succeeded by Samuel Simpson, whose ministry of 16 years was long remembered. The Bishop, in making these appointments, told Drury that until the church was consecrated he, as Bishop, had the right to appoint the chaplain, but Drury was not fully convinced, and only acquiesced through his respect for Auckland (which was shared by the whole Island) and by a natural desire for peace if possible. No steps had been taken to divide the parish as envisaged in the 1847 Act of Tywald, though there had been some abortive attempts. In August 1852 the Chaplains of St Matthew's, (Cannell), St George's (Forbes), St Barnabas'

(Gray), and St Thomas' (Simpson) wrote to the Bishop asking for Douglas to be divided into four parishes. Auckland approved the scheme, but nothing had been done when he was translated in 1854.

At a meeting on 10th December 1846 a subscription was started for a new vicarage, the existing one being little more than a cottage, but it was to be on the same site. In July 1847 it was finally decided to go ahead, Drury undertaking to cart all the required materials.

By 1847 the churchyard was very overcrowded, and far too many were being buried in the same grave. In March 1848 Tynwald passed a bill allowing the Vicar and Wardens to buy from the Trustees of the Impropriate Fund 4 acres of Ballafletcher, at a cost of £400, for a new burial ground. This was approved at a stormy Vestry meeting on Easter Monday, 24th April 1848, during which Drury's patience was widely noticed. The 4 acres were bought in October 1848, and it was planned to build a little chapel there. The new burial ground was consecrated by Bishop Auckland, assisted by Archdeacon Moore, on 11th June 1849, and in 1851 trees were planted around it.

BRIDE John Nelson died on 27th October 1847, aged 68, of typhus fever, contracted while visiting the sick. He was succeeded by his son, Daniel. While at Bride he lived in Ayre House, on the site of the present rectory, as there was then no rectory in Bride. He was much influenced by the Tractarian movement.

CASTLETOWN In 1849 Archdeacon Moore made a visitation, and although visitations had taken place from Bishop Crigan's time onwards, Parsons and his churchwardens protested that St Mary's was a Royal or Free chapel and not subject to the Bishop's or the Archdeacon's visitations, or to the authority of the church courts, but after some correspondence Parsons admitted that he was in error.

CRONK Y VODDY Before the chapel was built the schoolroom was used for services. Mrs Frances Hall, widow of Archdeacon Hall, built the Chapel, which cost £500, at her own expense and also built the parsonage and gave the trustees (the Bishop and the Archdeacon) £1,000 to be invested in land or on mortgage as an endowment for the chaplain. Mr Daniel Callow of Ramsey was the builder. Mrs Hall reserved the patronage to herself for her lifetime (she died on 3rd June 1888) after which it was to go to the Bishop. She laid the foundation stone on 17th July 1851, which was a fine day, in the presence of the Bishop, the Archdeacon and many of the clergy. There were two hymns, prayers and an address by Bishop Auckland, who afterwards provided lunch for everyone in the schoolhouse, and proposed Mrs Hall's health. The chapel was consecrated on 12th February 1852 by Auckland, but although it was a very wet day 13 of the clergy attended and the chapel was well filled. The chancel window commemorated Mrs Hall. The first Chaplain was John Fry Garde (1852-54).

ST JAMES' George Stephen remained chaplain under Auckland.

ST GEORGE'S Hartwell was succeeded in November 1847 by Edward Forbes. In 1847 he and the churchwardens made arrangements which gave nearly 200 extra seats for the poor. The Bishop's pew was moved to the side of the altar, thus giving more accommodation. Forbes was a kind and faithful man who was respected throughout the Island, and his departure in 1859 was deeply regretted. He worked tirelessly among the sick and poor, to an extent which affected his health, and in 1855 he had to take a year's holiday, on medical grounds in the south of France, Switzerland and Italy. He returned considerably improved.

On 19th November 1848 John Cowle, the Parish Clerk for over 40 years, died suddenly aged 80. He was also a Methodist local preacher. Forbes appointed in his place John Curphey, a tailor, but said that in future the responses, in accordance with ancient practice, would be given by the congregation alone, and not by the Clerk. In 1849 the Church was licensed for marriages and in April 1852 Samuel Harris gave two stained glass windows for the chancel in memory of his parents.

GERMAN On 13th April 1848 a Vestry meeting was held to discuss a new burial ground, and five sidesmen were appointed to help the Vicar and Wardens with the preliminaries. Things moved slowly and as the last rate assessment had been made in 1734 much of the rates fell on the old houses where the

people were often poor, and houses built since 1734 were exempt. As the churchyard was becoming a health risk, Bishop Auckland wrote to the Vicar and Wardens in September 1849 urging them to do something, and suggesting that the occupants of the new houses might make a donation equal to what would have been their rate. In October the cess payers decided to buy the present burial ground, each quarterland to be assessed for that purpose. The town of Peel was to pay two thirds of the sum required. On Easter Monday, 14th April, 1851, a Vestry meeting decided, at the Bishop's request, to build a small chapel in the new cemetery. By June 1853 the cemetery was ready for burials and it and the chapel were consecrated by Auckland on 22nd November 1853.

ST JOHN'S There was a church on the site in the 10th century, because when the building was demolished in July 1847 a broken shaft of a runic cross, dated about 950, was found. The 1699 Chapel, built by Bishop Wilson, was in design like a cross with equal limbs, and was set to the north east of the present church within a circular grass enclosure, surrounded by an earth fence, like that which now surrounds Tynwald Hill. In the centre of this cross was a small belfry. David Robertson, who visited the Island in Bishop Mason's time, said that St John's Chapel was desolate and ruinous, the roof off, and the walls simply a shelter for sheep. Feltham, who visited the Island in 1798 said that the chapel had lately been rebuilt, but that there were no pews and that it was only used occasionally, Vicar Corlett of German doing duty. The old chapel seated 174. For centuries St John's was a chaplaincy of German, but during the 17th century it became ruinous, and on Tynwald Fair Day 1697 a collection for urgent repairs was made among Members of the House of Keys. The main body of the Chapel, to which Wilson gave £40, was finished by August 1704 and in December 1706 a general assessment on land holdings was made to finish the north and south transepts, Tynwald Chapel being considered a national institution. Further repairs were made in 1739, but by 1792 it was ruinous, as the British Government, which had bought the Island in 1765, had let the chapel deteriorate. Until 1765 a small Poll Tax on everyone aged 16 and over maintained the chapel. Services had been held on Sunday afternoons by the Vicar or Curate of German.

In 1780 as a result of a dispute between the British Government and the 3rd Duke of Atholl, (who claimed that his father had not sold the Courthouses, and that they remained his property), the chapel which had been used as a courthouse was locked by the Governor, Richard Dawson, and although the parishioners offered to repair the chapel at their own expense he refused to return it. As a result the building soon became a complete ruin without roof, doors or windows, but in 1793 Atholl became Governor and repairs were started.

In 1793 Hugh Kennaugh, who lived at St John's, hanged himself in the church and it was at once put under an interdict. On July 20th 1793 Bishop Crigan issued a Deed of Reconciliation to free the chapel from this taint, and a service of reconciliation was held. The chapel was rebuilt in 1798 and further repairs were carried out in 1814 when Bishop Murray provided seats and some pews at his own expense. The first resident Chaplain was William Gill, later Vicar of Malew, who was appointed in October 1820, and stayed until 1824. He celebrated Holy Communion at long intervals, and at first performed baptisms, but the Vicar of German, James Gelling, objected to this, and they had to be discontinued.

He was succeeded by Samuel Gelling, the son of the Vicar of German and later Vicar of Santan, who was Chaplain from 1824-33. He lived in Peel. The stipend at this time was £5 per annum. William Drury followed (1833-34), but he was off the Island for part of this year. He lived at Snugborough. John Gell, whom we have met as Chaplain of St Mark's, followed, but he continued to live in Ballasalla, as there was no chaplain's house. He read Mattins alternately in Manx and English. In 1836 he applied to the Home Secretary, Lord John Russell, for an increase in stipend, and received £25 per annum, which he managed to increase to £40 in 1840. Next came William Bell Christian from April until August 1845, when he became Vicar of Lezayre. He had been Curate of German since 1840. John Fry Garde followed (August 1845) and remained until 1865. He was a graduate of Trinity College, Dublin, and it was in his time that the present church was built.

On 1st August 1840 the Diocesan Association voted the Chaplain £30 per annum, and the same year a chaplain's house was built at a cost of £300, £100 being given by Tynwald, and £200 by the Diocesan Association, which also bought the land. Further repairs to the chapel were made in 1840, but even so rain came through the roof on wet days. Manx services ceased at the end of Gell's chaplaincy. There was no font in the old chapel, but a basin of water placed on the altar was used instead. In 1865 the stipend was £67-16s-2d, but in 1868 Tynwald agreed to pay the stipend and raised it to £100.

On 12th February 1845 a new parish school was opened in St John's, and those who favoured the building of a new church felt that no better time could be chosen to launch a public appeal for the necessary funds. A meeting was addressed by Vicar Carpenter of St Barnabas' and raised £247. This was felt to be enough to start, and a motion was carried at a public meeting on 17th February that a petition for building a new church be forwarded to the Governor. A building committee was elected, of which the secretary was William Harrison, Rock Mount.

Meanwhile the Chaplain, John Gell, had died on 29th January 1845 and Vicar Stowell of German claimed the right to appoint his successor. This raised a delicate question, because it was the Government Chapel and the Government had promised £1,500 towards building a new church on condition that there were open seats instead of pews and that marble seats were built in the sanctuary. Many feared that if Stowell's claim was upheld the Government might withdraw their £1,500. To make sure that this did not happen, over a hundred landowners in the parish and district wrote to the Governor expressing the wish that the Government should retain the patronage and general control of the chapel. The Attorney General in England, and the Clerk of the Rolls for the Island (John MacHutchin) were consulted, and both upheld the Government's right to appoint the Chaplain. W. B. Christian was appointed.

A good deal of money was raised from individuals. Bishop Short sent £100, Governor Hope, £25, the Bishop £20, Deemster Christian £10, Deemster Heywood £5, Archdeacon £10, Vicar General Hartwell £1, the Revd G. S. Parsons £5, the Revd J. F. Garde 3 guineas, Speaker Gawne £25 and George Dumbell £5. It was decided that the church should be faced with granite, and the tender was given to Benjamin Hollins of Manchester, who gave an estimate of £2,000. The architect was Richard Lane of

Manchester, and the church is built in the 13th century style. On 17th July 1847, the Bishop and the Governor agreed to the demolition of the old church. When the roof timbers were exposed they were found to be so much decayed that only the mortar held them together.

On Thursday, 12th August 1847, after Morning Prayer in the school, Governor Hope laid the foundation stone at the south west corner of the tower, and the Bishop gave the address. The day had started wet, but the rain stopped during the service in the school. The total cost was £2,535-11s-0d. The spire is 100' high, the width of the transepts 53' and of the nave 22'. The tower is in three compartments, and the west end gallery is approached by a circular staircase in the angle of the tower. The organ was built by R. Jackson and Sons of Liverpool and cost £150. It was opened on 7th March 1852 and was originally in the gallery at the west end, but this proved to be too damp, so in 1907 it was moved into the north transept. The church seats 414 people and it was laid down that two thirds of the seats should be free.

By 1849 the church was still in debt, making consecration impossible, but Bishop Auckland took a bond for £2,000 to enable the consecration to proceed. This took place on 8th March 1849, when Auckland preached on II Samuel 6[11]. He was assisted by Vicar Brown of Kirk Michael (Episcopal Registrar), the Revd G. S. Parsons (Government Chaplain) and the Revd J. F. Garde (Chaplain of St Johns). People from all over the Island, including Members of the House of Keys and clergy, attended the consecration. A local poet summed up the proceedings in these lines:

"In faith the stone was laid by Hope,
Through Charity the funds were raised,
By Eden's lips the work was blessed,
By all assembled God was praised."

In June 1854 Garde refused to allow St John's Friendly Society to hold their annual service in the church and locked the door saying that he had not been properly asked in advance. William Boyde, the President of the Society, said that it had always been held in the church and hence had been taken for granted. In the end they held the service in the schoolroom. Boyde wrote a letter of complaint to the Governor and to the Archdeacon, but they felt that although locking the door was an error of judgement, the fault was not wholly Garde's, and they took no action in the matter.

In an old prayer book kept in the pulpit about 1849 were the words "Grant that from this place Thy Gospel may ever be faithfully preached, and also that Thy people in this parish may have grace humbly and thankfully to assemble themselves together in this Thy House to worship Thee and hear Thy Word".

One curious fact deserves mention. On 1st December 1846 a Tynwald Court was held in the old church, at which there were present Bishop Short, about to move to St Asaph, and Bishop-elect Shirley. This is probably the first and only time that two Bishops have been present at a Tynwald Court.

ST JUDE'S William Drury was succeeded as Chaplain by Daniel Nelson, but after a few months he was appointed Rector of Bride. He was followed by John Qualtrough who remained Chaplain until 1859. At his first Vestry meeting at St Jude's, Archdeacon Moore claimed to take the chair as Rector of the Parish, but Qualtrough, after some hot words, told Moore that as Chaplain he had the right to take the chair as the meeting was within the four walls of the church.

JURBY J. E. Harrison remained Vicar during Auckland's episcopate.

LEZAYRE In January 1849 Vicar Christian equipped at his own expense a barn in Bowring Road, belonging to John Taggart, a shipbuilder, as a chapel of ease, and he opened it with a service on Sunday evening, 21st January, preaching I Kings 18[21]. Though it was a bad night the place was filled. He said that there would be services at 6.30 p.m. on Wednesdays and Sundays. The chapel was on the first floor and the ground floor was a schoolroom, the teacher being the Curate of Lezayre in charge of North Ramsey. It was licensed for worship on 26th February 1849. These premises were used until St Olave's was built in 1870.

In 1851 Hugh Joughin, Parish Clerk since 1828, died, and on 2nd January 1852 William Caley, a weaver, was elected to succeed him. The election was disputed, as he was a Primitive Methodist, and there were allegations of bribery and undue influence, but the Bishop confirmed the election on 29th January. He was the last Parish Clerk to hold the office as a freehold. The 1880 Church Act ended the power of the Vestry to elect a Parish Clerk and laid down that at the next vacancy the Parish Clerk and the Sexton should be appointed by the Vicar and Wardens, and should be removable, (with the Bishop's consent), for misconduct. All glebe lands and other endowments pertaining to the office were vested in the Church Commissioners. Caley held the office until his death in 1896, aged 77.

LONAN Vicar Qualtrough's long incumbency ended with his death on 23rd June 1853, aged 72. He is buried in Lonan churchyard. He was succeeded by Thomas Caine, the Chaplain of St Luke's.

ST LUKE'S, BALDWIN Thomas Caine was succeeded as Chaplain by Hugh Stowell Gill, son of William Gill, Vicar of Malew, on 3rd November 1853, and he stayed until 1856 when he became Chaplain of Laxey. Gill became one of the outstanding clergy of his time in the Manx Church and in 1895 became Archdeacon. While at Baldwin, Gill lived at the parsonage with a housekeeper. Parson Drury and the Moore family at Cronkbourne, were very good to him and he was always welcome at either house.

The stipend in 1856 was £70 per annum.

MALEW A Vestry meeting held on 6th October 1847 decided that, as there was much begging in the parish, and as it was impossible to decide who were natives of Malew and who were imposters, in future the deserving poor of Malew would be given Testimonial cards, signed by the Vicar and at least one churchwarden, to be renewed monthly or quarterly according to circumstances.

In the Autumn of 1850 Pope Pius IX issued a Papal Bull for "re-establishing and extending the Catholic faith in England" and dividing the country into dioceses. Lord John Russell's Government was panicked into bringing in the Ecclesiastical Titles Bill, which made it illegal for Roman Catholic Bishops to take territorial titles. A Protestant Defence Committee was set up in the Island, which drew up two petitions, to the Queen and to the Archbishop of Canterbury, against what became known as the Papal Aggression. The committee asked Gill to sign the petitions and to obtain signatures in his parish, but with his usual commonsense, he refused.

ST MARK'S In 1847 Clarke completed the conversion of two cottages adjoining the church, which formed the original school, as a home for the chaplain, but the third was left unfinished until 1899 when it was opened by Mrs Straton, wife of the then Bishop, on 14th November. The rent of all three was for repairs to the church. Such repairs were carried out in 1853, and Clarke had enough money in hand to build four new bridges and to repair about 20 miles of road in the vicinity. All this made St Mark's much more accessible.

In July 1847 Clarke drew up a list of all he had done for St Mark's and ended "Though the labour entailed on me, owing to not having the least personal assistance in the discharge of my duty, has been unprecedently great; though my family have been compelled to endure many privations and my own mind often sank into the lowest depth of nervous despondency, yet, seeing the work now accomplished, and my children, after all my difficulties, so nobly taken by the hand by friends whose friendship the mercy of God exclusively has procured for us, my heart is so cheered, and full of gratitude to God and Man, that I would readily engage in the same work over again with as much devotion and energy as ever".

MAROWN The great event of William Duggan's incumbency was the building of the new parish church, which was authorised by an Act of Tynwald dated 26th February 1847. The foundation stone was laid by Auckland at 3 p.m. on Friday, 25th May 1849. The architect was Ewan Christian (1814-95). The Bishop consecrated the church at 11 a.m. on Tuesday 18th October 1853, the weather being favourable. After the consecration the Vicar read Mattins, the Bishop, the Archdeacon and Vicar Drury of Braddan also taking part. Auckland's text was Hebrews 10²⁵. The cost (£1,550) was met by an assessment on the ratepayers of the parish. People from all parts of the Island attended the consecration, and in addition to the clergy taking part in the service there were present the Vicar of Michael (Brown), the Vicar of German (Stowell), the Chaplain of St Luke's (Caine), the Vicar of Malew (Gill), the Chaplain of Castletown (Parsons), the Vicar of Rushen

(Corrin), the Principal of King William's College (Dixon) and Hugh S. Gill, not yet ordained.

ST MATTHEW'S In 1847 John Cannell began a weekly service at 6.30 p.m. on Tuesdays. In August 1841 Archdeacon Hall had instructed the Churchwardens to put posts and chains around the back of the church to prevent carts from being backed up against it. In October 1845 the parishioners presented Cannell with a valuable service of plate. In 1846 Archdeacon Moore presented a new font.

MAUGHOLD Bowyer Harrison's long incumbency continued under Auckland.

KIRK MICHAEL A Vestry meeting on 7th September 1853 agreed to remove the three decker pulpit. Auckland had agreed to preach the following Sunday and as there was no pulpit he preached from his pew adjoining the chancel. In 1854 a carved stone font was bought for £10 of which Auckland paid half. In January 1850 the Bishop provided a tea in the Sunday School for about 80 pupils, following which the parish provided an adult tea for about 120 people including the Bishop and his family.

ONCHAN Edward Craine was succeeded by John Howard (24th July 1847). He had great kindness of heart, a genuine love and sympathy for the poor, and great reverence in Church, but he also had a quick temper and was too ready to take offence. His readiness to resort to physical force often landed him in trouble, as he was a very strong man.

PATRICK On 28th September 1849 a day of humiliation and prayer was observed for the removal of a serious sickness prevailing in many parts of the parish. The Bishop preached in the morning on Amos 4[12], and the Vicar in the evening on Numbers 16[46-48]. The service used was that appointed for Ash Wednesday. The same day Archdeacon Moore preached at Dalby on Acts 27[31]. Generous collections were made at each service for the widows and children of the dead.

On 22nd August 1854 Vicar Holmes and his wife invited the children of the Day and Sunday Schools to tea. Although the weather was rather unfavourable, the children walked in procession from the schoolroom to the Vicarage, where tea, cakes and fruit were provided on the lawn. After tea, children and adults enjoyed sports, games and amusements on a meadow adjoining the vicarage until about 8 p.m. In July 1860 Holmes again entertained about 120 children to tea on the vicarage lawn, followed by games.

ST PAUL'S In 1848 £216 was raised to erect railings and gates opening onto the marketplace to safeguard the space between them and the church. The semi-circular extension at the east end was probably added at this time. It was at first used as a vestry, entered from outside the church. The reopening of the church after this work took place on Sunday 10th December 1848, the Bishop preaching in the morning on Psalm 65[4] and the Chaplain of St Barnabas' (Alcock) in the evening on Luke 4[18-19]. The services had been held in the Courthouse while this work was in progress.

St Paul's was licensed for weddings on 26th March 1849. The first organ, built by Forster and Andrews of Hull, was installed in 1852, and was first used on 18th July. Choir and organ were then in the gallery, but this was changed in 1874 when another organ was bought.

During the 1853 cholera epidemic Kermode won the respect and admiration of his people by his courage, and care for the sick and dying - often he and the Doctor were left to perform the last rites when fear of infection kept the relatives away. He often laid the dead in their coffins with his own hands when others were afraid to touch them. After the epidemic he took a leading role in improving the sanitation of Ramsey and in organising relief. The same devotion to his people was shown in later, less serious, cholera outbreaks, and he seemed regardless of his own safety.

In 1847 Kermode was appointed surrogate for Marriage licences for the northern parishes. He was the Secretary and Treasurer of the Health of the Town Association formed in October 1848 to cleanse the town of filth and to clean and ventilate the houses of the poor. He, with the churchwardens and the High Bailiff of Ramsey, visited the houses of the poor, and distributed lime for whitewashing, which was believed to make infection less likely. In July 1854 Kermode started a penny savings bank for the benefit of the poor.

Christmas Day 1853 was appointed by Auckland as a Day of Thanksgiving for the ending of the cholera. Kermode preached on Num. 16[48]. On 12th June 1854 the congregation presented Kermode with a tea and coffee service as a mark of their esteem for his work during the epidemic.

RUSHEN William Corrin's incumbency covered Auckland's episcopate.

SANTAN Samuel Gelling remained Vicar under Auckland.

ST STEPHEN'S John Qualtrough was succeeded by Edward Brailsford, who was appointed on 1st December 1847. A big man, he used to walk up the Glen to visit his people in all weathers. He returned to England in 1849 and died in 1893. He was succeeded on 6th August 1849 by Joseph Ward, who left in 1851 to become Vicar of St John's, Little Horbeck, Leeds. He was followed on 8th May 1851 by Matthew Thompson. He was Scottish, and had been introduced to the Island by Dr Carpenter of St Barnabas. He left in 1853, and eventually went to Canada. The next Chaplain, for a few months in 1853, was Edward Qualtrough, who left to become Curate of Kirk Michael (1853-56). The last Chaplain under Auckland was William Thompson, appointed on 18th December, 1853, who stayed until early 1855.

ST THOMAS' The building of St Thomas' originated in a sermon preached by Dr Carpenter of St Barnabas', lamenting the lack of church accommodation for the poor of Douglas. He was, soon afterwards, offered £250 if a site for such a church could be found, and a guarantee given of 500 free seats for the poor. The church, when completed, seated 1,021, of which 513 seats were free. Carpenter was the treasurer of the building committee, and by November 1846 £2,400 had been raised. The Governor gave £10, Bishop Short £250, the Archdeacon £25, Dr Carpenter £10, and the Revd W. B. Christian £5, but there were many donations of one shilling and half a crown from the poor. The total cost was £5,670. The foundation stone was laid by Governor Hope at noon on Thursday, 9th July 1846 following a service in St George's, which began with Psalm 84 and continued with prayers by Archdeacon Moore

and a sermon by Bishop Short, who had taken a great interest in the work. The actual stone-laying ceremony was curtailed because the day was showery. The architect of the church, which is in the early English style, was Ewan Christian. The original design was for a tower on which a spire was mounted, but this could not be built owing to difficulty in securing a sufficiently sound foundation. It was licensed and opened for worship on 1st August 1849, but was not consecrated, owing to a dispute over the patronage between Bishop Powys and Vicar Drury of Braddan. Prayers on this occasion were read by Dr Carpenter, the Bishop celebrated Holy Communion and preached on Psalm 5[12], while in the evening Carpenter preached on Psalm 68[10]. About 60 clergy and laymen dined with the Archdeacon, who also gave a dinner for the workmen. Bishop Short during his visit stayed part of the time with Deemster Heywood at Bemahague and for a short time with Mr Edward Gawne at Kentraugh.

Archdeacon Moore always felt that the church should have been built further up the hill. The original Communion Plate was given by Mrs Dorothea Smart, and the peal of eight bells was given in 1852 as a thanksgiving for the birth of a son by Richard Catley (Curate 1851-54) who stipulated that the Town must pay the cost of hanging them (£130). Catley left to become Curate of St Margaret's, Kings Lynn, and died in 1903 as a minor Canon of Worcester. The organ built by Forster and Andrews of Hull, was installed in 1852 and opened on 28th March. The clock was given by William Landor, who played a big part in founding St Thomas', and who died in 1860, in which year the chancel was re-tiled as a memorial to him. The quarter time attachment was added to the clock in 1897 to commemorate Queen Victoria's Diamond Jubilee. The rose stained glass window in the west gable was inserted in July 1850, paid for by the proceeds of a hymn written and composed by Mrs F. Garston. By this date the bell tower was being built. Bishop Short sent £5 towards the bells (June 1852) and many fishermen, boatbuilders and boatmen subscribed to them, as they would be very useful to boats when it was foggy. The bells were first rung on 4th December 1852 by professional ringers from St Peter's, Liverpool. They rang them again a day or two later, many people coming to hear them, but after one and a half hours a rope broke, and they had to stop, but next day they rang for two and three quarter hours. Mr Catley gave the ringers a supper.

The first Chaplain was W. D. Carter, who had been Curate of Lezayre with charge of North Ramsey, from 1847-9. He held services at 11 a.m. on Wednesdays and Fridays, and began a weekly lecture for working men at 7 p.m. on Fridays. He left in 1851, and was succeeded in May 1851 by Samuel Simpson, who began a ministry of 16 years which was long remembered. He was scholarly and refined and a very earnest preacher, and his wife was a wonderful help to him in the parish. He was unremitting in his care of the poor. In his time the Sunday services were at 11, 3 and 6.30, and those on the week were at 11 a.m. on Monday, Tuesday, Wednesday and Friday and every Festival and 7 p.m. on Thursday. He contributed largely to the building of the Vicarage which cost £1,500 and left it as a free gift to the parish. In the light of later events it is worth noting that in September 1853 Bishop Short wrote to Auckland saying that in his opinion the Patronage of St Thomas' should be vested in the Bishop. The stipend in 1868 was £200.

Chapter 9

BISHOP POWYS 1854-77

The new Bishop was Horatio Powys, the third of the six sons of Lord Lilford. He was born on 21st October 1805, and educated at Harrow and St John's College, Cambridge, where he took his degree in 1826. In 1833 he married Miss Percy Gore Curry, the eldest daughter of William Curry, of East Horsley Park, Surrey and they had two sons (Horatio and Henry), and four daughters, (Mary, Sophia, Maria and Laura). He was ordained in 1828 and after curacies at Burnley (1828-9) and St Helen's (1829-31) he became Rector of Warrington in 1831, where he remained until he became Bishop of Sodor and Man in 1854. In his later years at Warrington he was Rural Dean.

Powys was a man of great ability and personal energy, with a real love for his work and his people. He had indomitable perserverance, he was indefatigable and had the great gift of being able to inmpart his enthusiasm to others. He was an able and convincing preacher, usually preaching extempore. In character he was rather a mixture. Gentlemanly, dignified and pleasant in his manner, a devoted husband and father, most hospitable, and a faithful friend, he could yet be autocratic and even harsh on occasion towards the clergy, and took a rigidly legalistic view of any given case. This and his High Church leanings, soon involved him in disputes, and made him unpopular in the diocese. His temperament was cheerful, but he was sensitive and suffered greatly from the criticism and abuse to which he was subjected during the dispute over St Thomas'. Unfortunately most of these qualities were more than counterbalanced by his failure to understand the Manx people and their clergy.

As Rector of Warrington he proved to be a splendid parish priest. Almost immediately after his induction he was faced with a cholera outbreak, and the zeal and attention with which he visited the sick won the admiration and respect of the whole parish. He had places built at his own expense to accommodate the victims. In 1833 he built schools which had 900 pupils, at whose head he marched to church every Sunday. These schools had sick and clothing clubs which were a great help to the parents.

His next great work was to enlarge the parish church on the southside and instal an organ. He then raised funds to build Padgate church, vicarage and schools, and appointed the first incumbent. He then built large infant schools which were used as night schools for girls. He then built St Elphin's Girls School and was the main force behind the building of Chester Training College for teachers. He took a leading part in gaining support for the Ten Hours Bill of 1833 and gave the cause the influence of his name and the benefit of his purse. When the Bill passed, the workers held a tea party and presented Powys with a medal. These were for him, years of earnest, hard and tireless work.

Bishop Sumner of Chester once offered him an honorary Canonry, but Powys declined because "I have always shrunk from honorary distinctions among my brother clergy which carried with them no working responsibilities". A sidesman at Warrington Church wrote to the 'Manx Sun' in June 1854, "Powys has devotedly sacrificed his time, energy, private fortune, everything, indeed, which he had it in his power to bestow". He denied that Powys was a Tractarian and said that, had that been the case, Bishop Sumner would never have appointed him Rural Dean. The large congregation regretted his departure for the Isle of Man and presented him with a silver candelabrum, worth 100 guineas, to mark his faithful ministry of 24 years. The schools and various friends presented him with a service of plate costing £150. So anxious were people to subscribe generously that the amount that each person could give had to be limited.

Powys' appointment was announced early in June 1854. He said that it was unsought, and was not due to any political influence. He and Bishop Auckland had known each other for many years and it is possible that Auckland recommended him as a successor - at least, Powys thought that this was the case. On 13th June he crossed from Liverpool to Ramsey, and went to Bishopscourt where Auckland had arrived a few days earlier. On 15th June he returned to England, and was consecrated in York Minster on 25th July by Archbishop Musgrave. On Thursday evening, 27th July, he arrived on the 'Mona's Queen' and was met by the Archdeacon and several clergy. He went to Government House (then in Castletown) and next day was enthroned in St Mary's, Castletown, by the Archdeacon, who preached the sermon. That evening Governor Hope invited the clergy to meet the new Bishop at dinner. On 10th July Cambridge University conferred on him the degree of DD. His first confirmation was at Rushen and the 'Manx Sun' reported that he conducted the service in a "devout and solemn manner". The text was Titus 3$^{4-7}$.

He found Bishopscourt in a very indifferent condition. The chapel built by Bishop Murray was little more than a long room with one sash window. The floor was below the level of the surrounding soil and over the chapel were bedrooms. As 1855 approached plans were made to commemorate the centenary of Bishop Wilson's death, and the original idea was to build a cathedral on the Island. But Powys suggested that the memorial should take the form of enlarging and beautifying Bishopscourt Chapel. This was supported by the Governor, the Archdeacon, the Speaker of the House of Keys, the clergy and all the leading laity.

To meet the cost of all this, Tynwald, in 1855, allowed Powys to raise a sum not exceeding £2,000 on the security of the glebe tithes and profits of the see, one thirtieth to be paid off annually. In 1860 he was authorised to raise a further £1,000 in this way. Powys greatly improved the house and built the west wing, primarily for the domestic staff. Powys intended the new chapel to be the cathedral of the diocese, but this was not realised until the 1895 Church Act which made it the pro-cathedral.

The foundation stone of the new chapel was to have been laid on 25th August 1857, but had to be postponed owing to the death of the Bishop's elder son, Horatio, on board HMS Alarm off Panama on 24th July. It was consecrated on 24th August 1858, by which date only part of the nave and one of the transepts was completed. The window on the north side of the chancel was given by Mrs Hall, widow of Archdeacon Hall, whose gentle courtesy and devoted service were still remembered. The window on the south side was in memory of the Bishop's son. The

Revd S. Simpson donated a beautiful Communion Set, and the oak lectern was given by Mrs Hall. The organ, built by Mr Jackson of Ballaugh, cost £200 and was then the largest in the Island. Powys had announced that the gardens and glen would be open to the public for the day, and many took advantage of this for walks and picnics. Carriages from all over the Island began arriving about 9.30 and at 10.30 the clergy, led by the choir, came in procession across the front lawn, and circled the end of the chapel, while the choir sang Psalm 68. At the entrance to the chapel they began Psalm 24. Most members of Tynwald were there. For the consecration Powys used the form drawn up by Bishop Wilson for the consecration of St Matthew's. The anthem was "God is gone up" by William Croft. The first lesson (I Kings 8$^{22-62}$) was read by Rector Howard of Ballaugh and the second (Hebrews 10$^{19-26}$) by Vicar Corrin of Rushen. Powys then began the Communion Service, the Archdeacon reading the Epistle and the Principal of King William's College, Revd R. Dixon, reading the Gospel. After the Creed the formal sentence of consecration was read by the Episcopal Registrar. The Bishop preached from a temporary pulpit on Exodus 20^{24}, basing the address on Wilson's sermon at the consecration of St Matthew's. About 100 communicated and the offertory came to £47. After this a short Convocation of the clergy was held, then they and 60 lay people had lunch in a large tent erected in the garden. After the meal toasts were proposed by the Bishop, the Archdeacon and Deemster Drinkwater. Powys said that when he became Bishop he had determined to become a Manxman in heart and feeling. He said he had tried to revive some of Wilson's plans, but in deference to the expressed wish of the senior clergy he had dropped the idea of building a small Theological College. Later in the afternoon Mrs Powys provided tea for her guests and the day concluded with Evensong at 6.30. The 'Manx Sun' in its account of the occasion said that much of the pleasantness with which the day passed off was due to the unwearied attention and courtesy of Mrs Powys and members of her family. The chapel is in the Victorian Gothic style, with two transepts and an apse at the east end. Many friends of Powys in England helped with donations.

Powys had Wilson's 'Prayer for the use of Fishermen at Divine Service during the Herring Season' reprinted in 1855, and at 11 a.m. on Monday 23rd July he held a special service on Peel Castle Island to which he invited all fishermen and anyone interested in reviving the old custom of a special service for fishermen. The Bishop, and those of the clergy who attended, occupied the large mound near the ruins of St Patrick's Church, and in front of the Round Tower. Around the mound many visitors and residents, and about 100 fishermen, were seated. After a hymn they followed Wilson's beautiful simple service, which included Psalms 65, 78 [19 to end], and 104[24 to end]. The Bishop explained the purpose of the service and said that he would give the fishermen copies of Wilson's service to be used by them on leaving harbour. He expressed the hope that this service would be held each year, then he concluded with another hymn and the Blessing. The Archdeacon announced that a collection for expenses would be made and £6-14s-0d was given, but some of the fishermen disapproved of this, as they thought it was a charitable collection for them. A similar service was held on 23rd June 1856 attended by the Governor and the Archdeacon, but this, and to some extent the 1855 service, were just fashionable gatherings, and the fishermen tended to be crowded out. This caused much dissatisfaction and the service was never repeated.

Powys entered on his work in 1854 with missionary zeal, intending to devote all his energies to improving the diocese but it is probably true to say that it was too small for a man of his enthusiasm and energy. He was often injudicious, and this, with his High Church views, which were unpopular, made clergy and lay men look at him with suspicion and dislike. Some of his unwise actions only strengthened these feelings as the years passed. Some of his disputes with even the most respected of the clergy, like John Cannell of St Matthew's and William Hawley of St George's, were not really on matters of principle and could easily have been settled or avoided, and he did not always come out of them with dignity or success. He took a strictly legalistic view of everything and did not accept the fact that custom which had always worked well and kept the peace, was important in the Isle of Man. Gradually the opposition of both clergy and laity increased and his reaction to this was to drop all the aspirations with which he came and simply to discharge the duties which he could not avoid. In his later years he was away from the diocese for long periods, though after about 1873 this was mainly because his health was failing. Nevertheless these absences caused much dissatisfaction and it was thanks to Archdeacon Moore that the diocese continued to function.

The most serious dispute was that with Vicar Drury of Braddan over the patronage of St Thomas' Church. Taking his stand on the 1847 Act of Tynwald and probably following up the suggestion made to Bishop Auckland by the four Douglas clergy, Powys, in May 1859, introduced in Tynwald 'An Act for the Division of the Parish of Braddan' dividing Douglas into two parishes, St George's and St Thomas'. No district or cure of souls was assigned to St Matthew's, but it was implied that the Chaplain should continue. St Barnabas' was not mentioned. Vicar Drury, however, protested so strongly that the Bishop did not proceed, but when in November 1867 Mr Simpson resigned from St Thomas' for health reasons the matter came to a head, as a new Chaplain had to be appointed, and Drury determined to exercise what he considered to be his rights. Simpson had announced his impending retirement in July so on 1st August 1867 Drury wrote to the Bishop asking him to consecrate the church, and claiming the right to appoint the new Chaplain to which he said that he was entitled legally and morally. On 19th August Drury wrote again, saying that he had received no reply to his previous letter and adding that Simpson had agreed to defer his formal resignation until May 1868, and that Simpson's Curate, the Revd F. Grier, was also leaving. Under these circumstances Drury proposed to take charge of the services at St Thomas' as Vicar of the parish, either in person or by deputy, when Simpson left. He added "I omitted in my late Diocesan's (Auckland's) time to claim an incumbent's right to the church built in my parish. A sense of duty now impels me to act. Let me assure your Lordship that it is not in any spirit of antagonism". This letter also remained unanswered.

In the ensuing dispute Parson Drury was advised by Mr Alfred Adams, a Braddan parishioner, and one of the leading figures in the Manx Bar. The Bishop was advised by Mr (later Sir) James Gell, then Attorney General, later Deemster, and perhaps the greatest lawyer this Island has produced; and to a lesser extent by Vicar General Richard Jebb and by the Diocesan Registrar Samuel Harris, later for many years

Vicar General and High Bailiff of Douglas.

Vicar General Thomas Corlett died on 26th November 1861 at his home, Loughen-e-Yeigh, Lezayre, aged 69, following a stroke two weeks earlier. He was admitted to the Manx Bar on 7th December 1813, and was for some time High Bailiff of Ramsey before Bishop Ward appointed him Vicar General on 1st August 1835. His widow, Mary, died at Ramsey on 27th January 1868. Even before Corlett's funeral Powys nominated Jebb to succeed him. Jebb was born at Kilkenny on 27th January 1808, and after graduating at Trinity College, Dublin, he was called to the Bar in 1832. A sound lawyer and a worthy gentleman, he was very highly respected by the Bar and by the public, who recognised his basic kindness. He was sworn in on 16th December 1861 despite objections from the Manx Bar at an outsider being appointed. Being a bachelor, Jebb lived at the Castle Mona Hotel. He was very popular there and in the Island for his geniality and his quaint ways. On 26th August 1867 Harris wrote to him on behalf of Powys, enclosing a copy of the conveyance of the land on which St Thomas' was built; the licence granted by Bishop Auckland when the church was opened; the licence issued by him to Mr Simpson and Drury's two letters of the 1st and 19th August. Jebb was asked to give his opinion as to the rights (if any) of the Vicar of Braddan to nominate the chaplain of St Thomas'; whether the Vicar could inhibit anyone nominated by the Bishop from officiating in the church and for guidance regarding the respective rights of the Vicar and the Bishop generally.

Jebb replied on 30th August in a long and detailed letter. He expressed the view that as things stood the Vicar of Braddan could inhibit anyone appointed in future by the Bishop from officiating in St Thomas'. When the church was built the right of the Bishop and his successors to appoint the chaplain had not been secured **by Deed** and this being so, if the church were consecrated, the right of appointment would be vested in the Vicar. The only way to alter this and to exclude Drury and his successors from appointing the chaplain, was to execute a formal Deed to which the Patron of the living in which the church was situated (i.e. the Bishop, who is the Patron of Bradddan) and the Ordinary must be parties. The legal estate in the church was vested in the Bishop and his successors by the 1845 conveyance, but although no Trust had been declared by Deed, Jebb considered the Bishop to be a trustee for the people of Douglas, for whose benefit St Thomas' had been built, and he thought it likely that the founders of the church intended to vest the property and the patronage in the Bishop. The mistake had been made in 1849 of supposing that the reservation of the patronage to the Bishop and his successors could be done merely by licencing the church as a place of worship. In Jebb's opinion such reservation had no effect other than indicating the intention of Bishop Auckland and the founders, but added that such intention ought to be respected, especially as regards the founders, who, he said, had a right to prescribe the terms on which they presented St Thomas' to the people of Douglas.

Jebb therefore recommended that a Deed should be prepared declatory of the Trusts of the church, and giving the patronage to the Bishop and his successors. To this Deed Powys (as Ordinary and Patron of Braddan) and Drury should be parties, but if Drury refused to execute the Deed, the only alternative was for the Bishop to withdraw his licence for public worship in St Thomas' and close the church. In any case he advised Powys not to consecrate the church until Drury had executed the Deed, because after consecration Drury would have the right to appoint the chaplain.

In early October rumours began to spread that the church would be closed when Simpson left, so the churchwardens and most of the congregation drew up a memorial to Powys regretting this possibility, and urging him to appoint a chaplain as they believed that the patronage was his. Powys replied on 10th October 1867 saying that he would be sorry to close St Thomas' and that only an imperative sense of duty would make him do so. He could make no promise, as all depended on what Drury did. "Though ready to give Mr Drury credit for a sense of duty, I can see that he has mistaken his rights in this matter". He went on to say that he was satisfied that the founders wished the patronage to be vested in the Bishop, and that he felt it his duty to give effect to that wish - in other words, to give legal effect to the position which had existed since 1849. The district allotted to St Thomas' had, he went on, long ceased to be superintended by the Vicar of Braddan, and had been virtually a separate parochial district under its own chaplain. He therefore proposed to make it in law a separate parochial district, but as some time would elapse between Simpson's resignation and the completion of the necessary legal formalities, he ended the letter by agreeing to their wish to have a chaplain, adding that the only alternative was to close the church. It was perhaps unfortunate that the founders of St Thomas' had not left a record of their intentions regarding the patronage, but the weight of evidence is that they wished it to be vested in the Bishop. Archdeacon Moore, when asked for his views on the point by Powys in December 1867 said without hesitation that Bishop Short, in whose episcopate the idea of building St Thomas' had originated, intended the Bishop to be the Patron. He said that the church had not been consecrated in 1849 so as to keep it more completely under the Bishop's control and that Short had looked on it as the future parish church of Douglas. The Archdeacon considered that the original subscribers had never looked on the Vicar of Braddan as Patron.

In fulfilment of his promise Powys appointed as Chaplain the Revd H. R. Dodd, the curate of Warrington, and formerly a master at Charterhouse. On 23rd October Drury wrote to Dodd (and sent a copy to Powys) saying that as St Thomas' was in his parish, he claimed the right to officiate in (or nominate a person to officiate in) that church and that if he (Dodd) attempted to officiate there, he would take legal steps to inhibit him.

Powys was anxious to follow the law, so he would not let Dodd officiate until he had Drury's written permission. He wrote to Drury asking if he objected to Dodd personally or if, as rumour had it, he intended to nominate his elder son, the Revd W. F. Drury, as Chaplain. Drury did not reply. In a letter of 26th October to the memorialists at St Thomas', Powys expressed surprise that Drury had threatened legal action simply on the basis of a newspaper report, and without enquiring whether Dodd was a suitable man.

A personal meeting between Bishop and Vicar might have helped at this stage, but in view of their sharp differences over the appointment of the Revd William Hawley to St George's in 1859, Powys felt that a personal appeal to Drury was useless. He admitted the legal mistake made in 1849, and agreed that no legal effect had been given to the 1847 Act of Tynwald preceeding Drury's appointment to

Braddan, but he considered that its spirit had been recognised, because since August 1852 four parochial districts had been formed after a meeting between the Bishop, the Archdeacon and the Douglas clergy, who had administered their districts without any interference or supervision from Drury. There is no doubt that Douglas had, in fact, been separated from Braddan. Early in his episcopate Powys had introduced a Bill (drafted by Auckland), into the Legislative Council to carry out the intention of the 1847 Act, but was advised to withdraw it on the ground that it would never pass the House of Keys. Because of local feeling Powys was reluctant to appeal to London for the application of the provisions of an Act of Parliament which extended the powers of the English Church Commissioners to the Isle of Man and the Channel Islands in cases like that of St Thomas'.

Powys suggested to the St Thomas' memorialists that a settlement might be reached, without endangering Drury's legal rights, by the Vicar issuing a caveat against the Bishop's appointment of a chaplain, who would be allowed to officiate until the dispute was settled, but if this plan was ever put to Drury it was evidently rejected. Powys admitted in the same letter that Drury had the legal power to inhibit any chaplain appointed by him, but that he would do all in his power to save the Manx Church from such a scandal.

On 28th October 1867 Drury nominated his elder son as Chaplain of St Thomas'. This was certainly an error of judgement, as it gave the impression that the Vicar was joining issue with the Bishop to obtain preferment for his son rather than on the principle of his retaining control over the undivided parish of Braddan. Powys simply replied that this could not be, as the position was not vacant. This was only partly true, because although Simpson did not leave the Island until 15th November he had, in fact, resigned on 14th October. Simpson tried hard to persuade his people not to see him off at the pier, but many did, and the uncertainty over St Thomas' future made the parting all the more sad. The church was crowded with people of all denominations for Simpson's last service on 10th November, when he said that they might not be able to meet for worship the following Sunday. In fact the Revd J. B. Doyle (Curate of St Barnabas') and the Revd W. Hawley (Chaplain of St George's) officiated on 17th November, then the Archdeacon took the services for a few Sundays.

Dodd was on the Island on 3rd November and preached very effectively at Malew and Castletown. On 31st October 1867 Harris wrote to Drury on the Bishop's behalf stating that Dodd was to be appointed to St Thomas' subject to Drury's right to veto, but hoping that the Vicar would meet Dodd to ascertain his suitability. Drury replied on 2nd November, saying that he proposed to submit the whole case to Archbishop Thompson of York. On 9th December Powys wrote to Drury asking him to state whether or not he intended to veto Dodd, and Drury replied that Adams would answer the letter. Powys flatly refused to enter into correspondence with Adams, but nevertheless on 13th December Adams wrote to the Bishop saying that he had notified Harris of Drury's intention to veto Dodd.

While the church was unconsecrated Drury certainly had the power to veto, but not to nominate, hence it was that Adams advised him to have the church consecrated. By asking the Bishop to appoint a chaplain the churchwardens and congregation tacitly accepted him as Patron. Drury had refused to confer with Powys either in person or by letter, doubtless on Adams' advice. Powys had repeatedly urged Drury to withdraw his inhibition for the sake of the congregation, and said that this would be without prejudice to his rights as Vicar.

The prospect of the closure of St Thomas' was a matter of deep concern to many who had no part in the dispute, and various suggestions for a compromise were made. The most hopeful of these came from the Revd J. H. Gray, Chaplain of St Barnabas' (1852-70), who suggested that Jebb and Adams should try to work out a settlement, but that if they could not agree the case should be submitted to a mutually acceptable English Queen's Council (whose fees Powys offered to pay) but Drury would only agree to this if Powys consecrated the church unconditionally.

On 14th December 1867 Gell and Jebb advised Powys not to consecrate St Thomas' until a Court had decided that the original subscribers did in fact vest the patronage in the Bishop and until his right to appoint the chaplain had been secured by a proper Deed. Bishops Short and Auckland had, they recalled, asserted the principle of episcopal patronage

(after a counter-claim by Vicar Brown of Braddan) without any objection from the founders of the church or the people of Douglas. They ended by advising Powys to withdraw his licence from St Thomas' after proper notification to Drury unless he agreed to Powys' right of appointment, reserving to himself the legal right to displace such a chaplain should it be decided that the Bishop was in error regarding his rights. When Drury refused to accept this he was informed that St Thomas' would be closed and at noon on Thursday, 26th December 1867 a written notice, signed by the Bishop, was stuck onto the door, saying that the church would be closed indefinitely. The Sexton then locked the door and took away the key. The rumour that Powys was going to be there in person to close the church caused a considerable crowd to assemble.

Throughout the dispute the congregation at St Thomas' was almost wholly on the Bishop's side, due partly to churchmanship. Many of them were High Church, and they feared that Drury, a strong evangelical, would appoint a man of his own views. In the Island as a whole, however, opinion was against the Bishop and in December 1867 some of the windows at Bishopscourt were broken.

On 9th January 1868 St Thomas' congregation met to consider a letter from Dodd saying that he had been offered a living in England, but that he would take the Bishop's advice. A resolution was passed asking Powys to re-licence the church and instal Dodd as Chaplain, whether or not Drury agreed. To meet his stipend they pledged themselves to pay 6 months pew rent in advance. If Drury would not let him officiate in the parish of Braddan, it was proposed that their services be held in a properly licensed room in Onchan. They expressed the highest regard for Drury but felt that he was acting wrongly. A week later Dodd accepted the living of Stretton in the diocese of Chester.

Powys had closed St Thomas' reluctantly, and had hoped that the threat of closure would make Drury give in, but he was determined to separate Douglas from Braddan. He therefore, in November 1867, introduced a Bill into the Legislative Council to achieve this, which became known as the Parish of Braddan Bill, but this was not generally known, as the Council then met in private, and no account of its proceedings was made public. The Bill began by recalling the 1847 Act of Tynwald, then went on to form St George's, St Barnabas' and St Thomas' into three separate parishes. St Matthew's was not mentioned. It retained for ten years the right of Douglas people to be baptised and married at Braddan. Drury, for the rest of his incumbency, was to receive all fees and offerings from the existing parish of Braddan to which he was entitled by law and which he would have received had the present Bill not been passed. The Patron of the three new parishes would be the Bishop.

Despite the secrecy of the council's proceedings, the news leaked out and caused a storm of indignation. This was due less to the Bill itself than to the fact that many felt that Powys was making unfair use of his membership of Tynwald, and that his way of proceeding was contrary to all Manx custom. On 20th November a crowded meeting in the Wellington Hall condemned the Bill as needless and unfair, and passed a resolution to oppose it by petition to the House of Keys. An up and coming Douglas advocate, Alfred Nelson Laughton, was engaged to present the petition, and he did this so effectively that on 8th July 1868 the Keys rejected the Bill though it had passed in the Legislative Council.

The points which Laughton made in his speech to the Keys were:

(1) The summary and unjustifiable dismissal of John Cannell as surrogate for Douglas in 1866.
(2) Powys' unjustifiable and false attack on Vicar Gray at the Annual General Meeting of the Diocesan Association in 1861.
(3) Powys' unjustifiable and false attack on Vicar Hawley in 1861.
(4) Powys' extraordinary proceedings re St George's burial ground, and his renewed attack on Hawley's personal honour in 1862.
(5) The closure of St Thomas' and Powys' conduct in that connection.
(6) The scandal brought on the church by Powys' gross libel on Adams and Drury in the 1868 Convocation.
(7) The scandal brought on the church by Powys' treatment of, and continual squabbling with, the clergy.
(8) The scandal brought on the church by Powys' persistent discouragement of young Manxmen who wished to serve the Manx Church.

(9) Powys' general neglect of the diocese, his continual absences and failure to perform his duties, and having no Examining Chaplain resident in the Island.
(10) That Powys had completely lost the confidence of the diocese.
(11) That since 1854 the church had gone backward rather than forward.
(12) The scandal brought on the church by Powys' ordination of unsuitable men.

Except for numbers 8 and 12, Powys never attempted to disprove any of these charges. His attack on Hawley in 1862, was that he had obtained from Powys an induction to St George's instead of a licence by lying and trickery. The attack on Gray accused him of being guilty of conduct which, if true, would unfit him for being a clergyman or a gentleman.

Meanwhile the annual Convocation of the Manx Church had been held at Bishopscourt in May 1868. The Bishop, in his Charge, referred to the St Thomas' dispute, and some of his remarks led Drury to withdraw from the meeting. But Powys went too far in saying that "The Vicar of Braddan has displayed his imbecility by entrusting his case to a malicious and unscrupulous lawyer". The clergy must have been astounded, for Mr Adams was one of the most respected members of the Manx Bar. Adams felt that such a public attack on his professional integrity could not be allowed to pass and next day he retained Mr Richard (afterwards Deemster) Sherwood and Mr Laughton to institute an action for slander against the Bishop and formal proceedings opened before Deemster Drinkwater on 17th June.

Sherwood and Laughton then contacted Gell, who admitted that the words in question were indefensible, but said that they had been spoken without intended malice and that he had urged Powys to withdraw the remarks and make a full apology. Some days later Gell handed them a letter from the Bishop making a somewhat abject and unconditional apology, and offering to send a copy of it to every clergyman who had been at Convocation. Mr Adams, however, had no wish to put the Bishop into such a humiliating position with his clergy, so he waived the offer, and said that he would be satisfied with the letter of apology.

What followed showed Powys at his worst. He

at once wrote to all the clergy a letter marked "Private and Confidential" in which he said that as Adams had made a satisfactory explanation of his conduct as legal adviser to Drury, he was happy to withdraw the words he had used at Convocation. Despite the confidentiality one of the clergy did, in fact, show the letter to Adams, who could never afterwards respect the Bishop, and avoided any personal dealings with him.

In presenting his petition to the Keys against the Parish of Braddan Bill in July 1868 Laughton had clearly decided that the best course was to make a general attack, in no uncertain terms, on the Bishop's whole administration of the diocese, probably to represent him as an unsuitable person to have the patronage of the planned new parishes in Douglas. His speech, which lasted over 2½ hours contained the words "Has he not, by act after act, brought a foul stain and scandal on the church?" It was followed by an acrimonious debate, some of the members feeling that Laughton had made a wholly unprofessional use of his position as Counsel, but his eloquence, and Powys' unpopularity tipped the scales, and the Bill was rejected by 11 votes to 8. The diocese now wondered what Powys would do, but for nearly a year he was silent. There was no obvious way in which he could reply to Laughton, as anything he said in the Legislative Council would not be reported and for him to write to the newspapers was unthinkable. He could not bring an action for defamation against Laughton, as his address to the Keys was privileged. Convocation seemed to be the only possible place, and when the clergy gathered at Bishopscourt on Whit Thursday 1869 they heard a Charge devoted to the St Thomas' dispute and replying to Laughton. Once again Powys' language was unfortunate and, as many thought, rather unseemly in Chapel after a celebration of Holy Communion. Seven of the clergy, including Drury, did not attend this Convocation in view of the Bishop's remarks the previous year.

He began by criticising Drury and those who had opposed the Parish of Braddan Bill, accusing them of creating a public scandal and compelling him to break his silence. He then protested strongly against the way in which the Bill had been treated in the House of Keys, and against their allowing "a gross personal attack" to have been made in their presence on a member of the Council, thereby condoning the serious, but unproved, charges against him. So far his Charge was a reasonable reply, and was to some extent justified, but he then went on, without mentioning Laughton by name, to say that arguments and language had been used "not ordinarily used by any man of high professional repute" and to speak of "the entire disregard for truth which characterised the statements of which I complain". He ended by saying that he felt it his duty, for the sake of the church, to protect his office "from the assaults of wicked men". This Charge he sent to the 'Manx Sun' which, on 29th May 1869, published it in full. Laughton at once demanded an explanation and apology on the grounds that the Charge impugned his professional integrity, but as Powys declined to apologise or even to reply, Laughton instituted proceedings for libel, claiming £1,000 damages. Powys had shown the Charge to Gell, who had advised him to leave out a number of expressions.

The case came on at Ramsey before Deemster Stephen on 15th February 1870 and occupied 12 days until the 13th March. All sorts of wild rumours swept the Island in the preceding months, based mainly on Laughton's accusation in his speech to the House of Keys that the Bishop was seeking to introduce practices associated with the Roman Catholic Church by bringing in clergy of High Church views, whose qualifications were, in one or two cases, doubtful. The Court House, was therefore crowded, and many could not gain admission. Messrs. Adams, Sherwood and Alured Dumbell appeared for Laughton and the Attorney General (Gell) and Mr T. Callow for the Bishop - who did not attend the hearing.

The first day was mostly taken up with evidence from Vicar General Jebb. He said that Powys had submitted the Charge to him before delivering it to Convocation and again before sending it to the 'Manx Sun', with a request to strike out anything too strong or libellous. He admitted that he was not an expert on the law of libel, but he considered it contained nothing libellous and although he thought that parts of it were indiscreet and parts bad law, he had limited himself to crossing out a few too strong expressions.

On the second day the Court considered one of Laughton's main complaints, namely that young ordinands had to go away to be examined by the Bishop's Examining Chaplain, the Revd R. H. Gray, vicar of Kirkby (1850-1877) and Honorary Canon of Chester; but the Revd E. W. Kissack, then Chaplain of St Jude's, said that his expenses and those of others who went with him were paid by Powys, and that two young men, Meeres and Vesey, had to go away to be examined because the Archdeacon had declined to examine them.

Mr George Dumbell MHK, then gave evidence and said that he considered Laughton's language to the Keys violent and his attack on Powys disgraceful and he was followed by Mr E. C. Farrant, MHK, who considered Laughton's manner before the Keys improper and irregular.

Meeres, Vesey and a third man, Donaldson, had been trained at an Institution founded in 1866 by the Revd Thomas Mossman (1826-85) in his parish of Torrington, Lincolnshire, where he was Rector from 1859-85. He had at the same time founded the 'Order of the Holy Redeemer' to which his students belonged and the training was based on extreme Anglo-Catholic principles - confession, full vestments, Stations of the Cross, and acknowledgement of the Pope as Head of the Church, while the tonsure was adopted and the students dressed as monks. The English bishops seem to have been unwilling to ordain men from this Order because of their extreme views and practices and because it was doubtful whether the training they received fitted them for ordination in the Anglican Church. However early in 1867 Mossman announced triumphantly, in a letter to the 'Church Times' that Powys had ordained three of his men - Meeres, Vesey and Donaldson - to curacies at Patrick, Jurby and Kirk Michael respectively, where they soon became known as Mossman's monks.

This matter came to the forefront on the fourth day of the hearing, when the first witness was William Ingram, Vicar of Kirk Michael, 1864-74. He said that in 1867 he had obtained Alexander Donaldson as a Curate with the Bishop's consent, and that he had been made Deacon by Bishop Jacobson of Chester by letters dimissory from Powys, because Archdeacon Moore had refused to examine him, and could not conscientiously say in the ordination service that he had done so. Moore clearly considered that the Anglo-Catholic training at Torrington was totally unsuitable for a Manx Parish. Donaldson was Curate of Kirk Michael for 2½ years. On 27th May 1867 Powys had written to Ingram (and apparently to the Vicars of Patrick and Jurby also) to say that he had heard that Donaldson was a member of the Order of the Holy Redeemer and asking Ingram if he knew this when he applied to have him as a Curate, and whether he was still a member. Donaldson had told Ingram that he was not, and never had been, a member of the Order.

The next witness was Henry Hardy, Vicar of Jurby, 1858-75, who said that Arthur Vesey was his Curate from December 1866-July 1867. In August 1866 he was spending a few days at Bishopscourt, when Powys received a letter from Mossman, as a result of which Hardy wrote to Vesey in September inviting him to be his Curate. Hardy said that he did not know that Vesey was a member of the Order until he read it in the 'Church Times' but Vesey denied that he belonged to it.

Gell next called John Garde, Vicar of Patrick 1865-77. Strictly speaking the issue of Mossman's monks was not part of the libel action, but it was becoming clear that Powys' whole episcopate was on trial. Gell clearly thought that the Bishop was morally obliged to answer Laughton's allegations. It was not easy and the only practicable defence was the one Gell adopted, to prove that Powys did not know that the men concerned were members of Mossman's Order when they were ordained, even though this involved admitting that Powys had been negligent in ascertaining the background of his Ordinands. Garde said that he had applied to Mossman for a man ready for ordination and was put in touch with Meeres who, after being examined by Canon Gray, was ordained by the Bishop of Chester by letters dimissory and became his Curate in April 1867. Adams, in cross-examination, asked Garde if it was true that he had lamented to his parishioners that the Bishop had saddled him with a wholly incompetent man, and, although Garde denied this, there is little doubt that his initial approach to Mossman had been prompted or even ordered by Powys. Sometime after April 1867, the Bishop wrote to Garde, who asked Meeres if he was a member of the Order, but he denied that he was connected directly or indirectly with it. Garde admitted to Adams that he had expressed surprise to Powys that he should ask him to take a very High Church curate for a parish like Patrick. Meeres' stay was very short, as he resigned for health reasons in the autumn of 1867, and in January 1870 he was received into the Roman Catholic Church.

These three incumbents had not greatly helped the Bishop's case, and an astute lawyer like Gell must have realised it, as they had virtually admitted that Powys had prompted them to apply to Mossman, even though all three curates had denied membership of the Order. But Adams' first witness was little more help. He was Thomas Wheatley, now a Roman Catholic, and formerly a clerk in a Bank in Douglas, who appeared dressed as a monk. He had succeeded Mossman as Superior of the Order, and said that all three curates had been trained by Mossman, Donaldson being noted especially for his zeal in Catholic practices. Adams may not have known that he was a man of bad character but it is strange that he called him as a witness. Soon after succeeding Mossman he had been accused of homosexual conduct, and although the charges could not be proved, he had fled to France with such funds of the Order as he could collect. After this the Order broke up. Gell knew all this and it greatly reduced the value of Wheatley's evidence, but even so his revelations were serious if Adams could prove that Powys knew the nature of the Order, and that the three curates had belonged to the Training Institution when they were accepted.

The case resumed on 24th February. Mr J. Duggan, son of a former Vicar of Marown, said that he had applied for ordination in 1859 or 1860, as his father, then nearly 70, needed a curate. He had taken a degree at Trinity College, Dublin and had completed one of the two years necessary for the divinity testimonium, but could not afford the extra year. Powys refused to ordain him until he had the testimonium, adding, "Manxmen are better out of the district".

Archdeacon Moore was called next, and said that he had ceased to be the Bishop's Examining Chaplain in 1862 when he declined to examine Meeres and Vesey, and was never asked again. They had been private pupils of James Kelly, Vicar of Kirk Michael, 1860-64, a High Churchman and a friend of Powys - Moore had refused to examine them because he disapproved of ordinands being prepared by Kelly, he felt that the one year's preparation given to them was too short and he feared that the whole system was tending to make the diocese of Sodor and Man a back door into the Church of England. Moore recalled that under Bishops Short and Auckland it had been agreed that no-one should be admitted as a candidate for ordination until he had finished his University course. Kelly had started preparing men privately with the Bishop's sanction. The Archdeacon mentioned that Powys wished to establish a 'School of Pastoral Theology' near Bishopscourt, and had consulted him and some of the senior clergy - Dixon (King William's College), Howard (Ballaugh), Corrin (Rushen), and Gill (Malew) - but they could not support the idea, believing that it was best for young men to be trained out of the Island. Moore ended his evidence by saying frankly that he had been unhappy about some of the men whom Powys had ordained.

The Revd R. Dixon, Principal of King William's College (1841-65) was next examined but he added little to what the Archdeacon had said. When Moore declined to examine Meeres and Vesey, Powys wrote to Dixon on 3rd September 1862 asking him to examine them, but he conscientiously disagreed with Kelly's views, and resigned on September 9th from being Examining Chaplain to which he had been appointed in 1854.

On 25th February, Garde gave further evidence and cited as an example of Meeres' unsuitability that he was rarely in time for morning service. He felt, however, that he could not get rid of him without offending the Bishop who, he said, had conducted all the correspondence with Mossman concerning Meeres - in fact Garde said that he was unaware that he would have him as a Curate until after he was ordained. Meeres was, he added, unacceptable in Patrick on the grounds of his conduct, teaching, preaching and doctrine.

On 1st March Adams called Joseph Bellamy, Chaplain of Laxey, 1861-78, as an example of Powys' ordination policy. Bellamy said that he was a former Wesleyan Methodist local preacher and had no degree or divinity testimonium. Next came George Paton, then Curate of St Paul's, Ramsey. He was made Deacon in 1865 and ordained priest in 1867, both by letters dimissory to the Bishop of Chester. He too had no degree or divinity testimonium. He had studied with Ingram on Powys' instructions, and had been examined in Liverpool by Canon Gray, on which occasion his expenses were not paid.

The last witness was Mossman, who said that he

had never intended his Order to be run on monastic lines, and that this aspect was wholly due to Wheatley. He said that although the three curates had studied with him, they were not members of the Order - a rather fine distinction. He said that he had been introduced to Powys by Kelly, and in the summer of 1863 he had stayed at Bishopscourt and preached in the chapel. He maintained that in writing to Powys about Meeres he had stated the facts about his Order clearly, and that the Bishop had made no objection or query. In reply to a question from Adams he admitted that no English Bishop, other than Powys, had ordained any of his pupils. He said that as a result of the protests in the Island about 'Mossman's Monks', Powys had written to Bishop Jackson of Lincoln, who said that he disapproved of the Order. At the Church Congress in Wolverhampton in October 1867, Mossman tried to protest to Powys about his letter to the Bishop of Lincoln, but Powys refused to speak to him. A little later Mossman, feeling insulted by this incident, wrote threatening to publish the letters about Meeres, but Powys replied that in this case he would withdraw the Licences of the three Curates and write to every diocesan Bishop in England asking them not to ordain the three as priests, so Mossman did not carry out his threat.

Adams and Gell wound up the hearing, with speeches of marathon length. Adams based his case on Powys' bringing in Mossman's pupils, who were clearly unsuitable, and said that this alone justified Laughton's criticisms. Gell had to admit that Powys had been careless in enquiring into the background of his ordinands, but defended his use of a Liverpool clergyman as Examining Chaplain by saying that the Archdeacon's refusal to examine the men left him no choice. He added that, in his view, the Bishop's Charge to the clergy in Convocation was a privileged communication, and not subject to the law of libel.

The case ended on 15th March when Deemster Stephen summed up. After stating exactly what the law of libel was, he agreed with Gell that the Bishop's address at Convocation was privileged and told the jury that they had to consider whether he had brought in the three curates through carelessness, or as a deliberate attempt to introduce High Church clergy into the diocese. He added that it was up to Laughton to prove that the Bishop's Charge went too far in replying to his criticisms. The jury retired at 5

p.m. and before they returned at 7 p.m. the Court and surroundings were packed. The verdict was in favour of Laughton who was awarded £400 damages on the ground that the Bishop's Charge had been malicious.

By November 1869 St Thomas' had been closed for two years, and great hardship and distress was caused to the parishioners, especially during the visiting season, so Powys decided to re-open the church on Advent Sunday, 28th November 1869 and to take the services himself. Late on Friday, 26th November he received a legal notice, on Drury's behalf, inhibiting him from officiating, but, probably on Gell's advice, he ignored it and he also ignored an offer by Drury to arrange regular services if the Bishop would allow him. Efforts were made to persuade people to stay away and to incite the mob to resist any attempt to re-open the church, but it was crowded morning and evening. Uniformed and plain clothes police mingled with the crowd outside, but in the church complete order and reverence prevailed, and those who opposed the opening contented themselves with lounging and smoking in the approaches to the church. Before entering the reading desk Powys handed Vicar General Jebb a licence for the performance of the service. Adams applied to Harris (Episcopal Registrar) to see this licence, but was refused on Powys' orders. The Bishop preached on the text "Owe no man anything but to love one another" and made no reference to the dispute in the morning, but did so in the evening. He stayed at the Castle Mona Hotel while officiating at St Thomas' and attended at the Parsonage daily from 1-3p.m., not as Bishop but as Chaplain of St Thomas', to hear the views of the congregation on the services and to help individuals pastorally. On Monday many members of the church called on him there, and thanked him for having re-opened St Thomas' at great personal inconvenience. They expressed their utmost abhorrence and disgust at the slanders and criticisms that had been heaped on him, and said that they were resolved to uphold his good name, and to do all possible to keep the church open.

On the following Sundays there were large congregations and Powys showed himself to be an able and eloquent preacher. On 21st December he held a Confirmation for the parishes of St Thomas', Onchan, Braddan, St George's, St Barnabas' and Marown, at which the respective Vicars and their Curates were present. There were about 500 candidates. In mid-December Powys was affected by gout, and was in such pain that he could not preach in the morning, though he did in the evening, when men outnumbered women. Many were working men, with whom Powys was a great success - not for nothing had he been Rector of Warrington for 23 years. He was unable to officiate on 26th December and on 30th December he wrote to the congregation saying that owing to illness - which he felt had been caused by the worry over St Thomas' - he could no longer officiate and the church would be closed again, but he promised to consult the English Church Commissioners in the hope that they could settle the dispute. To prevent the church being closed again and the congregation scattered, Drury now wrote offering the services of his Curate, (Charles Langton, later Vicar of Arbory and Rector of Bride), but he received no reply. On 3rd January 1870 Powys left the Island and did not return until mid-May, considerably restored in health, after a serious illness.

After the verdict against him in the libel case the Bishop decided to appeal, doubtless on Gell's advice. The appeal was based on

(1) that the words in the Charge were no libel on Laughton personally
and
(2) that the damages were excessive.

The procedure for appeals had recently been changed by the Appellate Jurisdiction Act of 1867 which constituted the Governor (Loch) and the two Deemsters (Drinkwater and Stephen) as the Appeal Court. The Hearing was fixed for 9th June 1870, which was Convocation Day, but Powys, instead of giving a Charge, read from a printed slip, copies of which had previously been given to the clergy. This was partly on medical advice, and partly to avoid commenting on a matter which was *sub judice*. At this Convocation the clergy declared themselves opposed to Sunday funerals, and there was a discussion on the hardship they felt through the rent charge received by them being liable to be rated for the upkeep of the Lunatic Asylum. The clergy unanimously resolved to defend any suit which might be brought against them over this rate and Vicar Ingram of Kirk Michael said that proceedings were pending against him. The Bishop and the Archdeacon said that they

had paid the rate under protest. It was decided to appeal, and a fund was started for this purpose. All except Drury stayed for lunch. The business ended at 6 p.m. and the Bishop seemed very fatigued.

The Appeal was adjourned until 17th June and was heard at Castletown. It lasted three days, and was enlivened by a scene between Adams and the Governor. The Appeal was upheld and £100 costs awarded against Laughton on the grounds that the Bishop's address to Convocation was privileged, that there was no proof of malice and that Laughton's language before the House of Keys justified the Bishop's reply at Convocation. The verdict was very unpopular in the Island and Laughton decided to appeal to the Privy Council, the necessary money being raised by a subscription opened in February 1871 for people who disapproved of Powys as a Bishop. It was felt that the quashing by the Governor and Deemsters of the original verdict imperilled trial by jury. Laughton had obtained English Counsel's opinion that Deemster Stephen was substantially correct in his charge to the jury and in leaving to *their* consideration:

(1) the question of whether there was either malice on the part of the Bishop or an abuse of his privilege and
(2) the amount of damages due.

In July 1870 Archdeacon Moore said that Drury rested his case "on the technicality of one point of law which is the result of an accidental combination of contingent circumstances which technically would never have existed had the Act of Tynwald for the separation of Douglas from Braddan been passed. This combination was the translation of Short, the death of Shirley, the departure of Dr Carpenter, and the postponing policy of Auckland, in whose time the whole business ought to have been settled in accordance with the provisions of Governor Hope's Act of February 1847".

The appeal to the Privy Council came on in November 1872, when it was heard by five former colonial judges, and the parties were represented by Counsel. For Laughton, Sir John Karslake, QC, virtually admitted that the Bishop's Charge to Convocation was privileged, but he considered the language abusive, and said that the Bishop had sent the Charge to the 'Manx Sun' simply to discredit Laughton. Powys' Counsel, Mr Stephens, QC, pointed out that

Laughton's speech to the House of Keys had strayed far beyond his brief, which was to oppose the Parish of Braddan Bill, and that the Bishop was bound to reply to his attacks. On 14th December Laughton's Appeal was dismissed with costs, on the grounds that the Charge was privileged, that the clergy had an interest in hearing their Bishop's side of the case, and that the Bishop's language was an honest vindication and was not primarily intended to discredit Laughton. The case has ever since created a precedent in the law of libel. An article in the Solicitor's Journal of 21st December 1872 re the Privy Council's judgement said that Powys was justified in what he had said to the clergy in Convocation, even if he used defamatory language, but that to publish it in a newspaper was a "strong step". The article considered that the judgement had extended very considerably the doctrine of privilege in libel actions. 'The Law Times' disagreed with the judgement.

As a point of law, the Privy Council's decision was surely correct. Two such astute men as Laughton and Adams, with their training and experience, must have known this, even though they won the first hearing, and it is hard to see why they took their case so far, unless it was from a desire to harm Powys' standing in the diocese as much as possible. Laughton's speech to the House of Keys and the Bishop's Charge to the 1869 Convocation can now be read in full, and to do so with an open mind shows that Laughton went too far, as his speech was virtually an indictment of Powys' whole administration of the diocese, in addition to containing quite unwarranted abuse, whereas the Bishop carefully avoided personal criticism and confined himself to dealing with the actual speech which Laughton had made. There was certainly no malice in it, although to send a document of this kind for publication in a local newspaper was an error of judgement. It can also be admitted that Powys had often acted tactlessly, unwisely, and even tyrannically, and had engaged in far too many disputes with his clergy, while his choice of ordinands left much to be desired, but these matters were nothing to do with the Parish of Braddan Bill, to which Laughton should have confined himself, instead of attacking the Bishop personally.

To return to St Thomas', on 17th June 1870 Archdeacon Moore wrote to the Bishop saying that at all costs he wished to see St Thomas' re-opened, as the visiting season had just started, and he suggested that a chaplain should be nominated by the congregation, or, preferably, by the three Douglas Members of the House of Keys. Powys replied next day saying that although he had doubts regarding the principle, he would agree to the suggestion of the congregation choosing a chaplain being tried. He added that he had applied to the English Church Commissioners for help in settling the dispute but they were reluctant to take any steps which could be construed as interfering with Tynwald. He further said that if his health had permitted, he would have re-opened the church on Whit Sunday and that from the start he had sought every means of re-opening the church without compromising the rights of his successors, or going against the intentions of the Founders, and ended by saying that he had no **personal** object in claiming the patronage.

Moore then asked Drury to accept this suggestion and Drury replied that although Adams had advised him not to be drawn into correspondence, he would be happy to talk over the whole matter with the Archdeacon, Adams being present. The meeting took place in Adams' office in Athol Street on 30th June, but was fruitless. Moore said that he did not see how Powys could concede more than he had already offered, but the only concession Drury and Adams made was to be willing to refer the question "to whom the right of nominating will belong when the church is consecrated" to the Archbishop of York, or to two English Queen's Counsel, provided that the Bishop undertook to consecrate the church when the decision was known.

On 10th August 1870 a Committee of Tynwald was formed to draw up a Bill to separate Douglas from Braddan. It included the Archdeacon, who was then *ex officio* a member of the Legislative Council. They presented their report on 23rd February 1871, proposing that Douglas should be divided into districts and that the first appointment to St Thomas' should be made, neither by Powys nor Drury, but by either the Queen, the Archbishop of York, the three Douglas Members of the House of Keys, or the surviving subscribers of at least £5 to the building. This Bill passed the Council in March and on 29th March it came before the Keys, together with a petition from Drury, presented by Adams, who spoke for 3½ hours. It was, however, deferred, pending a

Bill introduced by Mr Sherwood for settling the presentation to St Thomas', but in June this Bill, and that of the Committee of Tynwald, were both rejected by the Keys, in each case by 10 votes to 9, due to four churchmen being absent, and a group of Methodist Members of the House of Keys wanting to keep St Thomas' shut.

Early in 1871 it was found that if any office holder in Church or State were absent from the Island for four months in any year, he should forfeit half his salary for the first offence and all his salary for subsequent offences. Powys returned hastily on 28th February. On 15th April a correspondent wrote to the 'Isle of Man Times' to say that the Bishop had not been to Kirk Michael Church since his return.

The situation was resolved in February 1872 when the English Church Commissioners, by Order in Council, assigned a parochial district to St Thomas' and vested the patronage in the Bishop. Powys offered the living to the Revd W. Baldwin, Organising Secretary of the Curates' Aid Society, but after visiting the Island in early May he declined it.

A few weeks later it was accepted by the Revd F.N.B. Hutton. He was inducted to St Thomas' on 31st July 1872 and was appointed surrogate for Douglas in 1872. Powys had consecrated the church on 28th May 1872, but no notice was given, so no robed clergy attended, though a few came without robing. On the day of the consecration Drury wrote to the Bishop saying that he had not been informed that St Thomas' had been separated from his parish and until this was done he could still inhibit anyone officiating in it. He also wrote to Hutton forbidding him to officiate without his permission, and inviting him to apply for his licence. The planned opening of the church on 2nd June had therefore to be postponed, but on 6th June the English Church Commissioners issued their official Instrument making St Thomas a separate parish with the Bishop as Patron. Their intervention in the dispute aroused widespread indignation in the Island, so unpopular had Powys become, and some even questioned its legality. On Saturday 29th June at 11 a.m. the church was re-opened by the Bishop in person with considerable ceremony and next day he preached to overflowing congregations both morning and evening. The sermon at the re-opening had been preached by Vicar Kermode of Maughold, one of the senior and most respected clergymen in the diocese.

In 1872 the church was in a bad state of repair and so were the gas fittings, the heating apparatus was out of order and the parochial organisation was in abeyance. Hutton's ministry, which lasted until 1877, brought peace and reconciliation, as his High Churchmanship suited the congregation. He made no changes except to wear a surplice throughout the services. On 25th August, 1872 the former Chaplain, the Revd S. Simpson, preached to a large congregation and presented a brass lectern inscribed "To the Glory of God, a thank offering on the opening of St Thomas' Church, Douglas by the Revd Samuel Simpson MA, August 1872".

Looking back over more than a century, there is no doubt that Powys and his predecessors were right in wanting to detach the growing town of Douglas from Braddan and divide it into separate parishes, as it was quite impossible, even for a man of Drury's ability and energy, to give such an unwieldy parish proper spiritual and pastoral oversight. The four Douglas parishes prospered greatly in the closing years of the century and the work of their clergy was much advanced by their status as vicars with full responsibility for their parishes. Powys had acted on the clear intentions of the founders and the wishes of the congregation.

The blame for this unhappy episode can be laid on no single person. Laughton was partly responsible through his speech to the House of Keys, and Drury may have been unwise to be guided so completely by Adams. It was unfortunate that Powys, still after 13 years evidently unacquainted with the manners and customs of his diocese, sought to achieve a desirable end by means which aroused general antagonism, but he must be given credit for standing firm through five of the most difficult and trying years that any bishop can have had to face.

The second major dispute concerned St George's Church and churchyard. In 1781 Vicar Woods of Braddan had agreed to the consecration of St George's on condition that Braddan should not be responsible for its support (which was to come from pew rents) and that the fabric should be maintained by the congregation. As a result of this Bishop Mason had, by a Commission dated 31st August 1781, nominated what were really Trustees, with powers to appropriate the funds from pew rents, etc., to the stipend of the minister and church officials, and the repair of the fabric. In 1859 Powys wished the Braddan Vestry to appoint churchwardens for St George's, not to spend the money of St George's, but the money of Braddan. The matter was discussed at Braddan Easter Vestry on 25th April 1859, as requested by the Bishop, but it was decided to adjourn for two weeks to give all parishioners notice of such an important question. It was then further adjourned because of the death of Drury's mother, and was eventually held on 23rd May, the Bishop being present. The Minister and people of St George's, had always elected what they called churchwardens, though they were not legally churchwardens, as St George's was not then a Parish Church. However the system had worked well, it had made St George's self-supporting, and had been tacitly accepted by every Bishop from Crigan to Auckland. If Braddan Vestry appointed the St George's Wardens, the people of Braddan would be responsible for the upkeep of St George's. On the motion of Mr Adams, seconded by Mr Dumbell, it was agreed unanimously not to elect wardens for St George's. Dumbell criticised the Bishop for attending the meeting, but Powys replied that he had only come as a matter of courtesy to provide any information needed. Henceforth Powys regarded everything done by St George's wardens as illegal.

On 27th May Powys wrote to Drury an open letter which began by complaining of the discourtesy shown to him at the 23rd May meeting, and that he had not been allowed to speak because he was not a ratepayer of the parish. He also protested about "offensive personalities and insinuations" to which he had been exposed, and ended with ominous hints of eventual legal proceedings, with heavy expenses. However the decision had been taken by the Vestry. The 'Manx Sun', in reporting all this, regretted the disputes in a once happy and united diocese, where disputes among clergymen were unknown and where all was peace.

There was also trouble over the appointment of William Hawley as Chaplain in 1859. Drury claimed the right to appoint, so Powys consulted two English Counsel, Mr A. J. Stephens and Dr Phillimore, both of whom said that he had the right to appoint, but as Vicar General Corlett and other Manx lawyers thought differently, Powys gave up his claim. The opinion of these two men was certainly based on part of the Consecration Deed of the Church dated 29th September 1781, which said "saving nevertheless and reserving to the Mother Church of Kirk Braddan and the Vicar thereof for the time being, all accustomed dues, privileges, profits and emoluments ecclesiastical; saving also to ourselves and successors, Bishops of Sodor and Man, the right of nominating and collating a proper and sufficient clerk or chaplain".

The dispute over the churchyard arose as follows. The original Trustees of St George's had not raised money by the sale of vaults and graves, but had borrowed £250 from the Trustees of the Academic Fund and built a wall around the churchyard. For a while interest was paid, but then no payment had been made of principal or interest and Bishop Mason had refused to consecrate the churchyard until the loan was repaid. Burials had continued, despite its being unconsecrated ground, and some of the parishioners asked Powys, in 1862, if this was being done with his knowledge and consent. The Bishop replied by banning any further burials in the unconsecrated ground and this caused a storm of indignation. In February 1859 Powys had written to Drury telling him to forbid any further burials, but Drury told him that this would create a major problem, so Powys agreed to let burials continue provided that the whole service was read in church and not partly at the graveside. In February 1861 Vicar General Corlett attended a funeral where the service was all read in church and was so pained that he protested to Powys.

In an open letter to Thomas Bridson, a pew holder, which appeared in the 'Manx Sun' on 19th April 1862, Powys criticised Hawley, the Chaplain, for inaccurate statements and said that he had done all in his power to settle the trouble, which he blamed on the "injudicious raising of questions by the Vicar of Braddan". On 10th April Powys had authorised Hawley to read the burial service "as formerly" but to make quite sure, Hawley wrote to him on 15th April asking him to confirm that he could read the burial service "in church and churchyard" according to the rubric. Powys replied on 17th April that the law gave him no power to permit the use of the burial service in unconsecrated ground, but that he could use it in church. Hawley laid the whole correspondence before the Easter Vestry on 21st April, and said that he would not read the burial service in the churchyard until the matter had been legally settled. He protested to the Vestry about the Bishop's aspersions on him, and was loudly applauded. Finally, after considerable criticism of the Bishop, a resolution was passed asking a committee of pewholders which had recently been set up

(1) to invite Powys to state clearly what were the inaccuracies of which he charged Hawley and

(2) to ask him how, and by whom, he could be legally enabled to consecrate the churchyard.

Powys replied to Bridson that he refused to have any communication with this committee. The adjourned Vestry meeting on 26th April passed a resolution deeply regretting the Bishop's attacks on Hawley, in whom they expressed complete confidence, and supporting his refusal to take any more funerals. On 10th May the 'Manx Sun' announced that, at the instance of the Bishop, burials would for the present be discontinued.

In 1825 Bishop Murray had personally read the burial service in St George's churchyard, and must have treated it as consecrated. On this occasion he wrote in the Vestry book "We, proceeding with our episcopal authority, do hereby pronounce decree and declare that the Trustees of St George's shall, and they are hereby empowered to, appropriate upon such terms as they think reasonable, all and any part of the churchyard or burial ground belonging or attached to the said chapel of St George's, for vaults or graves, or to dispose of the profits in supporting, repairing or ornamenting the said chapel, churchyard or burial ground". Murray, of course, may not have realised that the burial ground was unconsecrated, and simply acted as if it was. His entry in the Vestry book said nothing about consecration.

On Powys' behalf it might be said that his object was to make the church clear the debt on the churchyard and that he did not want clergy officiating in the churchyard to expose themselves unwittingly to the penalty which, according to Dr Phillimore (Hawley's Counsel) might be imposed on them for burying in unconsecrated ground. Phillimore agreed with Powys, saying that the churchyard was not consecrated and never could have been consecrated, from the legal tenure under which it was held.

On 7th July 1862 a meeting of pewholders was arranged by Mr Samuel Harris, at which Powys gave a full explanation of his actions re St George's and its churchyard, the drift of which was that his sole de-

sire had been to act legally and equitably and not to encroach on the rights of the Vicar of Braddan. After Evensong in the church he then consecrated the churchyard, new Trustees having been appointed by the Chancery Court. Much of the credit for the settlement goes to Vicar General Jebb, who had worked hard to overcome the legal difficulties.

On 15th March 1859 Powys attended a meeting in St George's Church to consider some proposed alterations and improvements, including painting the interior. He took the chance to say that the right which Drury had very properly asserted, to set aside the custom of the Bishop's patronage of St George's, necessitated a legal investigation. He thanked Drury and his legal advisers for the courteous manner in which the claim had been asserted, then went on to say that the church had been built and consecrated by the joint consent of the Ordinary and Patron (one person) and the Vicar of the parish. Records showed that Vicar Woods of Braddan, in 1781, had never been a consenting party to the reservation of the patronage to the Bishop. The present Bishop could not, therefore, legally maintain a right to act according to the custom of his predecessors if, as in the present case, the Vicar of Braddan objected. The Vicar, however, was only entitled to nominate a Chaplain, as he (the Vicar) was himself entitled by law to perform divine service in any consecrated building within his parish; but he could not appoint a permanent chaplain, as if to a benefice, so as to bind his successors. The chaplain was only an assistant curate to the vicar and, as such, removable. Hence all the property of St George's was as much under the control of the Vicar of Braddan and his churchwardens as Braddan Parish Church. Before the consecration of the church (it being the property of the Bishop, conveyed to him by the Deed), he could, by himself or his agent, arrange the letting of pews, though no power to alienate was given him by the Trust Deed. But when the Bishop consecrated the building he put it in the ordinary position of consecrated churches and chapels, relinquishing all his private rights as proprietor, and therefore ceasing to have power to let the pews. Hence, Powys continued, the Vicar and Wardens of Braddan must be consenting parties to the proposed alterations and improvements, the so called wardens of St George's, hitherto elected by the pewholders, having no legal status. As we have seen no wardens had been appointed by Braddan Vestry for St George's. Drury then said that he approved of the proposed alterations and improvements and Powys said that he would approve them when submitted to him in writing.

There had been a dispute when the church was consecrated between Bishop Mason and Vicar Woods of Braddan over the appointment of the first chaplain. The Vicar nominated Julius Cronahan, but the Bishop refused him a licence and nominated Charles Crebbin, Vicar of Santan (1st October 1781). Bishop Crigan seems to have assumed that St George's became vacant on Mason's death, and that no appointment should be made until the question of the patronage had been decided, so he appointed a temporary curate, but Crebbin refused to have him and continued as Chaplain.

The mandate for the induction of John Christian in 1817 described the Bishop as "the undoubted patron". He and his successor (Philpot) were collated by Murray as to a benefice. Howard was appointed in 1832 by licence directly issued by Bishop Ward and when he resigned the chaplaincy in 1836 it was to the Bishop. Hartwell's collation by Ward in 1836 was in the usual form of collation to a benefice, and it committed to him the cure of souls of St George's. Both Vicar Brown of Braddan and Hartwell died during the interregnum between Bishops Short and Shirley, and the appointments of Drury to Braddan and Forbes to St George's were made by the Crown. Forbes' Certificate of Institution from Auckland (1st November 1847) said that the appointment was in the gift of the Bishop. Howard, when Vicar of Braddan, protested to the Bishop when Christian and Philpot were appointed.

The Consecration Deed gave the Bishop the right to appoint both chaplain and organist, but no Deed of patronage had ever been made, hence it seemed that the right remained with the Vicar of Braddan and that the right of the Bishop to appoint in the Consecration Deed was illegal. Anyone appointed by the Vicar of Braddan however would have to be licenced by the Bishop.

Thus from 1781-1847, all the chaplains except Hartwell had been appointed in one way or another by the Bishop, without any legal suit being instituted by the Vicar of Braddan. In 1859, however, Drury told the Bishop that he intended to nominate the next

chaplain and that if Powys nominated he would start a suit in the Provincial Court of York. Powys suggested arbitration rather than litigation and it was agreed that advocates should be employed to prepare a case for the opinion of English Counsel, though Powys thought this unnecessary. The Bishop's advocate (probably Gell) and the Vicar General both supported Drury's right, so Powys asked Drury to nominate, and he nominated Hawley, whom Powys then licenced as chaplain. A case was, as originally intended, submitted to Dr Phillimore and Dr Twiss, who said that in their view the Bishop was the patron. They may have based their opinion on the fact that up to and including Forbes' appointment in 1847 St George's seems to have been treated as an incumbency, though the incumbents were called chaplains or curates and that various Commissions (of doubtful legality) had been issued by Bishops from time to time to regulate matters connected with the letting of the pews and the disposal of the proceeds.

Powys became involved in another dispute which added to his unpopularity when in April 1866 he dismissed John Cannell (Chaplain of St Matthew's 1835-73) from his office of Surrogate for Douglas, which he had held since 1849, on the ground of carelessness in issuing marriage licences. It was alleged that some marriages were within the prohibited degrees and some incestuous. The 'Manx Sun' upheld the Bishop's action, perhaps because two of the licences in question had been issued to the proprietor (Brown) and editor (Ousley) of their rival the 'Isle of Man Times', and said that Braddan was notorious for illegal marriages and had become the Gretna Green of the Isle of Man. The Vicar and Wardens of Braddan had refused to present the offender in perhaps the most notorious of the incestuous marriages, despite Powys' request. It was well known that when couples applied to Cannell for a marriage licence no questions were asked. On 1st March 1856 Powys asked Cannell to send the declarations made before him when granting three recent specified licences and these were sent. On 31st March Powys replied that "after a long and careful investigation of facts, confirmatory of the almost universal opinion respecting your lack of carefulness in granting marriage licences" he had decided to cancel his commission as Surrogate. He added that Cannell had not always confined himself to his Surrogate's district and that the Revd S.

Simpson had agreed to act as Surrogate as from 2nd April.

Cannell replied on 4th April saying that he had been dismissed without a hearing or chance of explanation and without the slightest information having been given as to the charges against him. He also said that his original licence as a Surrogate from Bishop Auckland did not limit him to a district and that he was made a Surrogate so that the fees would compensate him for those as Master of the Grammar School, which was temporarily suspended. These fees formed the chief part of his income. Powys replied that he did not know that the original licence did not limit him to a district, but had he known it he would have dissociated himself from it; but in any case a Surrogate's licence only lasted for an episcopate; that it was vital for a surrogate to be very careful; and that Braddan had become notorious for incestuous marriages. He also accused Cannell of showing the correspondence to Ousley, the editor of the 'Times'. On 12th April Cannell's advocate, Laughton, wrote to the Bishop denying this latter point, and the denial was accepted. Cannell replied to this letter saying that neither Powys nor any other Bishop had told him to limit himself to certain districts and that he had never had any complaint from anyone, or from Powys himself, regarding the discharge of his duties and that he was most anxious to produce all the documents if Powys would specify a particular case: and if incestuous weddings had taken place why had not Powys given him a hint or warning?

Cannell received no reply to this letter so he sought Laughton's advice, and sent to the 'Manx Sun' copies of the letters between him and Powys. The 'Sun' published the correspondence reluctantly on 28th April, believing that Cannell should not have employed Laughton, and reminding readers that a Surrogate was legally removable at the Bishop's pleasure. It also said that there had been many irregularities in Braddan weddings regarding the residence qualification of the couple concerned. On 14th April Laughton appealed on Cannell's behalf to Archbishop Thompson of York, who said that he had no jurisdiction in the matter.

Two of the marriages in question, as already noted, were those of the proprietor and editor of the 'Isle of Man Times'. The editor had married his deceased wife's sister, which was illegal. Powys' letters to Laughton had been leaked to Ousley, the editor, and made the basis of personal attack on his character and conduct as Bishop, so Powys said that he was only prepared to justify Cannell's removal "when a proper opportunity presents itself". Cannell wrote to Powys on 12th April saying that, on Laughton's advice, he had made no statement to any newspaper, and repeating his request for a hearing. Powys replied on 13th April that he could not take steps to justify his dismissal of Cannell in reply to anonymous writers in newspapers, or under pressure of personal attacks.

The matter ended there. On 5th May 1866 a meeting of Cannell's friends was held, and passed resolutions deploring Powys' refusal to state specific charges, or to give Cannell a hearing. It also started a public subscription for him. Later that month a 'Monster Indignation Meeting' attracted only 20 people. The subscription was widely supported and enabled a valuable service of silver plate to be bought, which was presented to Cannell on 24th December as a mark of sympathy on his dismissal as Surrogate. In his letter of thanks Cannell asked that the whole affair be allowed to drop, as Powys may have honestly believed the allegations to be true.

On almost all these points of dispute Powys was right, as can be seen now that the dust has settled, but his unconciliatory manner and rigid, legalistic attitude aroused antagonisms, and made him increasingly unpopular with both laity and clergy.

The 1863 Convocation was very harmonious. At Powys' request a resolution was passed asking him to prepare a Canon to restore the ancient custom of the Manx Church praying for the Legislature of the Island during divine service, and Convocation was adjourned until 6th July at St John's to enable him to do so. There Powys further proposed to add in the Litany, after the words "the Lords of the Council and all the nobility" "and with them the Lieutenant Governor, the Legislature, and all persons in authority in this Isle". Further, in the clause relating to "the kindly fruits of the earth" to which Bishop Wilson in the 1705 Convocation added the words "and restore and continue to us the blessings of the sea" Powys wished to omit the words "and restore". He said that as unanimity in a matter of this kind was essential, he would withdraw the suggestion if anyone was against it. He said that since the May Convocation he had received from the Archdeacon a letter dated 26th June 1863 containing a number of queries which amounted to serious doubt as to whether the Manx Convocation was competent to make canons on its own authority; whether the clergy's ordination declarations precluded them from adding to or altering the Liturgy and whether the Queen would have to be consulted? Powys maintained that the Manx Convocation did have the authority to make Canons and the Vicar General agreed, saying that, unlike an English diocese, Sodor and Man had retained the right of making canons without previous reference to the Crown. The Statute of Henry VIII 25c.9 (commonly called the Act of Submission of the Clergy) did not apply to the Isle of Man, where also the Prayer Book had only canonical authority (that of York Convocation) which ordered its use throughout the northern province prior to 1662. The Act of Uniformity did not apply to the Isle of Man.

Powys said that they must now wait and see what the Archdeacon felt, as he knew that the regard which they all felt for the position and person of Archdeacon Moore would add extra respect to any objection put forward by him - indeed, it would have such weight with him that if Moore remained dissatisfied he would drop the idea. The Archdeacon said that, much though he approved of the proposed Canon, he still felt that they had no power to do what was proposed. Opinion was divided, so Powys dropped the idea.

By ancient custom the Manx clergy formerly added to the prayer in the Litany for the Lords of the Council, etc., a prayer for the Lord and Lady and rulers of the Island. This prayer seems to have been printed in Manx Prayer Books until 1765, when the Island was sold to the Crown. In the 1777 edition this prayer was dropped - by whose authority no-one knows.

Some miscellaneous comments may conclude Powys episcopate. He preached his first sermon in St George's on 30th July 1854 on behalf of the Athol Street Day and Sunday Schools, the text being Acts 8[39]. On the same day he attended the Annual General Meeting of the Diocesan Association and took the chance to refute the idea that he favoured the Romanising party adding that no man hated or detested more than he the "damnable traditions of the Church of Rome". He had no sympathy with those who sought to introduce these ideas into the Church of England. On 6th August he preached his last sermon at Warrington.

22nd March 1855 was observed as a Day of National Humiliation and Prayer because of the Crimea War. Powys preached at St Mary's, Castletown, and shortly before he had sent to all the clergy a copy of Bishop Wilson's letter Ad Clerum (when a similar Day was observed on 7th January 1739) with the special collects, Psalms and lessons recommended by Wilson.

The Bishop's stipend in 1855 was a tithe commutation of £1,500 plus a glebe of about 500 acres. The Church Commissioners in England were precluded from applying in the Isle of Man any of their funds used in other dioceses to provide each Bishop with a fixed income and suitable residence, hence the constant translation of bishops to English dioceses. By 1868 the stipend was £3,000.

At a meeting of the Diocesan Association on 19th July 1855 it was stated that chaplains' houses were needed at Baldwin and Sulby. £234 had been raised in two years for a chaplain's house at Foxdale. The Dhoon Church was reported to be almost completed. Grants were made to Sulby, Foxdale, Baldwin, Cronk y Voddy, Laxey, Dhoon and Port St Mary and for Services at Oakhill.

Sundays 30th September and 7th October 1855 were Days of Thanksgiving, ordered by the Queen and the Governor for the success of our armies in the Crimea, especially the capture of Sebastopol.

In the spring of 1856 the Bishop and the Archdeacon made a visitation of the parishes to enquire into the state and efficiency of each church. The last visitation of this kind had been made by Bishop Ward.

As there was no Cathedral and no Cathedral property, Powys in April 1856 appointed the Archdeacon, the Revd R. Dixon (Principal of King William's College), Vicar Brown of Kirk Michael, Rector Howard of Ballaugh, Rector Nelson of Bride, Vicar Gill of Malew and Vicar Corrin of Rushen to form a Diocesan Chapter.

Whit Sunday, 11th May 1856 was a Day of Thanksgiving for the end of the Crimean War. Some of the Douglas churches kept it on the previous Sunday by mistake.

In July 1856 the clergy sent a request to the Governor that the new Act for the better Regulation of

Taverns and Tavernkeepers should prohibit Sunday opening and Tynwald agreed.

11th May 1859 was observed as a Day of Thanksgiving for the suppression of the Indian Mutiny. Powys suggested in a circular letter to the clergy that the collections that Sunday should be given to The Society for the Propagation of the Gospel.

On 20th April 1859 Tynwald passed the Glebelands Act, which enabled the clergy to lease glebelands for a maximum of 15 years, but eight acres were always to remain unlet.

At Easter 1860 Powys asked the clergy to give the Whitsun collections to the Diocesan Association, whose expenditure had exceeded their revenue. The response was good. At a meeting of the Association, on 21st August 1862, it was shown that the funds for 1861 were in deficit of £26-12s-6d, and it was feared that grants for outlying clergy would have to be cut. Receipts for 1861 were £334-17s-11d from 110 subscribers whereas in 1839 receipts had been nearly £900. The Association had lost money in the failure of Holmes' Bank, and it never really recovered.

Duties of churchwardens in 1860 were:

(1) If your Minister or Parish Clerk neglect the performance of any of their duties, or conduct themselves improperly, you are to present them.

(2) You are to present all Sabbath breakers, or such persons as misbehave in the churchyard during divine service.

(3) You are to present all persons who commit incest, adultery or fornication.

(4) You are to present all drunkards, cursers and swearers, and all who lead disorderly lives and commit offences against religion and morality.

(5) In case of children under 14 breaking the Sabbath, or committing immoral offences you are to present their parents or guardians.

(6) It is your duty to attend the church services on Sundays and Holy Days in order to see that all things be properly conducted therein, and to assist the clergyman in his lawful demands.

(7) It is your duty to see that the church and churchyard be kept in proper repair; that the church be provided with proper books and vestments for its service and that decent and proper vessels be found for the administration of the Holy Sacrament.

(8) If any person encroach on the churchyard or glebe lands of your parish you are to present them.

(9) It is your duty to balance and settle your yearly accounts every Easter Monday, in presence of your clergyman, as your authority to assess the parish ceases on that day.

(10) And in case you neglect any of these duties it belongs to the Minister to present you for such neglect.

On 11th November 1862 Powys appealed to the clergy to help the Lancashire cotton workers, many of whom were starving because the American Civil War had dried up the supply of cotton. There was a very good response through collections and donations, and in January 1863 Powys sent £768-13s-4d to the Relief Fund, but much more than this was raised in the Island in various ways.

On 21st December 1863 Powys held an ordination to which he invited the clergy, and any laity who wished to come. Bishopscourt Chapel was full and afterwards he entertained the clergy to lunch.

On 18th January 1864 a meeting was held in Douglas to form an Association for the Improvement of Church Music. Powys was elected President.

On 8th December 1868 a meeting was held to elect a Proctor for the diocese in York Convocation. Powys had ruled that only the Archdeacon and the incumbents of the seventeen ancient parishes could vote, although all the clergy were summoned. This led to much protest, and a formal resolution of protest against the Bishop's ruling was passed. Vicar Gill of Malew was elected. The Revd J. Qualtrough, Vicar of Arbory, said at this meeting that he was presenting a petition to the House of Keys asking that public notices of sales, etc. should not be posted on church doors, and those present fully supported him.

About 1865 there were signs that Powys' health was not good, the trouble, apparently, being gout. The 1865 Convocation had to be postponed, and when they eventually met on 29th June the main topic of Powys' Charge concerned the careful introduction of music as an aid to congregational participation in the service. After a sumptuous lunch some of the younger clergy paid croquet and bowls on the lawn.

At the 1866 Convocation Powys expressed his desire to stop irregular marriages and re ordination he said that in future he would require proper testimonials before ordaining or admitting men into the diocese. On 5th July 1866 Powys protested at so much secular business being transacted in St John's Church after the Tynwald ceremony. This year 'early closing' was in the air. Powys addressed a meeting of the "Early Closing Association" and agreed to be its Patron.

At the 1866 Convocation Powys said that because of poor support for the Diocesan Association he had applied to the Curates' Aid Society for help in making up the deficiency to maintain curates in rural areas, and they had agreed to send a large annual sum in return for a modest subscription. On 31st August 1866 a meeting of the Association was told that the annual income had sunk to £137, of which £110 had been given by four people. However the offer of help from the Curates' Aid Society was rejected as it was feared that it would give too much power to the Bishop, and that all future subscriptions would go to the Curates' Aid Society, thus ending the Diocesan Association. On 6th October 1866 Mr E. C. Farrant, of Ballakillingan, Lezayre, wrote to Powys saying that he and others accepted that Powys did not intend, in accepting the offer from Curates' Aid Society, to propose anything antagonistic to existing institutions; that it was clear that the Diocesan Association did not have enough public support to meet its commitments and that they were sure that Powys would adminster properly any aid sent from England. Powys replied on 8th October thanking him, hoping that it might yet be possible to accept the Curates' Aid Society offer and disclaiming any desire to overthrow the Diocesan Association, so as to gain power for the Bishop to promote a particular type of Churchmanship - which some of the Diocesan Association seemed to fear. He added that he had no wish to gain any independent control over money entrusted to him as Bishop. On 30th October 1866 a private meeting of friends of the Association was held. A deputation was sent to Governor Loch (President of the Association) to seek his good offices in obtaining an amicable settlement of the dispute so as not to endanger the Association's existence in its present form and that arrangements might be made to carry out the Bishop's suggestion, Powys having agreed to administer the Funds with the aid of a lay committee.

The meeting was adjourned so that Loch could see the Bishop and he spent a few days at Bishopscourt. The adjourned meeting was held on 6th November, with Deemster Drinkwater as Chairman, the Governor and the Bishop being present. Thanks to Loch's good offices it was agreed to accept the grant from the Curates' Aid Society. On 20th November a meeting of members and friends of the Association was held, which decided that all its funds be transferred to a committee of six (elected at the meeting) - Deemster Drinkwater, the Attorney General, the High Bailiff of Peel, Mr E. M. Gawne, Mr W. F. Moore and Mr E. C. Farrant - in order to obtain the grant from the Curates' Aid Society. The Association being now non-existent, the first Annual General Meeting of the Isle of Man Branch of the Curates' Aid Society was held on 6th August 1867, the Governor presiding, but it was poorly attended. There turned out to be no money in the name of the Diocesan Association, but rather a small debt. In eight months £191 had been subscribed to the new Curates' Aid Society, the aim having been to raise £200 in return for which the parent society would give £300, making £500 in all. Grants would only be made to properly appointed curates and the amount granted would be decided by the committee of six. A condition of a grant was that the church or chapel concerned should have Mattins and Evensong each Sunday.

In January 1867 Governor Loch made an Order (ratified by the Bishop) that special collections were to be made in churches to meet the expense of precautions to ward off human cholera and rinderpest in cattle. Loch and Powys were criticised for allowing a church collection for this purpose.

In November 1867 a rumour was circulating that Powys was to be translated to Lichfield but that the Queen had refused to sanction it.

On 20th March 1869 the 'Manx Sun' complained that the churchyards were mostly ill-kept and neglected and that neighbouring landowners would not let them be enlarged. A complaint was also made about the fees for funerals charged by the clergy. The Archdeacon raised this matter at the 1869 Convocation. There it was said that the clergy were sometimes kept waiting for funerals for up to four hours, and it was decided to give notice that they would only wait a reasonable time in future. It was also decided to enforce the law that no-one could dig a grave in the churchyard without the Vicar's permission, and that in all burials there was to be at least three feet of soil above the coffin.

Following the 'Manx Sun's complaint Tynwald appointed a committee to look into the state of the churchyards and they inspected them in May 1869. They found that the new regulation of three feet of soil over the coffin was generally observed, except at Lezayre, German, Patrick (especially bad), Lonan, Braddan, Malew, Rushen and Ballure. No burials seemed to have been made in churches during the 19th century. The custom was to bury still born and unbaptised babies at night (except in Lonan) nearly always without informing the Vicar, Parish Clerk or Churchwardens, but Vicar Hardy of Jurby had ruled that he must be informed. Since the enlargement of Malew Churchyard in 1865 there had been few burials in the ancient burial ground on Fort Island, where the soil was very shallow. Vicar Gill of Malew said that he had often officiated there, and had tacitly agreed to the burial of Roman Catholics there without a service. There were few permanent sextons. At German a Vestry meeting had agreed that all graves be dug to eight feet. The usual burial fees were one shilling for the parson and 1/6 for the clerk. No fees were paid for the erection of monuments in the churchyard, but only for monuments in the church. The committee advised that the churchyards around German parish church and in the Cathedral should be closed at once, and that strict regulations be made for future burials in the old churchyards at Braddan, Lezayre, Patrick, Lonan and Rushen. Extension of the burial ground was urgent at Lonan and Patrick, the latter being especially offensive, as there was often less than 12 inches of earth above the coffin. They recommended that in old churches burials should be banned within six feet of the wall of the church and, as laid down by Tynwald in 1830, and within twelve feet for new churches. The Ramsey people had asked for an extension of Ballure Churchyard. The committee recommended that St George's churchyard should be virtually closed. The report was signed by the Archdeacon, W. B. Stevenson, E. C. Farrant, J. S. Goldie Taubman (SHK) and W. B. Christian.

Detailed comments were:

MAUGHOLD
Pretty good. New wall in process of building by annual instalments. Some burial enclosures unreasonably large. Average yearly burials (AYB) 83

BALLURE
Gates and walls neat and good. AYB 7 or 8.

BRIDE
Walls very bad in places. AYB 23

ANDREAS
Walls good. Churchyard enlarged 1848. AYB 43. (at St Jude's AYB 2)

JURBY
Walls fairly good. Churchyard enlarged 1813. AYB 21.

BALLAUGH OLD CHURCH
Walls need some repairs. AYB 0

BALLAUGH PARISH CHURCH
Ground rather hard to dig until 4½ feet down. Some loss of ground through graves being widely spread. AYB 16.

LEZAYRE
Extended by ½ an acre in 1857. Gates and walls fairly good. Much of the old burial ground should not be used again for many years. Full time Sexton much needed. Rank grass and nettles were very bad and so were heaps of loose stones and broken monuments. AYB 47.

KIRK MICHAEL
Enlarged 1833. Parish Clerk was grave digger. Walls mostly good. AYB 24.

GERMAN
Walls and gates good. AYB 15

CATHEDRAL
Rarely 3 ft. of soil above the coffin. Burials close up to the church walls. No supervision whatever over opening graves. AYB 1

PATRICK
Bucket kept for baling water out of the graves. AYB 52.

LONAN PARISH CHURCH
Several burials within 12 ft. of the church walls on the south side. Walls good, churchyard well kept. AYB 57.

LONAN OLD CHURCH
Walls need repair. AYB 1

ONCHAN
Walls fairly good. Gates should be improved. AYB 37

BRADDAN OLD CHURCH
Churchyard slightly extended in 1836. Walls not good. Burials often close to the church wall. AYB 74.

BRADDAN CEMETERY AYB 83

BALDWIN

Walls and churchyard in good order. AYB 4

MALEW

Churchyard extended in 1865. Well kept, walls good. Some burials close to the church wall. AYB 80

ARBORY

Churchyard extended in 1863. Well kept, walls good. AYB 38.

RUSHEN

Walls of the old ground adequate, those of the new ground excellent. Old burial ground very crowded, not always three feet of soil on the coffin. AYB 61.

MAROWN PARISH CHURCH

Churchyard and walls in good order. AYB 14

MAROWN OLD CHURCH

Churchyard in great disorder, walls neglected, not always three feet of earth on the coffin. AYB 9.

ST MARK'S

Churchyard extended in 1865. All in good order. AYB 14

SANTAN

Churchyard extended in 1868. All in order. AYB 11

ST GEORGE'S

Recommended for closure. AYB 16

In many churchyards there were heaps of loose stones and accumulations of soil against the church walls.

At the 1871 Convocation Parson Drury's younger son, T. W. Drury, later Bishop of Sodor and Man, was made Deacon, the sermon being preached by Vicar Hutton of Lezayre on St Matthew 20[1] and after the service Powys suggested a vote of thanks to him for an excellent sermon. All present, except Parson Drury, stayed for lunch.

At a confirmation at Andreas on 25th July 1871, Powys, who had a bad cold, advised the candidates to use daily the prayer "Defend me, O Lord, with thy heavenly grace, that I may continue thine forever, and daily increase in thy Holy Spirit more and more, until I come to thine everlasting Kingdom". At a confirmation at St Thomas' on 1st November 1872 the 'Manx Sun' reported that Powys seemed much more feeble than on his last visit.

At the 1872 Convocation on 23rd May the Domestic Chaplain (Vicar Ingram of Kirk Michael) read Mattins, and the Archdeacon, Vicar Kermode of Maughold and Vicar Gill of Malew assisted the Bishop with Holy Communion. Powys said that he had given no Charge since 1869 because of the dispute over St Thomas'. He hoped that as both sides had conscientiously fought for what they considered to be right, all past differences would be forgotten and harmony restored. In response to a widely signed memorial from the clergy he promised to end his ban on ordaining non-graduates. He paid tribute to the Revd W. Gill who had died since the last Convocation. He ended by suggesting that all churches and parsonages should be insured against fire and that the premium would be a fair charge on the parish. The clergy elected Vicar Kermode of Maughold as Proctor in York Convocation in succession to Gill. The Bishop then provided an excellent lunch for the clergy in accordance with his customary generous hospitality.

At this Convocation Archdeacon Moore announced that he would visit all parishes during the summer to check the state of the church and buildings. He asked that parishioners be invited to join the visitation and that notice be given in church the previous Sunday. He asked the clergy for:

(1) A detailed report on the condition of the church, schools, etc., especially re the walls, roof, spouting, windows and doors.

(2) A detailed report of the burial ground - walls, gates, depth of graves, etc.

(3) A list of all articles needed for the proper performance of Divine Service - books, surplices, collecting boxes, font, Communion Plate, a clean linen altar cloth and the ordinary altar coverings.

(4) A catalogue of all registers, noting the date at which each begins and ends.

(5) A terrier of glebe lands, and any other emoluments attaching to the benefice.

(6) A Statement of any charities that had accrued to the parish since 1869.

(7) A report of the state and condition of the glebe house and premises.

(8) The amount of church insurance policies.

T. W. Drury was to have been ordained Priest at the 1872 Convocation, but a difficulty had arisen as he had recently preached in the Dalrymple Memorial Chapel in Union Mills. On the Tuesday before Convocation a clergyman in the diocese had written to Powys saying that Vicar Drury, (assisted by T. W. Drury) was in the habit of giving lectures in the Chapel. Powys said at Convocation that before ordaining him an inquiry would have to be made into the circumstances. Powys had formerly approved the practice, and so did the Archdeacon and many other clergy. T. W. Drury had just returned from seeing Canon Gray, Powys' Examining Chaplain, in Liverpool, and had been given high praise. He was ordained as arranged soon after Convocation.

At the 1873 Convocation, on the 4th June, Powys asked that when the clergy answered their names they should state whether or not they wanted a confirmation in their church during the coming year. He did not give a Charge, and said that he wished to make no reference to proceedings in the past. He suggested an annual gathering of church choirs, and offered Bishopscourt for the purpose. He envisaged a service during the day, and a large tea party in the grounds during the evening. He offered to contribute to the cost. This was agreed, and a clerical and lay committee was formed to make plans. The Bishop extended his usual hospitality after the most harmonious Convocation for years, a peace and harmony which, Powys observed, also existed in the diocese.

On 31st July 1873 the Bishop and Mrs Powys left for Harrogate and returned in late September. In July he had taken a Confirmation at Kirk Michael, and one who had not seen him for about three years thought that he had aged very much.

In 1873 the Bishop received £1,609-16s-9½d of the tithe, the Archdeacon £751-5s-2d, the Rectors of Bride and Ballaugh £321-19s 4½d each and the Vicars £150-5s-0¼d each.

Until 1783 there were two Ecclesiastical Courts holding separate jurisdictions. The Ecclesiastical Courts Amendment Bill (1873) abolished the Archdeacon's Court, and the various powers exercised in the past by the Vicar General and the Archdeacon's Official were vested in the Vicar General. This was one of Governor Loch's reforms. In December 1883 Jebb presented a petition to the House of Keys asking that the Bill should not become law until he retired as it altered the conditions on which he had accepted the post, gave him no remuneration for extra duties and because he had not been consulted about

it. The result was that his salary was raised from £400 to £500.

A visitor to Douglas in 1874 complained in a letter to the 'Manx Sun' that there was no weekly celebration of Holy Communion in the town. In only one church was there an early service and then only once a month. In all churches he found an absence of life and vigour and in two he saw irreverent behaviour by the choir.

The celebration of Holy Communion became much more frequent in the diocese during Powys' episcopate.

The 1874 Convocation on 28th May was Powys' last important engagement in the diocese. His health was failing as a result of incipient cancer. He and Mrs Powys left the Island in September and he spent the remaining three years of his life in Bournemouth. He arranged with Bishop Hobhouse (formerly Bishop of Nelson, New Zealand and now assistant Bishop of Lichfield), Bishop Selwyn of Lichfield and Bishop Goodwin of Carlisle to visit the Island when Archdeacon Moore needed them for a confirmation, ordination or consecration of a church. They stayed either at Bishopscourt or at Government House. Thus, Bishop Hobhouse took a confirmation at St Thomas' on Ascension Day, 1875, when his delivery was described as very indistinct and at times inaudible; Bishop Goodwin took a confirmation at St Thomas' for the Douglas parishes, Braddan and Santan on 4th July 1876 and on 6th July he confirmed at Lonan in the morning and at St Paul's Ramsey in the evening; on 12 July 1875 Bishop Selwyn confirmed at Malew and Rushen and in 1876 Bishop Goodwin did an ordination at Andreas and confirmed at St Paul's, Ramsey. In 1887, at Bishop Bardsley's request Goodwin sent his portrait to be kept at Bishopscourt. Bishop Selwyn preached once or twice each Sunday during his two months on the Island in 1876. He also visited the sick and poor around Bishopscourt and was much respected and valued. On 31st August Selwyn confirmed at Marown, on the following Sunday at Jurby, and on 5th September at King William's College. On 27th August he preached at Peel Sunday School Anniversary and in the afternoon confirmed candidates from Peel, Patrick, St John's and Foxdale in the parish church. On 10th September he took his last service in Bishopscourt Chapel and preached on St Mark 4[29]. Many could not get in. On

14th September he left for home.

In August 1876 a choir festival was held in Peel Castle, Miss M. L. Wood being the main organiser, helped by Ferrier (Chaplain of Castletown), Vicar Moore of Jurby and Vicar Gill of Malew. It was a very fine day and a choir of 200 assembled, drawn from St George's, St Matthew's, St Luke's, Rushen, Malew, German, Marown, Lezayre, Foxdale, Kirk Michael and Braddan. They sang from a temporary stage erected at the east end of the Cathedral, the reading desk and lectern being placed on the south side, and the conductor's stand on the north side. Vicar Hutton of St Thomas' read the service, Gill and Vicar Stowell of German read the lessons and Moore conducted. The Bishop of Lichfield preached on Revelation 10^9 and Mr J. Bamber, organist of St George's played the harmonium. Hundreds of people came from all parts of the Island, including most of the clergy. The service was fully choral, and the anthem was Barnby's 'Harvest Hymn'.

Bishop Powys wished to resign but Governor Loch wished to reduce the Bishop's stipend by £500, and use it to increase clergy stipends. This could not be done until a vacancy in the see arose, but it was long before the tedious formalities at the Home Office were completed. On 7th July 1876 in reply to a question in Tynwald, Loch said that he had asked the Bishop not to resign as he wished to secure for Tynwald the right to adjust the Bishop's stipend and that any appointment would be made on these conditions. Deemster Drinkwater and Mr G. W. Dumbell both said that they were glad that the Bishop was not retaining office by his own desire. It was probably in late 1874 or early 1875 that the first symptoms of the cancer, from which Powys died, appeared, and ever since then he had been anxious to resign in the interests of the diocese. Another cause for delay in appointing a new Bishop was the difficulty of arranging a pension for Powys from the small income of the see.

In October 1876 Mrs Powys and two of her daughters made a short visit to the Island, probably to collect personal belongings from Bishopscourt. While here she received a telegram saying that her eldest daughter, Mary, had been thrown from her carriage and killed while driving at Bournemouth. (11th October).

Powys was interested in farming and always at-tended the annual meeting of the Manx Agricultural Society. He had no great liking for Methodists and disliked the habit of turning to the east for the ascription after the sermon. In January 1877 Powys wrote to a friend in Douglas saying that he had resigned, but was holding the office nominally pending further arrangements and the appointment of a successor. Early in 1877 there was a rumour that the new Bishop would be T. H. Gill, then Rector of St Margaret's, Whalley Range, Manchester, and formerly chaplain of St Mark's. At the same time Vicar Hobson of St Barnabas' was canvassing support among the clergy for the next Bishop to be Vincent Ryan, DD, late Bishop of Mauritius and now Vicar and Rural Dean of Bradford, and Archdeacon of Craven, an evangelical.

Powys died at his home, 2 Richmond Terrace, Bournemouth, at 8 a.m. on Thursday, 31st May 1877, after being unconscious for three days. His death, had of course, been foreseen, but was rather sudden in the end. On 4th June his body was brought to Warrington for burial in the family vault; it remained overnight in the chancel and the funeral took place next day, taken by the Rector of Warrington, assisted by Canon Hopwood, who had been Powys' Curate at Warrington. He had not been forgotten by the people of the town, as hundreds of them filed past the vault before it was closed as a mark of respect, but only one of the Manx clergy, Vicar Airey of Kirk Michael, who had been Powys' last Domestic Chaplain, attended, though two former clergy, Kelly and Simpson, were there.

When the news of his death reached the Island, a Chapter Court for swearing in the churchwardens was in progress. Vicar General Jebb at once terminated it, as his office became vacant on the death of the Bishop (as did the office of Episcopal Registrar, held by Samuel Harris) but Governor Loch re-appointed them both the same day. The flags on all public buildings were flown at half mast. His death also meant that the Bishop's Temporalities Act, which Loch introduced in Tynwald on 1st May, fell through. It would have reduced the bishop's stipend by £500. Some members wished to reduce it by £750, but Loch said that the Home Office would never accept this. The Bill had passed the Keys on 16th May by 16 votes to 4, but there would have been difficulties as the proposals affected the rights of the Crown.

Mrs Powys had always, in a quiet way, been good to the poor people in Kirk Michael and around Bishopscourt and in December, 1877, as a last gesture, she sent £5 for Kirk Michael Coal Fund.

In 1875 it looked as if Bishop Ward's struggle to maintain the independence of the diocese would have to be fought all over again. On 8th January 1875 a meeting was held in Liverpool which proposed that a new diocese of Liverpool should be taken out of the diocese of Chester and would include Sodor and Man. A memorial to this effect was sent to the Home Office asking for this to take place when Bishop Powys retired, and that the stipend of Sodor and Man should go partly to increase clergy stipends in the Isle of Man and partly to fund the new diocese. Mr John Torr, MP, told the meeting that he had a letter from Powys favouring the proposed merger. Bishop Jacobson of Chester did not want Sodor and Man to be added to his diocese, but agreed to the new diocese of Liverpool being taken out of Chester.

The proposals aroused great indignation in the Island and its leading opponents were the Revd W. B. Christian, MHK, of Milntown, Mr E. C. Farrant (Ballakillingen) and the Revd G. Paton, Chaplain of St Paul's, the latter writing to each English bishop asking him to oppose the scheme, and expressing the grave concern of the whole Island. Most of them replied to Paton saying that they knew nothing about the scheme, but all said they opposed it. Although Paton's stipend was one of the lowest in the diocese, he denounced the proposed use of part of the bishop's stipend to increase clergy stipends as bribery. Public meetings to oppose the merger were held all over the Island.

The Revd Dr Joshua Jones, Principal of King William's College, 1866-86, was in Liverpool on the 8th January 1875 and was invited to the meeting on that date. He said that he favoured the idea of a merger, but he pointed out that Sodor and Man was poor financially, and that there was much opposition to the proposal, but he thought that this opposition might be reduced if £1,000 were deducted from the Bishop's stipend to augment the poorer livings. He added that he did not think the Bishop of Sodor and Man had enough to do. On 23rd January a letter from Jones appeared in the 'Manx Sun' saying that he had spoken at the Liverpool meeting in a purely private capacity, giving his personal opinion. He said that he understood the proposal was to add Liverpool to Sodor and Man, not vice versa, and said that he was totally opposed to Sodor and Man losing its independence.

The Archbishop of York (Thompson) and the Home Secretary (Cross) both favoured the scheme, but in the Island it was almost unanimously opposed, even by the Methodists. A clergy meeting on 23rd January asked Tynwald to oppose the scheme. It was called by Archdeacon Moore at the instigation of some of the clergy, but as he felt that it was improper for him as a member of the Legislature to attend, William Drury acted as Chairman. A resolution to oppose the scheme was carried without any dissentients, as was a motion to petition Parliament and Tynwald, which the Archdeacon did on 26th January.

Mr Farrant wrote to the Press saying that both the Bishop and Dr Jones favoured joining Liverpool to Sodor and Man and that the Bishop had, since his early years, thought of such a union as a possible way of raising clergy stipends, but he had realised that the Manx people would never accept it. On 25th January Mr G. W. Dumbell, MHK, called a public meeting, chaired by High Bailiff Harris, which was attended by about 500 people. Mr Dumbell pointed out that the clergy had said that they would not accept any increase in their stipends from money obtained by merging Sodor and Man with another diocese and the meeting decided

(1) To ask Tynwald to reject the scheme and
(2) To ask Mr Dumbell, when the matter came up in Tynwald next day, to move the adjournment of the debate until every town and village on the Island had been able to forward petitions to Tynwald stating their views.

Governor Loch had called a special sitting of Tynwald for 26th January, and he opened the debate by saying that it was essential to take some action to relieve the poverty of the clergy, but said that he had told the British Government that any union with an English diocese would be conditional on its clearly benefiting the church and the clergy, and that a Bishop would be on the Island for at least part of the year. He suggested a week's adjournment, but Dumbell successfully opposed this. The Keys had met before the debate, and had decided to reject the proposed merger. The Archdeacon duly presented the clergy's petition against the merger and said that he agreed with the clergy, but added that the British Government should be asked to sanction, at the next vacancy, part of the Bishop's stipend being used to augment the poorer livings, as he felt that otherwise it would be almost impossible to induce clergy to come to the Island. On this latter point he was supported by several members, but everyone spoke against the merger, and it was opposed unanimously. The Governor then successfully proposed the appointment of a committee to investigate the possible reduction in the Bishop's stipend as suggested by Moore.

Stipends in 1875 were Bishop £2,500, Archdeacon, £900, Ballaugh £360, Bride £308, and the remaining parishes £184-10s-0d each.

The proposed merger was also unpopular among the Liverpool clergy, and 175 out of 218 beneficed clergy in the Archdeaconry of Liverpool sent a protest to the Home Secretary that the merger would not give Liverpool proper episcopal oversight.

On 2nd February Tynwald met again and was told by Loch that he had informed the Home Secretary that, with Tynwald so strongly opposed to the merger, it was pointless to proceed with the plan, and the Home Secretary agreed. Thus the independence of the diocese was saved once again. On the same day Tynwald asked Loch to find out the terms on which the British Government would agree to any adjustments to the Bishop's stipend and how clergy stipends could be raised without a merger.

On 28th September 1875 the Archdeacon arranged a clergy meeting in St John's Church to ascertain their views on Loch's wish to use part of the Bishop's stipend to increase the value of the Livings. Most of the clergy attended, and after much debate a resolution was passed, with 4 or 5 against, that the

Governor should be asked to bring his proposals before Tynwald again. However 9 Vicars and Curates, including Paton, Kermode, Drury, B.P. Clarke, W. M. Hutton, Langton, S. N. Harrison and F. Hutton sent an open letter to the newspapers on 9th October saying that they would not agree to any scheme for augmenting stipends which involved union with any other diocese.

In 1876 Loch applied to the Home Secretary to obtain the consent of the Crown for him to introduce a bill into Tynwald saying that any future appointment to Sodor and Man should be subject to such measures as Tynwald may enact for the re-arrangement of the Bishop's stipend, and the application of part of this stipend to augment the livings; and to provide (in the case of a union of this diocese with an English see) what amount yearly should be paid to the Bishop of the united see from Manx Episcopal revenues. The British Attorney General and Solicitor-General replied that in their opinion Tynwald had not the power, even with the consent of the Crown, to pass such a measure, and that it would require an Act of Parliament. But the Manx Attorney General, Gell, in a closely-reasoned memorandum, caused them to reconsider, and in December 1876 they conceded that Tynwald had the authority to re-arrange the episcopal stipend, provided that "the operation of such a measure is confined to that object and is not made to affect, even indirectly, any English Bishopric". Gell then prepared a Bill entitled The Bishop's Temporalities Act 1878 which became law on 27th March. With the agreement of the Queen and Bishop Hill (Powys' successor) £500 of the revenue of the see was paid into a Clerical Endowment Fund to augment stipends.

The Parishes under Powys

ANDREAS In 1864-9 a major restoration of the church took place a a cost of about £2,000, of which Archdeacon Moore contributed £600, and the rest came from various contributions and an assessment of £3 per quarterland. The architect was Ewan Christian, who was for many years consultant architect to the English Church Commissioners. The work was given to Mr Radcliffe, the Andreas builder. Part of the restoration was to remove the low, plas-

tered roof (which, the Archdeacon thought, made the church look like a parlour) and to expose to view the interior woodwork of Swedish pine. In 1865 the church was re-roofed and to reduce the cost the old slates were used again. The east and west walls were raised to conform to the new roof. The foundation stone of the tower was laid by Mrs Frances Hall, widow of Archdeacon Hall on Ascension Day, 30th May 1867. The Archdeacon spoke, followed by

Bishop Powys, who was rather injudicious, as he charged the Manx people with being unfaithful to their parish churches and with being too easily drawn to Methodism. The choir then sang, tea was provided for the children of the church and the chapel Sunday Schools and for the Band of Hope. After tea the Band of Hope marched through the village, displaying flags and teetotal mottos. In the evening the Archdeacon preached to a large congregation. The tower is 130 feet high and a spiral stone staircase inside goes to a considerable height, then ladders lead to the top. The tower was completed in August 1869 and on 13th August the Archdeacon gave the workmen a substantial supper and next day their wives and children were treated to tea in the schoolroom. During the restoration a window in the south side of the chancel was built up, and the glass used for the window in the west wall. Massive ornamental abuttments were built, which counteracted the former barn-like appearance of the church. A circular cross was put on the east end of the roof. The east end received a magnificent ornamental circular window containing a large centrepiece with 14 small circles diverging from the centre - the gift of the Archdeacon's brother, Mr W. F. Moore of Cronkbourne. The six old plain windows were replaced by stone mullions filled with Cathedral glass and two stained glass windows were put in the west gable. This work necessitated the removal of the organ and the closure of the church for six months in 1864, during which time the services were held in the parish school. It was re-opened on 13th November 1864, when the Bishop preached in the morning and the Archdeacon in the afternoon. The Bishop was also to have preached in the evening, but the day was so wet that he thought it better to repeat the services on 27th November, when he came again and preached in the morning on St Matthew 21 [13and14] and in the evening on Acts 8[39].

A modern heating apparatus had been installed in 1860 and an organ in 1863. It was opened by Mr P. L. Garrett of Douglas on 12th April, when the preacher in the morning was William Kermode and in the evening James Sparrow, Curate of St Paul's, Ramsey and Headmaster of the Grammar School.

Moore gave an annual treat to the pupils of the Sunday and Day Schools on the rectory lawn, typical of his generous hospitality. On 23rd December he entertained the Members of the House of Keys to dinner and on 16th January 1869 the 'Manx Sun' said that Moore, "with his proverbial liberality" had spent a large sum on numerous articles of clothing and other necessaries to distribute among the poor of the parish at Christmas. In September 1873 he treated the 18 members of the choir to a day's outing. They left at 8 a.m. and stopped at Bishopscourt, where they spent some time in the chapel, the grounds and the glen. They then travelled by rail from Kirk Michael via St John's, to Peel, had lunch at the Peel Castle Hotel, visited the Castle and left for home at 6 p.m. Three cheers for the Archdeacon were given on their return. The 'Manx Sun' described Andreas Choir outing on 7th August 1876, when 26 members assembled on the rectory lawn before 7 a.m., and sang some sacred music, then set off in two wagonettes, the outward and return journeys being enlivened with singing. They stopped at Bishopscourt, where they joined Bishop Selwyn of Lichfield and his family at Mattins in the chapel. They spent two hours, and had lunch at Glen Helen, then went on to Peel where they visited the Castle, took boats on the bay, played games and had tea at Peel Castle Hotel. They left at 7.30 p.m. and on reaching Andreas they sang the National Anthem in front of the Rectory.

At the 1871 Easter Vestry the Archdeacon presented a hearse to the parish. Previously a cart had been used.

The population of Andreas in 1871 was 1,757.

ARBORY Alexander Gelling died on 7th July 1859, aged 74 after being Vicar for 43 years. He was succeeded by John Qualtrough, previously Chaplain of St Stephen's, Sulby and of St Jude's, Andreas. He was an excellent parish priest, always in his parish, and diligent in visiting. If anyone was missing from church on Sunday he would call at the house on Monday to ask why.

He was described as kind, upright and manly, and was both popular and esteemed by his people. A fluent Manx speaker, he held monthly services in Manx both when a Chaplain and for most of his time at Arbory. He found no choir, but quickly got one together. The churchyard was extended in 1863, but this extension, and the original burial ground, were closed in 1922. He built the vicarage in 1864 at a cost of £409, but must have neglected it, as his successor sued him successfully for repairs in 1875. The old vicarage, which was very small, stood just inside the gateway from the main road. In his time Holy Communion was only celebrated four times a year. The trees in the churchyard, and adjoining the road were planted about 1863. The first Harvest Thanksgiving service in Arbory was held on 28th September 1870.

In July 1875 Qualtrough was appointed Rector of Bride, and the parishioners gave him a silver salver as a leaving present. He was succeeded in Arbory by William Thomas Dinwoody, who had been Curate of Andreas since 1869. The parishioners of Andreas gave him a mahogany sideboard with an inscribed plate when he left.

Not being a Manx speaker he discontinued the Manx services. Unfortunately his incumbency was very short, as he died on 14th October, 1876, aged 38. He had been in delicate health for some time. He was much loved for his affability and his unremitting attention to the sick and poor. A large crowd attended his funeral at German although the day was wet.

The next Vicar was Frederick Grier who was appointed on 6th November 1876. At St George's, when he was Curate (1869-76) he was highly respected, as he had worked hard, especially among the poor and in the Sunday schools. He was presented on leaving with a purse of sovereigns. He resigned in February 1880 to become Priest in charge of Walton Breck, Liverpool. He was much loved in Arbory and when he left he was presented with a tea and coffee set. In 1908 his widow, in his memory, had the chancel panelled in oak, and gave the oak altar and communion rails. During the interregnum the services were taken by H. C. Davidson, a Master at King William's College, and B. Lupton, the Chaplain of St Mark's.

The population of Arbory in 1871 was 1,355.

BALLAUGH Thomas Howard's long incumbency ended with his death on 7th November 1876, aged 91. In 1868 a serious illness left him so impaired physically that he was only able to attend very occasionally to his parish duties, but he had a splendid Curate in his son-in-law, H. G. White. In his later years he was faithfully cared for by Sarah Kneale, who died in 1911. Until 1868 the service and sermon were in Manx on three Sundays in the month, but this had to end when White, who spoke no Manx, became virtually rector of the parish. The Sunday services at this time were at 11 a.m. and 3 p.m. Howard always prepared his confirmation candidates for three months, after Sunday afternoon service, and one night a week at the rectory. He visited the sick and brought them Holy Communion. He spoke to every child he met, and gave them one of the many tracts he always carried. He used to say to young people "In the time of youth is the time to begin serving the Lord. I am speaking from my own experience". Though feeble, latterly, he enjoyed good health to the last and when over 80 he copied out the old parish registers, which had become faded and tattered, in a beautiful hand. Those who knew him described him as quiet, peaceable, wise, patient, loving, courteous and charitable. He had a fine presence and a lovable face and was held in deep affection by the whole parish. He was perhaps the most popular Rector of Ballaugh. He was a total abstainer. He was buried at Ballaugh on 11th November, the Archdeacon taking the service.

For some years after 1832 when the new parish church was built, the old church was disused, and became dilapidated, but in 1849 it was rescued by Howard who re-roofed it, removed the galleries and took down the 1717 extension to the chancel, thus reducing the length by one third.

The population of Ballaugh in 1871 was 1,077.

ST BARNABAS' Vicar Gray remained until June 1870. He was very anti-Romanist and when a rumour went around Douglas in March 1856 that he had given half a crown towards a proposed Roman Catholic Cathedral in the town he wrote to the 'Manx Sun' indignantly denying it. In May 1859 the congregation presented him with a 14 day striking clock in black marble, and shortly before they had presented him with a purse containing 100 sovereigns. The Sunday services in Gray's time were at 11 a.m. and 6 p.m. and on Thursdays at 7 p.m. In the summer and Autumn of 1862 he had a serious illness. He had done much for Douglas charities and much preferred voluntary to compulsory poor relief. In his time a vicarage was built at a cost of £1,600 and the Widows' Houses in Fort Street were re-built. In late 1861 the organ was re-built and it was opened on 2nd February 1862 by Mr F. Gunton, organist of Chester

Cathedral.

The Trustees had appointed the incumbents since 1832, in accordance with the Trust Deed, and the incumbents had nominated their own curates, who were, if necessary, ordained and licenced by the Bishop. Bishop Powys, however, said that the incumbent was only a curate and as such had no power to nominate a stipendiary curate, this being the right of the Vicar of Braddan. Gray disputed this, and claimed the legal right to be treated in every respect as a beneficed incumbent. Powys therefore refused to grant a curate to St Barnabas, and asked the advice of a London barrister, Mr A. J. Stephens. The congregation vainly petitioned Powys for a curate, so they sought legal advice from Dr Robert Phillimore, Sir Travers Twiss and Mr James Gell.

All three said that St Barnabas' was an independent incumbency and had been treated as such by the present Vicar of Braddan (Drury) and his predecessors, hence the chaplain could appoint his own curate. They added that if the Vicar of Braddan nominated a curate the Bishop should accept him. Both felt that if the Bishop still refused to licence a curate the only course open was to submit the case to the Archbishop of York. Stephens quite independently also thought the matter should go to the Archbishop. Gell's opinion was that as the original Trust Deed (executed by the Bishop, as Patron in ordinary, and by Vicar Howard of Braddan) conferred the patronage on the trustees, the Bishop had nothing to do with the appointment and therefore nothing to do with the appointment of a curate, hence the incumbent could nominate his own curate.

Stephens added to his Opinion that Powys, in his efforts to maintain the rights of the Vicar of Braddan had not exceeded his authority, and that he was "legally and properly discharging the duties of his office in a diocese where in times past little regard seems to have been paid to order and law in the administration of ecclesiastical affairs".

On the basis of Stephen's advice, Powys told the Douglas clergy that to safeguard the rights of the Vicar of Braddan, curates must receive their nomination from the Vicar of Braddan, who alone had the cure of souls in the undivided parish, and not as hitherto from the chaplains or ministers of those chapels to whom no parochial district or cure of souls had ever been assigned. The ministers of St George's, (Hawley)

and St Barnabas' (Gray), strongly objected to this.

Powys' reason for refusing to grant a curate to St Barnabas' was that Drury claimed and maintained the right to nominate to St George's, and St Barnabas' was equally part of his parish, but it was felt that Powys' dislike of Gray personally operated as well. Eventually Gray and the congregation agreed to let Drury nominate someone to be ordained ostensibly as the Curate of Braddan, but when Powys found that he was to be attached to St Barnabas' he rejected the nomination. Powys had always been willing to accept the Trustees' nomination of the chaplain, provided the Vicar of Braddan agreed in writing. He said that the patronage of the Douglas churches was the last thing he wanted, and only wished to satisfy his own conscience, fortified by legal opinion.

The churchwardens of St Barnabas, in an open letter to Drury, printed in the 'Manx Sun' on 27th April 1861 said that the original Trustees had contributed £1,650 to building the church on condition of their being the Patrons in perpetuity, and they were not prepared to submit the matter to the arbitration of the Archbishop of York or anyone else. They added that the sooner the parish of Braddan, which had 1,500 people, was divided, and a district assigned to each of the Douglas churches, the better, especially as Drury had to leave all the spiritual work of the town to the Douglas chaplains. They said that the Douglas chaplains simply wanted a legal position and rights, and ended by appealing to Drury for help in dividing the parish.

A parochial district was assigned to St Barnabas' by Order of the Queen in Council on 7th October 1869, making it in every respect a separate parish, saving the rights of the present Vicar of Braddan during his incumbency. At the next vacancy in Braddan it would become a separate parish.

St Barnabas' sat 1,500 people plus 250 in the gallery. Gray preached his last sermon on 19th June 1870 and on 23rd June the parishioners presented him with a service of silver plate (kettle, stand, tea and coffee service) and a set of clerical robes and £50. He and his wife left the Island on 26th June. He was followed in May by Henry Sutton, but his ministry was very short as he became Priest in Charge of St Cleopas, Liverpool, early in 1872. He had the reputation of being a fine preacher. He was highly esteemed and founded the St Barnabas branch of the

YMCA. He preached his last sermon on 2nd June.

The next Vicar was William Thomas Hobson (November 1872). He took a full part in the life of the town, being chairman of the Douglas School Committee and was on the committee both of the hospital and the House of Industry. He was also Surrogate for Douglas.

In April 1875 a new organ was bought for £500, and on 18th September 1875 the choir celebrated it with a day's outing and picnic to Port Erin and Cregneash. The journey from Douglas took two hours. In April 1875 William Gell and Daniel Corrin were elected churchwardens, though they had no property or place of business in the parish and only rented pews in the church. In May Vicar General Jebb said that simply being pewholders did not entitle them to be churchwardens, and ordered that in future the Vicar should appoint one warden and the people elect the other.

In August 1875 the old pulpit and reading desk, which formed one central structure in the chancel were taken down, and the pulpit placed on the south side, the reading desk on the north side, and the lectern in the centre. These changes were made in connection with the new organ, which was opened on 7th September by Irvine Dearnaley, organist of Ashton-under-Lyne parish church, deputising for W. T. Best, who had eye trouble.

BRADDAN Bishop Powys came to preach at Holy Communion on Whit Sunday 29th June 1856. Long before the time of service the church was crowded, and many had to remain outside. Many had hoped that the service would be held in the churchyard, but although some of the local clergy had been preaching in the open air, it was not expected that the Bishop would do so. The day was fine, and the heat inside the church was so intense that several ladies fainted. At the end of the service those in the churchyard were surprised to see the Bishop, the Vicar and most of the congregation come out and it soon became clear that Powys had decided to repeat his sermon (of which the text was Acts 15[35]) under one of the fine trees on the south east side of the burial ground. He was preaching on behalf of the church schools in Braddan. His voice was described as strong and manly, and he was heard clearly. This was the start of Braddan open air services, which

were normally attended by several thousand people. In the churchyard there is a stone inscribed "Here the Rev. William Drury, for forty years Vicar of this parish, preached the Word of God". By 1857 Drury had greatly increased the congregation and even in winter the church was full.

On 22nd January 1861 Drury entertained the Choirs of St George's and Braddan to tea and supper at the vicarage. In 1861 he was appointed Chaplain to the Douglas Volunteer Rifle Corps, and he was also Chaplain to the Mental Asylum. In 1871 he was appointed translator of the Acts of Tynwald into Manx in succession to Vicar Gill of Malew. He used to say that the old Manx people in the Asylum enjoyed a prayer and a few words in their native tongue.

Drury raised money, not only for the new church but for Braddan school and house and Baldwin school. The former were built by a grant of £300 from the Government and by a parish effort held on the evening of 23rd May 1860 in a field adjoining the present cemetery, Drury being the chairman. The Bishop, who was present, congratulated the people of Braddan on having such an upright, honest and good man as their worthy Vicar. He said that his first impression on being introduced to Drury was "This is a big man, and he has a big heart" and he had never had occasion to alter the favourable opinion then formed. Ever since he came he had seen the straightforward course of usefulness Drury untiringly pursued and it would always be a delight to work with him for the spiritual and temporal advancement of the people of Braddan. It is sad that the subsequent dispute over St Thomas' Church completely soured their relations. The Bishop had laid the foundation stone of the school on 15th March 1859 in the presence of the Archdeacon, Deemster Drinkwater, Mr W. F. Moore of Cronkbourne and other notables.

Braddan was at this time the only parish where graves could be bought. Elsewhere all graves were the common property of the parish, and the vicar could bury anyone in them. This meant that families were split up.

The re-built organ, to which Bishop Powys had contributed generously, was opened on 19th February 1860. The Sunday services at this time were at 10.30 a.m. and 3 p.m. The stipend in 1868 was £175.

The total population of Braddan in 1868, including Douglas, was 14,287.

On 18th May 1860 three persons were presented in the Vicar General's Court for profane swearing and another for selling milk on Sunday. Three others - Mr E. P. Arthur (Port-e-chee), Mr Alcroft (Ballabeg) and Mr John Cormode (Pulrose) were presented for farming on Sunday. Mr Samuel Harris, who appeared for Arthur, said that the presentment should have been made by the churchwardens when they were in office, as they were now out of office. Drury said that he did not want to prosecute, as they were all worthy men, Arthur was a particular friend of his and he had only agreed to the presentment thinking that he could not refuse. Vicar General Corlett said that he could have refused, as the Vicar and Wardens could each prosecute independently. Drury then said that he did not wish to prosecute and as none of the wardens appeared the presentment was dropped.

As early as 1859 it was clear that something must be done towards enlarging the church or building a new one, as people often walked from Douglas and were unable to get in. The church held about 350, sitting five to a pew. In August 1859 it was planned to build a wing to seat 150 on the north side of the church. Deemster Drinkwater offered the land for a new church, but the Bishop preferred to enlarge the existing one. The plan for a new wing had to be given up because of objections from some people with whose rights of burial it interfered. Hence came the idea of a new church, and this was considered at a Vestry meeting on 9th November 1859. Drury said that he would agree to whatever was good for the parish. It was mainly in the summer that extra accommodation was needed, as only about 30 came to Evensong. When the vote was taken only about six in a full meeting favoured a new church, those against probably being influenced by the cost to the cess payer. The Deemster was thanked for his offer of a site.

On 3rd September 1868 a Harvest Thanksgiving was held in the afternoon, followed by a meeting in Douglas at which Mr W. F. Moore proposed that a new church should be built and offered £100 yearly during the building. Others promised lesser annual subscriptions during the building. Drury agreed, but said that he did not want the old church to be pulled down. Mr Moore stressed that the money should be raised by voluntary subscriptions, not by cess. A public meeting of parishioners on 14th November appointed a committee for building the new church and on 30th January 1869 they approved an appeal for subscriptions drawn up by Mr Moore. On 29th March 1869 a Vestry meeting voted formally to ask the Bishop for his consent, but he refused to consent or otherwise "under existing circumstances" (the dispute over St Thomas'). Another meeting on 28th August was told that enough money was available, but Powys' refusal embarrassed the Vestry, who had been told to approach Tynwald for a Bill and had only asked the Bishop as a matter of courtesy. On 25th October a special Vestry meeting rescinded the motion of 29th March and decided to apply direct to Tynwald. On 14th April 1870 the ground was given by Lady Buchan, the daughter of Colonel Mark Wilks, who built Kirby.

The foundation stone of the new church was laid by Lady Loch on 26th December 1871, and the Act of Tynwald authorising it came on 9th May 1872 and said

(1) that the new church must seat at least 500 people
(2) that there were to be no burials in or around the church.

It was the first church in the diocese to be built by voluntary contributions and cost £6,775-19s-7d. It was ready for consecration by late 1873 but this could not be done until it was clear of debt. The architect was Mr J. L. Pearson and the builders were Messrs. Wall and Hook of Briascombe, near Stroud. The original idea was to have a 130 foot spire, but when the temporary wooden spire (erected soon after the consecration) was blown down in a gale on 26th January 1884 the idea was dropped. An engineer's report said that it had been blown down because of poor timber and faulty construction.

Mrs Drury did not see the new church completed, as she died in the vicarage on 10th September 1872 after only a few days illness.

The church was finished in 1874, the tower was begun in 1883 and finished in 1884 but as the debt on the building was not paid off until 1876 the consecration had to be delayed. In 1875 Archdeacon Moore sent £100 to fence in the ground around the church to try and quicken things up. It was consecrated by Bishop Selwyn of Lichfield, with Powys' consent, on 31st August 1876 and despite torrential rain and gales all day about 200 people took part. A special train ran from Douglas. The Archdeacon (who acted as Bishop's chaplain), Drury and his son T. W. Drury (the Curate), Hutton, Hobson, Caine, Langton, Vicar General Jebb and Diocesan Registrar Harris were present. The proceedings began with Morning Prayer at 11 a.m. taken by the Vicar and his son. The lessons were Ezra 3 and I Peter 2 and the hymn was "We love the place O God". Holy Communion followed. The Bishop preached on St John 14^{17}, and after the service he and the clergy had lunch with Deemster Drinkwater at Kirby.

There was some opposition in the parish to the building of the new church, as many would have preferred the old church to be enlarged and many resented the abandonment of the old church. There was some friction over the allocation of pews in the new church. Some parishioners would not attend the new church and for them Drury held services in the old church from time to time, in addition to baptisms and weddings. It was discovered however that the Consecration Deed of the new church had transferred to it all the attributes of a parish church and the old church automatically ceased to be licenced for weddings, hence these weddings were declared illegal and had to be repeated.

Among subscriptions for the new church were Deemster Drinkwater £100, the Archdeacon £400, Bishop Short £50 and Bishop Powys £10, the latter being criticised by many as totally inadequate. One of the reasons for building it was public health, because at the north end of the old church many of the graves outside were almost on a level with the aisle.

Oakhill Chapel was licenced for worship by the Bishop on 6th December 1863. The Trust Deed was dated 24th January 1860 and was made between Robert and Sophia Crossfield on one hand and Powys, W. F. Moore and Drury on the other. Before it was built services were held in the barn of Oakhill, (Mr Crossfield's residence) which he had fitted out with a Reading Desk and seats. The chapel owed much to Mr Crossfield's liberality and exertions, but was never consecrated.

BRIDE Daniel Nelson was Rector for 28 years, and the main event of his incumbency was the building of the new church. In January 1865 a jury condemned the old church as unfit for use as the roof

was beyond repair and the galleries were unsafe. A Vestry meeting on 20th March was told by the jury that the site of the church was unsuitable for a new building as the graves were within two feet of the walls, so another Vestry meeting on 2nd April 1866 decided to build a new church on a different site. The new site was bought on 2nd May 1866 from Thomas and Catherine Lace for £100 of which Archdeacon Moore contributed £20. The Rector paid for the chancel and was allowed to borrow the money on the security of the glebe, tithe Rent Charge, profits and emoluments, to be a charge on the living for 30 years or until all was repaid. The Act to build the new church was passed by Tynwald on 9th July 1868 and received Royal Assent on 9th December.

The foundation stone was laid by Lady Loch at 4 p.m. on Friday, 30th July 1869, in the presence of about 300 people, including the Governor, the Bishop and the Arcdeacon, who all spoke. The architect was Ewan Christian and the builder Thomas Christian of Bride. The date was not known until the previous Wednesday and three of the four churchwardens were in Manchester. The day was dull and threatening at first but the afternoon was sunny. The proceedings began with Psalm 100, then the Rector read prayers and there followed a hymn with final prayers and blessing by the Bishop. After tea in the parochial schoolroom, Powys bought gingerbread and buns at a stall and scattered them among the children, who eagerly scrambled for them.

The date on the wall and tower is 1875. Although the church was not quite finished it was licenced for worship and formally opened on 4th February 1872. The services were well attended both in the morning (when the Archdeacon preached) and in the evening (when the Revd E. W. Kissack preached).

James Callow of Ramsey did the woodwork and the church was entirely the work of local craftsmen, the only imported material being the glazing. The estimated cost was £650, to be raised by assessment on quarterlands and the site was paid for by subscription. The final cost, however, was £950, and the tower was not completed until 1875. Miss Isabella Collister of Thornhill, later Mrs E. C. Farrant of Ballakillingan, paid the balance and also paid for the tower, the churchyard walls and the Rectory and gave four acres as the Rector's glebe. Because the ground was rather soft, and a firm foundation was needed, much of the large masonry from the old church was used for the purpose. When the old church was demolished it was found to have been partly built with material from an older church. The elm trees around the churchyard were planted by Rector Nelson in 1851 to shield the village from wind.

The 1872 Vestry meeting was lengthy, and there was considerable criticism of some of the bills paid for the new church. At the 1873 Vestry meeting the churchwardens, who had been in office since it was first decided to build a new church, all resigned. A Mr Joughin objected to the accounts, and had to be threatened with removal by the police. The church was now complete save for the tower, having taken a longer time to build through lack of funds than originally anticipated.

Rector Nelson died on 2nd April 1875, aged 68, at the home of his son, C. B. Nelson, in Waterloo Road, Ramsey, having been in failing health for some time. The funeral was on 5th April at Bride, and was attended by a large number of parishioners. There was a line of carriages from Ramsey and blinds were drawn in houses in the village. The service was taken by Archdeacon Moore, and at the end of it the choir sang the hymn "When our heads are bowed with woe" as Nelson had requested on his death bed. The Archdeacon was deeply affected at the graveside. Clergy present were Kermode, Drury, Caine, Airey, Paton, S. N. Harrison, Dinwoody, White and many well known lay people. Mrs Mary Nelson died in Douglas, on 24th August 1881, aged 66.

Towards the end of April a memorial signed by many parishioners (mainly Methodists) was sent to the Governor asking that Joseph Bellamy, the Chaplain of Laxey) and formerly a Methodist Minister, should be the new Rector, but in May the Governor replied that he could not conscientiously accede to the request.

The new Rector was the Vicar of Arbory, John Qualtrough. On his arrival he lived in the house by the village well, then was the first to occupy the new rectory. He held monthly Manx services, but about 1850 Manx services in many parishes dwindled from three Sundays in the month to every other Sunday and eventually stopped altogether. Qualtrough always preached in a black gown and once told the Bride people that if his successor preached in a surplice he must be a Jesuit.

The church was consecrated by Bishop Selwyn of Lichfield on 8th September 1876, a beautifully fine day. The Archdeacon acted as the Bishop's Chaplain. After the service 150 people had lunch, which went on until 4 p.m., in the schoolroom, provided by Mr E. C. Farrant.

The population of Bride in 1871 was 880.

CASTLETOWN   The Revd George Parsons died on 11th April 1855, aged 60, and was buried at Malew on 13th April. All shops in Castletown closed, and all business was suspended. A memorial tablet was erected in the church in 1856. He was succeeded by Edward Ferrier, who remained Chaplain until 1895. In Castletown he was Chaplain to the prison, then in Castle Rushen, and ministered daily to the prisoners. He was a leading Oddfellow, being Grand Master of the Isle of Man District, and was also a devoted Freemason. When Sir John Goldie-Taubman became Provincial Grand Master he appointed Ferrier as the First Provincial Grand Chaplain.

He started a Poor Relief Society in Castletown, and was always trying to build suitable houses for workers and poor people. He coached many young men without charge for the ministry and other careers. In 1857 he established a circulating library in the town. During his chaplaincy he installed four Bishops in St Mary's. Ferrier was a man of unfailing courtesy and sound judgement who was thorough and whole-hearted in everything he did. Canon Savage described him as wise in counsel, kind, unselfish and while always straightforward and outspoken, it was with the utmost consideration for the opinions of others. Archdeacon Gill said that he had never known a more upright man than Ferrier. He was a devoted and tireless parish priest and an eloquent, sometimes even flowery, preacher.

The population of Castletown in 1871 was 2,318 and the stipend £140.

CRONK Y VODDY   The stipend in the chaplaincies was so low that there was a rapid succession of chaplains. The first was John Garde, who was Chaplain of St John's from 1845-65 and who acted as Chaplain from 1852-54. Then came Charles Stewart. He had suffered from bronchitis for some time and his death was caused by bursting a blood vessel during a fit of coughing. The next Chaplain was

Christopher Taylor 1857-8, in whose time the organ, built by Jackson, the organ builder of Ballaugh, was installed. It was opened on 27th June 1858, the Bishop preaching both morning and evening. Next came Henry Hardy, who was appointed on 17th July 1858 and left in November to become Vicar of Jurby. He was followed by John Corlett (March 1859) who was Chaplain until November 1865 when he became Chaplain of St John's. James Edmunds succeeded him (1866-75). He died on 28th May 1875 aged 61 and was buried at Kirk Michael, John Corlett taking the service.

There was then an interregnum of four months, during which John Corlett walked from St John's to take the Sunday afternoon service. Mrs Hall, who had built the church, did a good deal of visiting while there was no chaplain and by her kindness of heart kept the congregation together. She also had the parsonage re-decorated and re-furnished and lived there herself for a short time. The next Chaplain was Edward Collet. He found that, due to Edmunds' illness and death and the interregnum, things were in a bad way. The churchyard was used as a children's playground and for drying clothes. The altar was ragged and dirty, the font encrusted with dust and dirt, the bell broken, many windows smashed, the stove out of repair (it had not been used for 10 years) and the walls dilapidated. The offertory averaged 1/10 a week. When he asked how often Holy Communion was celebrated no-one knew. He started a monthly celebration and introduced the eastward position. His views were High Church. In February 1876 he engaged a builder to do the repairs for which a considerable sum had been raised. The last Chaplain under Powys was Joseph Kyte, appointed in October 1876.

ST JAMES' Stephen was succeeded by Charles Hill, who was Chaplain for ten uneventful years (1858-68). In November 1859 he gave six evening lectures on astronomy to large audiences, the proceeds being for the Day and Sunday Schools. The last Chaplain under Powys was Joseph Kyte, 1868-72, after which there seems to have been no chaplain until 1881.

DHOON In 1853 William Carpenter, Vicar of St Barnabas' (1832-48), bought a piece of ground at Glen Mona for a new church with money he had received from the family of Mr C. Saltmarshe, who had recently died, as a thank offering for the spiritual benefits that he had received from Dr Carpenter's ministry at St Barnabas". The cost of the church was £730 and this was wholly met by Mrs Saltmarshe and her daughters. They also gave £200 towards a chaplain's house. Owing to legal difficulties the start of the work was held up until Whit Monday, 5th June 1854, when the foundation stone was laid by Governor Hope, who showed great expertise with trowel, square and plummet. It was a lovely day and many people attended. The Governor arrived at 2 p.m. and was met by the Archdeacon and Vicar General Corlett. Revd W. Kermode, Chaplain of St Paul's, made the opening remarks, Psalm 84 was sung by St Paul's Choir, and Vicar Harrison of Maughold took the prayers. An inscription on parchment, and some coins of the reign, were then put in a bottle which was sealed and placed in a groove prepared for it in the foundation. The Governor and the Archdeacon both spoke and the ceremony ended with prayers and blessing by the Archdeacon, who then provided a picnic lunch for the Governor and his wife near the waterfall in Ballaglass Glen, which they then explored. Mr William Haslam of Ballaglass, entertained many people at his house. The builders of the church were Messrs. James Callow and John Looney and the architect was Ewan Christian. The church was consecrated on 24th December 1855 and was licenced for marriages in 1897.

Meetings for worship had been held at Glen Mona since 1840, led by the Revd William Christian until his death in 1850, aged 59, and by the Revd Thomas Fenton. He was followed by Lloyd Bruce. After him came Samuel Hill. The next Chaplain was Hugh Stowell. Then came Jonathan Akroyd, who died on 1st November, 1872 and was followed by Stephen Nathaniel Harrison (1873) who had kept the services going after Akroyd's death. He remained Chaplain until 1889.

FOXDALE The present parish was formed out of Patrick, Malew and Marown, though Foxdale itself was in the parish of Patrick. The patrons are the Bishop and the Crown alternately. For 25 years before the church was built, services were held in the schoolroom, known locally as the Mines Chapel. In February, 1850 the people asked that their schoolmaster, Joseph H. Kewley, a graduate of St Edmund's Hall, Oxford, might be ordained as Curate of Patrick to give them a resident minister. Duties at Foxdale had been performed each Sunday by the Chaplains of St Mark's, St John's and the Vicar of Marown in rotation. Bishop Auckland agreed. The Diocesan Association had made a grant for a Chaplain at Foxdale. Kewley did much open air preaching and many came to hear him. In 1853 he became Diocesan Inspector of Sunday Schools. When he left in October 1854 he was presented with a pocket Communion set from the "Captains, miners and people of Foxdale". The next Chaplain was Francis Swallow.

Swallow was succeeded as Chaplain by John Leech (1859-64) then in December 1864 came Frederick James Moore, who was one of the outstanding clergy of the Manx Church. Moore was musical, so he acted as organist and choirmaster and formed a male voice choir. He was a thorough Manxman, respected by all, and was a great friend to the poor of Foxdale, besides visiting regularly in the parish. He was a fine preacher, with a special gift of preaching to children. He played a large part in obtaining a site for the church and in its building, and in this he was strongly supported by Mrs Kitto. He was also a great temperance worker. When he left to become Vicar of Jurby in 1875 the people presented him with a silver salver and a gold watch and chain.

Moore was succeeded by William Hart (1876-77) and the last Chaplain under Powys was Thomas Bates.

On 20th March 1854 a meeting was held in the schoolroom attended by the Archdeacon, Vicar Gill of Malew, Vicar Holmes of Patrick (Chairman) and Kewley, and it was resolved that as the schoolroom was inadequate for the spiritual needs of the district, plans should be made to build a church. A Committee was formed, with power to co-opt, consisting of Holmes (treasurer), Kewley (secretary), Gill, J. T. Clarke (Chaplain of St Mark's), Captain Bawden of the Foxdale mines and Messrs. H. Clucas, W. Pinder, J. Morcom, J. Johnson and R. Clucas, and they were asked to prepare a statement embodying the main facts of the case. The need for a new church was clear from the fact that in 1854 450 men worked in the Foxdale mines. By June 1872 £380 had been raised. A site was chosen at Ballameanaugh, the estate of Captain Bawden, who gave the ground at a much reduced cost. The churchyard was bought from Mr R. Clucas, Kionslieau. The church is 72 x 25 feet, and seats 250. As a result the foundation stone of the new church was laid on 7th May 1874 at 3 p.m. by Mrs Hall, widow of Archdeacon Hall. The Archdeacon gave the address, and the choir sang the anthem 'How amiable are thy dwellings'. The day was fine and people came from all over the Island, about 700 altogether. In the evening tea was provided in relays, and a concert was held at 8 p.m. preceded by prayers taken by Vicar Garde of Patrick, and during the concert short addresses were given by four of the clergy. A special train ran from St John's to Douglas at 10.30 p.m. The architect was James Cowle, and the builder was John Callister of Foxdale. The estimated cost was £630.

The church was opened for worship on 1st August 1876. Present were Mrs Hall and Vicars Garde (Patrick), Hutton (St Thomas'), Airey (Kirk Michael), Gill (Malew), Moore Jurby), Langton (St Luke's), Hawley (St George's), and Hart (Foxdale). Garde took the service and Moore and Hart read the lessons. The Archdeacon, in accordance with the terms of the Trust Deed, appointed two churchwardens, John Williams, Captain of the mines, and Thomas Hudson, schoolmaster. He also appointed John Kaye, a farmer and miner as sidesman. The Archdeacon preached on St Mark 11[17] and in his sermon he regretted the tendency of the time to attach too much importance to teaching and too little to public prayer and worship. At 8 p.m. there was a concert which lasted until 10 p.m. at which Garde was chairman.

One of the reasons why the church was built was the need for a churchyard, as until 1874 Foxdale people had to carry their dead to Patrick for burial, and as early as 1869 they asked for some provision to be made.

ST GEORGE'S Forbes, who died at Cannes on 12th May 1882, aged 68, was succeeded by William Hawley (1859). While Curate of Andreas (1847-52) he lived at Ballakaneen House.

The disputes with Bishop Powys over Hawley's appointment and over the churchyard have already been described.

In January 1860 the church was painted inside, but Powys refused to agree to the church being closed for a single Sunday so the work was done in a week, but the smell of paint was so overpowering that several ladies left on the two following Sundays to avoid fainting and Hawley was so affected by it that on the second Sunday, 29th January, he was too ill to take the services.

In 1864 the old semi-circular apse was pulled down and the present chancel, vestry and organ chamber were erected. The new organ was opened on 19th April 1865 by Mr George Hirst, organist of Liverpool Philharmonic Society, who played for both morning and evening services. There was a choir of about 30. The Archdeacon preached at both services as the Bishop was ill. There were fewer people than expected in the morning but in the evening the church was full.

The central chancel window was given by Mr Henry Bloom Noble in 1865 and the reredos on the east wall, given by Mrs Hawley's family, was erected. A new font was given by Miss Moore in 1872. The two stained glass windows in the chancel, given by Mr Samuel Harris, were removed when the chancel was enlarged in 1909 and set up in the new chancel. The side windows of the chancel were given by Mr Harris' daughters in 1910 in memory of their father. The pulpit was given in 1910 by Mrs Kendal, daughter of Commodore William Kermode of the Steam Packet.

In Hawley's time the stipend was £245 and the services on Sunday were at 11 and 6.30.

In February 1869 Robert Collister, who was the owner of a livery stable in Douglas, resigned as sexton after 30 years because of differences with Hawley. He was succeeded by William Kewley who had, for some time, been assistant sexton.

A proposal at the 1873 Vestry meeting that the Psalms should be sung at the morning service was defeated. On 20th Decmeber 1874, after a service of Holy Communion, a lady entered the Communion rails and threatened Hawley with an umbrella, saying that he was "taking them to Rome". Three choir men removed her from the church and Hawley remained completely calm throughout the incident. She also had a grudge against the Queen, and a few days previously had defaced references to her in a large and valuable Prayer Book. She came to Evensong but was turned away as it was feared that she would cause more trouble.

In December 1875 there was much controversy, due to misrepresentation over a proposal to have a surpliced choir. Hawley considered that most of the congregation favoured it and preached on the subject on 2nd January 1876, but all the old adult choir resigned and some leading members of the congregation left. In June 1875 Archdeacon Philpot, aged 84, visited Douglas, and preached to a large congregation in St George's.

In October 1877 Hawley accepted the living of Patrick and on 14th February 1878 the congregation presented him with an Address and £160, and gave Mrs Hawley a pedestal lamp. He also received an Address signed by all the nonconformist ministers in Douglas, and by about 50 leading nonconformists, something which he did not expect. At St George's and in his later parishes of Patrick and Kirk Michael Hawley was held in the highest esteem as a gentleman and for his quiet manner, upright character, personal piety, courtesy and ready sympathy.

GERMAN The 1871 Easter Vestry was marked by great noise and disturbance, and the High Bailiff of Peel, Mr R. J. Moore, more or less took over from the Vicar as chairman. There was doubt as to whether the wardens were properly elected and the case came on before the Vicar General at a special Court on 21st May 1872 when it was decided that they were properly elected. The 1873 Vestry meeting was well attended, many evidently expecting the kind of scene common in recent years. It was the custom in German for the retiring churchwardens to nominate their successors at the Vestry meeting. Four wardens were always elected for the country parts of the parish and two for the town of Peel. At this meeting Captain Cameron was elected a warden for Peel but the Vicar General disallowed it on the grounds that he was not resident in German, though he owned 10 acres in the parish but no building.

In August 1870 Mr James K. Ward of Montreal, while on a visit to his native town, presented the church clock and a Vestry meeting on 9th December 1870 decided to build a tower at the west end to house it. It is about 70 feet high, and replaced the old belfry. The clock is placed near the top of the tower and is reached by 67 steps. The bell is about halfway up the tower.

In April 1865 the parishioners presented Vicar

Stowell with a silk gown, hood and stole as a mark of their appreciation.

When Vicar Brown of Kirk Michael, who was Surrogate for the western area, died in 1860 it was felt that the Surrogate should be in Peel, so in 1864 the townspeople asked that Stowell be appointed Surrogate, as they had to walk to Kirk Michael to get a marriage licence. Marriage by licence was much commoner than by banns at this time. Powys replied that he had already offered the surrogacy to the new Vicar of Kirk Michael, Ingram. When Ingram left in 1874 a memorial was drawn up signed by about 100 people and sent to Powys, who was then at Bournemouth, by High Bailiff Moore. This time the request was successful and Stowell was appointed Surrogate.

In 1858 a committee was appointed to preserve the remains of the Cathedral from irreparable decay. Subscriptions were invited and in August 1859 a fair was held in the Castle grounds which raised enough money for urgent repairs. Further urgent repairs were done in 1877-79.

In 1860 a new organ was installed.

At the Easter Vestry meeting on 29th March 1875 Messrs. John Quine and J. S. Moore were elected as churchwardens for the Cronk y Voddy area. When Moore said that they were both Methodists Vicar Stowell said that they must become church-men and that he would see to it that they both attended church. Moore said that he would attend by proxy, to which the Vicar replied that under these circumstances he would arrange for the wardens to be sworn in by the Attorney General so that he would know the position.

On 11th June 1871 the Curate, Theophilus Talbot, complained from the pulpit that he had been publicly insulted by the Vicar by starting the service early.

In 1874 the churchwardens claimed the right to control and distribute the St John's offertory. Corlett, the Chaplain, resisted this, saying that St John's was a Government Chapel, hence the German churchwardens had no right to interfere. Governor Loch was consulted and wrote to the churchwardens supporting Corlett and telling them that they had no legal status in St John's Chapel.

In October 1876 Stowell authorised the use of Hymns Ancient and Modern instead of the collection called The Mitre, or Hall's Hymns, which had been used for many years.

The population of German in 1871 was 1,762.

ST JOHN'S Garde remained Chaplain until he became Vicar of Patrick in 1865. The chaplaincy was then offered to E. W. Kissack, Curate of Andreas, but he declined, so it was offered to John Corlett, Chaplain of Cronk y Voddy. His duties began on Christmas Day, 1865 and ended on Christmas Day 1908. He was a leading member of St John's Oddfellows, and was a genial man, full of humorous stories.

ST JUDE'S John Qualtrough was succeeded as Chaplain in October 1859 by George Bishop, who returned to England in 1865 and died in 1873. Then came Benjamin P. Clarke, an outstanding man who gave great service to the Manx Church and was one of the leading churchmen by the end of the century. The stipend of St Jude's was £100 per annum.

In 1865 he started evening adult classes where workmen could, for a nominal sum, learn the elements of education. He also began raising money to buy a harmonium. He left St Jude's in June 1869 to become Vicar of Marown. The next Chaplain was Edward W. Kissack, who also had a distinguished career in the Manx Church. The last chaplain under Powys was James S. Wilkinson (July 1872), who remained until 1888.

JURBY Vicar Harrison died very suddenly on 2nd November 1858 at Thornhill, the home of Mr William Collister. He was 74 and was buried at Jurby. He was succeeded by Henry Hardy, the Chaplain of Cronk y Voddy. He was a witness in the case of Laughton v. the Bishop of Sodor and Man, as he had Arthur Vesey, one of 'Mossman's Monks' as Curate from December 1866 until July 1867. In July 1869 Hardy announced that he would charge 2/6 for burials from another parish, 5/- for erecting a headstone and one guinea for covering a grave with brick, stone or slate. For some time before his death he suffered from a disorder of the brain and he was not always responsible for his deeds and sayings.

The next Vicar (September 1875) was F. J. Moore, the Chaplain of Foxdale, who left in December 1878 to become Vicar of Lonan.

The population of Jurby in 1871 was 788 and the value of the living was £167.

LAXEY Until 1856 Laxey was part of the parish of Lonan, with no church or chaplain of its own and services were held in the Schoolroom, but when Vicar Qualtrough of Lonan died in 1853 it was felt that something should be done towards building a church in the village with its own chaplain. The new Vicar of Lonan, Thomas Caine, was appointed on condition that the chaplains of the proposed church should be appointed by the Bishop and that although they would not be full incumbents they would be independent of the Vicar of Lonan and not just his curates. The foundation stone had been laid by Bishop Auckland on 12th March 1852, the ceremony being attended by Archdeacon Moore, Vicar Qualtrough, the Revd Edward Ford (Chaplain to the Laxey miners) and by the miners themselves led by Captain Rowe, who afterwards invited a large party to lunch. The architect of the church, which is in the early English style, was Ewan Christian and the cost was £550, of which the Laxey Mining Company gave £200, the remainder being made up by donations from the Commissioners for Woods and Forests, the Society for Promoting Church Building, the Bishop and the Archdeacon. The church was consecrated by Bishop Powys at 11 a.m. on 27th May 1856 - a beautifully fine day. The day began with Holy Communion at which the Bishop and the Archdeacon officiated. The Bishop preached on Nehemiah 8[8], saying that faithful exposition of Scripture was better than preaching about doctrinal points and striving for originality. The miners enjoyed a holiday for the day.

The land for the church had been given by Mr G. W. Dumbell, Chairman of the Laxey Mining Company. The indenture for this, which was signed by Mr & Mrs Dumbell and by the Bishop, said that no other building was to be erected within 60 feet of the church, that all seats were to be free, and that collections at the services of Mattins and Evensong should be held in trust by Mr Dumbell for the upkeep of the church. Mr & Mrs Dumbell also conveyed to the Bishop land for a chaplain's house and garden, a condition being that it was only to be occupied by a clergyman appointed by the Bishop.

The first Chaplain was Hugh Stowell Gill, who was appointed in 1856 and left to become Vicar of Rushen in 1859. He was succeeded by Matthew Pierpoint.

He came to Laxey after four short curacies in England, and left in 1861 to become Curate of St John's, Cardiff. Next came Joseph Bellamy, who was Chaplain from January 1861 until December 1878 when he became Vicar of Jurby. On 12th July 1863 Bishop Powys preached at the Anniversary in the evening, accompanied by the Governor and his wife, and as the church could not accomomodate everyone he preached on the lawn in front of Captain Rowe's house.

LEZAYRE W. B. Christian remained Vicar until 1861. After 1861 he gave up parish work but on 16th February 1866 he was co-opted as member for Ramsey of the self-elected House of Keys - the last member to enter in this way, as Governor Loch introduced the democratic system in 1867. The 1867 election was a triumph for Christian, as he was elected for Ramsey unopposed. He was escorted from Milntown to Ramsey Courthouse by the Volunteer Band, the Benefit Societies, the Amateur String Band, men on foot and on horseback and by numerous private carriages. While Member of the House of Keys he worked long and hard for the Queen's Pier and was, on several occasions, Deputy Speaker. He resigned his seat on becoming Receiver-General in 1883. In this post he was very successful, as he was a good administrator and although not eloquent, what he said was always sensible and carefully thought out. In 1866 he became a Justice of the Peace. He was taken ill suddenly on 7th July 1886 and was unable to speak for some time. He died at Milntown at 5.30 p.m. on Saturday, 31st July 1886, aged 70, and was buried at Lezayre on 4th August. Nearly all the Government officials attended, including the Governor and the Bishop. Governor Loch, in Tynwald, spoke of his invariable courtesy and unfailing good temper, while Mr E. C. Farrant spoke of his observance of the courtesies and amenities of a gentleman. Christian had an unsurpassed love for the Island. His sterling character and kindly manner won him universal esteem.

In 1856 half an acre was bought to extend the burial ground. The three-decker pulpit was removed to the north side of the church in Christian's time. It stood in the centre of the aisle completely hiding the altar. The reading desk was removed to the south side. The east window is in memory of Deemster John Christian, who died on 27th February 1852, and his wife, Susanna, who died on 14th March 1853.

Christian was succeeded by Edward Snepp, who was private chaplain to Governor Pigott. In June 1863 he exchanged livings with Thomas Henry, Vicar of St Paul's, Halifax, who was Vicar from 1863 to 1869.

In June 1869, with the approval of the Crown, Henry exchanged livings with William Hutton, Vicar of Tipton, Staffs, a brother of F. N. B. Hutton, Vicar of St Thomas'.

The population of Lezayre, including North Ramsey, in 1871 was 1,620.

LONAN Thomas Caine was Vicar from 1853-78. On New Year's Eve, 1862 he and his wife entertained the wardens and choir at the vicarage.

After the meal a pleasant evening was spent in cheerful conversation, interspersed with vocal and instrumental music, and ending with prayer. A similar gathering was held on 28th December 1865, from which the party returned home at 11 p.m.

In 1863 Caine held some weekday evening services at Beinn y Phott for the men building the mountain road. His first address, on St Luke 19^{10}, was well received.

On 31st May 1869 a special Vestry meeting decided to enlarge the burial ground by buying an acre of land, part of the Rhaa estate, for £100. It was on the east side of the old churchyard. The Vicar said that in his 16 years there had been about 900 burials and the old churchyard was full. The extension was consecrated by Bishop Powys on 28th July 1871, the ceremony lasting about an hour. Very few people, and only two clergy, attended, apart from Samuel Harris, the Diocesan Registrar.

Thomas Kerruish, for 50 years Parish Clerk and Schoolmaster, died on 26th November 1874, aged 75.

Mrs Caine died in the vicarage on 17th July 1869 and the Vicar on 15th November 1878 after nine days illness. The funeral was very large, there being nearly 50 carriages, while members of the Temperance Societies and the Rechabites turned out in force. The sale at the vicarage on 11th February 1879 included a brown mare, 2 cows, 17 sheep, 2 pigs, a few poultry, 2 carts, a roller, a turnip cutter, a wheelbar-

row, a grindstone, an iron cooler, a turnip drill, a gig and harness, and much cart harness. A memorial pulpit to Vicar Caine was installed in the church on 28th February 1880.

ST LUKE'S Gill was succeeded as Chaplain in September 1856 by George Dawes. The next Chaplain was Robert Airey, who, while at St Luke's lived at Bridgemount Cottage, Tromode. B. P. Clarke was Chaplain from 1864-65. W. F. Drury, elder son of the Vicar of Braddan followed (1866-68). Born in 1841 he graduated from Corpus Christi College, Cambridge in 1863 and was made Deacon (1864) and ordained Priest (1865) by Bishop Higgin of Derby. He returned to England in 1868 and eventually became Vicar of Holy Trinity, Burton on Trent. He died in 1913.

E. W. Kissack was Chaplain for a few months in 1869. The last Chaplain under Powys was Charles Thomas Langton (1869-80). He was known in Baldwin before becoming Chaplain and the Baldwin people were very anxious that he should be their chaplain. While at St Luke's he lived in Union Mills. Langton gathered a considerable congregation by his engaging manner to all people and ages and by his zealous, yet unobtrusive, discharge of duty. He worked among his people quietly and steadily, identifying himself with their interests, sharing their troubles and earning their confidence and respect.

On 29th September 1875 Langton entertained the churchwardens and choirs of St Matthew's and St Luke's and the St Luke's schoolchildren (about 60 in all) to tea at the parsonage.

MALEW On 5th April 1863 (Easter Sunday), William Clucas and James Dogharty opened the grave of a widow, Mrs Morrison, who had been buried the previous Sunday. Their object was to untie the strings of her cap and shroud, believing that unless they did so she would not rest in her grave but would haunt them. They had previously been refused permission by the Vicar, so they did it at 6 a.m. They were taken to court by the Vicar and Wardens and were severely reprimanded by the High Bailiff and ordered to pay costs.

The burial ground was extended in 1865 and was consecrated by Powys on 13th November.

At a Convocation held at St John's on 27th July

1865 William Gill was elected Proctor in Convocation for the clergy. On Sunday 8th October 1871 Gill preached twice, attended the Sunday School, took 2 funerals and joined in the evening service at Castletown, where his son, H. S. Gill, was the preacher. On Thursday 12th October he had a stroke while taking a wedding. As he pronounced the last words of the exhortation he fell back into the chair behind him. Although apparently fainting, he was anxious to complete the service, but after reading over part of it three times he said "I feel very unwell" but his speech soon failed and he sat down at the altar. Thomas Quilliam, the clerk, went to help him and in a few minutes he seemed a little better, but as he appeared to be in pain Quilliam ran to Mr Moore of Great Meadow, for brandy. Mr Moore quickly brought it and Gill took a little. Quilliam then went to Castletown for Dr Wise and to tell James Gell, (his son-in-law) and J. F. Gill (his brother) who at once started for the church, accompanied by Ferrier, the Chaplain of Castletown, who completed the service. The Vicar was taken home, but he never fully recovered consciousness although he recognised his family. It was clear that he would not recover though on Sunday morning he asked for his spectacles as if to complete the wedding service. He died peacefully at 6 p.m. on Tuesday, 17th October, aged 74. All the nearby shops in town and country at once closed and did not re-open until the following Monday. The parishioners draped the church in mourning and wreathed his coffin with flowers. His funeral was at 11 a.m. on Saturday 21st October and although it poured with rain all morning the church was full of people from all parts of the Island. The oak coffin had no fall as Gill disliked them. The funeral was taken by his former Curate, Gilmour Harvey, Vicar of Santan, and the hymn was 'O God our help in ages past'. On his memorial window in Malew Church are the words 'We preach Christ crucified' and on his tombstone is inscribed the text 'Blessed is that servant whom his Lord when he cometh shall find so doing.' Matthew 24[46].

He was succeeded by his son, Hugh S. Gill. On Sunday, 28th January 1872 he read himself in at Malew, having preached his last sermon in Rushen in the morning. There was a good attendance at Malew, despite a wet and stormy day. On Wednesday afternoon, 31st January, he was inducted to Malew by the Revd G. Harvey and the Revd E. Ferrier - again a wet day.

Gill's move to Malew caused great sorrow in Rushen but he accepted it in order to be near his mother, who went to live in Castletown, in the early years of her widowhood and so that his children could attend Castletown school. In 1875, as he had a growing family, he added to the vicarage a new dining room, 2 bedrooms, a study, a bathroom, a storeroom and attics. The stipend in 1875 was £200. Gill's health was not very good at this time so in 1874 various friends gave him and Mrs Gill the means to have a holiday in Italy, which did him much good. In later years he had a holiday in Spain, one in north Wales and many in Scotland.

By 1874 the church had been re-decorated and a pulpit and reading desk had been put on the south side. Mrs James Gell gave a brass bookstand for the pulpit and William Gill's widow gave a stained glass window for the sanctuary in his memory.

Gill was a small eater, and was never an early riser, so he breakfasted alone. At Malew he had a little den upstairs where he worked and smoked and read. He never wholly overcame a tendency to unpunctuality. He rode about the parish on horseback and kept a trap drawn by Jack at Rushen and Billy at Malew. Both were spirited horses, and although Gill was a good, if rather reckless, driver he was apt to forget the horse in conversation. He had large eyes and with his bushy eyebrows he could look very fierce. He could always keep order at crowded meetings and concerts. His stories were told with a wonderful imitation of the Manx dialect. Like his father he was very fond of children.

The population of Malew in 1871 was 2,466.

ST MARK'S J. T. Clarke's later work was to finish the buildings on the glebe, consisting of the dwelling house, the workman's cottage, stable, cowhouse, barn, loft, potato shed, carthouse (all slated except the cottage), the well, pigsty, and hen roost (both thatched), the garden with its pillars and gate, the pillars and gate at the entrance of the glebe road and the walls, pillars, gates and new fences on the old glebe. He also fenced and formed a mill dam in the old garey, which could also be used as a watering place for cattle and he drained and cultivated the old glebe lands. In 1855 a new bell, cast in Dublin, was obtained for the church and the floor was repaired. 1855 also saw the completion of 20 miles of high road, the building of four bridges, and the erection of ten milestones. This work meant that all the glebe, except what the chaplain needed personally, could be let, thus improving the stipend and giving the Chaplain more time for clerical duties, as he would not have to farm the glebe. In 1863 an infants' school was built. The granite font was a gift from Bishop Powys who, after preaching at St Mark's on 25th May 1856 afterwards baptised in it two boys, both named after the Bishop.

Clarke resigned in May 1864 mainly because of his bereavements and on the previous Shrove Tuesday, 9th February, he was presented by St Mark's people with a fine silver inkstand and a purse containing £30. His resignation was deeply regretted by everyone in St Mark's, as he was universally respected. He ministered to the people in Manx, and even treated their bodily ailments. At all times of the day or night he responded at once to any call from a sick person. He was known as 'The Patriarch of St Mark's'. In 1850, to help the poorer people he had founded a Benevolent Society called 'St Mark's Union Society' with 200 members. Clarke was a fluent Manx speaker and amid all his works, and at a time of severe domestic affliction, he found time to share with the Revd William Gill of Malew the editing of Kelly's Manx Dictionary. The stained glass window in the church was set up to his memory in 1899.

The new Chaplain was Thomas H. Gill. This appointment to St Mark's, by his father, was queried by Bishop Powys, as the Consecration Deed reserved the right of appointing the Chaplain to the Bishop, although no Deed had been executed by the then Vicar (Daniel Gelling) giving the Bishop this right. Powys consulted English Counsel, who said that he was the Patron, but his local advisers thought otherwise, so he dropped the claim, though previous Bishops had appointed the chaplain without any protest from the Vicar of Malew. Gill only remained Chaplain for a year and when he left the people were too poor to give him a present, so he absolutely declined one, but the farmers moved all his household goods to the boat without charge.

The main feature of his chaplaincy was a restoration of the church which was re-opened on completion of the work on 3rd August 1865. At 2.30 there

was a service, at which the Bishop based his address on Solomon's Prayer at the consecration of the Temple. At 4 p.m. he consecrated an addition to the churchyard made by Gill, using a consecration prayer of Bishop Wilson, then he led everyone around the ground singing Psalm 149, followed by a hymn. It was a day of sunshine and cool breeze and at 5 p.m. tea was served on the village green. The day concluded with addresses by the Bishop, the Archdeacon, the Vicar of Malew, and the Chaplain. The memorial tablet to T. H. Gill in the church was unveiled by Sir James Gell on 11th June 1899 when the Chaplain, Holmes, preached on St Luke 18[1].

He was succeeded by Robert Airey who was esteemed and respected by all, and was a great friend to the poor and sick, whom he helped up to, and beyond, his ability. The foundation stone of the school was laid just after he left, on 8th August 1874. He was followed by John Mitchell. The last Chaplain under Powys was Frederick B. Grant (December 1876) who was very popular.

MAROWN William Duggan died very suddenly on 2nd March 1862, his wife having died a few weeks before. He had his sorrows and troubles, for example on 26th June 1842 his barn and its contents were destroyed by fire, which spread to some other outbuildings and the horses were only removed from the stable with difficulty.

Although the property was insured, the period for renewing the policy had inadvertently been allowed to expire. Until 1850 he had kept up the tradition of reading prayers at Keeil Pheric on Ascension Day. He was succeeded by Robert Wesley Aitken, in April 1862. His father, an Anglican priest, adopted Methodist ideas and preached much in the open air. He was instrumental in building Crosby Methodist Chapel. He took charge of Marown in the spring of 1863 while his son was in Cornwall for his health, and attracted over-flowing congregations. He had married the daughter of a Warrington businessman named Eyres, and as his wife's mother had helped him financially he renamed his farm (Ballayemmy) Eyreton, in her honour. He had moved to the Island because of his wife's delicate health and had acted as honorary Curate of St George's, but gave this up after a dispute with Bishop Murray on a point of doctrine.

There was no vicarage in Marown at this time, so he lived in the big house on the bridge, now divided into two. He spent much time with his dogs and guns and owned a fine pair of hunting horses. He was a kindly man and a friend to the poor - for example on New Year's Eve 1867 he gave a number of widows and old folk in the parish a substantial dinner. He usually took his turn at shouldering the coffin at funerals. In his time the church was too small for the congregation. A new organ was installed in 1863 which was used until 1959. Before leaving in June 1869 the parishioners presented him with a large 14 day clock and his wife with a silver salver, each suitably inscribed.

Thomas Christian, for over 50 years Sumner and Parish Clerk, died on 22nd December 1867, aged 82.

Aitken's successor was Benjamin P. Clarke, Chaplain of St Jude's, who began a ministry at Marown of 33 years.

In 1870 Mr Samuel Harris, Episcopal Registrar, inspected the parish registers and found many inaccuracies in the past 10 years, and on 15th June 1871 a committee was appointed under Harris to consider the matter and report to Tynwald. In January 1871 a mourner at a funeral at the old parish church described it and the churchyard as being in a deplorable condition.

Marown glebe lands were scattered over the Ellerslie Estate and it was impossible to define their boundaries, so in 1876 Tynwald agreed to the Vicar's request to sell them for £450.

The population of Marown in 1871 was 1,121.

ST MATTHEW'S A new organ was obtained in 1863 and was first used on 1st November. The preacher for the occasion should have been James Bellamy, Chaplain of Laxey, but a storm on the previous day kept him in Liverpool, so Robert Airey, Curate of St George's took his place.

At the Chapter Court on 10th June 1870 Mr Archibald Clarke and Mr Caesar Quine were not sworn in, as a Mr Quane, for whom Mr Sherwood appeared, objected, saying that the only notice of the Vestry meeting had been given from the pulpit on the previous Sunday evening. Vicar General Jebb upheld the objection, saying that written notice had to be given at the church door.

In May 1871 the Chaplain, John Cannell, was recovering from a serious illness, so the services were taken by the Revd Hugh Derrig, Chaplain to the Mental Asylum. At the 1872 Easter Monday Vestry meeting on the 1st April only Cannell and the churchwardens were present. Cannell resigned in June 1873 due to age and failing health after a faithful ministry of thirty eight years, and he died at his home, 6 Auckland Terrace, on 8th March 1874, aged 73. He was buried at Onchan on March 12th, the funeral being attended by an immense crowd of people, 43 carriages were counted. In September 1873 Douglas Corporation discussed the possibility of moving St Matthew's church to enlarge the market place, but were unable to afford it.

From 1873-78 there was no chaplain, as Vicar Drury of Braddan, whose parish still included St Matthew's, felt that he could keep the services going, with the help of his Curate, Langton, Chaplain of St Luke's. Drury took Mattins (held early so that he could get back to Braddan) and Langton took Evensong. Langton came every Sunday evening from 1873, without pay, and attracted large congregations. At the 1876 Vestry meeting on the 1st April he said that it had been a strain on his health, and that he could only continue for a few more Sundays. He said that the pulpit was so high that it made him giddy, but Drury, the chairman, refused to have it made lower as he did not like these modern notions. It was suggested that Langton should preach from the Bishop's throne, which Cannell had done when he was too feeble to ascend the pulpit. In 1874 a week's mission was held in Douglas, and Drury held several well-attended mission services in St Matthews.

At a Vestry meeting held on 2nd May 1876, the question of a permanent minister arose. Drury, the chairman, said that he was very anxious to obtain one and it was decided to ask the Bishop to appoint Langton, who had proved very acceptable to the congregation. Powys replied on 4th May from his home in Bournemouth that the appointment rested with Drury, not with him, and this letter was read at the adjourned meeting on 16th May. By November 1877 no appointment had been made, mainly because of the small stipend (£120). Drury had offered it to Langton, who had private means, but he had been under some promise to Powys not to seek for a change, so he reluctantly declined.

In 1876 there was a dispute between the Braddan

Bishop Wilson 1698—1755

Bishop Wilson's birthplace at Burton near Neston, Cheshire. He was born there on 20th December, 1663.

A drawing of Bishopscourt by Daniel King in 1651. It would have looked much like this when Bishop Wilson first saw it in 1698.

Plate 1

The Revd James Wilks, 1719—1777,
Rector of Ballaugh and Vicar General

Bishop Hildesley 1755—1772

The Revd Philip Moore, 1705—1783,
editor of the Manx Bible

The Revd Evan Christian, 1744—1811,
Vicar of Patrick and Vicar General

Plate 2

Bishop Crigan 1784—1813

Bishopscourt after Bishop Crigan's alterations (between 1784—1788) which changed the roof line of the tower and included six new sash windows on the three main floors. The Bishop and his family lived in a small house in Peel during the alterations.

Bishop Murray 1814—1827

Bishopscourt after 1814 when Bishop Murray commissioned alterations including castellations and a Georgian gothic chapel

Plate 3

Bishop Ward 1828—1838

Revd J T Clarke, 1799—1888, Vicar of St Mark's

Revd William Drury, 1808—1887, Vicar of Braddan

Plate   4

The state of the Manx Church when Bishop Ward arrived in 1828

ST MARY'S CHAPEL IN CASTLETOWN
In the Parish of Malew.
Seat room for 1800. — Pop.n of town 2400.

PARISH CHURCH OF BRADDAN.
Seat room for 400. — Population 2434.

PARISH CHURCH OF KIRK ST ANNE
Seat room for 250. — Pop.n 280.

ST GEORGE'S CHAPEL IN THE TOWN OF DOUGLAS.
Seat room for 1000
Population 8350.

ST MATTHEW'S CHAPEL IN THE TOWN OF DOUGLAS
Seat room for 300
St George's 1000.
1300.

ST PAUL'S CHAPEL IN THE TOWN OF RAMSAY,
and Parish of Maughold
Seat room 800. — Pop.n of Town 1863.

PARISH CHURCH OF ONCAN.
Seat room for 150. Pop.n 1781

PARISH CHURCH OF LONAN.
Seat room for 300. — Pop.n 9280.

PARISH CHURCH OF KIRK CHRIST LEZAYRE.
Seat room for 250. — Pop.n 2709

PARISH CHURCH OF MAUGHOLD.
seat room for 360. — Pop.n 1837.

PARISH CHURCH OF BALLAUGH.
Seat room for 350. — Pop.n 1187

PARISH CHURCH OF KIRK ANDREAS.
Seat room for 650. — Pop.n 2729.

PARISH CHURCH OF KIRK CHRIST, RUSHEN.
Seat room for 200. — Pop.n 3154.

PARISH CHURCH OF KIRK PATRICK
Seat room for 500. — Pop.n 2485

PARISH CHURCH OF KIRK BRIDE.
Seat room for 250. Pop.n 1220.

PARISH CHURCH OF JURBY.
Seat room for 280. Pop.n 1518.

PARISH CHURCH OF KIRK MICHAEL.
Seat room for 300. — Pop.n 1737.

ST JOHN'S CHAPEL IN PARISH OF GERMAN.
Seat room 200.

PARISH CHURCH OF ST GERMAN
IN THE TOWN OF PEEL.
Seat room 500.
St John's 200.
700. — Pop.n 4608

PARISH CHURCH OF MAROUN.
Seat room for 250. — Pop.n 777.

ST MARK'S CHAPEL IN THE PARISH OF MALEW
Seat room for 200

PARISH CHURCH OF MALEW
Seat room for 550.
St Mark's 200.
750. — Pop.n 3239.

PARISH CHURCH OF ARBORY
Seat room for 500. Pop.n 1725.

Plate 5

A series of views of Manx churches built during the episcopacy of Bishop Ward (1828—1838). The prints were commissioned by Ward's successor, Bishop Bowstead (1838—1840) as a memorial to his work.

Kirk Lonan Church, with the Tomb of the Rev^d. Hugh Stowell, who preached the dilapidated state of the Manx Churches through England, & collected £4,000 there, towards the building of these new Manx Churches.

Baldwin Chapel, which, during the Week, serves, by means of screens, as separate School Houses.

Plate   6

Dawby Chapel, also used as a School House.

Kirk Onchan Church.

Plate 7

Ballaugh Church.

Sulby Chapel, also used as a School House.

Plate   8

Lezayre Church.

Kirk Michael Church, with the Tomb of the celebrated Bishop Wilson.

Plate   9

Bishop Short 1841—1846

Bishop Shirley 1847

Bishop Auckland 1847—1854

*Revd John Alcock, Chaplain
of St Barnabas', 1848—1852*

*Richard Jebb, 1808—1884,
Vicar General*

Plate 10

Bishop Powys 1854—1877

Bishop Hill 1877—1887

Revd William Gill, 1797—1871,
Vicar of Malew

Archdeacon Gill, 1830—1912,
Son of Revd William Gill

Revd Thomas Gill, 1836—1894,
Chaplain of St Mark's and of Malew.
Son of Revd William Gill

Revd J Hughes-Games,
Archdeacon, 1886—1895

Plate   11

Bishop Bardsley 1887—1892

Bishop Straton 1892—1907

Bishop Drury 1907—1911

Revd John Howard, 1817—1892,
Vicar of Onchan

Archdeacon Kewley 1860—1941

Canon Quine, 1856-1940, Vicar of Lonan, and Mrs Quine

Plate 12

and St Matthew's churchwardens over the claim by Braddan wardens that St Matthew's wardens should collect cess for Braddan in Douglas. For many years Douglas had paid one third of the cess for the undivided parish of Braddan. Early in May both sets of wardens met, and it was agreed that they should jointly collect the cess.

MAUGHOLD On 12th June 1860 a special Vestry meeting was summoned by order of the Bishop to consider building a new church. Most were opposed to this and finally it was decided to put on a new roof, to repair the pews and rough-dash the exterior. The north and south walls were rebuilt. The east window was not in line with the centre of the church and the east end of the south wall curved in to obviate this. When the chancel floor was lowered in 1865 a large quantity of bones was removed.

On 6th September 1865, after a confirmation, a Vestry meeting was held to consider the state of the churchyard and wall. There had been complaints of neglect and it was alleged at the meeting that bones, even with flesh still on them, had been found lying about. Archdeacon Moore, who was present, agreed that the churchyard was not what it should be. It was further said that graves were not deep enough and Powys suggested that the Vicar should not say prayers over any grave less than four feet deep. Finally it was decided that the Vicar and Wardens should employ a man two days a week, for the next year, and that a dry stone wall 5 feet high (including the coping) be built around the churchyard at the rate of 100 yards each year. The Bishop's conciliatory tone prevented the meeting from being stormy, as had been expected. He left the meeting for a short time to inspect the churchyard. Sheep had been freely kept in the churchyard, and in the centre various persons had enclosed large sections by chains and railings.

Vicar Harrison died at the vicarage on 20th April 1871, aged 79, loved and esteemed until the end. He was always on good terms with his parishioners. In the days of tithe he never put the tithes to auction but agreed in a few words with the farmers. He always allowed the Oiel Voirreys in Christmas week. He was friendly to the Methodists and gave a subscription to building Ballajora Chapel. By 1870 his infirmities were increasing and many parishioners felt that they would never get his like again. He left £80

for the poor of Maughold.

He was succeeded by William Kermode, Chaplain of St Paul's, Ramsey since 1843. Although he had moved to Maughold as a less exacting post, as his health had suffered from his hard work at St Paul's, he threw himself into the work with his usual energy.

About 1839 mining for iron had started in Maughold glebe under a mining lease from the Commissioners of Woods and Forests. This continued for years, and large royalties were paid to the Crown. Vicar Harrison had claimed the mines as his freehold and protested against the action of the Crown lessees, but took no steps to stop them beyond petitioning the Commissioners. They replied that their solicitor, and the Manx law officers, all said that the Vicar had no claim. Bishop Short had tried unsuccessfully to help the Vicar. A new mining lease was given to Richard Rowe and others, but Vicar Kermode threatened legal proceedings if they started mining. The case was heard by Deemster Stephen on 18th and 19th May 1875 and the verdict was for the Vicar as the glebe being freehold, the royalties belonged to the Vicar. The Maughold Vicarage Act of 1877 provided for the leasing of minerals in the glebe lands of Maughold and for the investment of royalties from these minerals for the purposes of the parish. This enabled Kermode to increase the stipend by £60 per annum and to enlarge the vicarage. This was a very old building, altered and added to from time to time. Originally it was a single storey thatched cottage, but in 1767 a second storey was added and it was slated. In 1834 two more rooms and a staircase were built. Kermode added a large new block of several rooms which juts out to form two sides of a square. He also improved the schools. Kermode was inducted by the Archdeacon on Monday afternoon, 19th June 1871 but few parishioners were present, as the occasion was not given much publicity.

Harvest Sunday 1871 was so wet and stormy that Kermode continued the services the following Sunday.

When Matthew Summers, Parish Clerk from 1833-75 died, his son gave the credence table in his memory. The election of a new Clerk took place on 30th March 1875 when Thomas Killip, who had been deputy Clerk for ten years, was elected by 453 votes to 193 for Edward Corteen. Election day being fine, there was great excitement and the road from Ramsey was thronged with cabs and carts all gaily decorated with flags, blue for Killip, Red for Corteen. All householders, and even occupants of apartments and owners of ploughs had the right to vote, and party feeling ran high, but there was no trouble. The local band played in the afternoon. After the result was declared a triumphal procession was formed with Killip in front and the band a mile behind. They paraded through Ramsey for half an hour, thousands gathered in Market Square and finally Killip's supporters unloosed the horses from his cab and drew him through the Town.

Kermode was elected Proctor for the clergy in Convocation in 1873, 1874, 1880 and 1886. In 1870 he was worshipful Master of Maughold Masonic Lodge of which he was a founder member.

The population of Maughold (including south Ramsey) in 1871 was 1,433.

KIRK MICHAEL Joseph Brown's long incumbency ended when he died in the vicarage on 27th January, 1860 aged 75. His funeral, on 2nd February, was taken by Archdeacon Moore. He had been Episcopal Registrar since 1818 and it was fully expected that he would be succeeded by his son, Robert, who had been helping his father for 20 years. Nearly all the members of the Manx Bar signed a petition to Powys that he should be appointed but the Bishop ignored it and appointed Mr Samuel Harris. Robert Brown had fully satisfied the legal profession in discharge of his duties and had been kind to everyone. Many felt that the Bishop had acted heartlessly in depriving him of an office he had held for so long, and it was attributed to the fact that Powys had not been on good terms with Vicar Brown. There was further criticism of the fact that all the documents and Deeds had been moved from the vicarage to Bishopscourt, under the supervision of Powys' butler, on a windy day, and instead of being put in bags, were put in carts, covered only by a sail. Upon these Deeds depended the title to much property in the Island. The deeds were now kept in a room at Bishopscourt reached only by an iron staircase, so there was no danger of fire. In answer to the criticism it was stated that the day for the removal had been fixed by the Vicar General, who had hired the carts for the day, and that no-one could help it being

windy. On being dismissed Brown had consulted a lawyer, who advised him to take no action. The matter was raised in the House of Keys, where there was some criticism of the Bishop and it was admitted that he was not popular and not on the best of terms with the clergy. Once again Powys was probably right, but was tactless in his methods. In May 1860 the Keys petitioned the Governor, in view of "recent circumstances" to have a proper Registry built.

The next Vicar was James B. Kelly (February 1860) who remained until June 1864. In the Autumn of 1861 he and Vicar Hardy of Jurby were accused by the Revd William Mackenzie, a Methodist minister, of hearing confessions. Both Kelly and Hardy were favourites of Powys, who supported them, but Archdeacon Moore did not support them. Kelly had published a booklet called 'Steps to the Altar' which contained very High Church views. At the 1861 Convocation the Archdeacon had preached a sermon enunciating sound Protestant principles, but Powys, in his Charge, made personal accusations against some of the Douglas clergy, and tried to extenuate Kelly's booklet. W. B. Christian moved a resolution, seconded by S. Simpson, supporting the Bishop, which was adopted after an animated discussion of one-two hours, during which Powys and Kelly withdrew from the meeting. It was, however, adopted in a rather watered-down version, so W. Gill proposed a more definitely worded address to the Bishop which some of the clergy, mainly from Douglas, refused to sign. Another meeting at St John's left things as unsatisfactory as before. On 13th November 1861 Kelly wrote to the 'Manx Sun' stating that he had never asked anyone to come to confession except in the words of the Prayer Book Exhortation and no-one had ever asked him to hear a confession. He wished neither to go beyond or fall short of the Prayer Book. He added that Mackenzie's accusation had weakened his influence in Kirk Michael and had sown suspicion and dissension in the parish, besides bringing aspersions on the Bishop who, he said, had always condemned Romanist teaching. In the end Kelly withdrew 'Steps to the Altar'. Kelly was a good parish priest, zealous in visiting the sick and helping the poor. In 1860 Powys presented the church with a new pulpit made from one of the chestnut trees planted by Bishop Wilson.

On 23rd October 1863 Kelly presented a churchwarden in the Vicar General's Court for non-attendance at church. Jebb dismissed the presentation with costs on a technicality - that the defendant's Christian name was not stated in the warrant.

The next Vicar was William C. Ingram who, from 1863-64 was Chaplain to H. M. Forces at Woolwich. On 12th October 1870 the first Harvest Thanksgiving was held in Kirk Michael. On 20th January 1873 the church was badly damaged by lightning in a thunderstorm.

Ingram refused to transfer the school property to the Education Committee when the 1870 Education Act came into force, hence the Act remained almost a dead letter in Kirk Michael.

At the Easter Vestry meeting on 1st April 1872, presided over by the Captain of the Parish (as Ingram never attended Vestry meetings) the following resolution was passed:

'That the churchwardens be ordered to take legal advice as to whether the Vicar of this parish can be presented for not attending Vestry meetings'.

At the Chapter Court in Peel on 15th May the wardens presented Ingram who said that he absented himself intentionally as he considered that he was not bound to attend. On 1st November 1872 the Vicar General gave his ruling that the Vicar was not obliged to attend or to state his reasons for absence (however desirable it might be that he should do so) and dismissed the presentment. Ingram did not attend the 1873 or the 1874 Vestry meetings. The 1873 meeting had been announced in Church as being at 11 a.m. on Easter Monday. For a long time neither Vicar nor Wardens appeared. Someone called out 'Every man to his tent O Israel' and the few who had come were about to go home when the wardens came with Mr Evan Gell, the Captain of the Parish, who took the Chair. There was indignation that the Vicar should treat his parishioners with so little respect. Despite this Ingram was popular, as he was good to the poor and did much for the Sunday School, though he was uncharitable to the Methodists. On leaving Kirk Michael he was presented with an ink stand, a dining room marble clock and vases. His sister, who kept house for him as he was unmarried, received a walnut work table from the Sunday School. Ingram left in June 1874 to become Vicar of St Matthew's, Leicester, a large and poor parish where he became widely known for his work in promoting religious education among the young. In 1887 he was made an honorary Canon of Peterborough, and from 1893 until his death on 25th April 1901, aged 64, he was Dean of Peterborough.

The last Vicar under Powys was Robert Airey, who had been Chaplain of St Luke's, and then of St Mark's. He resumed the practice of the Vicar chairing the Vestry meetings and at the meeting on 29th March 1875 he suggested a public subscription to provide a heating apparatus for the church. In 1877 the first ever Watchnight service was held in the church and was well attended. Airey left in 1878 to become Vicar of Santan.

The population of the parish in 1871 was 1,231.

Kirk Michael and Bishopscourt choirs had their annual picnic on 20th August 1874. Their first stop was at Peel where they heard Mattins in the old Cathedral, then they had lunch in the Castle grounds. They then went on to Glen Helen for tea. The Bishop's daughters went with them.

ST OLAVE'S We have seen how the Revd W. B. Christian had equipped a barn in Bowring Road for worship in 1849. The first Curate in charge (the Curate of Lezayre) was W. D. Carter (1847-8) who went to be Curate of St Thomas' and the second was Thomas Millington (1848-50) who had been ordained by Bishop Auckland (Deacon 1848, Priest 1849). He left to become Curate of St Sepulchre, Northampton. His successor was Robert Airey (1850-58), then came William Clay (1858-61). Next came J. J. S. Moore. He returned to England in 1863 and was followed by Thomas Lee, and when he left in 1865 George Paton became Curate in charge (1865-6). From 1866-7 the Curate in charge was Henry Barff. He returned to England and was succeeded by Walter Awdrey (1867-70).

The foundation stone of St Olave's was laid on 8th July 1861 by the Governor, Francis Pigott, after Mattins at which Bishop Powys preached. Archdeacon Moore was also present, but he always felt that the church was badly sited as regards the parish. The 'Mona's Isle' made the trip from Douglas for the occasion and the passengers swelled the crowd. The architect was Mr Michael Manning of London, and the builder Mr James Lambert. The church cost £1,500, to which the Revd W. B. Christian gave generously. It is in the early English decorated style and was licenced for worship on 12th September 1862, but the building was not finished until 1870, when the first chaplain was appointed in the person of Theophilus Talbot. The second Chaplain (1874) was Edward Curwen. The last Chaplain under Powys was Charles Buckley (1876-78). Buckley was unpopular with his congregation, as early in 1878 he announced that, on doctrinal grounds, he could no longer allow Hymns Ancient and Modern to be used, and replaced it by another hymn book.

At this time the only stipend for the chaplain came from pew rents, plus what was raised from private sources. In October 1876 a committee was formed to start an endowment fund for the church.

ONCHAN An extension of the burial ground was consecrated by Powys on 10th September 1857. A major restoration of the church was undertaken early in 1863 and was finished in July. At the east end the large unsightly pews were replaced by substantial open benches. The space occupied by the three-decker pulpit was given over to free seating for about 50 people. The chancel arches were erected and a new lectern and prayer desk of oak were given. The north chancel porch was opened out into the church by two arches, one facing the west end and the other the altar. The memorial window to three former vicars, (Gell, Cannell and Craine) made by Messrs. Forrest & Co., of Liverpool, was erected in the chancel and the walls and spire were put in order.

Vicar Howard's wife died in the vicarage on 17th July 1875. The services in his time were at 10.30 a.m. and 3 p.m. In January 1877 Mr Samuel Harris, the Episcopal Registrar, inspected the registers and, as at Marown, found many inaccuracies over the past ten years. Governor Loch took the same course as at Marown. In 1873 the Parish Registers Act was passed to remedy these defects at Marown and Onchan. In 1871 a new heating stove was put in the church.

Early in 1874 a dispute arose at a meeting of the School Committee when Henry Cadman, until then one of Howard's best supporters, accused the Vicar of saying that he (Cadman) wanted to levy a 2/6 school rate. The Vicar had certainly mis-quoted one of his speeches. Howard said that this was false and, after the meeting, assaulted Cadman with a walking stick. On the following Sunday, 8th March, he said

from the pulpit that should Cadman accuse him of lying again he would punish him more severely. Next day Cadman applied to the High Bailiff for Howard to be bound over to keep the peace and he was bound over in his own surety of £50 and two of £25. Howard refused to ask anyone to stand surety for him, and was committed to prison, but during the week two sureties came forward and he was released.

In March 1877 Richard Cowley, Headmaster of the Board School and Parish Clerk for 20 years until his recent resignation, refused to hand over to Howard the plan of the new churchyard, the account book of the sale of graves and the book of forms for the receipt of purchase money for graves. The matter came to court and Howard's petition to make Cowley hand them over was adjourned (27th March) so he pinned a notice on the church door saying that he would allow no burials in the new churchyard until Cowley handed them over to the Episcopal Registrar (Harris). The Easter Vestry on 1st April was stormy and a policeman was in attendance. Cowley was ordered to hand over the documents to the churchwardens and it was resolved that two copies of them should be made, one for the Vicar and one to be put in the vestry.

Meanwhile there was another dispute. In this same March 1877 Mr Daniel Christian of the Clypse told John Skillicorn, a labourer, to open the family grave for his dead sister, but Howard forbade him to do so as it was his freehold. Next day he started to open it and when Howard arrived there was an acrimonious discussion. Skillicorn however continued his work and Howard took the funeral on 6th March. The same day he put up a notice in the window of Mrs Kissack's hat shop saying that if anyone else opened a grave without his permission he would be proceeded against in both the civil and church courts. He headed the notice:

'Daring outrage in the parish churchyard of Onchan. Beware! Beware!! Beware!!!'

On 6th April Howard appeared in court as the result of a series of rows arising from the Vestry meeting on 1st April. John Skillicorn, Henry Cadman and Richard Cowley asked that he be bound over to keep the peace following a fight in the road between him and Skillicorn. A doctor said that Skillicorn had been badly beaten about the face and head. He was bailed to appear next day. At this adjourned hearing Howard described a statement of Mr A. N. Laughton (prosecuting) as a lie. On his refusal to withdraw this he was committed to Castle Rushen, then the prison, for five days. He was confined in what had been the Countess of Derby's room, his meals being sent across from the George Hotel. On 14th April Dr Mountford of Douglas and Dr Wood, who was in charge of the Mental Asylum, examined him. Mountford withdrew the next day, saying that he could not certify Howard insane, so Dr Clague of Castletown was called in, and on 16th April they certified Howard and he was moved to the Asylum. The court case resumed on 17th April when High Bailiff Harris said that he had received a letter from Governor Loch saying that it had been reported to him from Castle Rushen that Howard was of unsound mind and that he had committed him to the Asylum under the Lunatic Asylum Act of 1860. This action caused great consternation in Douglas, a subscription of £70 was raised for Howard's defence and it was suggested that Counsel be employed. Mr A. W. Adams was retained and on 20th April he lodged a petition to the Government praying that Howard be released and that his committal for contempt be declared illegal. This petition was heard the same day before a special Chancery Court consisting of Governor Loch, Deemster Drinkwater and the Clerk of the Rolls (Mr M. H. Quayle). Applause for Adams was so great that the Governor ordered the Court to be cleared and the hearing was adjourned until next day when the petition was dismissed. The judges slipped out of Court by side and back entrances, as a large crowd, sympathetic to Howard, had gathered outside the Court and greeted them with groans and hisses. On 25th April Adams went to London to submit Howard's case to Counsel and retained Mr Watkin Williams, QC, with a view to an appeal to the Queen.

Howard's health failed in the Asylum, he missed his children and was depressed. The Douglas clergy kept the services at Onchan going while he was away. On 16th April the adjourned Vestry meeting was held in the Vicar's absence, about 20 people attending and Messrs. Cadman, Daly, Quine and Christian were elected wardens, none well disposed to Howard. It was decided to sell the Parish school so that all the children could attend the Board school.

On Sunday 29th April some children from Onchan Sunday School walked to the Asylum and al-though they were not allowed to see the Vicar they left 14/8 which they had collected for the Howard Release Fund, which eventually reached £230. In July 1877 the Duke of Richmond, Lord President of the Council, said that Howard's case was not one which the Queen ought to recommend to the Judicial Committee of the Privy Council. Howard was eventually released on 7th August, thanks to the efforts of Mr Adams. He had started Family Prayers in the Asylum and was much loved by the other patients. He was greeted with great delight on his return to Onchan, and the church bell was rung for an hour. He was somewhat reduced physically, but was mentally alert and cheerful, not vindictive, but determined to have his rights.

Meanwhile things were not going smoothly in Onchan. Relying on Howard's declared wish for peace Mr F. Daly attended church and, at the proper time, he, as churchwarden, went forward to receive one of the offertory boxes, but the Vicar stalked past him and gave one box to the sexton and the other to a member of the congregation. Mr Daly returned to his seat and Howard kept the offertory without the usual checking by the wardens. Next Sunday Messrs. Quine and Christian were the wardens on duty but Howard gave the boxes to two boys, one his son. Mr Christian returned to his seat, but Mr Quine took the box from one of the boys and made the collection. Howard refused to count the collection with Quine and retained it. He then announced that he disputed the wardens' election and that he intended to test it in Court.

The population in 1871 was 1,620.

PATRICK Vicar Holmes died on 1st November 1865 and left £50 for a memorial window to him and his wife in the church. He was succeeded by J. F. Garde, the Chaplain of St John's, who was instituted at Bishopscourt on 1st December 1865, and inducted on 6th December by the Vicars of German (Stowell) and Kirk Michael (Ingram). His appointment was popular in Patrick. On 27th April 1869 he was married in Bishopscourt Chapel by Ingram to Miss Mary Birley of Ballacosnahan, Patrick. She left the Island after her husband's death and died at Exeter on 24th March 1884.

On 13th August 1874 a meeting was held under the Captain of the Parish, Mr R. Quirk, to consider whether to repair the parish church or build a new one. It was decided to ask the Bishop to appoint a special Vestry meeting to discuss the matter. This took place in September 1875 and decided that the church was unfit for further use, and that a new one should be built, without the choir gallery, to seat 200, on or near the present site.

Garde had bad relations with the Methodists and when the churchyard had to be extended in 1871 a meeting decided that half should belong to the church and half to the Methodists. On one occasion he threatened a group of Rechabites with legal proceedings because they sang a hymn over the grave of one of their members.

On 13th December 1873, the body of Robert Quayle of Peel was washed ashore at Glen Mooar. The inquest was on the following Monday, and orders were given to dig a grave at Patrick, but Vicar Garde said that if the burial could not take place on the Monday he could not allow the body to be left in the church all night. It was therefore kept in the family home overnight and the funeral was fixed for 2 p.m. next day, but the body was so decomposed after three weeks in the sea that Garde, using the discretion given to ministers in the rubric, conducted the whole service at the graveside. The family was very indignant over this and the service took place amid loud protests and remarks. After the Vicar withdrew an argument began between the family and the Parish Clerk, who was pelted with sods.

ST PAUL'S William Kermode built the vicarage in 1859 at a cost of £730, with the help of a grant from the Diocesan Association, on ground given by his parents, Thomas and Margaret Kermode of Claughbane. She was descended from the Callows, who had been owners of Claughbane since the 17th century. Kermode paid one third of the cost himself. Before moving into the new vicarage he had lived at 73 Parliament Street.

As far back as 1849 Kermode had suggested sanitary precautions against cholera and in 1856 he established the Ramsey Sanitary and Medical Dispensary. He also formed the Ramsey Health Association which was almost the start of self government in Ramsey. In 1868 he was largely responsible for providing free dinners for poor children.

In 1863 hot water heating was put into the church

and in 1864 the first organ, costing £78, was installed. In 1869 the pulpit was moved from the body of the church to its present position.

In 1865, while preaching on a Sunday morning, Kermode was suddenly seized with paralysis and his speech was affected, but he recovered fully. The Revd W. B. Christian took his place for some months. Kermode was one of the pioneers in forming the Ramsey Life-saving Corps, or Rocket Brigade. His splendid ministry of 28 years ended in February 1871 when he became Vicar of Maughold. Kermode, as Vicar of Maughold, claimed the right to appoint the next chaplain of St Paul's and, with Powys' agreement he nominated the Curate, George Paton, who had been for some time Chaplain of Taggart's Barn, later St Olave's. When H. G. White became Vicar of Maughold in 1878 he gave up the right to nominate and it passed to the Bishop. Paton was born on 11th October 1836 at Thurso and was educated at Edinburgh Academy, and later at Edinburgh University where he studied law and medicine. He came to the Island with his parents in 1853 and his father built Ormly Hall. He was made deacon by Bishop Jacobson of Chester on 11th June 1865, and was ordained priest by him on 11th March 1867, both by letters dimissory from Powys, who was ill on the first occasion. He was a keen Oddfellow and a lifelong supporter of the Lifeboat. His churchmanship was rather too high for many at St Paul's and many left the church, but his personality was such that the church was well attended. He and his wife were renowned for their kindness and generosity and were great friends of the poor. In 1887 he became the first Chairman of Ramsey Poor Law Guardians.

In 1874 extensive work on the church was begun. The old low ceiling was removed, thus exposing the massive roof timbers. A window was placed on either side of the gallery and the organ was moved from the gallery to its present place, thereby making the end gallery available for seats. A new chancel and three full length windows were added to the south side. Choir stalls were made and a new reading desk. The wooden rails in the south chancel chapel were from Ballure church. The wall separating the apse from the rest of the church was taken down, thus opening up the east end, and a new vestry was built on the north side.

A new pulpit, given by Bishop Powys, was sited

near the organ and the font was replaced by one of carved stone. In 1876 Paton added three stained glass windows to the chancel. The church had to be closed during this work but it was re-opened on 24th May 1874, Archdeacon Moore preaching in the evening.

In 1871 Paton caught typhus fever while visiting the sick. He did much for the Town of Ramsey. For 30 years he was either Secretary, Treasurer or Chairman of Ramsey Lifeboat and in 1875 he built the Old Cross Hall as an infants' school, but it was later condemned and he lost a large sum of money. Paton was a man of strong personality and was never afraid to express his views, however unpopular.

RUSHEN William Corrin's long incumbency ended with his death in the vicarage on 5th February 1859, aged 64. He had seen the death of five of his thirteen children. The memorial to him in the church was erected in 1860. He was succeeded by Hugh S. Gill, the Chaplain of Laxey, who remained until he was appointed Vicar of Malew in 1872. His Curate at first was B. P. Clarke, who had virtual charge of Port St Mary, though as yet there was no church there, and since 1848 services had been held in the school. Clarke was a diligent visitor, especially to the sick and aged, he was a good friend to the poor, and he had worked hard to educate both children and adults. Congregations at Port St Mary increased during his nine years curacy and when in 1864 he left to become Chaplain of Baldwin, he was presented on October 20th with 100 sovereigns, a gold watch, (suitably inscribed), a pocket Communion set and an Address. On 29th April 1862 he had been presented with Scott's Bible Commentary, a Greek New Testament with notes, Hayden's Dictionary of dates and Hook's Church Dictionary.

In June 1864 Richard Qualtrough was elected Parish Clerk in succession to his uncle, Thomas Qualtrough, for whom he had deputised for a year. He had 200 votes against 4 for his rival. Members of his family had held the post, with one short break, for 150 years. The Parish Clerk at this time announced the verses of the Psalms and raised the tune. The election by the parishioners always took place in the parish church and the candidate had to undergo tests in singing and reading. After the passing of the 1881 Burials Act Parish Clerks were appointed sexton by the Vicar and Wardens. Born in 1834 Richard

Qualtrough died at his home in Port St Mary on 28th September 1903 and was succeeded by his son, Evan, who held the post until 1947 when the family connection ended.

In May 1869 Vicar General Jebb refused to swear in the four churchwardens elected at the Easter Vestry, on the ground that the accounts for the past year had not been duly presented and passed by the Vestry. The Vicar was told to hold another meeting, which took place on 18th May, but this meeting decided to take the case to court to test the legality of Jebb's refusal. They won their case on 3rd June when Jebb's ruling was reversed and he was ordered to swear in the four wardens.

In 1864 Mr Edward Gawne of Kentraugh gave a heating apparatus (the first to be installed), and the lamps, to the church. During renovations in 1869 the three decker pulpit with its blue and black hangings, which stood halfway down the south side, was removed, and the Gawne pew (which had a canopy supported by 4 pillars and which stood on the north side facing the pulpit) was removed to its present position. The window on the right of the chancel was given by Mrs Gawne in memory of her eldest son, who died on 27th July 1869. She added the apse in September 1872 in memory of her husband who had been Speaker of the House of Keys until 1867. She also had the aisle and chancel paved with Minton tiles. In 1869 the damp and discoloured walls were stripped of their whitewashed plaster and coated with a light grey cement. The bare rafters were covered in with stained and varnished boards. In July 1875 Mrs Gawne gave the two side windows in the apse.

In 1869 about 1½ acres was added to the burial ground, the decision having been taken at a Vestry meeting on 10th December 1867, and authorised by Tynwald on 28th October 1868. The Vestry meeting instructed the churchwardens to buy from Mr J. T. Clucas a small field adjoining the glebe lands of the parish and to ask the Crown and the Bishop to agree to part of the glebe lands being exchanged for the said field. The price paid was £246 and a condition of the sale was that the Vicar should also convey a parcel of glebe land to the churchwardens to be added to the present burial ground and the wardens were to convey the field sold by Clucas to be added to the glebe lands of the parish. This 1869 extension was consecrated by Bishop Powys on 12th July 1869.

Gill used to hold a short week-night service at Cregneash, where Manx was mainly spoken, but he could not speak it fluently. Gill was fond of telling the story of a wedding in Rushen where the bridegroom, while taking his vows, said "With all my worldly goods I thee and thou". Gill said that in his time nearly the whole parish took Holy Communion at Easter. Baptisms at this time were performed during the morning service. The babies were brought into the vicarage kitchen to be got ready and the families sat around the fire until service time.

While Gill was Vicar there was a smallpox epidemic. The nearest doctor, in Castletown, was swamped with patients, so Gill obtained a supply of vaccine from him, with instructions on how to use it and, after preaching a sermon that it would be the people's own fault if they died of smallpox, said that he would vaccinate all who came to the parish school. Dozens came. There was also a terrible typhus epidemic which killed whole families and everyone was so terrified that no one would nurse the sick. Gill worked night and day among them, helped by one old woman who drank all she earned and presumably drowned her fears. Often he had to put bodies into a coffin with his own hands, the undertakers usually refusing to come beyond the garden gate. During both epidemics he always changed his clothes in the stable to protect his children.

While at Rushen Gill regularly visited his parents at Malew vicarage.

Gill was on good terms with the Methodists, but never gave in to them in any way, for which they respected him the more. Many of them were people who had been brought up in the church, but now wanted to become local preachers so that they could preach themselves. They came to church regularly, most communicated on Easter Sunday and the older ones communicated on Good Friday, when Holy Communion was at that time celebrated all over the Island. One old local preacher used regularly to borrow a sermon from Gill.

In 1864 Mr Gawne gave the church its first organ, which caused some opposition. Gill was the first parson in the Island to preach in a surplice instead of a black gown. It had been the custom to take off the surplice at the pulpit steps, put on a black gown, then put the surplice on again afterwards. One Sunday he became hopelessly entangled in the sur-plice while removing it, to the general amusement, and he angrily vowed that henceforth he would preach in a surplice. The parishioners objected strongly, and sent a deputation to tell him that such popish practices must cease. Gill pointed out that the black gown was very costly, it had to be worn at Convocation and he could not go on wearing it out each Sunday. He added that the clergyman had to preach in a decent gown provided by the parish and that if they bought him a new gown he would wear it. Nothing more was heard of the matter. Gill was succeeded early in 1872 by Edward Kissack, Chaplain of St Jude's, and on leaving for Malew the parishioners presented him with a silver tea service.

The population in 1871 was 3,660.

SANTAN Samuel Gelling died on 4th November 1865, aged 66, after being Vicar for 30 years, and was succeeded by Gilmour Harvey. On going to Santan he was presented with a gold watch.

On 26th February 1868 a Vestry meeting agreed to extend the burial ground from the Vicar's glebe, and the Vicar was to be compensated with part of the estate of Ballacrine, which was to be bought by the parish. The question also arose of a new vicarage, as the existing one was very dilapidated and for the site of a new one Vicar Harvey proposed that the parish should buy part of a field called Collister's Croft. Margaret and Esther Clucas of Ballavale, who had sold the part of Ballacrine, agreed to pay £88-1s-4d (being two thirds of the purchase price) to build a wall around the churchyard and to make certain repairs to the church. All this was approved by Tynwald on 28th October 1868 and on Monday afternoon, 12th July 1869, Powys consecrated the extension.

Before the new vicarage was built the vicar used to walk from the old vicarage in the glebe through a gateway in the wall (now built up) along the path on the other side of the wall, and enter the priest's door in the side of the church which took him right up to the altar. The new vicarage cost £693 of which Harvey paid £438.

In 1877 Harvey was appointed Vicar of Maughold, and before leaving he was presented with a clock and his daughter with a tea and coffee service as a token of the "universal respect" felt for him in Santan. He was succeeded by H. G. White, the curate of Ballaugh

The population of Santan in 1871 was 628.

ST STEPHEN'S From 1855-58 the Chaplain was William Kelly. He was remembered as a heavy smoker. Next came John Corlett (1858-9) the Chaplain of Cronk y Voddy. He gave to St Stephen's an altar chair once belonging to Bishop Wilson. James Wilson, who had been ordained by Bishop Davys of Peterborough, was Chaplain from 1859-60 and it was in his time that the title was changed from Chaplain of Sulby to Curate of Lezayre. His successor was Robert Aitken (1860-62) in whose time the parsonage was built. Then came Samuel Walker (1862-65) who had been curate of Andreas. He returned to England and was succeeded by J. E. Pattison (1865-78). He had been a Doctor in India and while at St Stephen's he acted as doctor for the Sulby district as well as being the minister. He would go anywhere, even up the mountain, to attend to the sick, and would take no payment except a fowl or a duck. He was an eccentric, and a great "character". He left in 1878 and went to Cornwall where he died soon afterwards.

ST THOMAS' We have already traced the long dispute between Bishop Powys and Vicar Drury over the patronage of the church.

In 1865 a hydraulic machine for blowing the organ was installed. The original reredos was erected in 1872 as a thank offering for the re-opening of the church and the lectern was given in 1875. Vicar Hutton was a man of integrity and truth, with great sweetness of character, diligent in his work and always a humble servant of God. He was beloved and respected at St Thomas' and in 1891 a memorial window was put in the church. He had begun his ministry at St James', Wednesbury, where his work among the poor in the terrible cholera outbreak of 1850 was typical of that self-denial which characterised his blamelesss life. At St Thomas' he was an unwearying visitor, and an unfailing friend of the poor.

The foundation stone of St Thomas' school was laid by Mrs Hutton on 31st July 1874. It was to have been laid by Mrs Hall (widow of Archdeacon Hall) who had contributed generously, but she was ill. Hutton organised the school on a sound basis before he left. Simpson had wanted to build a school, but the collapse of Holmes' Bank in 1851 ruined the project. The school was opened in 1875.

In 1877 Hutton accepted the living of St Saviour's, Leicester and on 17th August he was presented by the congregation with a silver tea tray costing £80, and a purse containing 36 guineas. He left on 29th September.

His reasons for leaving St Thomas' were:
(1) He felt happier with the working class congregation to which he was accustomed.
(2) He felt that he had accomplished the purposes for which he had been appointed to St Thomas'.
(3) He disliked pew rents.

Chapter 10

BISHOP HILL 1877-1887

Despite a rumour that Canon Bridgeman, the Rector of Wigan, had accepted the Bishopric, the new Bishop turned out to be Canon Rowley Hill. He was born in Londonderry on 22nd February 1836, the son of Sir George Hill and his wife, formerly Miss Elizabeth Rea. In 1859 he graduated from Trinity College, Cambridge, and was ordained by Archbishop Sumner of Canterbury (Deacon 1860, Priest 1861), he served curacies at Christ Church, Dover, (1860-1) and St Mary's, Marylebone (1861-3), then became Vicar of St Luke's, Marylebone (1863-8), Rector of Frant, Sussex (1868-71), Vicar of St Michael's, Pimlico (1871-73), then Vicar of Sheffield, where he was very popular (1873-77). In 1874 he became Rural Dean of Sheffield and in 1876 Canon of York. At Sheffield he did much for church extension, but his relations with the Methodists were not good. In 1863 he married Miss Caroline Mary Chapman, who was loved and respected in the Isle of Man. She died in London on 6th April 1882, after being in delicate health with a heart complaint for some years. Unlike her husband she was a total abstainer. On 11th June 1884 he married Miss Alice Eliza Probyn in Marylebone parish church, Archbishop Thomson of York performing the ceremony. Hill was genial, kind hearted, hard working and accessible to everyone, and quickly became popular.

His appointment to Sodor and Man was announced on 10th July 1877 and made him the youngest Bishop in the country. It was said that he owed his appointment to the Marquis of Abergavenny, whose Chaplain he had been and who was a member of his congregation at Pimlico. Abergavenny subscribed heavily to the Conservative Party, then in office under Lord Beaconsfield. When he left Sheffield to see the Prime Minister he had not made up his mind whether to accept the offer or not. He finally accepted, subject to a reduction of £500 in the Bishop's stipend to augment the stipends of the clergy. Hill's stipend was therefore £2,400. At this time the see was burdened with the remainder of a charge imposed in 1855 for improvements to Bishopscourt, repayable in 30 years by equal instalments plus interest. The Bishop's glebe then consisted of 245 acres in Kirk Michael and 365 acres in Ballaugh. On 25th July Loch told Tynwald that the Home Secretary would have agreed to receive a deputation regarding the revenues of the see, but could not do so now that Hill was appointed.

Hill was consecrated by Archbishop Thomson of York on 24th August 1877. The sermon was preached by Canon E. Hoare, Vicar of Tunbridge Wells on Acts 1^8, and the presenting Bishops were Durham and Rochester. 400 of his Sheffield parishioners attended. Hill and his wife had visited the Island from 16th-19th July, and were met on the pier by Vicar Hawley of St George's and Mr Samuel Harris. They stayed with the Governor. They inspected Bishopscourt with Mr J. Cowle, an architect and builder. Mrs Hill expressed a strong wish to live in Douglas, as her health was not good and Bishopscourt was badly in need of repair and was damp - it had only been occupied occasionally since Bishop Powys had left for the last time in late 1874. Hill decided to live in Douglas until the repairs at Bishopscourt had been completed and it was mid-December before they were able to occupy Bishopscourt. During this brief visit they went to Castletown and Ramsey.

On 26th August Hill preached his last sermons in Sheffield on II Kings 5^{19} in the morning and on Acts 8^{39} in the evening. The next evening he arrived in Douglas and was welcomed by Howard (Onchan), Langton (St Luke's), T. W. Drury, Samuel Harris and others before going to Government House. On 28th August he was enthroned by the Archdeacon in St Mary's, Castletown. The day was beautifully fine, all the ships in Castletown harbour were decorated with bunting and flags and flowers were everywhere. At 12 noon the Bishop arrived in an open coach and four with the Governor and Mrs Loch. Almost all the clergy attended and the hymns were 'Onward Christian Soldiers' and 'The Church's one foundation'. Hill was loudly cheered by the crowd when he left Castle Rushen after the legal formalities, then all the clergy and officials went for lunch to Westhill, the home of Sir James Gell, the Attorney General, who had recently been knighted with Deemster Drinkwater. Hill, Loch and many others hoped that the enthronement would be in St German's Cathedral in Peel Castle, but the repair work on the Castle, begun by Loch, was not sufficiently advanced. On 29th August Hill and Loch travelled by train to Peel to visit the Castle and Cathedral, in which the new Bishop showed great interest, and after having lunch in the railway refreshment room he went on to Bishopscourt. The Peel people regretted that the visit had not been announced so that they could have welcomed him. On 30th August he returned to Sheffield to arrange for his removal and finally took up residence in Douglas on 27th September.

Hill found that Powys had left all his books to his successor, in addition to a large painting of Bishop Wilson, which had been given to him by Lord Windmarleigh, a descendant of Wilson. In late August Powys' furniture was auctioned by Mr Raby, a Douglas auctioneer.

Hill preached his first sermon at Mattins in St George's on 30th September on Exodus 4^2 and preached again in the evening at St Thomas' on Psalm 55^{22}. He always preached without notes. He showed great energy in these early weeks in getting to know the diocese and his freedom from ritualistic tendencies made a good impression. He was, in fact, a member of the Church Association, which was anti-ritual. On 7th November he took his seat in the Legislative Council and on 6th December Cambridge University conferred on him the degree of DD. He appointed as his Examining Chaplains Dr Joshua Jones (Principal of King William's College from 1866-86) and the Archdeacon.

While on a short visit to Sheffield in February 1878, Hill was reported to have said that it would be the best thing for the diocese of Sodor and Man if it were joined to Liverpool, soon to become a separate diocese. In reply to a question in Tynwald about this on 20th February, Governor Loch said that no amalgamation with Liverpool would take place without Tynwald's consent and he was left in no doubt that this would not be given and that the merger would be opposed in every possible way. However on 18th March Hill invited the clergy to lunch at Bishopscourt and to a discussion on his proposal. The advantages he outlined would be higher stipends, a fund for the repair of churches and parsonages, and better hope of preferment. He said that several churches were in bad repair and that he could not attract men here with the low stipends. Some of the clergy said that stipends which were adequate some years ago were no longer so in view of the great rise in the price of food and other essentials. Hill offered to give £1,500 of his stipend to augment clergy stipends if the merger went through. A resolution was proposed that the union would be desirable if it could be made without any change in the constitution of the Island and on the basis of the terms put by the Governor to Tynwald in 1875. This was carried by 28 votes to 6, the minority being Kermode, Drury, B. P. Clarke, Paton, S. N. Harrison and Langton. The Vicars of Onchan and Lonan were absent. On 21st March Hill sent this resolution to the Governor, asking him to take steps to ascertain the views of church people. Loch replied that he would send the resolution to the Home Secretary, but declined to take any exceptional action to ascertain the views of Island Churchmen. He reminded Hill of the Home Secretary's letter of 29th January 1875 saying that he would only draw up a scheme in detail and that he would not do so without the consent of all parties. Lay opinion in the Island was totally opposed to the merger and the whole idea was dropped when in early April the clergy of the Archdeaconry of Liverpool (not yet a separate diocese) decisively rejected the idea of being linked to Sodor and Man.

On 5th March 1878, Shrove Tuesday, Hill revived the Peel Fishermen's Farewell Service, holding it at 6.30 p.m. so that the fishermen could attend. About 900 people crowded into the Parish church, which could only seat 650, and hundreds were turned away. Vicar Stowell led the service, Vicar Hawley of Patrick read the lessons and the prayers and the Bishop preached for 33 minutes on Acts 27^{11}. The hymns were 'Fierce raged the tempest', 'Eternal Father strong to save' and 'On the waters dark and drear'. The form of service was a shortened version of Wilson's Prayer for the Herring Fishing (1714). It was one of the most successful religious services ever held in Peel. A similar service had been held in Port St Mary, but not with the Bishop, on 1st March.

On 31st March Hill re-opened Bishopscourt Chapel and said that for the present there would be just one Sunday service at 3.30 p.m. Much work was done to the house and grounds in late 1877 and early 1878. The pillars, adorned with a mitre, at the entrance to Bishopscourt glen, replaced an old gateway. In May 1878 he bought a new organ for the chapel and gave the existing one to Kirk Michael church. He put a stained glass window in the ante-chapel in the wall formerly occupied by the fireplace and the stairs leading to the room above were removed, thus making more room for the clergy at Convocation. A curtain separated the chapel from the ante-chapel. Several hundred trees and shrubs were planted in the grounds.

The 1878 Convocation fell on 20th June and Hill said that he wanted to set up a Diocesan Conference to bring in the laity. He suggested a common hymn book for the diocese and said that he would like to restore St German's Cathedral and set up a Cathedral Chapter. He hoped to see more parishes created, and wished to improve the situation regarding church and parsonage dilapidations. He expressed surprise that many churches and vicarages were not insured.

On 28th June 1878 the House of Keys rejected a suggestion by Loch that the office of Vicar General should be abolished and his salary (£500 plus about £200 in fees) shared between the two Deemsters, to whom the Vicar General's secular duties would be transferred.

On the evening of 6th August 1878 the Bishop and Mrs Hill were driving from Peel to Bishopscourt in an open carriage, and on passing Ballagawne John Girven (one of several railway workmen standing by the road) threw a large stone at Mrs Hill and inflicted a fairly severe wound on her forehead. Joseph Scarffe, the coachman, stopped and Hill jumped out and gripped the man, who shook himself free and jumped the hedge. The Bishop chased him, then Girven turned and threatened to knife him. Mr Harrison, a grocer in Peel, then drove up and Hill got into his trap and they followed Girven towards Peel. He turned up a narrow road near Ballacarnane, followed by Hill and Harrison, whom he then threatened with a knife and a club, but the Bishop restrained Harrison from tackling him. Meanwhile the coachman had gone on to Kirk Michael where he met P.C. Cubbon of Ballaugh and P. C. Teare of Ramsey. They got into the coach and drove towards Peel where they overtook Girven and arrested him. He was commit-

ted for trial by the High Bailiff of Peel, Hill and Scarffe giving evidence. The coachman had previously driven Mrs Hill to the nearest cottage, where her wound, which was bleeding profusely, was dressed by Dr Anderson of Kirk Michael. The belief in the village was that Girven had aimed the stone, not at Mrs Hill, but at another workman who was getting the better of him in a quarrel.

On 14th August the Bishop wrote to all the clergy asking for their special prayers for him on Saturday, 24th August, the first anniversary of his consecration. He would have liked to have them all at Bishopscourt, but felt that a Saturday would not be convenient for them. On 26th August Hill preached to the Port St Mary fishermen, standing on herring boxes. Many local people came to listen.

Hill asked all the Douglas churches to hold a watchnight service in 1878.

Ascension Day 1879 fell on May 22nd, and Hill asked the clergy to keep it as a day of special prayers for missions. At Convocation on 5th June he announced that he had divided the Island into four Rural Deaneries and had appointed Drury (Braddan), Rural Dean of Douglas, Gill (Malew), Rural Dean of Castletown, Kermode (Ballaugh), Rural Dean of Peel and Kissack (Bride), Rural Dean of Ramsey. He suggested that Harvest Thanksgivings throughout the diocese should be held on the same day, but this received little support, though in the south this was already the case, and not a shop opened and no ship left port. To expedite Convocation Hill had asked the clergy to meet at Bishopscourt on the previous day to pass the accounts of the various charities. Many of the clergy expressed admiration for the great improvements the Bishop had made in the house and grounds. On June 12th, a beautifully fine day, he and Mrs Hill held a garden party at Bishopscourt.

On 17th July 1879 a special Convocation was held at Bishopscourt regarding the Bishopscourt Dilapidations Act. This allowed the recent work at Bishopscourt to be provided for by mortgage and to prolong the period in which the existing mortgage be paid, Mr James Cowle, architect and builder, was appointed Diocesan Surveyor.

In October 1879 Hill issued the rules and regulations for the Diocesan Conference which he proposed to set up. There were to be 36 members, lay and clerical, chosen by the four Rural Deaneries, and elections were to be held every three years. The Conference was to meet at least once a year and the Bishop was to have the right of veto on the discussion of any subject or the carrying of any resolution.

The Church Act 1880 had been introduced into Tynwald on 11th November 1879. One of the things which it did was to set up the Manx Church Commissioners, one reason being the heavy fees which had to be paid to the English Church Commissioners, e.g. when St Thomas' was made a separate parish. The Manx Commissioners were to be a body corporate, and were to be elected every three years. They had the power to create new parochial districts, though the right of people to go to the old parish church (e.g. in Douglas, Laxey, Ramsey and Castletown) for baptisms, marriages and burials was retained. It legalised the creation of rural deaneries and gave the Bishop the right to appoint rural deans. It authorised the Bishop to appoint curates in charge during a vacancy, and they were to be paid out of the sequestration fund. Pluralities were made illegal. The Episcopal Registrar was to be called the Diocesan Registrar. Parish Clerks were to be appointed by the Vicar and Wardens. Hitherto Parish Clerks had been elected. The Act vested all Parish Clerks' glebes in the Church Commissioners. In December 1902 they successfully applied to Tynwald for permission to sell them and invest the proceeds (The Clerks' Glebe Lands Act). Some were in very bad condition. The Maughold Clerk's glebe (60 acres) was larger than the Vicar's and in Jurby it was 30 acres, others were very small and there were none in Malew and Arbory. Part of the Clerk's glebe in Lezayre was just mountain.

The first meeting of the Manx Church Commissioners was held on 3rd November 1880. The three appointed by the Governor were Mr S. Harris (Secretary), Mr E. C. Farrant and Mr W. B. Stevenson, and the ex officio members were the Archdeacon, the Clerk of the Rolls (Mr A. W. Adams) and the Speaker of the House of Keys (Sir John Goldie-Taubman).

The first Diocesan Conference was held on 20th January 1880 in the Masonic Hall, Loch Promenade, preceded by Holy Communion at St Thomas' at 11.15. The Revd W. Kermode, as Secretary of Convocation, took a leading role in organising it. The Bishop in his address urged the restoration of St German's Cathedral. The meeting adjourned for lunch from 1 p.m. until 2.45 p.m. It was decided that members must be communicants, not simply churchmen. The main item was to discuss standing orders.

At Convocation on 20th May Hill said that he had been collecting money in England and on the Island to build churches and parsonages, and he hoped to have enough either to restore St German's Cathedral or to build a new one. Convocation had begun with Holy Communion at 11 a.m., followed by the Bishop's Charge. Lunch was taken at 3 p.m. after which the clergy and their ladies walked in the grounds or played tennis. Tea and coffee were served in the Library and everyone left about 7 p.m. Special trains, as usual, stopped for the clergy at Orrisdale. The Archdeacon and about six of the clergy, whose duty it was to administer certain charities, had been invited to dine and sleep and transact their business the previous day. The Governor joined the clergy at lunch.

Hill and Loch favoured the restoration of St German's Cathedral. Loch had had the central tower and the external walls repaired and secured and had obtained designs for a complete restoration at a cost of £10,000. It was also planned to raise £10,000 as an endowment. Mr W. E. Gladstone, after visiting the Island, wrote to the 'Manchester Guardian' commending the scheme to church people.

There was much criticism among tradespeople in May 1880 when it became known that Hill bought wine and groceries in bulk from the Army and Navy Stores, but a friend of the Bishop wrote to the newspapers explaining that for Holy Communion Hill used unfermented wine (unobtainable on the Island) and that the groceries concerned were delicacies also unobtainable here.

The second meeting of the Diocesan Conference was held in the Masonic Hall on 9th and 10th November 1880 after Holy Communion in St Thomas'. Standing Orders were approved and then several papers were read. Three were on the organisation of lay work in the parishes by Jones (who had changed his name to Hughes-Games), Principal of King William's College, Hobson (St Barnabas) and Mr R. Stephen. Three more followed on 'The Importance of a Cathedral in the Isle of Man as a centre of Church Work and Organisation in the Diocese', given by Mr E. C. Farrant, Vicar Gill of Malew and Mr A. N. Laughton. Finally three more papers were given by

Rector Kissack of Bride, Vicar Hawley of Patrick and Colonel Price on a composite subject:

(1) Are we doing all we can to retain as communicants those who are confirmed?
(2) What are the best means of increasing the number of communicants?

A motion was passed to build a cathedral in Douglas and a committee set up by the Diocesan Conference held their first meeting on 22nd February 1881. The committee consisted of the Governor, Sir James Gell, Vicar General Harris, Messrs. R. J. Moore, W. B. Stevenson, E. C. Farrant, Dr Hughes-Games and the four Rural Deans. Hill wanted to make St Thomas' the new Cathedral and to build a new church holding 700 for the congregation nearby. Others thought St George's more suitable and in the end it was decided to leave over the question of site and to ask several architects for plans.

Hill's early popularity remained, but he was criticised for appointing only Low Churchmen to parishes, for bringing men from England to fill vacancies and for not saying the words of administration to every communicant separately.

On Sunday 7th August 1881 the Annual Peel Fair was held in the grounds of Peel Castle under the patronage of the Bishop, who was President of the local branch of the Lord's Day Observance Society. He was criticised for this, even though he did not attend. There were other protests about rowdyism, all the travelling involved and the fact that the religious service was secondary to everything else.

The third session of the Diocesan Conference was held in the Masonic Hall on 25th and 26th October 1881, beginning with Holy Communion at St Thomas'. Papers, followed by discussion were given as follows:

(1) By what methods can we best attach our people to the church?
(2) Preaching - How best to adapt it to the present age to increase its usefulness?
(3) The Book of Common Prayer - How best to lead people to understand and value it?

(1) was given by Dr Hughes-Games, Colonel Price and Vicar Tracey of Rushen. (2) was given by Mr A. N. Laughton, Vicar Savage of Kirk Michael and Vicar Hobson of St Barnabas'. (3) was given by Revd H. Campbell, Curate of Braddan, Mr J. P. Stevenson and Mr G. A. Ring.

In 1881 Hill appointed Mr S. Harris as Surrogate for Douglas, passing over the Douglas clergy who were poorly paid. It was worth £50 per annum.

An important piece of legislation was the 1881 Burials Act, the main clauses of which were:

(1) The Governor could close any burial ground for reasons of public health, though he could grant a licence for burials in vaults after such closure if there was no risk to public health.
(2) No burial could take place in or under any church or chapel hereafter to be built, or within six feet of its walls.
(3) When a burial ground was closed the Governor could require the incumbent to summon a special Vestry meeting within six weeks, and they could levy a rate for a new or additional burial ground.
(4) The incumbent and wardens could appoint and dismiss the sexton.
(5) Tables of burial fees were to be provided.
(6) The clergy could refuse burials on Sunday, Good Friday and Christmas Day. No non-Anglican burial could take place on these days or before 1 p.m. on a Sunday, without the consent of the incumbent.
(7) Funerals could be conducted in the churchyard by ministers of all denominations.
(8) Burial Registers were to be kept.

In March 1882 Hill forbade holding Vestry meetings in church. Some of the clergy conformed, others, including the Archdeacon, did not. At German, Vicar Williams left the meeting when the Vestry refused to meet elsewhere than in church so the Chair was taken by Mr Laughton.

At the 1882 Convocation (June 1st) the Bishop gave no Charge owing to the recent death of his wife.

Hill had started open air services in Peel Castle and on 6th August 1882 he held one on Douglas Head in the afternoon, preaching on Isaiah 55[2]. Clergy and choirs of the Douglas churches took part and several thousand people attended. No collection was taken.

The fourth session of the Diocesan Conference was held in the Masonic Hall on 24th and 25th October 1882, after Holy Communion in St Thomas', at 11.15. Hill said that his first idea to restore St German's Cathedral was impracticable. His plan to make St Thomas' the Cathedral had not been accepted and he felt St George's to be unsuitable. He had now dropped the idea of having the Cathedral in Douglas and suggested that the proposed new church at Peel should be the Cathedral, with some enlargements. Mr A. W. Moore, the historian of the Isle of Man, suggested making Braddan church the Cathedral. The question of Lay Preachers was discussed and the report of a committee recommending their use was passed. A proposal for the conference to meet elsewhere than in Douglas was rejected. At the end of the meeting Dr Hughes-Games, taking up the Cathedral issue again, suggested that the new church at Peel could be the pro-cathedral, so that the Cathedral could be moved to Douglas at any time. The 'Manx Sun' considered that this Diocesan Conference had shown a decline in the interest and value of the papers and that the discussions following them had been very poor. It criticised Hill's chairmanship, considering that he had much to learn.

A public meeting was held on 28th November 1882 which passed a resolution saying that a Cathedral for the diocese was desirable, and appointed a committee to find a site. It was agreed that St George's should be the temporary pro-Cathedral.

At the 1883 Convocation several clergy protested that there was no proper accommodation for them in St John's church on July 5th and the Bishop undertook to see the Governor. It was pointed out that each year several clergy attended without robing and this was considered disrespectful.

On Sunday 5th August Hill held a service in the grounds of Peel Castle, which was well attended, despite indifferent weather. There was, however, criticism of the amount of Sunday work and travelling which this involved. Next Sunday he held another service on Douglas Head, preaching standing on a chair, on a very hot day.

There was no Diocesan Conference in 1883.

On Thursday night, 7th February 1884, Vicar General Jebb died at his home, Castle Lawn, in Castle Terrace, to which he had moved in early 1883 after living since his appointment in 1861 in private apartments in the Castle Mona Hotel. For two years his health and his wonderful memory had been failing. He had held a Court on 1st February and had worked at his papers all the week, though ill. He was a very learned lawyer and the soul of honour. In his last two or three years, probably because of

deafness, failing health and increasing age, his manner to the clergy, e.g. in Chapter courts, became very arbitrary and irascible and occasionally insulting. He was only ill for a few days and did not suffer, but from the start he said that he would not recover. He was buried at St George's on 13th February, the service being taken by the Vicars of St George's and St Barnabas'. Many people followed the hearse from the house to the church, despite drizzling rain, but there were fewer in church, mainly his friends and members of the Bar. A friend said 'He hasn't left a better man behind him'. Later in the month Hill appointed Samuel Harris, Diocesan Registrar, to succeed him.

The 'Manx Sun' observed that by 1884 Good Friday had come to be marked by festivities, concerts and amusements.

After the 1884 Convocation on June 5th the Bishop gave a Garden Party attended by about 400 people, including the Governor and Mrs Walpole. A band played, and tennis and croquet were played on the lawn. Special trains were run. The appearance of the aged Archdeacon Moore, who had been ill, caused great delight.

On 15th July 1884 Hill returned to the Island with his second wife. Kirk Michael was all bunting and evergreens to welcome them, and horns were blown. Their carriage was halted at the church gate and they drove on under a shower of rice. The Bishop handed over a generous sum for a treat for the children. At Bishopscourt tar barrels were burned and fireworks were let off. Many had gathered on the lawn to greet him, but unfortunately it began to rain heavily. Mrs Hill made a very good impression, and on 21st July she much pleased the Archdeacon by visiting him, without state or ceremony. Hill's sister had come to keep house for him when his first wife died, but she left when he re-married.

The fifth session of the Diocesan Conference was held in the Masonic Hall on 21st and 22nd October 1884, beginning with Holy Communion in St Thomas' at 11.15. Dr Hughes-Games and Vicar Bridgman of Lezayre gave papers on 'Religious Doubts and Difficulties and how to deal with them', Vicar Taggart of St Matthew's, Mr G. A. Ring and Dr Wood gave papers on 'Women's work in the church' and Paton (St Paul's Ramsey), Gill (Malew) and Mr A. N. Laughton gave papers on 'The Church in relation to Local Charities, Home and Foreign Missions'.

The Bishop's Temporalities Act (1878) had laid down that the Bishop had to pay £500 of his stipend to the Trustees of the Episcopal and Clerical Endowment Fund (Governor, Bishop and Clerk of the Rolls) to be distributed to the local clergy. This £500 was liable to certain deductions, e.g.

(1)   If the Bishop's stipend did not exceed £2,500
(2)   If the Bishop had to do repairs to chancels of which he was patron.

Moreover, this £500 would not be payable if an assistant Bishop had to be appointed or the previous Bishop took a pension. In 1884 the Clergy Temporalities Act said that in the event of an assistant Bishop being appointed or the previous Bishop taking a pension, the £500 would still be distributed to the clergy. This Act also took £250 off the stipend of Andreas (which stood at £707 in 1884) at the next vacancy, and put it into the Fund. Increases were given as follows: German £30, Marown £30, Lonan £40, Onchan £40, Jurby £20, Santan £20, Malew £40, Arbory £40, and Rushen £40. Bride, Ballaugh, Kirk Michael, Braddan, Patrick, Lezayre and Maughold (all good livings) were left unchanged. This brought all the livings up to £200. In Tynwald, Hill said that he only found out after accepting the see that the £500 would be deducted from his stipend, but that he had voluntarily agreed to it on finding out the level of clergy stipends.

The Ecclesiastical Civil Judicature Transfer Act (1884) ended the Bishop's jurisdiction and authority in civil matters, e.g. the estates of deceased persons and matrimonial matters.

On Friday evening, 12th December 1884 a public meeting was held in the parish school of Andreas to consider the proposal to reduce the stipend of the Rector by £250 and distribute it among the clergy. The meeting was called by Mr C. H. Cowle, Captain of the Parish, with the agreement of the Arcdeacon - who had not been consulted, and was opposed to the plan, even though it would not take effect until after his time. It was a full meeting and included the two Members of the House of Keys for Ayre. Before 1839 Andreas was worth £808 per annum, and this was the figure under the Tithe Commutation Act, but in 1839 £101 was deducted for the Chaplain of St Jude's. At the time of the tithe commutation all lands were taxed, to a certain extent, in proportion to their ability to grow wheat, barley and oats. Thus parishes like Andreas, which were good for growing cereals, were more heavily taxed than those which were not. Andreas was the only parish in the diocese which received all the tithes for its own use as Bride and Ballaugh had only two thirds of the tithes. Of the £250 which it was proposed to deduct from the £707 remaining, £40 was to go to the Chaplain of St Jude's. The motion at the meeting protesting about the £250 reduction was passed by a big majority and petitions to the Governor and the Home Secretary were drawn up. It was felt that Archdeacon Moore had spent all his income and much of his own money in the parish and for charitable purposes. The petitions proved unnecessary, however, because at a meeting of the Legislative Council on 16th January 1885 the Clergy Temporalities Bill was withdrawn.

The 1885 Convocation on 28th May was again followed by a garden party. In August 1885 Hill preached on Douglas Head each Sunday. On 30th December 1885 Hill summoned the clergy to meet in St George's Hall to elect a representative in York Convocation. The meeting was marked by a heated exchange between the Bishop and Vicar Howard of Onchan, who claimed that the meeting was irregular as it should have been called by the Archdeacon and that the Bishop had no right to be in the Chair. Howard also objected to the time and place of the meeting. Rector Kermode of Ballaugh was elected and Howard's nomination of Gill (Malew) found no seconder. Gill explained that he had heard the previous night that some of the clergy had received letters from Howard asking them to vote for him (Gill) and he deeply regretted it.

In June 1886 Hill preached in a Presbyterian church in the diocese of Aberdeen. Bishop Douglas of Aberdeen wrote complaining that he had not even been told of this, but received no reply, so he sent a registered letter to Hill, who replied asking by what authority he complained. Eventually Douglas sent a copy of the correspondence to each Bishop of the Anglican Communion, and said publicly that it was a Canon of the universal church that no bishop should intrude into the diocese of another. Hill replied to this by saying, rather lamely, that he was a Bishop of the Church of England, not of the universal church, but it was widely felt that he had treated Bishop Douglas with great discourtesy and even rudeness.

On 17th June 1886 the Press were admitted to Convocation for the first time. The ante-chapel was crowded to suffocation and there was a clear desire to get through the business quickly so as to join the ladies and the laity in the garden party outside. Many clergy looked back with regret to the days when Convocation was a quiet day for the Bishop and clergy alone. A proposal from Vicar Bridgman of Lezayre, seconded by Vicar Howard of Onchan, that the clergy should be allowed to sell their glebe, was lost.

On 22nd July 1886 Hill opened the Queen's Pier in Ramsey on behalf of the Governor, who had been called to England by the death of his mother. In August he agreed to become Patron of the local Society for the Prevention of Cruelty to Animals and on 29th August he became slightly indisposed after preaching on Douglas Head in a high wind and cancelled a preaching engagement in St George's that evening.

The most momentous event of 1886 was, however, the death of Archdeacon Moore, which ended an era. He once said that in 1879 he suddenly becaue an old man, though up until then he had carried out all his duties. Signs of failing health appeared in 1880, when he missed the Oiel Voirrey for the first time in 36 years, and earlier in the year he had missed King William's College Prize-giving for the first time, but he took part in the Christmas morning service of Mattins and Holy Communion. The day was frosty with snow and sunshine. At the 1881 Easter Vestry he was very different from what he used to be though, allowing for his age, he got through the duties of Chairman very well. Afterwards, as usual, he had the churchwardens and a few friends to lunch at the rectory. His inability to do regular duty in church was at first a great trial to him and his longing, in weaker days, to be there was strong up to the last month of his life. In November 1881, when about to celebrate Holy Communion in Andreas church, he bowed forward as if fainting, and was saved from falling by his Curate, the Revd F. Lamothe, who caught him and helped him to a chair in the chancel where he sat until the end of the service. For some time afterwards he was very weak and only partly recovered his former good health. There followed a few years of weakness, consciousness of failing powers and drooping hopes for the welfare of his beloved

Island. In early 1882 he was still unwell and unable to attend the College Prize-giving or the presentation of an Address from Tynwald to Governor Loch on his departure, but when Loch made his farewell visit to Ramsey he called on the Archdeacon to say goodbye.

On Saturday, 12th August 1882 Moore was 80, and about 8 a.m. the Sunday School children (about 60) came to the rectory with flowers and assembled in front of his window, singing hymns. The Archdeacon was visibly affected. The children and teachers then entered his breakfast room and put their bouquets on the table. The children were then given buns and milk on the lawn where Moore joined them and was said to look very well. Friends wished him many happy returns and the gathering closed with the doxology. He preached at the 1882 Sunday School Anniversary for the first time for a year or two and said that he felt much better. In 1883 he took his usual part in the service of Holy Communion and the proceedings at Convocation, attended King William's College Prize-giving as usual and again preached at Andreas Anniversary. On 5th August 1883 he preached in Andreas Church for Hospital Sunday on St Luke 10[36-7]. In mid-March 1884 he had a slight stroke but recovered well and presided at the Vestry meeting (his last), took his usual part at Convocation (also his last) where his appearance caused great delight. At Andreas Sunday School treat on the Rectory lawn (21st August) which was attended by the Bishop and Mrs Hill, he distributed the prizes sitting under a chestnut tree. On 7th September he preached at the Sunday School Anniversary on Psalm 107[43]. His bodily feebleness was manifest. He read most of the sermon and while some of it had the old power, the aged man striving to do his best for the Master he had served so long was as great an example as anything he said. He was unable to take part in the 1884 Harvest or Christmas services but in February 1885 the 'Manx Sun' said that he was fairly well and able to sit up in his room for most of the day. He could not attend the 1885 Vestry meeting (though he had the wardens to lunch) or Convocation, nor could he attend the Sunday School Anniversary on 6th September, but on the day before he had presented the prizes at the annual Sunday School treat on the rectory lawn. On 23rd July he had managed to do a wedding and on 27th December he was in church, but the Curate took the service and preached.

He died peacefully in the rectory at 1 a.m. on Friday, 26th February 1886, one of his last sayings being 'I rejoice with joy unspeakable and full of glory'. He had not been considered worse than usual until within the last few days. The funeral was at 1 p.m. on Wednesday, 3rd March. A snowstorm had begun on the Sunday evening after two very cold days and it fell heavily on the Monday and Tuesday. It was the worst snowstorm for about 30 years and it prevented many people from attending the funeral, as some roads and railways were completely blocked. March 3rd was a day of brilliant sunshine, with snow all around, and Moore was buried in a plot near the church door which he had chosen for himself, and at which he spent many hours in meditation over the years. When the coffin was brought to the front door the Bishop called on all to sing 'O God of Bethel by whose hand' one of the Archdeacon's favourites. The churchwardens then carried the coffin along the old familiar garden path on which he had for 42 years walked from the rectory to the church and at the church door some of the clergy shouldered it. The Bishop took the whole service and at the graveside he spoke of the Christian spirit in which the Archdeacon had borne his illness, what a valuable friend and counsellor he had been in church and state and how good and kind to others. The church was crowded with people from all over the north of the Island. On the following Sunday the church was draped in black and, in his sermon, LaMothe, the Curate, spoke of Moore's willingnesss to accept responsibility, his high sense of honour and his unselfish and God-fearing character. The Bishop preached in the evening.

Many tributes were paid to him. The Bishop said that he had lost 'a kind friend, a ready assistant and the best adviser'. The Revd W. Kermode said that Moore was a patriotic Manxman who took a deep interest in the welfare of both church and people. While maintaining his position as a churchman he was charitable, considerate and conciliatory to those who differed from him. He was straightforward, honest and outspoken, a warm friend and a wise and judicious advisor to the clergy. Dr Hughes-Games spoke of his love, admiration and veneration for Moore and said that he knew no-one wiser in counsel in all that he did or said. He had always received sound advice and kindly and fatherly sympathy and

said how much King William's College owed to Moore. Others spoke of his force of character, unswerving integrity, unsparing devotion to duty, sound judgement, inflexible honesty, personal charm and his willingness to give friendly help to young and inexperienced priests.

In April 1887 Hill preached in Kirk Michael Church and early in May he went to London, where he preached and attended meetings, and on 21st May he was present at a levee given by the Prince of Wales, but he was not feeling very well, having had a succession of colds. His illness was not looked on as serious, but by Friday, 27th May he was much worse and he died at 10.10 p.m. that evening, aged 51, at his London home, No 10, Hereford Square, Brompton, and was buried in Brompton cemetery with his first wife on 2nd June. The funeral service was at St Michael's, Pimlico, and was taken by the Archbishop of York (Thomson)

The news caused a great sensation in the Isle of Man. Hill left four sons, (George, Marcus, Alfred and Edmund) and two daughters, (Caroline and Elizabeth) by his first wife. His mother and second wife survived him. There was a large attendance of friends at the funeral, including the Governor, Dr Hughes-Games, the Revd W. Kermode, the Revd E. Kissack, the Revd W. Drury, the Revd H. S. Gill, Deemster Drinkwater and Mr A. N. Laughton. The sale of the contents of Bishopscourt which belonged to him personally was held on 8th August 1887 and lasted several days.

Some miscellaneous facts about his episcopate may be added here. He was very opposed to gambling and betting, but he was by no means an abstainer and often poked fun at those who practised abstinence or temperance - for example at a bazaar held at Bishopscourt he pinned a notice on the teetotal refreshment stall 'Here the wild asses quench their thirst'. Evening Communions began under Hill. There was much criticism of the long periods he spent in England, and of his practice of filling vacancies with men from England. He aimed at an annual confirmation in each parish and in his 10 years here he confirmed about 4,500 people. He made it a rule that no curate could leave the Island until 2 years (increased to three years in 1885) after his ordination. The second Mrs Hill, during the short time she was here, took a great interest in work for and among women, especially the YWCA. Hill's very low church views were unpopular, even among Methodists, and some thought that he was behind the disuse of Hymns Ancient and Modern in some churches. His good humour and Irish wit (he was fond of telling jokes) made him personally popular from the start, and he delighted in the company of the Manx countryfolk. A particular favourite was Thomas Caley, one of the gardeners at Bishopscourt, and verger of Bishopscourt Chapel, who died on 24th January 1911, aged 81, having lived under 7 Bishops and was buried at Ballaugh on 27th January. On his cottage at Ballarhenny, Kirk Michael, Hill set up the following verse:

This is the home of Thomas Caley
Who works within the garden daily.
If not within the garden found,
You'll look for him about the ground.
If not within the grounds when sought,

Enquire for him at Bishopscourt.

Dr Hughes-Games said that Hill's faults, such as they were, were those of a generous, impulsive, untiring, energetic man. He described him as an eloquent preacher, with a deep, sincere, manly piety. He loved giving and receiving hospitality, and was genial and kind, with a pleasant word and smile for the humblest folk. He was faithful to his friends and was the most generous and forgiving to his foes as any man Hughes-Games had ever known. At the same hour as the funeral on 2nd June, a service was held in German parish church at which Vicar Williams spoke of Hill's great earnestness and devotion to duty and how he would preach equally to thousands in the open air or to a few in a country church.

Hill never spoke much in Tynwald. It was during his episcopate that the Theological College was established at Bishopscourt, in conjunction with King William's College (1879).

The Parishes under Hill

ANDREAS Archdeacon Moore was succeeded as Rector and Archdeacon by Dr Joshua Hughes-Games, who was inducted to Andreas on 3rd June 1886, Ascension Day. After the induction there was a service of Holy Communion, the Bishop preached on Psalm 24[3], and the hymns were 'All people than on earth do dwell' and 'Where high the heavenly temple stands'. He did not take up residence until August, when the College term ended and when he had made some alterations to the rectory. Most people in the Island hoped that Vicar Gill of Malew would be appointed, but the fact that he was not was probably due to two of his near relatives (Sir James Gell and Deemster Gill) being already on the Legislative Council and if Gill had been appointed Archdeacon it would have made three. The 'Manx Sun' had hoped that a Manxman and a parish clergyman would have been appointed, but conceded that Hughes-Games was a good choice. The new Archdeacon was a profound, logical and very evangelistic preacher and usually preached without notes, while his personal integrity won him the respect of the whole diocese.

The stipend in 1881 was £707.

ARBORY Charles Langton was appointed to succeed Vicar Grier in April 1880 and remained for 10 years, living and working among his people in the same quiet way as he did at St Luke's and earning their confidence and respect. He was inducted by William Drury. He was the first Vicar of Arbory to wear a surplice when preaching. On 3rd July 1881 a new organ was opened, Bishop Hill being the preacher. In 1883 Colby Mission Church was licensed for worship and in 1884 a second hand organ was bought for it. On 23rd July 1885 Hill consecrated a new burial ground to the north of the church, the land being given by Thomas and Margaret Clucas of Parville. In the Autumn of 1886 extensive repairs to the church were carried out - re-flooring, re-roofing, the roof opened and boarded, stained and varnished, a new gallery, a new vestry and new pews. Bishop Hill withheld his sanction until he had scrutinised every item of the £129 estimate, and he preached morning and evening at the re-opening of the church on 24th November. The east window was given by Mr W. B. Stevenson of Balladoole.

The stipend in 1881 was £150.

BALLAUGH Rector Howard was succeeded by William Kermode, Vicar of Maughold, though there had been a rumour that the new Rector would be Ferrier, the Chaplain of Castletown. On his arrival Kermode found that the rectory adjoining the old church was too small for his large family, so he exchanged it and its glebe for the house (which he enlarged) and fields which remained the rectory until 1977. A new organ was opened on 7th April 1878 by Miss M. L. Wood, organist of St Thomas' and the Bishop preached in the evening. It had 9 stops and 312 pipes, cost £165, and was built by Foster and Andrews of Hull. Philip Teare of Ballaugh was appointed organist. Under Kermode a number of improvements were made to the parish church and the old church. In the parish church the font was moved from the chancel to the west end in 1879 and the Rector provided choir stalls and sanctuary chairs. In 1880 lamps replaced candles with a resulting improvement to the lighting. In 1881 a new heating apparatus and hot water pipes were installed and in 1882 a new table of benefactors was erected in the porch. In 1883 Mrs Freer gave the reredos of oak and pitch pine in memory of her brother, John Mylchraine, who died in America in 1882. At the same time an oak Communion rail was given and the sanctuary was panelled. This panelling was continued down both sides of the church in 1887.

On Thursday evening, 30th January 1879 the old church was re-opened for worship after restoration work, and despite a wet night it was full. The Bishop had been in Douglas all day, but reached the church just before 7 p.m. and robed in the rectory. The singing was led by an amateur choir of young people who had had little time for practice. Many had to listen outside the door. The Bishop preached on St Luke 4[16-20], and promised to give a carpet for around the altar. It was planned to hold a service each Wednesday evening.

When Hill introduced rural deaneries in 1879 Kermode became Rural Dean of Peel. In 1879 he was unanimously elected Secretary of Convocation, a post which he resigned in 1888 when he was succeeded by the Revd E. B. Savage, Vicar of St Thomas'.

The stipend in 1881 was £250.

ST BARNABAS'
Vicar Hobson remained throughout Hill's episcopate. On 6th April 1884 he fainted after reading the Litany but recovered in the vesty and went home; it was due to overwork, but he was soon back to normal. On 15th March 1885 he held a memorial service for General Gordon, who had, in January, been killed at Khartoum by the soldiers of the Mahdi. In 1882 a new reredos was erected. Hobson was one of the first in the diocese to hold services of Holy Communion in the evening.

The stipend in 1881 was £250.

BRADDAN
At a special Vestry meeting on 25th August 1879, called by order of the Bishop, it was decided to extend the existing churchyard and that in any such new ground Nonconformists should be allowed to be buried by their own ministers with their own rites. On 29th January 1885 the Bishop consecrated the new burial ground and he and the clergy had lunch at Kirby with Deemster Drinkwater. At the 1885 Vestry meeting on 6th April there were some complaints that the open air services in the churchyard desecrated the graves.

In June 1882 the tender of James Cowle, the builder, was accepted for the tower and spire, but they were blown down in a storm on 26th January 1884. They were re-built, but were again partly destroyed by another storm in December 1886.

By Hill's time services at Oakhill had dwindled to one a month.

The stipend in 1881 was £250.

BRIDE
Rector Qualtrough died on 27th February 1879 aged 64, after a painful illness which he bore with manly courage and Christian submission. The Bishop and the Archdeacon officiated at his funeral at Andreas and the coffin was carried by four of the clergy. The sale at the rectory after his death included 400 books, a strong and useful working horse, a cow due to calve in May, a pig, a covered car, a dogcart, two carts, a set of cart harness, plough, harrow, hay cutter, about a ton of meadow hay and the lease of a field of which there were still 3½ years to run. Mrs Qualtrough lived until she was 90 and died on 19th December 1907.

Bishop Powys once said that if every clergyman on the Island did his work as well as Qualtrough there would be fuller churches. When he spoke at clergy meetings everyone, including those who did not share his views, listened to him with respect, as all knew he would express his honest convictions even though he might be in a minority of one. All felt that he represented the views of the Manx people. He was, indeed, pre-eminently a man of the people and one of the few survivors of the old race of Manx clergy whose whole ministry had been in the diocese. More than any other of the clergy he had an instinctive and intimate knowledge of the Manx people, among whom he lived as one of themselves, and this, added to the fact that he spoke Manx, gave him a unique standing.

Qualtrough was succeeded by E. W. Kissack, who was instituted on 25th June 1879 and inducted the following week. A new organ was opened on 3rd September 1882, the cost being £65, less £15 which the organ builder (Hewitt of Leicester) allowed for the old one. On 22nd June 1870 Kissack had married the widow of a clergyman, Mrs Jane Arrowsmith, at Birkdale. She died in the rectory on 21st February 1887, aged 50, and the tubular bells in the tower were erected in her memory. They were first rung on 6th October 1890. On 29th November 1888 he married Miss Mary Murray of Ochrestyre, Perthshire, at St Columba's Episcopal Church, Crieff, the service being taken by the Revd B. P. Clarke and the Minister, the Revd A. Maitland.

Kissack was a fearless and able preacher and was kind and courteous as a man. He was a total abstainer and a tireless advocate of temperance. He added most of the stained glass windows in the church.

The stipend in 1881 was £303.

CASTLETOWN Ferrier's long chaplaincy covered the whole of Hill's episcopate. In 1877 the organ gallery was removed from over the altar to the south side of the church and the first Sunday in its new position (14th October) was marked by special services, morning and evening, at both of which the Bishop preached. The organist from 1878 to 1916 was Mr J. T. W. Wicksey (BMus, Dublin) the Master of Castletown Grammar School, a magnificent player whom the Choir (who then sat in the opposite gallery) held in awe. His arrival at church in top hat, frock coat and twirling a stick, was an imposing sight. He would climb the stairs and walk majestically around the gallery, while every face in the pews would be turned upwards to watch his progress. He died on 22nd July 1916, aged 65.

In June 1885 the choir began chanting the Psalms in the morning. They had chanted them in the evening for some time. In May 1880 the church was closed for a while for alterations and the services were held in the Town Hall. The panels containing the Creed, the Commandments and the Lord's Prayer were erected in 1880.

The stipend in 1881 was £140.

CRONK Y VODDY Kyte's chaplaincy ended in 1879, when he left to become Curate of Flixborough in the diocese of Lincoln. His ministry had not been a success as he was personally unpopular, and his sermons, always read, were barely audible and largely unintelligible. On his arrival there had been a fair choir, the church was well attended, and there was a good Sunday School, but by January 1878 all the choir had left, the congregation had dwindled to 2 or 3 and the Sunday School had ceased. He was succeeded by H. R. Finnis, formerly Headmaster of Wellington Road School in Douglas. At Cronk y Voddy he used to ring the bell, take the collection and play the organ. His successor was J B. Stephenson. The last Chaplain under Hill was Hugh Kinred, whose ministry lasted from December 1882 until 1895. He was quiet, unassuming, a good preacher and a fluent Manx speaker. On 19th December 1893 he married his housekeeper, Miss Bessie Bell, in German church by special licence. In 1885 he declined offers of both Sulby and Laxey.

The stipend in 1881 was £65.

ST JAMES' C. M. Barnes was Chaplain from 1881-88. During his chaplaincy a bogus clergyman preached in Dalby church. His name was John Lindsey, and he had spent 7 years travelling around England, taking services here and there under assumed names. He was eventually convicted at York Assizes for performing marriages when not in Holy Orders. Bishop Hill warned the clergy at Convocation to be very careful to examine the credentials of anyone offering to do locum duty.

On 28th November 1886 a new organ was opened. The stipend in 1881 was £120.

DHOON S. N. Harrison's chaplaincy covered the whole of Hill's episcopate.

FOXDALE Bates was succeeded by Eustace W. Cochrae in 1879. He stayed until 1900 and was the first Vicar of Foxdale, which was made a separate parish by the Church Commissioners on 21st October 1881. This new parish was taken out of Patrick and included parts of Malew and Marown with the agreement of the Vicars of these parishes. Cochran's kindly manner and keen interest in the spiritual and material welfare of his people earned him the love, confidence and esteem of the whole parish, and his wife, formerly Miss Margaret Lewin, was beloved in Foxdale as she visited the sick and did all possible to help others. A new organ was installed in November 1893.

The population of Foxdale was 1,500 and the stipend in 1881 was £160.

ST GEORGE'S Hawley was succeeded in December 1877 by H. Armstrong Hall. At a congregational meeting on 21st January 1878 it was announced that Hill and Drury had asked the Church Commissioners to make St George's a separate parish, and this was done in December 1878. A large scheme of alterations and repairs was planned during Hall's incumbency but there was so little popular or financial support that the 1879 Easter Vestry decided to drop the plan. There was also a difference of opinion over the form of some sample pews which had been set up.

Hall arrived in Douglas on 3rd January 1878 and was inducted on 29th January. In March 1879 he had to leave the Island for a short time owing to ill health but returned in mid-April. At the 1879 Vestry meeting he said that owing to a throat affection he had been medically advised to go somewhere less exposed to the east wind and would be leaving in September. He did not, in fact, leave until 13th May 1880 and preached his last sermon on 9th May on Numbers 10[29]. Hall was a good preacher, and a thorough gentleman and was very popular at St George's. Crowds attended his last services and assembled on the Victoria Pier to see him off.

Many hoped that the new Vicar would be the Revd T. W. Drury, son of the Vicar of Braddan, then Rector of Holy Trinity, Chesterfield, but Hill appointed J. E. Beauchamp George who was inducted to St George's by William Drury on 21st May 1880, having been instituted at Convocation the previous day. The induction had not been anounced, so very few were present. On 24th May he left the Island to help his Vicar at Clifton, until a new curate could be

obtained and returned in early July. The Curates looked after St George's during his absence.

The vicarage was bought in 1882. George collected enough money to repair and decorate the church. The chancel was tiled and ornamented with columns and the aisles were also tiled. Handsome gas fittings were provided, new stone windows replaced the rotten wooden sashes and three windows were filled with stained glass. A new screen was later erected in memory of the first Mrs George. The church was re-opened after this work on 27th February 1881.

The population of St George's in 1880 was 4,230 and the stipend was £276, but this had risen to £350 by 1885. The annual wages bill in 1886 was organist £40, organ blower £4-12-0, the Curate £61-18-10 and the Clerk £2-10 -0.

GERMAN Vicar Stowell's long incumbency ended when he resigned on 18th June 1880, owing to age and failing health and he then withdrew completely from public life. He was given a pension of £150 and allowed to stay in the vicarage until September 1st. He died at his home in Peveril Terrace, Peel, on 5th May 1884, aged 82 and was buried in Peel cemetery on 10th May. The funeral, held in the old parish church, was taken by Vicar Williams and by John Corlett, Chaplain of St John's, and was attended by many clergy and parishioners. Stowell was good, kind and genial and was much loved in Peel.

In January 1879 the Revd Pelham Stokes, apparently on the invitation of the Curate, the Revd H. Dening, began a Mission in German Church, at which, with the Vicar's approval, Sankey's Hymns were used instead of Ancient and Modern. The Sunday evening service was much curtailed to give more time for the Mission sermon and after-meeting. Prayers for the Mission replaced the state prayers. Several of the congregation objected to this and on 1st February about 20 of them handed the Vicar a protest about the omission of the state prayers and the nature of the after-meeting. Misinformed rumours got about over the nature of this protest and Stowell and Dening only with difficulty prevented a monster indignation meeting being held. There was no hostility to the Mission or to the parish clergy, simply a desire to keep the church services free from innovation. On the following Sunday Dening had the full service. The Mission was very successful, Dening's curacy lasted from 1878-1880 and in June 1880 he succeeded Stowell as Vicar. He was zealous in discharging his duties and this, with his kindness, gained him the respect and affection of everyone. He was a Londoner.

When Dening became Vicar Holy Communion was only celebrated once a month, on the first Sunday but he at once began an additional celebration on the third Sunday evening. On 18th January 1881 a Vestry meeting approved the sale of the old vicarage and the purchase of Glen View House, the difference between the sale and the cost price to be met from the stipend, spread over 30 years. Dening resigned in 1881 because of his wife's health, and from 1881-83 he was a missionary with the Church Parochial Missionary Society, then in 1883 he became Vicar of Baggotrath, near Dublin.

He was succeeded by James G. Williams, who was inducted on 16th April 1881 and remained Vicar until 1889. The stipend at this time was £216 and the population of German was 5,500. In Dening's time the General Thanksgiving had been said by the whole congregation but Williams returned to the previous practice of the Vicar saying it alone. He started a cricket club in Peel.

The main event of Williams' incumbency was the building of the new church. Forty years earlier Bishop Short had felt the parish church in the market place to be inadequate for the growing town of Peel, and had offered £300 of his own money and to pay for the chancel, but the parishioners refused and while Stowell was Vicar it often happened that all who wished to attend the services could not find seats. The church had been re-roofed and restored in 1844, but nothing could remove the unhealthy dampness caused by the ground outside being so high above the floor. Hill early recognised the problem and on 24th September 1878 he inspected a suggested site for a new church. Soon after his arrival he had begun raising money for church purposes in the Island by preaching in England and from friends there. He had proved very good at raising money during his years in Sheffield. From this money he offered £6,000 for a new church in Peel, and this was accepted by the 1879 Easter Vestry meeting.

Hill's original intention was to use this money to restore St German's Cathedral but there was little support for the idea, financial, or otherwise, so the money collected was used to build the new church. Hill's son said, after his father's death, that the restoration of the old Cathedral had been his dearest wish. Hill more than once made it clear that failing the restoration of St German's he would have liked one of the Douglas churches, preferably St Thomas', to be the Cathedral. Hill personally gave £100 to the building of the new church and Archdeacon Moore £50. At a bazaar held at Bishopscourt to raise money in August 1879, poetry by the Bishop and drawings by Mrs Hill, were on sale.

The site, selected by Hill, had been bought for £505 from Miss Elizabeth Graves and Mr Caesar Corris and the foundation stone was laid by Archdeacon Moore on 21st August 1879 in the presence of Governor Loch and the Bishop. The hymns at the service, held at 7.30 p.m. were 'The Church's one foundation', 'We love the place O God', 'Christ is our cornerstone' and 'Now thank we all our God'. The Psalm was 84, the lessons were I Kings 8²²⁻³⁰ and Matthew 7²¹⁻²⁹, and the anthem was Quitter's 'Non Nobis Domine'. The architects were Messrs. Thomas Barry and Son of Liverpool, but the building was done by local men - Thomas Radcliffe (stonemason) and Daniel Anderson (joiner).

On 20th September 1882 a meeting was held in Peel, attended by the Governor and local people to discuss making the new church the cathedral. The Governor would not commit himself, so Hill decided to call a public meeting in Douglas on the subject, but then changed his mind and said that he would bring it up at the October Diocesan Conference, on the ground that those who had no real interest in the matter could attend a public meeting.

On 6th August 1883 a bazaar was held in the grounds of Bishopscourt to raise money for the organ of the new church. It had been hoped that the church would have been ready for consecration by this summer, but there was delay in decorating the interior and in setting up the many gifts. By September 1883 the tower and steeple were making good progress and in March 1884 a peal of 8 bells was placed in the tower. The church was completed in 1884. Hill said that he had never intended German church to be the cathedral, and that it was larger and had cost more to build, than he had wished.

The church was opened by Archbishop Thomson of York. He reached Douglas on the evening of Saturday, 23rd August 1884, and was seen standing on the bridge with the Captain. He was met on the Victoria Pier by the Bishop, Gill (Malew), Ferrier (Castletown), Vicar General Harris, Colonel Paul (Chief Constable) and others. After the Bishop had introduced him to them he and the Archbishop were driven, amid the cheers of the crowd, to Government House, where a large party was held that evening. Next morning the Archbishop attended St George's (where Hill preached), on Monday he went to Bishopscourt and on Wednesday to Kentraugh. He then stayed overnight at the Peveril Hotel with the Bishop before returning home on the morning steamer. He opened the new church on Tuesday 26th August at 11 a.m. The weather was gloomy and threatening all day, but only a few showers fell and a great crowd assembled. Peel was all flags, banners and bunting. Peel Castle was illuminated in the evening, the ships in the harbour were decorated with flags and it was a general holiday in the town. All the clergy, including the aged Archdeacon, attended, robed. Miss M. L. Wood was the organist, the lessons were read by Gill and Kermode and the collection for the building fund came to £90. Gill (acting for the Archdeacon) read an Address from the clergy, signed by the Archdeacon, and the Rural Deans. The Archbishop, preaching on St John 1[46], referred to the church as 'possibly the future cathedral of the diocese and many of the later speakers made reference to this - received with applause by Peel people and in silence by the rest. The 'Manx Sun' considered that the Archbishop had been asked to say these words by Hill. Lunch was served in the Christian Street School to 170 people, a band played and speeches were made, among others by the Governor, the Archbishop, the Bishop, the Archdeacon, Sir James Gell, Dr Hughes-Games, Vicar Williams and Mr E C. Farrant. The church was not consecrated, simply licenced as a chapel of ease to the parish church. Hill preached morning and evening on the following Sunday. Vicar General Harris presented an Address to the Archbishop in which he expressed the hope that the new church would become the cathedral of the diocese, but the Archbishop in his reply made no reference to this. It was the first recorded visit by an Archbishop of York to the Isle of Man.

St German's Cathedral continued to be the legal parish church of German until the Church Act of 1880, which constituted St Peter's as the parish church. In 1871 Bishop Powys had introduced a Bill into Tynwald making St German's the Cathedral of the diocese, but it failed due to financial and other difficulties.

The Vicar's reading desk was given by Catherine White in memory of her parents in 1884. The memorial window to R. J. Moore, High Bailiff of Peel, was put in the south transept in 1895. The Adoration of the Shepherds window is in memory of Vicar Stowell, the Jacob's Dream window in the north transept is in memory of Bishop Hill and the tower, which cost £2,000, is a memorial to the first Mrs Hill. A plaque says 'Erected by those who loved her. She prayed and worked hard for the church in Peel. God puts to rest the workers, but carries on the work'. The Transfiguration, Resurrection and Ascension windows were installed in the chancel in January 1886 and the small stained glass window in memory of Robert Aitken (given by his son) was installed in December 1887.

On 10th December 1886 Hill received a petition, signed by 632 Peel people, asking him to make the new church the cathedral to mark the Queen's coming Golden Jubilee. He replied that he would do so if the debt could be cleared and the church consecrated, and offered £200 towards this. He said that he had taken steps to obtain the Royal Assent to this and added that the Governor favoured the idea. In January 1887 the Castletown Deanery approved the idea of making the new church the cathedral but the Douglas Deanery said that if a cathedral could not be made in Douglas, Bishopscourt Chapel should be made the pro-cathedral. This was what Bishop Powys had wanted.

Hill hoped to endow four canonries of £50 each in the new church for the benefit of Manx clergy, especially as, by 1887, clergy stipends had fallen with the value of tithe. On 14th April, 1887 The Cathedral and German Parish Act passed its second reading in the Legislative Council. It provided for a Chapter consisting of a Dean (who was to be the Bishop), the Archdeacon and six Canons, four stipendiary at £50 per annum and two honorary. Two of the stipendiary Canons and the two honorary Canons were to be appointed by the Bishop and the other two by the Crown. A canonry was to be declared vacant if the holder ceased to live in the diocese. The Cathedral Endowment Fund was to be administered by the Manx Church Commissioners. Bishop Hill's sudden death in May stopped further progress of the Act and put the church into financial difficulties, as he was a guarantor for £2,000, so the clock and chimes were silent, but after a meeting at St John's, Joseph Mylchreest, the Diamond King, offered to pay the £134 for the clock face, and other donations followed. The clock and chimes were eventually dedicated in 1888.

A clause in the Deed of Sale of the land for the new church said that this church was to be offered to the parish as a parish church. In 1885 it was so offered, but a special Vestry meeting declined it on the ground that it would be too costly to maintain. This reluctance caused the consecration to be postponed. The final cost of the church was £14,891.

ST JOHN'S John Corlett's long chaplaincy covered Hill's episcopate.

The stipend in 1881 was £120.

ST JUDE'S James Wilkinson remained the Chaplain under Hill.

The stipend in 1881 was £100.

JURBY Joseph Bellamy succeeded F. J. Moore early in 1879. Bellamy was a man of genial personality who was popular not only with his parishioners but with all who knew him. In January 1881 the old Vicarage and the 32 acre glebe (beside the church) were sold, as they were in bad repair and stood in a very thinly peopled part of the parish. The house and estate (36 acres) of Summerhill, were bought with Tynwald's approval. In 1881 it was proposed to build a new church nearer the centre of the parish and Mr W. Farrant of Ballamoar offered a site on his land. The idea came to nothing, probably because the Bishop was too pre-occupied with the idea of a cathedral to give any lead or help.

The stipend in 1881 was £150.

LAXEY Bellamy left to become Vicar of Jurby early in 1879. On 10th February 1879 a concert was held in the Victoria Hall, where he was presented with a fine drawing room clock, two purses of gold and a valuable inkstand. Reference was made to his great work for the schools and in the 1877 smallpox epidemic, to his instigating the building of the Working Men's Institute and Reading Room and to his creation of the Laxey Mines Poor Relief Fund. He was succeeded by Robert Brearey. He missed his train for Bellamy's presentation and did not arrive, but sent a telegram of explanation. He was a great friend to the poor of Laxey and was presented with a silver salver on leaving.

The next Chaplain was Theodore Chapman, a relative of Hill's first wife. The congregation at Laxey dwindled during his chaplaincy, the services being considered dull and unattractive and at the Sunday School Anniversary on 12th August 1883 less than 50 adults were present in either morning or afternoon. On two or three occasions in 1882 and 1883 it was announced that the Bishop would preach on the following Sunday, but in each case an indistinct notice was put up in an obscure place on the Saturday saying that he was unavoidably prevented from coming.

He was followed by Henry James in August 1884. On his arrival he added a wooden organ chamber to the parsonage to accommodate a large and valuable organ which he brought with him. On 24th May 1885 he said at the morning service that he would be making a statement in the evening and wanted as many as possible to attend, but there was only the average number at Evensong. The statement was that as his salary had diminished, and as he had much difficulty in getting it at all, he was returning to England. This may have been due to the fact that he made no collections for the Curates' Aid Society, hence they may have cut off their grant of £60 towards the stipend of £175. His kind and sympathetic manner made him popular in Laxey. He was a very good preacher and this took him out of Laxey too often for the liking of some. He even took preaching engagements in England. His practice of saying the words of administration once to each railful of people at Holy Communion was not liked.

The last chaplain under Hill was Claude Read (1885-87). He preached his last sermon on Acts 20[7] on 23rd October, 1887, many Methodists joining the congregation.

LEZAYRE Hutton was succeeded by Clement Shepheard, whose incumbency lasted only from December 1877 until December 1878. He came from Derbyshire, but owing to bad health he had not had charge of a parish for some time. There followed a long interregnum due, it was believed, to the reluctance of Moderate and High Churchmen and university men, to serve under a Low Church Bishop, but eventually Arthur Alexander Bridgman was appointed and remained Vicar for 30 years. Lezayre is a Crown living and it was Mr Richard Cross, the Home Secretary, a friend of many years, who nominated him. As a young man he joined the navy as an instructor, and saw several years of service, chiefly in the Mediterranean, where he explored the Holy Land. He was present at the naval bombardment of Acre in 1840 and received medals from both British and Turkish Governments. He was very interested in the volunteer movement and was a good linguist. On leaving the navy he studied for ordination. Bridgman read himself in on 6th July 1879, but did not preach at St Olave's in the evening, where a large congregation had assembled in the hope of hearing him. He did not preach in Lezayre church in the morning, but told the congregation that he was neither High nor Low church, but a Prayer Book man. Early in 1882 he re-introduced Hymns Ancient and Modern. In August 1882 he resigned from Ramsey Licensing Bench on the ground that it was ineffectual in preventing the spread of drunkenness. The windows in the church depicting Industry, Temperance, Charity, Truth and Modesty, Patience and Fortitude were given by Mr Cottier in 1884. A new pipe organ, to replace the 1874 harmonium, was opened on 18th January 1885, the preacher being Rector Kissack of Bride.

The stipend in 1881 was £173.

LONAN During the short interregnum after Vicar Caine's death the services were taken by James Bellamy, Chaplain of Laxey. The new Vicar was Frederick J. Moore, who had been Chaplain of Foxdale (1864-75) and Vicar of Jurby (1875-78). He remained Vicar until 1888.

The stipend in 1881 was £180.

ST LUKE'S Langton was succeeded as Chaplain by William Appleton who was appointed by Vicar Drury of Braddan in April 1880 but left after a few months to become Curate of Leverington, near Wisbech. The next Chaplain was Samuel Gasking. He was appointed in October 1880, but left early in 1882 to become Curate of Garston, Liverpool. Hugh Kinred was Chaplain for a short time in 1882 then came Richard Jones, who remained Chaplain until 1889. Jones had a strong Welsh accent.

MALEW H. S. Gill remained Vicar throughout Hill's episcopate.

The stipend in 1881 was £200.

ST MARK'S After Grant's return to England Vicar Gill of Malew, as patron of St Mark's, had difficulty in replacing him, due no doubt to the stipend being only £59, but in July he appointed Benjamin J. S. Lupton. For 13 years Lupton ministered faithfully in his quiet way, to his country congregation, whose spiritual welfare he had very much at heart.

MAROWN B. P. Clarke remained Vicar throughout Hill's episcopate.

The stipend in 1881 was £150.

ST MATTHEW'S The interregnum following the retirement of John Cannell lasted for 5 years, but a new era opened for St Matthew's with the appointment of Thomas A. Taggart in May 1878, who remained until 1909. In 1878 he became the Missions to Seamen Chaplain in Douglas, which brought in £120 per annum, but the stipend was only £81. The Missions to Seamen's grant ended in March 1886, as they wished to economise, but Mrs Hall then made up the deficiency in the stipend. On 16th March 1886 a crowded meeting was held in St Matthew's Hall, New Bond Street, to decide what to do about the stipend. Various individuals offered money and it was resolved to ask those who sent money to the Missions to Seamen to send it direct to 'St Matthew's Clerical Fund' of which the churchwardens were the treasurers. This would leave about £55 for the congregation to raise and the money came in well. As Chaplain to the Missions to Seamen, Taggart was expected to visit regularly the ships in the harbour and this he did, and up to the last he often had his breakfast on Sundays in the vestry so that he could visit the ships between the 8 o'clock and 11 o'clock services.

Until 1878 St Matthew's was only a chaplaincy,

but in 1879 it was made a parish and Taggart was the first Vicar. In 1878 there was no parsonage, Sunday School, Mission room or parochial organisation and the only permanent endowment was £20. Number 15 Derby Square eventually became the vicarage. There were 3,000 people in the parish.

Until 1878 all the pews were rented, 14 being owned by one man. This dated from the foundation of the church in 1708, when the seats had been permanently allotted according to the subscription given. Taggart determined to abolish pew rents, even though this would reduce his stipend by £30, but he assured the churchwardens that God would provide for him. They agreed to support him in abolishing pew rents and the extra money given in collections soon made up the deficiency.

St Matthew's held about 250. Soon after his arrival Taggart removed the old three decker pulpit, altar rails and reading desk and supplied new ones. The organ was repaired and a new lectern and font were given. Taggart used to hold 10-15 minute services in the lunch hour at the Gas Works. In 1890 he began weekly celebrations of Holy Communion at 8 a.m. on Sundays and on Saints' Days as the result of a visitor in July 1890 expressing regret that he had been unable to receive the Sacrament on the Sunday he was in Douglas.

Taggart lived a life of devotion to duty as a humble servant of his Master whom he delighted to serve. He began house to house visiting. Until the very end of his incumbency he worked to the full measure of his strength - and beyond it. His spirit was such that he concealed his physical exhaustion. He kept the church open every day (unusual at that time) for private prayer and encouraged the poorest people to love and use the church. He had a great love for the poor, he was very patient with their faults and he strongly denounced those who oppressed them. His memory for names and faces was remarkable. The loungers at street corners loved and feared him. He was very punctual and methodical, he forgot nothing and left nothing undone. Nothing would budge him on a matter of principle and he never seemed to tire. He would share his last penny with the humblest parishioner, never thinking whether he could spare it. When he came there had been no Sunday School for 40 years, so he held one in the church gallery. Eventually Mrs Hall bought back the old Grammar School

in New Bond Street and presented it to the church, after re-building and re-fitting it at her own expense. Taggart always gave a tenth of his income to God's service. He helped even those who never came to church. No sick person was ever unvisited. He always welcomed people in the church porch before the service.

His life was one of patient attention to duty, untiring industry, thoughtfulness for the poor and suffering, kindness of heart, loyalty to friends, care for the souls of men, and complete freedom from self-adverisement. No more familiar figure was to be met in Douglas. He seemed to be always at work, absorbed in his ministry, so intensely in earnest all the time that he seemed not to have a minute to spare for anything except duty. He was always cheerful and ready to speak the word in season whether of encouragement or rebuke. For him nothing was impossible and 'it must be done' was a characteristic phrase. He was confident that He who had called him to the work, great and difficult though it was, would give him the means to perform it. He took few holidays and when others would be enjoying change and rest he, whose need of them was far greater, toiled on. Faith and hope motivated his life. He gladly denied himself many things to be able to give to others. He was described as the hardest working parson on the Island. Taggart was a High Churchman, and this tradition began at St Matthew's while he was Vicar.

On 2nd February 1879 a heavy snowfall prevented the Bishop from coming for a confirmation and it was postponed for a week. 61 were confirmed, the text being II Timothy 2[1]. At the 1879 Easter Vestry it was decided to raise money for a vicarage and Taggart expressed the hope that all seats in the church would soon be free. In 1880 the church was licensed for weddings.

As early as 1878 Bishop Hill had advised Taggart to aim at a new church but this idea was not popular and at the 1881 Vestry meeting Taggart denied that there was any intention of demolishing the church and that all he wanted to do was enlarge it.

By 1881 the stipend had risen to £200.

MAUGHOLD William Kermode became Rector of Ballaugh in 1877 and was succeeded in March by Gilmour Harvey. He was appointed on the understanding that legislation was pending to separate Ramsey from Maughold, a matter which had been agitated for many years. Harvey wished this to happen and the 1877 Vestry meeting passed a resolution requesting it. His incumbency, however, was very short. While washing on the morning of 7th May 1875, he was taken ill with heart pains and, on returning to bed, he quietly died, aged 67. He had had an affection of the heart for some time but had seemed better at Easter, though not quite well. He was universally beloved and respected. He was buried at Malew.

His successor was Henry Grattan White. When he left Ballaugh he was presented with a handsome mantelpiece clock in Louis XIV style and a pair of matching vases. In his later years at Ballaugh he was virtually Rector as Thomas Howard was largely incapacitated by age and ill health. On 16th October 1856 he married Howard's second daughter, Catherine, the service being taken by Archdeacon Moore and thereafter he became like a son to his aged father-in-law. Mrs White died in Douglas on 21st September 1900, aged 87 and was buried at Ballaugh.

White impressed all with his courteous and gentle ways. He always judged others favourably, he was slow to take offence and never willingly gave it. In business matters he was scrupulously exact and punctual. He passed his life as a country parson without noise or excitement in the quiet, faithful discharge of duty; helpful to all who needed help and an example of Christian charity to all. He was very popular with everyone, including the Methodists. He was a lover of peace (but not at any price), conciliatory and most conscientious, the soul of honour and chivalry, with the inexpressible sweetness of his father-in-law. He confined himself to his own parish, and concerned himself very little with things outside it. T. E. Brown said of him 'He was not brilliant, but the most stainless and perfect gentlemen I think I ever knew'. White used to quote the Latin saying 'He has not lived amiss of whom the world has not heard'.

A new organ was opened on 16th June 1878. G. Paton of St Paul's preached in the morning and the Bishop in the evening. In 1881 the stipend was £170 and the population of the parish, 1,147.

KIRK MICHAEL Airey's successor in November 1878 was Ernest B. Savage. He was good, sincere, tolerant and broadminded. He maintained good relations with the Methodists and, in 1880, he contributed to the building of Baaregarroo Chapel. The 1878 Oiel Voirrey service was attended by Hill and his family and the domestic staff at Bishopscourt. At the 1879 Easter Vestry on 4th April the meeting accepted Savage's suggestion to renew most of the Church floors, to make the seats more comfortable and varnish them and to have a new heating apparatus. Bishop Hill attended as a parishioner, and spoke in support of the Vicar. This work necessitated the closing of the church, but it was re-opened on 21st September. On 8th June 1882 Savage and Vicar Williams of German revived the custom of walking the boundaries. There was thick mist and tea was taken in pouring rain. A plan to walk the boundary between Michael and Braddan was abandoned because of the mist. Savage became Vicar of St Thomas' in 1882, and was succeeded by Vicar Hawley of Patrick.

The stipend in 1881 was £200 per annum.

ST OLAVE'S Buckley was succeeded in 1878 by Robertson Bardell. Next came William Morris, who in 1881 became the first Vicar when St Olave's was made a separate parish. Soon after his appointment Hill had wanted to make St Olave's a separate parish. Bridgman, as Vicar of the mother parish (Lezayre) agreed to this, and also to Morris' appointment, but within a year differences had arisen between Bridgman and Morris, as the latter was acting independently and sometimes even in opposition to the Vicar. This situation was resolved in 1881 when the Church Commissioners made St Olave's a separate parish. In preparation for this, and in reply to a petition from the congregation, Hill consecrated the church at 11 a.m. on Wednesday, 20th April 1881. Perhaps because it was a weekday, the church was only half full. The Bishop preached on St John 20²⁴, 'But Thomas, one of the twelve, called Didymus, was not with them when Jesus came'. On 26th April Bridgman wrote to the 'Manx Sun' saying that many people took this to refer to him, as he was not present at the consecration. This, he said, was because he objected, not to the separation of St Olave's from Lezayre, but because he thought that the way it was done was neither straightforward nor honourable. This may refer to the fact that he thought the petition for consecration should have come from the Vicar and Wardens of Lezayre, as owners of the land, which had been sold to them in September 1862. However, Bridgman eventually accepted the situation. The vicarage, near the windmill, was bought in 1881. Morris remained Vicar until 1896 and was very popular.

ONCHAN John Howard remained Vicar under Hill. In 1880 he remarked that when he came to Onchan in 1847 there was not a single psalm chant sung in any church on the Island, nor was there any choral service until he started them. Except at Christmas there were no decorations. The service was just a dialogue between the parson and the clerk, who was the mouthpiece of the silent congregation. Extensive alterations and repairs were done to the church in 1885, which meant that it had to be closed, but it was re-opened on 22nd November.

The stipend at this time was £150.

PATRICK Garde was succeeded in December 1877 by William Hawley, the Chaplain of St George's. The main event of his incumbency was the building of the present parish church, something which Hawley very much wanted and for which he began planning in 1878. As far back as 19th August 1875 a vestry meeting had voted for the building of a new church. In 1878 the church was almost roofless and there was no spouting so it was very damp. The walls, windows and interior fittings were in ruinous decay, and for a long time services had been held in the parochial school room. The walls were not even upright and the churchyard was very neglected. The required Act of Tynwald allowed the churchwardens to raise £600 by cess. The Vestry's intention had been to build the new church on the same site, but Bishop Hill wanted it to be in Glen Maye, which was more a centre of population, and offered £1,500 towards the cost if it was built there. He had bought a one acre site in Glen Maye, but no money had been raised and nothing was done. The idea of building at Glen Maye did not find favour and a Vestry meeting on 25th November 1878 decided against it.

The foundation stone of the new church was laid by Mrs Hill at 3.30 p.m. on Wednesday, 30th April 1879, the Bishop's wedding anniversary. It was a very fine day. Before the laying of the stone Hawley held a service in the schoolroom attended by about 200 people. The estimated cost of the new church was £750 and it seats 120 people. In April 1879 the churchyard was enlarged and Hawley gave up part of his glebe for this purpose.

In November 1882 Hawley became Vicar of Kirk Michael and was succeeded in December by Hugh Davidson.

The stipend in 1881 was £100.

ST PAUL'S Soon after his arrival, Paton determined to end the system of pew rents, even though it would reduce his stipend. In wishing to make all the pews free, Paton was opposed by the Bishop and by some influential members of the congregation, including the Clerk of the Rolls, Alured Dumbell, but he carried his point at a meeting in 1879 and on 18th April 1880 he declared all seats free and open. On 20th November 1880 the High Bailiff of Ramsey, John Lamothe, successfully applied in the Vicar General's Court for a faculty to retain his pew for himself and his successors so long as they were parishioners.

In June 1881 Hill began a suit in the Chancery Court to have Paton's appointment declared null and void on the ground that it had been made illegally. In addition to their differences over pew rents, Hill and Paton disagreed over churchmanship. The churchwardens and sidesmen opened a defence fund and on 15th July 1881 the case came on in the Chancery Court (Governor Loch, the two Deemsters and the Clerk of the Rolls). It was a petition from the Bishop to have a certain Deed of Assignment, executed by Vicar White of Maughold, and dated 13th March 1879, transferring the patronage of St Paul's to the Crown, declared null and void. The original Trust Deed of 16th April 1821 had vested the patronage in the Bishop and had allotted the seats in perpetuity to the original subscribers. Until 1871 the Bishop had appointed the Chaplain, but in 1871 Kermode, as Vicar of the mother parish (Maughold), had claimed the patronage and, with Powys' agreement, had appointed Paton, who had been his Curate. In early 1878 Paton applied for a parochial district to be assigned to St Paul's, which was in the parish of Maughold, of which the patron was the Crown, and this was granted by Order in Council on 17th May 1879. The Deed of 13th March 1879 had vested the patronage in the Vicar of Maughold, then H. G. White, but he wished to have the patronage vested in the Crown, to which he resigned all his rights. Hill agreed to this, not knowing of the original Trust Deed, but he now rightly claimed that this gave him the patronage, and said that White had no right to execute the Deed. The judgement of the Chancery Court was that St Paul's was not a chapel of ease, and that the patronage was not, and never had been, vested in the Vicar, but in the Bishop, and that the Deed executed by White on 13th March 1879 was void.

Hill told Paton that his only intention in bringing the matter to court was to test the legal aspect and that a favourable judgement would not affect him, but Paton wanted an assurance that he would be reappointed unconditionally, especially as regards free pews. Despite this, Paton still felt that the Bishop had taken the action against him personally, even though Mr Sherwood, the Bishop's lawyer, agreed to have Paton's name removed from the petition to satisfy him.

Relations between Hill and Paton continued to be bad, mainly due to the free pews issue. In August 1882 Paton publicly appealed to St Paul's Church Workers' Guild to help with the Sunday School, as Hill had only offered him two curates, both strangers, and both totally unsuitable academically. Dr Hughes-Games, the Examining Chaplain, replied in the 'Manx Sun' on 19th August that several curates had been offered to Paton and that another, whom Paton wanted, Hill had refused to ordain as he would not take a course in Theological College. Hughes-Games said that there was no question of the Bishop being influenced against Paton by the pew rents issue and deplored Paton's making a public statement of this kind. To the undoubted fact that Hill had left several of Paton's letters on the subject unanswered, Hughes-Games replied that the Bishop had already given his decision on the points, directly, and through his Chaplain. In 1883 a good Curate was appointed in John Kewley, who, in November 1883, obtained the consent of a special Vestry meeting to the introduction of a robed choir which he agreed to train. They wore their robes for the first time on 20th April 1884, when the Bishop preached, but he made no reference to the robed choir, which would be contrary to his low church views. Kewley, while Curate, was one of the pioneers of the Ramsey Life-Saving Corps, or Rocket Brigade. He became a Captain, learned how to handle the equipment, fire the shot, etc. and

was a most efficient and enthusiastic member.

It was said that in 1879 Paton refused both Lezayre and Bride.

In 1881 the apse was panelled with walnut wood and a Bishop's chair was provided. The present organ was installed in 1883 and an organ chamber built. Before 1886 the church bell was situated in a bell turret on the roof, but in this year two bells were put in the tower as the nucleus of a future peal of bells which never materialised. In April 1888 the wooden tiles in the sanctuary floor were replaced by tiles and white marble steps, and new Communion rails of burnished brass were installed.

In 1879 the stipend was raised from £90 to £150.

RUSHEN E. W. Kissack moved to Bride in 1879 and on 18th February he was presented with a silver tea and coffee service by the parishioners. He said that his great desire had been to build a church in Port St Mary but although he had not succeeded, £400 had been raised towards it. Mrs Kissack had collected a large sum of money towards Cregneash church. Kissack's successor, Arthur Allwork, attended the presentation. Kissack had encouraged the people of Cregneash to build a church of their own and for many years a weekly service had been held in the village. They set to work with a will on a site given by Mr John Karran, and because labour was free, the only cost was that of the materials - £150. The foundation stone was laid by Mrs Gawne on Monday 12th August 1878, a beautifully fine day, after a short service. On Friday, 13th December 1878 Bishop Hill opened and dedicated the church, preaching on St Luke 23[42,] but only the chancel was consecrated so that the rest could be used as a school, but it was only used as a school for a short time. All seats were to be free.

Allwork was followed by Frederick F. Tracey. As he had a large family an extra floor was added to the vicarage in 1881 and while this was done he stayed at Kentraugh. On 23rd January 1885 a special Vestry meeting was held to put the church in proper repair and re-seat it. The contractor was Mr Robert Moore of Ballafesson. The old-fashioned high backed square pews were auctioned on 2nd July and were replaced by modern pews of pitch pine. The church was closed from 1st July until 23rd August.

At the Easter Vestry in 1885 there was some criticism of Tracey's management of the Milner Trust and a motion was passed to apply to Chancery Court to have the Trust vested in the Vicar and Wardens rather than in the Vicar alone. In April 1885 a libel action by Tracey against his former Curate, the Revd G. Mackey, was settled out of court after Tracey received a written apology.

The main event of Tracey's incumbency was the building of St Mary's Church, Port St Mary. On 27th February 1847 the 'Manx Sun' reported that a chapel of ease was to be built in Port St Mary, as the population of the parish was then 3,200 and the parish church only held 400. Bishop Auckland approved, Mr E. M. Gawne of Kentraugh gave the site and a donation and £300 was quickly raised. The plan foundered however and on 8th October 1848 the schoolroom in Port St Mary was licensed for worship by the Bishop until the new church was built. But the idea was revived and on 31st August 1880 a meeting was held to consider the necessary steps. Messrs. Barry of Liverpool were asked to draw the plans.

A bazaar was held in August 1881 and by February 1882 the plans had been accepted and the site cleared. In April 1882 Mr F. Stowell, joiner and builder of Castletown, was given the contract to build the church. The foundation stone was laid by Mrs Gawne at 12 noon on Monday, 15th May 1882, preceded by a service at which the Bishop preached. The weather was glorious and led the Bishop to remark that it was the first time he had officiated in Rushen on a fine day. Mrs Gawne gave £400 towards the building, which eventually cost £1,200. Forty of those present were invited to lunch at Kentraugh afterwards. Miss Caroline Hill, the Bishop's elder daughter, accompanied him, following the recent death of her mother. The Captain of the Parish and Mrs Clucas were absent owing to a family bereavement. By October 1882 the church was complete except for the roof and this was added in November. Hill presented the altar and sanctuary chairs, Mrs Gawne gave the Communion Plate, her daughters gave the font and the Vicar gave the pulpit. By August 1883 the spire, entrance gate, Prayer Books, Lectern Bible and the Table of Commandments were still lacking. By November 1883 the walls around the ground and the entrance gate were finished and the architects gave the lectern, but lighting, heating, porch and organ

were still required. The church was consecrated on Friday, 25th January 1884 at 11.30 a.m. There was only a moderate congregation in the morning, when Tracey took the service, H. S. Gill and E. W. Kissack read the lessons and the Bishop preached on Genesis 28[22], but the church was full in the evening when Hill's text was St Mark 14[14]. The aged Archdeacon Moore was not present.

Bishop Hill had always wanted a new large parish church at the Four Roads but he realised that the building of St Catherine's, Port Erin, put this out of court. There had been a church in Port Erin in Celtic times, dedicated to St Catherine, and when Mr William Milner died in September 1874, he left in his will a piece of land and £1,000 for the building of a church in memory of his wife, Jane (who had died earlier in the year), dedicated to St Catherine. Mr Milner, whose firm made safes, came to Port Erin each year, and was so good to the local people, especially the poor, that in 1871 the tower on Bradda Head was built by them in his honour. He did not specify a site for the church but this was chosen by Vicar Kissack, and was staked out on 15th October 1878. Milner's will laid down that a school was to be built as well as a church, but as a school was not needed, application was made to the Chancery Court for only the church to be built. The foundation stone was laid by Bishop Hill, in the presence of Governor Loch, at 3 p.m. on Thursday, 12th December 1878, the service being taken by the Vicar and his Curate, H. R. Finnis. The hymns were 'This stone to thee in faith we lay' and 'The Church's one foundation'. Building was completed by May 1880, the architect being Mr James Cowle and the builders Messrs. Moore and Costain. It was consecrated by the Bishop at 3.30 p.m. on Thursday, 3rd August 1880, a fine day, the text of the sermon being I Corinthians 3[16]. The collection was £8. Evensong was taken by Vicar Allwork and the lessons were read by Vicar Drury of Braddan and Dr Hughes-Games. Most of the clergy attended, in addition to Vicar General Jebb, Mr Samuel Harris and Sir James Gell.

The last Vicar of Rushen under Hill was Charles Dawes, who was inducted on Saturday 24th October 1885 by Vicar Gill of Malew.

The stipend in 1881 was £160 and the population of the parish 3,660.

SANTAN White was succeeded by Robert Airey, Vicar of Kirk Michael, who was inducted by Vicar Gill of Malew on 6th December 1878. In 1886 his health began to fail and he moved to a house in the Parade, Castletown, leaving his Curate, Archibald Clarke, in charge of the parish. Airey died on 8th November 1889, and was buried at Santan on 12th November, the service being taken by Bishop Bardsley and Gill. 'O God, our help in ages past' was sung outside the house. He left less than £200. His gentleness, kindness and unassuming and unobtrusive manner won him the respect and love of his people.

The stipend in 1881 was £150.

ST STEPHEN'S Pattison was succeeded by William Canton. He came to the Isle of Man when the Manx Northern Railway was being built and held a mission in Kirk Michael for the workmen. Bishop Hill was interested in him and appointed him to St Stephen's while still a Deacon. He was well liked and respected and so was Mrs Canton, who was a great friend to the poor. At Bishop Hill's suggestion St Stephen's was virtually re-built during his chaplaincy. The foundation stone was laid by Mrs E. C. Farrant on Friday 24th October 1879 in the presence of Governor Loch and the Bishop, and the work was completed by the following summer. The pulpit was given by Archdeacon Moore and the reading desk by Mrs Canton's mother.

In February 1887 a complaint was made to Vicar Bridgman of Lezayre (the Mother parish) that Canton had been letting pews. Bridgman said that it must stop as the original Deed of Gift conveying the site had stipulated that all seats were to be free, except the Staward family pew and one for the staff of the house and the farm.

Canton left in February 1882 to become Vicar of Dinting Vale, Glossop, then in the diocese of Southwell, where he remained until 1894. He preached his last sermons on 12th February, his text in the morning being I Thessalonians 5²³ and in the evening, Ephesians 6¹⁸⁻¹⁹· On the next evening he was presented with a silver salver.

In February 1881 the congregation asked the Manx Church Commissioners to make St Stephen's a parochial district. By December 1882 no appointment had been made and it was pointed out that if the appointment was not made by the patron (Bridgman) within 6 months the patronage would lapse to the Bishop. Bridgman said that he had nominated a chaplain in March but the Bishop would not accept him - rumour said because he had an ailing wife. Eventually Charles Bell became Chaplain (January 1883).

The last chaplain under Hill was William Blakeney (July 1885). He was formerly a soldier in a Canadian regiment and was a great horseman, frequently breaking in colts for the farmers. In his last months there was a fire in the church which did considerable damage.

The stipend in 1881 was £120.

ST THOMAS' Hutton was succeeded in November 1877 by Marmaduke Washington who was inducted and instituted by the Bishop on 9th November, when there was a large congregation despite a wet day. He took his first services on 11th November when Governor Loch and his wife attended.

It was not long before there was trouble between Vicar and congregation over church music. Washington was very evangelical and disliked ornate music and Hymns Ancient and Modern. In August 1877 Mr P. L. Garrett, the organist, had resigned for health reasons and on 9th September Miss M. L. Wood was appointed, as neither of the assistant organists, Messrs. Royston and Mylrea, wanted the post. On his arrival Washington said that he would not have a woman organist and Garrett was induced to return. Many of the congregation, including the two churchwardens, opposed the sacking of Miss Wood, as she had done so well.

Washington began children's services on the first Sunday afternoon of the month - soon changed to the last Sunday.

At the 1878 Easter Vestry (22nd April), Washington said that he proposed to substitute a hymn for the anthem on Sunday evenings and to make the services such that people could join in them more heartily. He had promised Mr Garrett, when he resumed after Miss Wood was dropped, that no change whatever would be made in the musical part of the service, and that Ancient and Modern would continue to be the Hymn Book and the choir (most of whom had resigned), agreed to return on hearing this. Soon afterwards they agreed, rather reluctantly, to say the

Creed instead of intoning it and to drop the playing of interludes between the offertory sentences. But at choir practice on 3rd May he said that there would be no more choral services, that the ladies in the choir would be replaced by boys and that the Hymnal Companion would be used instead of Ancient and Modern. Mr Garrett, Mr Mylrea and all the choir at once resigned. A memorial to retain Ancient and Modern, signed by 75% of the congregation was sent to Hill and Washington, but with no success.

At the 1879 Easter Vestry strong opposition was expressed to these changes. Both the churchwardens strongly advised Washington against them, but he said that he had the legal right to make them and would use his power. He had made a small concession in withdrawing an order to discontinue intoning the responses and for the organist to discontinue giving a note to the choir. The paid choir of boys had proved a costly failure as £50 had been spent in the year instead of £16 in the past, while offertories over the year had dropped by £50, as the congregation had dwindled. The meeting failed to get anything from Washington beyond a general assurance that he would meet the congregation's wishes. The Vestry also disputed a letter he had sent to the Bishop saying that the offertories had increased. On 2nd May 1879 an Address of Support was handed to Washington, signed by over 200 parishioners, but it was generally known that two ladies had touted for signatures among people who had only attended the church once or twice over the years.

In 1880 a Fund was started to build a spire but by March 1881 only £60 out of an estimated £1,000 had been subscribed so it was decided to have a new organ and to ask those who had subscribed to the tower to transfer their subscriptions to the organ.

Washington resigned on 31st March 1881 on the ground that circumstances might oblige him to be in England more than was right for the Vicar. He preached his farewell sermon on 27th March. His departure was not regretted as his policy over music had caused much unpleasantness. On 12th August he had married Miss Augusta Morley in Kent. Bishop Hill, who officiated, gave them a table, the Governor gave them a pair of bronze branch candlesticks and the people of St Thomas' gave them a silver tea service.

The next Vicar was John Quirk, son of Charles Quirk, who was inducted at St Thomas' by Vicar Drury, acting for the Archdeacon, who was ill, in June 1881. On 6th June an adjourned Vestry meeting voted 12 to 1 to restore Hymns Ancient and Modern and Quirk promised to consider it, but he took no action and at the 1882 Easter Vestry he said that Ancient and Modern would not be restored.

He was succeeded by Ernest Savage, Vicar of Kirk Michael since 1878, who began an outstanding ministry of 32 years. He was inducted by Drury on 21st December 1882 and at once said that he would restore Ancient and Modern. He came as a peacemaker after five years of dissension, which he overcame by kindly tact and sympathy. By 1885 the bells had become unsafe so they were re-hung and the two smallest were excluded from the peal as they were not in tune and were rarely used. The Revd R. Catley, who had given the bells, agreed to this.

A new organ, with 1,682 pipes, was designed by Mr W. T. Best, a personal friend of Mr Garrett and organist at St George's Hall, Liverpool, from 1855-94, who opened it on 1st August 1886. The builders were William Hill of London and the cost was £1,000, including the hydraulic blowing mechanism.

The stipend in 1881 was £330.

179

Chapter 11

BISHOP BARDSLEY 1887-1892

The new Bishop was John Wareing Bardsley, who accepted Sodor and Man the day after it was offered to him, (21st June 1887). He was born on 29th March 1835, the eldest of the seven sons of Canon James Bardsley, who in 1835 was Curate of Brierly, near Bradford and ended his ministry as Rector of St Anne's, Manchester (1857-79). John Bardsley was educated at Burnley Grammar School and Manchester Grammar School and graduated from Trinity College, Dublin in 1859. He was ordained by Bishop Graham of Chester (Deacon 1859, Priest 1860). From 1859-61 he was Curate of St Anne's, Sale, then, after a few months as Curate of St Luke's, Liverpool, he became secretary of Islington Protestant Institute (1861-4). He then became Vicar of St John's, Bootle (1864-71), which he found almost destitute of parochial organisations and where he established schools, lectures, a working men's club and a very large Bible class. He threw himself with characteristic energy into bringing the church into contact with the masses. While at Bootle he married Miss Mary Powell and had twin sons, Francis and Edward, and three daughters, Mabel, Helen and Edith. From 1871-80 he was Vicar of St Saviour's, Falkner Square, Liverpool, where he created a parish machinery and set up a home for aged widows. In 1880 he became a Canon of Liverpool, Archdeacon of Warrington and Chaplain to Bishop Ryle, the first Bishop of the newly-created diocese of Liverpool. He also became Chairman of the Diocesan Executive Council and the Liverpool clergy soon knew where there was an unfailing help in difficulty. From January to September 1887 he was Archdeacon of Liverpool. As Curate, Vicar and Archdeacon he won golden opinions. He had recently declined an invitation to be Vicar of Islington. He was very evangelical and was marked by sturdy commonsense, strength of character and sound judgement. He was the trusted friend and helper of Bishop Ryle who frequently consulted him.

On Wednesday, 22nd June he visited the Island and Bishopscourt, returning by the 4 p.m. steamer on Thursday. He admired Bishopscourt Glen and the surrounding scenery. On Thursday morning he met Vicar General Harris and some clergy in Douglas Courthouse and said that he strongly approved of the Douglas Head services. He had visited the Island in 1862 and had preached in St Barnabas'. In late June Mrs Bardsley and two of her daughters spent a week in Ramsey making arrangements for taking up residence on the Island.

He was consecrated by Archbishop Thomson of York, assisted by the Bishops of Liverpool, Chester and Manchester, at 11.30 a.m. on Wednesday, 24th August 1887. The sermon was preached by the Revd H. James, Rector of Livermere on I Corinthians 4[2], and the anthem was Wesley's 'Thou wilt keep him in perfect peace'. After lunching at the Railway Hotel with his relatives and friends he left York by the 5 p.m. train. He had asked his new diocese for their prayers on the preceding Sunday and hoped that at least some churches would hold a service at the same time as his consecration. Most of the churches did so. He planned to come to the Island as soon as possible and decided to occupy a temporary residence until Bishopscourt was ready.

On September 4th he preached at St George's in the morning on Exodus 3[12], and in the evening at St Barnabas', making a very good impression. In the afternoon he took a service on Douglas Head, attended by about 10,000 people, when his text was St Luke 14[23]. He was assisted at this service by the Vicars of St George's and St Barnabas'. On 9th September he went to Balmoral to pay homage to the Queen and on Tuesday, 20th September - a gloriously fine day - he was enthroned at Castletown. At Hill's enthronement Castletown was decorated and the lifeboat crew and rocket brigade turned out in honour of the occasion, but none of this happened for Bardsley. Archdeacon Hughes-Games preached on II Corinthians 1[11] and began by alluding to the recent death of Vicar Drury of Braddan. An Address from the people of Castletown was presented. The Bishop and most of the clergy lunched with Ferrier, Chaplain of Castletown.

Bardsley appointed as his surrogates Gill (Malew), Hobson (St Barnabas'), George (St George's), Paton

(St Paul's, Ramsey) and Williams (German). He appointed Gill and Savage (St Thomas') as his Examining Chaplains, and Hawley (Kirk Michael) as his Domestic Chaplain. He began by giving £100 towards clergy stipends, as the agricultural depression had reduced the value of the tithe by 25%. On 30th October 1887 he was presented with a set of episcopal robes and a signet ring by the Liverpool Clerical Society. On 25th September he had held his first ordination - at Andreas.

Bardsley quickly won the affection of all classes by his brotherliness, broadmindedness and lovable disposition. He was beloved by the clergy, who often sought his advice, and highly respected by the Methodists. He worked very hard - often too hard - from a high sense of duty and in summer he preached three times each Sunday. He was devoid of ambition and carried out his duties with painstaking simplicity. He would go to remote country churches to help the clergy, often staying with the curate and accepting cheerfully even the simplest hospitality. Often he would use the train instead of his carriage. He lacked Hill's physical vigour and restless energy and did not keep himself so prominently before the public, or attain Hill's unequalled popularity. He was a man of peace, with great consideration for the feelings and rights of others. His popularity among the ordinary people in the Island came from his great kindness, humility, gentleness of spirit, unfailing sympathy and quiet, unobtrusive piety.

He realised that Douglas was the centre of Island life, spending more time there than any of his predecessors. He considered that the Bishop should live in Douglas and that Bishopscourt should be made a Theological College. He had found the upkeep of Bishopscourt a strain, especially as the fall in the value of tithe had reduced his stipend, nominally £2,000 to £1,500. He continued to develop Bishop Wilson Theological College. Bardsley was a total abstainer, often acted as chairman at temperance meetings and, in 1887, became Vice-President of the Church of England Temperance Society. He was a frequent visitor to the Holy Land.

Bardsley was described as a man of loving sympathy and unostentatious simplicity, unvarying courtesy and quiet dignity. His kindness and practical sympathy were unequalled and he was always the courteous, kindly, approachable gentleman. Like Hill he was a conservative. He had exceptional qualifications as a thoughtful, eloquent preacher and parochial organiser, and in everything he showed calm judgement, wisdom in counsel, earnestness and force of character. He was equally at home in preaching to a few people in a small country church, or addressing thousands on Douglas Head.

There had been no Convocation in 1887 owing to Hill's death but the 1888 Convocation was held on 24th May. Bardsley, in his Charge, quoted figures to show that, even proportionately, Sodor and Man had less baptisms and fewer children in Sunday School than any English diocese. He felt that the remedy lay in "seeking by every allowable method to adapt our church system to the altered circumstances of changed times and by bringing home to every man's heart the conviction that we clergy are intensely in earnest, that we do love and seek to save souls and that as a body we exist only to care for and to do good to all those among whom we dwell". He urged visiting, more care of Sunday Schools (which the Vicar ought to open and close), more zeal and sympathy with young people at the difficult age - e.g. by communicants' unions. He said that a new cathedral would be too expensive a luxury for the diocese, but admitted that he had once thought Braddan suitable. He wanted to set up a Sustentation Fund to help clergy stipends and to create four canonries at £50 per annum each. He stressed the importance of their ministry to the visitors. He said that he at one time doubted whether he could keep up the grounds and gardens of Bishopscourt. In reply to a suggestion of a Mission to the Island he said "Our great want is that we clergy should be stirred up by a fresh outpouring of the Holy Ghost. The Ingathering for which we yearn depends upon ourselves. When we have been found worthy, God will use us as His instruments".

On three Sundays in August 1888 Bardsley preached to about 15,000 people on Douglas Head, helped by Vicar Hobson of St Barnabas'. At a confirmation at St Mark's on 18th November 1888 he said that the Isle of Man and its people had quite exceeded his expectations, except in attendance at Holy Communion.

On 4th April 1889 a deputation of clergy from the Douglas Deanery (Savage, Hobson, Taggart, Moore and Clarke) waited on Governor Walpole, to enlist his support to stop the increase in Sunday trading, but achieved little. The Governor simply said that the clergy were not doing enough by "moral persuasion".

On 5th April 1889 Deemster Drinkwater publicly rebuked the Bishop in Tynwald for his frequent absences in England. The 'Manx Sun', in reporting it, said that there was a widespread feeling about the perfunctory way in which the Bishop attended to his duties in the diocese and in the Legislative Council. It is possible that this was true of the Council, but contemporary evidence is over-whelming that Bardsley was a true Father in God and that he was most conscientious in the discharge of all his duties as Bishop.

Bardsley ordered the following prayer to be used in all Anglican places of worship as from 1st August 1889.

'A prayer for the Civil Government of the Isle of Man, to be used after the Prayer for the Royal Family at such times as the Litany is not appointed to be said.'

Almighty God, the Fountain of all wisdom, we humbly beseech Thee with Thy favour to behold the Governor and Legislature of this Isle; mercifully grant that Thy Holy Spirit may rest upon them, enlighten and guide them, that all their consultations may be directed and prospered to the advancement of Thy Glory and the welfare of Thy Church and People, through Jesus Christ our Lord. Amen.

In the Litany the clause was to read:

"That it may please Thee to endue the Governor and Legislature of this Isle, the Lords of the Council and all the nobility, with grace, wisdom and understanding".

This was approved by Governor Walpole and originated in a request at the 1889 Convocation that such a prayer should be authorised.

On each Sunday in August 1889 and on the 1st September the Bishop preached on Douglas Head. Early in December he was ill with pleurisy and he spent July and early August 1890 at Aix-les-Bains, which greatly improved his health. But in January 1890 there was still a feeling that the Bishop was off the Island too often. At the 1890 Convocation a resolution was passed deploring the increasing secularisation of Sunday. On 7th September 1890 Bardsley preached a sermon in St Thomas' in which he took a rationalistic view of the Flood and evoked a great deal of criticism. In November 1890 he took up residence in the south of the Island while alterations were made to the drainage at Bishopscourt.

Nearly all ordinations in Bardsley's time were in Bishopscourt Chapel. In 1890 he confirmed 558 people. He recommended that candidates should be 15 and over and under no circumstances under 13. He stressed that candidates should manifest simplicity of dress and so avoid the danger of distracting thoughts. Girls were to be confirmed first. He wanted each candidate to have a copy of the service and of the hymns, of which there were to be three. Two candidates were to be confirmed at a time. The Lord's Prayer was to be said by the Bishop alone.

On 20th March 1891 Bardsley invited the non-conformist ministers of the Island to spend a day at Bishopscourt and 16 accepted. They were welcomed by him at the railway stop for Bishopscourt then he took them for a walk along the cliffs. After lunch there was a service in the chapel, then they explored Bishopscourt Glen. The Archdeacon, Vicar Hawley of Kirk Michael and Rector Kissack of Ballaugh also attended. In April 1891 the Bishop received the President of the Primitive Methodist Society at Bishopscourt during his visit to the Island.

The 1891 Convocation fell on 21st May. The Bishop stressed that faculties must be obtained for work on churches and an inventory made of church plate. Faculties had been largely ignored. Since the last Convocation Bardsley had ordained 15 men and confirmed 542 people, this latter being the highest percentage of any diocese in the Province of York. It was suggested that a fund be set up to improve clergy stipends, which had been reduced to 75% of their nominal value by the fall in the value of the tithe.

In June 1891 there was again criticism in the 'Manx Sun' of the Bishop's absences in England.

On 23rd July 1891 Bardsley attended the opening of the first section of the Marine Drive Railway. On 2nd and 16th August he preached on Douglas Head to over 5,000 people. In November he moved to Douglas for the winter and rented Stanley House on Loch Promenade. On 4th January 1892 he entertained all 70 of the Postal and Telegraph Staff at Douglas to dinner at the Sefton Hotel, on which occasion a gramophone attracted much attention.

On 22nd December 1891 it was announced that

Bardsley had been translated to Carlisle, a move believed to have been due to the influence of his brother-in-law, Francis Powell, MP for Wigan. Bardsley had been very happy in Sodor and Man, and left with deep regret. By 26th December his successor was known. His last ordination was at Kirk Michael on 14th February 1892, and his last confirmation at St Matthew's on 17th February. On Wednesday, 9th March he received an Address from the clergy in Douglas courthouse which included these words "Your Lordship's unfailing kindness and sympathy, especially in times of trouble and perplexity, will leave an enduring remembrance among us; and the words of fatherly counsel you have addressed to us in our Convocation and elsewhere will often be recalled in the future. In every corner of the diocese Your Lordship is known and beloved, and by clergy and laity alike your readiness to preach even in the most remote churches has been greatly appreciated". He finally left Douglas on the 'Peveril' on the 11th March. In May 1893 Bardsley presented each of the engine drivers and stokers employed by the Isle of Man Railway with a handsomely bound New Testament. He returned for a short visit in September 1893 and preached on Douglas Head and at St George's on 6th September. He stayed part of the time with the Vicar of St George's and part with Deemster Drinkwater at Kirby.

By the summer of 1904 Bardsley was in very bad health. His trouble originated in eating unwholesome meat during a holiday in Egypt in 1901 and he had never been quite well since. He died on Wednesday, 14th September 1904, aged 69, and was buried on Saturday afternoon, 17th September, at Roughtonhead, near Carlisle, the funeral, by his own request, being very simple.

The coffin was carried from Rose Castle on an open hearse drawn by two horses, the bearers being workmen on the estate. At the same time as the funeral a memorial service was held in Carlisle Cathedral, attended by the Mayor and corporation. All Carlisle was in mourning. On his memorial in the Cathedral are the words "A man of rare humility and loving kindness".

The Parishes under Bardsley

ANDREAS The new burial ground was consecrated by Bardsley at 11 a.m. on Thursday, 19th March 1891, his text at the service being Genesis 23⁴. On 7th January 1889 Mrs Hughes-Games was badly hurt after being thrown out of a trap in Ramsey when the pony bolted. On 9th November 1890 the pulpit, reading desk and altar, given as a memorial to Archdeacon Moore, were dedicated by Bardsley. The lectern was given in Moore's memory by the Manx clergy.

The 1891 Choir outing lasted from 8.45 a.m. until 10 p.m. They had a picnic lunch at Knocksharry then went on to Peel, where they took boats out in the bay. The next stop was at Glen Maye, where they walked in the Glen, played games on the shore and had a meal in the cafe. They went home via Glen Helen.

ARBORY Langton was presented with a silver tea service by the parishioners on 12th March 1891, before his removal to Bride. He was succeeded by John Kewley who quickly won golden opinions in Arbory where he was a constant and sympathetic visitor. He was a moderate High Churchman of liberal views, anxious to uphold the best traditions of the Manx Church. It is said that during his curacy he turned down several good offers of livings in England so that he could serve his native diocese.

Kewley remained at Arbory until 1912 when, on 5th October, he was instituted and inducted as Rector of Andreas and Archdeacon. The Archdeaconry had first been offered to Canon Savage, Vicar of St Thomas', but he declined it, probably because his health was beginning to fail. So sure was Kewley that Savage would be the next Archdeacon that he wrote a letter of congratulation to him, but had waited to post it until the announcement had been made. Savage was one of the first to send congratulations to Kewley. On the Sunday before the appointment became public Bishop Denton Thompson (1912-24) was preaching in Arbory church and it was characteristic of him that he went to the vicarage and told Kewley's mother before telling the congregation.

Kewley's career as Archdeacon (1912-38) lies outside our period, but it is right that something should be said about the greatest figure in the Manx church in the 20th century. Preaching at his induction, Bishop Thompson said "No-one has more zealously toiled, in season and out of season, for the good of the church and the whole Island. Loyal and most helpful to my predecessors, he has a knowledge of Manx affairs unexcelled, and a patiotism that burns like fire". Kewley's first sermon at Andreas was on II Timothy 2⁴. He never married and after his mother's death his two sisters managed his household.

His profound knowledge, especially of Manx church law, history and custom, won him the respect and affection of all who met him. He was an encyclopaedia of Manx history, folklore, civil and ecclesiastical usages, antiquities and language. His learning was never paraded, but his knowledge and advice were available to all. He was man of very simple tastes and was equally at home with scholars or with the people on the farms of Arbory and Andreas. He had an inexhaustible fund of good stories about the "characters" of the past. His fine presence and commanding voice were for many years an outstanding feature of the Tynwald ceremony, where he read the laws in Manx. He was clever with his hands and when visiting farms he would help the men with whatever they were doing, in addition to being able to repair clocks and typewriters and to bind books. He undoubtedly learned much folklore when visiting his people, with whom he could converse in Manx. He revived Manx services at which he preached himself. Until the end of his life he firmly believed that the Manx language would survive. His remarkable memory was helped by a system of Pelmanism, which he worked out for himself. His freshness and simplicity of mind remained into his old age. He was devoid of ambition, and was content to carry out his duties as a parish priest to which he devoted love and care. The mainspring of his whole character was his simple, sincere faith in God, which found expression in love for all men.

On 8th December 1938 a presentation was made to the Archdeacon and his sisters. The Vicar General, (Ramsey Johnson) said "His great natural gifts, his warm sympathy, his desire to help others, coupled with his wide experience and his vast knowledge of ecclesiastical law and procedure have made his tenure of office memorable. He early acquired the distinction of possessing a wider knowledge of Manx ecclesiastical affairs than any other clergyman. Partly it comes from a quite exceptional memory and partly from the notebook which he always produced from his pocket when anyone questioned him on any matter. He has shown a high sense of duty and has rarely missed a meeting or an engagement. We will always remember him at inductions and at the after-proceeding and many a new man entering a living must have blessed the Archdeacon for making his introduction to his parish so easy". He went on to say that Kewley had brought to all his tasks industry and method, but he would never be hurried and disliked anything which seemed to be hasty or ill-considered. He would never claim to have been in the forefront of the fight for the great changes in the church which his tenure of office had seen, but when they became law it was he, more than anyone else, who had given the experienced guidance which made these measures so successful. Much of his vast store of accurate knowledge had come from Sir James Gell.

His successor as Archdeacon, the Revd C. V. Stockwood, said in the course of his address "His knowledge of all things pertaining to ecclesiastical law was encyclopaedic. The Church in Man has had, in the course of her long history, many far-seeing persons, but none, surely, could have been held in higher esteem than Archdeacon Kewley".

Bishop Stanton-Jones said that the diocese owed an incalculable debt to him for his splendid service of 55 years. He and the Archdeacon had worked together for 10 years and they had not had one single misunderstanding during the whole of that time. It was not until he actually laid down his task that they realised how closely his personality was identified with the Manx Church. He knew, as no-one else did, the history of the Manx Church and his knowledge of ecclesiastical law was of inestimable value.

In his reply the Archdeacon said that he had greeted six Bishops and served under seven, each of whom had his own gifts and talents. Often he (Kewley) did not see things from the point of view of the Bishop. That was a great misfortune but it was a greater misfortune that the Bishop did not see them from the Archdeacon's point of view. The Manx people were cautious and did not like things done in a hurry. They wanted to be sure that they were on the right track and were always suspicious of anything new. They would give it a fair trial but would not be hurried.

Archdeacon Kewley's retirement was short, as he died at his home in Castletown on 6th November 1941, aged 81, and was buried at Malew on 8th November. Tributes came in from all over the Island and a few, from the Manx Church Magazine, may be given as typical.

Bishop Stanton-Jones wrote:

"Since his retirement he has not been much in the public eye, but he loved to feel he was still one of us and that we could turn to him for counsel and help. Although he had laid down his task as a leader in our Church's life, he was deeply interested to the last in the church he had loved and served so long. The old Archdeacon had not only a great place in the hearts of the clergy and church people; he belonged in a unique way to the whole community and was universally respected. We are thankful he did not suffer and that he fell asleep in peace, tired but happy at the end of his long journey".

Archdeacon Stockwood wrote:

"The Manx Church has suffered an irreparable loss. He possessed almost a unique knowledge of Manx ecclesiastical law, which he was always willing to share with those who sought it".

Canon Rushworth, Vicar of Braddan, wrote:

"He had become not only a venerable but a venerated Manx institution."

The Revd E. L. Morris, Vicar of German, wrote:

"He was held in respect and affection by the whole Island - in respect, because of his great scholarship and ability; in affection, because of his kindly, friendly approachableness and his willingness to help and advise on any difficult matter that might arise".

The Revd J. H. B. Sewell, Vicar of Castletown, wrote:

"He was very much a part of the Island he loved so well. Some of my happiest memories are of sitting in his room while he puffed at his pipe and talked of old Manx customs and families, or discussed with real appreciation modern developments and their problems. His great disappointment latterly was that his infirmities prevented his taking a more active part in the life of the church. He will always remain an outstanding figure, a great scholar, and a wise counsellor, who loved above all things his Church and his Island home".

BALLAUGH The improvements to the parish church begun under Hill concluded with the installation of two 100 candle power lamps in 1889 at the cost of Rector Kermode. The total cost of these improvements was £386-8-10, of which Kermode personally gave £57-9-9. All his life Kermode's hobby was antiquarian research, as he was a man of scholarly tastes, much attracted to history and archeology. In 1876 he was made one of the Archeological Commission appointed by Governor Loch to report on the Island's Antiquities. He was a founder member and President of the Isle of Man Natural History and Antiquarian Society. His son, P.M. C. Kermode, first director of the Manx Museum, inherited these interests, and his daughter, Josephine, writing under the name Cushag, was perhaps the greatest Manx poetess. Kermode was a great friend of Arcdeacon Moore.

On Sunday, 22nd June 1890 Kermode fainted when kneeling at the altar in Ballaugh Church and never properly recovered. His interest in all around him, and the clearness of his mind, remained until the last. He made all his arrangements quietly and in detail, and during the last three months of quiet and patient waiting he gave full proof of his faith in the calm and settled peace and unfaltering trust in which he looked forward to his call. He gave the Archdeacon a message for the clergy "Tell them to be faithful; if I had my time over again I would try to be more faithful; it is a solemn office to which we are called; if they are faithful He will never forsake them in their ministry. I go in full trust in Him". He died on Friday, September 12th, aged 76, and was buried at Maughold on 16th September on a bright day in the presence of people from all over the Island, the service being very simple in accordance with his wishes. On his tombstone are the words "Let Israel hope in the Lord; for with the Lord there is mercy and plenteous redemption". Psalm 130[7]. His family presented a new altar to the church in his memory and this was dedicated by the Bishop on Sunday afternoon, 30th November. On 21st September the Bishop preached in the morning on Hebrews 13[7], and said what a loss Kermode was to him personally, as he could always go to him relying on his business capacity, ripe experience, wise counsel and personal sympathy. Archdeacon Hughes-Games preached in the evening on Revelations 7[13-15] and said "He was a man of much weight and dignity of character; unostentatious and unobtrusive; always calm and thoughtful; always to be depended on; always the same, wise, sagacious and practical. His influence among his brother clergy was deservedly great, and his counsel was always valued by them. He will be greatly missed by us; the Manx Church has lost in him not only one of its most valuable and useful servants, but also one of its wisest and most experienced counsellors".

He had six sons and eight daughters, into whom he instilled a love of learning, of country and of service. His eldest daughter, Minnie, married the Revd S. N. Harrison and was the mother of Canon Mark Harrison, Vicar of St Paul's, Ramsey from 1911-46.

His son, the Revd S. A. P. Kermode, looked after Ballaugh from June to December 1890, when E. W. Kissack, Rector of Bride, was appointed Rector. In February 1891 Kissack was appointed lecturer in Pastoral Theology at Bishop Wilson College. At this time the value of the living was £211-9-0, and the population of the parish 830. In 1878 the stipend had been £350, but it had been reduced by the fall in the value of tithe. Under Kermode and Kissack there were about 16 celebrations of Holy Communion annually, and communicants over the year ranged from 244-331.

ST BARNABAS'

Mrs Hobson died at St Barnabas' vicarage on 30th December 1891, aged 54, after some years of suffering. She was formerly Miss Eliza Anne Dalgleish of Liverpool, and married Hobson, when he was Senior Curate of St Paul's, Prince's Park, Liverpool. They had two sons and four daughters. Mrs Hobson was always ready to help the poor of St Barnabas' parish at the cost of considerable self-denial. She was buried at Braddan and hundreds of people from all parts of the Island attended her funeral on 4th January, which was taken by Archdeacon Hughes-Games, as the Bishop was engaged on an important Tynwald committee.

In Hobson's time Sunday services were at 11 and 6.30 with a children's service and baptism on the last Sunday of the month at 3 p.m. Holy Communion was celebrated at Evensong on the second Sunday, and at Mattins on the last Sunday. At 7.30 pm. on Wednesdays there was a service of prayer, with sermon.

BRADDAN

An era ended when Parson Drury died on 19th September, 1887, aged 79. He had preached on 21st August 1887, but was not very well. On 3rd September he was very unwell and the Doctor came twice. Next day, Sunday, he was despaired of, but by Tuesday he had improved. The Bishop called on the Saturday, but Drury was too ill to see him, but he came again and saw him on Monday 5th. The Governor called on Tuesday 6th, and his son, the Revd W. F. Drury crossed over from England. The news of his illness caused deep sorrow in Braddan and Douglas. On 17th September the 'Manx Sun' reported him to be much better, but he died at 6 a.m. on the Monday, 19th September, from Bright's Disease, from which he had suffered for some years. When his death became known flags on public buildings and on ships in

Douglas bay and harbour were flown at half mast. He was buried in Braddan cemetery, with his wife, at 11 a.m. on Thursday, 22nd September and nearly every place of business in Douglas was represented among the crowd of about 1,200 people. About 150 carriages were counted and most of the members of Tynwald and nearly all the clergy were present. The hymn 'There is a land of pure delight' was sung outside the vicarage, and as the coffin was carried from there to the church, the hymns sung were 'Come let us join our friends above', 'There is a fountain filled with blood', 'Crown Him with many Crowns' and 'O God our help in ages past'. There were no wreaths or flowers by Drury's request. Many harbour boat men and fishermen were present and, for hours before the funeral, old men, bent with age, dressed in black, could be seen making their way along the roads, anxious to be in time. The Bishop took most of the service and after the burial, the relatives and friends, in accordance with the old Manx custom, waited until the grave had been filled in.

Couples of all ages sought to be married by Drury and he nearly always gave them a few words of advice before leaving church. After a funeral he was always the first to offer consolation to the family. He was very fond of open air preaching. Although helped by curates in his later years, he still did most of the work, and in his last year preached as often as ever. When preaching he would often introduce Manx quotations or translate part of the sermon into Manx, and people flocked to hear the old tongue again.

He took a great interest in education and in the Mental Asylum, of which he was Chaplain. He was an evangelical of the old school, but was very tolerant and was popular with the Methodists. One of his chief cares was to provide for the old and poor Manx people at Christmas.

The Bishop licensed his son, W. F. Drury, as Curate in charge until an appointment was made. His name and that of his brother, T. W. Drury, were rumoured as successors, and another rumour said that the archdeaconry was to be moved to Braddan in the person of Dr Hughes-Games. In November it was rumoured that the living would be offered to Rector Kissack of Bride. The Bishop wished to appoint one of the local clergy and in December 1887 he offered it to Vicar Williams of German, but he declined it. He then offered it to F. J. Moore, Vicar of Lonan, who accepted it in January 1888 and was instituted and inducted on Ash Wednesday, 15th February. On this occasion the Bishop regretted that there was no memorial to Parson Drury, and shortly afterwards a new lectern was given in his memory. As the parish church did not have a bell, the part of the service in which the new incumbent tolls the bell had to be done in the old church. The congregation was only moderate. Vicar Moore thus began a distinguished incumbency of 24 years.

On 3rd January 1889 a parish meeting decided to restore the tower of the parish church, which had been damaged by storms and to have it (at least temporarily) roofed. On 2nd September 1889 the Drury memorial window, paid for by public subscription, was dedicated by the Bishop, who preached on Genesis 28[17]. The stone in the churchyard to mark the spot where Drury preached at open air services was given by Mr W. Kissack of Scarlett quarries and it was dedicated on Sunday, 9th June 1890 by the Bishop, who preached standing on the stone.

In 1888 the services were at 10.30 and 3 p.m. with 6.30 services at Oakhill and Cronkbourne. In 1890 6.30 Evensong at the parish church in the summer months was added, and Moore began a celebration of Holy Communion at 12 noon on the first and third Sundays of the month.

BRIDE In 1890 Rector Kissack moved to Ballaugh and was succeeded by Charles Langton, Vicar of Arbory. On Friday, 12th December 1890 the parishioners presented Kissack with a silver afternoon tea service, a tray and an illuminated Address and the Sunday School teachers and scholars gave him a pair of electroplated candle sticks. Langton was instituted on 20th December 1890 and in early January 1891 he was inducted by the Archdeacon. In 1891 the lighting of the church was much improved by the installation of eight 50 candle power lamps.

CASTLETOWN At the 1888 Vestry meeting Ferrier suggested that the old collecting boxes should be replaced by a wooden plate, but the idea was rejected. On 3rd October 1888 Ferrier, who was Second Officer of the Castletown Volunteer Life Saving Corps, was presented with a silver salver for his long and valuable service to the Corps.

CRONK Y VODDY Kinred remained Chaplain under Bardsley.

DALBY Barnes was succeeded by C. H. Brocklebank (1888-90) and he by H. C. Pigot. He embarked on an extensive repair and beautifying of the church which was completed in December 1890. The next Chaplain was Norman King. He filled Dalby church to overflowing and made the church a real power in the district. On 22nd November 1891 the first confirmation ever held in the church took place.

The stipend at this time was £92-3-0.

DHOON S. N. Harrison resigned in 1889 and was succeeded by Richard Jones, the Chaplain of St Luke's. He was appointed Vicar of Santon in 1891, and was followed on 4th February 1891 by William G. Rolston, who remained Chaplain until 1907. He was a man of deep spiritual character, who was a diligent visitor and gave unstinted service to his people. In 1891-2 the average number of communicants on a Sunday was 3 or 4, but by 1894 it was 12. The stipend was £113-2-0.

FOXDALE Vicar Cochran remained in office throughout Bardsley's episcopate.

ST GEORGE'S At this time the Sunday services were at 8, 11 and 6.30. The new bells were dedicated by the Bishop on 19th April 1891.

Vicar George had not been in good health for some years, and in the spring of 1891 he was not feeling well. He was a diligent visitor and on 12th May he called on Mr Robert Whiteside, who had a broken thigh, in Woodbourne Square. It was a hot day, and while there he complained that he was unwell. He set off for home, but collapsed and died on the way about 5.30 p.m., the cause being heart failure. He was 44. The news spread like wildfire and caused profound sorrow, as he was beloved and respected in Douglas. He was genial, friendly to all and unostentatious. He was chiefly instrumental in building the Allan Street Mission Hall. His last sermon, on 10th May, had been on St Luke 24[52]. Bardsley had made him an Examining Chaplain and he was Secretary of the local Church Missionary Society Branch, but in general he confined himself to his spiritual work. He had two children by each of his two wives. He was buried in St George's Churchyard, with his first wife, on 16th May, the Bishop officiating, in the presence of the Archdeacon and most of the clergy. Next day the Bishop preached in the morning and the Archdeacon in the evening. His second wife did not long survive him, as she died the following October.

There were many applications for St George's, but the Bishop chose Robert Benjamin Baron. The stipend in 1891 was £350. He had often preached in the Isle of Man so he did not come as a stranger. He was instituted and inducted on 16th September 1891. He began the custom of asking the congregation to stand when the clergy entered, but there was some opposition to this.

The services in Baron's time were at 11 and 6.30, with a children's service at 3 p.m. on the first Sunday of the month. There was a service at 7.30 p.m. on Wednesdays. Holy Communion was celebrated on the 1st and 5th Sundays at 12 noon, on the 2nd and 4th Sundays 8.15 a.m. and after Evensong and on the 3rd Sunday at 8.15 a.m. and 12 noon. In 1892 Baron began holding a service in the churchyard at 10 a.m. on Sundays during the summer months because of the difficulty in accommodating the large summer congregations in church.

GERMAN After the opening of the new parish church, services were held in both churches at 11 a.m. but this only reduced the attendance at both. The other services in the parish church in Williams' time were at 8.30 a.m. and 6 p.m.

A Chapter Court at Peel on 26th April 1888 upheld a claim by Mr James Morrison, who objected to being sworn in as a churchwarden because his duties as Harbour Master prevented his attending church regularly.

In October 1889 the Bishop appointed a committee consisting of the Archdeacon, Rector Kermode of Ballaugh, Vicar Clarke of Marown and three laymen to consider making German two parishes, one based at St John's, to include the country parts of the parish, and another consisting of Peel. Governor Walpole favoured the idea and so did John Corlett, Chaplain of St John's, who said that as Government Chaplain his duties were confined to the church. Most of the people of St John's favoured it. Bishop Bardsley felt that it was impossible for the Vicar of German to look after the country parts properly. Nothing came of it, however, and St John's did not become a separate parish until 1948.

In January 1889 Williams was presented with a silver pocket Communion set by his parishioners as a mark of their esteem. He preached his last sermon at the Harvest Thanksgiving on 29th September and on 5th November he was presented with an Address, a clock and a purse of gold at a meeting chaired by High Bailiff Laughton.

On 6th September 1891 the Bishop dedicated the chimes and clock of the new parish church which had been given by Joseph Mylchreest, the Diamond King, who had been born in Peel.

Williams was succeeded by Daniel S. Cowley. He often spent a holiday in Peel and on 23rd February 1890 he preached in German church and made a very good impression. He was inducted on 31st March 1890 by the Archdeacon. The Bishop, in his sermon, said that the long delay in filling the living was due to Vicar Williams' great love for Peel, which led him to ask the Bishop to put off an appointment as long as possible as he might change his mind and return.

Cowley was a great friend of the Peel fishermen and in May 1892 he went to Kinsale to spend a few days among them there. His last sermon in Peel was at the Fishermen's Farewell Service on 10th March 1895.

ST JOHN'S In 1888 John Corlett was appointed

Diocesan Inspector of Sunday Schools, but resigned for health reasons in September 1890 and was succeeded by the Revd A. S. Newton, Headmaster of Ramsey Grammar School.

ST JUDE'S James Wilkinson became Vicar of Lonan in March 1888 and was succeeded in April by Thomas Redfearn Kneale. Kneale was never a scholar and admitted that in his young days he was fonder of games than of books, though he had a certain talent for music. He never liked T. E. Brown's poetry. His life's purpose was to maintain the integrity of the Manx Church. He did good work at St Jude's. He drained the road, bought a new harmonium, heating stove and new lamps and panelled the walls, showing great energy in raising the money. The east window (Dorcas giving clothing to the poor) was given in the winter of 1890-91 by Mr E. Thellusson in memory of his mother.

JURBY In 1889 complaints were made about the state of the churchyard, where there was long grass, nettles, weeds and broken headstones. Bellamy exchanged livings with Henry Wilson, who was inducted on Easter Monday, 23rd March, 1891.

The population of Jurby in 1885 was 650.

LAXEY Read was succeeded as Chaplain on 30th October 1887 by John Morris Spicer. He was very popular in Laxey. On 27th September 1888 his 11 year old son was killed by being thrown out of a trap when the horse bolted. Bishop Bardsley assisted at the funeral.

LEZAYRE At the 1888 Vestry meeting on 2nd April Vicar Bridgman nominated two churchwardens, Mr F. G. Worrall and Dr H. H. Greenwood. Four others were proposed by the meeting and a motion protesting against the Vicar's claim to nominate two wardens was carried by 11 votes to 5. The matter came up at the Chapter Court in Ramsey on 24th August before Vicar General Harris. It was stated by Mr Cruickshank, on behalf of the parishioners, that the Vicar claimed, in case of dispute, to nominate two churchwardens (and had done so at the Easter Vestry) and asked the Vestry to elect two others. But the Vestry elected four, though the Vicar's return to the Court contained only the names of the

two he had nominated plus the two others who had obtained the most votes at the Vestry meeting. Mr Cruickshank objected to those nominated by the Vicar being sworn in, saying that such a practice was unknown and that the wardens should be elected by the Vestry as they had been from time immemorial. Bridgman contended that the canons of the church, having the force of statute law, would override any custom. The canon provided that in case of dispute in the election of wardens the Vicar should nominate two and the Vestry elect two. He went on to say that although the Isle of Man had Home Rule and its own Convocation, yet it formed part of the Province of York and sent representatives to York Convocation, so it came under English law. Furthermore, in case of appeal in a matter like this it would go to the Archbishop of York's Court. Cruickshank said that canon law had not the force of statute law and was only binding on the clergy, not on the laity. The Vicar General decided in favour of the parishioners, but said that the Vicar was right to have the case properly decided. The four elected by the Vestry were then sworn in.

In July 1888 Bridgman applied to have the old churchyard closed, not on sanitary grounds, but to expedite the purchase of a new burial ground. There were still 800-900 plots available in the old churchyard and Bridgman admitted that he personally did not want the old ground to be closed. The parishioners did not want it closed, so a committee was set up by the Vestry, which, after taking evidence, decided that there were no grounds for closure. An extension of the churchyard was consecrated on 18th March 1891 by Bardsley who, at the service in church, preached on Hebrews 11[13].

Until 1892 a morning service had always been held on Ash Wednesday, attended by about six people, but in that year Bridgman replaced it by an evening service of Holy Communion and hymns, and this was much better attended.

In 1892 Bridgman asked, unsuccessfully, that a law be passed to allow the clergy to sell their glebe land and to invest the money obtained to increase their stipends.

The stipend at Lezayre in 1892 was £171-14-0 and the population 1,412.

LONAN F. J. Moore was succeeded in February 1888 by J. S.. Wilkinson, the Chaplain of St Jude's, who was instituted on 28th March and inducted on 3rd April, Easter Tuesday, by the Archdeacon. Only a few attended. Moore, on leaving to become Vicar of Braddan, was presented on 28th February 1888 with an illuminated Address, a photograph of himself and one of Mrs Moore and a clock. Wilkinson was very evangelical. He was one of the old school of clergymen, always the Christian gentleman, and was loved and revered in Lonan. He ran the parish without a curate. In October 1888 the first Harvest Thanksgiving in living memory was held in the old church. The roof of the parish church was badly damaged by a violent storm on the night of 6th November 1890.

The population of Lonan, which then included Laxey, was 3,277, in 1892.

ST LUKE'S When Richard Jones left to become Chaplain of the Dhoon in August 1889 he was succeeded by George Thomson who remained until September 1891. In 1888 the services were at 11 and 6.30, but in 1891 the morning service was moved to 10.30.

He was followed in December 1891 by Mordaunt L Warren. While Warren was a Deacon, Vicar Moore of Braddan went to St Luke's once a month to celebrate Holy Communion.

MALEW By now Vicar Gill was probably the best loved and respected clergyman in the diocese. He paid his curates generously and showed great kindness to the poor. He remained a clergyman of the old school and was always a moderate churchman. In 1872 he had been made Surrogate for marriage licences for the south. In 1879 he was made Rural Dean of Castletown and in 1891 the clergy elected him as their Proctor in Convocation following the death of William Kermode. In December 1889 the Oiel Voirrey service was dropped. In 1892 Gill suffered a double bereavement when his daughter Helen died on the 9th June, aged 23 and his son Henry on 1st July, aged 16.

The population of the parish at this time was 2,280 and the stipend £244-9-0.

ST MARK'S Benjamin Lupton died on 16th September 1891, aged 59. He had only been ill for a week and his death was unexpected. He was buried at St Mark's on 18th September, the service being taken by the Bishop and Vicar Gill of Malew and the hymns being 'Brief life is here our portion', O God our help in ages past' and 'Lead kindly light'. On his tombstone are the words 'The greater the Cross, the brighter the Crown'. He was succeeded by Charles S. Kroenig who began work straight after his ordination and as he was a good preacher and a systematic visitor, he greatly increased the congregation.

The population of St Mark's in his time was 120 and in 1894 the stipend was £100 rising to £136 in 1896.

MAROWN In 1889 extensive alterations were made to the church and it was re-decorated. Special services were held to mark the completion of this work on 10th November, the Archdeacon preaching morning and evening. The morning was wet so the congregation was small, but the evening was fine and the service was well attended. Although by 1889 congregations had dwindled compared with the 1860's, (due mainly to a decreasing population), Marown church was described in 1892 as one of the best attended on the Island.

The population in 1892 was 961 and the stipend £131.

ST MATTHEW'S As far back as a Vestry meeting on 18th February 1830 there had been talk of moving the church to another site and the subject was raised again in 1873. By 1888 the church was wholly insufficient for large congregations as it only held about 250 comfortably - 300 with a crush - yet there were 3,000 people in the parish. This was especially noticeable in the evenings and for some time overflow services for young people had been held in the church hall, New Bond Street, attended by 200-300. On 4th December 1888 a meeting of laymen of the congregation was held in the vestry to consider the matter and they decided to call a meeting of parishioners, which was well attended. It was generally agreed that a new church on a new site was needed, rather than alterations or additions to the existing one and a committee was appointed. Bardsley promised £100 for a new church. It was said that the idea of building a new church was given to Taggart by the Revd W. J. Binder, who had worked a similar parish in Barnsley until his health failed.

The following figures for Holy Communion refer to 1892:

3rd July	(12 noon)39
7th August	(12 noon)39
10th July	(8 am) 24
14th August	(8 am) 12
17th July	(8 am) 18
21st August	(8 am) 7 (Anniversary)
24th July	(8 am) 21
28th August	(8 am)18
31st July	(8 am) 9
4th September	(12 noon)47
11th September	(8 am) 17
18th September	(8 am) 21
25th September	(8 am) 17

On Christmas Day 25 communicated at 8 am. and 46 at noon. 123 communicated on Easter Sunday 1893 and 130 on Easter Sunday 1897.

In 1888 the services were at 11 and 6.30 and in 1892 they were 8 a.m., 11 a.m. (Morning Prayer, Litany and Sermon) and Evensong 7.30, with Evensong on Wednesdays and Fridays at 7.30 in addition. In 1889 the endowment was £21 per annum plus a grant of £45, plus £87 from Mrs Hall's bequest of £2,000 for the stipend. In 1889 the congregation raised £250 for the stipend and to keep all seats free. The 'Manx Sun' reported that St Matthew's was much better attended than St Barnabas'.

MAUGHOLD In 1890 Vicar White was offered the Rectory of Bride, but declined it because of his age and health.

The population in 1892 was 982.

KIRK MICHAEL By November 1891 Vicar Hawley's health was failing. He was seriously ill in April and May, so he was given leave of absence and went to live with his niece, Mrs Callow, at Ballabrooie, Douglas. He resigned the office of Rural Dean of Peel to which he had been appointed in 1890. Until April 1892 S. A. P. Kermode, son of William Kermode, acted as Curate in charge, then T. R. Kneale, Chaplain of St Judes was asked, but he was unwilling, very reasonably asking for a promise of the living at the next vacancy. The Revd Alfred Morris then succeeded Kermode and the Bishop helped with the services.

In April 1889 Bishop Bardsley presented the clock in the church tower which cost £80.

Hawley's last appearance in the church was to preach at the Harvest Thanksgiving at the evening service on 9th October 1892. In 1892 congregations at Michael were described as fair in the morning and very good in the evening.

The population of the parish was 1,005.

ST OLAVE'S Vicar Morris, in May 1890, received an illuminated Address from the Fleetwood fishermen expressing their appreciation of all he did for them whenever they were stormbound in Ramsey. The Hall, originally a school, was built in 1887.

ONCHAN On 1st September 1889 Vicar Howard preached two heated and abusive discourses against the 'Manx Sun' and the churchwardens. The 'Sun' had queried what became of the evening offertories (said to be for oil for the lamps) and what had happened to money subscribed years ago for almshouses in Onchan. Howard claimed that the evening offertories were under his sole control. In the morning he spoke from the sanctuary and criticised one of the churchwardens who, he said, had aided and abetted the 'Manx Sun'. This left no time for the sermon and he refused to celebrate Holy Communion, which was always held on the first Sunday of the month. Many visitors were present and some of them, and some of the regulars, left in disgust. In the afternoon he harangued the mourners at the graveside of an 8 year old boy about the churchwardens and in the evening much of the sermon concerned Samuel's vindication of his conduct to the people (I Samuel 12).

On the following Sunday he again fulminated against the 'Manx Sun' to reduced congregations and the bad impression created was shown on 20th October when there were less than a dozen adults in church in the morning. In the midst of this trouble Onchan choir had their annual picnic at Bishopscourt by the Bishop's invitation. He met them in person at the station, and joined them for the day. Howard was with them and the Bishop told him that he was right to preach as he had done.

In November 1889 a certain John Hudson was convicted for assaulting Mrs Lewin, wife of the postmaster at Onchan. When Howard heard of this he took a pair of handcuffs, went to the post office and put them on Hudson, whom he then chastised with a stick until the police arrived. Late in 1890 it was found that Howard was suffering from an internal cancer and for most of 1891 he was confined to the house. Early in 1892 his condition worsened and he died in the vicarage on Sunday, 7th February, aged 75. He was buried at Onchan on 11th February, an immense crowd attended and the service was taken by the Bishop and the Archdeacon. Most of the clergy and many members of Tynwald were present, as were the Sunday School children, each wearing a small bouquet of snowdrops, Howard's favourite flower. Mrs Howard had predeceased him and he left 3 sons and 2 daughters to whom the Bishop-elect, Straton, sent a message of sympathy via the Vicar General.

Howard was, in character, a strange mixture. Generous to a fault, he was always ready to help weakness and distress. He was very unconventional and completely lacked the discretion of his father (Rector Howard of Ballaugh) nor did he share his father's very evangelical views. This lack of discretion overclouded his outstanding gifts. He was a conservative and a traditionalist and was out of sympathy with his time. His charming personality made him loved, but his kindness to others sometimes took the form of condescension and this was disliked. He had a fearless spirit and a manly independence, refusing to bow down to men of power. The poverty which he shared with the Manx clergy (he left £350) fettered his energies and dampened his genial spirits.

PATRICK In May 1890 Vicar Davidson retired from active work, through age, and went to live in Castletown, where he died of cancer on 6th January 1897. The parish was looked after by the Curate, the Revd A. J. Makepeace from 1890-95 and by his successor as Curate, the Revd H. Kinred from 1895-7. Makepeace went to be Curate of Holy Trinity, Hull, with Archdeacon Hughes-Games.

ST PAUL'S Paton remained Chaplain throughout Bardsley's episcopate.

RUSHEN Dawes was succeeded by Blundell Browne who was beloved by all in Rushen for his sympathetic and kindly disposition and for his faithful discharge of his duties. He was a moderate churchman of liberal views, who disliked extreme opinions,

especially when those holding them formed themselves into parties. On 16th August 1891 the Bishop preached in Rushen church and as so many could not get in he directed the Curate, R. H. Bellamy, to conduct a service in the churchyard, while he took the service and preached in church, his text being II Thessalonians 2^1. He then preached to those in the churchyard on Psalm 4^6. The Vicar was taking Mattins at St Catherine's, Port Erin.

Browne greatly increased the congregations in Rushen with the aid of two curates. The Additional Curates Society made a grant of £140, the stipend of each curate being £70 per annum, but they usually cost Browne more, and the balance had to be paid from his own pocket. The population of the parish in Browne's time was 3,401 and the stipend £195-8-0.

The Sunday Services were as follows:
Parish Church
    10.45 am and 3 pm (Holy Communion on the 1st and 3rd Sundays)
St Catherine's
    10.45 am and 6.30 pm (Holy Communion at 8 am on the last Sunday)
St Mary's
    10.45 am and 6.30 pm (Holy Communion on the second Sunday after Mattins).
Cregneash
    3 pm and Thursdays at 7.30pm

SANTAN On the death of Vicar Airey, John Kirkby, the Curate who had looked after the parish during Airey's illness, was appointed Vicar (December 1889). He was genial, firm and tactful, an excellent parish priest, who won the love and respect of all by his devotion to duty, earnestness and kindly, sympathetic manner. He was a good preacher and a regular visitor. He was succeeded by Richard Jones, who began a dedicated ministry of 39 years until his retirement in 1931.

The population of the parish at this time was 510 and the stipend £133-13-0.

ST STEPHEN'S Sidney Swan succeeded Blakeney and although Chaplain for only a year he was very popular. He was a man of great physical strength and on one occasion he rode from the Point of Ayre to the Sound and reached home the same night. He left in December 1890 to become a missionary in Japan for the Church Missionary Society and remained there until 1898. On Wednesday, 26th November 1890 a meeting was held in the Board School, Sulby to say goodbye to Swan and his wife. The room was packed and the Bishop, on behalf of the parishioners, presented them with a silver tea tray. Afterwards Vicar Morris of St Olave's showed views of Japan by means of an oxy-hydrogen lantern. After several of these had been shown the apparatus exploded loudly and as the room was in darkness there was panic. Women and children shrieked and there was a rush for the door. The Bishop and other clergy present did their best to restore calm and shouted to people to resume their seats, matches were struck, men ran for lamps and the confusion gradually calmed down.

The last Chaplain under Bardsley was James S. Gardiner. Bardsley had known him in Liverpool and had valued his abilities so he ordained him (Deacon 1888, Priest 1889). He was a liberal churchman and a good visitor, marked by sympathy, tact and discretion.

ST THOMAS' Savage's long incumbency continued under Bardsley. The stipend was £317-10-0. There were 2,659 communicants in 1887 and 251 at Easter 1888. In 1892 the services were at 11 and 6.30. There was a children's service at 3.30 on the 1st Sunday of the month. Holy Communion was normally at 8 a.m. but on the 1st and 3rd Sundays it was at 12 noon. Morning Prayer was said daily at 10 a.m. and on Wednesdays at 4.30 there was Evensong and sermon. On 7th February 1888 Bardsley unveiled and dedicated the two stained glass windows in the south wall, one in memory of Mrs Hall (widow of Archdeacon Hall), given by some parishioners and one given by Mrs Dalby in memory of her parents. From May to November 1891 Savage went to Kirby Lonsdale for the sake of his health, which gradually improved.

Chapter 12

BISHOP STRATON 1892-1907

The new Bishop was Norman Dumenil John Straton, who was born on 4th November 1840, the son of the Revd G. W. Straton, Rector of Aylestone, Leicestershire. He graduated from Trinity College, Cambridge, in 1862 and while there he was a captain in the University Volunteer Corps. He was made Deacon by Bishop Graham of Chester on 12th March 1865 and was ordained Priest on 21st December 1865 by Bishop Lonsdale of Lichfield. After a curacy at Market Drayton (1865-6) he was Vicar of Kirby Wharfe, Yorkshire, (1866-5), then Vicar and later Rural Dean of Wakefield. In 1883 he was made a Canon of Ripon and, on the creation of the diocese of Wakefield in 1888, he became Archdeacon. He was one of the main creators of this new diocese and had taken a prominent part in raising the large sum (£94,000) needed to form it. The Wakefield diocese elected him Proctor in York Convocation, in which he played a prominent part. In 1873 he married Miss Emily Jane Pease, youngest daughter of the late Mr J. R. Pease of Hesslewood, near Hull. After they left the Island she continued to receive the Manx Church Magazine until her death. Her life was marked by simple faith, untiring devotion and orderly activity. She was always ready to help others and had a great love for flowers and animals. She was very fond of entertaining and held a monthly At Home at Bishopscourt. Although she never interfered in diocesan administration she did her full share of diocesan work, especially in the spiritual welfare of women and girls and all her life she worked hard for the Girls' Friendly Society.

Straton was no scholar, but he was characterised by manliness, good commonsense and administrative and business ability. He performed his duties faithfully and methodically and was always in earnest and sincere. His preaching was plain, practical and impressive, enhanced by his fine presence, though slightly marred by a rather harsh and nasal voice. Those in sorrow or distress never came to him in vain. He stated and held his opinions without fear or wavering, but was always fair to those who disagreed with him. He was never a party man and was popular with men of all schools of thought for his courtesy and fairness. In everything he was conscientious and just and when he had decided on the right course of action nothing could make him deviate from it. His strong reserve veiled a kind and sympathetic nature, but by many who did not know him intimately he was rather misunderstood and never attained the personal popularity of Hill and Bardsley. He held daily prayers for his household in Bishopscourt Chapel at 9 a.m.

Straton is said to have owed his promotion to Lord Abergavenny, one of the closest friends of the Prime Minister, Lord Salisbury. Straton was a great friend of Bishop Hill, but this would hardly have influenced his selection. There had been great hope in the Island that a Manxman would have been chosen to succeed Bardsley. Straton was appointed on Christmas Eve, 1891 and he announced it at the Christmas morning service in Wakefield Cathedral. He and Mrs Straton crossed to the Island on 8th January 1892, leaving Wakefield on a cold, wet morning, and embarked on the 'Fenella' at Liverpool in a blinding snowstorm at 11.30 a.m. They did not reach Douglas until 6 p.m. and both were very seasick. It was their first visit to the Island. They were met on the pier by Bishop Bardsley and Vicar General Harris. A carriage took them to the station and they travelled by train to Bishopscourt, where they stayed as Bardsley's guests. Straton was very pleased with Bishopscourt. Archdeacon Hughes-Games called on him next day and on Sunday 10th he and Mrs Straton attended Kirk Michael church. They left the Island on 13th, having stayed overnight at Bardsley's house in Douglas. He was consecrated in York Minster by Archbishop MacLagan of York on 25th March 1892, the assisting Bishops being Carlisle (Bardsley), Liverpool (Ryle), Wakefield (Walsham How), Beverley (Crosthwaite), and Hull (Blunt). He was attended by Hughes-Games and E. W. Kissack whom he had appointed as his chaplains and the diocese was also represented by Harris and Vicar Baron, of St George's. The sermon on Revelation 12[11] was preached by Dean Lefroy of Norwich.

Straton arrived in Douglas on Thursday 7th April 1892, this time after a good crossing, but Mrs Straton, who had a heavy cold, joined him later. He stayed at the Peveril Hotel until 25th while Bishopscourt was being decorated and the furniture installed. He was met on the pier by a large crowd and several of the clergy. On Sunday morning he preached at St George's on Exodus 3[1] and in the evening he confirmed 16 candidates at St Barnabas, preaching on II Peter 1[5,6]. He appointed two more Examining Chaplains, the Revd G. A. Schneider, Vice-Principal of Ridley Hall and the Revd W. E. Hancock, Vicar and Rural Dean of Knaresborough. The 'Manx Sun' felt that these posts could have been given to Manx clergy. Perhaps because of this, Straton added Gill (Malew), and Clarke (Marown), to his list of chaplains. He appointed as his Domestic Chaplain the Revd H. E. T. Barlow, Principal of Bishop Wilson College. On 16th April the Bishop and Mrs Straton visited the Archdeacon and his wife at Andreas, and stayed overnight, preaching in Andreas church next morning (Easter Sunday) and at St Paul's, Ramsey in the evening.

His enthronement had to be postponed as the Queen was in the south of France and he was unable to pay homage until 10th May. He was enthroned in St Mary's, Castletown on Saturday, 28th May. He arrived on the 10.35 train from Douglas. The morning was threatening but the rain held off until 4 p.m. The Archdeacon preached on St Matthew 28[20].

Straton was even more Protestant than Hill and Bardsley and was a founder-member of the Churchman's Protestant Alliance. His early sermons made a good impression, as his subject matter was good and his manner quiet and dignified. Early in 1892 he said 'I believe that the observance of the Lord's Day has made England great. I want to see the sanctity of the Sabbath preserved'.

His first Convocation was on 9th June 1892. He said that he would like to have the authority to confer some mark of distinction on long-serving clergy. He recognised that the stipends were low and said that he would like to have a fund to enable aged and infirm clergy to retire. He commented adversely on their being no Diocesan Conference, which had lapsed since 1884. He said that he would like to raise the academic standard of the clergy and ended by suggesting the creation of four Canonries for long-serving clergy, each endowed with £50 per annum and hoped that the Diocesan Conference would be revived

so as to give the laity a voice in church affairs.

On 12th June he held his first ordination in German church, even though it was not consecrated. On 21st August he preached to about 7,000 people on Douglas Head. In October he sent a pastoral letter to the clergy asking that a Communicants' Union be formed in each parish. In January 1893 the Bishop, the Archdeacon and certain laymen drafted a provisional constitution for a Diocesan Conference and the Rural Deans were instructed to arrange for the election of lay members from the parishes.

In 1893 some stipends in the diocese did not exceed £150 and some were less than £100 due to the falling value of the tithe. The Bishop's stipend was nominally, but not actually, £2,000 and if it reached £2,000, £500 had to go to the poorer clergy.

The Bishopcourt Improvement Bill (1893) enabled the Bishop to put the glebe buildings and lands into proper order and a clause enabled the Governor to order a survey every three years and oblige the Bishop to carry out such repairs as were ordered. In Straton's time there was an indoor staff of twelve and six gardeners.

On 17th March 1893 the revived Diocesan Conference met in Douglas and passed, with some amendments, the constitution which had been drawn up in January. Sir James Gell, Mr A. W. Moore and Mr R. S. Stephen were elected lay representatives in York Convocation.

On Tuesday 16th May 1893 occurred the disastrous fire at Bishopscourt. On the Monday evening a Mr Aspinall had arrived for the examination of ordination candidates arranged by the Archdeacon for the Tuesday. A fire had been lit for him in the study (the Bishop being in London on diocesan business and Mrs Straton in Bath) but as the evening was rather warm and close he went for a walk and did not return until bedtime. About 10 p.m. Spencer, the butler, had checked on the fire and found it practically out, yet it was believed that it was a spark from it which started the fire. It was discovered about 3 a.m. on Tuesday. The housemaids, who slept on the top floor of the central block, were awakened by the smoke, and their screams aroused the butler and George Batley, the footman, who went for a ladder, but Mary Gardner, the head maid, jumped in terror about forty feet from the top window facing the road onto the lawn and injured her spine. The other maids

(Louisa Batley, Kitchen maid, Maria Fisher, under housemaid, who was the last to leave, and Maria Cutts, the cook) escaped by knotted sheets onto the ladder which Spencer held for them. All had come with Straton from Wakefield. George Batley, on Spencer's instructions, rang the bell vigorously and this brought the neighbours who started rescuing the furniture. Barlow and some of the students and locals, did what they could with a hand pump, while others brought buckets of water from the river and from taps so the fire was confined to the central part. George Storr, the coachman, set off on horseback to Ramsey, where he arrived about 6.30 a.m. He asked a man where to find the fire brigade and, by great good fortune, this man happened to be Mr W Boyde, the brigade's superintendent. Within 15 minutes it was on its way, drawn by 2 horses, but did not reach Bishopscourt until about 7.30 a.m. They found that the study floor had burned through and that the burning timbers had fallen into the dining room below and set it on fire. Between the study floor and the dining room ceiling there was a stuffing of straw to deaden the sounds. The fire brigade saw that it was hopeless to save the central block and concentrated on preventing the fire from spreading. The study, central rooms, dining room and main hall were completely destroyed, as was some of the furniture and a number of heirlooms, but portraits of the Bishops were saved. All papers, books and documents in the study were destroyed, though most of the Bishop's most valuable papers were in the safe. Most of the furniture, except that in the study, was saved. The chapel and the library were not affected but the west wing was damaged by water. Many came to see the ruins which smoked all day, but the fire was finally put out about 10.30 p.m. Mr James Cowle arrived from Douglas to do a structural report on the building and the Archdeacon arrived about 10 a.m. to examine the ordination candidates and both were surprised to find the house in ruins.

Mary Gardner was taken to the coachhouse and cared for by Mrs Storr, the coachman's wife, as she was too ill to be moved and there she died, after much pain, on Friday evening, 19th May, aged 26. She had been unconscious since Thursday evening. She came from Shipston on Stour in Worcestershire and had been with the Stratons for a long time. Her parents crossed over to Douglas on the Friday, and were met by the coachman, but were just too late to see their daughter alive. A sad feature of the tragedy was that the staircase by which she could have reached the ground floor was not damaged. Her Bible was found on her pillow. Straton was at once informed by telegram of the fire, and it was characteristic of him that when he wired back it was only to ask after Mary Gardner. Her death was due to compression of the brain following spinal injuries. This was the diagnosis of the cause of death given in 1893, but when I asked the opinion of Dr Cyril Partington, whose extensive medical knowledge is well known, he said death would be due to extra dural haematoma, a collection of blood between the dura and the skull, and he considered that the delay in losing conciousness was consistent with this view. He thought that it would be due to her head hitting the ground when she fell, and not the spinal injuries. She was buried at Ballaugh on Monday, 22nd May. Mr & Mrs Gardner went in the coach with the Bishop and Mrs Straton, followed by many people, including the staff and students of Bishopscourt. The Bishop, Rector Kissack and Principal Barlow shared the service in church but the Bishop took the whole committal part and threw the earth on the coffin with his own hand. Mrs Straton was very distressed. Straton paid for the funeral and erected a headstone on which was written "Erected by the Bishop of Sodor and Man and Mrs Straton in memory of their faithful servant".

The damage was estimated at £2,000-£3,000 but the furniture was insured for £3,500 and the house and outbuildings for £5,000. The restoration work was given to Kelly Bros. of Kirk Michael and the mason's work was entrusted to Mr George Crowe. They decided to pull down the walls facing the road and rebuild them in block stone to harmonise with the chapel and west wing. By September the re-building was making good progress. About 40 workmen were engaged on it and on 13th October the Bishop entertained them all to dinner. Some of them sang after the meal. During the re-building some fragments of old stained glass windows were found in a built-up recess and these were set in the stairs window, together with other fragments, possibly from the old chapel demolished in 1815. After the fire the Bishop asked to be excused from preaching engagements for a few weeks.

In August 1893 the Principal of the College,

Barlow, left to be Curate in charge of Workington Parish church and in 1894 became a Bishop in Japan. He was succeeded as Principal by the Revd H. Geldart.

The 1893 Convocation on 25th May was held at St George's for the first time since Bishop Murray's episcopate, because of the fire. Straton repeated his wish to create four Canonries. He wanted to set up a Manx Church Sustentation Fund to try and raise all stipends to a minimum of £200 per annum. Convocation passed a resolution of sympathy with the Bishop and Mrs Straton for what they had lost in the fire - proposed by the Archdeacon and seconded by Vicar Hobson of St Barnabas'. Afterwards the Bishop entertained the clergy to lunch at the Sefton Hotel.

In June 1893 Tynwald passed the Glebelands Bill enabling an incumbent to sell part (not all) of his glebe with the consent of the Bishop and the Church Commissioners. The proceeds of the sale were to be vested in the Church Commissioners who would pay the interest to the incumbent. On 6th and 7th November 1893 the Diocesan Conference met in St George's Mission Hall, Allan Street.

Early in 1894 and again in 1896 and 1898, Straton requested that Easter offerings be given to the incumbent as the decrease in stipends through the falling value of the tithe was causing great distress among the clergy. On 22nd February 1894 a well-attended meeting was held in Allan Street Mission Room to consider the best means of forming a Sustentation Fund to augment permanently the poorer livings and provide for the present distress. The Governor, the Bishop and the Attorney General (Gell) were present. A committee was formed to manage the Fund consisting of:
(1) The Governor, the Bishop, the Archdeacon and the Attorney General.
(2) Five clergy, one from Douglas, one from the country parts of the Douglas deanery and one from each of the three other rural deaneries, to be elected triennially by the deaneries.
(3) Five laymen, two from the Douglas deanery and one from each of the other three deaneries to be elected triennially by lay subscribers of not less than one guinea per annum and donors of not less than £10 per annum in each deanery.
Straton gave £500 to the Fund, Sir James Gell and Mr W. B. Stevenson £100 each, Deemsters Drinkwater and Gill, Ferrier (Castletown), the Governor, Vicar

General Harris and the Revd F. B. Walters (Principal of King William's College), £50 each. Some of the clergy gave their Easter offerings to the Fund and by November 1894 it had reached £2,755.

The value of the livings in 1894 was as follows:

Braddan:	£187-1-0.
St Luke's:	£77-11-0.
St Barnabas':	£183-6-0.
St George's:	£406-7-0.
St Matthew's:	£193-3-0.
St Thomas':	£317-10-0.
Lonan:	£152-17-0.
Laxey:	£145-0-0.
Marown:**	£131-0-0.
Onchan:	£153-0-0.
Arbory:	£149-19-0.
Malew:	£244-9-0.
Castletown:	£140-0-0.
St Mark's:	£100-0-0.
Rushen:	£195-8-0.
Santan:	£133-13-0.
Ballaugh:	£211-9-0.
German:	£157-13-0.
St John's:	£120-0-0.
Cronk y Voddy:	£129-10-0.
Kirk Michael:	£190-0-0.
Patrick:	£145-0-0.
Dalby:	£92-3-0.
Foxdale:	£160-0-0.
Andreas:	£546-16-0.
St Jude's:	£103-0-0.
Bride:	£233-19-0.
Jurby:	£149-18-0.
Lezayre:	£171-14-0.
Sulby:	£130-10-0.
Maughold:	£144-10-0.
Dhoon:	£113-2-0.
St Paul's:	£143-0-0.
St Olave's:	£67-11-0.

** (Marown) which had no vicarage.

The 1894 Convocation was on 17th June, a dull day at first, then very sunny. Trains stopped at Bishopscourt siding as usual. Straton urged the clergy to have their parsonages surveyed regularly by the Diocesan Surveyor. On 21st June Straton arranged a Quiet Day for the clergy at Bishopscourt from 11 a.m. until 5.15 p.m. It was conducted by the Revd H. G. Moule, Principal of Ridley Hall, Cambridge, and later Bishop of Durham. On October 25th and 26th the Diocesan Conference met. Apart from business there were papers and discussions on Sunday observance and on Holy Communion. On 18th December 1894 Straton moved in Tynwald the first reading of a Bill to create four Canonries and to legalise the Manx Sustentation Fund. The second reading passed on 15th January 1895 when a clause was added saying that a Canonry automatically became vacant six months after a holder left the Island. This became the 1895 Church Act, which said that until St German's Cathedral was restored, or a new one built, Bishopscourt Chapel should be the Pro-Cathedral and that a Chapter should be appointed consisting of the Bishop, (who was also Dean), the Archdeacon and four Canons. An amendment in the House of Keys that German parish church should be the pro-cathedral was defeated.

At the 1895 Convocation on 6th June Straton advised the clergy to publish all accounts for which they were responsible. In his Charge he said "Of all the gifts which you and I need for the right discharge of our high calling, sanctified commonsense is perhaps the choicest. The ministry of many a good man is ruined for the lack of it".

On Friday 25th October 1895 the first four Canons were installed in Bishopscourt Chapel - Clarke (Marown), Hobson (St Barnabas'), Kissack (Ballaugh), and Ferrier (Castletown). The sermon was preached by the Dean of Norwich, and light refreshments followed the service. In 1896 Straton, on legal advice, asked Archbishop MacLagan of York to summon the Chapter to appear at York Convocation by its lawful representative. MacLagan agreed and in November 1896 Ferrier was elected Proctor.

In December 1895 Straton asked each Deanery Chapter to meet twice a year and, if possible, to hold an annual devotional meeting.

The Snaefell mine disaster occurred in May 1897 and the Bishop and Mrs Straton at once visited the bereaved families and prayed with them. They never forgot his kind, sympathetic and helpful words and his heartfelt kindness of manner.

In January 1898 Straton had a narrow escape when walking with the Revd F. B. Walters in Bishopscourt Glen near some trees which were being felled. One fell on him and knocked him down, but it caught on an iron railing and he escaped with only an injury to his leg.

In February 1898 Tynwald passed an amendment to the 1879 Ecclesiastical Residences and Dilapidations Act, laying down a compulsory three-yearly inspection of parsonages, including Bishopscourt. In this same year Church rates (cess) were abolished by Tynwald.

By 1898 the average stipend in the diocese had fallen to £150 due to the falling value of the tithe. The Bishop's stipend was just under £2,000, but he had to pay one third of his official expenses himself.

In 1899 Tynwald removed the restriction in the 1881 Burials Act on the sale of graves in the free half of the churchyard. Henceforth plots in the ground hitherto free could be sold with the consent of the Vicar General.

The failure of Dumbell's Bank in 1900 caused much suffering among the clergy as well as many other people on the Island, so in March Straton opened a Clergy Relief Fund. Later in the year he asked that one offertory each year should be given to the curate. In 1901 he said that how the Manx clergy lived was a mystery to him. At the 1902 Convocation Straton advised the clergy to have lay readers and at the 1903 Convocation he expressed disappointment that no-one had yet been presented for admission as a lay reader. By the end of his episcopate the idea had still not been much adopted, though on 24th July 1904 he licensed 10 lay readers in St Matthew's, the first service of its kind in the Island. They were chosen on the basis of the work they did in their parishes and after an examination.

On 2nd July 1902 Straton conducted the funeral of the Governor, Lord Henniker, at Thornham, Suffolk.

By 1901 twenty six years of conscientious work began to tell on Straton's health, and in August, on medical advice, he began a three months' holiday in Scotland which greatly refreshed and strengthened him. His return voyage to the Island took from Saturday afternoon, 16th November until 5.15 p.m. on Sunday morning because of fog.

At the 1903 Convocation Straton said that he aimed at a minimum stipend of £200 for incumbents and £150 for chaplains. His own stipend in 1903 was £1,500. In 1906 Cyril Hughes-Games succeeded Samuel Harris as Vicar General. Harris was born on 6th November 1815 and died on 9th June 1905. He is buried in St George's churchyard. He was High Bailiff of Douglas from 1864-1905.

On 27th June 1907 Straton was translated to Newcastle, where he was enthroned on 9th October. He left Bishopscourt on 29th August, accompanied by his Domestic Chaplain, the Revd W. I. Moran. His lasting monuments here were the Manx Church Sustentation Fund and the setting up of a Dean and Chapter. He resigned in 1915 and died in 1918. Mrs Straton had died on Good Friday 1916.

The Parishes under Straton

ANDREAS Archdeacon Hughes-Games attached great importance to the Watchnight Service, which always ended with the Te Deum at midnight. His text in 1892 was Exodus 3^{12}. In 1893 the service consisted of part of the Commination Service, the General Thanksgiving, selected collects, hymns and address. On 12th June 1892 he preached at an ordination in German Church on I Timothy 4^{16} and his sermon was described as forcible and thoughtful, full of practical useful hints for the ordinands and setting forth unmistakably the difficulties, responsibilities and duties of a minister. In July 1892 he was elected a Vice-President of the Church Missionary Society in recognition of his long support for the society - a distinction nearly always reserved for Bishops. He was much loved in Andreas and was respected by all churchmen because of his intellectual gifts and preaching powers and for his saintly character.

On 10th November 1894 the 'Manx Sun' announced that he was resigning as Archdeacon and Rector to become Vicar of Holy Trinity, Hull, the old parish church of Hull and one of the most important livings in England, worth £350 per annum. It made him the patron of six parishes. On 31st December a public tea and concert was held in the parochial schoolroom to present him with a folding illuminated Address enclosed in an artistic album. Among other things it said 'You have at all times been kindly and energetic in your ministrations among us, prompt to visit the sick, to relieve the needy and to cheer and console the mourners, while you have guided our more secular affairs with wisdom and discretion'. In his reply the Archdeacon said that whenever he was in the parish he had spent part of each afternoon in visiting. He said that on two occasions he had been pressed to be Vicar of Hull and looked on it as a call from God.

On Tuesday, 8th January 1895 an Address was presented to Hughes-Games from the clergy in the Courthouse at Douglas. The Bishop spoke of his happy personal relations with the Archdeacon and of his valuable help when he first came to the diocese. Hughes-Games in reply said that in many ways he was sorry to be leaving and had hoped to end his days in the Isle of Man. At the 1895 Convocation on 6th June Straton spoke of Hughes-Games as one held in esteem by the clergy, as a wise and judicious Archdeacon, a parish priest of great spirituality and earnestness, a ripe theologian and scholar and a able man of business. He referred to his personal kindness and help to him on his arrival as Bishop and his sympathy after the fire at Bishopscourt.

In September 1903 Hughes-Games had a serious illness and his health began to fail, but he still took the deepest interest in his old pupils at King William's College and in the diocese of Sodor and Man. He died at 8 a.m. on Friday, 25th March 1904, aged 73, at Holy Trinity Vicarage, and was buried in Spring Bank cemetery, Hull, on 28th March. He left £13,508. In Hull he had been highly respected by all who knew him. At the 1904 Convocation members mentioned his learning, activity in all good works, wisdom, piety, kindness, singleness of purpose, strong sense of duty, understanding of the needs of the Manx Church and his unfailing courtesy. All the clergy felt that in him they had had a friend.

On 29th December 1894 the 'Manx Sun' announced that H. S. Gill, Vicar of Malew, would be the next Archdeacon and rumours of this had swept the Island since early November. It was a very popular appointment as he was only the third Manx Archdeacon since 1787. The Archdeaconry had been offered to T. E. Brown, who declined it. He was appointed on 20th February 1895, moved to Andreas after the Big Snow of that month had cleared, was inducted as Rector on 14th March and installed as Archdeacon on 25th October in Bishopscourt Chapel with the four new Canons. Gill's health was much better at Andreas. He had to go to Tynwald by train, but when motor cars came in he was usually

199

driven back by someone. He always kept bees, and was fearless, never wearing veil or gloves, but smoking his pipe all the time he was taking the honey or handling a swarm. In his later years he was a great friend of the Governor, Lord Raglan.

In 1898 a new organ was installed, built by Morgan and Pollard of Douglas and it was opened on 24th November by Miss McKnight, FRCO. The service was shortened Evensong and the Bishop preached on Psalm 107 verse 8.

Frederick Radcliffe, Parish Clerk for nearly 50 years, died in January 1906. The office had been in the family for over 200 years. Like many other Manx Parish Clerks he was a prominent Methodist and was the last surviving Clerk elected by popular vote. Originally all householders in the parish - all those sending out smoke from their chimneys - were entitled to vote for the clerk, but in recent years he had often been appointed by the incumbent.

On June 17th 1906 the Archdeacon and his wife celebrated their golden wedding.

The stipend in 1903 was £546.

ARBORY In 1892 the chapel which once stood at the foot of Fisher's Hill was built by Mr W. B. Stevenson of Balladoole for his farmers and workmen. In 1894 Vicar Kewley began holding services at Ronague Old Schoolhouse. In Balladoole schoolhouse, built in 1893, services were held on the 2nd, 3rd and 5th Thursdays of the month, and on Wednesdays at Colby Mission Church. In 1896 Miss Stevenson became organist of the parish church and remained so until 1912. In October 1896 a man in the parish with an infectious fever was attended unremittingly by his brother and by Kewley, who continued alone when the brother also contracted the fever. When the man died no-one would put him into the coffin, so Kewley did this as well. In 1905 the lectern was made by Kelly Bros. of Kirk Michael and is decorated about the centre of the support with bog oak, dug up on Ballaugh Curraghs. It was given in memory of Mr W. B. Stevenson, who died on 5th February 1905, by his daughters.

The stipend in 1903 was £115.

BALLAUGH Kermode had been succeeded by E. W. Kissack, Rector of Bride. He had been Rural Dean of Ramsey since 1888 and became Rural Dean

of Peel in 1893. In 1892 the stone pulpit was given by Mrs Rowley Hi2541l and the prayer desk, given by Bishop Bardsley, was set up the same year. On the pulpit, after the reference to Hill is written "Thy word have I hid in my heart that I might not sin against Thee". In 1893 a major restoration of the church was begun. It was re-floored and re-seated with pitch pine pews and the chancel and sanctuary were given tiled pavements and marble steps. A new lectern was set up and the old windows were replaced by stained glass. The church was also re-decorated and was opened again on 8th November 1893.

At the 1892 Vestry Meeting Kissack asked to be allowed to use the gallery (which was never used) for the Sunday School as there was nowhere to hold it except in church and parishioners had complained of their books and seats being disarranged. This was agreed unanimously. He also asked to be allowed to move the font, as it was so near the door that several people on passing through the curtains had tripped over the base. It was proposed that the font be moved one seat further eastward and some discussion ensued as to the owners of the seat, who would be deprived of their place in church. The rector said that the seat was never used and as no-one knew who the owners were the motion was put and carried.

In January 1897 Kissack left to become Vicar of Chillenden, near Dover, and there he died after a long cancer illness on 29th April 1901, aged 63. One of his last acts was to write to Straton expressing the deep interest which he felt to the end in the welfare of the Manx Church. He was succeeded by the Vicar of Rushen, T. R. Kneale, who was inducted on 25th January 1897 and began a faithful incumbency of 37 years.

The stipend in 1903 was £203.

Philip Boyde, Parish Clerk from 1857-901, died on 25th March 1901, aged 85, and was buried at Ballaugh.

ST BARNABAS' Canon Hobson left in November 1895 to become Rector of Playden with East Guildford, near Rye, in the diocese of Chichester. On 28th November the parishioners presented him with a purse containing £100. The text of his farewell sermon was I. Corinthians 2¹⁻². He had been one of Straton's Examining Chaplains. He was one of the first of the clergy to start evening Communions. His health had not been good and was one reason for taking this lighter parish. Another was that he was a cousin of the previous Rector (the Revd C. M. Ramus) who expressed a wish to his son, who succeeded as patron of the living, that Hobson should succeed him. In manner Hobson was abrupt, and apparently haughty, but beneath a stern exterior was a warm heart and a kindly disposition. Straton had a high opinion of him. He came of a Northern Ireland Presbyterian family and was always a gentleman - scrupulous, straightforward, honest and, it must be conceded, a martinet. He sought neither friendship nor popularity, but was excellent company and a charming companion. He was good and clever, but his goodness was not always made obvious by his words. He was a militant Low Churchman and resented anything else. His sermons were skilful essays, spoiled by a tedious delivery.

The new Vicar was F. J. Lansdell, who was inducted on 11th March, 1896, when the Bishop preached on Revelations 2[1]. He was offered St Barnabas' in December 1895 and on 8th December he visited Douglas and read the lessons at Evensong, making a very favourable impression. His induction was delayed by the death of his wife in January 1896, five days after the birth of her son. Lansdell quickly became popular in the parish. He was a member of the Church of England Temperance Society. In his time the services were at 11 and 6.30 on Sundays, with a children's service at 3 p.m. on the first Sunday of the month. Holy Communion was celebrated after Mattins or Evensong.

Lansdell resigned in November 1903, preaching his last sermon on 8th November. He was succeeded at St Barnabas by George E. Craven, who was inducted on 1st June 1904 by the Rural Dean, Vicar Moore of Braddan.

BRADDAN The open air service on Sunday 31st July 1892 attracted nearly 5,000 people, though 2,000 was the average. At the service on 14th August 1892 Vicar Moore successfully appealed to the people not to smoke. In October 1892 a two day bazaar was held at the Palace, opened by Governor Walpole and raised the necessary £500 for a new organ.

On 12th November 1891 a meeting had been held to consider buying a new organ. Seventeen attended, and it was then that the decision was made to hold a bazaar, and a committee was elected to organise it. Mr H. B. Noble refused a request to hold the bazaar in the grounds of the Villa Marina. Hiring the Palace cost £25 (including lighting), erection of stalls cost £52, and Mr Harry Woods charged £12 for his five man orchestra. After all expenses had been paid £751 remained. It was decided that the organ was not to cost more than £500 and Dr E. H. Turpin, FRCO was asked to give advice. It was built by Brindley and Foster and was first used on 21st May 1893. The old organ had been taken to St Luke's under the impression that the people there would pay the removal and re-assembling cost of £31. Contributions from Baldwin however came to only £5-8-6 and the Vicar thought that the organ committee should pay the difference. Eventually they paid £10. The balance in the organ fund £130 was then spent on the chancel of the parish church.

In 1894 there were 84 children in the Sunday School.

In October 1895 a special Vestry Meeting was called to discuss the urgent need to extend the churchyard. Only 4 or 5 parishioners, plus the Vicar and wardens, turned up, but the wardens refused a suggested adjournment and it was decided to purchase extra ground at a cost of £750. The Clerk of the Rolls, Alured Dumbell, strongly condemned the way this had been done at the Easter Vestry on 6th April 1896.

The services in Moore's time were at 10.30, 3 and 6.30, the latter service being held only in the summer months. A children's service was held on the 2nd Sunday at 3 p.m. Holy Communion followed Mattins or Evensong. The news of the relief of Mafeking in May 1900 reached Douglas late at night. In order that Braddan church bells could be rung a cyclist hastened to the vicarage, and at midnight the Vicar and his family and many parishioners joined in solemn thanksgiving to God.

In 1901 new flooring was put in the chancel and in 1905 Miss M. L. Wood was appointed organist.

In 1903 the stipend was £187 and the population was 2,041.

BRIDE In September 1892 Langton was appointed Rural Dean of Ramsey, but by 1894 his health had begun to fail and late in the year he announced his resignation. There had been some failure of strength and energy but the end came suddenly and it was only a few days before his death on 14th December 1894 in the rectory that the case was seen to be hopeless. He was 64 and unmarried. He was buried at Bride on Monday, 17th December and on his tombstone are the words "Now Lord, what is my hope? Surely my hope is even in Thee". He left money to provide a new oak altar, prayer desk and pulpit and the prayer desk is his memorial. An eagle lectern had been bought in 1893. Langton never sought applause and had no unworthy fear of men. He was quiet and consistent, always courteous, sympathetic and helpful.

Langton was succeeded by the Vicar of German, Daniel Cowley. John Sayle, who was Parish Clerk from 1854-1901, died in October 1901, aged 80. Under the 1880 Church Act the freehold office of Parish Clerk died with him. He is commemorated by a baptismal ewer. He was succeeded by his son Henry, who died in 1933.

The stipend in 1894 was £233-19-0, but by 1902 it had fallen to £212. The population of the parish in 1892 was 640.

CASTLETOWN   Ferrier died on 14th March 1899 and was buried at Malew on 18th March. The Bishop was unable to attend his funeral, but was represented by his Domestic Chaplain (Moran). The pallbearers were Moore (Braddan), Kermode (Onchan), Walters (King William's College), Kewley (Arbory), Kneale (Ballaugh) and Locke (his successor at Castletown).

The success of the Diocesan Magazine, which started in 1891 and of which Ferrier was editor, was largely due to him. On news of his death places of business in Castletown closed down. Archdeacon Gill said he had never known a more upright man.

In 1892 a new altar replaced the marble one given to the old church by Lord Derby in 1704.

On 28th June 1895 the Manx Church Commissioners, including the Bishop and Archdeacon, met in Castletown Courthouse to hear objections, if any, to the proposal to make Castletown a separate parish and detach it from Malew. Feeling on the subject had been growing since Douglas had been separated from Braddan. Opinion was strongly divided in Castletown and Malew, but the speakers at the meeting were all against the proposal. One said that the

annual Government grant of £140 to St Mary's might be lost. As a result nothing was done, and Castletown did not become a separate parish until 1921.

Ferrier's successor was E. H. L. Locke, who had been Chaplain of Dalby since 1895. He was inducted on 1st February 1896. There was some criticism of the Bishop for appointing such a junior clergyman to Castletown. He was steady and painstaking, but no scholar. He reversed his first two initials on ordination. During his chaplaincy (1896-1921) various needlework societies and charitable organisations in the town began to bring clergy and laity into closer cooperation. His manner of preaching and speaking was oratorical and during vigorous denunciation of faults and offences he seemed to stare straight at individual members of the congregation.

In 1896 the large old pulpit was removed from the central space in front of the altar and was replaced by a smaller and lighter one. In 1898 the congregation voted to adopt 'Hymns Ancient and Modern'. In 1899 a fine new organ was installed at a cost of £500. It was said to be the nearest to the sea of any in the British Isles. The church lost a faithful servant in 1901 by the death of Mr W. H. Cudd, who had been a churchwarden since 1869.

The stipend in 1903 was £200.

CRONK Y VODDY   Kinred went to Patrick as Curate in 1895, and was succeeded by Alfred G. Bowerman. He was a very little man and was very difficult to deal with, especially in his later years. He was soured by losing his money in the failure of Dumbell's Bank and by never being given a parish. (He was Chaplain of St Stephen's Sulby from 1906 until his retirement in 1929). He always pleaded poverty, but left over £4,000. The stipend in 1902 was £120. In January 1904 Bishop Straton gave the church the oak lectern which had been presented to Bishopscourt Chapel by the widow of Archdeacon Hall. In September 1906 Bowerman was succeeded by W. K. Smyth.

ST JAMES'   The chaplains succeeded one another quickly in Straton's time. Norman King was succeeded in 1892 by William Callahan. On 5th March 1893 the Bishop preached to a large congregation at the Fishermen's Farewell Service. In 1894 extensive repairs were made to the parsonage which had become very dilapidated. The roof and chimneys were renewed, some new windows put in, much plastering and papering carried out and a new range put in the kitchen, as the old one was useless. The roofs of the outhouses were also repaired. Callahan left in October 1894 to take a curacy in Cambridge and was presented with a pocket Communion Set by the people of Dalby. Next came E. H. L. Locke (1895-6) and he was followed by William H. Gibson. He left in 1899 and was followed by William H. Whalley. In his place (March 1904) came Thomas H. Williams, who stayed until August 1907 and was the last Chaplain under Straton.

The stipend in 1896 was £90 and had risen to £97 in 1902.

DHOON In 1901 a Watchnight Service was held for the first time and although it was a wild night about 40 people attended. A Mission was held in late November and early December 1903. About 200 attended on the two Saturday evenings and the average week night attendance was 60. Rolston left in 1907 and went to be Curate of Stokesby, Norfolk, then in 1908 until his retirement in 1924 he was Rector of Cantley. He left the Island mainly because of his wife's ill-health. His own health was bad in his later years, and he died at Lowestoft on 1st June 1940.

The stipend in 1903 was £138.

FOXDALE On 4th November 1894 the Bishop dedicated the stained glass window in memory of Mrs Kitto. Cochran was succeeded by George F. Packer. He was inducted on 1st November 1900 and afterwards tea was served at the home of Captain Kitto. Packer had been a travelling architect for the Church Missionary Society and had travelled over much of the world designing churches, but being abroad did not suit his wife and young children so he returned home. He was a scholar who knew many languages and was an accomplished preacher who never used notes. His parishioners found him kind, courteous and quiet and he was very popular in Foxdale, especially with the young men.

He was succeeded by Frederick W. Stubbs in October 1903. On 16th May 1901 the Queen Victoria memorial clock was erected.

The stipend in 1903 was £160 and the population of Foxdale in 1900 was 1,500.

ST GEORGE'S Vicar Baron, who was very well liked in the parish, died suddenly on 4th November 1906, aged 59, and was buried in the churchyard. His headstone was erected 'by his parishioners and friends in grateful appreciation of his faithful and large-hearted labours of love for the welfare of others'.

The stipend in 1902 was £400.

The most important event of Baron's incumbency was the building of All Saints as a daughter church in the parish. On 2nd November 1896 the Bishop, the Archdeacon, Vicar Baron and several local residents met to discuss the offer of a site from Mr Quayle Farrant and his sister, of Greeba Towers. There was some difficulty regarding handing over the freehold so the land would have to be held on a lease. This would prevent a permanent church being consecrated, but would not prevent the opening and licensing of a temporary church. The decision to build was partly due to a resolution of the 1897 Diocesan Conference that another church was needed in Upper Douglas. The Revd J. B. George, while Vicar of St George's, had collected some money for a church in this part of the parish which he felt was needed. In Bishop Hill's time Vicar Savage of St Thomas' was willing to erect a chapel of ease to St Thomas' in the Murray's Road area but the plan fell through because Hill insisted on the new building being given a separate parish. The foundation stone was laid on 8th February 1898 by Mrs Straton and the weather just kept fine for the ceremony. The builder was Mr J. B. Hawes, an iron building manufacturer of Deptford, London. The Bishop was absent as he was unwell, but he preached at the opening and licensing of the Church on 14th July 1898. The church seated 500. The first organist was Miss Lizzie Cannell.

GERMAN On 10th October 1892 a meeting of German parishioners was held in St John's schoolhouse to consider setting up a repair fund of £250 (in lieu of cess) for the new church so that it could be consecrated as the parish church. The old church had been condemned as insanitary. A committee was appointed to raise the money. Mr Joseph Mylchreest gave £50 and the Bishop £10, adding that he thought the new church the most beautiful in the diocese. On 23rd January 1893 a special Vestry Meeting was held in the old church which approved, with minor alterations, the draft Bill to make the new church the parish church. It also set up a repair fund of £400. In Tynwald next day discussion on the German Parish Church Act was adjourned after the Clerk of the Rolls, Alured Dumbell, questioned the competence of Tynwald to deal with a church matter of this kind, but on 11th April 1893 the Legislative Council passed the Act, both the Governor and the Attorney General (Sir James Gell) saying that Tynwald was not exceeding its powers - otherwise most of the church legislation of the last 40 years was null and void. The Act abolished cess (by which the old church had been maintained) but stipulated that a minimum repair fund of £400 had to be set up before consecration. It forbade burials around the church. It also confirmed the system by which six churchwardens were elected (unique in the diocese) namely one appointed by the Vicar, one by the seat holders and four by the parishioners. On 16th and 17th August 1893 a bazaar was held, patronised by the Governor and the Bishop, to raise the £400 repair fund and this was achieved in time for the consecration on Thursday afternoon, 5th October 1893. The Archdeacon and many of the clergy were present, Miss M. L. Wood was at the organ, and the hymns were 'The Church's one foundation', 'Lord of the worlds above', 'Oh Lord of heaven and earth and sea' and the Te Deum. The lessons were read by Archdeacon Hughes-Games and Vicar Gill of Malew and the Bishop preached on I. Chronicles 29$^{9-13}$. Had the church become a cathedral there was a plan to extend the chancel and build a Chapter house. This accounts for the disproportionately small chancel.

The population of the parish in 1892 was 5,079 and the stipend £157-13-0.

2nd November 1893 was observed in Peel as a day of Thanksgiving and Prayer for the safe return of the Herring Fleet.

Vicar Cowley moved to Bride in March 1895 and was succeeded by George Ensor. He was inducted to German on 5th April 1895 and soon afterwards he leased Glenfaba House, Patrick, as the vicarage was too small for his numerous household. He preached his first sermon on Revelations 20 $^{11-12}$ and made a good start, but his attempts to force his ideas on the congregation soon made him unpopular. He and his Curate, W. H. Gibson, disagreed doctrinally and often they preached different doctrines on the same Sun-

day. This led to Ensor forbidding him to preach, to the annoyance of the congregation. On the Bishop's advice, Gibson asked to be allowed to preach on alternate Sundays, but when this was refused, Straton appointed him to Dalby and replaced him by A. J. Holmes. In June 1896 Ensor changed from Hymns Ancient and Modern to the Hymnal Companion (which was used in Bishopscourt Chapel). Hymns Ancient and Modern was too High Church for him and he disagreed with its doctrinal teaching.

The next Vicar was Edward Rainbow. In December 1901 he began a restoration of the Old Parish Church, which had been kept open (only for Mattins) for some time after the opening of the new church, then had fallen into disuse. It was hoped to use it for Mission purposes. This involved the removal of the pews, pulpit, reading desk, font and gas brackets and the laying of a new floor. Straton agreed to issue a faculty for this as there was no opposition to the plan, on condition that the services to be held in the old church should be religious services and in connection with the Church of England.

Heathfield House was the vicarage at this time.

On 26th and 27th February 1903 a great gale blew in most of the roof of the new church and the fine west window was destroyed. This window depicted 'The house at Bethany' and had been given by Miss Gell, Kennaa, at a cost of £500. The roof timbers of the central nave and the north aisle fell on to the pews, smashing many of them and forced out the west gable and windows. The font was broken but the organ, reredos and pulpit were undamaged. Services were held in the old church until the damage was repaired at a cost of £3,000. A subscription list was opened, headed by the Bishop and by April £1,440 had been raised. In addition there were many offers of practical help. In 1906 signs of insecurity had appeared in the spire. The foundations of the tower had slipped severely and the spire was taken down stone by stone in 1907, each stone being marked, but only the tower was re-built. The original foundations had been laid for the tower alone, and were insufficient for the spire as well. The cost of taking down the tower and spire was £2,000. The church was re-opened after the restoration work in July 1904.

The window depicting 'The Adoration of the Infant Saviour' was given by Dr Malius of Birmingham in memory of his sister, Mrs Katherine Adams, and was dedicated by Bishop Straton on 22nd April 1905. 'The Light of the World' window is in memory of the Revd Robert Aitken.

ST JOHN'S John Corlett remained Chaplain under Straton.

The stipend in 1903 was £120.

ST JUDE'S T. R. Kneale left to become Vicar of Rushen in May 1893 and was succeeded by R. B. Blakeney. Early in 1894 it was decided to move the Ballachurry and parsonage pews and to renew the pulpit, the reading desk and the altar, which latter was put on an oak platform. The next chaplain was Adrian S. Rolleston. He was marked by habitual courtesy, a kindly disposition and steadfast loyalty to friends. He was devoted to his chaplaincy and, ably supported by his wife, worked for it without thought of self.

The stipend in his time was £103.

JURBY In March 1894 there was trouble between Vicar Wilson and the churchwardens over the distribution of money for the poor.

The Bishop and the Archdeacon both came to try and restore peace but several parishioners absented themselves as a result of the dispute. Wilson died at the vicarage, Summerhill, on 12th June, 1895, aged 45, after a rather long illness and was buried at Jurby on Saturday 14th June. The Bishop, the Archdeacon, Rector Cowley of Bride and the Revd A. E. Clarke (Chaplain of St Stephen's Sulby) shared in the funeral service, which was attended by many clergy and parishioners. On his tombstone are the words "Fear not, for I have redeemed thee".

The population of Jurby in 1891 was 543 and the stipend £150.

He was succeeded by Frederick W. Stubbs, who was inducted on 14th October 1895. He was a man of great enthusiasm, a sense of humour and unquenchable optimism. He was very evangelical and a churchman of the old school. He had an alert mind, and never seemed to grow old. He was a lifelong supporter of the Church Missionary Society. He brimmed over with life and energy and infused this into whatever he did. After his death on 19th June 1937 aged 79, Bishop Stanton Jones wrote "To the end of his long life he retained a remarkable boyish-ness of spirit and radiated the joy of his religion. He had his cares and sorrows, as all men have, but he never allowed any of these to daunt him, so, to the last Sunday of his life, although his health was broken and the end not far off, his one thought was to finish the work God had given him to do". He left in October 1903 to become Vicar of Foxdale and was succeeded by William H. Whalley. The population in 1900 was 491.

The next Vicar was Henry F. Shenston. He was inducted on 23rd November 1905, but did not take up residence until January 1906. About 200 people attended the Harvest Thanksgiving in 1906 but on Christmas Day 1906 there were only 10 communicants.

LAXEY Spicer became Vicar of Malew in April 1895 and was succeeded in May by Charles H. Leece, who became one of the leading Manx Churchmen in the early 20th century. He was succeeded in April by William E. Davies. Within a month of becoming Chaplain he was faced with the Snaefell mine disaster on 10th May 1897. He lectured on Church History at Bishop Wilson Theological College. He was well liked in Laxey for his kindness and unassuming manner and when he left to become Vicar of St Olave's in April 1904 he was presented with a silver tea urn by the parishioners. The last Chaplain under Straton was William N. Gibson.

The stipend in 1903 was £140 and the population in 1911 was 1,198.

LEZAYRE Brigdman strongly objected to the establishment of a Poor Law, which involved the creation of a Poor Relief Committee in Lezayre and he told the 1894 Vestry Meeting that he would apply the Sunday morning collections, hitherto given to the poor, to church purposes.

In 1896 William Lace (born 15th October 1856, died 9th November 1940) became Parish Clerk. He was devoted to the church, to which he gave freely of his time and money. He paid for installing electric light in the church and left his house for future sextons. He and his wife, Ellen, known as Lonnie, were both in the choir for over 60 years. She was born on 23rd March 1858 and died on 21st August 1938.

In 1897 six churchwardens were elected at the Vestry Meeting but the Vicar General ordered a fresh election, when four were elected.

The news of Queen Victoria's death on 22nd January 1901 reached the vicarage at 8 p.m. and Mr Lace mounted the belfry and tolled the minute bell.

At a Vestry Meeting in December 1901, presided over by Dr Tellet, the Captain of the Parish, the Vicar and Wardens gave notice that all gravestones without inscriptions would be removed from the churchyard, but that the Wardens would attend on New Year's Day to hear any objections.

The stipend in 1902 was £150.

In April 1902 Bridgman had the idea of forming a Parish Council, but finally decided against it. He wrote to a meeting to elect sidesmen "At my age, knowing that I cannot be with you for a long time now, I think it better that things should go on as they are, and leave changes and innovations to the next Vicar. We have had a very peaceful and united parish for many years and are generally considered to be not behind the times and I think it is in the interests of all parties that things should go on quietly as they are".

LONAN Vicar Wilkinson moved to Maughold in April 1895 and on 6th May the parishioners bade farewell to him in the old parochial schoolroom at Ballabeg, and presented him with a clock and a lamp.

The stipend in 1894 was £152-17-0 but by 1903 it had fallen to £126.

The new Vicar was John Quine, whose long and memorable incumbency lasted until his death on 29th February 1940 and made him one of the best known clergymen on the Island. From 1883-95 he was Headmaster of Douglas Grammar School, where he wrote his novel 'The Captain of the Parish' which appeared in 1897, and gives an authentic picture of life in the Island in the second half of the 19th century.

Quine was instituted by the Bishop in Douglas Courthouse on 24th April 1895 and was inducted on 30th April. The date of the induction was not generally known so the congregation was small. On 18th December 1895 the Masters and boys of the Grammar School presented him with a brass drawing room lamp, the presentation being made by Vicar Taggart of St Matthew's.

The stipend in 1902 was £126.

Quine at once began raising money for the restoration of the old church, the east end of which was being used as a hen house. The font was brought from old St Matthews' church, which was being demolished at this time. Quine designed the north window. In 1896 an ancient window was opened on the north side, dated 12th century at latest and intended to light the altar from the north side. The lepers' hole was carefully preserved. On 9th July 1899 a wedding was held in the old church, the first since 1st October 1734.

On 13th May 1897 the funeral took place of the 17 victims of the Snaefell mine disaster. It was held in the open air because of the huge crowd.

ST LUKE'S Warren left for a parish in Brighton in April 1894 and was presented by his congregation with a pocket Communion Set in silver. He was succeeded by Robert W. Watson. His vigorous personality soon made itself felt, and he organised a bazaar and entertainment at Injebreck House on 27th December 1894 to pay off the debt on the parsonage. In 1895 the lamp over the main door was set up. On 14th May 1896 the 60th anniversary of the church was kept. There were services at 3.45 p.m. at which the preacher was Vicar Baron of St George's and at 6.30 p.m., when the preacher was Vicar Kermode of Onchan. Between the services tea was provided in a nearby field. The normal services were at 11 a.m. and 6.30 p.m. Watson did much to restore and improve the church. He left in February 1899 to be Curate of Driffield in the diocese of York.

He was followed by Samuel R. Butterton. He took great interest in the spiritual welfare of the hundreds of workmen building Baldwin reservoir.

Francis Iles came in April 1903. The last Chaplain under Straton was Robert L. Cain.

In 1896 the stipend was £77-11-0 but this had risen to £107 in 1903.

MALEW Vicar Gill was appointed Archdeacon in February 1895, and preached his last sermon in Malew on 24th March on the text, 'finally, my brethren, farewell' (II Corinthians 13[11]). On 26th March a presentation was made to him in Ballasalla schoolhouse - a purse of gold containing £143 and an illuminated Address. The choir gave him a marble clock. Gill expressed his thanks in a short speech given in spite of his having a heavy cold.

On 23rd March 1893 a meeting was held, chaired by the Bishop, at which a committee was appointed to promote the building of a church in Ballasalla. The site had been conveyed in 1853 to the Vicar and Wardens by the Revd W. P. Ward, son of Bishop Ward, but owing to lack of funds nothing had been done. The church, of which the architect was Ewan Christian, was to hold up to 200 people and the estimated cost was £1,400. Preliminary work began in January 1894 and several farmers lent horses and carts to bring sand and gravel from the shore to make cement and stone from Scarlett. The builder was James Cooper from Castletown. Lady Ridgeway, wife of the Governor, laid the foundation stone on 20th June 1895 in brilliant sunshine, and the church was opened and licensed by the Bishop in a continuous downpour of rain on Thursday, 14th October 1897. The Archdeacon preached.

The tower is a copy of the old tower of Rushen Abbey. The cost was £1,500 and at the opening £320 was still owing so the consecration did not take place until Monday 12th August, 1907. On the same day the new organ at Malew, given by Mr T. Moore of Billown, was dedicated, these two being Straton's last episcopal acts. The old organ went to St Mark's. At the opening in 1897 the Archdeacon read the first lesson, the Revd F. B. Walters (Principal of King William's College) read the second lesson and the Bishop preached on Ephesians 2²². There followed a public tea, and Evensong at 7 p.m. when the Archdeacon preached. The day was a holiday in Ballasalla, the streets and station being lined with bunting. The pulpit was given by descendants of Bishop Ward, as a memorial to him, in 1895 and the organ was opened in March 1898. On 10th November 1895 the gable of the church was badly damaged by a gale.

Gill's successor as Vicar was the Chaplain of Laxey, John M. Spicer, who preached his last sermon in Laxey on 7th April and was instituted and inducted at Malew on 9th April 1895. He preached his first sermon on Easter Sunday evening, 14th April on St John 11³⁹. In the morning he had read the Thirty-nine Articles instead of a sermon. On 15th April the people of Laxey presented him with a clock and some ornaments. Spicer was kind and genial and never spared himself where the welfare of his people was concerned. He was a vigorous, courageous and very evangelical preacher and was in demand as a preacher at missions, sometimes in England. He was a member of the Malew Board of Guardians, of the School Board and of the Southern Higher Education Board.

He was Treasurer of the Police Court Mission and was Surrogate for the southern deanery. From 1903-12 he was Bishop's Chaplain and in 1913 succeeded Canon Moore as a member of the Cathedral Chapter. He strongly advocated the use of Lay Readers. He entered on his duties with great zeal and spirit. The Sunday School, which had gone down considerably in teachers and pupils, was re-organised, a weekly Bible class was started and Mattins was moved from 10.30 to 11 a.m.

In September 1895 a Vestry meeting decided to extend the churchyard westwards, the necessary £400 being borrowed, repayable over 20 years. This extension was consecrated by Straton on Thursday 16th July 1896. In December 1897 some alterations were made to Malew church. A new vestry was made and the font was removed to the west end, which meant that some pews had to be removed. The organ was re-built and enlarged and moved from the gallery to the south side. Choir seats and a prayer desk were installed. The door in the south wall was closed up and a new one opened. In May 1898 a subscription was started for a lectern in memory of William Christian (Illiam Dhone) who is buried under the church, and this was installed later in the year.

At the Easter Vestry meeting on 19th April 1897 six Methodists were elected as churchwardens as a result of many Methodists attending. This was because a 1½ penny rate had been levied in 1896 to pay for the new burial ground. It was later found that three of them had not been legally nominated and objection was made to them at the Chapter Court for swearing in the wardens.

Vicar General Harris ordered another Vestry meeting to be held on 7th July when three churchmen were elected, but there was much bad feeling in the parish over the whole affair.

On 30th January 1898 the church at Derbyhaven, built by Messrs. Cannell and Corrin, was opened and licensed for worship. Only the sanctuary was consecrated.

The stipend in 1903 was £144.

ST MARK'S Kroenig left in September 1896 to take a parish in Southampton and was succeeded by Arnold J. Holmes in June 1897. Holmes was beloved and respected by his people and did a splendid work, considerably increasing the congregation. The church, parsonage and outbuildings were extensively repaired and restored, a new floor was put in the chancel and a lamp was erected in the churchyard. In 1900 he visited the farms to bless the harvest and cut the first sheaf. Miss Holmes acted as organist and superintendent of the Sunday School while her brother was Chaplain. He wrote a little book entitled 'A Homely Talk with Homely People' dealing with the need for baptism and the responsibility of Godparents.

In 1903 the stipend was £125.

Holmes left in June 1903 for the parish of Broomfield in Yorkshire.

The next Chaplain was Robert Halstead who was Chaplain from November 1903 until November 1904 but things seem to have gone down under him, as at Easter 1904 there were only 3 communicants. He returned to England to take a curacy.

The last chaplain under Straton was Henry Hickin, who began on 3rd March 1905 and his ministry at St Mark's was well received. He started a singing class, which met in the winter, for young people.

MAROWN   On 12th June 1895, at a clergy meeting at St George's, Vicar Clarke was elected as Proctor for the clergy in York Convocation in place of Gill, who had resigned on becoming Archdeacon. Hobson (St Barnabas') was also proposed, but Clarke was elected on a show of hands. He proved to be most assiduous in his duties. He became ill with pneumonia on 25th August 1903 which started with a chill contracted while taking a funeral on a wet day. On 4th September his condition was critical, he was attended by Dr Pantin, and two nurses were engaged. He died the next day, Saturday, 5th September and was buried at Marown on the 8th September. The committal was taken by the Archdeacon and Canon Moore read the lesson. The hymn was 'Now the labourer's task is o'er'. Almost the whole parish attended the funeral. The Bishop could not attend as he was on holiday in the north of Scotland.

As there was no vicarage Clarke had lived at The Laurels in Crosby, with his sister. He was a man of quiet disposition who devoted his life to his duties as a parish priest. His wisdom and unfailing courtesy made it a pleasure to deal with him and he was always willing to give help and advice. Bishop Straton said "Everyone who knew him must have respected

him and felt him to be an earnest, faithful servant of Christ". Archdeacon Gill singled out his remarkable blamelessness of life and his quiet, unostentatious devotion to duty. Canon Taggart said that there was no man in the diocese whom he respected more and described him as a man of very great judgement, true-hearted, upright, honest and hard-working and added that no greater loss could have happened to the diocese.

Clarke had his own strong opinions and would declare them plainly when occasion required, but no-one was more free from anything like self-assertion or self-advertisement. John Corlett, Chaplain of St John's, said that his worth was not sufficiently known by those around him.

Joseph Lewin, Parish Clerk since 1868, when he was elected at a Vestry meeting, attended by Bishop Powys, died on 26th October 1901, aged 70. He was the blacksmith at Glen Vine. His son, Thomas, succeeded him.

The stipend in 1903 was £135.

The new Vicar was Archibald Edward Clarke. He left Andreas in June 1892, but on 28th December a parochial tea was held at which the people presented him with a handsome solid silver teapot. In his reply of thanks, Clarke said that he had received a very good training from Archdeacon Hughes-Games. In 1903 a house was bought in Station Road, Crosby, for the Vicar, this being the first vicarage in the history of the parish.

Clarke was the son of a banker and was meticulous regarding figures, accounts and correspondence. His poor eyesight meant that he was not a scholar. By tradition and inheritance he was a conservative, but not to the point of timidity. He believed that the Prayer Book was unequalled as a guide in daily life. He was unswerving in his loyalty to the church which he loved, faithful as a friend, generous to a fault and although he had a quick temper it was soon over. He was every inch a Manxman, he loved tradition and disliked any innovation which displaced time-honoured custom. He was an excellent friend and minister to the sick and was Chairman of Marown School Board from 1904-20.

He was inducted on 31st December 1903 by the Rural Dean, Canon Moore of Braddan, but did not move into the vicarage until March 1904. His mother was present at his induction but she died five days later on January 4th, aged 62, at Sulby parsonage and was buried at Lezayre on 7th January. The offer of Marown had come in mid-October 1903 and on 5th November Clarke and his mother had come to look around the parish.

On Easter Sunday 1904 Clarke held a service at 3 p.m. in the Old Church (St Runius) which had only been used for funerals since the new parish church had been built in 1853. The service was combined with a baptism and there was an overflowing congregation.

One of Canon Clarke's last acts had been to give land on his glebe, and £100, for the building of a church hall. This was opened on 7th February 1905.

ST MATTHEW'S The great event of Taggart's later years was the building of the new church. The site was bought in August 1894 for £5,000 from Douglas Corporation and the foundation stone was laid by Governor Ridgeway on Thursday, 23rd August 1895 in the presence of the Bishop, the Archdeacon, most of the clergy and many people. The hymns were 'Blessed city, Heavenly Salem', 'The church's one foundation' and 'In the name of earth and heaven'. The Psalm was No. 84 and the lesson was Ezra 3$^{10-13}$. The nave was consecrated by Straton on 10th July 1901, though it had been in use since 1897, having been opened and licensed for worship on 10th August 1897, when the Bishop preached on Haggai 2^9 and the lessons were read by the Archdeacon and Canon Clarke. The delay in the consecration was due to the fact that £1,500 was still owing. By 1901 only the nave, aisle and first storey of the tower had been completed, so the church still lacked a chancel. At the consecration Vicar Hopkins of St Olave's preached on Ephesians 2^{22}. The foundation stone of the chancel was laid on 25th July 1907 and during the ceremony Straton said of Canon Taggart 'I have never known a more indefatigable, hard-working and well-beloved incumbent'. The chancel was consecrated by Bishop Drury on 21st September 1908. The builders were Messrs. Kelly and Preston, the final cost was £8,700 and all seats in the church were to be free. The architect was Mr J. L. Pearson. The east window, by Morris, is in the style of his master, Burne-Jones.

A Vestry meeting on 25th January 1898 approved the sale to Douglas Corporation of the site of Old St Matthew's for £2,500 and Tynwald sanctioned this on the 12th April.

On 4th April 1893 a purse of gold was presented to Taggart by the people of St Matthew's in recognition of his work as Vicar. On Good Friday 1898 the Three Hours Service was held for the first time, and was attended by 100 or more people throughout. In 1898 the services were at 8, 11 and 6.30 with a 7.30 service on Wednesday and Friday evenings. In 1899 the stained glass window of Christ stilling the storm was given by Mr H. S. Clarke, the advocate, in memory of his father. On 19th June 1902 the new organ was opened by Miss McKnight, FRCO.

The following figures show the value of Taggart's work. 400 attended the Watchnight service in 1903, there were 74 Christmas Communicants in 1904, 220 Easter communicants in 1906 and attendance at the 1906 Anniversary was 200-300 in the morning, the same in the afternoon and about 500 in the evening.

The stipend in 1894 was £193-3-0, and had fallen to £180 in 1902.

MAUGHOLD Vicar White died rather suddenly, aged 75, on Thursday, 31st May 1894 soon after going to bed. He was ill for only half an hour and had suffered for some time from a heart disease. He was buried at Ballaugh on 5th June, a wet and stormy day, the service being taken by Vicar Moore of Braddan and Vicar Gillof Malew, as the Bishop and the Archdeacon were both on holiday. White had preached at the re-opening of Ballaugh church, where he had been so long the curate, in 1893, and said that he felt he would never preach in the church again. There followed a long interregnum, during which the services were taken by the Revd A. S. Newton, Headmaster of Ramsey Grammar School. The new Vicar was J. S. Wilkinson, Vicar of Lonan, since 1888, who was instituted by Straton in Douglas Courthouse on 24th April 1895 and inducted to Maughold by Archdeacon Gill on 29th April in the presence of a large congregation. Unfortunately his health was not good, so he could not visit about the parish as much as he wished. He had a quiet and retiring disposition, had many friends and was very highly respected. He died in the icarage on 25th January 1898, aged 70, just when arrangements had been made to give him a curate. Straton said that he had left the memory of a life marked by conscientious self-denial and devotion to duty. He is buried at Lonan. His successor was Robert D. Kermode.

The stipend in 1902 ws £194.

The foundation stone of the Church Hall was laid by Straton on Thursday, 24th May 1900, and was followed by tea on the vicarage lawn and Evensong at 6.30 p.m. when Vicar Baron of St George's was the preacher. In October 1900 it was decided to renew all the internal woodwork and flooring in the church, at a cost of £1,250. The church was re-opened on 7th March 1901, when the Bishop preached on I Timothy 2³⁴.

KIRK MICHAEL Vicar Hawley died early on Friday 22nd December 1893, peacefully but rather suddenly. After moving to Douglas the rest had improved his health and as late as the 10th December he had preached on the text "Prepare to meet thy God" at a service of Holy Communion in St George's, and had helped to administer thesacrament. He was buried at St George's on 24th December, a very wet day, hence there were fewer people than expected. Archdeacon Hughes-Games took most of the service and the committal. The Bishop read the lesson. The hymn was 'Hush, blessed are the dead in Jesus' arms who rest'.

His successor, Alfred Morris was instituted on 1st March 1894 at Bishopscourt as the Bishop was kept to his room with a heavy cold. Morris quickly made himself popular, and was respected for his integrity - for him principles meant everything, consequences little or nothing.

Since 1894, money had been collected for a church hall and Morris was the driving force behind this - the first in the diocese. It was opened on Easter Monday, 6th April, 1896, by Straton. On Whit Sunday 1894 the choir chanted the Psalms for the first time for many years. In 1898 the centre chancel window, reredos and wainscotting were erected in memory of the Diamond King, by his widow.

The stipend in 1902 was £145.

In February 1893 James Cannell, Parish Clerk since 1878, died aged 87. He was the last to hold the office which his brother, father, grandfather and great-grandfather had held for 200 years. Miss A. M. Crellin, organist of Bishopscourt Chapel since 1897, died on 13th May 1906. She was marked by faithfulness to friends, devotion to duty and unswerving straightness.

ST OLAVE'S Vicar Morris resigned in March 1896, and at a gathering on 7th April he and Mrs Morris were presented with a silver salver and an afternoon tea service.

The stipend in 1896 was £67-11-0.

He was succeeded by Charles Hopkins, who was inducted on 27th May. His labours at Oundle (1871-96) had undermined his health and this led him to take the smaller parish of St Olave's. He lectured on Pastoral Theology at Bishop Wilson Theological College.

In 1899 a new organ was installed, built by Morgan and Pollard, and ws opened on 18th May by Edward Watson, FRCO, of Liverpool. Bishop Straton attended the opening. An organ chamber to accommodate it had been built in 1898, and at the same time the vestry was enlarged. A new pulpit was installed in 1900. In 1899 Hopkins succeeded F. B. Walters, Principal of King William's College, as Examining Chaplain to the Bishop.

Hopkins resigned in April 1903, and went to live in St Alban's, where he acted as honorary Curate of St Peter's. On leaving he and Mrs Hopkins were presented with a silver bowl and flower vases. On 29th April 1908 they had just returned from London, and he was apparently in the best of health but he collapsed on St Alban's Station and died almost at once. He was 74. On the anniversary of his death, 29th April 1909, an oak screen over the north door was dedicated to his memory by Archdeacon Gill.

H was succeeded by A. K. Dearden, who, since his ordination by Straton in 1898, had been Curate of Rushen. In June 1903 he introduced a surpliced choir, to which there were mixed reactions from the congregation. He worked hard and made a good impression, but his health was not good and in May 1904 he went to England. The next Vicar was the Chaplain of Laxey, William Davies, who was inducted on 9th June 1904.

ONCHAN Howard was succeeded by Stanley A. P. Kermode, son of the late William Kermode, Rector of Ballaugh. On 21st March 1892 Governor Walpole, who took a great interest in Onchan parochial affairs, called a meeting to decide how to finance the dilapidations on the vicarage. He hoped to raise a hundred pounds for repairs and decorations. The meeting was not well attended, but a committee was elected to raise the money.

Kermode was inducted to Onchan on 30th May 1892, when the Bishop preached on Isaiah 40[11]. He preached his first sermon on 5th June on Ephesians 4[3].

At this time the stipend was £153, but by 1902 it had risen to £164 and Kermode also received £50 as Chaplain to the Prison (1893-1904). The population in 189 was 1,890. Sunday services were at 11 a.m. and 6.30 p.m.

Onchan choir, at the end of their annual outing, used to stop on Whitebridge Hill and sing 'Son of my soul'.

A new pulpit, costing £27, was installed in 1894.

Kermode was a thorough Manxman and a Manx speaker. He had been well liked in Kirk Michael, where he considerably increased the congregation by constant visiting. He was a cultured man, with a taste for theology and the classics, and while at Onchan he was Vice-Principal of Bishop Wilson College. He was a moderate Churchman. He was of slender build, with a pleasing, courteous manner, and quickly became popular in Onchan. In Howard's time it had been the custom for the evening offertory to go to the vicar, as Onchan was not a good living and this was continued under Kermode. To the great surprise of all he announced from the pulpit on 13th December 1903 that he would be leaving at the end of January to assist the aged Archdeacon Gore of Chester, who was Vicar of Bowdon.

He was followed by Walmisley Stanley who was inducted to Onchan by Archdeacon Gill on 7th March 1904.

PATRICK On the death of Vicar Davidson in January 1897, Hugh Kinred, who had acted as Curate in charge since April 1895, was appointed Vicar, and began a faithful ministry of 26 years. The memorial window to Richard Qurk, who died in 1892, was erected early in 1893 and dedicated by the Rural Dean of Peel (Rector Kissack of Ballaugh) on 25th April. It is on the south side behind the reading desk.

The population of Patrick in 1892 was 2,228 and the stipend was £145.

ST PAUL'S George Paton died on 13th January 1900, aged 63. He had been in the town two days earlier, but later that day (Thursday), was unwell and went to bed on Friday. By Saturday he was unconscious and he died at 5.45 p.m. in the presence of his wife, son and two daughters. Next day all the flags in the town and on ships in the harbour were at half mast. He was buried at Ballure on Tuesday, 16th January, thousands lining the route from the parsonage to St Paul's, where the funeral service was held, taken by Canon Kewley, Vicar of Arbory, who had been his curate and who said that Paton had spent himself for his people and the church. Archdeacon Gill took the committal and the Bishop gave the blessing. Paton was described as "a friend of the friendless, a nurse of the fever-stricken and dying, and the one person to whom the poor and destitute could turn in their sorest need, knowing that he would not fail them".

On 23rd January 1895 the trustees appointed under the Trust Deed of St Paul's (the Bishop, Deemster J. F. Gill, the Archdeacon and Mr J. C. Lamothe), who were represented by Sir James Gell, who also represented the Queen, lodged a petition before the Clerk of the Rolls, asking that the Order in Council of 17th May 1879 be declared invalid on the ground that St Paul's could not legally become the church of a parochial district. The English Church Commissioners were the defendants. Gell contended that St Paul's was a private chapel according to the original Trust Deed, that the Bishop was owner of the site and therefore it could not be a chapel of ease or parish church. It was intended for the use of the subscribers, not for the general public. Bishop Murray had made over the property to trustees to carry out the wishes of the subscribers. The Act of Consecration did not convert private property into public property and as it was private property the Vicar of Maughold had no control over St Paul's. The Church Commissioners argued that the original Trust Deed had made it clear that St Paul's was for the Ramsey people and that it had replaced Ballure, which was undoubtedly either a chapel of ease or a parochial chapel - probably the latter, as it had a burial ground. On 6th February the Clerk of the Rolls, Alured Dumbell, decided that it was a private chapel, that the Order in Council of 17th May 1879 was invalid and that St Paul's was part of Maughold.

In February 1900 a petition was sent to the Bishop, signed by about 800 people, asking him to appoint as Chaplain Paton's son, the Revd E. C. Paton, who had been the Curate since 1894. Straton allowed him to continue as Chaplain provided that he resigned voluntarily at Easter 1901, but in March 1900 Straton declined to receive a deputation to ask for his permanent appointment. Many felt strongly about this and threatened to resign from all church work if someone else was preferred. This was probably an error of judgment on Straton's part, but his attitude was due to the fact that George Paton, a very High Churchman, had given him certain promises on the subject of Churchmanship which he had failed to keep. Their different approaches to certain doctrinal points were irreconcilable, but the congregation argued that if E. C. Paton was fit to have charge of a church for a year he should have been appointed permanently. While he was Curate in charge the average evening congregation was about 400 and at Easter 1901 he received an offering of £50. The 1901 Vestry meeting refused to elect churchwardens "not knowing their position and having no permanent Vicar". Paton finished on Whit Sunday, 26th May 1901, and went to be Curate of St James', Kensington, The Revd A. S. Newton, Headmaster of Ramsey Grammar School, then became Curate in charge.

The bad feeling aroused by this episode made things difficult for the next chaplain, Henry T. Devall, who was inducted by Archdeacon Gill on 31st July 1901. On coming to St Paul's he found that many of the best workers for the church and leading members of the choir had resigned, that some of the parish organisations (e.g. the Girls' Friendly Society) had disbanded and that the parish magazine had ceased. However by patient work he was able to hand over a united and revived parish to his successor in 1911. The main event of his incumbency was the passing of the South Ramsey Church Act in 1904, which made St Paul's a separate parish, hence Devall was the first Vicar.

The stipend in his time was £143.

RUSHEN Vicar Browne left in April 1893 to be senior Curate of St Paul's, Southwark, under Arthur Allwork, who had been Vicar of Rushen from 1879-81. On 28th April Browne was presented with a silver salver and a purse of gold. The members of the Ladies Sewing Party, which met at the vicarage, gave Mrs Browne a set of silver spoons and sugar tongs and a brooch, but unfortunately she was unable to attend the presentation, due to illness. Browne was beloved in Rushen for his kindly disposition, sympathetic manner and sense of duty. He left the Island on 4th May, and died young on 17th September 1902, after an illness of three days.

His successor was Thomas R. Kneale, the Chaplain of St Jude's, who was instituted and inducted by the Bishop and Archdeacon Hughes-Games on 31st May 1893. He began with a dispute at St Mary's, Port St Mary, as his insistence on choosing the hymns was rejected by the organist (Mr Clague) and the choir, who said that they had always chosen them. They all resigned and Kneale appointed Arthur Cregeen as organist.

On 15th January 1894 a meeting was held to discuss enlarging St Catherine's, Port Erin, which only held 200 people and was too small for the growing number of summer visitors. It was agreed to extend the nave westward by about 25 feet, providing 70 extra seats, and to build a small tower. The cost was £355, most of which was raised by donations and by a two day bazaar in August 1895, opened by Governor Ridgeway, deputising for his wife, who had a heavy cold. The additions were dedicated by Bishop Straton on 1st August 1894.

In 1896 the old font of the parish church, which had lain buried in the churchyard for many years until it was discovered during the opening of a grave, was set up at the west end of St Catherine's.

In 1891 Arthur Cregeen began his long years as organist of St Catherine's, which extended until 1920. He was also organist of the parish church from 1901-20).

The reredos and mosaic tiling in the chancel of St Mary's (a memorial to Bishop Hill) were dedicated by Straton on 22nd August, 1893 and on 19th April 1896 he dedicated the porch. In April 1896 the first wedding in St Mary's took place, that of Mr & Mrs F. Poulson of Bootle.

In April 1895 there was a dispute over Vicar Kneale's refusal to lay before the annual Vestry meeting an account of the church collections. He said that only the cess accounts had to be presented. The matter came up at the Diocesan Conference in October 1895, when Kneale was supported by both the

Bishop and the Archdeacon, but the Bishop said that as a matter of expediency, as apart from law, all accounts should be presented.

The stipend in 1894 was £195-8-0, and by 1902 it had risen to £205.

In January 1897 Kneale was appointed Rector of Ballaugh and in March he was succeeded by Charles H. Leece, the Chaplain of Laxey, who began an outstanding ministry of 30 years. In August 1901 a two-day bazaar, opened by Sir James Gell, was held in Port Erin to raise money for the building of St Catherine's Hall, the foundation stone of which was laid on 28th March 1902. It was opened by the Vicar on 5th August 1902. The cost was £520, and the architect was Mr Armitage Rigby.

In August 1902 Leece was prosecuted by Port Erin Commissioners for carting sand off the beach, and was fined.

Leece was an energetic and tireless worker, a diligent visitor and a preacher who stated the gospel in plain language. His invariable courtesy, tact and discretion enabled him to avoid making enemies and to keep his friends.

The clock in St Mary's was started at noon on 25th March 1904 and the bell was installed at the same time. The tower had recently been built. Both clock and bell were given by Mr Farnsworth of Manchester. On 30th November 1904 the church was lit by gas for the first time. The pulpit and prayer desk were dedicated on 10th May 1905 by Rector Cowley of Bride. In 1905 a new pulpit, lectern and prayer desk were put in Cregneash Church, and the floor within the communion rails was lowered. The churchyard around the parish church was closed for burials on 29th September 1904 and on 9th May 1904 an extension of the newer churchyard was consecrated by Straton.

In 1906 Straton set up a commission of enquiry consisting of the Vicar General, the Archdeacon and the Rural Dean (Vicar Kewley of Arbory) to consider a division of the parish and a public enquiry was held on 1st May 1906. Vicar Leece said that it was impossible to work the parish properly with its four churches and a mission room at Ballakilpheric with only himself and two curates, who might not be in priest's orders. The population of the parish was 3,200, swelled by visitors in the summer. He suggested that Rushen be divided into two parishes, centred on Port Erin and Port St Mary. He said that there were 9 services each Sunday in the visiting season, though in winter there were no early Celebrations. Before any decisions could be reached Straton was translated to Newcastle and the matter was shelved indefinitely.

The Annunciation window in the parish church was given by the daughters of Mrs Emily Gawne, of Kentraugh, who died in 1889, and the Ascension window was given by her sons. The window depicting the raising of Dorcas by Peter was also given in her memory. The two small west end windows were given in 1887 by Miss Annie Gawne.

SANTAN Richard Jones was Vicar throughout Straton's episcopate. A new organ, costing £150 was installed in 1895.

The stipend in 1902 was £94.

ST STEPHEN'S Gardiner was succeeded in June 1892 by A. E. Clarke, the Curate of Andreas. The stipend in his time was £130. In 1815 Clarke revived the Watchnight Service and about 30 attended. Several improvements and additions were made to the church while he was Chaplain. The oak porch was erected in March 1894 and the organ was installed in 1899. Choir stalls, a reredos, a brass stand for the pulpit, an oak cover for the font and a new stove and heating apparatus were added. On February 5th 1904 he left to become Vicar of Marown and was presented with a solid silver sugar basin and a silver pocket Communion set.

During the short interregnum the services were taken by the Revd W. I. Moran, Straton's Domestic Chaplain and by the Revd S. N. Harrison. The new Chaplain was Percy H. Brown who began work as Chaplain following his ordination and left in May 1906 to take a curacy in England. He was succeeded by A. G. Bowerman, the chaplain of Cronk y Voddy.

ST THOMAS' E. B. Savage was Vicar throughout Straton's episcopate. The Sunday services in 1898 were at 8, 11 and 6.30 and at 7.30 p.m. on Wednesdays. Until 1893 the church was lit by gas standards but in that year they were replaced by pendants from the roof. The oak Communion rails, paid for by those who had been confirmed in the church, were installed in 1897 and the chancel screen and pulpit, both of carved oak, in 1898. The stipend in 1904 was £318.

213

Chapter 13

BISHOP DRURY

Straton was succeeded by Thomas Wortley Drury, younger son of Parson Drury of Braddan, and was born in Braddan Vicarage on 12th September 1847. He was educated at King William's College and graduated from Christ's College, Cambridge in 1871. In 1901 he took the BD degree. He was made Deacon by Bishop Powys at Convocation on 1st June 1871, when Vicar Hutton of Lezayre preached on St Matthew 20[1]. He was licensed as Curate of Braddan and preached his first sermon at St Luke's, Baldwin on 11th June. He was ordained Priest in St Thomas' on 29th June 1872. In April 1872 he became Chaplain to the Mental Asylum. From 1874-76 he was Mathematics master at King William's College. In January 1876 he became Rector of Chesterfield, where he held open air services on Sunday evenings in the summer in different parts of the parish. About 200 attended the first one. In April 1882 he became Principal of the Church Missionary Society College, Islington and in 1892 he became Examining Chaplain to Bishop Ryle of Liverpool. In 1899 he was appointed Principal of Ridley Hall, Cambridge, where he remained until he became Bishop of Sodor and Man in 1907, when he was, according to custom at the time, awarded the degree of DD by Cambridge. He married at Braddan on 28th November 1872 Miss Catherine Dumerque, daughter of Captain Dumerque, of Douglas, formerly of the Madras Army. Parson Drury married them, assisted by his elder son, the Revd W. F. Drury, Vicar of Holy Trinity, Burton. Only a limited number were invited owing to the death of Mrs Drury, nee Wortley, the bridegroom's mother in September. They spent their honeymoon at Brighton. They had two daughters. Mrs T. W. Drury, died in 1914.

Drury was a man of sincere and fervent piety, kind and sympathetic to all. As a Bishop he was conscientious and devoted to his work. In his long and busy life he had his share of anxieties, disappointments and sorrows, but he endured them with patience and courage. The graceful courtesy which he and Mrs T. W. Drury extended to everyone endeared them to the whole diocese. He once said that knowledge, sympathy and character were the three essentials for a clergyman.

Drury was the fifth Manx Bishop, the previous ones being Hamond (1100), Michael (1195), William Russell (1348) and John Donkan (1374), and he was the first Manxman to become a Bishop since Charles Crowe was made Bishop of Cloyne in 1702. Drury was consecrated in York Minster at 11 a.m. on Saturday, 30th November 1907 by Archbishop MacLagan, and was enthroned in St George's on 9th January 1908. Reginald Collins, Principal of Bishop Wilson College became his Domestic Chaplain. In October 1912 Drury asked him to join him at Ripon as Chaplain-missioner. Collins' unselfish devotion, unwearying enthusiasm and unwavering loyalty earned him the respect of the whole Island.

In March 1908 Drury asked everyone to protest about a proposal to run a Sunday steamer from Fleetwood. On 14th June 1908 he preached at St Luke's, Baldwin and before the sermon he asked anyone who could join him in saying the Lord's Prayer in Manx to do so. About six of the older people did so.

The 1908 harvest was very difficult owing to wet weather. In 1909 Drury hoped to revive "the old spirit, at least of the old Rogation Days, which were simply days of Prayer for God's blessings on the harvests of earth and sea". On 28th June 1908 he preached at Arbory Anniversary and on the previous Saturday and following Monday he and Mrs Drury visited several aged and sick parishioners, who long remembered their kind and sympathetic words. On 31st January 1909 he preached at St Mark's on Philippians 3[20] and 1[27]. On his arrival he offered a kindly greeting to those who were in the road and in the churchyard, shaking hands warmly, and talking of his young days when he knew St Mark's. He celebrated Holy Communion and after the service took a baptism, to the great delight of the parents. Drury paid two visits to the Calf of Man, on 17th August 1909 and on 11th August 1911, and on each occasion went out to the Chicken Lighthouse where he conducted a short service for the keepers, who were very pleased with his visit and kindly interest in their welfare.

Early in 1910 he obtained a motor car. On 15th August 1910 he preached for the Childrens Special Service Mission on Port Erin shore. The organiser was Mr Henry Steward, who had held Children's Special Service Mission services in Port Erin since about 1890.

On 9th November 1911 Drury was translated to Ripon. He neither expected nor wanted the move but felt that he should not shirk a call to more arduous duties. He was enthroned at Ripon on 14th February 1912. He remained there until 1920 and for the last six years of his life he was Master of St Catherine's College, Cambridge. He died on Friday 12th February 1926 after a short illness and on the memorial plaque to him in the college Chapel are the words "AMOREM SIBI OMNIUM AMANDO CONCILIAVIT" - he gained for himself the love of all by loving.

We have travelled a long way since Bishop Wilson landed at Derbyhaven in 1698 and we have met some of the finest men the Manx Nation has produced, others who were not Manx who gave wonderful service to the Church of their adoption and a few who were unworthy of their calling. The Manx Church had its ups and downs in these two centuries but it was always guided by the God whom it served. With all our modern expertise and technology we can learn much from these men, who brought the Gospel to the people of this Island by their teaching and, more important, by their life and example. The later 19th century was the Golden Age of the Church in Sodor and Man, and though it will be said that things have changed, the eternal truths of God never change and the qualities of faithfulness, integrity, and love for God and man are what the church still needs if it is to bring men and women to the Gospel and to the knowledge and love of God.

The Parishes under Drury

ANDREAS On 17th June 1906 the Archdeacon and Mrs Gill celebrated their golden wedding. On 26th March 1910, his 80th Birthday, he was presented by the parishioners with a barograph, which, in returning thanks, he said that he had long wished to have, and his friends gave him 100 guineas. It was becoming clear, however, that his health was failing and by 1912 his parishioners were prepared for his death. His last illness, which began in late April 1912, was not really an illness - just a sudden failure of strength. Until the last few hours his mind was clear and he faced death, which he knew was near, with serene happiness. It was a period of beautifully fine weather and he had his bed moved near to the window where he could look on the garden. He died peacefully on Monday morning, 13th May, aged 82. Mrs Gill died on 3rd August 1912, aged 80. She had accepted her husband's death bravely and even cheerfully, but in July she was taken ill. Gill was buried at Malew, where he had been born, baptised and married, at 4.30 p.m. on 6th May, Canon Savage taking the committal. Bishop Denton Thompson, who was present, considered Gill one of the greatest men produced by the Manx Church. He later described him as "tall and stately, brave and courteous, strong and generous. His exceptional knowledge, his practical

wisdom, his unfailing sympathy and his untiring devotion earned for him the gratitude, the reverence and the affection of all in the Island. Speaking for myself, the heartiness of his welcome, the loyalty of his support and the sincerity of his spirit will never fade from my grateful memory".

Gill was honoured and beloved by the whole Island. He had great force of character, and was striking in appearance, with a voice which filled the church. He was very thorough in everything he did. He carried on the traditions of an earlier generation and would deplore the ways of his own time. Like so many of the older Manx clergy he had a fund of good stories which he told inimitably. He was good and kind, and his whole life was a witness to the faith which sustained him and to the Divine Presence in which he lived. To him, God was everything and everywhere. On his tombstone are the words "When the days of his ministration were accomplished he departed to his own home", and under his wife's name "They were lovely and pleasant in their lives and in their death they were not divided".

ARBORY In 1908 occurred the death of Dr John Clague, who regularly worshipped at Arbory, and who was the best known and best loved Doctor on the Island. The tower of the church was built in 1915 as a memorial to him and was dedicated by Bishop Thompson on 22nd August 1915. His text for the occasion was "The name of the Lord is a strong tower; the righteous runneth into it and is safe". On Dr Clague's tombstone are the words "He went about doing good." and "POST MORTEM VITA EST".

BALLAUGH On 6th July 1909 the foundation stone of the Church Hall was laid by the Governor, Lord Raglan, in the presence of Bishop Drury. The Hall was opened in 1910 and was partly paid for by money left by Rector William Walker.

The stipend at this time was £203.

Rector Kneale's health had begun to fail some time before his retirement in June 1934. He went to live at Yn Druin, Lezayre, where he died on 29th July 1935, aged 77.

ST BARNABAS' Vicar Craven left in April 1909 and returned to England. He was succeeded by F. W. Stubbs, the Vicar of Foxdale, who remained until December 1912 when he was appointed Vicar of Arbory, where he exercised a memorable ministry until his death on 19th June 1937, aged 79. St Barnabas' was closed in 1957 and later demolished.

BRADDAN The foundation stone of the new Church Hall was laid on 5th October 1911 and it was opened by Bishop Thompson on 10th July 1912. It cost £1,300.

Mr A. W. Moore, the Manx Historian and Speaker of the House of Keys (1898-1909) died in 1909, aged 53. On the Sunday after his death Canon Moore preached on Hebrews 13[14] and said "We remember his exemplary life; we think of his learning in many departments of knowledge, of his abilities, of his patiotism; of the services he rendered to his country; of his unfailing courtesy to all. In all his life and actions he was completely straight. He loved the House of God and its worship. In his early days as Sunday School Teacher, Churchwarden and Lay Reader, he set an example of faithful discharge of duty". On his memorial in the church are the words "The path of the just is as the shining light, that shineth more and more unto the perfect day". (Proverbs 4[18]).

For some years indifferent health had handicapped Canon Moore's work. He had undergone an operation and for a while improved, but he was left in a weak state and gradually worsened. He took the services on Sunday, 8th September 1912, but on the following Wednesday he became seriously ill and thereafter his condition varied until he died quietly and consciously at 2 a.m. on Friday, 4th October, aged 74. The funeral was held at Braddan on 7th October, and was attended by the Bishop, the Archdeacon, many clergy and by a vast crowd, mainly from Braddan,but some from all parts of the Island. The Bishop and the Archdeacon shared the service in church, at which Psalm 90 and the hymns "Through all the changing scenes of life" and "On the resurrection morning' were sung. To the last Moore had been keenly interested in every detail of the parish, and he had his wish 'to be at work in the Master's service to the end". His 47 years in the diocese made him the oldest and longest serving of the clergy. He was Rural Dean of Douglas and the senior member of the Cathedral Chapter, which he represented in York Convocation. In his address at the funeral, the Bishop said that Moore "was a strong and sturdy Manxman of the highest order, devoted to his church and her Lord, resolute in the defence and proclamation of the Gospel'.

Moore was a faithful, courteous, industrious parish priest, always ready to identify himself with his parishioners in joy and in sorrow. His sound judgement, genial and sympathetic manner, kindly smile, moral courage and spiritual culture won the respect of all, and in his last years he was a venerable figure. The pulpit in the church was given in his memory.

In Moore and Archdeacon Gill, 1912 saw the loss of two of the most distinguished members of the Manx Church.

BRIDE Rector Cowley was elected Proctor for the clergy in Convocation on 1st February 1910, but in 1911 his health, which for many years had been delicate, deteriorated, and in 1912 he had to take a long holiday, returning in June. Early in 1913 a long illness began and he died on 19th April aged 60. He was buried at Bride on 22nd April, and on his tombstone are the words "The memory of the just is blessed". Cowley was a man of marked ability, an attractive speaker and a strong personality with decided views. In pastoral and parochial work he showed such sympathy, singleness of aim, and steadfastness of purpose as to gain the lasting love and esteem of his people.

CASTLETOWN When Castletown was made a separate parish in 1921, St Mary's ceased to be the Government chapel.

The stipend in 1902 was £200.

CRONK Y VODDY Smyth was succeeded in April 1908 by Henry Eaves. The last Chaplain under Drury was Samuel Sidebotham, who was Chaplain from January 1910 until July 1913 when he left to become Vicar of St Jerome's, Ardwick, Manchester. Total attendance at the three services of the 1910 Anniversary was about 300.

ST JAMES' Williams was succeeded on 18th August 1907 by Hampton Robinson. He left in October 1909 to be Curate of St Thomas' and his place was taken by Frederick W. Shippam, who started in November 1909 and stayed exactly a year until November 1910. On 10th July 1910 Drury dedicated a memorial window to Archibald Holmes, Vicar of Patrick from 1842-65 and his wife. The last Chaplain under Drury was Arthur P. Bradshaw.

DHOON Rolston was succeeded by George W. Gregson, who stayed at the Dhoon from September 1907 until February 1913 when he became Vicar of Jurby. Gregson was loved by his people for his unfailing sympathy and kindly disposition, which made him a real friend to all in sorrow or sickness.

FOXDALE Stubbs was succeeded as Vicar by the Chaplain of St Luke's, Robert L. Cain, who was inducted on 2nd September 1909 and stayed until he became Vicar of Laxey in 1917. He resigned in 1926 and died on 28th June 1932, aged 67. On his memorial in Laxey church are the words "He that winneth souls is wise".

ST GEORGE'S Baron was succeeded in May 1907 by John Campbell but he left in June 1908 to take a post with a missionary organisation in Liverpool. His successor was R. D. Kermode, Vicar of Maughold, who was inducted on 1st October 1908. A major restoration of the church was carried out while he was Vicar, the roof being renewed and additional vestries built. At Bishop Drury's request the chancel, originally a semi-circular apse, was extended by 18 feet and raised 4 feet above its former level. Stalls were built in it for the Bishop, the Archdeacon and the four Canons, showing clearly that Drury hoped that it would be eventually the cathedral church of the diocese. This hope was never realised and German Church was made the Cathedral in November 1980. The church was closed for several months for this work and was re-opened on 5th May 1910, when the Bishop dedicated the restored church. The preacher was Archbishop Lang of York who spoke that evening at a meeting in the Palace for the Manx Church Sustentation Fund. Kermode remained Vicar until 1920, when he became Vicar of Lezayre. He resigned in 1939 and died on 29th May 1948, aged 79. He was Canon of St Patrick.

GERMAN Rainbow's successor was Walter A. Lewis. When he came there was little peace or harmony in the congregation and his great achievement was to leave a peaceful and united church when he left in June 1914 to become Vicar of Fordleigh, near Barnstaple.

ST JOHN'S John Corlett's long and faithful chaplaincy ended with his death on Tuesday, 23rd February 1909, aged 77. His last services were on Christmas Day, 1908. He was buried at Peel on 27th February, the service being taken by Archdeacon Gill, as the Bishop had a heavy cold. The next Chaplain was Sidney B. Botwood who left St John's in 1913 to become Rector of Bride.

ST JUDE'S Rolleston remained Chaplain during Drury's episcopate.

JURBY The church was renovated in Shenston's time, and was re-opened on 19th April 1912. Two new windows were put into the east end, and the stained glass window was set in stone instead of wood. There was a new altar, credence table, communion rails, choir stalls, pulpit and prayer desk, all in oak. The old door on the north side was closed up, a porch was added, providing a good shelter against the weather and a new vestry was made. The seats were made more comfortable and the font was moved to a more suitable position. The two standard lamps in the chancel were given by Shenston and his predecessor, Whalley. Shenston left in 1912 to become Vicar of St Barnabas'.

LAXEY   Gibson remained Chaplain under Drury. He left in 1916.

LEZAYRE   Vicar Bridgman died early on Thursday, 14th January 1909. aged 94, and was buried in the churchyard at 12 noon on 16th January. Bishop Drury attended.   Two of his favourite hymns 'All people that on earth do dwell' and 'O God our help in ages past' were sung at the graveside. Mrs Ellen Bridgman died very suddenly on Monday, 3rd July, 1911.   Although she had not been quite well during the previous winter, she had been in church the day before she died.

Bridgman was succeeded by James H. Cain. He was Curate of Lezayre from 1907-9, and had been virtually Vicar, as Bridgman was prevented by age from taking any active part in the parish. He had an almost unique knowledge of Church law, history and custom and throughout his life he worked for the interests of the Manx Church.

LONAN   Canon Quine's long ministry ended with his death on 29th February 1940, aged 81. He was buried at Lonan on 3rd March. Mrs Quine died on 30th March 1942. He had planned to retire at the end of March.   He was a true friend to all and he won and retained the friendship of all.   He showed his sympathy for those in trouble or distress by prompt practical help.   Quine was a scholar and had many and varied scholarly interests, but these all came second to his work as a parish priest.   He found the church rather ugly, but he left it a church of dignity and simple beauty and more worthy of the worship of God.   His loyalty to the Manx Church and his determination to uphold its interests, were unsurpassed.   At the funeral Bishop Stanton Jones spoke of his devotion to the Island, to Lonan, to the Manx Church and to his home and family.   His rather rough exterior concealed a kind heart.   His knowledge of Manx history was profound and he fought all his life to keep alive Manx literature and folklore.   The Bishop ended by saying that, like many of the Manx clergy, he had a struggle to make ends meet but "we are thankful to know that, although life had its crosses,

its disillusionments and its disappointments, the closing years were marked by a tenderness of heart, and a graciousness and mellowing of the spirit."

ST LUKE'S   R. L. Cain left in September 1909 to be Vicar of Foxdale and was succeeded in January 1910 by Frank R. Whittaker.   He left in 1913 to be Curate of Faversham.

MALEW   Spicer died suddenly at the vicarage on Tuesday, 12th August 1919, aged 69, and Bishop Thompson took the funeral at Malew on 15th August.   Spicer had lately been feeling his age and was under Doctor's orders not to overtax his strength. His widow, Mrs Emma Spicer, died on 13th January 1928, aged 80.

ST MARK'S   The stile in the west wall was built in 1908.   Hickin resigned in July 1912 because of failing health and went to London to be nearer his sons.   Mrs Hickin died on 3rd November 1912 after a short illness.   Her health had never been good and this prevented her from making many friends but those who really knew her spoke of her gentle disposition, loyal friendship and constant thought for others.   She was a loyal helpmate to her husband and the beauty of her married life was only partly known even by those closest to her.

MAROWN   On 4th September 1910 Clarke held a service in the ruined St Trinian's Church at which Bishop Drury preached and Lord Raglan, the Governor, read the lesson.   It was probably the first service held there since before the Reformation.

James Cottier of Ballavitchell, who had been sexton, bell-ringer and sacristan since 1862, died in November 1910, aged 70.

Vicar Clarke had completed exactly 30 years in the parish when he died on Monday 1st January 1934, aged 72.   He had been ill for many weeks, but seemed to be recovering.   He was buried at Lezayre on 4th January, nearly all the clergy attending.   He was loved and respected throughout the Island.

ST MATTHEW'S   In his 31 years of incessant work Canon Taggart had scarcely taken a rest or a holiday and this led to a serious illness.   As early as 1903 twenty-five years of single-handed work was tell-

218

ing on his health. On 15th February 1909 he resigned, feeling that St Matthew's needed a stronger man, and took the small parish of St Maurice, Horkstow, in the diocese of Lincoln, but in October 1911, feeling his strength failing, he resigned and moved to London where he died on 1st June 1912, and was buried in High Barnet Cemetery on 3rd June. He was unwell when he left Douglas and missed the farewell gathering in the hall on 29th April.

In 1909 Mr James R. Fielding, who had been a churchwarden since 1874, resigned on account of age and failing health. He devoted his life to works of mercy in the town and it was said of him "the poor of Douglas can never have had a better human friend, nor the church of St Matthew's a more diligent and devoted servant". In his last years he was unable to attend church, though his mind was clear, and he was kept to bed. He was looked after by his daughter, who rarely left his bedside. He live at 57 Derby Square. He died on Sunday, 11th February 1912, aged 94, and was buried in old Braddan churchyard.

Taggart was succeeded by his son, Hugh S. Taggart. At St Matthew's he continued the devoted work of his father and was universally loved. He built new schools which were opened by Lady Raglan on 7th March 1912, the Lady Chapel was consecrated by Bishop Thompson on 5th February 1914, and in March 1916 Archdeacon Kewley dedicated the reredos in memory of Canon Taggart. The strain of Hugh Taggart's faithful and unceasing work began to tell, however, and in October 1926 he felt it right to hand over to a younger man. He then became Rector of Sedgbrook, near Grantham.

MAUGHOLD In the autumn of 1908 Vicar Kermode moved to St George's and was succeeded by John G. Pope who held the living until 1920. Pope was the best type of parish priest - fond of children, generous and dignified.

KIRK MICHAEL The lych-gate which was designed by Mr Armitage Rigby, was opened by Lady Raglan on 16th October 1907. The foundation stone had been laid by Lord Raglan on the previous Easter Monday. In 1910 the burial ground around the church was closed, and the new extension to the west was consecrated by Bishop Drury on Easter Sunday, 16th April 1911, at 3 p.m.

Vicar Morris resigned in May 1913. Mrs Morris survived him and on 5th December 1926 she erected the memorial to him directly over the vicarage pew. The carving of the Four Evangelists was her work.

ST OLAVE'S Vicar Davies left in December 1917 to become Rector of Compton Valence in the Salisbury diocese (1917-23) and then Rector of Norton Fitzwarren in the diocese of Bath and Wells (1923-31).

ONCHAN Stanley was succeeded by Robert Wakeford, who was inducted on 16th September 1908. In 1910 Lord Raglan appealed for funds to obtain a curate to help the Vicar of what was even then a growing parish. Wakeford retired in October 1933 and returned to England.

PATRICK Vicar Kinred retired in 1921 due to failing health and went to live in Peel, where he died on Sunday, 13th May, 1923, a few days short of his 80th birthday.

The stipend in his time was £145.

ST PAUL'S Vicar Devall left in 1911 and was succeeded by Mark Wilks Harrison. At St Paul's, to which he was inducted on 30th August 1911, he aimed at making the church and its services more beautiful. He continued the Soup Kitchen, the Clothing Club and the Penny Bank.

Like his father and grandfather he was a knowledgeable antiquarian, and in his later years he was a Trustee of the Manx Museum. His interests were scholarly. His conduct and policy as Vicar were guided strictly by what was right or wrong, never by what might prove popular or even expedient. He remained a humble man, and though rather shy and reserved he was a devoted and conscientious parish priest, who worked a demanding parish single-handed, though in his later years he had considerable assistance from Canon E. C. Paton. In a memorable ministry of 35 years he unquestionably deepened the spiritual life of St Paul's and made its influence felt in every phase of the civic and social life of Ramsey. Early in 1946 he underwent an operation and after a long and painful illness he died on 11th October 1946, and was buried at Maughold on 13th October. A huge gathering of people attended his funeral, including representatives of all organisations in the town, and was proof of the love and respect in which he was held by the whole community. Ramsey was almost at a standstill on the day of the funeral because of the crowds.

RUSHEN The larger bell in the tower of St Catherine's was for many years the fog bell at the Chicken lighthouse. It was given to the church by the Commissioners of Northern Lights in 1909. The organ, built by Mr Morgan of Douglas, at a cost of £520, was dedicated on 5th March 1913.

SANTAN Vicar Jones retired in 1931 and died on 5th February 1937, aged 82. He is buried at Santan.

ST STEPHEN'S Mrs Amy Bowerman died on 18th August 1909, aged 59 and was buried at Lezayre. Bowerman's health failed in his last years at St Stephen's, but he could not be persuaded to resign until 1929. He died on 10th August 1932 and was buried with his wife.

ST THOMAS' The choir stalls and chancel panelling were given at Easter 1910 by Mrs Mylchreest in memory of her husband, Thomas Mylchreest, who was a churchwarden for 13 years. The decoration of the walls and chancel by Mr J. M. Nicholson took two years and was completed in 1910. In 1912 a fire destroyed or damaged the clock, bell and organ, but all were restored by 1913. The organ had to be rebuilt and the opportunity was taken to add a third manual (the choir).

Savage resigned in April 1914 following a serious illness and went to live in Ambleside, where he died on Saturday, 22nd May 1915, aged 66. While Vicar he had lived at 'Woodside'. He had inherited a parish torn by dissension but left it united and happy. He left two sons and four daughters.

APPENDIX I
BIOGRAPHICAL DETAILS OF THE CLERGY

This includes all clergy (apart from Bishops) mentioned in the History, except a few to which only passing allusion is made.

ABBREVIATIONS

b	= born
Bp	= Bishop
C	= curate
Cantab	= Cambridge
Coll	= college
Chap	= Chaplain
C in C	= Curate in charge
CGS	= Castletown Grammar School
CMS	= Church Missionary Society
D	= Deacon
Dio	= Diocese
DGS	= Douglas Grammar School
grad	= graduated
GS	= Grammar School
KWC	= King William's College
M	= married
Oxon	= Oxford
P	= Priest
P in C	= Priest in charge
PGS	= Peel Grammar School
R	= Rector
RD	= Rural Dean
RGS	= Ramsey Grammar School
SM	= Sodor and Man
TCD	= Trinity College, Dublin
V	= Vicar
VG	= Vicar General

AIREY, Revd Robert: b 5 Apr 1815; Assistant Master at Cheltenham Coll; D 1850; P 21 Dec 1851 (Bp SM) in St Paul's, Ramsey; 1850-58 C of Lezayre, with charge of Taggart's Barn, Bowring Road, which Vicar Christian of Lezayre had fitted up as a chapel of ease; C of Jurby 1858-59; Chap of St Luke's 25 Mar 1859-64; Chap of St Mark's 1865 - June 1874; V of Kirk Michael June 1874 - Aug 1878; V of Santan 17 August 1878 - 8 Nov 1889 when he died; buried Santan; M Jane, daughter of John Teare, Glentramman 16 Sept 1852; she died 18 June 1860; 11 Aug 1864 M Charlotte Farrant in St Mary's Rochester.

AITKEN, Revd Robert Wesley: b 1836; D 1858; P 1859 (Archbp. Musgrave of York); M Mary Tregise of Pendeen, Cornwall, 29 May 1862; Chap of St Stephen's Sulby 1860-62; V of Marown Apr 1862 - June 1869; V of St Paul's Penzance, 1869 until death 9 Feb 1911 aged 75.

AKROYD, Revd Jonathan: Chap of the Dhoon 1869 until death 13 Nov 1872.

ALCOCK, Revd John: b Kilkenny 1805; TCD grad 1827; D 1828. P 1829; M Jane McKenny in St Peter's, Dublin 10 Jan 1849; Chap of St Barnabas' 27 July 1848 - April 1852; P in C of Bethesda Dublin 1852-66; R of St Patrick, Waterford and Archdeacon of Waterford 1866-7; Chancellor of Waterford Cathedral 1867.

ALLEN, Revd Henry (1): b 1677; D 22 Sept 1706; P 30 Mar 1712 both in Ballaugh Church; C of Ballaugh Sept 1706 - Apr 1714; V of Lezayre 13 April 1714 - Oct 1726; V of Maughold 24 Jan 1727-1746 (resigned); died 18 June 1748 aged 71; buried Maughold; nephew of Thomas Allen (4).

ALLEN, Revd John (2): C of Lonan; V of Kirk Michael 21 May 1735 until death 10 July 1735; buried Maughold; M Jane Corlett; accepted Kirk Michael against Bp Wilson's advice and wishes; brother of Henry Allen (1).

ALLEN, Revd Thomas (3): b 1709; C of Andreas 1739-46; V of Maughold 2 June 1746 until death 7 April 1754 aged 44; buried Maughold.

ALLEN, Revd Thomas (4): V of Maughold 5 June 1666 until death 8 Mar 1726, aged 83; buried Maughold 11 Mar.

ALLWORK, Revd Arthur: b 2 Nov 1853; Corpus Christi Cantab grad 1877; D 1877; P 1878 (Bp Jackson of Chester); C of St Silas, Liverpool 1877-8; C of Dunstable 1878-9; V of Rushen July 1879 - June 1881; left Rushen because of wife's health; C of St Peter's, Tunbridge Wells 1881-7; V of Donington, Lincs, 1887-90; V of St Paul's, Southwark 1890-97; R of Whickham, Durham 1897 until death 8 Dec. 1912.

APPLETON, Revd William: D 1860, (Bp of Nova Scotia); P 1862 (Bp Philpott of Worcester); Chap St Luke's for few months from Apr 1880; C of Levengton, Dio Ely 1880.

AYNSLEY, Revd Lord Charles: Youngest brother of 4th Duke of Atholl; changed name from Murray to Aynsley; R of Andreas and Archdeacon 16th July 1803-1808; also Dean of Bocking, Essex, where died 5 May 1808 aged 36.

BARDELL, Revd Robertson: Owen's Coll Manchester, grad 1877; D 1878; P 1879 (Bp SM); C of Lezayre (for St Olave's) 1878-25 Oct 1879; C of Kirk Michael Oct 1879-80; C of Macclesfield Parish Church 1880-82; C of West Kirby 1882-3; V of Christ Church, Liverpool 1883.

BARFF, Revd Henry Tootal: Trinity Hall Cantab, grad 1858; D 1858 P 1859 (Archbp Musgrave of York); C of Church Fenton 1858-62; P in C Hawkley 1862-65; C of Lezayre (for St Olave's) 1866-7; C of Holy Trinity, Maidstone 1868-70; C of Hythe 1870-72; Assistant Chap at Nice 1872-5; Chap at Naples 1875.

BARNES, Revd Charles Marston: Bishop Wilson Theological Coll 1879; D 1881; P 1886 (Bp SM); Chap of Dalby 1881-88.

BARON, Revd Robert Benjamin: b 1847. D 1871; P 1873 (Bp Fraser of Manchester); C of St Anne's, Manchester under Bp Bardsley's father 1871-3; V of Annscroft, nr. Shrewsbury 1873-6; Secretary of C of E Temperance Soc 1876-9; V of St Cleopas, Liverpool 1879-91 where he was very popular; V of St George's 16 Sept 1891 until sudden death 4 Nov 1906 aged 59; buried St George's Churchyard; M

Catherine Carr.

BATES, Revd Thomas Storey: D 1875; P 1877 (Bp Jacobson of Chester); C of St James', Toxteth Park, Liverpool 1875-77; Chap of Foxdale 1877-9; C of Ince in Makerfield 1879-80; Organising Secretary for Chester and Liverpool C of E Temperance Society 1880-83; V of St Jude's, Ancoats, Manchester 1883.

BELL, Revd Charles: Univ of London grad 1875; D 1877; P 1878 (Bp Jacobson of Chester); Headmaster of March GS 1867-77; 3 short curacies in England; Chap of St Stephen's, Sulby Jan 1883-1885 when took curacy in London.

BELLAMY, Revd Joseph: Formerly Methodist Minister; D 6 May 1860 in Bishopscourt Chapel; P 1861 (Bp SM); May - Dec 1860 C of Kirk Michael; 6 Jan 1861 - Dec 1878 Chap of Laxey; V of Jurby Dec 1879-1891; V of Holme, nr Carnforth 1891 until death in Mar 1906; M by Bp Powys in Bishopscourt Chapel on 13 Aug 1860 to Anna Rowe sister of Captain Rowe of the Laxey mines; she died in Jurby Vicarage on 26 Jan 1889 aged 48 and was buried in Lonan.

BIRKETT, Revd Thomas: Chap of St Matthew's and Master of DGS 1732-36.

BLAKENEY, Revd R. B. (1): Peterhouse Cantab; grad 1889; D in St George's 20 Dec 1891; P in Bishopscourt Chapel 18 Dec 1892; C of Malew Dec 1891-93; Chap of St Jude's 1893-6 June 1894; R of Wombwell, Dio York June 1894.

BLAKENEY, Revd William (2): Gonville & Caius Coll Cantab; D 1884; P 1887 (Bp SM); C of German 1884-85; Chap of St Stephen's July 1885-89; V of Thorpe Sallein, Dio York 1889.

BOTWOOD, Revd Sidney B.: D 1907; P 1908 (Bp SM); C of German 1907-9; Chap of St John's 1909-13; R of Bride 1913-19.

BOWERMAN, Revd Alfred George: D 24 Dec 1893 in St George's; P 23 Dec 1894 in St George's; C of St George's Dec 1893-95; Chap of Cronk y Voddy 11 Apr 1895 - June 1906; Chap of St Stephen's, Sulby June 1906-1929; died 10 Aug 1932 aged 59; buried

Lezayre.

BRADSHAW, Revd Arthur P.: D Apr 1911 (Bp Drury); P 21 Dec 1913 (Bp Thompson) in German Church; Chap of Dalby Apr 1911-1914 when he went to England.

BRAILSFORD, Revd Edward: D 4 July 1847 (Bp SM); P 1848 (Bp SM); C of St Matthew's July 1847-48; Chap of St Stephen's, Sulby 1848-49.

BREAREY, Revd Robert Gawne: b Douglas 1848; Sidney Sussex Coll Cantab D 20 Dec 1874 (Bp Jacobson of Chester) (letters dimissory from Bp Powys); P 9 July 1876 (Bp Goodwin of Carlisle) in Andreas Church; C of Malew Dec 1874-9; Chap of Laxey Dec 1879 - May 1881; Chap of HM Reform Ship Akbar in the Mersey 1881 until death on 14 Mar 1895.

BREW, Revd Robert: C of Andreas then V of German 15 Apr 1758 until death in 1760.

BRIDGMAN, Revd Arthur Alexander: b London 21 Dec 1814; Educated in France; Gonville & Caius Coll Cantab grad 1836; At his death he was the oldest member of the College. D 1844; P 1845 (Bp. Copleston of Llandaff); C of Llanfihangel Mon 1844-46; C of Warrington under Rector Powys 1846-52; Perpetual C of Padgate 1852-79; V of Lezayre 5 July 1879 until death 14 Jan 1909; buried Lezayre.

BRIDSON, Revd John (1): Son of William Bridson (2); Chap of Ballure 1771-83 and again from 1785-88; C of Marown 1788-99; V of Marown Sept 3 1799 - Nov 1808; R of Bride 8 Nov 1808 until death 22 Nov 1816.

BRIDSON, Revd William (2): b 1672; son of a former V of Braddan; D 30 Mar 1712 in Ballaugh Church; P 1713; C of Marown Mar 1712-13; V of Marown 13 Apr 1713 - Jan 1727; V of Lezayre Jan 1727 - Feb 1729; R of Bride May - Oct 1729; R of Ballaugh 17 Oct 1729 until death 7 Feb 1751; buried in Ballaugh Church; he was rough, coarse and ignorant and was Bp Wilson's leading enemy among the clergy, hence his appointment by Derby, 10th Earl to the richest livings in the Diocese.

BROWN, Revd Joseph (1): b London 26 Dec 1785; D 1 Oct 1807; Chap of Castletown and Master of CGS Oct 1807-1818; V of Kirk Michael 4 April 1818 until death 27 Jan 1860 aged 74; Episcopal Registrar 1818; he and his wife Janet had six children but by 1851 only two, Robert and Matilda, were still alive; Mrs Brown died 5 Apr 1853 aged 67.

BROWN, Revd Percy H. (2): b 29 Jan 1878; D 29 Mar 1904; P 18 June 1905 both in Bishopscourt Chapel; Chap of St Stephen's, Sulby Mar 1904 - May 1906.

BROWN, Revd Robert (3): b Douglas 1792; educated at CGS and Master of DGS; D 7 Mar 1816 in St George's; Chap of St Matthew's and Master of the GS Mar 1816 - Apr 1832; then C at Braddan 1832-1836; V of Braddan Apr 1836 until death 28 Nov 1846; M Dorothy Thompson, a Scottish lady living in Douglas, at Braddan on 21 Apr 1819; she died 7 Mar 1875.

BROWNE, Revd Blundell: b 10 July 1855; D 25 May 1880 in KWC Chapel; P 25 Nov 1881 in St Thomas'; M Lucy Reynolds at Pennachno Church, N Wales on 27 Aug 1884; C of Rushen May 1880-82; C of Braddan 1882-84; C of St Thomas's 1884-7; on leaving St Thomas's he was presented with a black marble clock; V of Rushen 1887-3 May 1893; left to become senior Curate of St Paul's Southwark under Arthur Allwork.

BRUCE, Revd Lloyd Stewart: TCD grad 1854; D 1852; P 1854 (Bp SM); Chap of Dhoon 3 Jan 1853-1855; Chap to Bp Auckland of SM 1852-54; C of Aynhoe, Northants 1855-62; R of Hale, Hants 1862-5; R of Barton in Fabis 1865-72; V of Scalby 1872-5; R of Charlton in Lindrick, Notts 1875-83; R and RD of Stokesly, Dio York 1883; Canon of York 1873.

BUCKLEY, Revd Charles: D 9 July 1876 in Andreas Church (Bp Goodwin of Carlisle); P 21 Dec 1877 in St Thomas' (Bp SM); Chap of St Olave's July 1876-8; C of Sancreed, Dio Truro 1878-9; C of Burgate, Dio Norwich 1880-83; C of Perranzabuloe, Dio Truro 1883-4; C of Beere Ferrers, Dio Exeter 1884.

BUTTERTON, Revd Samuel R.; D 6 Aug 1899

in Braddan Church; P 2 June 1901 in Bishopscourt Chapel; Chap of St Luke's Aug 1899 - Nov 1902; left to become C of St John's, Sheffield.

CAIN, Revd James H. (2): b 1873; D 1907 (Bp Straton); P 1909 (Bp Drury); C of Lezayre 1907-9; V of Lezayre 6 May 1909-1919; R of Bride 1919-41; Died 1943; his wife died 1937; Secretary of the Diocesan Conference 1915-33; RD of Ramsey 1918-41; Canon of St Columba 1926; Proctor for the Clergy in York Convocation 1931.

CAIN, Revd Robert (1): b 1865; D 9 Sept 1906 in Braddan Church; P 11 June 1909 in St Thomas's; previously a grocer in Douglas for many years; Chap of St Luke's Sept 1906 - Sept 1909; V of Foxdale 2 Sept 1909-17; V of Laxey 1917-26; died 28 June 1932 aged 67; his memorial in Laxey Church has the text "He that winneth souls is wise".

CAINE, Revd Thomas: b 21 Dec 1809, son of a Douglas innkeeper; began life as a farmer but educated himself in his spare time; D 1835; C of Ballaugh 1835-40; first Chap of St Luke's 13 Nov 1840 - Oct 1853; V of Lonan 7 Oct 1853 until his death 15 Nov 1878; M Jane Creer at Braddan on 7 Sept 1841.

CALLAHAN, Revd William: D Sept 1892; P 24 Dec 1893 in St George's; Chap of Dalby Sept 1892 - Oct 1894; left to take a curacy in Cambridge.

CANNELL, Revd John (1): V of Onchan 27 Apr 1798 until death 29 Dec 1809 aged 38; buried Onchan 2 Jan; M Margaret Moore who died Aug 1804.

CANNELL, Revd John (2): b 9 Jan 1801, son of John Cannell (1) V of Onchan; D 1824 (Bp Murray) P 30 Nov 1828 (Bp Ward) in St George's; C of Santan 1824-28; C of Bride 1828-32; C of Ballaugh 1832-35; M Catherine Brew who died young, leaving 2 sons and 2 daughters; 16 Sept 1833 M Sophia, daughter of James Gelling (3) V of German; she survived her husband and died 9 Sept 1884 aged 84; Cannell was thus brother-in-law to Samuel Gelling (4) (V of Santan); Chap of St Matthew's 24 June 1835 - June 1873 when he resigned due to age and failing health; died at home 6 Auckland Terrace, 8 Mar 1874 aged 73.

CANTON, Revd William: D 21 Sept 1878 in St George's; P 23 May 1879 in KWC Chapel; M Helen Hick at Blackburn 25 Nov 1879; Chap of St Stephen's, Sulby Sept 1878 - Feb 1882 when he became V of Dinting Vale, Glossop where he remained until 1894.

CARPENTER, Revd William: b Ireland 1806; TCD Hon DD 1840; originally planned a legal career and studied at Gray's Inn before being ordained; D 19 June 1831 (Bp Fowler of Ossory); P 27 May 1832 (Bp Lindsay of Kildare); June 1831 - Dec 1832 C of Odogh, Co Kilkenny; this area was then in a very disturbed state, but Carpenter became very popular in the parish of which he had full charge; while at Odogh M the daughter of Sir William Forbes of Craigiever, Aberdeenshire - he is said to have eloped with her; she proved a faithful helper to him; she died 23 Oct 1876 aged 82; C of St Barnabas' 12 Dec 1832 - 19 Mar 1848; V of St Jude's, Liverpool Jan 1849 - Feb 1850 where his ministry was less successful than at St Barnabas'; Feb 1850 - June 1864 V of Christchurch, Moss Side, Manchester; June 1864 until death 24 Dec 1865 V of St Paul's, Penzance, where he completely restored the church, largely at his own expense; he moved to Penzance due to failing health as he had had heart trouble for a long time; he had preached as usual on the Sunday before he died.

CARTER, Revd William D.: C of Lezayre with charge of North Ramsey 1847-9; Chap of St Thomas' 1849-51.

CASTLEY, Revd Thomas: 31 Jan 1758-1807 Chap of Castletown and Master of CGS; died 1807.

CHAPMAN, Revd Theodore Charles: Corpus Christi Coll Cantab grad 1877; D 1878; P 1880 (Bp SM); 3 Aug 1881 M Alice Keith in St Stephen's, Kensington (Bp Hill took part of the service); Chap of Laxey May 1881 - 25 May 1884 then became V of St John's, Lowestoft.

CHRISTIAN, Revd Evan (1); V of Patrick 9 Oct 1769-1808; 1769 became one of the Vicars General.

CHRISTIAN, Revd John (2): R of Bride 1687-

98; V of Jurby 1698 until death early in 1747.

CHRISTIAN, Revd John (3): son of Nicholas Christian (6); D 1811; P 7 Mar 1816 (Bp SM); C of St George's 1811 - 11 Dec 1817 when he became C; died 24 July 1827 at Ballasalla.

CHRISTIAN, Revd John (4): V of Arbory 20 Oct 1791 until death 9 Apr 1815 aged 53; his widow Jane died 14 Mar 1842.

CHRISTIAN, Revd John (5): one of the Christians of Ballakilley, Marown and son of Thomas Christian (9) (V of Marown 1734-52); D Oct 1751 in Bishopscourt Chapel; V of Marown 27 Feb 1753 until death in Sept 1779 aged 51; buried Marown 29 Sept; his wife Elizabeth died 19 Nov 1777 aged 47.

CHRISTIAN, Revd Nicholas (6): P 20 Sept 1734 in Kirk Michael Church; C of Rushen Sept 1734-48; V of Rushen 23 June 1748 until death Mar 1782; buried at Rushen 1 Apr; One of the Vicars General; his first wife, Jane Tyldesley, died after the birth of twins on 10 Oct 1744 and on 17 Dec 1746 M Catherine Hanley in Arbory Church by the Curate, John Moore (4); he had 10 children.

CHRISTIAN, Revd Nicholas (7): Chap of Ballure 1789-90; Chap of St Matthew's 1791-7; V of Kirk Michael 15 Mar 1802 - Nov 1808; V of Patrick 8 Nov 1808 until death 29 Dec 1811 aged 45; VG 1808.

CHRISTIAN, Revd Robert (8): D 1750 (Bp SM); C of Ballaugh 1750 - Nov 1752; V of German 11 Nov 1752 until death 26 Dec 1754 aged 27.

CHRISTIAN, Revd Thomas (9): D 1733; P 25 Mar 1735 at the consecration of Lonan Church; V of Marown Mar 1734 until death 1752; he owned Ballakilley, now called Ellerslie.

CHRISTIAN, Revd Thomas (10): son of John Christian (5) (V of Marown 1753-79); V of Marown 24 Nov 1780-1799.

CHRISTIAN, Revd Thomas (10a): V of Rushen 1713-27

CHRISTIAN, Revd William (11): V of Malew 18 Apr 1817 until death 22 Mar 1830 aged 39.

CHRISTIAN, Revd William Bell (12): b 17 Aug 1815, third son of Deemster John Christian of Milntown; Trinity Coll Cantab grad 1840; D 14 June 1840 (Bp Pepys); P 1 Aug 1841 in St George's (Bp Short); C of German, June 1840 and in charge of St John's April - Aug 1845; V of Lezayre Aug 1845-1861; M (1) Charlotte Brine at Castletown in 1840 (2) Emma Du Bulay at St Peter's, Eaton Square, London (3) Maria Johnson (4) Sophia Schlat at Schwerin, Germany; died 31 July 1886 aged 70; buried Lezayre.

CLAGUE, Revd John: b 1750; pupil of Bp Hildesley; D 1772 (Bp SM); C of Kirk Michael 1772-82; V of Rushen 22 May 1782 until death 9 Mar 1816; M Esther, daughter of William Crebbin (3) (V of Jurby); she died 29 Dec 1812 aged 58.

CLARKE, Revd Archibald Edward (3): b 20 Mar 1861; nephew of Revd Edward W. Kissack; St Aidan's Theological Coll, Birkenhead; D 21 Dec 1884 in German Church (Bp Hill) P 25 Sept 1887 (Bp Bardsley); C of St Matthew's 1884-6; C of Santan 1886-9 (where he was virtually in charge of the parish as Vicar Robert Airey was incapacitated); C of Andreas 1889 - June 1892; Chap of St Stephen's Sulby June 1892 - Dec 1903; V of Marown 31 Dec 1903 until death 1 Jan 1934.

CLARKE, Revd Benjamin Philpot (1): b 23 Sept 1831, son of J. T. Clarke (2) (Chap St Mark's 1827-64); godson of Archdeacon Philpot; TCD; D 2 Sept 1855 in Bishopscourt Chapel; P 21 Dec 1856 in St John's Church; C of Rushen Sept 1855-64 with special responsibility for Port St Mary; Chap of St Luke's 1864-5; Chap of St Jude's 1865-69; V of Marown June 1869 until death 5 Sept 1903; RD of Douglas 1888-1903; 25 Oct 1895 installed as one of the four original Canons.

CLARKE, Revd John Thomas (2): b Jurby 1799 at The Nappin which his father farmed; D 1822 (Bp SM); C of Andreas 1822-27; Chap of St Mark's 29 July 1827 - May 1864; M in Santan Church on 26 Sept 1822 Betsy Clucas and after her death on 2 Sept 1862 M Catherine Clucas of Kionslieau; his first wife was buried St Mark's with a son and a daughter who died young; May 1864 left to become C of the Mariners' Church in Swansea; 1872 C and in 1876 V of Caerleon near Dolgelly, Dio Bangor where he died 2 Feb 1888 aged 89.

CLAY, Revd William: D 1858; P 1859 (Bp SM); C of Lezayre with charge of North Ramsey 1858-61; Secretary of CMS 1861-67; emigrated to Australia.

CLUCAS, Revd William: b 1742; one of the Clucas family of Ballanicholas, Marown; D 1767 SM: C of Marown 1767-71; C in C of Ballaugh 1771-2; C of Kirk Michael 1772-78; V of Malew 31 Mar 1778 - May 1783; R of Bride 31 May 1783 until death in Aug 1798; buried at Bride 6 Aug; 1780 VG; M Elizabeth sister of Thomas Christian (10) (V of Marown 1780-99), she died Mar 1837 aged 80; while C of Marown he translated the Song of Solomon for the Manx Bible.

COCHRAN, Revd Eustace William: D 1876; P 1878 (Bp Jacobson of Chester); C of St Martin's, Liverpool 1876-8; C of Widnes 1878-9; V of Foxdale 1879-1900; died June 1928; his wife Margaret Lewin died in 1915.

COLLET, Revd Edward: D 1870 (Bp Mackarness of Oxford); P 1871 (Bp Philpott of Worcester); served 4 curacies in England; Chap of Cronk y Voddy Sept 1875-1876 when he returned to England.

CORLETT, Revd Henry (1): b 1736, son of Thomas Corlett, the Sumner General (n.b. not Revd Thomas Corlett (4); D 1755 (Bp SM); C of Ballaugh 1755-61; V of German 4 Mar 1761 until his death 15 Nov 1801.

CORLETT, Revd John (2): b Cumberland; D 1855; P 1856 (Bp Longley of Ripon); C of St Matthew's, Leeds 1855-7; Chap of St Stephen's, Sulby 14 Apr 1858-59; Chap of Cronk y Voddy 25 Mar 1859 - Nov 1865; Chap of St John's Dec 1865 until death 23 Feb 1909; M Harriet Marsh at St Clement's, Leeds on 3 May 1869; for many years, until 1905, he was Clerk to German Parish Commissioners and to German Poor Law Guardians.

CORLETT, Revd Philip (3): b 1795; D 21 Mar 1819 in Kirk Michael Church; Chap of Ballure Mar 1819 until death 1 Oct 1825; First Chap of St Paul's Ramsey 1822-25.

CORLETT, Revd Thomas (4): D 16 June 1764; P 14 Mar 1772 (Bp SM); C of Bride 1764-73 where he translated Job for the Manx Bible; V of Lezayre 13 Sept 1773 until death from dropsy on Sun 2 Jan 1803; buried Lezayre 7 Jan.

CORRIN, Revd William; b Arbory 1795; educated at CGS; an excellent classical scholar; D 24 Aug 1817 in St George's P 21 Mar 1819 in Kirk Michael Church; C of Kirk Michael Aug 1817 - Mar 1824; V of Rushen 1 Apr 1824 until death 5 Feb 1859 aged 64; he had 5 sons and 8 daughters; his wife died on 5 Sept 1850 aged 55; buried at Rushen 7 Sept Vicar Gill (5) of Malew taking service.

COSNAHAN, Revd John (1): b 1693, son of John Cosnahan (2) (V of Santan); C of Santan 1731; V of Braddan 30 Oct 1733 until death June 1750 aged 57; buried Santan 29 June; M Ann Corrin and had 6 children, Joseph (who succeeded him as Vicar), Hugh, Ann, Jane, Catherine and Margaret; VG 1731.

COSNAHAN, Revd John (2): V of Santan 12 July 1691 until death 14 April 1724 aged 56; buried Santan 16 April under the great stone, weighing 1.5 tons which covers the Cosnahan family grave.

COSNAHAN, Revd Joseph (3): D 20 Sept 1747 (Bp SM); V of Braddan 4 Oct 1750 until death Sept 1768 aged 43; buried Santan 22 Sept; M Margaret Caesar who died Feb 1760 leaving a son Julius (4) and 3 daughters, Margaret and Ann (twins) and Jane; 22 July 1760 M in Bishopscourt Chapel, Ellinor, daughter of Robert Radcliffe (V of Patrick); the apparent haste of his second marriage was doubtless due to his needing a mother for his children.

COSNAHAN, Revd Julius (4): son of Joseph Cosnahan (3) and nephew of T. W. J. Woods (3); C of St George's, then V of Braddan 21 Mar 1786 until death 5 months later; buried Santan 26 Aug; M Margaret, daughter of Deemster Moore.

COTTIER, Revd John: V of Patrick 3 Jan 1812 until unfrocked for drunkenness in June 1827; M a Miss Moore in Oct 1810.

COWLEY, Revd Daniel Scurr: b Hull 1852; St John's Cantab; D 1877; P 1878 (Bp Bickersteth of Ripon); C of Great Horton, Bradford 1877-9; Chap to Farnley Iron Co, Leeds 1879-83 with charge of Parish of New Farnley. C of High Harrogate 1883-4; V of Christchurch, Wakefield 1884-90; V of German 31 Mar 1890 - Mar 1895; R of Bride 14 Mar 1895 until death 19 Apr 1913 aged 60; 1897 RD of Ramsey; Feb 1910 Proctor for the Clergy in Convocation.

CRAINE, Revd Edward (1): Chap of St Mark's 1814-20.

CRAINE, Revd Edward (2): V of Onchan 29 Mar 1810 until death 26 Apr 1847 after an illness of 6 months; buried Onchan 1 May; he had resigned on 7 Feb; 2 Nov 1812 M Isabella Moore of Douglas at Onchan; she died 9 Oct 1863 aged 88; a Manx speaker.

CRAINE, Revd John (3): V of German 28 July 1741 until death 4 Apr 1742 aged 26, less than 3 months after his marriage to Margaret Woods, who also died young in 1747.

CRAINE, Revd Robert (4): Chap of Ballure 1804-07.

CRAVEN, Revd George E.: Grad King's College, London; D 1890 (Bp Carpenter of Ripon); P 1891 (Bp Temple of London); C of St David's Holloway 1890-4; British Chap at S. Paolo, Brazil 1894-97; Secretary of South American Missionary Society 1897-1901; V of St Barnabas 1st June 1904 - Apr 1909, then returned to England.

CREBBIN, Revd Charles (1): Chap of St Matthew's 1765-69; V of Santan 1769-1817; also Chap of St George's 1 Oct 1781 until death 4 Dec 1817 aged 81; son of Paul Crebbin (2).

CREBBIN, Revd Paul (2): D 20 April 1729; V of Santan 2 July 1731 until death 26 Aug 1764 aged 59; buried Santan 29 Aug; M Jane Cubbon on 30

May 1730 Bp Wilson taking the service; she died in 1799 aged 100.

CREBBIN, Revd William (3): lived with Bp Wilson for a year before his ordination; D 1743; C of Jurby 1743-51; V of Jurby 9 Aug 1751 until death on 19 Nov 1803 aged 86; he was one of the best Manx scholars of his time and was a man of great energy, taking regular duty up to his death; M Esther Brew who died 2 Oct 1771 aged 50; both are buried at Jurby.

CRELLIN, Revd John: Chap of Ballure July 1761 - Oct 1771; V of Kirk Michael 4 Nov 1771-98; R of Bride 1798 until death in 1808; he died in Liverpool and was brought home for burial at Kirk Michael on 11 June 1808; he was Episcopal Registrar and in 1800 became one of the two Vicars General. His wife, Margaret Frissell, a grand-daughter of Deemster Christian, died on 18 Aug 1770, aged 31, and is buried at Ballure, where her stone reads, "To the memory of the best of women and wives"

CUBBON, Revd Thomas: b 1739; educated at Castletown GS and was for a time in the service of the Clerk of the Rolls; M Elizabeth, daughter of the Revd James Wilks (who took the service) on 29 Aug 1769 in Kirk Michael Church; their son Mark was Governor of Mysore 1834-61; V of Santan 1765-9; V of Maughold 7 Mar 1769 - Apr 1814; V of Lonan 3 May 1814 - Mar 1817; R of Bride 18 Apr 1817 until death Jan 19 1828 aged 89; VG 1808-27; buried at Maughold; his wife died 4 Sept 1829 aged 80.

CURGHEY, Revd John (1): b 1657, one of the Curgheys of Ballakillingan, Lezayre; V of Braddan 4 Sept 1704 until death 6 Oct 1733 aged 76; buried in the chancel of Braddan Church; with his fellow VG, William Walker, he shared Bp Wilson's imprisonment in Castle Rushen.

CURGHEY, Revd Matthias (2): b 1668, younger brother of VG John Curghey (1); D 25 Sept 1698 at Bishopscourt; C of Ballaugh Dec 1698 - June 1703; V of Patrick 24 June 1703-29 and also of German 10 June 1710-29; the last Vicar of German and Patrick combined; R of Bride 21 Nov 1729 until death 31 Jan 1754 aged 85; his wife Dorothy died Apr 1749;

both are buried at Bride.

CURGHEY, Revd Matthias (3): son of VG John Curghey (1); b 1699; D 1725; C of Lonan 1725-28; V of Marown 18 Sept 1728-29; V of Lezayre 12 Feb 1729 - Feb 61; R of Ballaugh Feb 1761 until death 19 Jan 1771 aged 71; buried at Ballaugh; his wife Catherine died June 1781 and was buried with him; he was described on his tombstone as "humble, meek, pacific, a sound divine, learned and exemplary".

CURGHEY, Revd Matthias (4): V of Rushen 24 June 1703-13.

CURGHEY, Revd Nathaniel (5): b 1710; D 25 Mar 1735; C in C of Lonan Mar 1735 - July 1753; V of Lonan 6 July 1753 until April 1759; died 9th June 1759, buried at Lonan.

CURWEN, Revd Edward: Graduate of Durham; D 1870; P 1871; (Bp Goodwin of Carlisle); C of Grasmere 1870-2; C of Harrington, Cumberland 1872-4; Chap of St Olave's 1874-5; R of Plumbland, Carlisle 1875.

DAVIDSON, Revd Hugh C.: Master at KWC 1845-82; D 26 Jan 1851 as C of Castletown, in Bishopscourt Chapel; P 27 Dec 1854; V of Patrick Dec 1882 until death on 6 Jan 1897; M Anne Gelling in St Mary's, Castletown on 5 Feb 1851; she died 31 Jan 1856 aged 31 (her daughter had been born on 24 Jan and died on 14 Feb); then M Harriet Watson who died in Patrick Vicarage 10 Aug 1888 aged 65.

DAVIES, Revd William E.: University of Durham grad 1895; BD 1901; DCL 1906; D 1887 (Bp Temple of London); Missionary at Multan, India 1887-94; C of Braddan 1895-7; Chap of Laxey 1897-1904; V of St Olave's 9 June 1904 - Dec 1917; R of Compten Valence, Dio Salisbury 1917-23; R of Norton Fitzwarren, Dio Bath and Wells 1923-31.

DAWES, Revd Charles (1): Corpus Christi Coll Cantab grad 1876; D 1876; P 1877 (Bp Browne of Winchester); C of Sandown, Isle of Wight 1876-79; Chap to the Tyne Missionary Ship, South Shields 1879-80; V of the Fishermen's Church, Hastings 1880-85; V of Rushen 24 Oct 1885 - Apr 1887 when he took a parish in Portsmouth.

DAWES, Revd George (2): TCD grad 1855; D Sept 1856 in Braddan Church; P 4 June 1857 in Bishopscourt Chapel; Chap of St Luke's 2 Sept 1856-59; C of Beeston, Derbyshire 1859-65; V of Ash, Somerset 1865.

DEARDEN, Revd A. K.: C of Rushen 1898-1903; V of St Olave's 1903-04.

DENING, Revd Henry: b London; D 1878 in Bishopscourt Chapel; P 1879 in KWC Chapel; C of German 1878-80; V of German June 1880-81.

DEVALL, Revd Henry T.: D 1889; P 1890 (Bp Ryle of Liverpool); C of St Matthew, Liverpool 1889-91; C of St George's, Everton 1891-8; Senior C of St George's with special charge of All Saints 1898-1901; Chap of St Paul's, Ramsey 31 July 1901-04; first Vicar of St Paul's 1904-1911; V of Kirk Michael 1914-22.

DINWOODY, Revd William Thomas: C of Andreas 1869-75; V of Arbory July 1875 until death 14 Oct 1876 aged 38; buried at German; M on 14 Nov 1865 Emily, eldest daughter of Frances Matthews of Glenmoar, St John's.

DRURY, Revd William: b Port Erin 4 June 1808 son of Thomas Drury who belonged to an old Derbyshire family and who M Mary Oates; baptised privately and received into the congregation at Onchan 9 April 1809; D 1832; P 1833 (Bp SM); Chap of St John's Oct 1833 - Oct 34; C of Andreas 1834-41 and Chap of St Jude's 26 Nov 1841 - Mar 1847; V of Braddan 1 Apr 1847 till death 19 Sept 1887; M Jane Wortley from Ridlington, Rutlandshire; they had two sons, W. F. Drury (2), T. W. Drury (Bp Drury) and a daughter who died in infancy.

DUGGAN, Revd William: D in Kirk Michael Church 21 Mar 1819; Chap of St Mark's 1820-27; V of Marown 7 Dec 1827 until his sudden death on 2 Mar 1862; his wife had died a few weeks before; he was a farmer and as there was no vicarage in Marown he lived at Middle Garth Farm.

EAVES, Revd Henry: D Kirk Michael Church

19 Apr 1908; P in German Church 13 June 1909; Chap of Cronk y Voddy Apr 1908 - Nov 1910 when he went to a parish in Oldham.

ENSOR, Revd George: Queen's Coll Cantab grad 1867; D and P 1868 (Bp Tait of London); CMS Missionary at Nagasaki, Japan 1868-72; returned to England for health reasons; he could speak and write Japanese; C of Ashton-Flamville 1872-4; Associate Secretary of CMS 1874-8; 1878-95 V of Rendham, Dio Norwich; V of German 5 Apr 1895 - Nov 1896; 1896 RD of Peel; V of Heywood, Wilts Oct 1896; preached his last sermon at Peel on 1 Nov and left next day; the Bishop did not receive his resignation until 1 Dec; died at sea in 1910; buried on Gibraltar.

FENTON, Revd Thomas: TCD; D 12 Oct 1850 in St Barnabas; P 21 Dec 1851 in St Paul's Ramsey; Chap of Dhoon 1850-52; left to become R of Waterfall and V of Cauldon, Staffs.

FERRIER, Revd Edward: b Great Yarmouth 1827; Pembroke Coll Cantab grad 1850; D 1850; P 1851 (Bp Blomfield of London); C of St Martin's in the Fields 1850-52; C of St James', Southampton 1852-54; Chap of Castletown 21 July 1855 - 19 Jan 1896 (retired through ill health); died 14 Mar 1899; buried Malew 18 Mar; Secretary to Board of Education 1874-95; 1863 Chap to House of Keys; Diocesan Inspector of Religious Education in Schools; Surrogate for Marriage licences for Malew, Santan and Arbory; his wife Elizabeth died 3 Mar 1873 and on 8 Jan 1877 M at Malew Margaret Cunningham a widow; 1895 RD of Castletown; Oct 1895 one of the four original Canons; after his resignation he took a long holiday in England but continued as RD and as a member of the Cathedral Chapter; resigned as RD Mar 1897; 1896 unanimously elected Proctor in Convocation for the Dean and Chapter.

FINNIS, Revd H. R.: D 21 Sept 1878 in St George's; P 22 Feb 1880 in St Thomas's; C of Rushen Sept 1878-79; Chap of Cronk y Voddy 1879 - 17 July 1880; July 1880 R of Rokeby, Tasmania; returned as Canon Finnis to preach at Cronk y Voddy 18 June 1893.

FLETCHER, Revd Robert (2): V of Braddan 14 Nov 1696 until 9 Apr 1704 when he was unfrocked for misconduct; buried at Braddan.

FLETCHER, Revd Robert (2): V of Marown 20 June 1686-1701.

FORBES, Revd Edward: TCD grad 1838; Hebrew Prizeman; D 1840 (Bp Law of Bath and Wells); P 1841 (Bp Allen of Ely); C of St Mark's Bath 1840-41; V of Ramsey, Hants 1841-47; C of St George's 1 Nov 1847-59; died at Cannes 12 May 1882 aged 68.

GARDE, Revd John Fry: D 1845; Chap of St John's 1845-65; Chap of Cronk y Voddy as well 1852-4; V of Patrick 6 Dec 1865 until death 22nd Sept 1877 aged 63.

GARDNER, Revd James S.: b 1854; D 1888 P 1889 (Bp SM); 1875-87 a solicitor in Liverpool and for many years Superintendent of the Sunday Schools at St Cleopas, Toxteth Park under R. B. Baron; C of Kirk Michael and Domestic Chaplain to Bp Bardsley 1888-9; C of St Thomas' 1889-91; Chap of St Stephen's, Sulby 13 Apr 1891 - 20 Apr 1892 when he left to join Bardsley in Dio Carlisle and there became V of Ireleth; later V of Clauston, nr Melton Mowbray where he died 15 Aug 1924; He and Margaret McDonald of Edinburgh were married by Bardsley in Bishopscourt Chapel 29 Oct 1890.

GASKING, Revd Samuel: D 1879; P 1880; (Bp Jacobson of Chester); Chap of St Luke's 1880-82; then became C of Garston, Dio Liverpool.

GELL, Revd John (1): b 1761, only son of Samuel Gell (2) (V of Lonan); Chap of St Mark's 1783-1809 with a short break 1796-7; then left to serve a curacy in Liverpool; Chap of St John's Oct 1834 - April 1835.

GELL, Revd Samuel (2): b 1720, son of William Gell (3) (V of Onchan); D 1744; C of Onchan 1744-47; V of Jurby 1747-48; V of Onchan 13 Mar 1748-1759; V of Lonan 19 Apr 1759 until death January 1802; buried at Lonan; M Catherine Cosnahan (died Jan 1789) daughter of John Cosnahan (1) (V of Braddan).

GELL, Revd William (3): D in Bishopscourt Chapel 25 Sept 1698 (Bp Wilson's first ordination); V of Onchan 11 Sept 1701 until death 31 Mar 1748 aged 72; buried Onchan; M Isobel Moore who died 2 Jan 1756 aged 80; they had 12 children.

GELLING, Revd Alexander (1): D 1809 (Bp SM); Chap of Ballure 1809-16; V of Arbory 4 Mar 1816 until death 7 July 1859 aged 74; M on 10 Oct 1811 Susan Clucas, daughter of William Clucas, R of Bride; she died at Ballavagher Marown 3 May 1860 aged 72.

GELLING, Revd Daniel (2): D 1750 (Bp SM); C of Andreas 1750-56; Chap of Ballure 27 Oct 1756 - July 1761; V of Malew 8 July 1761 - Dec 1777; R of Ballaugh 16 Dec 1777 until death 23 Aug 1801; buried at Ballaugh 25 Aug; M Elizabeth Lace.

GELLING, Revd James (3): b 1772; ordained as Chap of St Mark's but his stay there must have been very short; V of German 23 Nov 1801 until sudden death 8 July 1838; his wife Sophia died Santan 17 Dec 1844. Daughter, also Sophia, married John Cannell (2)

GELLING, Revd Samuel (4): b 1799, son of James Gelling (3) V of German; D 1824; Chap of St John's and Master of Peel GS 1824-35; Chap of St Matthew's May - June 1835; V of Santan 24 June 1835 until death 4 Nov 1865 aged 66.

GEORGE, Revd J. E. Beauchamp: St John's Coll Cantab D 1872; P 1873 (Bp Ellicott of Gloucester and Bristol); C of the Temple, Bristol 1872-78; Assoc. Secretary of Colonial and Continental Missionary Society 1878-79; C of Emmanuel, Clifton, Bristol June 1879-80; V of St George's 21 May 1880 until sudden death 12 May 1891; M Annie Davies who died 18 Aug 1884 then on 28 Apr 1886 M Marian Steeman who died Oct 1891.

GIBSON, Revd William Henry (1): D 23 Dec 1894 in St George's; P 22 Dec 1895; C of German Dec 1894-6; Chap Dalby 1896-99.

GIBSON, Revd William N. (2): D 1898 (Bp SM); C of St Thomas's 1898-1904; Chap of Laxey Sept 1904-1916.

GILL, Revd Evan (1): V of Onchan 20 June 1686-1701; V of Marown 11 Sept 1701 until death early in 1713.

GILL, Revd Hugh Stowell (2): b 26 Mar 1830, son of William Gill (5) (V of Malew); TCD grad 1853; D 30 Oct 1853 (Bp Auckland) in Malew Church (the last ordination there until 1908); P 21 Dec 1854 (Bp Powys) at St John's; a keen mathematician and a good classical and Hebrew scholar; 17 June 1856 he was married by his father, William Gill (5) in Malew Church to Margaret, daughter of John Llewellyn who was High Bailiff of Peel until his death in 1839; she was born 8 Feb 1832 and died 3 Aug 1912; Chap of St Luke's 3 Nov 1853-56; first Chap of Laxey Apr 1856-59; V of Rushen 5 Mar 1859-71; V of Malew 1872-1895; R of Andreas and Archdeacon 20 Feb 1895 until death 13 May 1912; buried Malew; 1872 Surrogate for marriage licences for the southern parishes.

GILL, Revd John (3): b 1708; D 24 Oct 1751; P 24 Sept 1752 (Bp SM); C of Andreas Oct 1751 - Apr 1759; V of Malew 19 Apr 1759 - Mar 1761; V of Lezayre 2 Apr 1761 until death Oct 1772.

GILL, Revd Thomas Howard (4): b 28 June 1836, son of William Gill (5) (Vicar of Malew); KWC and TCD grad 1859; D in Bishopscourt Chapel 3 Sept 1859; P 1860; C of Malew with his father Sept 1859 - June 1864; Chap of St Mark's June 1864 - Aug 1865; 7 Sept 1859 M Isabella Mondes from Co Sligo at Riverstone Parish Church, the service being taken by his father, William Gill (5); his later career was in England and he died 5 June 1894 as V of Tonbridge after some years of bad health; buried at Malew.

GILL, Revd William (5): b 30 July 1797 in the parish of German, son of Henry Gill, not Revd Gill, a customs officer at Peel and Marcia, daughter of Henry Corlett (1) (V of German); his family had farmed Kennaa for generations; D 1820; P Dec 1824 in Bishopscourt Chapel; Chap of St John's (then a chapel in the parish of German) 1820-24; C of Ballaugh 1824-27; after the suspension of Vicar Christian (11) of Malew in 1827 Gill was appointed priest in charge and became Vicar in 1830 until death 17

Oct 1871.

GRANT, Revd Frederick B.: D 1 Nov 1872 in St Thomas'; P 18 May 1875 (Bp Hobhouse acting for Bp Powys) in St Thomas's; [Hobhouse had been Bp of Nelson, New Zealand and on his return to England became assistant Bp of Lichfield]; Nov 1872-6 C of Rushen; Chap of St Mark's Dec 1876 - Feb 1878 when he returned to England.

GRAY, Revd Joseph Henry: TCD grad 1835; D 1837; P 1838; (Bp Blomfield of London); Principal of CMS Coll, Madras 1838-48; Chap of St Barnabas' 24 June 1852-70; V of Keynsham, nr Bristol 1870 until death on 29 Oct 1893; 5 Sept 1854 M in St Barnabas' by Revd E. Forbes to Emilie Jane Awdry, daughter of the late Major John Awdry of the 1st Madras Infantry and Judge Advocate of the Madras Army; she died 5 May 1889.

GREGSON, Revd George W.: D Dec 1896; P 1897 (Bp SM); C of Andreas Dec 1896 - Sept 1900; Curacy in London 1900-03; C of Lezayre 1903-7; Chap of Dhoon Sep 1907 - Feb 1913; V of Jurby Feb 1913-31; V of Crosby Ravensworth, Dio Carlisle 1931 until death after a long illness in 1935.

GRIER, Revd Frederick: TCD; D 1859; P 1860 (Bp Lonsdale of Lichfield); C of Heath and Hault Hucknall 1859-62; C of Enfield 1862-4; C of St Thomas' 1864-67; C of St Mary's, Hulme, Manchester 1867-69; C of St George's 1869-76; V of Arbory 6 Nov 1876 - Feb 1880; 1880 P in C of Walton Breck Liverpool; M Helen Phythian at Braddan 5 Jan 1876.

HALL, Revd Henry Armstrong (1): TCD; D 1876 (Bp Claughton of Rochester); P 1877 (Bp Thorold of Rochester); C of Holy Trinity, Lee, Kent 1876-7; V of St George's Dec 1877 - May 1880; V of Holy Trinity, Bristol 1880-92; V of St John's Episcopal Church, Perth 1892; M Catherine Hutchinson at Lee 14 Feb 1898.

HALL, Revd John Cecil (2): b 1804; R of Andreas and Archdeacon 19 Sept 1839; M Frances Amelia, daughter of Colonel the Honourable J Wingfield Stratford of Addington, Kent; she died 3 June 1888 after an illness of six months; Hall died 8

Feb 1844 and after his death Mrs Hall lived in Finch Road and attended St Thomas' Church; she used her wealth to help the diocese, notably in building Cronk y Voddy church.

HALSALL, Revd Anthony: D 24 Mar 1716 (Bp SM); Chap of St Matthew's and Master of DGS Nov 1716-32; in 1732 he became Master of the GS at Crosby, Liverpool where he remained until death in 1755 aged 62, gaining the reputation of a faithful and hard working parish priest; V of Crosby 1735-55; at St Matthew's he was involved in many unfortunate disputes.

HALSTEAD, Revd Robert: grad Durham 1891; D 1891; P 1892 (Bp Moorhouse of Manchester); served 3 short curacies, the last at St Margaret's, Whalley Range, Manchester; Chap of St Mark's Nov 1903 - Nov 1904.

HARDY, Revd Henry: b 1821; St John's Coll Cantab; D 1850 (Bp Bagot of Bath and Wells); P 21 Dec 1851 (Bp SM) in St Paul's, Ramsey; C of Jurby 1850-58; Chap of Cronk y Voddy 17 July - Nov 1858; V of Jurby 20 Nov 1858 until death at 10 Waterloo Road, Ramsey on 19 Aug 1875; 1854 appointed Diocesan Inspector of Sunday Schools; buried at Windsor; his widow died at Gainsford, nr Doncaster in Oct 1876.

HARRISON, Revd Bowyer (1): b 9 Mar 1792, son of David Harrison (2) and grandson of T. W. J. Woods (3); D 30 Nov 1815 in Kirk Michael Church (Bp Murray's first ordination); P 3 Nov 1816; Chap of Ballure Nov 1816 - Mar 1818; V of Maughold 4 April 1818 until death on 19 Apr 1871 aged 79; M (1) Ellinor Cosnahan at Braddan 29 Aug 1826 and after her death on 26 Sept 1828 aged 31 (2) Theodosia Rimmer at St Nicholas Liverpool on 23 June 1832; she died 3 Apr 1853 aged 50.

HARRISON, Revd David (2): First Chap of St Mark's June 1772 - June 1783; V of Malew 25 June 1783 - Apr 1817; V of Lonan 18 Apr 1817 until sudden death 27 Feb 1824 aged 77; M Anne, daughter of the Revd T. W. J. Woods; she died 10 May 1840 aged 88.

HARRISON, Revd John Edward (3): b 1784; D 1 Oct 1807 (Bp S&M); C of Ballaugh Oct 1807-14; V of Maughold 20 Apr 1814 - Apr 1818; V of Jurby 4 Apr 1818 until sudden death 2 Nov 1858; buried at Jurby.

HARRISON, Revd Mark Wilks (4): b 1881 at the Dhoon Parsonage, son of the Revd S. N. Harrison (5), grandson of Bowyer Harrison (1); his mother was a daughter of the Revd William Kermode (3); Emmanuel Coll Cantab grad 1899; a teacher before ordination; D 1905; P 1906 (Bp Paget of Oxford); C of Stoke Poges (famous for Gray's 'Elegy') 1905-08; C of St George's 1908-11; V of St Paul's, Ramsey 1911 until death 30 Aug 1946; Chairman of Ramsey Lifeboat Committee 1927-46; elected to Ramsey Commissioners in 1928 and was twice chairman, dying in the middle of his third term.

HARRISON, Revd Stephen Nathaniel (5): b in Maughold Vicarage 28 Sept 1836, son of Bowyer Harrison (1); grad Durham 1861; D 1862 (Bp Lonsdale of Lichfield for the Bishop of Worcester); P 1863 (Bp Perowne of Worcester); served curacies at Dudley and Redditch before returning to the Island; Chap of the Dhoon 1873-89; JP 1904; Canon 1920; died 23 Nov 1925; buried Maughold; M Mary, eldest daughter of William Kermode (3), who performed the ceremony in Maughold church on 29 Aug 1876; she died 13 Oct 1886 aged 38.

HARRISON, Revd Thomas (6): V of Kirk Michael 25 Nov 1808 until death 2 Feb 1818; Episcopal Registrar.

HARTWELL, Revd Francis: Oriel Coll Oxon; D 27 July 1829 in Bishopscourt chapel; Chap to Bp Ward Feb 1831; 1 June became one of the Vicars General but resigned this post for health reasons in Jan 1846; Chap of St George's 2 Apr 1836 until death 27 Dec 1846 aged 63; his wife, Elizabeth, died 15 Oct 1843 after an illness of 10 days.

HARVEY, Revd Gilmour: D 15 Nov 1840 in St Barnabas'; Master at KWC 1833-65 and from 1855-65 was Bursar and Chap; also acted as C of Malew Nov 1840-54; V of Santan Nov 1865 - Mar 1877; V of Maughold Mar 1877 until death 7 May 1878.

HAWLEY, Revd William: b 15 Jan 1817; came to the Island as a Master at KWC and studied with the Principal of KWC, the Revd R Dixon; D 1847; P 1849 in Andreas church; C of Andreas 1847-52; C of St George's 1852-59; Chap of St George's 21 Mar 1859 - Dec 1877; V of Patrick Dec 1877 - Nov 1882; V of Kirk Michael Nov 1882 until death 22 Dec 1893; on 18 June 1849 M Catherine Jefferson in St George's by Archdeacon Moore (6).

HENRY, Revd Thomas: After being a missionary in Japan and V of St Paul's, Halifax became V of Lezayre 1863-9 then V of Tipton Staffs.

HICKIN, Revd Henry: b London where he served 3 curacies the last at St James', Rentonville; Chap of St Mark's 3 Mar 1905 - July 1912; returned to England.

HILL, Revd Charles (1): Chap of St James', Dalby 1858-68.

HILL, Revd Samuel (2): D 21 Dec 1855 in St Thomas's; Chap of Dhoon Dec 1855-58; returned to England.

HOBSON, Revd William Thomas: b 1833; TCD grad 1858; D 1859 (Bp Fitzgerald of Cork); P 1860 (Bp Singer of Meath); C of Monkstown, Co Dublin 1859-63; C of St Paul's, Prince's Park, Liverpool 1863-67; Assoc. Secretary of the Colonial and Continental Church Society 1867-72; V of St Barnabas' June 1872 - Nov 1895; installed as one of the first four Canans in Oct 1895; R of East Guildford, nr Rye Mar 1896 until death 3 May 1897.

HOLMES, Revd Archibald (1): Chap of St Paul's Ramsey 1825-42; V of Patrick 5 Oct 1842 until death 1 Nov 1865; M Charlotte Tellet at Malew 10 Apr 1845; she died at Castletown on 12 Apr 1879.

HOLMES, Revd Arnold John (2): D 22 Dec 1895; P 19 Dec 1897 (Bp SM); originally a medical student; C of German Dec 1895 - June 1897; Chap of St Mark's June 1897 - June 1903; M Kathleen Mills at Southport 1 July 1903.

HOPKINS, Revd Charles: b 1834; grad from

St Catherine's Coll Cambridge 1857; D 1858; P 1859 (Bp Davys of Peterborough); C of Aylestone, Leics (then Dio Peterborough) 1858-9; Bp Straton's father, Revd G. W. Straton, had been R of Aylestone and Hopkins had been Bp Straton's tutor; C of Broseley, Salop 1859-60; V of Dudington, Northants 1860-63; R of Polebrook, Northants 1863-71; V of Oundle 1871-96 where he was a faithful and much loved parish priest; he had been Domestic Chap to Bps Davys and Jeune of Peterborough; V of St Olave's 27 May 1896 - 3 Apr 1903; died 29 Apr 1908.

HORROBIN, Revd Robert: ordained C of Warrington; R of Andreas Oct 1719-16 May 1727; from 1719-25 he was also Government Chaplain at Castletown during which period his curate, Charles Wattleworth (1), was in charge of Andreas; 1727 R of Winfrith, Dio Salisbury where died 1729.

HOWARD, Revd John (1); son of Thomas Howard (2); b 3 Feb 1817 Braddan Vicarage; D 1 Aug 1841 in St George's; P 1842 (Bp SM); C of Castletown and Master KWC 1842-47; V of Onchan 24 July 1847 until death 7 Feb 1892; M Sabrina McHutchin daughter of the Clerk of the Rolls, John McHutchin.

HOWARD, Revd Thomas (2): b 29 Sept 1785; educated in Ramsey under Henry Maddrell, Chap of Ballure, then at Peel Academy (Peel Grammar School), then at St Bee's; From 1804-6 was officer in the Manx Fencibles, saw service in Ireland and was much loved by his men; D 1 Oct 1807; P 4 May 1809 (Bp SM); Chap of Ballure Oct 1807-09; C of St George's 1809-10; V of Braddan Apr 1810 - Apr 1836 and from 1832-36 also Chap of St George's; R of Ballaugh 1836 until death 7 Nov 1876 aged 91; M 4 June 1810 at Braddan Nessy, daughter of Thomas Stowell (not Revd Thomas Stowell), Clerk of the Rolls, when she was only 16; of their 14 children 8 died before him.

HUGHES-GAMES, Revd Joshua: b Bristol 1830; grad from Lincoln Coll Oxon with 1st Class degree in Mathematics 1852; D 1854; P 1855 (Bp Graham of Chester); C of Doddleston, Cheshire 1854-55; C of Holy Trinity, Hulme, Manchester 1855-57; Vice-Principal York Training Coll 1859-62; Head-master of Liverpool Institute 1862-66; Principal of KWC 1866-86; Examining Chaplain to Bps Hill, Bardsley and Straton; 1879 Principal of Bp Wilson Theological Coll; changed his name from Jones to Hughes-Games in 1880; R of Andreas and Archdeacon 21 May 1886 - Jan 1895; 1895 V of Holy Trinity, Hull; 1859 M Mary Helena Yates in Onchan Church; she returned to the Island after his death and lived in Homefield, Woodbourne Road, Douglas.

HUTTON, Revd F. N. B. (1): b 1826; St John's Coll Cantab; D 1849 Lichfield; 1869-72 V of St James', West Bromwich; V of St Thomas' 31 July 1872 - 29 Sept 1877; V of St Saviour's, Leicester 1877 until death 22 Oct 1884 aged 58, after a short but severe and painful illness; buried in Humberstone churchyard; his last sermon had been on the text "Prepare to meet thy God"; on the Sunday after his death the bells of St Thomas' rang a muffled peal.

HUTTON, Revd Wyndham M. (2): b 1826, brother of F. N. B. Hutton (1); St John's Coll Cantab grad 1849; D 1849 (Bp Lonsdale of Lichfield); served curacies at Wednesbury and Ely and was for some time Chap to an iron works; a high churchman; V of Lezayre 1869-77; V of Hungarton Leics, 1877.

ILES, Revd Francis: b 27 Sept 1871; Corpus Christi Coll Cantab grad 1900; Chap of St Luke's 7 Apr 1903-1906; left to take a curacy in Leeds.

INGRAM, Revd William C.: b 11 Aug 1836; Jesus Coll Cantab grad 1857; Mathematics Master at Lancing Coll 1858-60; D 1859; P 1860 (Bp Gilbert of Chichester), then took private pupils; V of Kirk Michael and Chaplain to Bp Powys 30 June 1864 - Mar 1874; V of St Matthew's, Leicester 1874-93; honarary Canon of Peterborough 1887; Dean of Peterborough 1893 till death on 25 April, 1901, aged 64.

JAMES, Revd Henry Lionel: D 1880; P 1881 (Bp Pelham of Norwich); C of St Clement's Ipswich 1880-84; Chap of Laxey 1884 - Aug 1885; appointed V of Walberswick, Dio Norwich June 1895, but stayed at Laxey until Aug.

JONES, Revd Richard: b 20 Nov 1855; trained at Bp Wilson Theological Coll; D 1881; P 23 Dec

1883 in Rushen Church; C of Arbory 1881-82; Chap of St Luke's 1882 - Aug 1889; Chap of Dhoon 1889-91; V of Santan 1891-1931; died 5 Feb 1937; his wife died Apr 1895; buried at Santan.

KAYE, Revd John: b 1795; Chap of Ballure 1818 until death 17 Mar 1819 after a long and painful illness.

KELLY, Revd James Butler (1): Clare Coll Cantab grad 1854; D 1855; P 1856 (Bp Davys of Peterborough); C of Abington, Northants 1855-56; Domestic Chap to Bp Powys 1856-64; V of Kirk Michael Feb 1860 - June 1864 then went to Newfoundland where he became successively Archdeacon, Assistant Bishop and Bishop (1876); Consecrated 1876 by Archbishop Longley of Canterbury; returned to England in 1877 as V of Kirby; Bp Jacobson of Chester appointed him Suffragan Bp of Liverpool (then in Dio Chester); Archdeacon of Macclesfield 1880-84; later he administered the Dio of Salisbury for Bp Moberly who had been ill for a year, then acted as coadjutor Bp to Bp Eden of Moray, who had also been ill and whom he succeeded in 1886; died 1904.

KELLY, Revd William (2): b 1830, son of High Bailiff Kelly of Castletown; TCD grad 1852; D 1852; P 1854 (Bp SM); C of Andreas 1852-55; Chap of St Stephen's 14 May 1855-58; then went to England where he died 1860.

KERMODE, Revd Robert Daniel (1): b Douglas 22 Nov 1869; Gonville & Caius Coll Cantab; D 1892 (Bp Temple of London); C of St George in East London 1892-96; Senior C of St George's Douglas 1896-98; V of Maughold 6 June 1898-1908; V of St George's 1 Oct 1908-1920; V of Lezayre 1920-39; served as a Chaplain in the Boer War; a Freemason and for many years provincial Grand Chaplain; M in St Olave's 2 Sept 1908 Bertha, daughter of J.T. Clucas, Thornhill; Canon of St Patrick; died 29 May 1948.

KERMODE, Revd Stanley A. P. (2): b March 1862, son of William Kermode (3); Queen's Coll Cantab grad 1884; D 1885; P 1886 Archbp Benson of Canterbury; C of Margate 1885-88; C of Chelsham, Surrey 1888-90; C of St Peter's, Chester

1890-91; C in C of Kirk Michael 1891-92; V of Onchan 30 May 1892 - 5 Feb 1904; M Lucy Lynam on 23 Apr 1889 in Stoke on Trent Parish Church, the service being taken by his father and the Vicar, the Revd Sir Lovelace Stamer, Suffragan Bp of Shrewsbury; worked in England from 1904 until death Sept 1925.

KERMODE, Revd William (3): b 3 July 1814 in Ramsey; TCD; D 1839; P 1840 (Bp SM); Chap of Dalby 28 Mar 1839-1840; C of Lezayre 1840-43; Chap of St Paul's Ramsey 12 Oct 1843-1871; V of Maughold 19 June 1871 - 20 Feb 1877; R of Ballaugh Feb 1877 until death 12 Sept 1890 aged 76; 1880 RD of Peel; M (1) Mary Ann Griffith who died 14 Jan 1844 (2) on 8 Oct 1846 at St Giles', Northampton Jane Bishop, who died 29 Sept 1858 aged 39 (3) Margaret Pizey who died 8 Mar 1901 aged 74.

KEWLEY, Revd John (1): b 1 May 1860; Sidney Sussex Coll Cantab, grad as 34th Wrangler 1883; D 23 Sept 1883 in St Mary's, Castletown; P 21 Sept 1884 in KWC Chapel; C of St Paul's Ramsey 1883 - Dec 1890; V of Arbory 19 Jan 1891 - Oct 1912; appointed Canon 1899; R of Andreas and Archdeacon 5 Oct 1912 - 1938; died 6 Nov 1941, buried at Malew.

KEWLEY, Revd John (2): b Ballafreer, Marown 1772; Chap of St Matthew's and Master of DGS 1802 until death 3 Nov 1810; buried at Marown.

KEWLEY, Revd Joseph H (3): b 1826; grad from St Edmund's Hall, Oxford; D 1 Nov 1850 in St John's; P 19 Dec 1852 in St Mary's Castletown; Chap of Foxdale Nov 1850-54; 1853 Diocesan Inspector of Sunday Schools; M Sarah Ellis 15 Sept 1853; Oct 1854 R of Waterfall and perpetual C of Cauldon nr Leek; died 1907.

KEWLEY, Revd Thomas (4): D 1819 (Bp SM); C of Patrick 1819-27; V of Santan 12 Apr 1827 until death 12 Apr 1835 aged 39; M Anne Moore in Braddan Church 11 Sept 1820; she died 16 Feb 1836 aged 35.

KING, Revd Norman: D in Bishopscourt Chapel 1 June 1890; P St George's 20 Dec 1891; Chap of Dalby 1890 - Sept 1892; then took a curacy in

Birmingham.

KINRED, Revd Hugh: b Lezayre 1843; Bp Wilson Theological Coll; D 1881; P 1882 (Bp SM); C of Braddan with charge of Oakhill 1881-82; Chap of St Luke's for a few months in 1882; Dec 1882-1895 Chap of Cronk y Voddy; 1895-97 C of Patrick; V of Patrick 1897-1921.

KIPPAX, Revd Archippus (1): Chap to 8th Earl of Derby at Ormskirk; R of Andreas and Archdeacon June 1696-1700; V of Ormskirk 1700 until death 6 May 1718; buried at Ormskirk.

KIPPAX, Revd John (2): Chap to 10th Earl of Derby; Chap of Castletown Aug - Sept 1727; R of Andreas and Archdeacon 6 Oct 1727 until death 1760.

KIRKBY, Revd John: St Catherine's Coll Cantab; D 1886; P 1887 (Bp Ryle of Liverpool); C of St Cleopas, Toxteth Park, Liverpool 1886-89; C of Santan 1889-90; V of Santan 3 Feb 1890 - Jan 1891; V of St Catherine's, Edgehill 1891.

KISSACK, Revd Edward William: b 27 Aug 1837; TCD; D 4 May 1862; P 21 Dec 1863, both in Bishopscourt Chapel; C of Andreas May 1862-69; Chap of St Luke's for a few months in 1869; Chap of St Jude's Aug 1869 - Feb 1872; V of Rushen 21 Feb 1872 - May 1879; R of Bride 25 June 1879-1890; R of Ballaugh 15 Dec 1890 - Jan 1897; V of Chillenden, Dio Canterbury Jan 1897 until death after long illness 29 Apr 1901 aged 63; RD of Ramsey 1888; 1893 RD of Peel; 1895 one of the four original Canons.

KNEALE, Revd Thomas Redfearn: b Ramsey 6 Feb 1858; Emmanuel Coll Cantab, grad in Mathematics; 1882-84 Assistant Master at a school in Epsom; Headmaster of Ramsey GS 1884-88; D 21 Dec 1884 in German Church; P 18 Dec 1887 in Bishopscourt Chapel; C of St Paul's Ramsey Dec 1884 - Apr 1888; Chap of St Jude's Apr 1888 - May 1893; V of Rushen 31 May 1893 - Jan 1897; R of Ballaugh 25 Jan 1897 - June 1934; 1909 RD of Peel; Diocesan Inspector of Religious Education in Schools 1888-1913; Secretary of the Diocesan Conference 1893-1913; M Mary Augusta Sumner in St Mary's, Mosely, Birmingham on 29 Mar 1884; she died 6 Sept

1945 aged 86; he died July 1935.

KNIPE, Revd James: Schoolmaster at Ballure and although not ordained was licensed by Bp Wilson to take the services (1712-47).

KROENIG, Revd Charles S.: Corpus Christi Coll Cantab; D 20 Dec 1891; P 23 Dec 1894 both in St George's; Chap of St Mark's Dec 1891 - Sept 1896.

KYTE, Revd Joseph: D 1865; P 1867 (Bp Jacobson of Chester); after curacies in England he was Chap of St James, Dalby, 1868-72 and Chap of Cronk y Voddy Oct 1876-79.

LAMOTHE, Revd John Henry: b 23 July 1812, youngest son of Dr Lamothe of Glentramman; TCD; ordained as C of St Paul's, Preston then R of Walton, nr Warrington; V of Lezayre 5 Dec 1842 until death 6 June 1845; buried at Lezayre; M Eliza McHutchin, eldest daughter of John McHutchin, Clerk of the Rolls, in Malew Church 9 Feb 1841; she died 1 May 1850 aged 35.

LANCASTER, Revd Peter: Chap of St Matthew's 1714-16

LANGTON, Revd Charles Thomas: b 1830; came to the Island for health reasons and lived in Braddan where he did church work as a layman; D 21 Dec 1869 in Onchan Church; P 21 Dec 1878 in St Thomas's; 1869-77 Chaplain to Bp Powys; Chap of St Luke's Dec 1869 - Apr 1880; V of Arbory 30 Apr 1880-90; R of Bride 1890 until death 14 Dec 1894.

LANSDELL, Revd F. J.: St John's Coll Cantab; D 1894 (Bp Temple of London); C of St John's, Streatham 1894-6; V of St Barnabas' 11 Mar 1896 - Nov 1903 when he returned to his curacy at Streatham; he became Vicar of that parish in 1905.

LEECE, Revd Charles Henry: b 11 Mar 1852; Churchwarden at Braddan; D 1889; P 1891 (Bp SM); C of Rushen 1889-91; C of Braddan 1891-95; Chap of Laxey 1895-97; V of Rushen 1 Apr 1897 - June 1927; 1902 President of the IOM Natural History and Antiquarian Soc; RD of Castletown 1912; Canon of St Maughold 1915; retired after a stroke, lived at

Laurel Mount, Lezayre, died Friday 17 Jan 1930 aged 77; buried at Rushen 20 Jan.

LEECH, Revd John: Chap of Foxdale 1859-64.

LEWIS, Revd Walter A.: V of Tynmouth, Dio Exeter; V of German 6 June 1907 - June 1914.

LOCKE, Revd E. H. L.: D 23 Dec 1894 in St George's; P 22 Dec 1895 in Bishopscourt Chapel; Chap of Dalby Dec 1894 - Jan 1896; Chap of Castletown 1 Feb 1896 - 1921.

LOWCAY, Revd Henry: Master of Castletown GS; V of German 1661-80; R of Ballaugh Sept 1687 until death in Douglas 24 June 1700; buried at Braddan; as he was non-resident at Ballaugh, the Curate, Thomas Christian (10a) looked after the parish.

LUPTON, Revd Benjamin J. S.: b Leeds 1832; taught in various schools in England; Master of Castletown GS 1861-78; D 1878; P 1882 (Bp SM); Chap of St Mark's July 1878 until death 16 Sept 1891; buried at St Mark's; first wife, Emma, died suddenly 5 Sept 1870, aged 35; then M Laura Coates in Castletown Church on 26 July 1871; she died Southport 24 Feb 1893.

MADDRELL, Revd Henry: Chap of Ballure 1790-1803; V of Lezayre 22 Mar 1803 until death 23 July 1842 aged 76; buried at Arbory 29 July.

MAKON, Revd James: First Chaplain of St Mary's Chapel in Castletown, consecrated by Bp Wilson on 11 Apr 1701; died 1719.

MARSDEN, Revd Christopher: R of Andreas and Archdeacon 10 June 1700 - 3 Oct 1701 when he was drowned in a shipwreck during violent storm near Liverpool.

MITCHELL, Revd John: D 1840; P 1841 (Archbp Vernon Harcourt of York); Chap of St Mark's 1874-76 and from Feb - July 1878; died 13 June 1889 as V of Pentney, Dio Norwich.

MOORE, Revd Edward (1): elder brother of Philip Moore (7); D 1725; C of Arbory 1725-26; C of Andreas 1726-35 where he was criticised for neglect of duty; V of Lonan in 1735 for a few months, then V of Kirk Michael 8 Nov 1735 until Sept 1751 when he died after a rather long illness; buried at Malew; he and his brother and Henry Corlett (1) were the chief companions of the aged Bp Wilson in his last years; one of the Vicars General.

MOORE, Revd Frederick James (2): b Douglas 25 Aug 1838, son of Nicholas Moore, a grocer in King Street, who was a Methodist and brought up his four sons as Methodists; educated in Douglas and at TCD; D 1863; P 1864 (Bp Graham of Chester); C of St Paul's, Chester 1863-64; Chap of Foxdale 1864-75; V of Jurby 11 Sept 1875 - Dec 1878; V of Lonan Dec 1878 - Jan 1888; V of Braddan 15 Feb 1888 until death Friday 4 Oct 1912; buried at Braddan 7 Oct; 5 Mar 1896 succeeded to Hobson's canonry; 15 Sept 1897 elected as Proctor for the Chapter in York Convocation; 1903 RD of Douglas; M Emily, eldest daughter of Capt Kitto of Foxdale Mines (the ceremony being performed by Archdeacon Moore (6) and Vicar J. F. Garde of Patrick) 17 Apr 1877.

MOORE, Revd J. J. S. (3): TCD; D 1855; P 1856 (Bp Graham of Chester); C of Lezayre with charge of north Ramsey 1861-63; then returned to England.

MOORE, Revd John (4): D 20 Sept 1746 (Bp SM); C of Arbory Sept 1747 - July 1748; V of Arbory July 1748 until death Sept 1791 aged 77; buried at Arbory; one of the Vicars General.

MOORE, Revd John (5): b 1754, son of John Moore (4), V of Arbory; Chap of St Mark's 1783-86; V of Braddan 1786 until death Dec 1791; Vicars General; Buried Arbory 17 Dec.

MOORE, Revd Joseph Christian (6): b Douglas 12 Aug 1802, eldest of the seven sons of James Moore of Cronkbourne; educated at Douglas GS under Joseph Qualtrough, then Chap of St Matthew's; on leaving school he went into business, but strongly wishing to be ordained he became a pupil of the Revd W. H. Havergal, V of Shareshill, Staffs who prepared him for Oxford and whom he always held in the highest esteem; grad 1827 from St Edmund Hall, Oxon; D 1828 (Bp Ryder of Lichfield); P 1829; C of Measham, Derbyshire 1828-9; V of Measham 1829 - Apr 1844; R of Andreas and Archdeacon Apr 1844 until death 26 Feb 1886; buried Andreas.

MOORE, Revd Philip (7): b Douglas 5 Sept 1705; educated at DGS; D 20 Apr 1729; P 23 Sept 1739 in St Matthew's; after curacies at Bride and Marown he became Chap of St Matthew's and Master of DGS 1736-65; R of Ballaugh 1751-60 and R of Bride 1760 until death Douglas 22 Jan 1783 after a few hours illness; buried Braddan 25 Jan, all the Island clergy attending his funeral; his wife died in 1768; a very good classical scholar; did most of the work in producing the Manx Bible, work which ruined his health which was not good after 1773; before ordination he had studied with Bp Wilson; Chaplain to the various Bishops and to the 3rd Duke of Atholl; Non-resident at Ballaugh and Bride, the parishes being run by Curates.

MORRIS, Revd Alfred (1): b 24 June 1859; Headmaster of PGS then D 21 Dec 1890 in St Thomas'; P 12 June 1892 in German Church; C of German Dec 1890 - May 1892; C in C of Kirk Michael May 1892 - Mar 1894; V of Kirk Michael 1 Mar 1894 - May 1913; left the Island in 1913; died 23 Feb 1923 at Lingfield, Surrey after a long illness.

MORRIS, Revd William (2): Sidney Sussex Coll Cantab grad 1869; D 1869; P 1870 (Bp Baring of Durham); C of Holy Trinity, Darlington 1869-72; C of Thurlby, nr Newark 1872-79; Chap of St Olave's 1879-20 Apr 1881; first V of St Olave's 20 Apr 1881 - 31 Mar 1896.

MURRAY, Revd Lord George: brother of 4th Duke of Atholl; R of Andreas and Archdeacon Nov 1787; 1801 appointed Bp of St David's after which he was non-resident in Andreas; died 1803.

MYLREA, Revd Daniel (1): son of Archdeacon William Mylrea (2); Chap of Ballure 1783-5; C of Andreas 1785-99; V of Kirk Michael 1799-1802; R of Ballaugh 17 Feb 1802 - Apr 1814; R of Andreas and Archdeacon 16 Apr 1814 until death 29 Mar 1832; M Susannah Curphey of Ballakillingan who died Ram-

sey 24 Feb 1839.

MYLREA, Revd William (2): b 1721, son of Deemster Mylrea of Ballaugh; d 1747 (Bp SM); C of Andreas 1747-54; R of Bride 24 July 1754-60; R of Andreas 1760 until death 14 Sept 1787 aged 65; buried Andreas 18 Sept; his appointment as Archdeacon was said to be due to his father's friendship with the 2nd Duke of Atholl; his wife Ellinor Gill died 6 Feb 1795 aged 66.

NELSON, Revd Daniel (1): son of John Nelson (2); D 1835 (Bp SM); C of Andreas 1835-40; C of Kirk Michael 1840-47; Chap of St Jude's Oct - Nov 1847; R of Bride 19 Nov 1847 until death 2 Apr 1875; M 8 May 1843 Mary Bell of Kirk Michael in Bishopscourt Chapel; she died in Douglas 21 Apr 1881 aged 65.

NELSON, Revd John (2): V of Jurby 20 Dec 1803-1818; V of Santan 4 Apr 1818-1827; Vicar General; R of Bride 19 May 1830 until death 27 Oct 1847 aged 68; he seems to have resigned as V of Santan after supporting Bp Murray in the tithe dispute as on 12 Apr 1827 Thomas Kewley succeeded him; M Anne Allen of Ballavarrey, Andreas in Andreas Church on 21 Nov 1801; she died on 17 Apr 1845 aged 63.

NORRIS, Revd Henry: V of Kirk Michael 8 July 1686 until death 23 Jan 1717; buried Kirk Michael 25 Jan, Bp Wilson taking the funeral; M (1) Christian Fletcher who died in 1695 leaving a son and (2) Mary Berkenhide by whom he had a daughter.

PACKER, Revd George F.: D 20 Dec 1896 in Bishopscourt Chapel; C of St Olave's Dec 1896-99; C of Braddan 1899-1900; V of Foxdale 1 Nov 1900-1903; V of Llanvetherine, Abergavenny 1903; V of Holy Trinity, Swansea 1905.

PARR, Revd John (1): Chap of Ballure 1688-91; V of Rushen 1691 - Oct 1700; R of Bride 25 Oct 1700 until death 1723.

PARR, Revd Robert (2): V of Lezayre 20 June 1686 until death Dec 1712; buried Lezayre; VG 11 June 1698.

PARR, Revd Robert (3): V of Arbory 13 Apr 1713 - Mar 1723; R of Bride 29 Mar 1723 until death in 1729; VG.

PARSONS, Revd George Stickler: b 31 Oct 1795 at Petersfield, Hants; Chap of Castletown Nov 1827 until death 11 Apr 1855; M Ann Evans, daughter of Capt John Evans of Castletown at Malew on 25 June 1827; she died on 17 Mar 1837 9 days after the birth of a daughter; Parsons lost his elder daughter, aged 2, in the same month; Master of CGS 1823-27; Government Chaplain 1849.

PATON, Revd George (1): b 11 Oct 1836 at Thurso; D 11 June 1865; P 11 Mar 1867 (Bp Jacobson of Chester); C of Lezayre with charge of North Ramsey June 1865-6; C of St Paul's 1866-71; Chap of St Paul's Ramsey 3 July 1871 until death 13 Jan 1900; M at Lezayre 22 Aug 1865 Ellen, 4th daughter of the late William Farrant of Ballamoar, Jurby; Bp Powys married them; they had 2 sons and 4 daughters.

PATON, Revd E. C. (2): C St Paul's 1894-1900; Chap of St Paul's 1900-01; assisted Revd Mark Wilks Harrison (4).

PHILPOT, Revd Benjamin: b 9 Jan 1791 at Laxfield, Suffolk; Christ's Coll Cantab grad 1812, Fellow of Christ's 1814; D 1815; P 1817 (Bp Bathurst of Norwich); Chap of St George's 10 Aug 1827 - 22 May 1832; R of Andreas and Archdeacon May 1832 - Aug 1839; he then returned to England and was R of Lidney in the Forest of Dean (1860) and R of Denington, Norfolk (1872); he retired to Putney in 1874 and in 1878 moved to Surbiton; Philpot had been orphaned early and was brought up by an uncle from whom he inherited land near Southwold; his first wife died young and in 1822 he M Charlotte Vachall, daughter of a clergyman, who was the mother of 14 of his children and who died 17 July 1876 aged 74; Philpot died in 1889 and was buried with his wife at Lidney.

PIERPOINT, Revd Matthew: D 1850; P 1851 (Bp Pepys of Worcester); after 4 short curacies in England he was Chap of Laxey 1859-61; C of St John's, Cardiff 1861.

PIGOT, Revd H. C.: D 1889; P 1890 (Bp SM); Chap of Dalby 1890; then C of St Thomas's.

POPE, Revd John Grasett: D 1900; P 1901 (Bp SM); C of St Barnabas' 1900-01; C of Braddan 1901-08; V of Maughold 27 Oct 1908-20.

QUALTROUGH, Revd John (1): Born 25 Dec 1813, son of Joseph Qualtrough (2); D 1837 (Bp Sumner of Chester); P 1839 (Bp SM); Chap of St Stephen's 12 Dec 1839 - Feb 1848; Chap of St Jude's 10 Feb 1848 - Aug 1859; V of Arbory 16 Aug 1859 - June 1875; R of Bride 3 July 1875 until death 22 Feb 1879 aged 65; M (1) Elizabeth Leatham, a widow, on 11 Aug 1840, she died young (2) Emma Thompson on 29 Apr 1845 in Lezayre Church, his father taking the service, she died 15 Jan 1857 (3) Margaret Paton in Ballaugh Church on 21 Sept 1859.

QUALTROUGH, Revd Joseph (2): Chap of St Matthew's 1810-16; V of Rushen 13 Apr 1816 - Mar 1824; V of Lonan 1 Apr 1824 until death 23 June 1853 aged 72; M Agnes McColoch of Dumfries, who died 29 May 1854 aged 61.

QUAYLE, Revd John (1): V of Arbory July 1728 until death June 1748 aged 72; buried Arbory 7 June.

QUAYLE, Revd John (2): V of Rushen 26 Mar 1729 - Mar 1739; V of Malew Mar 1739 until death June 1758 aged 72.

QUAYLE, Revd Robert (3): Chap of St Matthew's 1770 - Dec 1791; V of Braddan 19 Jan 1792 - until death 3 Dec 1809 aged 68; buried Braddan.

QUAYLE, Revd Thomas (4): V of Onchan 14 Apr 1759 until death 9 Mar 1798; buried at Onchan; M (1) Grissel, daughter of William Ross, Chap of Castletown, she died 28 July 1768 (2) Jane, daughter of John Oates of Bibaloe, she died Apr 1794 aged 66.

QUINE, Revd John: b 5 May 1856, son of William Quine of Silverdale; grad in Mathematics from Merton Coll Oxon in 1881; D 1881 (Bp SM); P 23 Sept 1883 in St Mary's, Castletown; C of Kirk Michael and domestic Chap to Bp Hill 1881-83; Master of

Douglas GS 1883-95; V of Lonan 30 Apr 1895 until death 29 Feb 1940; 1907-24 Chaplain to the House of Keys; succeeded to Taggart's (2) Canonry in 1909; M Mary Jane Lindsay (B 13 Apr 1858 died 30 Mar 1942).

QUIRK, Revd John Nathaniel: son of Revd Charles Quirk (R of Golborne 1854-85); St John's Coll Cantab grad 1873; D 1874; P 1875 (Bp Atlay of Hereford); C of Bridgnorth 1874-78; C of Doncaster Parish Church 1878-81; V of St Thomas' Douglas June 1881 - 29 Oct 1882; V of Rotherham 1882-89; V of St Mary's, Beverley 1889-94; Canon of York; V of St Paul's, Lorrimore Square, London 1894-95; R of Bath 1895-1901; Suffragan Bp of Sheffield 1901, later Suffragan Bp of Jarrow.

RADCLIFFE, Revd Robert: b 1703; D 20 Apr 1726; P 20 Feb 1729 (Bp SM); V of Patrick 22 Feb 1729 until death 2 Oct 1769; one of the Vicars General.

RAINBOW, Revd Edward: Corpus Christi Coll Cantab; Chap for Missions to Seamen at Yarmouth until 1897; V of German 13 May 1897-1907 when he went to work at Church Army HQ in London as Warden of the Church Army Training Houses.

READ, Revd Claude: D 1882; P 1893 (Bp Jayne of Chester); C of St Mary's, Birkenhead 1882-85; Chap of Laxey 1885 - Oct 1887; V of Chevington, Northumberland 1887.

ROBINSON, Revd Hampton (1): D 1907; P 1908 (Bp SM); Chap of Dalby 18 Aug 1907 - Oct 1909; C of St Thomas Oct 1909.

ROBINSON, Revd Samuel (2): Born in Scotland, spoke no Manx so never preached; Master of Castletown GS then V of Arbory 23 Apr 1680 until death in 1712 for part of which period he was schoolmaster at Arbory; M Bridget Crowe; he and Revd William Bridson (2) were the only two clergy who supported the 10th Earl of Derby in his dispute with Bp Wilson; he was twice suspended, the first time for a year for calling the highly respected Deemster Parr a church robber and the second time for conducting a secret marriage between Thomas Steich and Susan Rose, neither of whom lived in Arbory and for drunkenness (Aug 1708); this time it was for 3 years but he apologised to Wilson and the suspension was lifted after a month.

ROLLESTON, Revd Adrian S.: D 12 June 1892 in German Church: P 27 May 1894 in Bishopscourt Chapel; C of Rushen June 1892 - June 1894; Chap of St Jude's 12 June 1894 - Dec 1913; V of Congerstone, Atherstone 1913.

ROLSTON, Revd William George: b 7 Nov 1855: D 1883; P 1886 (Bp SM); Bp Bardley's Domestic Chaplain 1887-91; Chap of Dhoon 4 Feb 1891-1907.

SAVAGE, Revd Ernest Bickersteth: b 1849; Emmanuel Coll Cantab grad 1871; D 1872; P 1873 (Bp Selwyn of Lichfield); C of Perry Bar, Birmingham 1872-75; C of Shrewsbury 1875-77; C of Easington, Gloucs 1877-78; V of Kirk Michael Nov 1878 - Nov 1882; Domestic Chap to Bp 1878-82; V of St Thomas' 21 Dec 1882 - Apr 1914; succeeded to Kissack's Canonry Mar 1897; for many years Secretary of Convocation; Proctor for clergy in York Convocation 1904; Proctor in Convocation for the Dean and Chapter 25 Jan 1909; RD of Douglas 1912; for many years Chap to IOM Volunteers; resigned after serious illness, moved to Ambleside and died there 22 May 1915 aged 66.

SHENSTON, Revd Henry F.: D 21 Dec 1902 (Bp SM); C of Malew Dec 1902 - Nov 1905; V of Jurby 23 Nov 1905-12; V of St Barnabas 1912-17; M Lily Osborne in June 1906.

SHIPPHAM, Revd Frederick: D 1905; P 1906 (Bp Hoskyns of Southwell) after a period with the Church Army; Chap of Dalby Nov 1909 - Nov 1910.

SIDEBOTHAM, Revd Samuel: b 1879; had been a workhouse official and Lay Reader: D 21 Dec 1908 in St George's; P 25 Jan 1910 in Bishopscourt chapel; C of Malew Dec 1908 - Jan 1911; Chap of Cronk y Voddy Jan 1911 - July 1913; then V of St Jerome's, Ardwick, Manchester.

SIMPSON, Revd Samuel: D 26 Jan 1851 in

Bishopscourt Chapel; P 21 Dec 1851 in St Paul's, Ramsey; C of St Matthew's Jan - May 1851; Chap of St Thomas' May 1851 - Nov 1867; died at Chester 2 July 1881 aged 78.

SMYTH, Revd W. K.: D 1906 (Bp SM); after a few months as Chap of St Luke's he became Chap of Cronk y Voddy 1906 - Apr 1908; C of Rushen 1908-9 then became C of Stowell Memorial Church, Salford.

SNEPP, Revd Edward: Private Chap to Governor Pigott; V of Lezayre 1861-63; V of St Paul's, Halifax 1863.

SPICER, Revd John Morris: D 31 May 1885 in St George's; P 25 Sept 1887; C of Kirk Michael May 1885-87; Chap of Laxey 1887 - Apr 1895; V of Malew 9 Apr 1895 until death in 1919; from 3 Feb 1886-1919 he was Secretary of the local branch of the C of E Temperance Society.

STANLEY, Revd Walmisley: Peterhouse Cantab; D 12 June 1892 in German Church; P 27 May 1894 in Bishopscourt Chapel; C of St Barnabas' June 1892 - Mar 1895; C of Wombwell, Yorks 1895 then V of Bengeworth, Dio Worcester; V of Onchan 7 Mar 1904 - May 1908 then returned to England.

STEPHEN, Revd George Caesar (1): D 14 June 1840 (Bp Pepys); P 1 Aug 1841 in St George's (Bp Short); M Mary Grindley of Liverpool 1844, she died in 1865; Chap of Dalby 15 June 1840-58; died in Douglas 13 Aug 1864.

STEPHEN, Revd Thomas (2): b 16 Jan 1776 into a well known Ballaugh family; D 1799 (Bp S&M); C of Bride 1799-1802; C of Ballaugh 1802-09; V of Marown 27 Mar 1809-1827; V of Patrick 9 July 1827 until death Fri 30 Apr 1842 after a very short illness as he had taken the services and preached the previous Sunday; M Charlotte, daughter of Rector Daniel Gelling of Ballaugh on 13 Apr 1801, she died in 1811 aged 32; VG 1812-24; Father of Deemster Stephen; for some years he was editor of the Manx Advertiser; buried at Ballaugh; on his tombstone are the words (in Manx) "All the days of my appointed time will I wait till my change come". (Job 14¹⁴).

STEPHENSON, Revd John Burnaby: D 1874; P 1875 Archbishop Thomson of York; after several short curacies in England he was Chap of Cronk y Voddy 1880 - Nov 1882 then returned to England.

STEWART, Revd Charles James: b 1821, son of Major Stewart of Ballavale, Santan; D 1846; P 1848 (Bp SM); one of the oldest members of the Manx Bar; Chap of Cronk y Voddy 1854-57 then C of St James', Burnley; died 29 Mar 1881 as V of New Bury, Farnworth.

STOWELL, Revd Hugh Ashworth (1): D 1853; P 1854 (Archbishop Sumner of Canterbury); Chap of the Dhoon 28 Aug 1858-69; C of Wardslow, Staffs 1869.

STOWELL, Revd Hugh (2): b Douglas 18 Nov 1768; educated at Ramsey under the Revd John Crellin, then in 1781 at CGS under the Revd Thomas Castley; D 1791; P 23 Apr 1793 at Bishopscourt; C of Arbory 1791-7; Chap of St Matthew's and Master of DGS 1797-1802; V of Lonan 15 Mar 1802 - Apr 1814; R of Ballaugh 20 Apr 1814 until death 14 Oct 1835; M 1796 Amelia Callow, who died at Lonan on 9 Jan 1814 aged 36 and was buried in the churchyard.

STOWELL, Revd John Lamothe (2): b Peel 18 June 1801, son of the Revd Joseph Stowell (4) (Master of PGS) and Elizabeth, daughter of Dr Lamothe Stowell of Castletown; Queen's Coll Oxon grad 1825; D 1825 (Bp Legge of Oxford); P 1826 (Bp Barrington of Durham); C of Egglingham, Dio Durham 1825 and later Chap in the household of Mr George Raikes; Chap of St Matthew's 14 June 1832 - Mar 1839; V of German 28 Mar 1839 - 18 June 1880; died 5 May 1884, buried in Peel Cemetery 10 May.

STUBBS, Revd Frederick William: D 20 Dec 1885 in KWC Chapel; P 18 Dec 1887 at Bishopscourt; C of Rushen Dec 1885-89, then served short curacies in Doncaster, York and Sheffield; V of Jurby 14 Oct 1895 - Oct 1903; V of Foxdale Oct 1903 - June 1909; V of St Barnabas' 1 July 1909 - Dec 1912; V of Arbory Dec 1912 until death 19 June 1937 aged 79.

SUTTON, Revd Henry: TCD; D 1858; P 1860 (Bp Jackson of Lincoln); before coming to the Island had been P in C of St Augustine's, Everton, Liverpool; V of St Barnabas' 1870-2; V of St Cleopas, Liverpool 1872-9; Secretary of the CMS (of which he had been an associate secretary 1861-64) 1879.

SWALLOW, Revd Francis: D 30 Mar 1856 in Patrick Church; Chap of Foxdale Mar 1856 - June 1858; C of Hepworth, Dio York 1858.

TAGGART, Revd Hugh Selwyn (1): b 21 Mar 1874; son of Revd Thomas Arthur Taggart (2); grad Oxford; D 1899; P 1900 (Bp Talbot of Rochester); C of Emmanuel, Camberwell 1899-1901; after 3 further curacies he became R of Stowell Memorial Church, Salford (1905-09); V of St Matthew's 27 Apr 1909 - Oct 1926.

TAGGART, Revd Thomas Arthur (2): b Kansas, educated Washburn Coll; D 1873 (Bp of Kansas); P 1876 (Bp Selwyn of Lichfield); Assistant minister in Bp's Chapel, Topeka, Kansas 1873-5; came to England 1875; C of Ilkestone, nr Nottingham 1875-8; V of St Matthew's May 1878 - 15 Feb 1909; became Canon 1903; V of St Maurice, Horkstow, Dio Lincoln Feb 1909 - Oct 1911; died 1 June 1912 in London; buried High Barnet Cemetery 3rd June.

TALBOT, Revd Theophilus: D 1869; P 1871 (Bp SM); formerly a Methodist; C of German 1869-70; First Chap of St Olave's 1870-74; well known as an antiquary; died 12 Mar 1908.

TAUBMAN, Revd John: V of Lonan 20 June 1686 until death 16 Feb 1720 aged 59.

TAYLOR, Revd Christopher: D 1848; P 1849 (Bp Hampden of Hereford); Chap of Cronk y Voddy 11 Feb 1857-58 then returned to England.

THIMBLEBY, Revd Thomas: Sidney Sussex Coll Cantab; Chap of Castletown 1818 until death 18 Sept 1827; Master of Castletown GS 1818-23; died at Ballasalla, buried at Malew; M Hannah Gibson at Santan 25 June 1823.

THOMSON, Revd George: D 16 June 1889; P 24 May 1891 both in Bishopscourt Chapel; M Lucy Ward of Glasgow in St Barnabas' on 23 Apr 1891; Chap of St Luke's June 1889 - Sept 1891 then C of Ulverstone under Canon C. W. Bardsley, brother of Bp Bardsley.

TRACEY, Revd Frederick Francis: b 1829; Christ's Coll Cantab; D 1853; P 1857 (Bp Gilbert of Chichester); after several curacies he became R of St Pancras, Chichester 1865-72 and R of Beccles, Suffolk 1872-81; V of Rushen 1881 - 30 Sept 1885.

WAKEFORD, Revd Robert: TCD; D 1882; P 1884; (Bp Temple of Exeter); served 8 short curacies, one of which was assistant chaplain at Smyrna; V of Onchan 16 Sept 1908 - Oct 1933; returned to England.

WALKER, Revd William: b in Ballaugh 18 Feb 1679; D 11 Mar 1700; P 31 May 1702 (Bp SM); R of Ballaugh 10 June 1703 until death 18 June 1729 aged 50; buried in chancel of Ballaugh Church; VG 1712; shared Bp Wilson's imprisonment in Castle Rushen.

WARREN, Revd Mordaunt Laidlaw: D 20 Dec 1891; P 24 Dec 1893, both in St George's; the service in which he was ordained priest had to be postponed from 10.30 to 11 because of the Revd William Hawley's funeral; Chap of St Luke's Dec 1891 - Apr 1894.

WASHINGTON, Revd Marmaduke: Trinity Coll Cantab grad 1868; D 1869; P 1870 (Bp Gilbert of Chichester); C of Frant, Sussex 1869-71; C of St Michael's, Chester Square 1871-73; C of Sheffield Parish Church (Rowley Hill was his Vicar) 1874-76; V of Neen Savage, Salop 1876-77; V of St Thomas' 9 Nov 1877 - 31 Mar 1881; V of St George's, Tufnal Park, London and finally became a Canon of Norwich.

WATSON, Revd Robert William: D 1894; P 22 Dec 1895 (Bp SM); Chap of St Luke's 1894 - Feb 1899;

WATTLEWORTH, Revd Charles (1): son of Archdeacon Samuel Wattleworth (2) D 25 Sept 1698 in Bishopscourt Chapel (Bp Wilson's first ordination) as C of Andreas; V of Arbory 21 June 1726 until death 26 May 1728 aged 52; buried in St German's Cathedral; he seems not to have been very satisfactory and was once reproved for falsifying the register.

WATTLEWORTH, Revd Samuel (2): V of Kirk Michael 1672-77; V of Patrick 27 Mar 1677-91 and also V of German 5 July 1682 - July 1703; R of Andreas and Archdeacon 10 July 1703 until death 20 Dec 1718 aged 72; buried in St German's Cathedral; VG 1694-1703 and Diocesan Registrar 1684-94; [N.B. Patrick and German shared a Vicar at this time]; his wife, Jane Barton died 5 Aug 1721 and was buried with him.

WHALLEY, Revd William H.: b 12 Jan 1864; D Dec 1898; P 23 Dec 1900 in Bishopscourt Chapel; Chap of Dalby Dec 1898 - Dec 1903; V of Jurby 15 Dec 1903 - Dec 1905; V of the Mariners' Church in Gloucester 1905.

WHITE, Revd Henry Grattan: b Ireland 11 June 1819; D 24 Sept 1854 in Ballaugh Church (Bp Powys' first ordination); P 21 Dec 1855 in St Thomas'; C of Ballaugh Sept 1854-55; C of Andreas 1855-8; C of Ballaugh 1858-77; V of Santan Mar 1877 - Aug 1878; V of Maughold 17 Aug 1878 until death 31 May 1894.

WHITTAKER, Revd Frank R.: D 25 Jan 1910 in Bishopscourt Chapel; P 11 June 1911 in St Thomas'; Chap of St Luke's Jan 1910-13; then C of Faversham 1913-14; V of Little Waldingfield (Suffolk) 1914-18; C of Walkden Moor 1918-19; R of Rockhampton, Dio Gloucester 1919-32; V of Ullenhall with Aspley, Dio Coventry 1932-42; V of Garway with Orcop, Dio Hereford 1942-51.

WILKINSON, Revd James Seely: b 27 Jan 1827; St Edmund's Hall Oxford grad 1849; D 1850; P 1851; (Bp Gilbert of Chichester); 3 short curacies in England then a Missionary in Madras 1860-70; C of St Thomas' Wigan 1870-72; Chap of St Jude's July 1872 - Mar 1888; V of Lonan Mar 1888 - Apr 1895; V of Maughold 24 Apr 1895 until death 25 Jan 1898; his wife, Emma Jane, died in Lonan Vicarage 29 Apr 1891 aged 55 and was buried at Lonan 4 May.

WILKS, Revd James: D 1742; P 1743 (Bp SM); C of German 1742-44; V of German 1744-52; V of Kirk Michael 16 Mar 1752-71; R of Ballaugh 16 Sept 1771 until death 21 June 1777 aged 58; buried at Ballaugh; at various times he was Archdeacon's official, Episcopal Registrar and VG; M Margaret Woods, daughter of T. W. J. Woods (3) and had 2 daughters, Deborah and Elizabeth and a son, Mark, who was Governor of St Helena 1813-16 when Napoleon was in exile there, and who built Kirby Mansion on his return to the Island; his second wife was Elizabeth Christian of Ballamoar, Jurby, who died 8 Jan 1779.

WILLIAMS, Revd James George (1): D 1879; P 1879 (Bp Ellicott of Gloucester and Bristol); C of Christchurch, Bristol 1879-80; C of St Luke's, Ramsgate 1880-81; V of German 16 Apr 1881 - Sept 1889; V of Ranmoor, Nr. Sheffield 1889 until death 3 June 1913.

WILLIAMS, Revd Thomas H. (2): D 29 Mar 1904; P 10 Mar 1906, both in Bishopscourt Chapel; Chap of Dalby Mar 1904 - 11 Aug 1907; went to a curacy in Salford.

WILSON, Revd Henry (1): b 3 Apr 1850; D 1877; P 1878 (Bp Baring of Durham); C of Hetton le Hole, Dio Durham 1877-78; R of Kirklington, Dio Carlisle 1878-80; R of Pinxton, Derbyshire 1880-85; V of Holme, Dio Carlisle 1885-91; V of Jurby 23 Mar 1891 - 12 June 1895.

WILSON, Revd James (2): ordained in Peterborough; Chap of St Stephen's 2 May 1859-1860.

WOODS, Revd John (1): b 1695 son of John Woods (2) (V of Malew); D 1717 (Bp SM); C of Kirk Michael 1717-35; also V of German 20 Sept 1730 until death after illness of 2 years, on 17 April 1740.

WOODS, Revd John (2): V of German 1680-82; V of Malew 2 Dec 1696 until death 1739; Episcopal Registrar.

WOODS, Revd Thomas William Joseph (3): son of Revd John Woods (1); D 1746; P 20 Sept 1747 in Kirk Michael Church; Chap of Ballure and Schoolmaster Sept 1747-54 (the first ordained chaplain); V of Maughold 6 Aug 1754 - Dec 1768; V of Braddan 23 Dec 1768 until death Feb 1786.

APPENDIX II
PARISH CLERGY

Rectors of ANDREAS and Archdeacons of Man

				Curates		
	1696-	1700	Archippus KIPPAX	Charles WATTLEWORTH Sep1698-Jun 1726		
Jun	1700-Oct	1701	Christopher MARSDEN			
Jly	1703-Dec	1718	Samuel WATTLEWORTHa			
Oct	1719-May	1727	Robert HORROBIN	Edward MOORE	1726-	1735
Oct	1727-	1760	John KIPPAX	Robert BREW		1758
Jly	1760-Sep	1787	William MYLREA			
Nov	1787-	1803	Lord George MURRAY	Daniel MYLREA	1785-	1799
Jly	1803-May	1808	Lord Charles AYNSLEY			
Sep	1808-Mar	1814	George MURRAY			
Apr	1814-Mar	1832	Daniel MYLREA	J T CLARKE	1822-	1827
May	1832-Aug	1839	Benjamin PHILPOT	William DRURY	1834-	1841
Sep	1839-Feb	1844	John Cecil HALL	Daniel NELSON	1835-	1840
Apr	1844-Feb	1886	Joseph C MOORE	William HAWLEY	1847-	1852
				William KELLY	1852-	1855
				Henry G WHITE	1855-	1858
				Edward W KISSACK	May1862-	1869
				William DINWOODY	1869-	1875
Jun	1886-Jan	1895	Dr Joshua HUGHES-GAMES			
Feb	1895-May	1912	Hugh Stowell GILL	Archibald E CLARKE	1889-Jun 1892	
			George W GREGSON	Dec1896-Sep 1900		

Vicars of ARBORY

				Curates	
Apr	1680-	1712	Samuel ROBINSON		
Apr	1713-Mar	1723	Robert PARR	Edward MOORE	1725- 1726
Jun	1726-May	1728	Charles WATTLEWORTH		
Jly	1728-Jun	1748	John QUAYLE	John MOORE	Sep1746-Jly1748
Jly	1748-Sep	1791	John MOORE		
Oct	1791-Apr	1815	John CHRISTIAN	Hugh STOWELL	1791- 1797
Mar	1816-Jly	1859	Alexander GELLING		
Aug	1859-Jun	1875	John QUALTROUGH		
Jly	1875-Oct	1876	William DINWOODY		
Nov	1876-Feb	1880	Frederick GRIER		
Apr	1880-	1890	Charles LANGTON	Richard JONES	1881- 1882
Jan	1891-Oct	1912	John KEWLEY		
Dec	1912-Jun	1937	F W STUBBS		

Rectors of BALLAUGH

				Curates	
Sep	1687-Jun	1700	Henry LOWCAY	Thomas CHRISTIAN	1687- 1698
			Matthias CURGHEY		1698- 1703
Jun	1703-Jun	1729	William WALKER		
Oct	1729-Feb	1751	William BRIDSON	Robert CHRISTIAN	1750-Nov 1752
	1751-	1760	Philip MOORE	Henry CORLETT	1755- 1761
Feb	1761-Jan	1771	Matthias CURGHEY	William CLUCAS	1771- 1772
Sep	1771-Jun	1777	James WILKS		
Dec	1777-Aug	1801	Daniel GELLING		
Feb	1802-Apr	1814	Daniel MYLREA	Thomas STEPHEN	1802- 1809

Apr 1814-Oct 1835	Hugh STOWELL	John HARRISON	Oct 1807- 1814
May 1836-Nov 1876	Thomas HOWARD	John CANNELL	1832- 1835
	Thomas CAINE		1835- 1840
	Henry G WHITE		Sep 1854- 1855
	Henry G WHITE		1858- 1877
Feb 1877-Sep 1890	William KERMODE	S A P KERMODE	Jun 1890- Dec1890
Dec 1890-Jan 1897	Edward KISSACK		
Jan 1897-Jun 1934	Thomas R KNEALE		

Chaplains of BALLURE

1712-	1747	James KNIPE *	
Sep 1747-	1754	T W J WOODS	
Oct 1756-Jly	1761	Daniel GELLING	
Jly 1761-Oct	1771	John CRELLIN	
1771-	1783	John BRIDSON	
1708-	1785	Daniel MYLREA	
1785-	1789	John BRIDSON	
1789-	1790	Nicholas CHRISTIAN	
1790-	1803	Henry MADDRELL	
1803-	1804	William STURT	
1804-	1807	Robert CRAINE	
Oct 1807-	1809	Thomas HOWARD	
1809-	1816	Alexander GELLING	
1816-	1818	Bowyer HARRISON	
1818-Mar	1819	John KAYE	
1819-	1822	Philip CORLETT	then CHAPLAIN OF ST PAUL'S

*Schoolmaster, not ordained, but licensed by Bishop Wilson
Then see ST PAUL'S, RAMSEY

Chaplains of ST BARNABAS'   Curates

Dec 1832-Mar 1848	William CARPENTER
Jly 1848-Apr 1852	John ALCOCK
Jun 1852- 1869	Joseph Henry GRAY

Vicars of ST BARNABAS'

1869- 1870	Joseph Henry GRAY		
1870- 1872	Henry SUTTON		
1872- 1895	William T HOBSON	W STANLEY	Jun 1892- Mar1895
Mar 1896-Nov 1903	F J LANSDELL	John G POPE	1900- 1901
Jun 1904-Apr 1909	George E CRAVEN		
Jly 1909-Dec 1912	F W STUBBS		
1912- 1917	Henry SHENSTON		

Vicars of BRADDAN   Curates

Nov 1696-Apr 1704	Robert FLETCHER
Sep 1704-Oct 1733	John CURGHEY
Oct 1733-Jun 1750	John COSNAHAN
Oct 1750-Sep 1768	Joseph COSNAHAN

Dec 1768-Feb 1786	T J W WOODS	
Mar 1786-Aug 1786	Julius COSNAHAN	
1786-Dec 1791	John MOORE	
Jan 1792-Dec 1809	Robert QUAYLE	
Apr 1810-Apr 1836	Thomas HOWARD	Robert BROWN 1832- 1836
Apr 1836-Nov 1846	Robert BROWN	
Apr 1847-Sep 1887	William DRURY	Charles LANGTON 1873? 1878?
Feb 1888-Oct 1912	F J MOORE	Hugh KINRED 1881- 1882
		Blundell BROWNE 1882- 1884
		Charles H LEECE 1891- 1895
		William E DAVIES 1895- 1897
		George PACKER 1899- 1900
		John G POPE 1901- 1908

Rectors of BRIDE

Curates

1687- 1698	John CHRISTIAN	
Oct 1700- 1723	John PARR	
Mar 1723- 1729	Robert PARR	
May 1729-Oct 1729	William BRIDSON	
Nov 1729-Jan 1754	Matthias CURGHEY	
Jly 1754- 1760	William MYLREA	
Nov 1760-Jan 1783	Philip MOORE	Thomas CORLETT 1764- 1773
May 1783-Aug 1798	William CLUCAS	
1798- 1808	John CRELLIN	Thomas STEPHEN 1799- 1802
Nov 1808-Nov 1816	John BRIDSON	
Apr 1817-Jan 1828	Thomas CUBBON	John CANNELL 1828- 1832
May 1830-Oct 1847	John NELSON	
Nov 1847-Apr 1875	Daniel NELSON	
Jly 1875-Feb 1879	John QUALTROUGH	
Jun 1879- 1890	E W KISSACK	
Dec 1890-Dec 1894	Charles LANGTON	
Mar 1895-Apr 1913	Daniel COWLEY	
1913- 1919	Sidney BOTWOOD	
1919- 1941	James H CAIN	

Chaplains of CASTLETOWN

Curates

Apr 1701- 1719	James MAKON	
1719- 1725	Robert HORROBIN	
Aug 1727-Sep 1727	John KIPPAX	
1727-Oct 1754	William ROSS	
Jan 1758- 1807	Thomas CASTLEY	
Oct 1807-Apr 1818	Joseph BROWN	
1818-Sep 1827	Thomas THIMBLEBY	G S PARSONS -Nov 1827
Nov 1827-Apr 1855	George S PARSONS	John HOWARD 1842- 1847
Jly 1855-Jan 1896	Edward FERRIER	
Feb 1896- 1921	E H L (H E L) LOCKE	

Chaplains of CRONK Y VODDY

1852- 1854	John Fry GARDE	
1854- 1857	Charles James STEWART	

Feb	1857-	1858	Christopher TAYLOR
Jly	1858-Nov	1858	Henry HARDY
Mar	1859-Nov	1865	John CORLETT
	1866-May	1875	James EDMUNDS
Sep	1875-	1876	Edward COLLET
Oct	1876-	1879	Joseph KYTE
	1879-Jly	1880	H R FINNIS
	1880-Nov	1882	John B STEPHENSON
Dec	1892-	1895	Hugh KINRED
Apr	1895-Jun	1906	Alfred G BOWERMAN
Sep	1906-Apr	1908	W K SMYTH
Apr	1908-Nov	1910	Henry EAVES
Jan	1911-Jly	1913	Samuel SIDEBOTHAM

Chaplains of ST JAMES' DALBY

Mar	1839-	1840	William KERMODE
Jun	1840-	1858	George C STEPHEN
	1858-	1868	Charles HILL
	1868-	1872	Joseph KYTE
	1881-	1888	Charles M BARNES
	1888-	1890	C H BROCKLEBANK
	1890-	1890	H C PIGOT
	1890-Sep	1892	Norman KING
Aep	1892-Oct	1894	William CALLAHAN
Dec	1894-Jan	1896	E H L LOCKE
	1896-	1898	William H GIBSON
Dec	1898-Dec	1903	William WHALLEY
Mar	1903-Aug	1907	Thomas WILLIAMS
Aug	1907-Oct	1909	Hampton ROBINSON
Nov	1909-Nov	1910	Frederick SHIPPHAM
Apr	1911-	1914	Arthur P BRADSHAW

Chaplains of DHOON

	1840-	1850	William CHRISTIAN
	1850-	1852	Thomas FENTON
Jan	1853-	1855	Lloyd BRUCE
	1855-	1858	Samuel HILL
Aug	1858-	1869	Hugh Ashworth STOWELL
	1869-Nov	1872	Jonathan AKROYD
	1873-	1889	Stephen N HARRISON
	1889-	1891	Richard JONES
Feb	1891-	1907	William G ROLSTON
Sep	1907-Feb	1913	George W GREGSON

Chaplains of FOXDALE

Nov	1850-	1854	Joseph H KEWLEY
Mar	1856-Jun	1858	Francis SWALLOW
	1859-	1864	John LEECH
Dec	1864-	1875	Frederick J MOORE
	1876-	1877	William HART

1877-		1879	Thomas BATES
1879-Oct		1881	Eustace W COCHRANE

Vicars of FOXDALE

Oct	1881-	1900	Eustace W COCHRANE
Nov	1900-	1903	George PACKER
Oct	1903-Jun	1909	F W STUBBS
Sep	1909-	1917	Robert L CAIN

Chaplains of ST GEORGE'S

			Curates		
Oct 1781-Dec	1817	Charles CREBBIN	Thomas HOWARD	1809- 1810	
		John CHRISTIAN		1811-Dec1817	
Dec 1817-Jly	1827	John CHRISTIAN			
Aug 1827-May	1832	Benjamin PHILPOT			
May 1832-	1836	Thomas HOWARD			
Apr 1836-Dec	1846	Francis HARTWELL	William McGILL	? ?	
Nov 1847-	1859	Edward FORBES	William HAWLEY	1852- 1859	
Mar 1859-Dec	1877	William HAWLEY			
Jan 1878-Dec	1878	H Armstrong HALL			

Vicars of ST GEORGE'S

		Curates		
Dec 1878-May 1880	H Armstrong HALL			
May 1880-May 1891	J E Beauchamp GEORGE			
Sep 1891-Nov 1906	Robert Benjamin BARON	Alfred G BOWERMAN	Dec 1893- 1895	
	Robert D KERMODE		1896- 1898	
May 1907-Jun 1908	John CAMPBELL	Henry T DEVALL	1898- 1901	
Oct 1908- 1920	Robert D KERMODE	Mark W HARRISON	1908- 1911	

Vicars of GERMAN

			Curates		
Jly	1682-Jly 1703	Samuel WATTLEWORTH			
Jun	1710-Nov 1729	Matthias CURGHEY			
Sep	1730-Apr 1740	John WOODS	Thomas CHRISTIAN	1733-Mar	1734
Jly	1741-Apr 1742	John CRAINE	James WILKS	1742- 1744	
	1744- 1752	James WILKS			
Nov	1752-Dec 1754	Robert CHRISTIAN			
Apr	1758- 1760	Robert BREW			
Mar	1761-Nov 1801	Henry CORLETT			
Nov	1801-Jly 1838	James GELLING	Wiliam BELL		
Mar	1839-Jun 1880	John La Mothe STOWELL	CHRISTIAN*	Jun 1840-Aug1845	
			Henry DENING	1878- 1880	
Jun	1880- 1881	Henry DENING			
Apr	1881-Sep 1889	James G WILLIAMS	William BLAKENEY	1884- 1885	
		Alfred MORRIS		Dec 1890-May1892	
Mar	1890- 1895	Daniel S COWLEY	William H GIBSON	1894- 1895	
Apr	1895-Nov 1896	George ENSOR	Arnold J HOLMES	Dec 1895-Jun1897	
May	1897- 1907	Edward RAINBOW			
Jun	1907-Jun 1914	Walter LEWIS	Sidney BOTWOOD	1907- 1909	

* in charge of St John's

Chaplains of ST JOHN'S

1820-	1824	William GILL
1824-	1833	Samuel GELLING
Oct 1833-Oct	1834	William DRURY
1834-Apr	1845	John GELL
Apr 1845-Aug	1845	William Bell CHRISTIAN
Aug 1845-	1865	John Fry GARDE
Dec 1865-Feb	1909	John CORLETT
1909-	1913	Sidney BOTWOOD

Chaplains of ST JUDE'S

Nov 1841-Mar	1847	William DRURY
Oct 1847-Nov	1847	Daniel NELSON
Feb 1848-Aug	1859	John QUALTROUGH
Oct 1859-	1865	George BISHOP
1865-	1869	Benjamin P CLARKE
Aug 1869-Feb	1872	Edward W KISSACK
Jly 1872-Mar	1888	James S WILKINSON
Apr 1888-May	1893	Thomas R KNEALE
1893-Jun	1894	R B BLAKENEY
Jun 1894-Dec	1913	Adrian ROLLESTON

Vicars of JURBY

1698-	1747	John CHRISTIAN
1747-	1748	Samuel GELL
Aug 1751-Nov	1803	William CREBBIN
Dec 1803-Apr	1818	John NELSON
Apr 1818-Nov	1858	John HARRISON
Nov 1858-Aug	1875	Henry HARDY
Sep 1875-Dec	1878	F J MOORE
Jan 1879-	1891	Joseph BELLAMY
Mar 1891-Jun	1895	Henry WILSON
Oct 1895-Oct	1903	Frederick W STUBBS
Dec 1903-Dec	1905	William WHALLEY
Nov 1905-	1912	Henry SHENSTON
Feb 1913-	1931	George W GREGSON

Curates

William CREBBIN	1743-Aug1751
Henry HARDY	1850- 1858
Robert AIREY	1858- 1859
Arthur VESEY	Dec 1866-Jly1867

Chaplains of LAXEY

Apr 1856-	1859	Hugh Stowell GILL
1859-Jan	1861	Matthew PIERPOINT
Jan 1861-Dec	1878	Joseph BELLAMY
Dec 1879-May	1881	Robert G BREAREY
May 1881-May	1884	Theodore C CHAPMAN
1884-Aug	1885	Henry L JAMES
1885-Oct	1887	Claud READE
1887-Apr	1895	John Morris SPICER
May 1895-	1897	Charles H LEECE
1897-	1904	W E DAVIES
Sep 1904-	1916	William N GIBSON
1917-	1926	Robert CAIN

Vicars of LEZAYRE			Curates	
Jun 1686-Dec 1712		Robert PARR		
Apr 1714-Oct 1726		Henry ALLEN		
Jan 1727-Feb 1729		William BRIDSON		
1729-Feb 1761		Matthias CURGHEY		
Apr 1761-Oct 1772		John GILL		
Sep 1773-Jan 1803		Thomas CORLETT		
Mar 1803-Jly 1842		Henry MADDRELL	William KERMODE	1840- 1843
Dec 1842-Jun 1845		John Henry LA MOTHE		
Jly 1845-	1861	William Bell CHRISTIAN	William D CARTER	1847- 1849
1861-	1863	Edward SNEPP	Robert AIREY	1850- 1858
1863-	1869	Thomas HENRY		
1869-	1877	Wyndham M HUTTON		
Dec 1877-Dec 1898		Clement SHEPHEARD		
Jly 1879-Jan 1909		Arthur BRIDGMAN	George W GREGSON	1903- 1907
		James H CAIN		1907- 1909
May 1909-	1919	James H CAIN		
1920-	1939	Robert D KERMODE		

Vicars of LONAN			Curates	
Jun 1686-Feb 1720		John TAUBMAN		
1725-	1735	Robert RADCLIFFE	John ALLEN	May 1735
1735-	1735	Edward MOORE	Nathaniel CURGHEY	Mar 1735-Jly1753
VACANCY				
Jly 1753-Apr 1759		Nathaniel CURGHEY		
Apr 1759-Jan 1802		Samuel GELL		
Mar 1802-Apr 1814		Hugh STOWELL		
May 1814-	1817	Thomas CUBBON		
Apr 1817-Feb 1824		David HARRISON		
Apr 1824-Jun 1853		Joseph QUALTROUGH		
Oct 1853-Nov 1878		Thomas CAINE		
Dec 1878-Jan 1888		Frederick J MOORE		
Feb 1888-Apr 1895		James S WILKINSON		
Apr 1895-Feb 1940		John QUINE		

Chaplains of ST LUKE'S, BALDWIN		
Nov 1840-Oct 1853		Thomas CAINE
Nov 1853-	1856	Hugh Stowell GILL
Sep 1856-	1859	George DAWES
Mar 1859-	1864	Robert AIREY
1864-	1865	Benjamin P CLARKE
1866-	1868	W F DRURY
1869-	1869	Edward W KISSACK
Dec 1869-Apr 1880		Charles T LANGTON
Apr 1880-	1880	William APPLETON
Oct 1880-	1882	Samuel GASKING
1882-	1882	Hugh KINRED
1882-Jun 1889		Richard JONES
Jun 1889-Sep 1891		George THOMSON
Dec 1891-Apr 1894		Mordaunt L WARREN
1894-Feb 1899		Robert W WATSON

Aug	1899-Nov 1902	Samuel BUTTERTON			
Apr	1903- 1906	Francis ILES			
Sep	1906-Sep 1909	Robert L CAIN			
Jan	1910- 1913	Frank WHITTAKER			

Vicars of MALEW

			Curates		
Dec	1696- 1739	John WOODS			
Mar	1739-Jun 1758	John QUAYLE			
Apr	1759-Mar 1761	John GILL			
Jly	1761-Dec 1777	Daniel GELLING			
Mar	1778-May 1783	William CLUCAS			
Jun	1783-Apr 1817	David HARRISON			
Apr	1817-Mar 1830	William CHRISTIAN			
		William GILL			1827-Sep1830
			Gilmour HARVEY		1840- 1854
Sep	1830-Oct 1871	William GILL			
Jan	1872- 1895	Hugh S GILL	Thomas H GILL	Sep	1859-Jun1864
		Robert G BREAREY			1874- 1879
		R B BLAKENEY		Dec	1891- 1893
Apr	1895- 1919	John M SPICER	Henry SHENSTON	Dec	1902-Nov1905
		Samuel SIDEBOTHAM		Dec	1908-Jly1913

Chaplains of ST MARK'S

Jun	1772-Jun 1783	David HARRISON
	1783- 1786	John MOORE
	1786- 1809	John GELL
	1809- ?	Patrick KNEALE
	? 1814	John COTTIER
	1814- 1820	Edward CRAINE
	1820- 1827	William DUGGAN
Jly	1827-May 1864	John T CLARKE
Jun	1864-Aug 1865	Thomas H GILL
	1865-Jun 1874	Robert AIREY
	1874- 1876	John MITCHELL
Dec	1876-Feb 1878	Frederick GRANT
Jly	1878-Sep 1891	Benjamin LUPTON
Dec	1891-Sep 1896	Charles KROENIG
Jun	1897-Jun 1903	Arnold J HOLMES
Nov	1903-Nov 1904	Robert HALSTEAD
Mar	1905-Jly 1912	Henry HICKIN

Vicars of MAROWN

			Curates	
Jun	1686- 1701	Robert FLETCHER		
Sep	1701- 1713	Evan GILL		
Apr	1713-Jan 1727	William BRIDSON		
Sep	1728-Feb 1729	Matthias CURGHEY		
Mar	1734- 1752	Thomas CHRISTIAN		
Feb	1753-Sep 1779	John CHRISTIAN	William CLUCAS	1767- 1771
Nov	1780-Jan 1799	Thomas CHRISTIAN	John BRIDSON	1788- 1799
Sep	1799-Nov 1808	John BRIDSON		

Mar 1809-	1827	Thomas STEPHEN
Dec 1827-Mar	1862	William DUGGAN
Apr 1862-Jun	1869	Robert W AITKEN
Jun 1869-Sep	1903	Benjamin P CLARKE
Dec 1903-Jan	1934	Archibald E CLARKE

Chaplains of ST MATTHEW'S   Curates

Sep 1708-	1714	Samuel ROBINSON			
1714-	1716	Peter LANCASTER			
Nov 1716-	1732	Anthony HALSALL			
1732-	1736	Thomas BIRKETT			
1736-	1765	Philip MOORE			
1765-	1769	Charles CREBBIN			
1770-Dec	1791	Robert QUAYLE			
1791-	1797	Nicholas CHRISTIAN			
1797-	1802	Hugh STOWELL			
1802-Nov	1810	John KEWLEY			
1810-	1816	Joseph QUALTROUGH			
1817-May	1832	Robert BROWN			
Jun 1832-Mar	1835	John La Mothe STOWELL			
May 1835-Jun	1835	Samuel GELLING			
Jun 1835-Jun	1873	John CANNELL	Edward BRAILSFORD	Jly	1847-Feb1848
			Samuel SIMPSON	Jan	1851-May1851
May 1878-	1879	Thomas A TAGGART			

Vicars of ST MATTHEW'S

1879-Feb	1909	Thomas A TAGGART	Archibald E CLARKE	
Apr 1909-Oct	1926	Hugh S TAGGART		1884- 1886

Vicars of MAUGHOLD

Jun 1666-Mar	1726	Thomas ALLEN
Jan 1727-	1746	Henry ALLEN
Jun 1746-Apr	1754	Thomas ALLEN
Aug 1754-Dec	1768	T W J WOODS
Mar 1769-Apr	1814	Thomas CUBBON
Apr 1814-Apr	1818	John E HARRISON
Apr 1818-Apr	1871	Bowyer HARRISON
Jun 1871-Feb	1877	William KERMODE
Mar 1877-May	1878	Gilmour HARVEY
Aug 1878-May	1894	Henry G WHITE
Apr 1895-Jan	1898	James S WILKINSON
Jun 1898-	1908	Robert D KERMODE
Oct 1908-	1920	John G POPE

Vicars of KIRK MICHAEL   Curates

Jly 1686-Jan	1717	Henry NORRIS	
		John WOODS	1717- 1735
May 1735-Jly	1735	John ALLEN	
Nov 1735-Sep	1751	Edward MOORE	

Mar 1752-	1771	James WILKS	William CLUCAS		1772- 1778
Nov 1771-	1798	John CRELLIN	John CLAGUE		1772- 1782
1799-	1802	Daniel MYLREA			
Mar 1802-Nov 1808		Nicholas CHRISTIAN			
Nov 1808-Feb 1818		Thomas HARRISON			
Apr 1818-Jan 1860		Joseph BROWN	Daniel NELSON		1840- 1847
			Edward QUALTROUGH		1853- 1856
			Joseph BELLAMY		Jun1861-Dec 1878
Feb 1860-Jun 1864		James B KELLY			
Jun 1864-Mar 1874		William INGRAM			
Jun 1874-Aug 1878		Robert AIREY			
Nov 1878-Nov 1882		Ernest B SAVAGE			
Nov 1882-Dec 1893		William HAWLEY	John M SPICER		May1885-1887
			James GARDNER		1888- 1889
			Stanley KERMODE		1891- 1892
		Alfred MORRIS			May1892-Mar1894
Mar 1894-May 1913		Alfred MORRIS			

Curates-in-charge North Ramsey LEZAYRE

Curates

1847-	1848	W D CARTER
1848-	1850	Thomas MILLINGTON
1850-	1858	Robert AIREY
1858-	1861	William CLAY
1861-	1863	J J S MOORE
1863-	1865	Thomas LEE
1865-	1866	George PATON
1866-	1867	Henry BARFF
1867-	1870	Walter AWDREY

Chaplains of ST OLAVE'S

	1870-	1874	Theophilus TALBOT
	1874-	1875	Edward CURWEN
Jly	1876-	1878	Charles BUCKLEY
	1878-Oct	1879	Robertson BARDELL
	1879-Apr	1881	William MORRIS

Vicars of ST OLAVE'S

Apr 1881-Mar 1896	William MORRIS		
May 1896-Apr 1903	Charles HOPKINS	George PACKER	Dec 1896- 1899
Jun 1903-May 1904	A K DEARDEN		
Jun 1904-Dec 1917	William E DAVIES		

Vicars of ONCHAN

Curates

Jun 1686-Sep 1701	Evan GILL	
Sep 1701-Mar 1748	William GELL	Samuel GELL 1744- 1747
Mar 1748- 1759	Samuel GELL	
Apr 1759-Mar 1798	Thomas QUAYLE	
Apr 1798-Dec 1809	John CANNELL	

Mar 1810-Apr 1847	Edward CRAINE	
Jly 1847-Feb 1892	John HOWARD	
May 1892-Feb 1904	Stanley KERMODE	
Mar 1904-May 1908	Walmsley STANLEY	
Sep 1908-Oct 1933	Robert WAKEFORD	

Vicars of PATRICK

Curates

Jun 1703- 1729	Matthias CURGHEY		
Feb 1729-Oct 1769	Robert RADCLIFFE		
Oct 1769-Jun 1808	Evan CHRISTIAN		
Nov 1808-Dec 1811	Nicholas CHRISTIAN		
Jan 1812-Jun 1827	John COTTIER	Thomas KEWLEY	1819- 1827
Jly 1827-Apr 1842	Thomas STEPHEN		
Oct 1842-Nov 1865	Archibald HOLMES		
Dec 1865-Sep 1877	John F GARDE		
Dec 1877-Nov 1882	William HAWLEY	A J MAKEPEACE	1890- 1895
Dec 1882-Jan 1897	Hugh DAVIDSON	Hugh KINRED	Apr 1895- 1897
Jan 1897- 1921	Hugh KINRED		

Chaplains of ST PAUL'S, RAMSEY

Aug 1822-Oct 1825	Philip CORLETT		
1825- 1842	Archibald HOLMES		
Oct 1843- 1871	William KERMODE	James SPARROW	c.1860
		George PATON	1866- 1871
Jly 1871-Jan 1900	George PATON	E C PATON	1894-May1901
Jly 1901- 1904	Henry T DEVALL	A S NEWTON	1901- 1901

Vicars of ST PAUL'S

1904- 1911	Henry T DEVALL	
1911-Aug 1946	Mark W HARRISON	

Vicars of RUSHEN

Curates

Jun 1691-Oct 1700	John PARR		
Jun 1703- 1713	Matthias CURGHEY	Thomas CHRISTIAN	1703- 1711
1713- 1727	Thomas CHRISTIAN		
Mar 1729-Mar 1739	John QUAYLE	Nicholas CHRISTIAN	Sep 1734-Jun1748
Jun 1748-Mar 1782	Nicholas CHRISTIAN		
May 1782-Mar 1816	John CLAGUE		
Apr 1816-Mar 1824	Joseph QUALTROUGH		
Apr 1824-Feb 1859	William CORRIN	Benjamin P CLARKE	Sep 1855- 1864
Mar 1859- 1871	Hugh Stowell GILL	Frederick GRANT	Nov 1872- 1876
Feb 1872-May 1879	Edward KISSACK	H R FINNIS	Sep 1878- 1879
Jly 1879-Jun 1881	Arthur ALLWORK	Blundell BROWNE	May 1880- 1882
1881-Sep 1885	Frederick F TRACEY		
Oct 1885-Apr 1887	Charles DAWES	F W STUBBS	Dec 1885- 1889
1887-May 1893	Blundell BROWNE	Charles H LEECE	1889- 1891
	R H BELLAMY		c.1891
May 1893-Jan 1897	Thomas R KNEALE	Adrian ROLLESTON	Jun 1892-Jun1894
Apr 1897-Jun 1927	Charles H LEECE	A K DEARDEN	1898- 1903

Vicars of SANTAN				Curates		
Jly	1691-Apr 1724		John COSNAHAN			
			John COSNAHAN		?	1731
Jly	1731-Aug 1764		Paul CREBBIN			
Feb	1765-	1769	Thomas CUBBON			
	1769-Dec 1817?		Charles CREBBIN			
Apr	1818-	1827	John NELSON	John CANNELL	1824-	1828
Apr	1827-Apr 1835		Thomas KEWLEY			
Jun	1835-Nov 1865		Samuel GELLING			
Nov	1865-Mar 1877		Gilmour HARVEY			
Mar	1877-Aug 1878		Henry G WHITE			
				Archibald E CLARKE	1886-	1889
Aug	1878-Nov 1889		Robert AIREY	John KIRKBY	1889-	1890
Feb	1890-Jan 1891		John KIRKBY			
	1891-	1931	Richard JONES			

Chaplains of ST STEPHEN'S SULBY

Nov	1839-Feb 1848		John QUALTROUGH
Feb	1848-	1849	Edward BRAILSFORD
Aug	1849-	1851	Joseph WARD
May	1851-	1853	Matthew THOMPSON
	1853-	1853	Edward QUALTROUGH
Dec	1853-	1855	William THOMPSON
May	1855-	1858	William KELLY
Apr	1858-	1859	John CORLETT
May	1859-	1860	James WILSON
	1860-	1862	Robert AITKEN
	1862-	1865	Samuel WALKER
	1865-	1878	J E PATTISON
Sep	1878-Feb 1882		William CANTON
Jan	1883-	1885	Charles BELL
Jly	1885-	1889	William BLAKENEY
	1889-Dec 1890		Sidney SWAN
Apr	1891-Apr 1892		James GARDNER
Jun	1892-Dec 1903		Archibald E CLARKE
Mar	1904-May 1906		Percy BROWN
Jun	1906-	1929	Alfred G BOWERMAN

Chaplains of ST THOMAS'   Curates

	1849-	1851	William D CARTER
May	1851-Nov 1861		Samuel SIMPSON

Church closed during dispute

Vicars of ST THOMAS'

Jly	1872-Sep 1877	F N B HUTTON		
Nov	1877-Mar 1881	Marmaduke WASHINGTON		
Jun	1881-Oct 1882	John N QUIRK		
Dec	1882-Apr 1914	Ernest B SAVAGE	Blundell BROWNE	1884- 1887
			James GARDNER	1889- 1891
			Hampton ROBINSON	Oct 1909-?

Index

A

Academic Fund 22, 118
Act of Settlement, 1703 5
Adams, Alfred
    106, 109, 110, 111, 113, 114, 115, 116, 117, 151
  Clerk of the Roles 159
Additional Curates Society 192
Airey, Robert
  Chaplain 143, 145, 149
  Vicar 149, 174, 178, 192
Aitken, Robert Wesley 146, 205
  Chaplain 155
  Vicar 146
Akroyd, Jonathan, Chaplain 138
Albert, Prince Consort 92
Albert Tower 92
All Saints' Church, Douglas
  building of 203
  laying of foundation stone by Mrs Straton 203
Allan Street Mission Hall, Douglas 188
Allcock, John, Vicar 95
Allen, Henry (1), Vicar 23, 26
Allen, John (2), Vicar 27
Allen, Thomas (3), Vicar 26
Allen, Thomas (4), Vicar 26
Allwork, Arthur, Vicar 176, 212
Anderson, Daniel 169
Anderson, Doctor 158
Andreas 16, 47, 58, 66, 82, 94, 165, 183, 199, 215
  building of new church 58
  choir 131
  church
    confirmation at 126
    dedication of gifts, by Bishop Bardsley 183
    major restoration of 130
    new organ installed, 1898, 200
  consecration of new burial ground, 1891, 183
  parish population in 1871, 131
  public meeting, 1884 162
  rectory 67
Anglo-Catholic principles 112
Anglo-Catholic training 112
Apocrypha 34
Appellate Jurisdiction Act of 1867, 115
Appleton, William, Chaplain 172
Arbory 17, 32, 38, 42, 47, 59, 68,
    84, 94, 131, 165, 183, 200, 215
  Ballacross, well 17
  Balladoole Schoolhouse, building of, 1893. 200
  building of new church 36
  chapel 200

  church 28
    building of tower, 1915, 216
    consecration of new burial ground 165
    discontinuation of Manx Services 132
    repairs to, 1886, 165
  parish population in 1871, 132
Archbishop of Canterbury 1, 18, 32
Archbishop of York 1, 7, 8, 15, 48, 78, 116
  Court 189
Archdeacons 15, 17, 62, 70
Archdeacon's Court 127
Association for the Improvement of Church Music 123
Athol Street Day School, Douglas 122
Athol Street Sunday School, Douglas 122
Atholl, Duke of 25, 62
  1st Duke of Atholl 65
  2nd Duke of Atholl, James Murray
    13, 16, 21, 29, 36, 38
  3rd Duke of Atholl 32, 46, 98
    Dowager, wife 41, 46
    sale of Island to British Crown 32
  4th Duke of Atholl
    42, 43, 44, 47, 48, 52, 58, 59, 63, 64
    offer to commute tithes 55
    transfer of tithes 58
  5th Duke of Atholl 65
Auckland, Bishop Robert John Eden
    90, 91, 101, 108, 109, 113,
    115, 120, 121, 139, 142, 149
  appointed inspectors of parish schools 93
  attended prizegiving, King William's College 93
  Chaplain to King William IV 92
  Chaplain to Queen Victoria 92
  consecrated at Whitehall Chapel 92
  donations to Church building funds 93
  enthroned at St Mary's, Castletown 92
  granted licence to Samuel Simpson 107
  member of Tynwald and House of Lords 92
  Patron, Scripture Readers Association 93
  services to education 94
  Vice-Patron, Scripture Readers Association 93
Awdrey, Walter, Curate 149
Aynsley, Lord Charles, Archdeacon 47, 52

B

Baldwin 153
  Chaplain's house required 122
  grants to 122
Baldwin Reservoir, building of 206
Baldwin, Revd W. 117
Balfour, Henry 11
Ballachurry 2

Ballacrine, Santon 154
Ballafletcher, Braddan 96
Ballaglass Glen 138
Ballajora Chapel 147
Ballakilley 21, 32, 45, 50
Ballakillingan 23
Ballakilpheric Mission Room 213
Ballasalla Church, Malew
  damaged by gales, 1895, 207
Ballaugh 2, 17, 37, 42, 47, 59, 64, 68,
    84, 94, 132, 165, 185, 200, 216
  church
    additions to 37
    completion of improvements 185
    improvements 42
    major restoration, 1893, 200
    Manx Services 132
    repairs to church 94
    services in Manx 37
  church hall
    laying of foundation stone, 1909, 216
  improvements to both churches, 1879, 166
  old church 42, 132
  parish population in 1871, 132
  parish population in 1891, 186
  rectory 42
  reopening of Ballaugh Old Church 166
  shore 42
Ballure 37, 47, 59
  Chapel of Ease 59
  church 19, 42
Balnahowe 77
Banks, John 75
Bardell, Robertson, Chaplain 174
Bardsley, Bishop John Wareing 180, 194
  committee to review dividing of German 188
  consecration of, 1887, 180
  death of, 1904, 183
  enthroned at St Mary's, Castletown 180
  gift of prayer desk, Ballaugh Church 200
  invitation to nonconformist ministers 182
  presentation of clock to Kirk Michael 191
  presentation to drivers and stokers 183
  proposal for Bishopscourt as a Theological College 181
  reception of President of Primitive Methodist Soc. 182
  respected by Methodists 181
  translated to Carlisle 182
  Vice-President, Church of England Temperance Soc.
    181
Bardsley, James, Canon 180
Barff, Curate Henry 149
Barlow, H. E. T. 195
Barnes, Charles Marston, Chaplain 167, 187
Baron, Robert Benjamin, Vicar 183, 188, 194, 206, 217
Barrow, Bishop 13, 22, 65
Barrule 24
Barry, Messrs of Liverpool 177
Bates, Thomas, Chaplain 139, 167
Bayliss, John, Vicar 88

Bell, Charles, Chaplain 178
Bellamy, Joseph
  Chaplain 113, 137, 142, 171, 172
  Curate 142
  Vicar 171, 189
Bellamy, R. H., Curate 192
Bennet, Revd Thomas 2
Best, W. T. 179
Betham, Elizabeth 44
Big Tree House, Castletown 50
Binder, Revd W. J. 190
Birkett, Chaplain Thomas 26
Birley, Mary 151
Bishop Barrow's Fund 81
Bishop, George, Chaplain 141
Bishop Wilson Theological College 181, 205
Bishops 32, 33, 70
  1st Manx Bishop
    Hamond (1100) 214
  2nd Manx Bishop
    Michael (1195) 214
  3rd Manx Bishop
    William Russell (1348) 214
  4th Manx Bishop
    Donkan, John (1374) 214
  5th Manx Bishop
    Drury, Thomas Wortley (1907-1911) 214
Bishop's Charge 114
Bishops of
  Carlisle 29
  Chester 1, 29, 41, 112, 113
  Durham 41, 156
  Ely 41, 78
  Hereford 78
  Lincoln 29, 78
  London 81
  Norwich 1
  Ripon 81
  Rochester 156
  St David's 46
Bishop's Temporalities Act (1878) 162
  becomes law 130
Bishopscourt 6, 13, 18, 38, 41, 46,
    63, 75, 112, 114, 124, 127
  attack on, 1825, 57
  chapel 12, 13, 30, 36, 40, 123
    choir formed 31
    consecrated, 1858, 105
    Family Prayers 15
    ordinations in Bardsley's time 182
  clergy gathering at 111
  dilapidated state 41
  farm 4, 30
  fire, 1893, 195
  glen 36
  Improvement Bill, 1893, 195
  mortgage, extension of 158
  mortgage on 156
  need for completion of repairs 156

poor state of repair 52
renovation to house and grounds 157
reopening of Chapel, 1878, 157
repairs and improvements, 1787, 46
ruinous state 2
windows broken, 1867, 109
Bissett, Captain 56
Blakeney, R. B. (1), Chaplain 205
Blakeney, William (2), Chaplain 178, 192
Bligh, Captain 44
Bluett, Mr 88
Botwood, Sidney B., Chaplain 217
Bowerman, Alfred George
Chaplain 213, 220
Curate 202
Bowerman, Amy 220
Bowstead, Bishop James 67, 72, 78
Diocesan Association, formation of 79
enthroned, St Mary's, Castletown 78
raising of educational standards 79
Bowstead, James
Bishop of Lichfield 90
Boyde, Henry 202
Boyde, Philip 200
Braddan 3, 19, 25, 37, 42, 48, 59,
68, 69, 84, 95, 114, 117, 134,
136, 166, 186, 201, 216
church 12, 119
consecration of new churchyard, 1849, 96
consecration of new churchyard, 1885, 166
inadequate churchyard 84
open air services 201
organ fund-raising bazaar 201
raising of money for new organ, 1892, 201
thefts and vandalism 85
church hall
laying of foundation stone, 1911, 216
new church
consecration of 135
erection and destruction of tower and spire 166
foundation stone laid 135
new flooring, 1901, 201
opposition 136
proposed 135
subscriptions to building fund 136
old church
major restoration, 1774, 42
parish population in 1903, 201
parishioners meeting, 1842
refusal to allow corpses in church 84
population in 1868
including Douglas 134
separation from Douglas 108
Sunday School 201
vestry 118, 120
vicars 107, 119, 120
Bradshaw, Arthur P., Chaplain 217
Brailsford, Edward, Chaplain 102
Bray, Dr Thomas 3

Brearey, Robert, Chaplain 171
Brenainn 19
Brew, Robert, Vicar 38
Bride 19, 20, 22, 32, 37, 42,
48, 59, 69, 85, 96, 166, 187, 201, 216
building of new church 136
church
gallery given by Bishop Hildesley, 1772, 42
improvements to lighting 187
laying of foundation stone 136
new organ opened, 1882, 167
new church
funding 136
parish
population in 1871 137
population in 1892 202
Bridgman, Arthur Alexander, Vicar
172, 174, 178, 205, 206, 218
application to close old churchyard 189
paper at fifth Diocesan Conference, 1884 161
proposal for sale of glebe land 163
reintroduced Hymns Ancient and Modern 172
Bridgman, Bishop 2, 18
Bridgman, Mrs Ellen 218
Bridson, Christopher of Ballavervane (3) 39
Bridson, John (1)
Chaplain 42, 47
Curate 50
Rector 48
Vicar 50
Bridson, Thomas 118, 119
Bridson, William (2)
Vicar 8, 11, 17, 19, 21, 22, 23, 25, 50
Brindley and Foster 201
Brine, Thomas 52
British and Foreign Bible Society 34, 66
British Hotel, Douglas 63
Brocklebank, C. H., Chaplain 187
Brown, Ann 49
Brown, Joseph (1)
Vicar 48, 56, 59, 60, 61, 78, 141
church building 61
collection of funds - new vicarage 88
Episcopal Registrar 78
Brown, Percy H., Chaplain 213
Brown, Robert 148
Brown, Robert (3) 49
Chaplain 61
principal of Douglas Grammar School 88
Vicar 69, 74, 84, 109
death of 91, 120
Manx speaker 69
Brown, T. E. 49, 189
'Betsy Lee', Parson Gale 62
Manx National Poet 49
offer of Archdeaconry 199
Browne, Blundell, Vicar 192, 212
Bruce, Lloyd, Chaplain 138
Buchan, Lady 135

Buchan, Sir John 84
Buckley, Charles, Chaplain 150, 174
buggane 19
Burials Act, 1881, 153, 160
Butler, Weeden 33
Butterton, Samuel R., Chaplain 206

C

Cadman, Henry 150
Cain, James H. (2), Vicar 218
Cain, Robert L. (1)
  Chaplain 206
  Vicar 217, 218
Caine, Philip (3) 72
Caine, Thomas
  Chaplain 87, 100
    Manx services 72
    Mrs Caine, death of 143
  Vicar 100, 142, 143
Calcraft, Mrs 46
Caley, Thomas 165
Caley, William 99
Callahan, William, Chaplain 202
Callister, Esther 87
Callister, John 87
Callow, Daniel 96
Callow, James 136, 138
Callow, Mrs 191
Callow, Robert 45
Callow, T., lawyer 111
Cameron, Captain 140
Campbell, H., Curate
  paper at third Diocesan Conference, 1881, 160
Campbell, John, Vicar 217
Cannell and Corrin 207
Cannell, James 210
Cannell, John (1), Vicar 150
  fluent Manx speaker 51
Cannell, John (2), Chaplain 88, 101, 110, 121, 146, 172
  dismissal of 120, 121
  dispute with Bishop Powys 106
  principal of Douglas Grammar School 88
Cannell, Lizzie 203
Canonry of Wilford 63
Canons - Ten 5
Canton, William, Chaplain 178
Carpenter, William
  Chaplain 68, 69
    departure of 115
    founder of institutions for the poor and sick 69
  Vicar 67, 79, 84, 86, 93, 98, 138
    departure of, 1848, 94
    founded Christ Church, Maughold 95
    founded House of Industry 95
    founded St Barnabas' Schools 95
    founded St Thomas' Church 95
    proposed building of St Thomas' 102
  Carter, William D.

Chaplain 96, 103
  Curate 149
Castle Mona Hotel, Douglas 114
Castle Rushen 8, 11, 33, 70
  treatment of prisoners 7
Castletown 1, 21, 37, 41, 43, 48, 59,
    70, 85, 96, 137, 167, 187, 202, 217
  chapel 8, 21
  church
    building of 3
    Caley, Philip, first organist 48
    new altar, 1892 202
  deanery 170
  Grammar School 18, 21
  Poor Relief Society 137
  population in 1851, 70
  population in 1871, 137
  separate parish, 1921, 217
Castley, Thomas
  Chaplain 43, 48
    Master, Castletown Grammar School 37
Catechism 34
Catechism in Manx, 1707, 5
Cathedral Endowment Fund 171
Catholics 15
Catley, Richard 102
Chancery Court 10, 46, 176
Chancery Court, 1881, 175
Chapel Royal, Whitehall 41, 81
Chaplains
  appointment of, 1781-1847, 120
  request, division of Douglas and Braddan parishes 96
Chapman, Caroline Mary 156
Chapman, Theodore, Chaplain 171
Chapter Court 13
  Peel, 1888, 188
  Ramsey 189
Chapter Quest 10, 33, 39
Chibbyr Vreeshey 21
Children's Special Service Mission 215
cholera epidemic
  1831, 64
  1832, 62, 70, 77
  1849, 92
  1853, 101, 102
Christ Church, Laxey
  building of 142
Christchurch, Oxford 52
Christian, Daniel 150
Christian, Deemster 54, 63, 79
Christian, Deemster John 143
Christian, Evan (1), Vicar 40, 44, 51
Christian, Ewan 100, 102, 130, 136, 138, 142, 207
Christian, James 23
Christian, John (2), Vicar 14, 21, 22
Christian, John (3), Vicar 60, 70, 120
Christian, John (4), Vicar 47, 59
Christian, John (5), Vicar 15, 25, 35, 39, 44
Christian, Major General John 27

Christian, Nicholas (6)
  Vicar 28, 35, 40, 44, 61
  Vicar General 48
Christian, Nicholas (7)
  Chaplain 47, 50
  Vicar 50, 51
Christian, Robert (8), Vicar 22, 38
Christian, Susanna 143
Christian, Thomas (10), Vicar 44, 50
  translated Milton's 'Paradise Lost' to Manx 44
  unfrocked, 1799 50
Christian, Thomas (10a), Vicar 28
Christian, Thomas (10b), Vicar 28
Christian, Thomas (9), Vicar 15, 23, 25
Christian, William (11), Vicar 61, 72
  complaints against 61
Christian, William (13), Sumner General 11
Christian, William (14), Vicar 12
Christian, William Bell (12)
  Chaplain 98, 138
  Vicar 86, 142, 148, 149, 152
    opened Chapel of Ease in barn, Ramsey 99
Church Act
  1880, appointment of Parish Clerks 100
  1895, Bishopscourt as Pro-Cathedral 105, 198
Church Association 157
Church Building Society 64
Church Commissioners
    100, 115, 116, 117, 122, 159, 197, 211
  proposed extension of powers 108
Church Courts 7, 8, 9, 10, 11, 12
Church Enlarging Society 64
Church Missionary Society 188, 193, 205
Church of England Temperance Society 201
Churchwardens 13, 134
  duties of 3, 123
  Onchan
    Cadman 151
    Christian 151
    Quine (2) 151
Churchyards, state of 125
Circuit or Chapter Court 33
Civil Courts 11
Claghbane estate, Ramsey 89
Clague (2), Doctor 151
Clague, Doctor John 215
Clague, John
  Curate 44
  Vicar 44, 51, 62
    preservation of Manx Gaelic 44
    translation of Psalms into Manx 45
Clague, Mr 212
Clarke, John Thomas (2), Chaplain 74
Clarke, Archibald Edward (3)
  Chaplain 205, 213
  Curate 178
  Vicar 208, 218
    induction of, 1903, 209
Clarke, Benjamin Philpot (1)
  Canon
    gift of land for church hall 209
  Chaplain 141, 143, 195
    initiated adult evening classes 141
  Curate 153
  installed as Canon, 1895 198
  Vicar 146, 167, 172, 188, 208
    elected as Proctor, 1895, 208
Clarke, H. S. 209
Clarke, John Thomas (2)
  Chaplain 72, 73, 74, 87, 100
    building of Chaplain's house 100
    founder of country library and post office 87
    founder of schools for adults 73
    improvements to St Mark's Parish 100
    legal battle to recover land 87
    Manx speaker 145
  editor, Kelly's Manx Dictionionary 145
  Vicar 144
    resignation 145
Clay, William, Curate 149
Clergy Meeting 1875 130
Clergy Relief Fund 198
Clergy Temporalities Act, 1884, 162
Clergy Temporalities Bill, 1885 162
Clerical Endowment Fund 130
Clucas, Thomas and Margaret 165
Clucas, William
  Rector 48
  Vicar 44, 50
  Vicar General 41
Cochran, Eustace William
  Chaplain 167
  Vicar 167, 187, 203
Cochrane, Basil, Governor 13, 16, 32, 36, 37
Colby Mission Church 165, 200
collapse of church discipline 31
Collet, Edward, Chaplain 138
Collins, Reginald 214
Collister, Robert, Sexton 140
Collister's Croft, Santon 154
Commissioners for Woods and Forests 142, 147
Commissioners of Northern Lights 220
Confirmation, for Parishes 114
Consecration Deed 120, 145
Consistory Court 8, 12, 13, 33, 74
Convocation 5, 6, 34, 110, 111, 114, 115, 189
  1703, 5
  1721, 8
  1722, 8, 11
  1731,
    responsibility for parish library 3
  1755, 33
  1758,
    limited use of English in services 33
  1861, 148
  1863, 121
  1865
    postponement of 123

1866, 123, 124
1868, 110
1869,
  Bishop's Charge to 116
1871, 126
1872, 126
1873, 127
1874, 127
1878, 158
1879, 158
1880,
  collection of money for Churches and Parsonages
  159
1882,
  no charge by Bishop 160
1883
  no proper accommodation for clergy, St John's 161
1884, 161
1885, 162
1886,
  admittance of press for first time 163
1888, 181
1889,
  approval of Bardsley's prayer 182
1890, 182
1891, 182
  Election of Vicar Gill (2) as Proctor 190
1892, 195
1893,
  Bishop Straton's desire to create four Canonries 197
1894,
  urge for clergy to have parsonages surveyed 197
1895,
  advice to clergy, re publishing of accounts 198
  tribute to Hughes-Games by Bishop Straton 199
1902,
  use of lay readers 198
1903, 198
  minimum stipends 198
1904,
  tribute to Hughes-Games by Bishop Straton 199
1910,
  Rector Cowley, elected Proctor 216
Bishop's Charge to 115
special, 1879
  Bishopscourt Dilapidations Act 158
Convocation Day 115
Cook, John 48
Cooper, James 207
Corlett (5)
  Vicar General 107, 118, 138, 148
Corlett, Henry (1), Vicar 16, 21, 35, 36, 38, 43, 48
  defiance of Mason's ban on Wesley 42
  preached at St John's Chapel 97
  preaching of Wilson's Manx sermons 43
  unfriendliness to Methodists 48
Corlett, John (2), Chaplain 138, 141, 171, 205, 208, 217
  benefactor of St Stephen's, Sulby 155
  Diocesan Inspector of Sunday Schools 188

Government Chaplain 188
Corlett, Philip (3)
  Chaplain 59
  Vicar 62
Corlett, Thomas 68
Corlett, Thomas (4)
  Parish Clerk 38
  Vicar 34, 43
    corrector of proofs for Manx Bible 44
    criticism of his record keeping 49
    excommunication, 1780, 44
Corlett, Thomas, Sumner General 10
Corn Laws 55
Corneil ny Killagh 75
Cornish, Dorothy 28
Corrin, William, Vicar 62, 76, 102, 105, 113
Corris, Caesar 169
Cosnahan, Deemster 55
Cosnahan, Hugh, MHK (5) 39
Cosnahan, John (1)
  Vicar 20, 28
  Vicar General 25, 40
Cosnahan, Joseph (3), Vicar 20, 35, 37
Cosnahan, Julius (4)
  Chaplain 43
  Vicar 48
Cosnahan, Revd John (2) 12
Cottier, James 218
Cottier, John
  Chaplain 61
  Vicar 51, 76
    unfrocked for drunkenness 62
Countess of Derby
  rebellion against 1651 2
Court of Chancery 13
Court of Enquiry, 1824, 60
Courtney, William 58
Cowell, James 177
Cowell, John 41, 42
Cowle 97
Cowle, C. H., Captain of Andreas Parish 162
Cowle, James 158, 196
Cowley, Daniel Scurr
  Rector 205, 213, 216
  Vicar 188, 202
    sailed to Kinsale with Peel fishermen 188
    succeeded by Vicar George Ensor 204
Cowley, Thomas (2) 42
  Churchwarden 68
Craine, Edward (2)
  Chaplain 61
  Vicar 61, 76, 88, 101, 150
Craine, John (3), Vicar 22
Craine, Robert (4), Chaplain 48
Cranston, James, Governor 13
Craven, George E., Vicar 216
  induction of 1904, 201
Crebbin, Charles (1)
  Chaplain 39, 43, 48, 120

Curate 35
Vicar 40, 45, 51, 60, 62
    rebuilding of Church and Vicarage 45
Vicar General 41
Crebbin, John 51
Crebbin, Paul (2), Vicar 12, 28, 40, 51
Crebbin, William (3), Vicar 22, 33, 35, 38, 43, 49
Creer, John 69
Cregeen, Archibald 34, 56, 60
Cregeen, Arthur 212
Cregeen, James 94
Cregneash Church
    building of 176
    improvements, 1905, 213
    opening and dedication, 1878, 176
Crellin, John
    Chaplain 35, 37
    Rector 48
    Vicar 44, 50
Crellin, Miss A. M. 210
Crigan, Bishop Claudius 27, 31, 46, 52, 60, 120
    death of, 1813, 47
    Deed of Reconciliation, St John's Chapel 98
    Perambulating Parish Boundaries 47
Crimean War 93, 122
Cromwell, Oliver 2
Cronahan, Julius 120
Cronk y Voddy 96, 137, 167, 187, 202, 217
    church
        dilapidated state of 138
        presentation of oak lectern by Bishop Straton 202
    grant to 122
Crowe, George 196
Crown lessees 147
Cruickshank, Mr 189
Cubbon, constable 158
Cubbon, Pat 37
Cubbon, Thomas (2) 33
    Rector 59, 69
    Vicar 39, 40, 44, 50, 60, 61
    Vicar General 55
Cudd, W. H. 202
Cunningham grave 17
Curates Aid Society 124, 171
Curghey, John (1)
    Vicar 12, 20, 23
    Vicar General 8, 9, 10, 22, 33
        imprisonment in Castle Rushen 8
Curghey, Matthias (2)
    Curate 18
    Rector 15
    Vicar 21, 22, 27
Curghey, Matthias (3)
    Rector 42
    Vicar 23, 25, 35, 37, 38
    Vicar General 34
Curghey, Matthias (4), Vicar 28
Curghey, Nathaniel (5)
    Deacon 23

Vicar 24, 38
Curghey, Robert 23
Curlett, Edmund 23
Curlot, Thomas, Sumner General 18
Curlot, William 18
Curphey, John 97
Curry, Miss Percy Gore 104
Curwen, Edward, Chaplain 150

D

Dalby 76, 187
Dalby, Mrs 193
Dalrymple Memorial Chapel, Union Mills 126
Daly 151
Davidson, Hugh C. 132
    Vicar 175, 192
Davies, William E.
    Chaplain 205
    Vicar 210, 219
Dawes, Archbishop of York 9
Dawes, Charles, Vicar 177, 192
Dawes, George (2), Chaplain 143
Dawson, Richard, Governor 50, 98
Day of Thanksgiving 64
Dearden, A. K., Vicar 210
decline of Manx in Church Services 35
deeds and documents
    moved to Bishopscourt 148
Deemsters 11
Dening, Henry
    Curate 168
    Vicar 169
Derby, Earls of 13, 15
    5th Earl of Derby 65
    6th Earl of Derby 7
    7th Earl of Derby, Stanley, James 2, 13
    8th Earl of Derby 13
    9th Earl of Derby, Stanley, William George Richard
        1, 2, 4, 21, 24
    Stanley, James 10th Earl of Derby
        5, 7, 9, 10, 11, 12, 13, 17,
        19, 20, 21, 22, 26, 27, 28
Derbyhaven Church, Malew
    opened, 1898, 207
Derrig, Hugh, Chaplain
    Chaplain to Mental Asylum 146
Devall, Henry T.
    Chaplain 212
    Vicar 219
Dhoon 167, 187, 203, 217
    church 122
        building of 138
    grant to 122
Dinwoody, Thomas, Vicar 132
Diocesan Association 72, 98, 110, 124, 139, 152
    Annual General Meeting 122
    Committee 124
    funds for St Jude's parsonage 86

meeting of 122
provision of Chapels of Ease 79
provision of Chaplains houses 79
provision of grants 79
Whitsun Collection to 123
Diocesan Chapter, formation of 122
Diocesan Conference 198
   1879, format for rules and regulations 158
   1880
      Kermode, Revd, Secretary of Convocation 159
      proposed restoration of St German's Cathedral 159
   1881, committee to consider Cathedral in Douglas 160
   1895, 213
   1897, need for church in Upper Douglas 203
   fifth, 1884, 161
   fourth, 1882
      considerations for new Cathedral 160, 169
   inaugral meeting, 1880 159
   revived, 1893 195
   second, 1880 159
   third, 1881 160
Diocesan Inspector of Schools 72
Diocese
   proposed change in 129, 130
   threat of merger with Carlisle 64
   visitations by Vicars General 32
dispute, maintainance for rural curates 124
Dixon, Revd R.
   Principal, King William's College 105, 113
   Vice-Principal, King William's College 65, 79
Dodd, H. R., Chaplain 108, 109
   preached at Malew and Castletown 109
Donaldson, Alexander, Curate 112, 113
Douglas 19, 32, 43, 108, 160
Douglas, Bishop of Aberdeen 162
Douglas Deanery 170, 181
Douglas Grammar School 19, 61
Douglas Head
   open air service, 15,000 present 181
Douglas, parish of 117
Douglas School Committee 134
Doyle, J. B., Curate
   officiated at St Thomas' 108
Dreem-freaie 38
Dress of clergy 154
Drinkwater, Deemster
   94, 105, 110, 115, 124, 134, 151, 157, 182, 183
Drinkwater, Sir George 84
Drummond, Archbishop of York 34, 41
Drury, Bishop Thomas Wortley 209, 214
   against proposed Sunday steamer from Fleetwood 214
   Curate 187
   difficulty concerning Ordination 126
   Manx speaker 214
   Services at Chicken Lighthouse 214
   son of Vicar Drury 126, 186, 187
Drury, William
   Chaplain 69, 86, 99, 143
   Vicar 95, 96, 98, 108, 109, 110,

      111, 114, 115, 116, 117, 118,
      119, 120, 134, 146, 155, 172
   action against H. R. Dodd 108
   benefactor 134
   church, parsonage, school 86
   dispute with Bishop Powys 106
   Manx speaker 96, 186
   nomination of elder son as Chaplain 108
   Rural Dean of Douglas 158
Dublin, Trinity College 1, 46
Duggan, William
   Chaplain 61
   Vicar 74, 100
      Duggan, J. (2) son of 113
Dumbell, Alured 111, 118, 175, 201, 204, 211
Dumbell, George W., MHK 112, 142
Dumbell's Bank failure 198
Dumerque, Catherine 214

E

Eaves, Henry, Chaplain 217
Ecclesiastical Civil Judicature Transfer Act 1884, 162
Ecclesiastical Constitutions 5, 31
Ecclesiastical Court 42, 61
   Amendment Bill (1873) 127
Ecclesiastical Titles Bill, 1850, 100
Edmunds, James, Chaplain 138
Education Act
   1703, 4
   1870, 149
Elliot, Captain 36, 37
Ensor, George, Vicar
   dispute with Curate W. H. Gibson 204
   induction of, 1895, 204
Episcopal Registrars 105
   renamed Diocesan Registrars 159

F

Faragher, Thomas 39
Farrant, E. C., MHK 112, 124, 129, 137, 159
Farrant, Mr W, of Ballamoar
   offer of site for new Jurby Church 171
Farrant, Mrs E. C.
   laying of foundation stone, St Stephen's, Sulby 178
Farrant, Quayle 203
Farrant, Robert 54
Farrant, William 55
Feltham, John 22, 50, 97
Fenton, Thomas, Chaplain 138
Ferrier, Edward
   Chaplain 137, 167, 180, 187
      benefactor 137
      Chaplain to Castle Rushen Prison 137
      First Provincial Grand Chaplain 137
      Oddfellow and Freemason 137
   installed as Canon, 1895, 198
Fielding, James R. 219
Finnis, H. R.

Chaplain
    ex Headmaster, Wellington Road School 167
Curate 177
First Lord of Admiralty, Earl de Grey 65
Fisherman's Service 14
Fishermen's Farewell Service, 1893, 202
Fitzsimmons, William, Minister of Episcopal Chapel 35
Fletcher (2), Archdeacon 13
Fletcher, Robert (1), Vicar 20, 25
Fleury, Cardinal 16
floating chapel for seamen, Douglas harbour 65, 69
Forbes, Edward, Chaplain 97, 120, 139
Ford, Edward, Chaplain
    Chaplain to Laxey miners 142
Forrest & Co. 150
Foster and Andrews 101, 166
Foxdale 39, 76, 138, 167, 187, 217
    church 39
        dedication of stained glass window 203
        need for graveyard 139
        new organ installed, 1893, 168
        opening 139
    erection of Queen Victoria memorial clock 203
    formation of parish 138
    funds for chaplain's house 122
    grant to 122
    new Parish, 1881, 167
    population in 1881, 168
    population in 1900, 203
    proposed church 139
Funerals 124
Furness Abbey 26

G

Garde, John Fry
    Chaplain 97, 98, 137, 141
        dispute over use of Church 99
    Vicar 112, 113, 151, 175
        dispute over burial 152
        dispute with Methodists 152
Gardner, James S., Chaplain 193
Garrett, P. L. 131, 178, 179
Garston, F. 102
Gasking, Samuel, Chaplain 172
Gawne, Edward, JP, SHK 56, 153
Gawne family 76
Gawne, Mrs 177
Geldart, Revd H. 197
Gell, Evan 149
Gell, James 106, 109, 110, 111, 112, 113,
    114, 115, 120, 133, 141, 157, 165,
    184, 195, 197, 204, 211
Gell, John (1)
    Chaplain 61
        death of 98
        end of Manx services 98
        Matins in Manx and English 98
    Vicar 50

Gell, Kennaa 204
Gell, Samuel (2), Vicar 22, 27, 35, 38, 39, 44, 49
    poor record-keeping 49
Gell, William (3), Vicar 11, 15, 27, 150
Gelling, Alexander (1)
    Chaplain 48
    Vicar 59, 84, 94, 131
Gelling, Charlotte 42
Gelling, Daniel (2)
    Rector 42, 47
        defied Mason's ban on Wesley 42
    Vicar 37, 38, 44, 145
Gelling, James (3)
    Master of Peel Grammar School
        complaints against 60
    Vicar 48, 60, 71, 86, 98
        petitioned for new church at Peel 48
Gelling, John Caesar 42
Gelling, Samuel (4)
    Chaplain
        principal of Douglas Grammar School 88
    Vicar 77, 89, 98, 102, 154
        accomplished Hebrew scholar 77
George, J. E. Beauchamp, Vicar 180, 203
    Examining Chaplain 188
German 3, 21, 27, 32, 38, 43, 48,
    60, 71, 86, 97, 140, 168, 188, 203, 217
    bazaar held, 1893 to raise funds for church 204
    building of new Church 169
    church 14, 27
        became Cathedral in 1980 217
        erection of clock tower 140
        opening of, and protest against Mission 168
        opening of new Church, 1884, 170
    Great Gale, 1903
        damage to New Church 204
    meeting to consider repair fund for new church 203
    parish
        dispute, election of churchwardens 140
        population in 1831, 60
        population in 1871, 141
        population in 1881, 169
        population in 1892, 204
    Parish Church Act 204
    restoration of old parish church 204
Gibson, William Henry (1)
    Chaplain 203
    Curate 204
Gibson, William N. (2)
    Chaplain 205, 218
Gill, Evan (1), Vicar 25, 27
Gill, Hugh Stowell (2)
    Archdeacon
        137, 205, 207, 208, 211, 212, 213, 215, 217
        death of, 1912 215
        Golden Wedding, 1906 200
    Chaplain 100, 142, 143, 195
    Vicar 126, 144, 153, 165, 172, 190, 206, 209
        appointment as Archdeacon, 1895, 199

bereavements 190
Examining Chaplain to Bishop Bardsley 181
good terms with Methodists 154
Manx services at Cregneash 154
paper at fifth Diocesan Conference, 1884, 161
paper at second Diocesan Conference, 1880, 159
Rural Dean of Castletown 158
smallpox and typhus epidemic 154
Surrogate 190
translator of Acts of Tynwald into Manx 134
Gill, J. F., Deemster 165, 211
Gill, John (3), Vicar 35, 38, 43
Gill, Mrs 215
Gill, Thomas Howard (4)
  Chaplain 145
  Rector 128
Gill, William (5)
  Chaplain 98
  Vicar 72, 73, 87, 113, 123, 145, 172
    accomplished Manx scholar 72
    editor, Kelly's Manx Dictionary 72, 145
    illness and subsequent death 143
    improvements to Malew Parish 72
    translator of Manx Laws 72
Girls' Friendly Society 212
Gladstone, W. E. 159
Glen Maye 175
Glen Mona 138
Glenfaba House 204
Goldie-Taubman, Colonel Sir John, SHK 85, 137, 159
Goodwin, Bishop of Carlisle 127
Gordon, Thomas 11
Goverment Chapel, St John's 98
Government House 127
Governors 11, 121
Graham, Doctor John 90
Grant, Anne Charlotte 52
Grant, Frederick B., Chaplain 145, 172
Graves, Elizabeth 169
Gray, Canon (2) 112, 113
Gray, Joseph Henry
  Chaplain
    suggested solution to St Thomas' dispute 109
  Vicar 95, 110
Gray, R. H., Vicar 132
  Bishop's Examining Chaplain 111
Greenwood, Doctor H. H. 189
Gregson, George W., Chaplain 217
Grier, Frederick
  Curate 106
  Vicar 132, 165
Grissell, Mrs 40
Groudle 71

H

Hall, Frances 96, 97, 105, 130, 138, 173, 191
Hall, Henry Armstrong, Vicar 168
Hall, John Cecil (2), Archdeacon 77, 80, 81, 82, 84, 101

Halsall, Anthony, Chaplain 12, 26
Halsall, Henry 11
Halstead, Robert, Chaplain 208
Hammersley, Anne 63
Hampton, Christopher 6
Harcourt, Vernon, Archbishop of York 52, 63, 80, 81
Hardy, Henry
  Chaplain 138
  Vicar 112, 141, 148
Harley, Thomas 8
Harmon, Mary 46
Harris, Misses 140
Harris, Samuel 119
  appointed as Surrogate for Douglas 160
  benefactor, St George's Church 97, 140
  Diocesan Registrar 106, 143
    wrote letter to Drury, dispute at St Thomas' 109
  Episcopal Registrar 114, 150
    inaccuracies in parish registers 146, 150
  High Bailiff 151
  Secretary, Manx Church Commissioners 159
  Vicar 148
  Vicar General 161, 180, 189, 192, 194, 205, 207
    death of 198
Harrison, Bowyer (1) 50
  Chaplain 59
  Vicar 61, 75, 88, 101, 138, 147
Harrison, David (2)
  Chaplain 39
  Vicar 44, 50, 60, 61
Harrison, John Edward (3)
  Vicar 61, 71, 78, 86, 99, 141
    Manx scholar 60
Harrison, Mark Wilks (4)
  Vicar 186, 219
Harrison, Mr. 158
Harrison, Stephen Nathaniel (5) 213
  Chaplain 138, 167, 186, 187
Harrison, Thomas (6), Vicar 61
Hart, William, Chaplain 139
Hartwell, Francis
  Chaplain 86, 97, 120
  death of 120
Harvey, Gilmour, Vicar 87, 144, 154, 173
Haslam, William 138
Hastings, Lady Elizabeth 4
Hawles, J. B. 203
Hawley, Mrs 140
Hawley, William 108
  Chaplain 118, 120, 139, 140
    dispute with Bishop Powys 106
    officiated at St Thomas' 108
  Domestic Chaplain to Bishop Bardsley 181
  Vicar 110, 133, 157, 168, 174, 175, 182, 191
    paper at second Diocesan Conference, 1880, 160
Hay-Drummond, Lady Sarah 52
Health of the Town Association, Ramsey 101
Henniker, Lord, Governor 198
Henricks, Mary 6

Henry, Thomas, Vicar 143
herring fishing failure, 1825, 55
Hewetson, Revd Michael 1
Heywood, Mrs 16
Heywood, Peter 44
Heywood, Thomas 10, 12
Hickin, Henry, Chaplain 208, 218
Hickin, Mrs 218
High Bailiffs
    of Peel 57
    of Ramsey 62
High Court 11
Hildesley, Bishop Mark
        5, 14, 17, 19, 20, 27, 29, 41, 42, 43, 44, 49
    attempts to maintain discipline 31
    death of wife 30
    directives to Chapter Quest 31
    directives to churchwardens 31
    encouraged use of Manx language 33
    enthroned in St German's Cathedral 29
    failing health 36
    great interest in Kirk Michael 31
    isolation at Bishopscourt 30
    proposed Cathecism in Manx 33
    standards of clergy 32
    translation of Bible into Manx 33
    translation of Prayer Book into Manx 33
Hildesley, Hester 38, 42
Hill, Bishop Rowley 73, 156, 158, 177, 203
    consecration of 156
    death of 164, 171
    death of wife, 1882 160
    enthroned at St Mary's, Castletown 156
    first Manx service at St George's 157
    forbidding of Vestry meetings to be held in Church
        160
    friend of Bishop Straton 194
    ordained by Sumner, Archbishop of Canterbury 156
    patron of SPCA 163
    petitioned to make Church into Cathedral for Queen
        170
    poor relations with Methodists 156
    revival of Peel Fishermen's Farewell Service 157
    start of Evening Communions 164
    started open air services 160
    started Theological College at Bishopscourt 165
    suggested amalgamation of diocese 157
Hill, Charles (1), Chaplain 138
Hill, Mrs Rowley 200
Hill, Samuel (2), Chaplain 138
Hill, Sir George 156
Hill, William, of London 179
Hillary, Sir William 71
Hirst, George 140
Hobhouse, Bishop 127
Hobson, Eliza Anne 186
Hobson, William Thomas 198
    Canon 200
    Vicar 128, 134, 166, 180, 181, 186

paper at second Diocesan Conference, 1880, 159
paper at third Diocesan Conference, 1881, 160
proposed Proctor 208
Hollins, Benjamin, of Manchester 98
Holmes, Archibald (1)
    Chaplain 65, 88
    Vicar 60, 62, 76, 88, 101
        dedication of window, 1910, St James', Dalby 217
        marriage of 151
Holmes, Arnold J. (2),
    Chaplain 207
    Curate 204
Holmes Bank, failure of 123
Holmes, Miss 208
Holy Trinity 27
Hope, Charles, Governor 90, 99, 122
    Act, of February 1847, 115
    laid foundation stone, Dhoon Church 138
Hope, John, Governor 32, 42, 105
Hopkins, Charles, Vicar 209
    lecturer at Bishop Wilson Theological College 210
    resignation of, 1903, 210
Horne, Alexander, Governor 6, 7, 8, 9, 10, 11, 24
Horne, Jane 7
Horrobin, Robert
    Archdeacon 17
    Chaplain 7, 8, 9, 21
        controversial sermon 7
Horton, Thomas, Governor
        2, 10, 11, 12, 20, 22, 24, 28
Hospital Dispensary 69
House of Industry 69, 134
House of Keys 7, 9, 11, 111, 112, 115, 116
    criticism of Bishop Powys 148
    Laughton's speech to 116, 117
    Members of 131
    Parish of Braddan Bill 111
    petition to 123
    Registry 148
    rejection of suggestion to abolish Vicars General 158
    Speaker Gawne 105
Howard, John (1), Vicar 101, 175, 191, 211
    committal to mental asylum 150
    discourses against Manx Sun and churchwardens 191
    heated exchange with Bishop Hill 162
    imprisonment in Castle Rushen 151
    release from mental asylum 151
Howard, Mrs 192
Howard, Thomas (2)
    Chaplain 17, 48, 86, 120, 132
    Father of Vicar Howard (1) 192
    Rector 68, 79, 84, 105, 113, 165, 174
    Vicar 48, 59, 61, 69, 70, 85
Howley
    Archbishop of Canterbury 65, 67, 78
    Bishop of London 63
Huddleston, Thomas 21
Hudgeon, William 57
Hudson, John 191

Hughes-Games, Cyril, Vicar General 198, 213
Hughes-Games, Joshua
    Archdeacon 73, 180, 182, 185, 186, 187,
        188, 190, 192, 194, 204, 208, 210, 211, 212
    Chaplain 176
    importance of watchnight services 199
    induction of, 1886, 165
    paper at fifth Diocesan Conference, 1884, 161
    paper at second Diocesan Conference, 1880, 159
    paper at third Diocesan Conference, 1881, 160
    Vice-President, Church Missionary Society 199
Hughes-Games, Mrs 183
Hunt, Mary 92
Hutton, Archbishop of York 29
Hutton, F. N. B. (1), Vicar 117, 155, 178
Hutton, Wyndham M. (2), Vicar 126, 143, 171
Hymn tunes
    'Braddan' 61
    'Hatford' 61
Hymnal Companion 204
Hymns
    The Mitre, or Hall's Hymns 141
Hymns Ancient and Modern 141, 150, 168, 178, 204

I

Iles, Chaplain Francis 206
Impropriate Fund 96
Impropriate Tithes 13, 38, 65
Incorporated Society for the Enlargement of Church 62
Indian Mutiny 123
Ingram, William C., Vicar 112, 113, 115, 141, 149, 151
    Domestic Chaplain 126
    refusal to recognise Education Act 149
Isle of Man Railway 183

J

Jackson, Bishop of Lincoln 114
Jackson, Mr 105, 138
Jackson, R. and Sons 99
Jacobson, Bishop of Chester 112, 129
James, Henry, Chaplain 171, 213
Jebb, Richard, Vicar General
        107, 111, 114, 119, 120, 122, 134, 146
    adviser to Bishop Powys 106
    burial at St George's 161
    death of, 1884, 161
    dispute over churchwardens 153
Jeffcott, Mr 88
John Sumner, Bishop of Chester 63
Jones, Bishop Stanton 218
Jones, Dr. Richard 70
Jones, Joshua
    Examining Chaplain 157
    later became Hughes-Games, Joshua 159
Jones, Richard (1)
    Chaplain 172, 187, 190
    Vicar 192, 213, 220
Joughin, Hugh 99

Jurby 21, 22, 32, 38, 43, 49,
        60, 71, 86, 99, 141, 171,
        189, 205, 217
church
    complaints regarding condition of churchyard 189
    improvements to, 1751, 38
    renovation to, 1912, 217
parish
    population in 1831, 60
    population in 1871, 142
    population in 1885, 189
    population in 1891, 205
    population in 1900, 205
proposal to build new church 171
purchase of house and estate, Summerhill 171
sale of vicarage and glebe 171

K

Karran, John 176
Kaye, John, Chaplain 59
Kelly & Preston 209
Kelly Brothers 196, 200
Kelly, Doctor 34
Kelly, High Bailiff 56
Kelly, James Butler (1), Vicar 113, 114, 148
Kelly, William 88
Kelly, William (2), Chaplain 155
Kemp, Doctor 91
Kendal, Mrs 140
Kennaugh, Hugh 98
Kennedy, Mr 57
Kentraugh 76
Kermode, John (4) 57
Kermode, Josephine 185
Kermode, Minnie 186
Kermode, P. M. C. 185
Kermode, Revd S. A. P. (7) 186
Kermode, Robert Daniel (1), Vicar 210, 217, 219
Kermode, Stanley A. P. (2)
    Curate 191
    Vicar 206
    Vice-Principal, Bishop Wilson Theological College 211
Kermode, Thomas and Margaret 152
Kermode, William (3)
    Chaplain 59, 85, 88, 89, 101, 138
        builder of Parsonage 88
        founder of a penny savings bank 101
        founder of Ramsey Health Association 88
        rebuilder of Ballure Church 59
    Deacon 79
    Rector 165, 185, 188
        death of, 1890 185
        exchange of Rectory for house 166
        member of Archaeological Commission 185
        President, I.O.M.N.H.A.S. 185
    Vicar 117, 126, 131, 147, 173, 200
        building St Paul's vicarage 152
        Master, Maughold Masonic Lodge 148

Proctor for York Convocation 126
Rural Dean of Peel 158
sanitary improvements; free meals 152
sudden illness 152
threatened legal action 147
Kerruish, Daniel 39
Kerruish, Thomas 143
Kewin, William 15
Kewley, John (1)
  Archdeacon 216
  Curate 176
    ecclesiastical knowledge 184
    pioneer of Ramsey Life-Saving Corps 176
  Vicar 183, 211, 213
    knowledge of all aspects of Manx life 184
    services at Ronague Old Schoolhouse 200
    services to fever victims 200
Kewley, John (2), Chaplain 50
Kewley, Joseph H. 139
Kewley, Thomas (4), Vicar 62, 77
Kewley, William, Sexton 140
Killey, Phillip, of Douglas 88
Killip, Thomas, Sumner 23
King George I 9
King in Council 11
King, Norman, Chaplain 187, 202
King William III 1
King William's College 65, 75, 79
  Chapel 73, 84
  The Great Fire 85
Kinnoull, 10th Earl of 52
Kinrade, Catherine 6
Kinred, Hugh
  Chaplain 187
    Manx speaker 167, 172
    married Bell, Miss Bessie 167
  Curate 192, 202
  Vicar 211, 219
Kippax, Archippus (1), Archdeacon 17
Kippax, John (2), Archdeacon 17, 21, 36
Kirby House, Braddan 135
Kirk Michael 2, 22, 26, 36, 39, 44,
    50, 61, 64, 75, 88, 101, 141,
    148, 174, 191, 210, 219
  church 16
    closure of burial ground around church 219
    extension of western burial ground 219
    memorials to 'Diamond King' 210
    petition for services in Manx, 1840, 88
    struck by lightening 149
  Church Hall opened, 1896 210
  confirmation at 127
  dispute over Protestant principles 148
  fishermen 33
  population in 1871 149
  population in 1892, 191
  Vicar's lack of attendance at Vestry meetings 149
  Watchnight Service, first 149
Kirkby, John, Vicar 192

Kissack, Edward William
  Chaplain 112, 141, 143, 194
  Curate 141
  installed as Canon, 1895, 198
  Rector 136, 167, 182, 186, 187
    lecturer at Bishop Wilson College 186
    marriage to Arrowsmith, Mrs Jane 167
    marriage to Murray, Miss Mary, 1888, 167
    paper at second Diocesan Conference, 1880, 160
  Vicar 176, 200
    Rural Dean of Ramsey 158
Kissack, Mrs 176
Kissack, W. 187
Kitterland, Rushen 93
Kitto, Captain 203
Kitto, Mrs 139, 203
Kneale, Mr 67
Kneale, Patrick, Chaplain 61
Kneale, Stephen 68
Kneale, Thomas Redfearn
  Chaplain 205
  Curate 191
  Rector 216
  Vicar 189, 200, 212
Knipe, James 19
Kroenig, Charles S., Chaplain 190, 207
Kyte, Joseph, Chaplain 138, 167

L

La Mothe, John Henry, Vicar 86
Lace, Ellen, (Lonnie) 205
Lace, William 205
Lambert, James 149
Lamothe, F. (2), Curate 163
Lamothe, J. C. 211
Lamothe, John 175
Lancaster, Peter, Chaplain 26
land tenure, system of 2
Landor, William 102
Landsdell, F. J., Vicar 201
Lane, Richard 98
Lang, Archbishop of York 217
Langton, Charles Thomas
  Chaplain 143, 146, 172
  Curate 115
  Rector 187
  Vicar 183
    benefactor 202
Laughton, Alfred Nelson
    110, 111, 112, 114, 115, 116, 117, 121
  accusation against Bishop Powys 110, 111
  action for slander against Bishop Powys 110, 111, 112
  High Bailiff of Peel 188
  paper at fifth Diocesan Conference, 1884, 161
  paper at second Diocesan Conference, 1880, 159
  paper at third Diocesan Conference, 1881, 160
  prosecutor 151
Laxey 122, 142, 171, 189, 205, 218

parish population in 1911, 205
Laxey Mining Company 142
Lee, Thomas, Curate 149
Leece, Charles Henry
    Chaplain 205
    Vicar 213
Leech, John, Chaplain 139
Legislative Council 111, 116, 182
    German Parish Church Act 170, 204
    intention of 1847 Act 108
    Parish of Braddan Bill 109, 110
Levinz, Bishop 2, 16, 21
Lewin, Joseph 208
Lewin, Juan 60
Lewin, Miss Margaret 168
Lewin, Mrs 191
Lewis, Walter A., Vicar 217
Lezayre 22, 38, 43, 49, 60, 64,
        86, 99, 142, 171, 189, 205
    church 172
        alterations to 142
        improvements ordered by Bishop Crigan 49
        neglect of church building 71
        opening of new organ, 1885, 172
        poor conditions, 1762, 38
    dispute over election 99
    formation of Poor Relief Committee 205
    population in 1871, 143
    population in 1892, 189
    ruinous state of Vicar's house and outbuildings 86
Lezayre Cross 23
Lindsay, Patrick, Governor 13
Lindsey, John 167
Lingague, Rushen 28
Litany, addition to 122
Liverpool Clerical Society 181
Lloyd, John, Governor 10
Loch, Lady 135
Loch, Lord Henry Brougham, Governor
        115, 124, 129, 142, 150, 151, 156, 177
Locke, E. H. L., Chaplain 202, 203
Loe, John 58
Lonan 14, 23, 27, 32, 38, 44,
        49, 60, 64, 71, 87, 100, 143,
        172, 189, 206, 218
    Beinn y Phott
        evening services 143
    church
        badly damaged by storm, 1890, 190
        consecration, 1735, 25
        extension of graveyard 143
    old church
        funeral of victims, Snaefell mining disaster 206
    parish
        population in 1831, 72
    parish, (incl. Laxey)
        population in 1892, 190
Looney 10
Looney, John 138

Lord Cobham 29
Lord Goderich 63, 65
Lord John Russell 100
Lord Melbourne 65
Lord Sidmouth 55, 58
Lord's Day Observance Society 160
Lowcay, Henry, Rector 18
Lowey, Isobel 28
Lunatic Asylum 115
Lunatic Asylum Act 151
Lupton, Benjamin J. S., Chaplain 132, 172
Lushington, Doctor Stephen 68

M

MacHutchin, John, Clerk of the Rolls 70, 98
Mackenzie, William, Methodist Minister 148
MacLagan, Archbishop of York 194, 198, 214
Macnameer, Jane 11
Maddrell, Henry
    Chaplain 48
    Vicar 49, 60, 71, 86
Magher y Raad Vooar 68
Makepeace, Curate A. J. 192
Makon, James, Chaplain 21
Malew 24, 36, 38, 44, 50,
        61, 72, 87, 100, 143, 172, 190, 206, 218
    church
        alterations to, 1897, 207
        extension of burial ground 143
        Gell, Mrs James 144
        Gill, Mrs William 144
        rebuilding and enlarging of organ 207
        redecorated 144
        unauthorised grave opening 143
        William Christian (Illiam Dhone) 207
    laying of foundation stone, Ballasalla Church, 189 207
    meeting to promote building of church, Ballasalla, 206
    opening of new Church, Ballasalla, 1897, 207
    population in 1871, 144
    population in 1892, 190
    vicarage, extensions 144
Malew Street Chapel, Castletown 50
Malius, Doctor 204
Manning, Michael 149
Manx Agricultural Society 128
Manx Bible 34, 35
Manx Catechism 14
Manx Chancery Court 41
Manx Church Commissioners 159, 178, 202
Manx Church Magazine 185
Manx Church Sustentation Fund 197, 199, 217
Manx Convocation 122
Manx Court of Exchequer 54, 55
Manx Fund for Bibles and Prayer Books 35
Manx Gaelic 1, 2, 5, 11, 12, 14, 17, 18,
        26, 27, 32, 33, 34, 35, 36, 37,
        39, 42, 43, 44, 45, 48, 49, 50, 51, 53,
        56, 60, 66, 67, 69, 71, 72, 74,

76, 77, 81, 86, 88, 90, 91, 96, 98,
122, 131, 132, 134, 137, 145, 167,
184, 186, 211, 214, 226, 227, 237, 240
Prayer for the Herring Fishery 5
translation of Bible and Prayer Book 5
Manx Northern Railway 178
Manx Prayer Book 34, 35, 71
translators
Christian, John 34
Christian, Nicholas 34
Crebbin, Paul 34
Crebbin, William 34
Curghey, Matthias 34
Moore, Phillip 34
Mylrea, William 34
Radcliffe, Robert 34
Wilks, James 34
Manx Prayer Books 122
Manx ways and customs recorded 67
Manx Wedding, The (song) 72
Marine Drive Railway 182
Marown 19, 24, 38, 39, 44, 50,
61, 74, 88, 100, 114, 145,
172, 190, 208, 218
church
Christian, Thomas 146
dilapidated state of 39
first vicarage, 1903 208
population in 1796, 44
population in 1871, 146
population in 1892, 190
Marriage Act, 1753 32
Marriage by licence 141
Marsden, Christopher, Archdeacon 17, 21
Mason, Bishop George 41, 46, 50, 52, 118, 120
appointment of Trustees for St George's 117
burial in Kirk Michael churchyard 42
opposition to Methodists 41
Maughold
19, 26, 32, 39, 44, 50, 61, 75, 88, 101, 147, 173, 191, 209, 219
appointment of Parish Clerk 147
church
gallery erected, 1774, 50
new organ opened, 1878, 174
rebuilding programme 147
renewal of interior woodwork, 1900, 210
ruinous state, 1780, 50
church hall
foundation stone laid, 1900, 210
mining rights on glebelands 147
population in 1831, 61
population in 1871, 148
population in 1881, 174
population in 1892, 191
vicarage
extension to 147
rebuilding of 39
Maughold Vicarage Act 147
Mawdsley, Robert, Governor 11, 13, 14

McCrone, James 54, 55, 56, 58
McGill, William, Curate 86
McKnight, Miss, FRCO 200, 209
Meeres, Curate 112, 113, 114
Memorial for use of Manx in services 81
Methodism 91, 131
Methodist Minister 76
Methodist revival 35
Methodists 15, 32, 41, 53, 59, 67,
69, 76, 82, 83, 94, 137, 141, 147, 171, 174
Michael 32, 42
Millington, Thomas, Curate 149
Milner, William 177
Milntown, Lezayre 87
Mines Chapel, Foxdale 138
Mitchell, John, Chaplain 145
Moore, A. W. 195, 216
Moore and Costain, Messrs 177
Moore, Deemster 7, 11, 12
Moore, Edward (1)
Vicar 24, 27
Vicar General 25, 40
Moore, Frederick James (2)
Canon 208, 209, 216
Chaplain 139, 189
outstanding clergyman 139
Vicar 141, 171, 172, 190, 201, 209
Moore, J. J. S. (3), Curate 149
Moore, J. S., Churchwarden 141
Moore, James (8), Churchwarden 71
Moore, John 43
Moore, John (4), Vicar 17, 36, 37, 42, 47, 50
Moore, John (5), Vicar 44, 48
Moore, Joseph Christian (6), Archdeacon
36, 67, 82, 88, 93, 96,
101, 102, 105, 106, 108, 112, 113, 115,
116, 122, 126, 127, 130, 134, 137, 138, 140,
142, 145, 147, 149, 159, 165
adviser to Bishops Eden and Hill 84
attended opening of German new Church 170
benefactor 83, 131, 135, 136
control of diocese 106
donated stipend to charity 83
Examining Chaplain 157
founder of schools 82
involvement in Church building 84
laying of foundation stone, German new Church 169
officiated at St Thomas' 109
plea to Tynwald 129
presented to Queen Victoria, 1885, 84
raising of funds for poor 94
repairs to Church buildings 83
requests details of church property 126
restorer of Andreas Church 82
uninfluenced by Tractarian Movement 83
Moore, Margaret 22
Moore, Mrs Emily 190
Moore, Philip (7)
Chaplain 16, 19

269

translator of Manx Bible 26
  Rector 16, 22, 30, 34, 35, 36, 37, 38, 42, 48
Moore, R. J. 170
Moore, Robert 176
Moore, T. 207
Moore, W. F. 131, 134, 135
Moran, W. I., Chaplain 199, 202, 213
Moreton, Bishop, of Kildare 1
Morgan and Pollard 200, 210
Morgan, Mr 220
Morris 209
Morris, Alfred (1)
  Curate 191
  Vicar 210, 219
Morris, E. L. (3), Vicar 185
Morris, Mrs 219
Morris, William (2)
  Chaplain 174
  Vicar 174, 191, 193, 210
Morrison, James 188
Mosely, Canon 94
Mossman, Revd Thomas 112, 113, 114
Moule, Revd H. G. 197
Mountford, Doctor 151
Murray, Bishop George 31, 43, 47, 49, 52, 63, 65,
    70, 71, 73, 76, 119, 120, 146, 211
  appointed Dean of Worcester 58
  Cobb, gardener 56
  decline in church discipline 58
  dispute - cost of improvements 53
  enthronement in St George's 53
  lack of popularity 56
  leaving of Island 57
  lime kiln, jetty, new road improvements 53
  opposition to Corn Laws 53
  relations with Methodists 58
  remittance of potato tithe, 1825, 56, 57
  revival of tithes 54
  wife 53
Murray, Captain James, Governor 13
Murray, Lord George 46, 47
  Archdeacon 47, 52
  Rector 47
Mylchreest, Joseph 171, 188, 203
Mylchreest, Mrs 220
Mylrea, Daniel
  Chaplain 47
Mylrea, Daniel (1)
  Archdeacon 58
  Rector 47, 66
  Vicar 50
Mylrea, Deemster 7, 18
Mylrea, William (2)
  Archdeacon 35, 36, 42, 50, 53, 63, 65
  Rector 21, 35, 37, 42, 47

N

Nelson, C. B. (3) 137

Nelson, Daniel (1)
  Chaplain 99
  Rector 136
    death of 137
  Vicar 96
Nelson, John (2)
  Rector 69, 78
  Vicar 49, 53, 55, 60, 61, 62, 74, 85
New Testament, revised edition 34
Newchurch 15
Newspapers
  'Church Times' 112
  'Isle of Man Times' 117, 121
    Brown, proprietor of 120
    Ousley, proprietor of 120, 121
  'Manchester Guardian' 159
  'Manx Patriot' 59
  'Manx Sun' 70, 81, 82, 86, 87, 92, 93, 104,
    105, 111, 115, 118, 119, 120, 121, 124,
    125, 126, 127, 129, 131, 132, 148, 161,
    165, 170, 174, 176, 182, 186, 191, 195, 199
  'The Independent Whig' 11
  'The Law Times' 116
Newton, A. S., Curate 189, 209, 212
Nicholson, J. M. 220
Noble, Henry Bloom 140, 201
Norris, Henry, Vicar 13, 19, 22, 26, 27
Northern Deemster 62

O

Oakhill Chapel, Braddan 122, 136
Ogden, Attorney General 95
Oie'll Voirrey 36, 147, 190
Onchan 27, 32, 39, 44, 50, 61, 64, 75,
    88, 101, 114, 150, 175, 191, 211, 219
  church
    decision to build new church, 1829, 75
    dilapidated state, 1760, 75
    dispute over offertory 151
    dispute re churchyard and graves 150
    extensive alterations to church, 1881, 175
    grounds, restoration and extension 150
    major restoration, 1757, 40
    new pulpit, 1894, 211
  dispute over opening of family grave 150
  dispute over school rate 150
  population in 1871, 151
  sale of parish school 151
Order of the Holy Redeemer 112, 113, 114
organ builders
  Brindley and Foster 201
  Forster and Andrews of Hull 101, 102, 166
  Hewitt of Leicester 167
  Hill, William of London 179
  Jackson of Ballaugh 105, 138
  Jackson, R. and Sons of Liverpool 99
  Morgan and Pollard of Douglas 200, 210
  Morgan, of Douglas 220

organists
    Bamber, J. 128
    Best, W. T. 179
    Cannell, Miss Lizzie 203
    Clague, Mr 212
    Cregeen, Arthur 212
    Crellin, Miss A. M. 210
    Dearnaley, Irvine 134
    Finnis, H. R. 167
    Garrett, P. L. 178, 179
    Gunton, F. 132
    Hirst, George 140
    Holmes, Miss 208
    McKnight, Miss 200, 209
    Moore, Frederick James 139
    Mylrea, Mr 178
    Philip Caley 48
    Royston, Mr 178
    St George's 168
    Stevenson, Miss 200
    stipends 43
    Teare, Philip 166
    Watson, Edward 210
    Wicksey, T. W. 167
    Wood, Miss M. L., ARCO 166, 170, 178, 201, 204
organs
    Andreas 131, 200
    Arbory 165
    Ballaugh 166
    Ballure 47
    Bishopscourt 105, 158
    Braddan 20, 69, 85, 134, 201
    Bride 167
    Castletown 48, 167, 202
    Colby Mission Church 165
    Cronk y Voddy 138
    Foxdale 168
    German 141, 169, 204
    Laxey 171
    Lezayre 172
    Malew 207
    Marown 146
    Maughold 174
    Michael 158
    Rushen 154, 177, 220
    Santan 213
    St Barnabas' 84, 132, 134
    St George's 43, 48, 140
    St James', Dalby 167
    St Johns' 99
    St Luke's 201
    St Mark's 207
    St Matthew's 146, 173, 209
    St Olave's 210
    St Paul's 101, 152, 176
    St Stephen's, Sulby 213
    St Thomas' 102, 155, 179, 220
Ormly Hall, Ramsey 152

P

Packer, George F., Vicar 203
Page, Samuel 65
Parish boundaries, beating of 14
Parish Clerk 100
Parish Clerks, appointment of 159
Parish of Braddan Bill 110
Parish Registers 3
Parish Registers Act 150
Parr, Bishop 2, 19
Parr, John (1), Vicar 21, 28
Parr, Robert (2)
    Vicar General 17, 21, 22
Parr, Robert (3)
    Vicar General 18, 23
Parsons, George Stickler
    Chaplain 60, 64, 78, 85
    Curate 60
    Vicar 70, 78, 96
Parville, Malew 17
Paton, E. C.
    Canon 219
    Chaplain 212
Paton, George
    Chaplain 152, 174, 175, 192, 211
    Curate 113, 149, 152
    paper to fifth Diocesan Conference, 1884, 161
    Vicar 59, 152, 153
Patrick 3, 27, 40, 44, 51, 62, 76,
    88, 101, 151, 175, 192, 211, 219
    building of Patrick Church 175
    population in 1892, 211
Patten, Mary 15
Pattison, Doctor J. E., Chaplain 155, 178
Pearson, J. L. 135, 209
Pease, Emily Jane 194
Peel 1
Peel Castle 10, 22, 128
Peel Castle, Constable of 9
Peel fishermen 33
Peel meeting 169
Peel, Sir Robert 81
Pepys, Bishop Henry 78, 80
    consecrated in Whitehall Chapel 80
    donation of tithe 80
    enthroned, St Mary's, Castletown 80
    made Bishop of Worcester 81
    revival of S.P.C.K. 80
Pettman, William 58
Phillimore, Doctor Robert 118, 119, 120
Phillimore, Doctor Robert, 133
Phillip, Bishop 34
Phillips, Revd A. 79
Philpot, Benjamin
    Archdeacon 64, 66, 68, 69, 75,
    76, 78, 79, 82, 140
    Chaplain 66, 70, 86
    Rector 66

Vicar 120
Vicar General 70, 71, 74
    chose site for King William's College 70
    revival of St George's Parish 70
Philpot, Mrs 67
Pierpoint, Matthew, Chaplain 142
Pigot, H. C., Chaplain 187
Pigott, Francis, Governor 143, 149
Poole, Sir James 7
poor crops, 1825-1826 55
Pope, John Grasett, Vicar 219
Pope Pius IX 93, 100
Port Erin Commissioners 213
Port St Mary, grant to 122
Port St. Mary 153
Porteus, Bishop of London 63
Powell, Miss Mary 180
Powys, Bishop Horatio 104
    appeal against libel verdict 115
    appeal to assist cotton workers 123
    condition of Bishopscourt 105
    conducted Fishermans Service, Peel Castle 105
    conducts open air service 134
    consecrated in York Minster, 1854, 105
    death of 105, 128
    departs Island in September 1874, 127
    dispute over St Thomas' Church 106
    enthroned at St Mary's Castletown 105
    friend of Bishop Auckland 104
    improvements to Bishopscourt 105
    introduction of church music 123
    lack of popularity 106
    left his books to successor 157
    Methodists 128
    offers resignation 128
    Rector of Warrington 115
    response to Drury regarding Dodd 108
    the case against 111
    treatment of clergy 110
    wife of 128
Powys, Mrs 129
Prayer Book 34
Price, Colonel 160
Privy Council 9, 10, 41, 55, 58, 115, 116
Probyn, Alice Eliza 156
Proctor, election of 123
Protestant Defence Committee 100
public houses 67
publications
    'Atholl Papers' 58
    'Diocesan Magazine' 202
    'Island Minstrelsy' 49
    'Kelly's Manx Dictionary' 33, 72
    'Kelly's Manx Grammar' 72
    'Manx Bible' 53
    'Manx Prayer Book' 53
    'Matthew Henry's Commentary on the Bible' 67
    'Scott's Commentary on the Bible' (six volumes) 87
    'Steps to the Altar' 148

Puller, Mrs Rebecca 8

Q

Quakers 15
Qualtrough, Evan, Rushen Parish Clerk 153
Qualtrough, John (1)
    Chaplain 50, 89, 99, 102, 141
    Rector
        conducted Manx services 137
        death of 166
        Manx speaker 167
    Vicar 35, 79, 123, 137
        as Parish Priest 131
Qualtrough, Joseph (2), Vicar 61, 62, 71, 87, 100, 142
Qualtrough, Richard 153
Qualtrough, Thomas 153
Quayle, John (2), Vicar 17, 24, 28, 38
Quayle, M. H. (5) 151
Quayle, Robert (3)
    Chaplain 39, 44
    Curate 35
    Vicar 48, 50
Quayle, Thomas (4), Vicar 35, 39, 44, 50
Quayle, Thomas (5) 30
Queen Victoria 92, 116, 180, 195, 206
Queen's Pier, Ramsey 163
Quilliam, Thomas 144
Quine, Caesar 146
Quine, John 141
Quine, John, Vicar 206, 218
Quine, Mrs 218
Quine, Thomas 37
Quirk, High Bailiff 63
Quirk, Richard 151, 211

R

Radcliffe, Frederick 200
Radcliffe, Mr. 130
Radcliffe, Robert
    Vicar 24, 35, 40
        owner, Knockaloe 27
    Vicar General 16, 32
Radcliffe, Thomas 169
Raglan, Lady 219
Raglan, Lord 200, 216, 218, 219
Rainbow, Edward, Vicar 204, 217
Ramsey 32
Ramsey Health Association 152
Ramsey Life-saving Corps, or Rocket Brigade 152
Ramsey Literary Institution and Reading Room 93
Ramsey Sanitary and Medical Dispensary 152
Rea, Miss Elizabeth 156
Read, Claude, Chaplain 171, 189
Ready, Colonel John, Governor 81
Revestment Act, 1765 42, 43
Richmond, Bishop Richard 38, 41, 46, 48
Ridgeway, J. W., Governor 197, 209, 212
Rigby, Armitage 213, 219

Ring, G. A. 160, 161
Ripon, Earl of, formerly Lord Goderich 65
Robinson, Hampton (1), Chaplain 217
Robinson, Samuel (2)
    Chaplain 26
    Vicar 15, 17
Rolleston, Adrian S., Chaplain 205, 217
Rolston, William George, Chaplain 187, 203, 217
Roman Catholic Church 111
Roman Catholics 94
Roper, William, Vicar General 54, 55, 58, 60, 61, 70
Ross, William
    Chaplain 26, 37, 40
    Revd 11, 12, 21
Rowe, Captain 142, 147
Rowe, John, Comptroller 7, 8
Royal Bounty 14
Royal Commission of Enquiry 48
Rushen 28, 32, 36, 40, 44, 51, 62, 76,
    89, 102, 153, 176, 192, 212, 220
    Abbey 23, 65
    church
        Clucas, J. T. 153
        extension to burial ground 153
        extensions and alterations, 1775, 44
        Gawne family 44, 153, 154, 213
    commission of enquiry 213
    dispute, collections against Vicar Kneale 213
    enlargement of vicarage, 1881 176
    new vicarage built, 1839 89
    parish
        population in 1831, 76
        population in 1841, 76
        population in 1871, 154
        population in 1881, 177
        population in 1891, 192
        population in 1906, 213
    replacement of vicarage, 1839, 77
    St Catherine's Hall 213
Rushworth, Vicar 185
Russell, Lord John MP 73
Ryan, Vincent, Vicar of Bradford 128

S

Sailing vessels
    'Ben my Chree' 91
    'Fenella' 194
    'King Orry' 90
    'Lily', wreck of 93
    'Lucy' 28
    'Majestic' 63
    'Manx Fairy' 94
    'Mona's Isle' 80, 81, 149
    'Mona's Queen' 105
    'Peveril' 183
    'Queen of the Isle' 78, 79
    'William Leece' 53
Sailors' Home 69

Saint Conchenn 27
Saltmarshe, Mr. C. 138
Saltmarshe, Mrs 138
Sankey's Hymns 168
Sansbury, Richard 62
Santan 32, 38, 40, 45, 51, 62, 77,
    89, 102, 154, 178, 192, 213
    church 51
        building of new vicarage 154
        Clucas family 154
        dilapidated state 40
        installation of new organ, 1895, 213
        rebuilding of church and chancel, 1774, 51
    parish
        population in 1831, 77
        population in 1871, 155
        population in 1889, 192
    vicarage
        rebuilding of, 1769, 40
Savage, Ernest Bickersteth
    Canon 137, 215
    Vicar 160, 166, 174, 181, 183, 193, 203, 213, 220
Savage, Mary 21
Savoy Chapel 1
Sayle, John 202
Scarffe, Joseph 158
scholastic society 81
schoolmaster libraries 81
Scripture Readers Association 93
Secker, Archbishop of Canterbury 29
Selwyn, Bishop of Lichfield 127, 131, 135, 137
Sewell, J. H. V., Vicar 185
Sharp, Archbishop of York 1
Shenston, Henry F., Vicar 217
Shepheard, Clement, Vicar 171
Sherlock, Dr, Rector of Winwick 1
Sherwood, Richard 110, 111, 117, 146, 176
Shimmin, John, schoolmaster 44
Shippam, Frederick, Chaplain 217
Shirley, Bishop Walter Augustus 88, 90, 91, 115, 120
Short, Bishop Thomas Vowler
    78, 81, 82, 86, 95, 109, 113, 115, 120, 147
Sidebotham, Samuel, Chaplain 217
Simon, Bishop 2, 7
Simpson, Samuel
    Chaplain 96, 103, 106, 107, 108, 117, 120
    Revd 105
Skeeylley Mayl 26
Skillicorn, John 150
smallpox epidemic
    1817, 53
    1887, 171
Smart, Mrs Dorothea 102
Smelt, Cornelius, Governor
    53, 54, 55, 56, 60, 63, 65, 70
smuggling 2, 4, 32, 43
Smyth, W. K.
    Chaplain 217
    Curate 202

Snaefell mine disaster, 1897, 198, 205
Snedden, William 7, 11
Snepp, Edward, Vicar 143
Society for Promoting Church Building 142
Society for the Propagation of Christian Knowledge
    34, 53
Society for the Propagation of the Gospel 123
South Ramsey Church Act,1904, 212
Sparrow, James, Curate 131
Spicer, John Morris
    Chaplain 189, 205
    Vicar 207, 218
Spicer, Mrs Emma 218
Spittall, Alex 88
St Patrick's Isle 27
St Abban 72
St Andrew's Church, Douglas 54
St Barnabas' Church, Douglas 64, 68, 69, 84, 94, 106,
    114, 132, 166, 186, 200, 216
    building of 68
    churchwardens 133
    closure of, 1957, 216
    foundation of YMCA 134
    Gordon, Mr., of London, trustee 68
    land bought for Vicarage 95
    new organ installed 134
    parochial district 133
St Barnabas' Day 68
St Barnabas' Schools 69
St Bridget 20
St Cairbre 17
St Catherine's Church, Port Erin 177, 192, 212, 220
St Columba 17
St George's Church, Douglas 25, 41, 43, 48, 60, 63,
    70, 86, 97, 106, 114, 120, 133, 139, 168, 187, 203, 217
    alterations to 140
    and Churchyard 117, 119
    Bishop's patronage, legal investigation 119
    building of church, 1781, 43
    burial ground 110
    clearance of debt on building 48
    controversy, surpliced choir 140
    dispute, apppointment of incumbents 133
    dispute over churchyard 118
    extra seats for poor 97
    first organ on Island, 1778, 48
    licensed for marriages, 1849, 97
    major restoration, 1908, 217
    meeting of pewholders 119
    meeting to consider improvements 119
    new bells dedicated by Bishop Bardsley 187
    parish 168
    purchase of vicarage 168
    repairs to, and decoration of Church 168
    separate Parish, 1878, 168
    temporary Pro-Cathedral 161
    vandalised, 1845, 86
    windows broken, 1846 86
St George's Church, Peel 47

St German's Cathedral 2, 21, 27, 41, 47, 65, 170
    consideration of rebuilding 159
    crypt 6, 8
    damage to, 1815, 60
    improvements to 2
    Manx Services, 1798, 48
    proposed preservation of 141
    ruinous state 2
St German's new Church 170
St German's Prison, Peel Castle 23
St James', Dalby 64, 85, 97, 138, 167, 202, 217
    extensive repairs to parsonage, 1894, 202
    new organ installed, 1886, 167
    repairs and improvements, 1890, 187
St John's Chapel 97, 141, 188, 205, 217
    building of Chaplain's house 98
    commencement of building, 1847 99
    consecrated, 1849, 99
    dispute over appointment of successor 98
    donations to rebuilding fund 98
    fund raising for new Church 98
    Government Chapel 141
    parish 171
    rebuilding of, 1798, 98
    repairs to, 1814, 98
    repairs to, 1840, 98
    ruinous condition of 97
    secular business 124
St John's Friendly Society 99
St John's Oddfellows 141
St Jude's 86, 99, 141, 171, 189, 205, 217
St Luke's, Baldwin
    20, 64, 72, 87, 100, 143, 172, 190, 206, 218
St Mark's Church
    38, 44, 50, 61, 73, 87, 100, 144, 172, 190, 207, 218
    building of new parsonage, 1830 74
    dispute over appointment of Chaplain 145
    improvements to chaplaincy 87
    parish population in 1776, 39
    parish population in 1891, 190
    poor state of parsonage 73
    received old organ from Ballasalla Church 207
    repairs to church and outbuildings 207
    restoration and reopening 145
    unfinished state, 1772, 73
St Mary's Church, Castletown
    8, 21, 38, 60, 63, 70, 81, 202
    adoption of Hymns Ancient and Modern 202
    alterations to 167
    building of 59
    Governor's pew 60
    installation of new organ 202
    no longer Government Chapel, 1921, 217
    removal of large old pulpit 202
    repositioning of organ gallery 167
    starting of clock and installation of bells, 1904, 213
St Mary's Church, Port St Mary
    building of, 1880, 177
    dedication of memorial to Bishop Hill 212

St Olave's
    1896, 210
St Paul's
    1825, 62
    1881, 176
    1904, 212
St Stephen's
    1881, 178
St Thomas'
    1868, 103
    1881, 179
    1891, 193
Stockwood, C. V., Archdeacon 184, 185
Stoker, Elizabeth 29
Stoker, Hester 30, 36
Stokes, Revd Pelham 168
Stowell, F. 177
Stowell, Hugh
    Chaplain 138
    Rector 64, 65, 68, 72, 75
    Vicar 49, 50, 59, 60
Stowell, J. E. 79
Stowell, John La Mothe
    Chaplain 88
    Vicar 74, 86, 98, 141, 151, 157, 168
Stowell, Thomas 75
Stratford, Bishop of Chester 2
Straton, Mrs 199
Straton, Norman Dumenil John, Bishop 194, 203
    Churchman's Protestant Alliance 195
    enthroned at St Mary's Castletown 195
    licensing of 10 lay readers 198
    translated to Newcastle, 1907, 199
Straton, Revd G. W. 194
Stubbs, Frederick William, Vicar 203, 216, 217
Sturt, William, Chaplain 48
Sulby 122
Sullivan, Maria 80
Sumner, John 59
Sumners 3, 27, 74
Sumners General 10, 12
Surrogates 121, 134, 141, 180
Sutton, Henry, Vicar 133
Swallow, Chaplain Francis 139
Synods, 1239, 1291 and 1350, 5

T

Taggart, Hugh Selwyn (1) 219
Taggart, John 71, 99
Taggart, Nicholas 38
Taggart, Thomas Arthur (2)
    Canon 208, 218
    Chaplain 172
    Vicar 161, 173, 190, 206, 209
Taggart, William (3) 39
Taggart's Barn, Bowring Road, Ramsey 99, 152
Talbot, Theophilus
    Chaplain 150

Curate 141
Taubman, John, Vicar 14, 24
Taylor, Christopher, Chaplain 138
Teare, David 51
Teare, Philip 166
Teare, Police Constable of Ramsey 158
Tellett, Doctor 206
Tellett, High Bailiff of Ramsey 92
temperance 70
The Laurels, Crosby 208
The Prayer Book 34
Thellusson, E. 189
Theological College 176
Thimbleby, Thomas
    Chaplain 59
    Vicar 59, 70
Thomas Barry and Son 169
Thompson, Bishop Denton 183, 215
Thompson, Matthew, Chaplain 102
Thompson, William, Chaplain 102
Thomson, Archbishop of York 109, 121, 129, 170, 180
Thomson, Chaplain George 190
Thornton-Duesbery, Bishop 27
Thurot
    Captain 36, 37
    Cottage 48
Tithe Commutation Act 64, 162
tithes 12, 13, 19, 41, 56, 64, 65, 69, 76, 170, 182
    agents, lack of attendance 56
    agreements with farmers 147
    Andreas 86
    attempts to extend 52
    collections 56
    commutation of 122
    dispute 53, 62
    falling value of, 1893, 195, 197, 198
    fish 42
    glebe 105
    lapsed 3
    on calves 55
    on cocks and hens 55
    on colts 55
    on fish 42, 54
    on geese 55
    on green crops 54
    on potato crop 54
    raising of, by Bishop Murray 54
    reduction of 55, 181
    refusal to pay 6, 33
    Rent Charge 136
    revived old claim 54
    riots, Patrick Parish 57
    up for public auction 41
    valuation of 58
Tobin, Caesar 54, 55
Toleration Act, 1689 6
Tower of Refuge 71
Tracey, Frederick Francis, Vicar 160, 176
Trevor, Bishop of Durham 29

Trevor, Edward 21
Trinity College, Cambridge 29
Turpin, Doctor E. H., FRCO 201
Twiss, Doctor Sir Travers 120, 133
Tynwald 11, 23, 25, 27, 64, 65, 71, 116
    1847, division of Douglas & Braddan 91
    Acts
        abolition of corbs, 1734, 13
        Act of Settlement, 1704, 5
        approval to build Marown Church, 1847, 88, 100
        approval to build Onchan Church, 1830 75, 76
        Authorisation of Braddan New Church 135
        Ballaugh New Church, 1830, 68
        Bishop's Temporalities Act 128
        building of Lonan New Church, 1830, 71
        building of new Arbory church, 1757, 36
        Building of St Jude's Church, 1839, 86
        Burials Act, amendments to 198
        Church Act, 1879, 159
        clergy to live in parishes, 1696, 3
        division of Douglas and Braddan parishes, 1847,
        95, 106, 108, 110
        division of Douglas and Braddan parishes, 1859 106
        Ecclesiastical Residences and Dilapidations Act 198
        enlargement of Andreas Churchyard, 1847, 94
        Glebelands Act 123
        Kirk Michael New Church, 1834, 75
        new Andreas Church, 1800, 59
        parochial libraries, 1734, 3
        petition to build Andreas Church, 1800, 47
        petition to build Jurby Church, 1806, 49
        raising of funds by churchwardens, 1878, 175
        raising of funds for Bishopscourt, 1855, 105
        remuneration on leaving parish, 1734, 3
        simplification of canon law 5
        special licences to marry, 1757, 32
        tenancy of land, 1645, 5
        The Clerks' Glebe Lands Act, 1902, 159
    Bills 135
        Bishop's Stipend 130
        Canonries Bill 198
        commutation of tithes, 1839, 78
        enlargement of Braddan graveyard, 1848, 96
        levying and payment of tithes 55
        Manx Church Sustentation Fund 198
        need to separate Braddan from Douglas 115, 116
        The Glebelands Bill, 1893 197
    building of Bride New Church 136
    debate, poverty of clergy 129
    petition to, from clergy, 1838, 78
    plea to, by clergy 129
    question re amalgamation of diocese 157
    questioning of competence of Tynwald 204
    refusal to allow sale of tithes 52
    Sunday opening prohibition 122
Tynwald, Committee of 116, 117
Tynwald Court 8, 9
Tynwald Fair Day 97
Tynwald Hill 12, 72

U

Uniformity, Act of 122

V

Vesey, Arthur, Curate 112, 113
Vestry Meetings
    Ballaugh, 1892
        use of gallery for Sunday School 200
    Braddan
        care of poor in the parish 84
    Braddan, 1846
        proposal to extend burial ground 84
    Braddan, 1879
        extension of churchyard 166
    Braddan, 1885
        complaints against open air services 166
    Braddan, 1895
        discussion on extension to churchyard 201
    Bride, 1872
        criticism of bills paid 137
    Castletown, 1888, 187
    German, 1848
        discuss new burial ground 97
    German, 1851
        decision to build Chapel in cemetery 97
    German, 1881
        sale of old Vicarage, purchase of Glen View House
        169
    German, 1893
        draft bill, new parish church 203
    Kirk Michael
        decision to build new church 75
        poor state of church 75
    Kirk Michael, 1857
        decision to build new pulpit 101
    Kirk Michael, Easter, 1879
        improvements to church 174
    Lezayre
        new church considered 71
    Lezayre, 1888
        dispute regarding nomination of two churchwardens
        189
    Lezayre, 1894
        Bridgman's objection to creation of Poor Law 205
    Lezayre, 1897
        dispute over election of churchwardens 205
    Lezayre, 1901
        dispute over gravestones 206
    Lonan, 1829
        ruinous state of church 71
    Malew, 1847
        testimonial cards for deserving poor 100
    Malew, 1895
        extension of churchyard 207
    Malew, 1897
        election of churchwardens - dispute 207
    Marown, 1841

decision to build new Church 88
Maughold
  to consider building of new church 147
  to consider state of church grounds 147
Maughold, 1877
  resolution to separate Maughold from Ramsey 174
Rushen, 1832
  decision to extend churchyard 77
Rushen, 1885
  repairs to church 176
Rushen, Easter, 1885
  criticism of management of Milner's Trust 176
St Mark's, 1828
  Purchase Manx Bible and Register 74
St Mark's, 1898
  sale of old St Matthew's site 209
St Matthew's, 1873
  consideration of new site 190
St Matthew's, Easter, 1879
  decision to raise money for vicarage 173
St Paul's, Ramsey
  extensions to Church 88
St Paul's, Ramsey, 1883
  introduction of robed choir 176
St Paul's, Ramsey, 1901
  refusal to elect Churchwardens 212
St Thomas', 1881
  vote to restore Hymns Ancient and Modern 179
St Thomas', Easter 1878
  substitution of a hymn for anthem 178
St Thomas', Easter 1879
  opposition to changes made by Washington 179
Vicar General 1, 5, 9, 10, 15, 18,
    20, 22, 23, 31, 33, 37, 38, 41,
    42, 48, 50, 54, 55, 58, 59, 60,
    61, 70, 72, 74, 93, 98, 106, 107,
    111, 114, 118, 119, 120, 127, 128, 134,
    135, 136, 138, 140, 146, 153, 158, 160,
    161, 170, 177, 180, 184, 189, 194, 197,
    198, 207, 224
  clergy 237
Vicar General's Court
    19, 23, 24, 27, 36, 51, 85, 135, 149, 175
Viscount Bolingbroke 29

W

Waddington, Maria 90
Wainwright 10
Wake, Archbishop of Canterbury 18
Wakeford, Robert, Vicar 219
Walker, Samuel, Chaplain 155
Walker, Thomas 18
Walker, William
  Rector 5, 15, 17, 18, 216
  Vicar General 8, 31, 33, 34
Wall and Hook 135
Walpole, Sir Spencer 16, 186, 188, 201, 211
Walters, F. B., Revd 207, 210

Ward, Bishop William 38, 49, 62, 63, 78, 120, 122
  founded King William's College 65
  founder of St James', Dalby 85
  inadequate accomodation 64
  inception of St Stephen's, Sulby 89
  questionnaire to clergy 66
Ward, James K. 140
Ward, Joseph, Chaplain 102
Ward, Revd W. P. 207
Ward's (building) Fund 64, 71, 75, 88
Warren, Mordaunt Laidlaw, Chaplain 190, 206
Washington, Marmaduke, Vicar 178, 179
Watson, Edward, FRCO 210
Watson, Robert W., Chaplain 206
Watterson, William 11
Wattleworth 10
Wattleworth, Charles, Vicar 17
Wattleworth, Samuel (2) 21, 22
  Archdeacon 6, 17
  Vicar 1
  Vicar General 1
Wellington Hall, Douglas 95
Welsh, John 68, 71, 75, 76
Wesley, John 32, 41, 42, 43
Wesleyan Methodist 113
Whalley, William H.
  Chaplain 203
  Vicar 205, 218
White, Henry Grattan
  Curate 132
  Vicar 152, 154, 174, 175, 178, 191
Whitehall Chapel 29, 52
Whiteside, Robert 188
Whittaker, Frank R., Vicar 218
Wicksey, J. T. W. 167
Widows' Houses, Fort Street 132
Wilkinson, James Seely
  Chaplain 141, 171, 190
  Vicar 189, 206, 209
Wilks, Colonel Mark 135
Wilks, Elizabeth 42
Wilks, James
  Episcopal Registrar 32
  Rector 42
  Vicar 16, 22, 33, 36, 39
Wilks, John 22
Williams, James George (1), Vicar 174, 187, 188
Williams, Thomas H. (2), Chaplain 203, 217
Williams, Watkin, Q.C. 151
Wilson, Bishop Thomas 1, 16, 26, 30, 31, 32,
    33, 36, 38, 42, 64, 68, 77, 122, 155
  advice to Clergy 1
  alleviation of food shortage 4
  basic knowledge of Manx language 5
  beginning of translation of Bible into Manx 33
  building and restoration of church buildings 3
  charitable work 4
  church discipline 6
  complaint against clergy conduct 14

confirmation, minimum age 14
contributions to churches' funds 15
death of 16
denouncement of smuggling 4
dispute with Governor Horne 6
dispute with Governor John Lloyd 10
education 4
fining and imprisoned in Castle Rushen 8
improvements in farming 4
improvements to Bishopscourt 2
improvements to standards of clergy 2
introduced potato tithe, 1712, 54
medical aid to the poor 4
need for Manx speakers 2
observations on state of the see 2
poor relations with Derby Governors 13
Prayer for the Herring Fishery 34, 45, 105, 157
started parochial libraries 3
translations into Manx 5
Wilson, Dr. Thomas 4, 26, 27

Wilson, Henry (1), Vicar 189, 205
Wilson, James, Chaplain 155
Wilson, Revd E. 65
Winwick Church 15
Wood, Doctor 151, 161
Wood, John, Governor 32, 38, 48
Wood, Miss M. L. ARCO 166, 170, 178, 201, 204
Woods, John (1), Vicar 22, 27
Woods, John (2), Vicar 8, 11, 12, 21
Woods, Margaret 22
Woods, Thomas William Joseph (3), Vicar
    19, 37, 39, 42, 43, 48, 117, 119, 120
Worcester 80
Worrall, F. G. 189
wrecking 67

Y

Yn Druin, Lezayre 216
York Convocation 123
Young, Doctor 91